More praise for *Sometimes Madness Is Wisdom*

"Kendall Taylor's new biography of [Zelda and F. Scott Fitzgerald] is the first to provide adequate groundwork for a thorough account of literary custody."
—Salon.com

"Drawing on every source available to her for this unflinching portrait of the Fitzgerald marriage, Kendall Taylor gives us a disturbing story that bears retelling."
—FRANCES KIERNAN
Author of *Seeing Mary Plain: A Life of Mary McCarthy*

"There are those whose lives resemble novels, and there are those who write novels, but however you categorize the singular Mrs. Fitzgerald, she could not be better served than with this exhaustive and highly readable biography."
—*Flaunt* magazine

"Well-written, comprehensive . . . Taylor charts this complex story of frenetic spiritual squalor and mutual doom with curiosity and insight."
—*Library Journal*

"A library of books has been published about the legendary Fitzgeralds whose lives were filled with epic drama and tragedy. But Kendall Taylor proves that the best account of Zelda Sayre Fitzgerald—smart, beautiful, and ambitious—was still waiting to be written. . . . Moving beyond the 'last of the flappers' clichés, *Sometimes Madness Is Wisdom* threw me into Zelda's world, where I could not help marveling, gasping, and shuddering."
—MARION MEADE
Author of *Dorothy Parker: What Fresh Hell Is This?*

Sometimes Madness
Is Wisdom

SOMETIMES MADNESS IS WISDOM

Zelda and Scott Fitzgerald
A MARRIAGE

KENDALL TAYLOR

BALLANTINE BOOKS | NEW YORK

*In memory of Alex Finne and David Garner
and for Sophie*

CONTENTS

ACKNOWLEDGMENTS

By its very nature, a biography takes a long time to write. The research required is painstaking and each life uniquely woven of circumstances, influences, and relationships. Peoples' lives follow uncharted routes with numerous turns, detours, and dead ends. That certainly was the case with the Fitzgeralds, who lived out of suitcases and wandered from Montgomery to Westport, Hollywood to Wilmington, and Paris to Antibes. Complicating matters is the biographer's temptation to digress and explore the interesting at the expense of the relevant. To maintain coherence, biographers must maintain a rigorous point of view, staying fully committed to their subjects or at least remaining fascinated by their natures. Along the way, many people help and the list of those to whom I owe thanks is a long one.

Several libraries and archives held collections without which this biography could not have been written. For assisting with original materials and allowing me to quote from the unpublished writings of F. Scott Fitzgerald, Zelda Sayre Fitzgerald, Sara Mayfield, and Sara Haardt, I am grateful to: the Special Collections Division in the Firestone Library of Princeton University, especially Anna Lee Pauls in Photoduplication and Margaret Sherry, who made available—at the precise moment I needed them—recently acquired Craig House medical records documenting Zelda's confinement; Clarke E. Center, Jr., curator, W. S. Hoole Special Collections Library, the University of Alabama at Tuscaloosa; the librarians at Goucher College, Vanderbilt University, Rare Book Department of Cornell University, Beinecke Rare Book and Manuscript Library of Yale University, the Huntington Public Library, Motion Picture Division of the Library of Congress, National Portrait Gallery of the Smithsonian Institution, Enoch Pratt Free Library, New York Historical Society, Tenafly Public Library, the Museum of Broadcasting Library, Fashion Institute of Technology, the Westport Historical Society, Alabama State Department of Archives and History, the F. Scott and Zelda Fitzgerald Museum, and the Montgomery Museum of Art. My particular thanks to Julia Courtney and the interlibrary loan staff of Saint Lawrence University and Jennifer Maine at the SLU bookstore, the librarians at the University of Alabama at Tuscaloosa for making available the Sara Mayfield Archive, Stephen Nonack of the Special Collections Division of the Boston Athenaeum for allowing me to see Robert Edward Francillon's *Zelda's Fortune* (1874), the research staffs of the American Psychiatric Association Library, New York Psychiatric Hospital at Ogdensburg, and Sheppard Pratt Hospital.

A portion of this book was written while I was a graduate student in the English Department of Vanderbilt University, and in its early stages my research benefited greatly from suggestions made by Professors Walter Sullivan and Harold Weatherby. Another initial key influence was Andrew Turnbull, who introduced me to Zelda's daughter, Scottie Lanahan, and sister Rosalind Smith. Two of my most important interviews were with them. Scottie was reluctant to discuss her parents but, as a favor to her childhood friend Andrew, finally agreed. Turnbull had just completed his own biography of Fitzgerald, was teaching at MIT, and living on Brattle Street in Cambridge. He willingly shared his research materials with me and spent numerous hours sharing his observations and knowledge of the Fitzgeralds.

Over the years I conducted interviews with many others who shared their recollections of Zelda and Scott's life together. I am indebted to Archibald MacLeish, Tom Johnson, Lillian Gish, C. Lawton Campbell, Tom Daniels, Charles Angoff, Helen Blackshear, Mrs. H. L. Weatherby, Anne Tillinghast, Landon Ray, Dr. Otto

Billig, Dr. Basil T. Bennett, Helen Hopkins, Mrs. George Hickson, Mary Porter, and Laura Kahler, daughter of Pauline and George Brownell.

Several Fitzgerald scholars contributed to my understanding of Zelda's life, including: Nancy Milford, Sara Mayfield, Andre Le Vot, Henry Dan Piper, Jeffrey Meyers, Eleanor Lanahan, Scott Donaldson, Morrill Cody, and Hugh Ford. I am particularly indebted to James R. Mellow, who shared his ideas about the difference between fame and celebrity as relevant to Zelda and put me in touch with Alexander McKaig's nephew, Robert Taft. I owe him a debt of gratitude for allowing me to hand-copy the entire diary of Alexander McKaig in his Peterborough, New Hampshire, law office and for providing original photographs. Arthur Mizener met with me at Vanderbilt and Cornell, sharing his observations about Zelda's relationship with George Jean Nathan. C. Lawton Campbell agreed to be interviewed several times at his Bronxville home and gave me full use of his unpublished essay "The Fitzgeralds Were My Friends." Carolyn Shafer shared information about Dr. Frederick Wertham, included in her thesis for the University of South Carolina, and shared photographs of the artwork Zelda created for Wertham's therapy sessions. Richard and Nat Ober scoured their photo collections for fresh images of Scottie with their family.

My literary agent, Betsy Nolan, believed in this book from the beginning, and her practical advice and steadfast support helped keep me writing. I was very fortunate to have my book purchased by Ballantine Books at Random House, and to work with Leona Nevler, a highly experienced and skilled editor. I owe her, and her assistant, Louis Mendez—who spent much effort helping bring my manuscript to production—my sincere appreciation. My thanks to Nancy Delia, production editor on this book, and to Diana Frost of Random House's legal department. I am indebted to Upton Birnie Brady for superbly editing the manuscript by employing his keen intelligence and editorial experience to make the story come alive. Elizabeth Lustig is to be thanked for her line edit and Joyce Lilholt for her typing. Robert Best provided valuable aid with word processing and printing. Carol Hindle, Joanne Pritchard-Sobhani, and Dr. Ralph Johns were of tremendous assistance and gave me the courage to weather difficult times. Closely following my work were relatives and friends who sustained me with continual encouragement. I thank: Ronald Finne, Maria Della Schiava, Maureen Seccombe, Craig Taylor, Philip Kokataillo, Richard Kuchta, Nelly Case and Stephen Ledoux, Henry Button, Diane Gingold, Barbara Brennan, Ann Ratner, Julia Rubin, Gary L. Smith, Mary Burgess Avrakotos, Dave Brown, Beverly and Stuart Denenberg, Amy Henderson, Bill Cody, Debra McCord, and Deede Tonelli. My appreciation also to Marc Pachter at the Smithsonian Institution, who invited me to participate in the Washington Biography Group and whose members offered insightful commentary. And to Carol Mitchell and Denise McMahon of the Marco Island, Florida, Collier County Library, for arranging the C-SPAN "BOOK-NOTES" taping of my lecture on this book. If I have inadvertently left someone out, I offer my apologies and the assurance that I valued their assistance.

Most important, this book could never have been written without the help of my father, Alexander Finne, and my husband, David Russon Garner. I only wish they could have lived to see it published. For years, my late husband lived with this biography on a daily basis. He provided unfailing support and made countless helpful suggestions. Always encouraging, he coped with my long hours at the computer and indulged endless years of manuscript writing and editing. I could never have completed this project without his love and support. It is to him, our wonderful daughter, Sophie Alexandra, and my beloved father that this book is dedicated.

PREFACE

Years ago I began this book fascinated by the legend that had grown up around Zelda Fitzgerald. Finishing it, I have come to better understand my own intense interest and the ongoing curiosity of others. While the initial fascination may rest with the twenties flapper or the tantalizing nature of madness, it is the innate intelligence and ability of this enigmatic and remarkable woman that ultimately captures the imagination.

Anyone who met the beautiful, young Zelda was immediately struck by her spirited self-confidence, energy, and determination; a person so absolutely sure of herself that anything seemed possible. Spontaneous and exciting, she shone in any situation. With talent and the will to succeed, she should have accomplished much. How was it, then, that in an age of opportunity she failed to find her own voice?

What Zelda always wanted was equal footing and an identity apart from her famous husband. But she was thwarted in that goal by an initial lack of direction. Ironically, she needed Scott to show her the way. Like many women of her era, she began her adult life with little idea about how to apply her numerous abilities. She married Fitzgerald expecting he would lead her to realms she could not enter alone, following the path many women of her class took. Talented, and with similar goals to her own, Scott appeared capable of guiding her, but was focused on his own career and offered little help. Occasionally he tried, but it was an unnatural role at cross purposes with his own intentions. Their unconventional marriage and hedonistic lifestyle did not help matters. Co-creators of their own legend, in which fantasy and fact often blurred, they found it increasingly difficult to perceive or accept reality. Instead, as husband and wife, they alternatively bolstered each other then cruelly wrenched away—love, mistrust, and competitiveness permeating their relationship.

Nowhere is the reality of the Fitzgeralds' marital situation more evident than in Zelda's superbly crafted letters to Scott. These number in the thousands, and Fitzgerald saved all of them. Much of my book has been drawn from them, because they provide the greatest understanding of Zelda's character. Other insights come from interviews with family members, friends, and colleagues, along with a careful perusal of diaries, photo albums, notebooks, scrapbooks, news clippings, medical records, and minutiae: bills, contracts, passports, and Zelda's red Moroccan leather address book. And from earlier biographers.

Matthew Bruccoli, who devoted his entire career to writing about the Fitzgeralds, recalled how his interest began on March 27, 1949, when he heard a radio dramatization of "The Diamond as Big as the Ritz" and was inspired to read *The Great Gatsby*. A decade later, I had a similar experience. On June 26, 1958, I was introduced to F. Scott Fitzgerald through a television adaptation of *The Great Gatsby* on "Playhouse 90" with Robert Ryan as Jay Gatsby and Jean Crain in the role of Daisy. An impressionable teenager, I was struck by the poignancy of Gatsby's romantic idealization of Daisy and the intensity of his love. I went to the local library to borrow the novel and Arthur Mizener's biography of Fitzgerald, *The Far Side of Paradise*. After reading both, it was Zelda whom I found most intriguing—my interest heightened by Mizener's omission of Zelda's story after Fitzgerald's death.

By the time Mizener corrected this oversight in his 1965 edition, I was well along in my own investigation. I had read everything Scott and Zelda had written, as well as everything written about them. In graduate school, I wrote my master's thesis on Zelda's life

and work, and was aided by Tom Johnson, a fledgling poet and protégé of Archibald MacLeish. The former Poet Laureate and his
wife, Ada, were friends of Zelda during the twenties, and MacLeish
shared his recollections of the Fitzgeralds with me. Andrew Turnbull also became an important resource. He had met Zelda at La
Paix when the Fitzgeralds rented a cottage on his parent's estate.
Having recently completed his own biography of Scott Fitzgerald,
he became a continual source of assistance. He put me in touch
with Zelda's sister Rosalind Smith in Montgomery and Fitzgerald's
daughter, Scottie, then living in the Georgetown section of Washington, D.C.

I drove from graduate school at Vanderbilt south to Alabama and
spent five days talking with Rosalind and others who had known
Zelda. Newman Smith, Rosalind's husband, was seriously ill and
died soon after, so it was a difficult time for Rosalind. In spite of
this, she spent many hours with me, speaking openly about her sister and Fitzgerald. Upon my departure, she presented me with a
collection of Zelda's paper dolls.

Scottie was equally generous, providing me access to Zelda's letters, scrapbooks, and photo albums, and talking with me about her
childhood. She seldom discussed her parents, even with her own
children, and had erected a wall of denial about them. At first, she
was disinclined to relive childhood memories. "I knew there was
only one way for me to survive [my parents'] tragedy," she wrote in
an introduction to her father's letters. "And that was to ignore it."
After her initial reluctance to see me, she finally agreed—with the
warning: "If you come to Washington I would be delighted to see
you, but I must warn you that I am invariably disappointing to people who hope to find out more about my father and mother than
has already been in print. Time and again I have watched faces fall
as scholars like yourself come to the inevitable realization that I
really have nothing new to add. Daddy died when I was only 18 and
I had hardly seen him over the previous five or six years so that
what memories I have are so confused by what has been written and
said they no longer seem real, even to me."

But that week with Scottie proved critically important, for she
added much to my understanding of her mother. Equally valuable
was her letter of support that introduced me to friends of the family
and encouraged them to share recollections. "Kendall Taylor has

asked me to write her a covering letter stating that I have no objections to her obtaining any material concerning my father or mother, F. Scott and Zelda Fitzgerald, which she deems relevant to her work. I am counting on her tact and taste to edit whatever seems 'sensational.' But I am not concerned with suppressing facts which might be useful to her."

With my work proceeding well, I was acquiring an ever-deepening understanding of Zelda. Then I received a call from Nancy Milford. It seemed she was also writing about Zelda and interviewing the same people. Emphasizing that she was far along in her research with a publisher in hand, she also implied she had Scottie's backing.

I telephoned Scottie to ask if something had changed in her resolve to help me and was reassured. But three days later, I received a letter from her that showed how emotionally charged the memories of her childhood were. "I went to bed for two days after I saw you, I was so unstrung by our conversation. Now do you begin to understand why I avoid, like one of the 'ten most wanted' this sort of thing? Perhaps I am not very balanced about it, to put it mildly. However, you were charming and I'm glad I met you. If past experience holds true, however, you will have thought me so normal and natural about my parents that you will—as you should, you being normal and natural—assume that now we're friends, I will answer letters, phone calls, etc. I do want to warn you that I probably won't, and there won't be anything personal about it. I think you are a *sensational* girl. But I am not 'normal' on this subject. I'm allergic, you might say. I'm like somebody who breaks out inexplicably in a rash. I hate talking about my parents. I suppose it is foolish and possibly a $20,000 psychoanalysis would clear it up, though I doubt it. I think probably most people who had a grubby growing up feel this way, except they usually can get away with not talking about it. I can't—I'm surrounded on all sides by it. Call it a kind of claustrophobia, if you will. It was just perfectly terrible, that's all, and I just barely survived it, and the idea of re-living it is awful for me. I'm telling you all this so you won't feel hurt, and I won't feel guilty when you want me to read your manuscript and I put it off for two and a half years. It will have nothing to do with you. Just self-preservation."

At that time, writing about Zelda without Scottie's cooperation seemed daunting, though it would not stop me now. Assuming Milford was far along in her work, I put aside my own research. But it would be five more years before her *Zelda* was published, and Scottie would also withdraw her support from Milford.

So distressed was Scottie by the *Zelda* manuscript, she refused to speak with Milford directly, demanding through Matthew Bruccoli that all materials be returned, and all conjectures about Zelda's sexuality deleted. An extremely private person, Scottie resolutely protected her family history, and from the time of Mizener's research until Scottie's death in 1986, biographers were forced to censor certain materials. Only after her daughter Eleanor's biography, *Scottie, the Daughter of . . . : The Life of Frances Scott Fitzgerald Lanahan Smith*, has previously supressed information become available. That, along with the recent release of Zelda's medical records from Craig House, a private mental institution in Beacon, New York, and newly discovered biographical material at Princeton, has opened unexplored avenues of research, making a new book on Zelda not only feasible but desirable.

Still, one might question whether the Fitzgeralds haven't been "done to death," given the numerous studies to follow Arthur Mizener's *The Far Side of Paradise*. As the first full-length Fitzgerald biography, published one decade after Scott's death and three years following Zelda's, Mizener's effort is an honest and sympathetic book. But the Fitzgeralds' personal life was of secondary interest to him. Andrew Turnbull's *Scott Fitzgerald* is fairer to Zelda, adding important material Mizener was forced to omit. It is a compassionate book focusing on Fitzgerald's emotional life and the complex relationship between Scott and Zelda. Third on the list of biographies was Matthew Bruccoli's thirty-year effort, *Some Sort of Epic Grandeur*. Exhaustively researched, it presents a treasure-trove of new facts but gives readers little sense of Fitzgerald as a person and even less of Zelda. More interpretive, and perhaps the most adventurous and sensitive Fitzgerald biography, is Andre Le Vot's *F. Scott Fitzgerald*. Published in French in 1979 and later translated into English (1983), it delivers an excellent account of the man and the artist. Out that same year and concentrating almost entirely on Scott, *Fool for Love* by Scott Donaldson examines Fitzgerald's inferiority complex and obsessive need to please others as the key to his personality. The sixth major biographical study to appear since

1970, James Mellow's *Invented Lives* is a very good, impartial, and controlled critical study. Well-documented and constructed, it explores how the Fitzgeralds created themselves and the circumstances that inevitably destroyed them.

The best study of Zelda to date is Nancy Milford's *Zelda*, an engaging but evasive book that poses as many questions as it answers. Sara Mayfield's *Exiles in Paradise*, published only a year after Milford's *Zelda*, provides some additional insights, being a sympathetic book based on personal recollections. Sara had known Zelda since childhood days in Montgomery and maintained contact with her during ensuing years. When her book finally was published, Mayfield was sixty-six and living in Alabama after years of confinement in a mental institution. Most noteworthy among the extensive interviews Mayfield conducted with Zelda's family and friends are a series of lengthy questions posed in writing to Zelda's sister Rosalind, who had known Mayfield for years. Rosalind answered those queries in great detail, but her own bias against Fitzgerald, coupled with Mayfield's negative feelings about Scott, only reinforced the author's opinion of him as a selfish and weak alcoholic responsible for Zelda's breakdown. Flawed by a one-sided viewpoint and sweeping generalizations, the book is a highly biased account by a childhood friend. Nevertheless, because of rather than despite its idiosyncrasies, the book is an interesting read.

Two recent biographies, Jeffrey Meyers's *Scott Fitzgerald* and Eleanor Lanahan's *Scottie, the Daughter of . . .* , have added fresh material. Meyers's compassionate, though occasionally condescending, study contains some new facts about Zelda's confinements in various institutions. Lanahan's biography includes personal family information heretofore unavailable, and is particularly revelatory about Scottie's feelings toward her parents, children, and husband. Acknowledging that her tell-all biography "exposes, bleeds, mourns, whines, brags and complains," Lanahan openly admitted, "My mother would flip." As a detailed exposé of Scottie's life, it provides some raw material for scholars, but needs to be read objectively.

With these and other biographical works on the Fitzgeralds available, I still felt compelled to pursue Zelda's story. As to why, I find a clue in Archibald MacLeish's comment to me about Zelda's impact on Scott's life and work. "I don't think that any woman really affects the kinds of things a man writes," he said, "because what he writes and how he does it come from inside him; they are stored up there and arrive at the surface as a product of the man nobody ever knows. She can seriously affect his production; how much he writes and when he does, but I think with any other wife, Scott would never have written as much as he did during those times, or really had any measure of happiness at all."

In other biographies, Zelda has been primarily considered in relation to Scott Fitzgerald. Even in Milford's *Zelda*, the index entry for Zelda is headed "Fitzgerald, Mrs. F. Scott (Zelda Sayre)." The woman who held my attention was the Zelda who gave life to all of Fitzgerald's heroines, then struggled to go beyond that persona. Was Zelda *only* to be researched as the wife of Scott Fitzgerald?

Zelda died when I was a child, so we never met, but I have always identified with her struggle to succeed on her own. Mirroring other women of her generation caught between old notions of subservience and new ideas of equality, Zelda's story remains relevant to today's women who face similar challenges. This explains why her determination to find valuable work and establish an identity apart from Fitzgerald still intrigues us. Ultimately, the glory of her life rests on the fact that she accomplished as much as she did— despite the odds stacked against her, the most powerful impediment (to use her own words) being that she *was* Mrs. F. Scott Fitzgerald.

Emblem and Era

Every decade has a writer who emerges as spokesperson for his or her age. During the fifties and sixties in twentieth-century America, it was Jack Kerouac and J. D. Salinger. F. Scott Fitzgerald briefly held that exalted position in the twenties, capturing the tenor and tempo of his time in a series of stories and novels about brash, independent, self-centered young women called flappers. They were girls whose personalities all were based on his highly original wife, Zelda Sayre.

Fitzgerald met Zelda during the summer of 1918 in Montgomery, Alabama, then a genteel, quiet community of forty thousand. When the United States entered World War I, it had been designated an air depot to serve southern training contingents. The town was a natural choice because of its already-existing airfields. Seemingly overnight, Montgomery swirled with activity as it was inundated with soldiers from nearby Camp Sheridan, which housed more than half as many people as the town itself. Zelda later fictionalized this sudden transformation in her novel *Save Me the Waltz*, describing officers from the nearby base. "There was the little major who stormed around like a Japanese warrior flashing his gold teeth, and an Irish captain with eyes like the Blarney stone and hair like burning peat, and aviation officers, white around their eyes from where their goggles had been, with swollen noses from the wind and sun; and men who were better dressed in their uniforms than ever before in their lives." In an interview with childhood friend Sara Haardt, who also had escaped the suffocation of small-town life by marrying a famous writer, Zelda recalled Montgomery prior to World War I and just after. "Before 1905 or 1906, there was scarcely a ripple in our lives. Life itself seemed serene, almost smugly secure. Mothers in the South scarcely worried about what would happen to their children. We wandered out in the streets and the parks to play, and took care of ourselves, with the exception of a sleepy old mammy or two . . . then the war came and we had the inescapable feeling that all this beauty and fun—everything—might be over in a minute. We couldn't wait, we couldn't afford to wait, for fear it would be gone forever, so we pitched in furiously, dancing every night and riding up and down the moonlit roads and even swimming in the gravel pools under that white Alabama moon that gives the world a strange, lovely touch of madness."

Not since the Civil War had there been so many northerners in Alabama. Though some hostility toward the "Yankees" still lingered, a modest cordiality had been initiated at Saturday night dances held in the Beauvoir and Montgomery Country Clubs for officers from Camp Sheridan and Camp Taylor. When the governing board of the Montgomery Country Club extended occasional invitations to officers from nearby camps, Fitzgerald managed to secure a member's card enabling him to enter at will. On one particular Saturday evening in July of 1918, he was escorting senior officers to the club as his guests. His responsibility for the evening, they were quickly forgotten when he encountered Zelda Sayre.

Just weeks shy of her eighteenth birthday and recently graduated from Sidney Lanier High School, where she had been voted prettiest and most popular, Zelda was noticeably different from other local girls and the most sought-after of Montgomery's young women. Recalling her elevated position, a friend described that extraordinary popularity: "As long as I can remember and long before that I have been told, Montgomery always had at least one girl who either purposely or unintentionally stood out as a target of town-talk. In the spring of that year, Zelda was that target."

Even before meeting Scott, she had begun exploring ways to expand her popularity beyond Montgomery's confining borders. But Fitzgerald presented a new and interesting challenge. He seemed more sophisticated than her southern beaux, one of those "men from Princeton and Yale who smelled of Russian Leather and seemed very used to being alive." With his blond hair parted down the middle and heavily lashed lavender eyes, Fitzgerald presented a jaunty confidence that suggested he belonged among an intellectual and social elite. Exuding an Ivy League charm, and smartly dressed in a Brooks Brothers uniform, he could dance the trendy Maxie, Turkey Trot, and Aeroplane Glide. Princeton had given him an urbanity against which young men from Auburn and Tuscaloosa could not compete. And though Zelda was pursued by numerous boys from better families with more money, none superficially were as impressive as Fitzgerald, or possessed such lofty ambitions. She was flattered to hear that she resembled the heroine of his novel-in-progress, and impressed by his conviction that he would soon be a famous author.

Although the promise of his potential fame piqued her interest, Zelda needed more than vainglorious bragging; she required solid proof that he could provide the type of life she wanted. Caught up in a frenzy of dating, she was immersed in a game to collect men's hearts along with their regimental insignia. "Through the summer Alabama collected soldiers' insignia," Zelda wrote of the heroine in her novel. "By autumn she had a glove box full. No other girl had more and even then she'd lost some. So many dances and rides and so many golden bars and silver bars and bombs and castles and flags and even a serpent to represent them all in her cushioned box. Every night she wore a new one."

The competition for her attention was staggering. Discharged on Valentine's Day, 1919, from his Montgomery Division, Fitzgerald realized he must act quickly or lose Zelda. He went home to St. Paul to rewrite his manuscript, *This Side of Paradise*, which finally was accepted by Scribner's for its spring 1920 publication list. With his book sold, he convinced Zelda to marry him. But not until the novel was in bookstores did the ceremony occur, taking place in the rectory of Manhattan's St. Patrick's Cathedral on Easter Sunday, April 3, 1920. In its wedding announcement, the *Montgomery Advertiser* prophesied accurately: "Montgomery friends yield most reluctantly this beautiful and fascinating young girl to her new home in New York City, feeling assured she will soon be surrounded by the same admiring atmosphere as that left in this section of the picturesque South."

With Scott's novel a runaway best-seller, the Fitzgeralds immediately became Manhattan's most sought-after couple, in demand at chic gatherings, parties, and theater openings. Acknowledged leaders of the twenties lifestyle, they were, John Dos Passos recalled, "celebrities in the Sunday supplement sense of the word. They were always where the action was." Lillian Gish agreed: "They didn't make the twenties; they WERE the twenties." No couple drank more, went to as many parties, or so willingly abandoned themselves to having a good time. Propelled into the limelight, they were expected to remain outrageous. The columnists' best friends, everything they did made good copy. To stay newsworthy, they continually had to outdo themselves, and so frequently were they in the gossip columns, that William Randolph Hearst assigned a reporter solely to cover their activities. Seemingly overnight, they became high priest and priestess of the era. Mingling freely with the theater crowd, they befriended Lillian Hellman, Helen Hayes, and Lillian Gish, attended opening nights with George Jean Nathan and his actress girlfriend Ruth Findlay and had their images emblazoned on the overture curtain of the Greenwich Village Follies.

But it would prove a brief reign, for within eight years Zelda would be hospitalized in a Swiss sanitarium and Fitzgerald on his way to becoming an alcoholic. Looking back on the decade, in an effort to unravel the tapestry of her decline, Zelda listed the critical events that had sealed her destiny:

> *My marriage, after which I was in another world, one for which I was not qualified or prepared because of my inadequate education.*
>
> *A love affair with a French aviator in St. Raphael. I was locked in my villa for one month to prevent me from seeing him. This lasted for five years. When I knew my husband had another woman in California I was upset because the life over there appeared to me so superficial, but finally I was not hurt because I knew I had done the same thing when I was younger.*
>
> *I determined to find an impersonal escape, a world in which I could express myself and walk without the help of somebody who was always far from me.*

*I am lost about anything with him, with his life in which there is
nothing for me except the physical comfort . . . I must add another thing:
this story is the fault of nobody but me. I believed I was a Salamander
and it seems that I am nothing but an impediment.*

Her reference to the salamander—that domestic deity that Plato
said could pass through fire unscathed—is the key to understanding Zelda's personality and ultimate downfall. She alludes here
to Owen Johnson's 1914 best-seller *The Salamander*, a novel that
permanently affected her attitude toward life. Wildly popular, the
book was purported to have reached over ten million readers, pre-
dominantly women under twenty-five, and the Broadway play
based on it, starring Nathan's girlfriend Ruth Findlay, opened to
appreciative audiences on October 23, 1914, at the Harris Theatre.
It was so successful that *Motography* magazine, in its August 21,
1915, issue, announced that a movie version was fast approaching
completion with Findlay again in the lead role. With 360 scenes, 14
big stars, and a production budget of over $100,000, the film
opened in January of 1916 to rave reviews: The *Evening Journal*
called it "The classic of the year," *Review* labeled it "A great success," and *Billboard* acclaimed it "The hit of the year."

Zelda was entering her junior year at Sidney Lanier High School
when *The Salamander* opened in Montgomery, and like the film's
heroine, was already renowned for her conquests of men. An avid
reader who loved discussing the year's popular novels, she had read
James Branch Cabell even before Fitzgerald, as he acknowledged.
Even more than novels, Zelda loved the movies, often sitting
through features twice. "Darling, I nearly sat my seat off in the
Strand Theatre today," she wote Fitzgerald, and "all because T. E.
Lawrence of Arabia is your physical counterpart." Movies were one
of her favorite pastimes, and in 1918, Montgomery housed four
motion picture theaters—the Strand, Plaza, Empire, and Orpheum—
along with the Grand and the Majestic theaters, which presented
burlesque and stage plays.

When *The Salamander* heroine Dore Baxter declares on screen:
"I am in the world to do something unusual, extraordinary. I'm not
like every other little woman. . . . I adore precipices! It's such fun
to go dashing along the edges, leaning up against the wind that
tries to throw you over," it is easy to imagine Zelda's delight and instant identification with the character. For both, ordinary life "was

too permissible and lacked the element of danger, of the forbidden." In the film, Dore plays off one man against another at places like the Jungle Club with its "barbaric swinging music of stringed instruments . . . and the laughing, swaying gliding confusion of the dancers." Modeled after one of New York's most popular speakeasies of the same name, the Jungle Club was notorious for the rough crowd it attracted. Zelda would later precipitate a brawl there between Fitzgerald and the club's bouncer. "It had a large and brazenly well-stocked bar," Fitzgerald's Princeton classmate Lawton Campbell later recalled, "a dancing floor with dimly lit tables, a famous orchestra with popular entertainers, headwaiters in white tie and tails and many liveried attendants"—the sort of place where anything could happen . . . and did.

Like other women from her generation unwilling to settle for boring lives, Zelda identified with the salamander's desire to experiment and experience everything. As Owen Johnson described his heroine: "She comes from somewhere out of the immense reaches of the nation, revolting against the commonplace of an inherited narrowness, passionately adventurous, eager and unafraid, neither sure of what she seeks nor conscious of what forces impel or check her." A girl who knows what she wants and possesses the self-confidence to achieve it, "She [Dore] can meet what men she wishes," Johnson wrote. "Men of every station [were] drawn to her by the lure of her laughter and tantalizing arts, men who simply wish to amuse themselves, or somber hunters who have passed beyond the common stuff of adventuresses and seek with a renewal of excitement this corruption of innocence."

Unafraid of consequences, the daring girl of Johnson's novel employed any tactic to win. Her basic strategy was "acceptance that raises hopes, then an excuse that brings tantalizing disorder but whets the appetite." The whole process was an elaborate game—the prize being the right man at the right time. But no ordinary man, as Dore makes unabashedly clear: "The man I marry has got to be able to give me everything I see other women have—dresses, jewels, automobiles—or I should be miserable. You see I don't spare myself. I tell you the truth; I've got to have money, and I've got to have New York." Like her fictional counterpart, Zelda also disdained the ordinary and shared Dore's sentiments about money. When she initially ended her engagement to Fitzgerald, she very coolly explained it was simply because he could not adequately support her.

For salamanders, all men were props, a term derived from the theatrical word *property*. "A prop is a youth," Johnson explained, "not too long out of the nest to be rebellious, possessed of an automobile . . . and agitated by a patriotic craving to counteract the evil effects of the hoarding of gold." Salamanders considered all men fair game, even unworthy men, and Zelda agreed with the fictional Dore that "she had met few real men. She had played with idlers, boys of twenty, or boys of forty, interested in nothing but an indolent floating voyage through life."

The original novel had a more complex storyline than the six-reel adaptation. It traced Dore's search for the right marriage partner through associations with some of New York's most influential and dangerous men. A diverse group of suitors, these included a judge, a newspaper editor, a stage director, a racketeer, an actor, wealthy old men, and wealthy young ones—a game identical to the one Zelda was playing in Montgomery. "It was not simply three or four intrigues that she drove at once but a dozen," Johnson wrote, "keeping the threads from tangling, adding new ones each night for a few days mystification and abandonment." So captivating is Dore that, by the novel's conclusion, each man will do anything to possess her. In the end, she chooses the one who truly needs her affection and with whom she stands the best chance of combining love and financial security.

Zelda's romantic intrigues mirrored Dore's identically. And she would later draw on those experiences for a series of short stories about twenties' flappers. In "The Girl the Prince Liked," Zelda writes of the variety of men pursuing her heroine. "She went through her wintertime beaux with the same air of impassibility and detachment. On the list of her admirers there were sober, efficient young men who organized balls, and middle-aged men with five figures and a devoted reticence, and tall, trim men from New Orleans, and two or three admirable pianists, and an almost magnificent tenor. She had around her too, lots of young boys still in college—very attractive, straight young athletes, mostly who were afraid of the difficulties that lay in sentimental relations with girls their own age."

As every salamander acknowledged, choosing the right man to

marry was pivotal, and Zelda considered marriage the most momentous decision of her life. Her determination to pick carefully so impressed Fitzgerald that he incorporated entire sections from her diary on this topic into *The Beautiful and Damned*. Having his heroine Gloria express what Zelda in many cases actually stated, he wrote: "What grubworms women are to crawl on their bellies through colorless marriages! Mine is going to be outstanding. It can't, shan't be the setting—it's going to be the performance, the live, lovely glamourous performance, and the world shall be the scenery. I refuse to dedicate myself to posterity."

This critical choice of husband was to become the driving force in all of Fitzgerald's heroines, most clearly articulated through Daisy in *The Great Gatsby*. "She was again keeping half a dozen dates a day with half a dozen men . . . all the time something in her crying for a decision. She wanted her life shaped now, immediately— and the decision must be made by some force—of love, of money, of unquestionable practicality—that was close at hand." Although Zelda intellectually accepted being dependent on a man for security, on an emotional level she resented it. And Fitzgerald voiced her frustrations through Eleanor in *This Side of Paradise*: "Rotten, rotten old world . . . and the wretchedest thing of all is me— oh, why am I a girl? Why am I not a stupid [boy]? Look at you; you're stupider than I am, not much, but some, and you can lope about and get bored and then lope somewhere else, and you can play around with girls without being involved in meshes of sentiment, and you can do anything and be justified—and here am I with the brains to do everything, yet tied to the ship of future matrimony."

The salamander prototype had predated Fitzgerald's flapper by six years, a fact Owen Johnson continually emphasized. The publisher, Robert McAlmon, recalled how annoyed Johnson was that Fitzgerald was always credited with putting the flapper into fiction, arguing that he had accomplished this years earlier. However, in naming the 1920s the Jazz Age, and capturing its prevailing atmosphere of nervous stimulation in his writing, Fitzgerald was more alert than Johnson to the revolution taking place, and more precisely defined the era's changing manners and morals. Fictionalizing Zelda as the prototypical salamander and flapper, Fitzgerald captured the decade's youthful delirium full of "discovery and sensational exploits, all high-lighted by the challenge of Prohibition and the determination to forget the effects of the war."

Fitzgerald's Jazz Age spanned eleven years, beginning with the Armistice in 1918, and ending with the Wall Street crash in 1929. Characterized by flappers and Prohibition, it was a cynical period in which young people were unmoved by the previous generation's patriotic idealism. With old tenets abandoned and values shifting, concerned with manners and not morals, the era took on a strained, hysterical quality. As Zelda described it, "They were having the breadline at the Ritz that year. Everybody was there. People met people they knew in hotel lobbies smelling of orchids and plush and detective stories, and asked where they'd been since last time. Charlie Chaplin wore a yellow polo coat. People were tired of the proletariat—everybody was famous."

Youth-centered, fueled by illegal alcohol, and exploding with vitality, those under thirty pursued two major interests: socializing and making money. People wanted instant wealth and overnight sophistication. "Smart" was the buzzword. You were "smart" if you owned a radio and refrigerator, "smarter" still if you had a car. Automobile manufacturers scrambled to supply the newly wealthy with stylish ones—the Stutz-Bearcat, Marmon roadster (Zelda and Scott's first car), Pierce-Arrow, Essex, Cord, Maxwell, Franklin, Kissel, and Oakland. Many had rumble seats in the back where young couples could neck. It was thrilling to see how far one could go—without going all the way, and flappers played the game to perfection. Encouraging this behavior were popular films like the 1923 movie *Alimony*, which advertised: "Brilliant men, beautiful jazz babies, champagne baths, midnight revels, and petting parties in the purple dawn—all ending in one terrific smashing climax that makes you gasp."

Automobiles made petting epidemic, as Fitzgerald explained in *This Side of Paradise*. "None of the Victorian mothers—and most of the mothers were Victorian—had any idea how casually their daughters were accustomed to being kissed. . . . Amory saw girls doing things that even in his memory would have been impossible: eating three o'clock, after-dance suppers in impossible cafes, talking of every side of life with an air half of earnestness, half of mockery. . . . Amory found it rather fascinating to feel that any popular girl he met before eight, he might quite possibly kiss before twelve." The era's promiscuity was further encouraged by musical and theatrical offerings glorifying flappers' behavior. A wave of erotic plays opened in Manhattan, attracting girls from finishing schools who packed the balconies to hear about the romance of being lesbian.

What contributed greatly to this new promiscuity was the Volstead Act, making the manufacture and sale of alcoholic beverages illegal. Signed into effect in January of 1919, and not repealed until December 1933, it proved impossible to enforce. If anything, Prohibition *encouraged* drinking. It was thrilling to break the law for a drink, and New York's speakeasies did a booming business. The Fitzgeralds' favorite watering holes were the Rendezvous, Bearnaise, Montmartre, and Dizzy Club. Jack Shuttleworth, editor of the humorous magazine *Judge*, recalled running into Fitzgerald and John Held Jr. at the Bearnaise during the fall of 1925. "The basement was bedlam. . . . Actors and actresses, artists and writers, brokers and debutantes, judges and gangsters, college boys and flappers, were all laughing and shouting over their Pink Ladies, a disastrous concoction of bathtub gin, applejack, grenadine and egg white served in fancy, long-stemmed glasses. John Held, Jr. was there, . . . tall, dark, and tweedy, and I found him sitting with F. Scott Fitzgerald. I didn't know it then, but there I was smack in the middle of the Jazz Age with its two creators."

Relieved of inhibition by alcohol and advocating Freud's new sexual theories, flappers became overnight role models for the era's modern women. Though Freud had published his work on psychoanalysis and human sexuality at the end of the nineteenth century, his writings were not widely available in America until after World War I. Following their publication, enthusiastic flappers embraced his theories about unmet sexual needs precipitating psychological problems, and applauded Rosalind's and Eleanor's protestations in *This Side of Paradise*: "Oh, just one person in fifty has any glimmer of what sex is. I'm hipped on Freud and all that, but it's rotten that every bit of '*real*' love in the world is ninety-nine percent passion and one little soupçon of jealousy."

The flapper movement was at its peak when Fitzgerald introduced Rosalind to the reading public, making her the year's most widely known and imitated exemplar. Possessing Zelda Sayre's courage and first love Ginevra King's cool reserve, Rosalind's attitude became the flapper's credo. As Zelda would later explain, "the flapper awoke from her lethargy of sub-deb-ism, bobbed her hair, put on her choicest pair of earrings and a great deal of audacity and rouge and went into battle. She flirted because it was fun to flirt and wore a one-piece bathing suit because she had a good figure, she covered her face with powder and paint because she didn't need it, and she refused to be bored chiefly because she wasn't boring. She was conscious the things she did were the things she had always wanted to do." The average man was confused and intimidated by this independent woman, who, as columnist Dorothy Dix pointed out, "could play golf all day, dance all night, drive a motor car, and give first aid to the injured if anybody gets hurt." Considering Fitzgerald spokesman for their generation, they avidly read about his flappers' exploits as they galumphed around in unfastened galoshes agitating every male in sight. Zelda's alter ego, Gloria, in *The Beautiful and Damned* was a prime example. She was a girl who "took all the things of life for hers to choose from and apportion, as though she were continually picking out presents for herself from an inexhaustible counter." When Fitzgerald has husband Anthony inquire, "Aren't you interested in anything except yourself," Gloria's cynical answer said it all: "not much."

Before encountering Zelda, Fitzgerald already was writing about flapper behavior. But she more precisely embodied the heroine he wanted to define, a girl who embraced the salamander philosophy and brought it to life. Encouraging her daring antics and clever chatter, he scribbled down her spontaneous witticisms and incorporated her mannerisms into his fiction, telling one reporter, "I married the heroine of my stories." Created entirely from Zelda's personality, Rosalind so instantly defined the twenties' flapper that the Louisville *Courier-Journal* promptly dispatched a reporter to ask Zelda what it was like being her model. "I love Scott's books and heroines," she replied. "I like the ones that are like me! That's why I love Rosalind in 'This Side of Paradise.' I like girls like that. I like their courage, their recklessness and spendthriftiness."

Actually, it was H. L. Mencken, married to Zelda's childhood friend Sara Haardt, who had coined the term *flapper* fifteen years earlier. Originating in England, it described teenage girls who "flapped" awkwardly while walking—British stores selling "flapper" dresses with long, straight lines to hide this gracelessness. When the term crossed the Atlantic, it defined thrill-seeking city girls who did not have to work and instead spent time at parties and sporting events, and driving around in fancy cars. Describing the flappers' attitude with keen observation, Zelda wrote: "If you could afford to take her out, she was yours for the evening . . . If you are famous or rich or very, very handsome, she will annex you and give you a good time and hurt your feelings. If you just meet her because chance has thrown you into her path without exciting her curiosity about you, she will simply hurt your feelings." For out-of-town, would-be flappers starved for excitement, the quest for entertainment was even more obsessive—targeted toward anybody even moderately attractive: college boys in bell-bottom trousers and school sweaters; fellows who played the ukulele or jazz saxophone; or guys, like Fitzgerald, who wore a Brooks Brothers suit and carried a flask in their back pocket.

However, Zelda was somewhat of a contradiction. While yearning for independence, she also expected to be protected and made that clear from the beginning. Fitzgerald infused Rosalind with that contradiction. "You know I'm old in some ways—in others— well, I'm just a little girl. I like sunshine and pretty things and cheerfulness—and I dread responsibility. I don't want to think about pots and kitchens and brooms. I want to worry about whether my legs will get slick and brown when I swim in the summer." That self-absorption initially held irresistible appeal for Fitzgerald, who told his Princeton classmate Edmund Wilson that any girl who made a living directly on her prettiness interested him immensely. "The most enormous influence on me in the four and a half years since I met her," he wrote Wilson, "has been the complete, fine and full-hearted selfishness and chill-mindedness of Zelda." But it would not take long for his attitude to change.

And Zelda could not know the toll her role as Scott's fictional heroine would take. Only later, when she fought for personal freedom and self-expression, would she understand that it would not be *through* Scott, like a good salamander, but in *spite* of him that she would find fulfillment. When she confessed, "I am nothing but an impediment," implying she could no longer keep up the pace, she could not fathom—what we perceive at this distance— that her greatest accomplishment in life would be her contribution to Fitzgerald's oeuvre. Far from being an impediment, she provided the backbone for Fitzgerald's fiction, irreparably damaging in the process her own fragile psyche. Her retreat into madness was how she arranged herself, as she said, "in a condition to be able to breathe freely." And it was what she meant when she wrote, about her art and, by extension, her life: *parfois la folie est la sagesse*—sometimes madness is wisdom.

CHAPTER 1

Montgomery and All That Jazz

Born on Tuesday, July 24, 1900, when her mother was nearly forty, Zelda was the youngest of Anthony and Minnie Sayre's six children. She was named for the gypsy heroine in Robert Edward Francillon's 1874 romantic novel *Zelda's Fortune*. Describing his heroine, Francillon could have been speaking of Zelda Sayre when he wrote, "Zelda's heart was of July, but her tears were of April, when her sun rose. There was more than a little of Marietta in her besides her trick of stamping on the floor. But it must not be thought that rippling waves are always the sign of a shallow sea. She had her mother's quickness and impulse, but her depths were her own." She was baptized in the Episcopal Church of the Holy Comforter along with her three sisters: Marjorie, the oldest, born in 1882; Rosalind (called Tootsie), eleven years older, born in 1889; and Clothilde (called Tilde), nine years older and born in 1891. Her brother Daniel died of spinal meningitis at eighteen months, which left Anthony D. Sayre Jr., born in 1894, the only boy.

By the 1600s, Sayres were prominent on Long Island and then in New Jersey and Ohio. They moved to Alabama in 1819 and became large landowners and prosperous planters, merchants, and respected citizens. Many streets bore their surnames, including a prominent one named for William Sayre, Zelda's great-uncle, who came to Montgomery with his brother Daniel in 1819 and played a leading role in the growth of the town. Daniel became a newspaper publisher in Tuskegee and Montgomery, and his private residence at 644 Washington Street was later used as the first White House of the Confederacy. Zelda's mother's family, from the Scottish MacHen clan, had emigrated to Virginia early in the seventeenth century and changed their name to Machen. They were prominent statesmen, farmers, and politicians. A descendant of early Maryland and Virginia settlers, Minnie Machen's father was an attorney and tobacco planter who owned three thousand acres on the Cumberland River, and represented Virginia in the Confederate Congress. After the Civil War he served as a U.S. senator.

The Sayres had always resided in the western section of Montgomery, the oldest part of town, convenient to schools and serviced by the streetcar. While wealthier families built new homes in other sections, many of the old families remained rooted there. Though the Sayres moved several times within that neighborhood, Zelda's childhood was spent at 6 Pleasant Avenue in a rented gray frame house. It was built by one of the Judge's friends, whose family's pre–Civil War plantation had occupied that part of town. The square home faced their landlady's large white house across the street, left to her by ancestors; it was set amid a huge garden dotted with fruit and shade trees, boxwood, crepe myrtle, camellias, and kiss-me-at-the-gate that had been planted before the Civil War. At the rear of the Sayre house was a grassy, field-sized lot bordered by a ravine laced with wild grapevines on which Zelda spent hours climbing, and a great oak tree between whose roots spread carpets of moss on which she played endless games. It was a comfortable house surrounded by a spacious porch curtained with clematis vines and smilax to shield it from the western sun. On one side was a bench and chairs where Zelda and her friends gathered after supper; on the other hung a vine-laced swing where she and her sisters entertained male suitors. The large informal rooms were tastefully papered, and downstairs, furniture was set on polished pine floors centered with rugs. An expert gardener, Zelda's mother placed fresh flowers everywhere, and the rooms were always cheerful with sunlight and color. Tall glass-doored bookcases filled with Daniel Sayre's library lined the hallways. A piano, on which Zelda was given lessons, dominated the living room, on whose walls hung an oil painting of Minnie Sayre's mother and a hand-colored mezzotint of Napoleon bidding his wife and infant son good-bye.

Zelda's sister Rosalind recalled how "the door was always open to those of all ages, friends of each of us who were always dropping in and were welcome to meals when they wanted to stay for them. Even with his dislike of organized social activity, Papa did not mind this visiting influx but was a gracious host. He was always hospitable to callers who visited his daughters and would say a few words to them before making a hasty retreat." Zelda's room above the porch on the second floor was the smallest and coziest; the sound of the rain hitting the porch's tin roof remained forever in her memory. It was papered in a pink floral design that matched a chintz-covered dressing table, and the view from its two windows, curtained in white muslin, was of the luxuriant gardens across the street. A smoothly woven straw mat covered the floor, and the simple furnishings included a small white desk, slender rocking chair, and white-painted iron bed.

The valedictorian of his class at the University of Virginia, Judge Anthony Dickerson Sayre was a formidable man, president of the Alabama State Senate, and a circuit court judge at the time Zelda and Scott met. He later served as associate justice of the Alabama Supreme Court. A brilliant lawmaker—often referred to as "the brains of the bench"—he was famous in legal circles for never having his opinions overturned. He neither smoked nor drank and was usually in bed each night by eight-thirty. Every morning he walked to the corner and caught the tram to the capitol. Because of poor eyesight (which Zelda inherited), he had never learned to drive. "He was considered a great Judge, so much so that when it rained, the conductor of the streetcar which ran down to the Supreme Court building, and which he caught every morning, would stop the streetcar and walk for two blocks with an umbrella to fetch him." Dignified and reserved, he could become an animated conversationalist when the mood struck him, and shared a gentle sense of humor with his family. Though he had many friends, he cultivated no particular intimates. Like Zelda, who was exceptional in the way she drew young people to her, he, too, possessed an affinity for small children. The son of Daniel Sayre, editor of the *Montgomery Post* and an influential figure in Masonic politics, Anthony Sr. was not interested in acquiring material things. He so disapproved of debt that he refused to purchase a house because it meant carrying a mortgage. Yet, while they never became wealthy, the Sayres always had a cook, laundress, handyman, and, when necessary, a nurse to care for infants. Zelda's nurse had been a large, handsome black woman called Aunt Julia who lived in a small house in the rear yard and dressed in a starched white apron and cap. Totally absorbed in his work, Judge Sayre provided a strong, assuring presence to his family but little warmth or affection. Zelda tried piercing his remoteness by capturing his attention with her antics; when this proved unsuccessful she determinedly sought the attention of other men.

Zelda inherited her father's keen intelligence. Her ability to use words and witty metaphors, however, came from her mother, who had aspired to be an actress or opera singer and had studied elocution in Philadelphia during the winter of 1878. Thwarted by her own father, who considered a theatrical career socially unacceptable, Minnie placated her creative ambitions by writing poetry for local newspapers, giving singing lessons, and producing plays and skits for community theater. She wanted her daughters to have the opportunities denied her, and especially encouraged Zelda's creative endeavors by making her costumes for local charity productions and encouraging her interest in ballet. One astute reporter for the *Montgomery Advertiser*, commenting on Zelda's dancing, observed: "Already she is in the crowd at the Country Club every Saturday night and at the script dances every other night of the week. . . . She might dance like Pavlowa [*sic*] if her nimble feet were not so busy keeping up with the pace of a string of young but ardent admirers set for her." The paper dispatched a photographer to take Zelda's picture. At fifteen, in a ballerina's tulle dress and ornate headpiece, her arms gracefully uplifted, she already appeared supremely confident.

As the youngest child, Zelda was always called "baby" by her parents. Pampered and indulged, she developed finicky eating habits and became petulant whenever food was not to her liking. "I never considered Zelda especially spoiled by Mama, except about food," Rosalind recalled. "If she did not like what the meal offered, she would refuse to eat and become cross or insistent, then Mama would produce something from the icebox or pantry that was acceptable. Not the proper feeding, but it had no bad effect, for she was a healthy child and teenager, stronger than the rest of us." Accustomed to eating only what she wanted and determined to remain slim, she practically lived on tomato sandwiches. On dates, she was partial to midnight suppers of fresh spinach and champagne. The specificity of her culinary likes and dislikes so fascinated Fitzgerald that he later incorporated them into the character of Gloria in *The Beautiful and Damned*. "There was, for example, her stomach. She was used to certain dishes, and she had a strong conviction that she could not possibly eat anything else. There must be a lemonade and a tomato sandwich late in the morning, then a light lunch with a stuffed tomato. Not only did she require food from a selection of a dozen dishes, but in addition this food must be prepared in just a certain way."

Encouraged by a mother who believed she could master anything, Zelda grew fearless in her approach to life, tackling even the most dangerous feats without hesitation. Unconventional and independent, capricious and imaginative, she possessed enormous stamina and performed even the most elementary tasks with competitive drive. Sara Haardt recalled that "She had . . . a great deal more than the audacity or the indestructible vitality of those war generations. In addition, she had a superb courage—the courage that is not so much defiance as a forgetfulness of danger, gossips or barriers." She was drawn to excitement and danger as a child, climbing trees that others shunned, teasing boys mercilessly, and seldom encountering anyone she could not out-distance. Once, when forced to baby-sit her cousin Noonie, she placed the little girl high in the oak tree near the back of her house and said, "Stay right there until I get back." Then she ran off with friends, returning in an hour with a candy stick and the warning, "Don't you dare tell on me."

At ten she was interviewed by Tallulah Bankhead's aunt Marie for an article entitled "Children of the Alabama Judiciary" to appear in the *Montgomery Advertiser*. Describing Zelda as a friendly and candid child, Bankhead took her at her word. Zelda asserted that Robber and Indian were her favorite games because they involved running, and that she admired the Indians for their fearlessness and because they were "such great riders and swimmers." While claiming reading and geography were her favorite school subjects, and drawing and painting favorite pastimes, it is clear that as a child she was always more interested in playing outdoors. A typical tomboy, she'd swing from the magnolia tree in her yard or run barefoot at breakneck speed down the street after a dog. "I was very active as a child and never tired, always running with no hat or coat . . . ," Zelda recalled. "I liked houses under construction and often I walked on the open roofs; I liked to jump from high places . . . I liked to dive and climb in the tops of trees. When I was a little girl I had great confidence in myself, even to the extent of walking by myself against life as it was then. I did not have a single feeling of inferiority, or shyness, or doubt, and no moral principles." One of her favorite pranks was to call out the fire department on false alarms. She once telephoned the fire station to say her cousin Noonie was stuck on the roof, then climbed up herself so they would have someone to rescue.

Younger by nine years than her nearest sister and six years younger than her brother, Zelda was never really close to any of her siblings, but saw more of Rosalind than anyone else. Both Tootsie and Tilde were attractive and popular in Montgomery society long before Zelda. Tilde was a classic beauty with lovely soft-cut features, creamy skin, and large dark eyes, but reserved. Marjorie was artistically inclined and excellent at pen-and-ink drawings. But she was a sickly child and prone to depression during much of her life. Anthony was as mischievous as Zelda and always a troublemaker; at two years old, he lined the chamber pots up on the front porch and filled them with coal to welcome the governor's wife. Also a talented artist, he became an aimless and rebellious youth who dropped out of Auburn, suffered a nervous breakdown, and eventually took his own life. He was the third member of Zelda's immediate family to do so: Zelda's maternal grandmother and her sister had both committed suicide. When Zelda entered high school there were no other children living at home. Anthony was employed in Mobile as a civil engineer. Rosalind, after working for six years as society editor and general reporter for the *Montgomery Journal*, had married Newman Smith. Marjorie had quit teaching school to marry Minor Brinson. As the first girl from a respected family to take a job other than teaching, Clothilde raised eyebrows by working as a teller in the First National Bank, where men lined up outside to stare at her. She held that job until marrying John M. Palmer.

Compared to her more stylish sisters, Zelda was uninterested in clothes or fashion. "During those days, she cared very little for clothes, was even slouchy at times," one classmate recalled. "Her two older sisters were 'out' and the new clothes and family's attention went to them. Zelda's dresses were often hand-me-downs. Maybe that is why she preferred to wear her middy blouse and skirt, the uniform of high school girls at the time. However, if she had cared enough for pretty clothes to demand them, she could have had them, I'm sure. Old Judge Sayre, as we called him, was comfortably fixed. They lived in a big two-story home just off Mildred Street. Judge Sayre was always immaculately dressed and dignified; Mrs. Sayre seemed to be a nonconformist."

Since childhood, Zelda had always dreamed of becoming a ballerina. She began taking dance lessons at the age of six and continued training with several good teachers. In 1917 she enrolled in a new dancing class offered by Professor Weisner, a talented coach who had suddenly appeared in the city. "The Gentiles thought he was Gentile and the Jews thought he was a Jew; and no one could say where he had come from or why a dancing master as talented as he should come to Montgomery." Under his skillful tutelage, Zelda starred in numerous pageants and entertainments, receiving top billing in ballet recitals at the Grand Theatre. The *Montgomery Advertiser* of 1917 noted one such performance: "A feature of the evening was the exquisite solo dance given by Miss Zelda Sayre, a pretty and popular member of the younger set. Miss Sayre wore a costume of blue and gold tarleton, and gave the dance in a spotlight." Another event did not go as well. Sara Haardt recalled how, portraying Mother England in a wartime pageant, "in a resplendent costume of crimson and white, with a shining helmet and sword, [Zelda] marched on the stage and faced the tense, waiting crowd. The moment before, in the dressing-room, she had recited her speech letter perfect: '. . . Interrupted in these benevolent pursuits for over three years, I have been engaged in bloody warfare and the end is not yet. O, America, young republic of the West, blood of my blood and faith of my faith, for humanity's sake together we fight! . . . The Stars and Stripes on the battle lines of glorious France have strengthened my hand and filled my heart with cheer. In this hour of great peril, the young manhood of your great Republic is needed in all its strength!' But now, as she stood there, her tongue was suddenly paralyzed. 'Interrupted—' she began. 'Interrupted—' she began again. 'Interrupted—' It was hopeless. With a shrug of her shoulders, she said in a clear voice, 'I'm sorry, I've been permanently interrupted,' and walked off the stage with great dignity."

Seizing every opportunity to improve her singing and dancing talents, Zelda kept a series of scrapbooks documenting her achievements—dance cards, school photos, complimentary reviews of dance recitals, newspaper clippings, and letters from admirers. Upon seeing her photo in the newspaper, one stranger wrote: "Dear Miss Sayre, I saw your picture in the Montgomery paper, which my parents sent to me here at school and I wonder if you would care to correspond? Your picture was lovely." She pasted this missive in her scrapbook with all the others, and while relishing the adoration of strangers, never considered providing a reply.

Days were filled to overflowing with activities, and later she recalled how, "In the afternoons, after we snatched a mouthful to eat, we went swimming in some inconceivably muddy hole—and at night we were [roller] skating again, in mad, milling crowds, or dancing violently. For us, life had become spectacular, bombastic, almost unbearably exciting. There were places to go, and everybody was in glowing spirits." Delighted by her audacity and nerve, girlfriends followed her lead, swearing each other to silence in fear their parents would learn of Zelda's behavior and forbid them to see her. As to whether Judge Sayre and his wife knew the extent of Zelda's outrageous conduct, her sister Rosalind always believed the secrecy worked: "I do not believe that he [Judge Sayre] and mama were aware of Zelda's young antics; they were old people still living in the way of their own era, out of touch with youth but for Zelda's flitting presence and a small grandchild or two, not knowing what young people were doing or how war was changing them. Even to me Zelda was just a girl having a good time, as I had done but in the more formal way of my time, and if she was 'talked about' —this did not reach us."

Voted champion swimmer and diver of her senior class, Zelda was compulsive about the sport and would sneak into the Huntington College pool, dive from the highest boards at the YWCA and Bell Street pools, and swim longer and faster than anyone else. For shock value, she wore a flesh-colored, silk jersey Annette Kellerman bathing suit that from a distance made her appear nude. Mother of synchronized swimming and creator of the one-piece bathing suit, the Australian-born Kellerman championed less restrictive swimming attire and was arrested in Boston for wearing a one-piece swimsuit. In 1914, when she told the press "I can't swim wearing more stuff than you hang on a clothesline," girls like Zelda applauded her audacity. One of Zelda's favorite swimming spots was Roquemore's gravel pit, where she would dive from the high crane others were afraid even to climb. One classmate remembered how "she swam and dove as well as most of the boys and better than many. She was absolutely fearless; there was a board rigged up at the swimming pool from which everyone was afraid to dive, but Zelda did it without a thought." Once, while swimming with girls at the pool behind the chemical plant, she was preparing for a shallow dive from the high board when her arms became entangled in the straps of her suit. Without a second thought, she shed her suit and naked "stood poised for an instant like a water nymph, rose upon her toes, and leaped from the board."

In addition to swimming, Zelda also roller skated better than anyone else. In 1918 it was the latest craze and she practiced on the Whitfield's paved backyard. It was thrilling to skate down Sayre Street hill from Chilton School to the synagogue, turning only at the last moment to avoid the cobblestones and traffic. Recalling those days with amusement, she told Sara Haardt: "I remember playing tag and police and Robber lazily in our yard around the Old Ship Church one day—and suddenly, almost the next day, it seemed—everything was changed. Life had suddenly become exciting, dangerous; a crazy vitality possessed us, and I felt it as I leaned over to fasten the straps of my skates the moment before I went sailing wildly down the middle of Perry Street hill, screeching at the top of my lungs and catching hold of the backs of automobiles as they dashed up the hill again."

Zelda had a way of emboldening her friends. Sara Mayfield, Zelda's childhood friend and author of *Exiles from Paradise*, once tried copying Zelda's roller-skating tactics, forcing Zelda to rescue her from disaster. "Listen, you'll break your neck," admonished Zelda, pulling Sara from the stream of traffic. "Wait until a dray comes along to pull us back up the hill; then you can go down holding on to me until you learn how to make the turn." Her sister Rosalind recalled that "she was exceptional in the way she drew other children about her by the imaginative amusements she devised. They always liked her and she them." One day Zelda convinced Eleanor Browder to talk the streetcar conductor into letting them drive the trolley. Of course it went off the tracks and the man was almost fired. And though her father decried such irresponsible acts and chastised her for them, Zelda continued doing as she pleased.

From childhood on, she consciously set out to rebel against custom—refusing to cross her legs at the ankle, revealing her developing bosom, and saying whatever came to mind. "When we were in our teens," her friend Eleanor Addison recalled, "Zelda dived off the highest boards, skated at break-neck speed down the Perry Street hill, with passing automobiles making the descent doubly hazardous, and urged more and more speed from her swains as they drove to and from parties while the rest of us contented ourselves with a quieter pace. By day she was healthy and hoydenish, a veritable dynamo, by night a beautiful enchantress. . . . When she commandeered a streetcar bright and early one Sunday morning and went clanging down Court Street with the befuddled motorman practically hanging on the ropes, the town criers lifted their eyes to the heavens and said 'disgraceful.' When she danced like an angel in a pink ballet costume at some charity affair, the same town criers murmured 'beautiful.' "

While her mother allowed her free rein and her father complained to no avail, her rebellious personality by sixteen was firmly established. Recalled one friend, "Zelda lived just around the corner from me on Pleasant Avenue. She went in our crowd and was my friend in high school days although she was different from us even then—not so different by nature, perhaps, as by the fact that she was unsupervised. The rest of us went directly home from school unless we had permission from home to do otherwise; Zelda could go to town or home with someone without contacting her mother. The rest of us stayed home and studied on school nights, but Zelda went at will, often dropping in after supper to talk. She was smart but never studied regularly. Her grades were passing but seldom above average. She was amiable, kind, happy-go-lucky, uninhibited and undisciplined. She followed her own interests to the neglect of duties. She was calm, soft-spoken and even-tempered, but talked lots."

Her exploits were matched only by Tallulah Bankhead. Two years older than Zelda, Tallulah was also an athletic tomboy who performed somersaults and handstands in front of the capitol building and cartwheeled before the great circular staircase of its rotunda. Her mother, Adelaide Eugenia Sledge Bankhead, had died at twenty-one from blood poisoning just three weeks after Tallulah's birth. The newborn was shuffled between her grandmother's house in Jasper and her aunt Marie Bankhead's home in Montgomery. A successful career woman, Marie Bankhead directed the Department of Archives and History with her husband, Dr. Thomas Owens, a cousin of Sara Mayfield. Tallulah grew up with progressive ideas about what women might achieve. She was born in Jasper, a small town north of Birmingham, and like Zelda, was the daughter of an attorney and statesman. Her father, William Brockman Bankhead, was a U.S. congressman and former Speaker of the House of Representatives. Her uncle and grandfather were both U.S. senators and influential politicians in Washington and Alabama. The Bankheads were better known than the Sayres, and their exalted status in Montgomery gave Tallulah and her sister, Eugenia, the same privileges accorded Zelda. The sisters did as they pleased, but Eugenia, older by one year and the prettier of the two, was more exuberant and boisterous. Tallulah, like her grandmother before her, was named for North Georgia's Tallulah Falls in Tallulah Gorge State Park, spanning the border between Habersham and Rabun Counties.

The two Bankhead girls competed with Zelda for the honor of being "the most talked about girls in town." Their scorn of convention made them symbols of the emacipated woman, and Tallulah's antics became known as "tallulabaloos." Montgomery residents were constantly astonished by the three girls' behavior on Goat Hill, the grassy slope leading down from the capitol. "Even in those days," Sara Mayfield recalled, "both of them had dash, a style and daring that left me wide-eyed and open-mouthed with admiration. For Zelda and Dutch, as we called Tallulah, were personalities and performers long before they became famous; Tallulah specializing in cartwheels, backbends, mimicry and song-and-dance routines." Zelda and Tallulah routinely performed song-and-dance numbers, gymnastics, and dramatic sketches on the steps of the capitol. Tallulah was so limber she could do a back-bend (often exposing the fact that she wore no underclothes) and pluck a scarf from the floor with her teeth. Her best routines were hilarious parodies of Miss Gussie Woodruff, the prim, white-haired spinster who ran a private girls' school in Montgomery and always wore long black dresses with high collars.

Tallulah was as uninterested in schoolwork as Zelda. After dropping out of Margaret Booth's School for Females at 117 Sayre Street (near Zelda's home), she suffered additional educational trials in New York, with Eugenia, at the Academy of the Sacred Heart, then at Mary Baldwin Academy in Staunton, Virginia, and finally at Fairmont Seminary in Washington, D.C. But after that she'd had enough. "If you know your Bible and your Shakespeare and can shoot craps," she said, "you have a liberal education."

Throughout her teenage years, Zelda dreamed of becoming a professional dancer or an actress like Tallulah. Her disdain for school was evident in her lackluster academic record. Because of her father's membership on Montgomery's Board of Education and his support of public schools, she attended Sayre Street Grammar School and Sidney Lanier High. Girls from Zelda's social class generally attended Miss Booth's, the private academy owned by Lawton Campbell's aunt. Founded in 1914, it was housed in a private home and limited its enrollment to one hundred girls from Montgomery's wealthier families. Its aim was to prepare students for southern women's colleges training schoolteachers, but these private academies also served as excellent places to house young women until they made good marriages. At the coeducational, public Sidney Lanier High School, Zelda took four years of what was termed classic curriculum—English literature, history, French, Latin, geography, mathematics, physics, chemistry, and physiology. With the exception of English and math, she found school boring and had no interest in going on to college. Most of her studies seemed irrelevant to her, and, like Scott, she seldom did homework, cut classes, and did just enough work to pass. Her best friends, Eleanor Browder and Livyre Hart, followed her every move. "We played hookey almost every day from school," Zelda readily admitted, "straggling along the streets in a kind of dare. We didn't know—or care—where we were going. Sometimes we'd stop at old Mr. McCormack's grocery store at the edge of Boguehomme and buy a lot of loose crackers and dill pickles and chocolate nigger babies [a type of candy] and eat them as we walked along. It always seemed to be Spring, as I look back now, with the whole town filled with this smell of kiss-me-at-the-gate and the red-bud blooming. When we were tired, if we were near town, we would go in a picture show and sit in the dark of the theater while the janitor swept around us and picked up peanut shells and tin foil we dropped in the aisles." Inscribed under her unflattering 1917 yearbook photograph was the revealing epigram: "What would happen if—Zelda Sayre ever said anything serious—and Eleanor Browder came to school on time?"

No photograph ever captured Zelda's unique, unusual beauty. Ring Lardner Jr. agreed: "I have never seen a photograph of her that conveyed any real sense of what she looked like, or at least the way she looked to me. A camera recorded the imperfections of her face, missing the coloring and vitality that transcended them so absolutely." Her flawless skin tanned in summer to a deep brown, and her high cheekbones gave her the look of a fair-haired Cherokee crowned with a full head of silky, honey-gold hair. There was a stubbornness in her face and a piercing quality in her gray-green eyes. "She was not a legitimate beauty—thank God," recalled Gerald Murphy, who later became one of the Fitzgeralds' closest friends, "her beauty was not legitimate at all. It was all in her eyes. They were strange eyes, brooding but not sad, severe, almost masculine in their directness. She possessed an astounding gaze, one doesn't find it often in women, perfectly level and head-on." Her eyes suddenly could become intent and piercing, a glare caused in part from poor eyesight. Scott noticed it early in their relationship and later told her doctor, C. Jonathan Slocom, at Beacon House, that she was "almost totally blind in one eye from some childish accident." Her sister Rosalind had another explanation, remembering, "The specialist to whom Mama took her for her sinus trouble discovered that she had no retina in one eye. He told Mama about it, but I feel sure that Mama did not tell Zelda, or that Zelda ever realized it. I did not know until long after Zelda's death, when the doctor told me. It may have accounted for her squinting at times when she looked closely at things."

Her expression was so animated that no two photographs of her appear alike. "Zelda was really a great beauty," recalled John Biggs, Scott's Princeton roommate and later Zelda's lawyer, "but her pictures never showed this because she was terribly unphotogenic." Yet everything about her—from the long lashes of her deep-set gray-green eyes, down to her evenly tanned and shapely legs—was captivating. The Montgomery newspaper agreed: "Of bright, vivacious intellect, unusual beauty and charming manners, she was unusually admired." Endowed with an exceptionally lovely figure, Zelda once boasted she could sell it "to Cartier's for a gold mesh sweat shirt." The neighborhood boys spied on her from bushes around the Sayre's back porch, but when Minnie was warned about these peeping Toms, she remained unconcerned. Proud of her daughter's beautiful body, she saw no cause for embarrassment, a remarkable attitude to possess in an ultra-conservative southern town.

Designated Alabama's state capital in 1846, Zelda's hometown of Montgomery combined the two rival settlements of East Alabama and New Philadelphia, serving briefly as the capital of the Confederacy. The town's center was Court Square at the intersection of Dexter, Commerce, and Court Streets. There, vendors sold their goods, auctioneers hawked cotton and cattle, and volunteers were recruited for war. By 1900, many impressive structures loomed over Court Square, including the Italianate Winter Building and Central Bank. The Old Exchange Hotel was a popular meeting place for businessmen and politicians and its ballroom the site of Montgomery's most prestigious celebrations.

Not since the Civil War had there been so many outsiders in town, as nearby Camp Sheridan and Camp Taylor filled with new recruits to undergo training for World War I. On Friday evenings at the Old Exchange Hotel, where Mrs. Jefferson Davis had been received as First Lady of the Confederacy, Montgomery's young women welcomed the visiting soldiers. As Ida and Sara Haardt danced nimbly up and down the hotel's steps with their partners, Zelda circled the Old Exchange floor from midnight until dawn with scores of officers from surrounding encampments. Sara Haardt, who later married H. L. Mencken, recalled Zelda's extraordinary appearance there at one holiday ball. "I saw her as she had looked at that last Christmas dance we were together, wearing a flame dress and gold-laced slippers, her eyes starry and mocking, flirting with an immense feather fan. Her bronze-gold hair was curled in a thousand ringlets, and as she whirled about, they twinkled enchantingly like little bells. Around her flashed hundreds of jellybeans—the Southern youth of the day—in formal black broadcloth and pearl-studded fronts and hundreds of other flappers in gold slippers and rainbow-colored skirts, but they seemed somehow vain and inarticulate beside her. Beauty they had, and grace, and a certain reckless abandon—yet none of them could match the glance of gay derision that flickered beneath the black edge of her eyelashes—and none of them could dance as she did, like a flame or a wind."

Full of energy even after dancing all night, Zelda would be up early the next morning working as a volunteer for the Service League, distributing coffee and doughnuts to soldiers in the train station canteen. At other times she rolled bandages for the Red Cross or sold tags on downtown streets for the innumerable benefits supporting the war effort. "Some of the girls who were heads of the committees, thought that because we talked so much, we of the younger generations would never get any work done, but we sold more tags and folded more bandages than all the rest of them put together. It was as if we were possessed with an insatiable vitality."

By eighteen, Zelda had already dated the city's wealthiest and most well bred young men: Peyton Spottswood Matthis, Dan Cody, John Sellers, Lloyd Hooper, and Leon Ruth. Matthis, one of her favorites and Montgomery's most eligible bachelor, was popular with women because of his gracious manners and sense of humor. Later fictionalized as the "Dayton Bee" in John Kohn's book *The Cradle*, Matthis was blessed with a multitude of talents. Proprietor of the Montgomery Marble Works and possessing a maturity beyond his years, he was highly artistic, creating two sculptural masterpieces for the town's cemetery—*The Wings of Death* and *The Broken Column*. Matthis and John Sellers became known as "the Gold Dust Twins" because of their knack for making money, and each was renowned for giving their dates a good time. It is likely that Sellers seduced Zelda while they were still in high school.

Zelda was the most sought-after girl at gatherings for northern soldiers, and young aviators soon took to doing air stunts over the Sayre's house on Pleasant Street, looping and barrel-rolling their planes to win her attention. The daily flybys continued until two second lieutenants, Henry Watson and Lincoln Weaver, crashed on the nearby Speedway while attempting a tailspin. Camp Taylor's commanding officer immediately issued orders that such frivolous activities cease. On another occasion, infantrymen from Camp Sheridan paraded before her house and executed a drill in her honor. Zelda loved the attention.

Her behavior embarrassed and infuriated Zelda's father, whose frequent attempts to discipline her failed utterly. Recalling that wild year, Zelda told Sara Haardt: "I danced every night . . . through the late spring and summer until the Lenten season of another spring. There were Country Club dances, college and Pan-Hellenic dances, benefit dances for the Red Cross and Liberty Loan drives, officers' dances, Jackson Club and Beauvoir Club dances where mostly only officers went, Camp Sheridan dances, Beauty Balls and Folly Balls. . . ." But it was the enlisted men's dances, which often ended in scuffles, that provided the element of danger she found most exciting. "The ones I enjoyed the most were the privates' dances down in the dirty old City Hall auditorium. Only a few girls went, because it was supposed to be rough, and there were no officers present—there weren't even any intermissions because there weren't enough girls to go around. We danced from nine until one, without once stopping, to the most marvelous music in the world—their bands were always better than the officers' . . . and somehow it brought the War, in all its tragedy and waste and horror, much more vividly to us. I'll never forget the way they used to play 'No Name Waltz,' 'Road to Home' and 'Rose of No Man's Land.' " Another girl might have been ostracized for such behavior, but because she was a Sayre, Zelda's social position in Montgomery was firmly established according to southern society. As a member of one of Alabama's best families, related to many other distinguished families, including that of Senator John Tyler, one of the state's best-known politicians, Zelda could bend the rules without jeopardizing her social position. In addition to being the daughter of Judge Anthony Sayre, who would later become an associate justice of the Alabama Supreme Court, Zelda was considered southern aristocracy.

Scott Fitzgerald was eagerly awaiting embarkation for the European front when he and Zelda met. He had applied for his commission in the spring of 1917 following three weeks of military training at Princeton, having unearthed a federal statute authorizing officer status for those speaking French. It was a proficiency he did not really have. Nevertheless, that summer he underwent examinations at Fort Snelling for a provisional appointment as a second lieutenant in the regular army. Returning to Princeton, he planned on remaining only until his infantry commission arrived. Most of his friends had already enlisted and left the campus: Alex McKaig was an ensign in the navy; John Peale Bishop, his closest buddy, was in the infantry; and Edmund Wilson, who had joined the Hospital Corps, awaited orders to France.

Scott's commission came on October 26, and on November 20

he received orders to leave for Officers' Training Camp at Fort Leavenworth, Kansas. The young captain in charge of his platoon was an ambitious West Pointer named Ike Eisenhower, but Fitzgerald was unimpressed. As poor a soldier as Princeton undergraduate, Scott was more interested in writing than military training. During lectures on trench warfare, he made voluminous notes for his novel-in-progress, "The Romantic Egoists," and during evenings and weekends worked on the manuscript at the officers' club. "Every Saturday at 1 o'clock, when the week's work was over, I hurried up to the Officers' Club and there in a corner of a room filled with smoke, conversation and rattling newspapers, I wrote a 120,000-word novel on the consecutive weekends of three months."

In February of 1918 he took leave and, sequestering himself in Princeton's Cottage Club, polished his novel about a young man coming of age. When it was finished, he sent it to John Biggs's father's law office in Wilmington, Delaware. Biggs had briefly been his Princeton roommate and had offered the typing services of his father's secretary, Mrs. Bradford. Scott instructed her to make only one typed copy, which she did, sending it back to him along with his original longhand manuscript. The package never arrived. This was the first of two mishaps connected with his manuscript. (The second occurred a year later when he sent the revised version to Scribner's via Tom Daniels.) Upset but undaunted, Fitzgerald rewrote an entire second version from notes and memory, and once again sent it to Biggs with the same instructions. The new manuscript was much improved. This time, however, Biggs kept a second typed copy in the office, posting the original to Fitzgerald, who forwarded it to Shane Leslie, a Scribner's author and former teacher at Fitzgerald's prep school, Newman. On May 16, 1918, Leslie sent it on to Charles Scribner II, commenting that it expressed an authentic sense of America's youth. "In spite of its disguises, it has given me a vivid picture of the American generation that is hastening to the war. I marvel at its crudity and its cleverness."

Fitzgerald's Princeton English professor, Christian Gauss, had suggested Scribner's because Charles Scribner and his younger brother Arthur were Princeton graduates—Charles the class of 1875 and Arthur the class of 1881. Fitzgerald had known Charles's son on campus and there were other Princeton graduates working as Scribner's editors who Fitzgerald felt would enjoy those chapters dealing with their alma mater. But Scribner's editor in chief, William Crary Brownell, took an instant dislike to the manuscript, as did many of his colleagues. Only Maxwell Evarts Perkins, who had joined the firm in 1910 and was Brownell's apprentice, recognized the manuscript's potential. It was five months before Fitzgerald heard from Perkins, who rejected it but encouraged Scott to try another revision. His primary complaints were that the story did not advance to a conclusion, and that the hero drifted from one situation to another with no real awareness or understanding. Writing Fitzgerald, "The story does not culminate in anything as it must to justify the readers' interest," he suggested changes for a revised submission. "We hope we shall see it again and we shall then reread it immediately." In two months an improved version arrived on Perkins's desk. Charles Scribner II liked it, but the older editors still voted no, and again it was returned to Fitzgerald who, disappointed and temporarily dejected, put the manuscript away.

Scott had not anticipated this second rejection and was upset not only by the delay in finding a publisher but also by the interminable time it was taking to see military action. In February of 1918 he was transferred with the Ninth Division of the Forty-fifth Infantry to Camp Zachary Taylor near Louisville, Kentucky, then posted to Camp Gordon in Georgia, and finally in April of 1918 sent to Camp Sheridan near Montgomery. His Princeton classmate John Peale Bishop impatiently wrote from France, "When are you coming? God I wish you'd hurry up. Aren't you almost a soldier now? We'll get a room in town the first night you are here, and read Brooke and Keats all night."

Princeton had given Fitzgerald an air of sophistication that made him appear very different from the southern boys to whom Zelda was accustomed. He stood out from fellow soldiers, "better dressed in their uniforms than ever before in their lives." Attired in his hand-tailored uniform, he represented a world Zelda sought to enter. "He smelled like new goods," Zelda later wrote in her thinly veiled, autobiographical novel, *Save Me the Waltz*, and "being close to him with her face in the space between his ear and his stiff army collar was like being initiated into the subterranean reserves of a fine fabric store exuding the delicacy of cambrics and linen and luxury bound in bales." With hundreds of soldiers in town and not enough girls, Zelda recalled in her story "Southern Girl" how "girls too tall or too prim for the taste of Jeffersonville [Montgomery] were dragged from their spinsterly pursuits to dance with the soldiers and make them feel less lonely through the summer nights. You can imagine how the popular ones fared!"

Since he was assigned to Headquarters Company, First Lieutenant Fitzgerald was allowed to wear a custom-designed Brooks Brothers uniform and, instead of puttees, cream-colored boots extending up to just below his knees. With his chiseled nose, green eyes, and blond hair parted down the middle, he made an impressive appearance despite his modest height of five feet eight and a half inches. Handsome in a pretty way and projecting excitement and optimism, Fitzgerald seemed confident around women, though he was fully aware of his shortcomings: "I didn't have the two top things; great animal magnetism or money. I had the two second things though: good looks and intelligence. So I always got the top girl."

Before he met Zelda, Fitzgerald had dated some other local girls. He had gotten their names from Montgomery native Ludlow Fowler, a Princeton classmate. Even after meeting Zelda, he continued to see May Steiner, a popular date of several camp officers. But Steiner's relationship with Fitzgerald was never serious, in part because of Fitzgerald's continuing melancholy over Ginevra King's impending marriage to Ensign William Mitchell, an instructor at the Naval Air Station in Key West, Florida. Fitzgerald had been introduced to Ginevra King, a debutante from Lake Forest, Illinois, and daughter of the fabulously wealthy Charles Garfield King, by his St. Paul friend Marie Hersey in January 1915. Along with a host of other suitors, he had pursued Ginevra the following year. Just sixteen when they met, Ginevra visited Scott at Princeton and rendezvoused with him in New York at the Midnight Frolic and Ritz Roof. But it was a superficial romance that Fitzgerald fantasized out of proportion. And there was unpleasant gossip. Scott overheard somebody remark at a house party they attended in Lake Forest that "poor boys shouldn't think of marrying rich girls" and believed the comment was directed at him. Ginevra's indifference toward the relationship finally registered when he asked for his letters back and discovered she had not kept them. "I'm sorry you think that I would hold them up to you as I never did think they meant anything," she wrote, offering instead to return his Triangle pin. Fitzgerald, for his part, had not only kept her letters, but had had them typed and bound in a volume numbering three hundred pages.

Ginevra would always represent the unattainable girl. He would use elements of her personality to create Isabelle Borge and Rosalind Connage in *This Side of Paradise* and his most famous heroine, Daisy Buchanan in *The Great Gatsby*: "Her voice . . . was full of money—that was the inexhaustible charm that rose and fell in it, the jingle of it, the cymbals' song of it. . . . High in a white palace the King's daughter, the golden girl. . . ." As a member of the privileged class, Ginevra represented a world Fitzgerald envied, and his conviction that the rich were a breed apart was born of this rejection. "Let me tell you about the very rich," he wrote. "They are different from you and me. They possess and enjoy early, and it does something to them, makes them soft where we are hard, and cynical where we are trustful, in a way that, unless you were born rich, it is very difficult to understand. They think, deep in their hearts, that they are better than we are because we had to discover the compensations and refuges of life for ourselves. Even when they enter deep into our world or sink below us, they still think that they are better than we are. They are different." His brief sojourn in King's world of privilege forever altered his attitude toward the poor, which he described in his first novel. "Never before in his life had Amory considered poor people. He thought cynically how completely he was lacking in all human sympathy. O. Henry had found in these people romance, pathos, love, hate— Amory saw only coarseness, physical filth, and stupidity. . . . 'I detest poor people,' thought Amory suddenly. 'I hate them for being poor.' "

After rejections by both Scribner's and Ginevra King, Fitzgerald was primed in the summer of 1918 for a new emotional attachment. But it would take the sparkle of Zelda Sayre to reenergize him. When he met Zelda that July in Montgomery, Fitzgerald recognized her as another golden girl and was absolutely determined not to lose her. One of the youngest to date northern soldiers, she was also their most popular choice. Sara Haardt recalled her precocious entry into the debutante's social circle. "One day, a lady who was on the committee arranging a Beauty Ball for the entertainment of the soldiers, offered little Zelda Sayre, whom she still regarded as a school-girl, a dollar if she would dance a ballet she had learned at dancing school. Zelda danced—in silver slippers and spangled skirts—and later when she appeared on the ball-room floor for her first, formal, grown-up dance, she had the most thrilling 'rush' of her life. The next night was the formal Saturday-night dance at the Country Club where, according to tradition, only very grown-up debutantes and very dignified married people danced, but Zelda had received her first invitation during a magical waltz at the Beauty Ball—and Zelda went."

Thereafter, the country club, where she frequently was asked to perform dance solos, became her domain. On the warm July evening Fitzgerald first saw her there, she was performing "Dance of the Hours" before the crowded ballroom. Afterward she was surrounded by a swarm of admirers. No sooner would one officer dance off with her than another would cut in. Fitzgerald introduced himself, then swirled her around the dance floor and tried mightily to charm her. He was promptly rebuffed, however, when he suggested a midnight date. "I never make late dates with fast workers," she laughingly told him. He called the next day only to learn that she was booked for weeks. An expert at making suitors jealous, she heightened Fitzgerald's interest to a frenzied state within days. By the following Saturday, he found himself enormously agitated by the sight of her kissing a date under the overhanging gas lamp of a telephone booth near the club. Accelerating his pursuit, Scott convinced her to see him, and on July 24 hosted a country club party in honor of her eighteenth birthday. It was a magical evening she never forgot. "Remember there were three pines on one side and four on the other the night you gave me my birthday party and you were a young Lieutenant and I was a fragrant phantom, wasn't I? And it was a radiant night, a night of soft conspiracy and the trees agreed that it was all going to be for the best."

Though a year had passed since Ginevra King's rejection, Scott was not entirely over her, and Zelda reminded him of the Chicago debutante. Fitzgerald told Zelda how closely she resembled Isabelle (modeled after King) in his unfinished novel. Two weeks into their courtship, he gave her the chapter entitled "Babes in the Wood," in which Isabelle was prominent. Never having been courted in this way, Zelda was swept off her feet. By fall, Fitzgerald also admitted to being in love, noting the exact day in his ledger as September 7. Just five days later, Zelda presented him with a silver flask bearing the inscription: "Forget Me Not, Zelda. 9/13/18."

One of Zelda's high school classmates recalled that romantic autumn: "We were more closely supervised than girls of our age today. For one of us to date a soldier was unthought of. Not only were these boys soldiers, they were 'Yankees,' foreign enemies. Scott Fitzgerald was one of them. I think it was through her older sister's friends that Zelda met him. We were a little shocked, but admired her for her conquest. They began going steady immediately. She was always more interested in the boys than the rest of us, and she liked to keep her favorite boy guessing by teasing and embarrassing him, good-naturedly on her part—in public. Scott fared as the others had. When he could be in town to see her, instead of keeping him to herself, she would bring him around the corner and join us on the wall in front of our house, the place where we gathered to talk. Scott was good-looking, quiet and sweet. Zelda did enjoy making him blush. He seemed to fit in with our crowd and they would join us in walking back to school meetings and games on Friday and Saturday nights."

Although only five feet five inches, Zelda seemed much taller, and in shoes stood almost eye level with Scott. With a dancer's grace, she appeared to float across a room. Fitzgerald, too, seemed to have "some heavenly support beneath his shoulder blades that lifted his feet from the ground in ecstatic suspension, as if he secretly enjoyed the ability to fly but was walking as a compromise to convention." From the start, they were a matched pair.

But Zelda was not only beautiful; she also possessed the courage and self-confidence Scott lacked. Fitzgerald was determined to impress her, though enticing a girl so tantalizingly elusive, a girl exuding such cool reserve, was no easy task. Years later, Sara Murphy, Gerald's wife, recalled: "I don't believe she liked many people although her manners to everyone were perfect. Her dignity was never lost in the midst of the wildest escapades. No one ever took liberty with Zelda."

Using highly original phrases and syntax, she spoke with a southern accent in a low and husky voice. Only those who knew her best appreciated her unique sense of humor. Sara Haardt described it as a "devastating wit—yet not so much wit as philosophy—so peculiar to the South. . . . When Montgomery was swarming with soldiers' wives as well as soldiers, one particular grand lady was inexplicably annoyed by her high spirits. 'Who is that wild Comanche you've been dancing with?' she asked Fitzgerald during an intermission at a Jackson Club dance. Almost the next moment she had turned to Zelda and inquired in a syrupy voice, 'I don't suppose you wear fur coats very often in this climate.' 'Fur coats?' Zelda Sayre repeated, her soft voice suddenly as sharp as a blade. 'I've never *seen* a fur coat.' "

But that would not be true for long. Zelda's yearning for sophistication and glamour so paralleled Fitzgerald's own desires that Edmund Wilson observed, "If ever there was a pair whose fantasies matched . . . it was Zelda Sayre and Scott Fitzgerald." Zelda once wrote Scott what a psychic had intuited about their relationship: "Mrs. Francesca—who never heard of you—got a message from Ouija for me. Nobody's hands were on it—but hers—and it told us to be married—that we were soul-mates. Theosophists think that two souls are incarnated together—not necessarily at the same time, but are mated—since the time when people were bisexual." For a time, Zelda's mother had been a theosophist, and she and Fitzgerald discussed the philosophy. Later, in *The Beautiful and Damned*, Scott would have Gloria express her beliefs about some people being mirror reflections of each other. "We're twins. . . . Mother says that two souls are sometimes created together—and in love before they're born." Those were also Zelda's thoughts, which she expanded on in *Save Me the Waltz*, having her heroine Alabama explain, "So much she loved the man, so close and closer she felt herself that he became distorted in her vision, like pressing her nose upon a mirror and gazing into her own eyes."

Oddly, the Fitzgeralds looked enough alike to be taken for brother and sister. Scott, with his classical features, was so handsome as to be pretty. Zelda, with her gorgeous coloring and golden hair so vivid that Fitzgerald recalled, "The glow of her hair and cheeks, at once flushed and fragile, made her the most living person he had ever seen." Admittedly, she used rouge and lipstick to heighten her coloring, and was the first in her group to use mascara, but she was also naturally beautiful and always appeared fresh and healthy-looking. Both of them had that well-scrubbed look suggesting youthful innocence. "We were at a large round table with them, Fannie Hurst and other writers in New York at that time," Lillian Gish recalled. "They were both so beautiful, so blond, so clean and so clear—and drinking strait [*sic*] whiskey out of tall tumblers."

Obsessed with cleanliness, Zelda took three or four baths daily. Her high school friend Julia Garland recalled that "she was one of the cleanest people I've ever known. She looked like she'd always just had a bath." Fitzgerald infused Gloria in *The Beautiful and*

Damned with Zelda's predilection for cleanliness. "Always intensely skeptical of her sex, her judgments were now concerned with the question of whether women were or were not clean. By uncleanliness she meant a variety of things, a lack of pride, a slackness in fibre, and most of all, the unmistakable aura of promiscuity. 'Women soil easily,' she said, 'far more easily than men. Unless a girl's very young and brave it's almost impossible for her to go down-hill without a certain hysterical animality, the cunning dirty sort of animality." As casual as she felt about sex, she always took a bath after it, and like Scott associated with intercourse some element of soiling.

Zelda had always preferred men to women, not only because they were less bound by convention but also because women often seemed unclean to her. "You like men better, don't you?" Anthony asks Gloria in *The Beautiful and Damned*. "Oh, much better. I've got a man's mind," she replies. When Anthony counters, "Don't you ever intend to see any women?" Gloria responds: "I don't know. They never seem clean to me." Then, when asked why she wants to marry him, Gloria answers: "Because you're so clean. You're sort of blowy clean like I am. There's two sorts, you know. One's like Dick: he's clean like polished pans. You and I are clean like streams and winds. I can tell whenever I see a person whether he is clean, and if so, which kind of clean he is."

George Jean Nathan revealed Scott's own fixation on women and cleanliness. "During his undergraduate days [Fitzgerald] sent out questionnaires to prospective female dates as to: (1) Whether they had had their hair washed during the day and (2) how many baths they had taken. I can testify from personal observation," he wrote, "that it was his habit, to their consternation, to demand of any female companions in taxicabs that they open their mouths so he might determine that the insides of their teeth were free of tartar."

In the competition to win Zelda—his golden girl—Fitzgerald faced an uphill battle. Her parents strongly opposed the match—he came from a middle-class family, had no money, drank too much, and might easily become a negative influence. Zelda's parents really did not know what to make of the midwesterner who seemed determined to outdistance her other suitors.

Christened Francis Scott Key Fitzgerald, after the composer of America's national anthem, Scott was a distant second cousin of his famous namesake—three times removed on his maternal side.

What many don't know, and it's ironic in Fitzgerald's case, is that "The Star-Spangled Banner" was a set of new words applied to an old drinking tune. Fitzgerald was Irish-Catholic on both sides of his family. His mother, Mollie McQuillan, was the eldest daughter of Philip McQuillan, an Irish immigrant from County Fermanagh who had settled in Illinois with his parents in 1843. Trading supplies to the Indians for furs and hides, McQuillan soon established a thriving grocery business that eventually grew into one of the Midwest's largest wholesale companies. When he died prematurely at forty-three of Bright's disease, he left an estate of nearly $300,000, which enabled his widow to raise their five children comfortably.

An unattractive woman, Mollie McQuillan was twenty-nine when she wed Edward Fitzgerald, manager of a small wicker furniture business in St. Paul, Minnesota. Born near Rockville, Maryland, Edward always considered himself a southerner. He was descended on his mother's side from Marylanders who had served in the Colonial legislatures. A small, quiet man with good manners, he was every inch a gentleman. But throughout his life he lacked energy and ambition. The couple had two daughters who both died in an epidemic three months before Scott's birth on September 24, 1896. Fitzgerald was always convinced the trauma suffered by Mollie Fitzgerald during the last months of pregnancy had permanently affected his mother's emotional well-being. "Three months before I was born," he wrote, "my mother lost her two other children and I think that came first of all though I don't know how it worked exactly." A third daughter, born in 1900, lived only one hour. Fitzgerald's sister Annabel arrived in July of 1901.

Because of the tragic losses she had suffered, Mollie Fitzgerald became an overly protective mother. She kept Scott out of school whenever he had a cold and so pampered him, he later admitted, "I didn't know till 15 that there was anyone in the world except me." Afraid he might contract tuberculosis, which had infected her father and sister, Mollie worried over Scott's every ailment. At an early age, he became a borderline hypochondriac. When it was time to start school and Scott resisted, his mother held him back a year—a reprieve identical to the one accorded Zelda. But spoiled as he was, Scott's sense of his place in the world was clouded by his father's repeated business failures. When Scott was a year and a half, Edward Fitzgerald's wicker factory went bankrupt. He went to work as a salesman for the Procter & Gamble Company and moved the family to Syracuse in upstate New York. But Edward's lack of aggressive energy made him an ineffectual seller of soap, and he was fired in March 1908. Scott always remembered the terrible day. "His father had gone out a comparatively young man, full of strength, full of confidence. He came home that evening an old man, a completely broken man. He had lost his essential drive, his immaculateness of purpose. He was a failure the rest of his days."

From then on Scott paid careful attention to life's circumstances, documenting important events in his ledger book, as though by doing so he could avert failure. In it, he noted that "his father used to drink too much and play baseball in the back yard." And he admitted embarrassment about his feet, writing: "There was a boy named Arnold who went barefooted in his yard and peeled plums. Scott's Freudian shame about his feet kept him from joining in." The second and third toes on his right foot were so bunched and disfigured at the first joint, he seldom allowed them to be seen and wore socks and shoes even on the beach. When Zelda playfully took a photo of his feet and pasted it in her scrapbook, he stealthily ripped the offending portion away.

Scott commented in his ledger that, at seven, he had befriended "Dodo" Clifton (Zelda would later call Scott "Do-Do") but made scant other friends. The family was still living in Syracuse but had been uprooted again, "this time to a flat on East Willow Street. He begins to remember many things, a filthy vacant lot, the haunt of dead cats, a hair-raising buck-board, the little girl whose father was in prison for telling lies, a Rabelaisian incident with Jack Butler, a blow with a baseball bat from the same boy—son of an Army officer—which left a scar that will shine always in the middle of his forehead."

From one rented house to another the Fitzgeralds moved, living for a time in Buffalo before finally returning to St. Paul where Mc-Quillan money became their primary support. Here they occupied a series of rented houses and apartments within blocks of Summit Avenue, St. Paul's most fashionable street. Using her dwindling inheritance, Mollie was able to provide private schooling for her two children. But Scott was continually ashamed of his family's circumstances and his father's failures. At the core, he felt weak and ineffectual, believing that, like his father, he lacked the qualities necessary for success. As a teenager he admitted, "I knew I was 'fresh' and not popular with the older boys. . . . Generally—I knew that at bottom I lacked the essentials. And at the last crisis, I knew I had no real courage, perseverance or self-respect."

In September 1908, Fitzgerald entered St. Paul Academy, a private high school for the wealthy, where he became a rebellious show-off and continually was in trouble with teachers. Bossy, arrogant, and contentious with classmates, his reputation as a bully made him the school's most unpopular boy. His ledger told it all: At seven his mother gave him a birthday party "to which no one came," and at nine the boys at a potato roast told him "they didn't want him around." He would later recount these boyhood rejections and feelings of inferiority in the Basil Duke Lee stories—most vividly in "The Freshest Boy." The school magazine sarcastically implored students to find some way to poison Scott or shut his mouth. He so detested his classmates and teachers that he convinced his mother to let him remain home whenever he liked. To her, he was "just a bad brownie." Not until well into adolescence did he recognize how he rubbed people the wrong way, noting in his journal, "Growing unpopular." Writing was the only thing he did easily and well. His English teacher recalled him as "a sunny light-haired boy full of enthusiasm who fully foresaw his course in life even in his schoolboy days. . . . I helped him by encouraging him to write adventures. It was also his best work; he did not shine in his other subjects." At thirteen he published his first writing (a detective story) in the academy's newspaper.

Generally, Scott ignored boys and turned to girls for consolation and validation. Girls liked Scott. He was attractive in a refined way, dressed nicely, and was a flatterer. Sensitive to layers of meaning and innuendo, in an effort to understand them, he listened carefully to their conversations. Most fascinating to him were their discussions of feelings. But he could also become confrontational with them, and it was not untypical for him to inquire "Are you really the richest girl in your boarding school?" or "Do you believe in God?" Only the most attractive were asked "What sort of heroine would you like to be?" as a way of suggesting he might portray them in fiction. That intrigued even the most popular girls, and it was those he pursued, for only by winning the girl blessed with beauty and position could he gain self-respect.

His father always emphasized the importance of good manners and refinement. To attain both, Scott attended Professor Baker's dancing classes in 1909, held in the ballroom above Ramaley's

Caterers at 668 Grand Avenue. Here, St. Paul's elite delivered their white-gloved children in chauffeured limousines to learn ballroom dancing and etiquette, the boys lining up on one side and girls on the other. One of his fellow students, Tom Daniels, lived near Scott and occasionally offered him rides to lessons. Daniels was the son of the highly successful founder of Archer-Daniels-Midland, and Fitzgerald was ever conscious of their divergent backgrounds. (Daniels had moved to St. Paul in 1901 at the age of eight and attended St. Paul Academy with Fitzgerald.) He went on to the Hill School before attending Yale where he became friends with Archibald MacLeish, a fellow member of Skull and Bones. Tom would later carry Scott's manuscript of *This Side of Paradise* to Scribner's in New York City. Fitzgerald considered dancing an important social grace, and soon became Baker's star pupil, taking advanced lessons at Mr. Van Arnum's dancing academy. His mother was proud of his ability. She loved to watch him demonstrate new steps in their front parlor and encouraged him to perform the popular songs and poems he memorized. An excellent mime, Scott developed a passion for the stage. His Saturdays were spent watching vaudeville shows and operettas at the Orpheum Theatre in downtown St. Paul.

Because his grades at St. Paul Academy were so poor, his parents feared he would not be admitted into a good college. So when his aunt Annabelle offered additional money for private school tuition, he was sent east to Newman, a small Roman Catholic boarding school sixty miles from New York City in Hackensack, New Jersey. The strict Newman School was founded in 1890 by Cardinal Gibbons of Baltimore. Highly selective, it accepted sixty students annually from wealthy Catholic families across America to prepare them for prestigious secular universities. Once again Scott was the poorest boy in a rich man's school. He felt alienated from his classmates and was unsure how to act; either he worked too hard to impress people or refused to impress them at all. Rather than cultivate friendships among fellow students, he forged important relationships with two adults: Father Cyril Sigourney Webster Fay, a Roman Catholic convert and Newman trustee who subsequently became its headmaster, and Fay's Anglo-Irish friend the novelist Shane Leslie, a cousin of Winston Churchill. Fitzgerald was fifteen when he arrived at Newman and Father Fay was twenty-one years older, but the two became good friends. Fay was soon devoted to

Scott's welfare. In many ways he acted as a surrogate father for Fitzgerald, encouraging his writing and introducing him to influential friends in Washington, D.C., including the historian Henry Adams, whom Fitzgerald later portrayed as Thornton Hancock in his first novel, *This Side of Paradise*, which he dedicated to Fay.

Fitzgerald was tolerated only slightly better at Newman than he had been at St. Paul Academy. He had already started to smoke and drink and, perhaps because of some genetic disposition or because the idea of drinking disoriented him, got drunk on only one drink. Always late for classes and meals, he exhibited a bossy, mercurial attitude and routinely engaged in fistfights with fellow students. Within weeks he found himself ostracized by most classmates. His January 1912 grades showed the result: unsatisfactory work in history, English, Latin, Latin composition, French, algebra, and trigonometry; an 87 in Christian doctrine, and a 76 in English composition. Scrawled on the report was the headmaster's admonition: "Naturally bright and with sufficient application could attain a high rank."

Fitzgerald kept to himself much of the time but managed to develop a superficial acquaintance with Stephen Parrott. He made only one real friend, Sap Donahoe, who was from Seattle and among the school's most popular boys. Excelling in both academics and sports, Donahoe appreciated Fitzgerald's interest in literature and the stage. Whenever the two boys won an evening's leave, they headed for Broadway's musicals, spending hours drinking and talking at Reisenweber's or Bustanoby's. Fitzgerald enjoyed seeing Gertrude Bryan in *Little Boy Blue* and became immediately infatuated with Ina Claire in *The Quaker Girl*. He was determined to meet her after graduation. Both Donahoe and Fitzgerald took Princeton's entrance exams at Manhattan's YMCA during the summer of 1912. Princeton was Scott's only choice; he never considered another college. For years he had fantasized about being on their football team after watching their star player, Sam White, score a winning touchdown. But he foresaw real success at Princeton linked to his writing ability, and planned to write lyrics for Triangle, Princeton's theatrical society. Apprehensive about Princeton's high tuition, he dreaded the possibility of having to settle for the University of Minnesota. His financial situation radically improved, however, when Grandmother McQuillan died leaving an estate of $125,000. But while Sap Donahoe got into Princeton easily, Fitzgerald did not; even after cheating on the multiple choice questions he failed the essay section. Though he spent the summer studying for a makeup examination, he failed a second time. His last hope was a personal interview with Princeton's Board of Appeals. The meeting was scheduled on his seventeenth birthday, and, impeccably dressed in clothes from Brooks Brothers and Jacob Reed's, he rode the train to Princeton, New Jersey, resolute in his ability to convince admissions officers to take him. Largely by virtue of his extraordinary charm, Fitzgerald was accepted into the class of 1917.

Through his work writing scripts and lyrics for Triangle and contributing humorous pieces to the *Princeton Tiger*, he got to know Edmund Wilson, who edited the *Nassau Literary Magazine*. Wilson was a true intellectual, so withdrawn as to be thought reclusive. A student of classics, he was considered the campus eccentric. He and Fitzgerald, however, got along well and took to going into Manhattan to see the newest shows. Scott occasionally dated Ruth Sturtevant, a student at Miss Porter's School in Connecticut and classmate of his childhood friend Alida Bigelow from St. Paul, with whom he went to dances and boat club races. But his closest Princeton friend and greatest influence became John Peale Bishop, who introduced him to the poetry of John Keats and the French Symbolists.

Born in West Virginia's Shenandoah Valley, Bishop attended boarding school in Mercersburg, Pennsylvania, before entering Princeton in 1913, where he was elected president of his club. While he was still a freshman, his English professor observed he had a "self possession and self mastery which gave him the poise and bearing of a young English lord," and "a more carefully thought out and more accomplished mastery of the technique of English verse than any other undergraduate." Bishop won all of Princeton's literary prizes and supervised Fitzgerald's reading program, teaching him more about literature than most of his instructors. He admired Scott's writing talent, but remembered him as the eternal adolescent. "Long afterwards, I complained to him that I thought he took seventeen as his norm, making everything later a falling off. For a moment he demurred, then said, 'If you make it 15, I will agree with you.' "

Fitzgerald's work on Princeton's literary magazine also led to his friendship with John Biggs, who recalled their first meeting in the

Nassau Lit office. "I was a sophomore at Princeton. It was a winter night in 1916. . . . I walked out on campus and went over to the *Nassau Lit* office which was in Old North. Fitzgerald was in the office dressed in a sweatshirt. He was sitting at a desk with a little stub of pencil, working away, writing a poem. First time I ever saw him. He was shorter than I am, had blonde hair and a very cold blue eye. We sat and talked for about half an hour, he telling me what a good poet he was." Biggs had entered Princeton in 1914, the year before Edmund Wilson became managing editor of the *Lit*. Wilson and Biggs had been students at the Hill School in Pottstown with Tom Daniels, who had also attended St. Paul Academy with Fitzgerald, and struck up an easy friendship because of their shared interests. Like Fitzgerald, Biggs was the only son of a doting mother. He had a poor relationship with his father, a successful attorney who always thought his son lacked intelligence. Actually, Biggs was dyslexic, which, to his parent's embarrassment, made academics difficult and caused him to be dismissed from the Wilmington Friends School. Although he managed to finish Princeton and later Harvard Law, his father's underlying contempt persisted and forever troubled him. Beneath Biggs's calm exterior seethed an explosive anger, which Zelda Fitzgerald later would observe with alarm.

During his sophomore year, Fitzgerald, along with Sap Donahoe, was selected for Cottage, the most sought-after eating club on campus. His other Princeton friends—Townsend Martin, Alex McKaig, and Ludlow Fowler—were relegated to the less prestigious Quadrangle. Making Cottage was critically important to Scott because its president, Walker Ellis, was his hero and role model. A wealthy and cosmopolitan junior from New Orleans, Ellis was also president of Triangle. The prestigious eating clubs along Prospect Avenue attracted class leaders, and only the most popular boys were elected to them in the middle of sophomore year. At that time there were ten clubs. They provided a place to eat, drink, play billiards, socialize with classmates, and take girls on weekends. Making the right club was a badge of honor and an important achievement in an undergraduate's social life. It was where one acquired the manners and attitudes of the privileged class, as well as making friends with people who would later be useful in professional and business life. Success on campus was measured by the club to which one was elected, and Fitzgerald was determined to join the best. Because of his success in writing for the *Tiger* and

Nassau Lit, and the use of his lyrics for Wilson's 1915 Triangle club musical *The Evil Eye*, Fitzgerald also received bids from Quadrangle, Cap and Gown, and Cannon. But there was never any doubt; Cottage was the most sought-after, its building the most architecturally impressive, its members on the highest rung of the social ladder. Founded in 1887, it accepted only the most popular men, who were expected to bring the most attractive girls to club functions. Fitzgerald was ecstatic when he was chosen. Even after leaving Princeton, he returned many times, and over the years frequently mentioned his affiliation with Cottage.

Cottage was what Princeton was all about for Fitzgerald. Like Zelda, he remained wholly indifferent to academics. His interests lay in making social connections and writing for Princeton's dramatic club and literary magazines. In 1915, by the end of his sophomore year, he had failed so many courses he was ineligible to be an English major, and six weeks into his junior year was barred from all extracurricular activities. In December he dropped out for the balance of his junior year and was told he would have to repeat it. He reregistered in the fall of 1916, joining John Biggs's class of 1918 and rooming with him in Campbell Hall. On academic probation and unlikely to graduate, he stayed on campus only to await his army commission. The day it arrived, he packed his bags and left, never receiving his Princeton undergraduate degree.

The glib charm that had gotten Scott into Princeton and given him an air of unlimited potential was the same quality that ultimately kept him in the running with Zelda. And run he did. Long before she and Fitzgerald met, Zelda had begun to disdain ordinary activities. It was an effort to keep up with her, and while her outrageous behavior shocked other young women, it drew admiration from men. One of the few girls in Montgomery to ride boys' motorcycles, she chewed gum, smoked in public, danced cheek-to-cheek, and drank corn liquor and gin. The first to bob her hair, she habitually sneaked out of her room at midnight to swim in the moonlight with boys at Catoma Creek, then showed up for breakfast as though nothing had happened. Her escapades became legendary. At one Auburn prom she flouted convention by executing a wild highland fling. On another occasion, after complaining of blisters, she borrowed her date's oversized tennis shoes and flopped around the dance floor. There were numerous similar stories— weekends at Tuscaloosa and Sewanee where she would break with convention to satisfy a whim or attract the attention of a particular boy. She scorned chaperones, left dances during intermission to neck in parked cars, was unconcerned when people called her a "speed," and ignored the double standard by using her social prerogative to do as she pleased. "The fun in those first years came from being yourself," she recalled. "We were never conscious of chaperones or disapproval of any sort. If we were criticized one place we simply went to another. We had no social sense, and consequently no sense of guilt. In our vivid good times, nothing seemed unnatural. It was only when the older generations made us conscious of what we were doing that we grew confused and wild."

Zelda always believed sex had little to do with love. By the time she met Fitzgerald, she was well on the way to becoming the most sought-after girl in the Alabama-Georgia area. She relished leaving "the more or less sophisticated beaus and belles of Atlanta gasping for air when she struck the town." Once, after a dance at the University of Alabama in Tuscaloosa, she and her date returned to the sorority after everyone had gone to bed, and in a fit of drunken hilarity, broke the sorority's record collection over each other's heads. The angry housemother, awakened by the disturbance, sent the boy back to his fraternity and soundly reprimanded an unconcerned Zelda. When one chaperone complained about her dance-floor behavior, she pinned a sprig of mistletoe to the seat of her dress and twirled boldly in front of her. There was a contagious quality about Zelda's antics. "Many of those older people who came to chaperone our dances, and to disapprove of them found themselves getting interested, even thrilled. The next thing we knew they were out on the floor dancing and consciously copying the gestures that had been perfectly unconscious with us. Then they started giving parties and running around wilder than we had ever thought of doing. But they were always conscious and calculated and it wasn't like the glorious times we had had."

She took great pleasure in telling Scott about the wild things she and Eleanor Browder did. "Last night a small crowd of practical jokers reversed calls to the University of Alabama, Sewanee and Auburn—telegraphed collect all over the U.S. and were barely restrained from getting New York on the wire. . . . Our lives are in continual danger, and our mothers are frantic, but Eleanor and I are enjoying the sensations we create immensely." While extremely feminine, she also believed she possessed a man's mind and was attracted to the daring quality of their lives. "I have always been inclined towards masculinity. It's such a cheery atmosphere boys radiate—and we do such unique things together." Unpredictable, she was as likely to break a window and run as to shine a spotlight on boys as they entered the local whorehouse. Most of her admirers found it impossible to keep up and gave up the chase.

Popularity was the highest status symbol for young women in Montgomery, therefore Zelda was reluctant to link herself exclusively with Fitzgerald. Even while the two dated, she continued to encourage more weekend invitations than she could possibly accept. It was common knowledge that only the most eligible boys might expect a positive response, and convincing her to attend your Senior Hop or commencement ceremony was considered a great accomplishment. Throughout their courtship, Zelda kept Scott continually off-balance by telling him about her other suitors. "Yesterday Bill Le Grand and I drove his car to Auburn and came back with ten boys to liven things up—of course, the day was vastly exciting—and the night even more so. . . . Red said last night that I was the pinkest-whitest person he ever saw, so I went to sleep in his lap—Of course you don't mind because it was really very fraternal and we were chaperoned by three girls." (Leon "Red" Ruth was far too tame to be any threat to Scott. After graduating from Columbia University, he returned to Montgomery to lead a sedate life as owner of a successful jewelry store.)

Taking Zelda out for the evening generally proved to be an exciting experience. Once, when John Sellers and some other Auburn undergraduates were home, and ran short of transportation money to return to campus, they turned to Zelda for help. Dressed in black and sitting in a wheelchair, she had them push her through Montgomery's train station to beg alms. It was a prank repeated several times. A classmate recalled her delight over a similar episode. "Zelda was interesting, attractive, popular and pretty. . . . My classmates and I loved her and thought she was beautiful. She often thought of things she might do but seldom did. These things were not bad but a little shocking. I think our routine lives bored her although she went in our crowd and seemed to accept and return our friendship. One time on a dare, she dressed as a beggar, old long skirt, floppy hat pulled low, dark glasses—and with a tin cup went up and down the benches at the railroad station waiting room. She got quite a good collection and enjoyed to the fullest recounting this exploit." Reprimanded by the police, she was elated over the attention, telling Scott, "yesterday, when the university boys took their belated departure, John Sellers wheeled me through a vast throng of people at the station crying intermittently, 'the lady hasn't walked in five years.' 'God bless those who help the poor,' the lady would echo much to the amazement and amusement of the station at large." Yet, while determined to rebel against convention, Zelda also had a conservative side to her nature. At the age of twenty, she acknowledged this duality in her personality: "One . . . wants to have a law to itself and the other . . . wants to keep all the nice old things and be loved and protected."

She attracted both types of female friends—Sara Martin Mayfield and Sara Powell Haardt being among her closest. Both got involved in Zelda's pranks. Haardt's mother, Venetia, was a strict disciplinarian who set stringent rules for her two daughters. On Friday nights, they were not permitted to return home separately, which would have implied they had been out on dates rather than at a dance. Outsmarting Venetia, Ida and Sara Haardt conspired with Zelda to meet under a tree at the edge of Oak Park and wait for each other before returning home.

Both Sara Haardt and Sara Mayfield had graduated from Miss Booth's school and met Fitzgerald in September of 1918. They encountered him on the steps of Montgomery's capitol building, an impressive Greek Revival structure with twelve Corinthian columns supporting an enlarged dome. Zelda had taken Scott there to see the gold star near its entrance where Jefferson Davis had been sworn in as president of the Confederacy. Mayfield recalled his eagerness to impress them. "She introduced him to us, and he told us that his name was Francis Scott Fitzgerald and that he was a great-grandson of Francis Scott Key, who had written 'The Star-Spangled Banner.' " It was a slight exaggeration, but no matter.

Mayfield was also from a prestigious family. Her father had served with Zelda's on the Alabama Supreme Court for twenty years, and his office was on the second floor of the capitol, next to Judge Sayre's. For years both men kept a chessboard in the anteroom between their offices. They played only between cases and each game could last months. The Mayfields lived on Court Street just a few blocks from the Sayres' Pleasant Street house, and the two girls knew each other well. But Zelda was almost five years older than Sara, and so wild that Judge Mayfield had serious misgivings about his daughter growing too friendly with her. He never forgot the day Zelda had jumped into his new brougham and taken the carriage for a wild ride down the street. Nevertheless, Zelda and Sara remained friends and even shared boyfriends. Sara actually married one of Zelda's former beaux—John Sellers—in November 1924. The marriage proved brief; Mayfield divorced him in March 1927 because of "too many parties, too many hangovers, too much money." Sara had ambitious plans and studied in Paris at the Sorbonne, attended the University of Chicago during 1927, and graduated from Goucher College in 1928. She received a master's degree from the University of Alabama in 1931 and pursued a career in journalism and theater, working as a correspondent for the *New York Herald Tribune*, *Paris Herald*, and *Baltimore Sun*. As a fledgling writer herself, what struck Mayfield that day on Montgomery's capitol steps was how fascinated Scott was with Zelda's thoughts, mannerisms, and unique speech patterns.

In contrast to the unfortunate traits inherited from her parents (the most serious being a propensity toward schizophrenia), Zelda also acquired her mother's outstanding vocabulary and her father's razor-sharp mind and memory. Scott immediately recognized her keen intelligence and superior powers of observation. He particularly appreciated her ability to formulate strange connections and develop original figures of speech. Encouraging her to express herself in unconventional ways, he mentally noted things she said— writing them down so he could later incorporate them into his writing. Zelda possessed incredible conversational stamina and she and Scott would engage in marathon conversations, "long talks throughout the night, those joint monologues like shared dreams." Though others sometimes found her verbal associations difficult to follow, Fitzgerald tracked them easily and with immense interest.

Sara Powell Haardt also recalled meeting Fitzgerald that September day and his boastful reference to a famous ancestor. The Haardt family owned a Montgomery department store and lived in a large corner house at 903 South Perry Street. Sickly from birth, Sara had barely survived infancy and subsequently battled smallpox, typhus, appendicitis, and the removal of a kidney. Also a victim of tuberculosis, she spent part of 1924 and 1925 in a Maryland sanitarium. Frequently in and out of hospitals, she died at thirty-seven of meningitis and a tubercular infection of the spine. It was a tragically short life, for she was an exceptionally gifted student and a writer with extraordinary interpretive capabilities. Two years older than Zelda, she had decided early to leave Montgomery. And though she dated several men, including John Sellers, she was more interested in intellectual pursuits than marriage. Whereas Zelda's rebelliousness against southern conservatism took a social path, Haardt's was expressed intellectually and politically. A star pupil at Miss Booth's school, she applied to the best colleges and was accepted at Goucher near Baltimore. It was precisely the intellectual environment she craved and in which she excelled. Goucher's faculty was so impressed with Haardt that she was invited to teach there following her graduation. During 1923 and 1924, she corresponded with Peyton Matthis, who had also dated Zelda and was rumored to be Sara's true love (the two almost married). Mayfield later told Zelda how "Peyton wired Sara [Haardt] that he was coming to Baltimore to marry her . . . [but] . . . took a few drinks on the train and ended up in Charleston, South Carolina married to another girl." Zelda's prophetic response was that marriage and drinking don't mix.

After Sara Haardt married H. L. Mencken, she and Zelda shared a unique bond as wives of literary figures. Each felt she had narrowly escaped the South. And Zelda's alter ego, Alabama, in *Save Me the Waltz* admits that when she went North, she left behind "the sense of suffocation that seemed to be eclipsing her family, her sisters and her mother." And in "Commencement," published by Mencken in the August 1926 issue of *The American Mercury*, Sara wrote of her own determination to flee the South in a thinly veiled narrative about an intelligent girl "doomed to stay in Meridian [Montgomery] because her father cannot send her to the school she deserves." Haardt's father died while she was still a teenager, and only with the assistance of her grandmother, replicating Fitzgerald's situation at Princeton, could she afford Goucher's tuition.

Haardt was hardly a flapper in the twenties model, but she was following her own path. In contrast, Zelda personified the twenties' icon who defied convention and broke men's hearts. With Ginevra King as his first literary model, Fitzgerald already had begun writing about flappers. But after meeting Zelda, he recognized she more precisely embodied the heroine he wanted to create. Quickly, he altered Rosalind's character in *This Side of Paradise* to reflect Zelda's personality. Sending her the rewritten sections of his manuscript from Camp Sheridan, he said, "Here is the mentioned chapter . . .

a document in youthful melancholy. . . . However . . . the heroine does resemble you in more ways than four." Making her the heroine of his novel served two purposes: winning her affection and enhancing his story line. Eager to enter Scott's creative world, Zelda allowed him full use of her letters and diaries, which Fitzgerald immediately incorporated into his draft. In spring of 1919, Zelda wrote of a day spent in Montgomery's cemetery and her little vignette made its way into his book—verbatim. "It isn't really a cemetery, you know—trying to unlock a rusty iron vault built in the side of the hill. It's all washed and covered with weepy, watery blue flowers that might have grown from dead eyes—sticky to touch with a sickening odor—the boys wanted to get in to test my nerve—to-night—I wanted to feel 'William Wrenford, 1864.' Why should graves make people feel in vain? I've heard that so much, and Grey is so convincing, but somehow I can't find anything hopeless in having lived. All the broken columns and clasped hands and doves and angels mean romances, and in an hundred years I think I shall like having young people speculate on whether my eyes were brown or blue—of cource [sic], they are neither."

Out of high school only six weeks when they first met, Zelda was already exploring ways to expand her horizons outside the South. Perhaps sensing this longing, Fitzgerald was eager to advance the relationship quickly. But while Zelda admitted to being in love, she also knew she would be financially dependent on her husband for the rest of her life, so money was an important prerequisite for marriage. She demanded a standard of life far beyond what Fitzgerald could then provide, and while his monthly army pay of $141 might entertain her in Alabama, it was insufficient to support her in a comfortable lifestyle elsewhere. Montgomery's modest leisure attractions then included several theaters and restaurants, a country club, the zoo at Oak Park, and an amusement arcade at Pickett Springs where, on Sunday afternoons, crowds hovered near the merry-go-round, popcorn stands, and barbecue pits. Scott's courtship consisted of dinners at the Pickwick Cafe or Elite restaurant, then a dance or movie. Occasionally there were touring musical comedies and vaudeville shows at the Grand Theater where the couple sat holding hands and kissing in one of the gilt-and-red-plush boxes.

They often strolled together in the honeysuckle and wisteria-scented moonlight, and Zelda remembered the night they carved their names in the country club doorpost—his larger than hers. Impressed by his assurances of fame then, the incident was reinterpreted differently by Zelda in *Save Me the Waltz*. "Alabama and the lieutenant lingered beside the door. 'I'm going to lay a tablet to the scene of our first meeting,' he said. Taking out his knife he carved in the doorpost: 'David,' the legend read, 'David, David, Knight, Knight, Knight, and Miss Alabama Nobody.' 'Egotist,' she protested. . . . She was a little angry about the names. David had told her about how famous he was going to be."

Scott was naturally extravagant and enjoyed giving Zelda whatever she wanted. She interpreted this generosity as a sign of future success, and his potential for fame held her interest. But she would not agree to marriage until it was absolutely proven he could provide an exceptional life. Accepting her future status as "wife," Zelda nevertheless was unwilling to play the passive role prescribed by southern society. Throughout their courtship she never fully committed to Scott and continued dating a variety of men. Fitzgerald later recalled that reluctance with resentment: "She was not perfectly sure—except for the sexual recklessness. She was cagey about throwing in her lot with me before I was a money maker, and I think by temperament she was the most reckless of all the women I had known." Yet while unwilling to marry him, she feared losing Scott to someone else. "When she saw him leave the dance floor with other girls, the resentment she felt was not against any blending of his personality with theirs, but against his leading others than herself into those cooler detached regions which he inhabited alone." Scott felt equally possessive about her and wrote Edmund Wilson, "I wouldn't care if she died, but I couldn't stand to have anybody else marry her." By keeping Fitzgerald jealous and all her options open, Zelda increased her chances of obtaining what she wanted most: the salamander's dream of the right man and the right life.

In September of 1919, when Sara Haardt returned to Goucher for her junior year, Zelda again began dating John Sellers. The son of a wealthy cotton broker, John Allen Sellers Jr. was being trained to class and staple cotton in his father's firm, Sellers-Orum. He possessed two advantages—both of which Fitzgerald by his own admission lacked and envied—animal magnetism and money. Owning a nice car and having money to spend made Sellers a serious threat.

Fitzgerald would always harbor anger over Zelda's involvement with the tall blond southerner, and remained convinced that their relationship had been sexual. He complained bitterly about Sellers in a letter written much later to Zelda but never mailed, accusing her of being seduced at fifteen by him. "The assumption is that you were a great prize package. By your own admission many years after (and for which I never reproached you) you had been seduced and provincially outcast. I sensed this the night we slept together first for you're a poor bluffer.... There was an elaborate self-consciousness about our seduction which told of deep intuition that you were playing a role, though my one-track mind didn't choose to notice it, and I should have guessed ... there had been an old emotional experience for you had learned to feel before I did." In another unsent letter to Zelda's sister Marjorie, his outrage was even more vehemently expressed: "Your mother took such rotten care of Zelda that John Sellers was able to seduce her at fifteen and she was so drunk the first time I met her at the Country Club that her partners were carrying her around in their arms."

Sellers may well have seduced Zelda; Mayfield was certainly in a position to know, since she married him. But Sara interpreted Zelda's dance-floor antics differently, recalling how Zelda often played drunk, then slipped to the floor so she could be romantically carried off in the arms of an escort. Once, when Zelda was dancing with Lloyd Hooper, Mayfield remembered that she "pretended to be drunk and fell down on the floor. Since Lloyd could not rouse her, he picked her up and carried her to his car. Before he could open the door, she doubled up laughing at him for being taken in by her joke."

In the fall of 1918, while Scott and Zelda's relationship was still highly unsettled, Fitzgerald was reassigned to Hoboken, New Jersey, as a supply officer. On October 26, 1918, in preparation for embarkation to France, he received orders to join the 67th Infantry at Camp Mills, Long Island. Sellers's initial elation at having Zelda's complete attention was short-lived, for the November 11 armistice brought Fitzgerald back to Camp Sheridan for demobilization.

Fitzgerald's Princeton education and charm won him the easy job of aide-de-camp to General J. A. Ryan of the 17th Infantry Brigade, where he primarily functioned as the commandant's social secretary. Now he could court Zelda in style. "You invited me to dine and I had never dined before but had always just 'had supper,' " she later wrote. "The General was away. The night was soft and gray and the trees were feathery in the lamp light and the dim recesses of the pine forest were fragrant with the past, and you said you would come back from no matter where you are. So I said and I will be here waiting. I didn't quite believe it." However, as the general's aide, Fitzgerald was required to appear beside him on horseback in dress parades. Never an equestrian, he was quickly thrown off, which did not impress his commanding officer. As one of the most expendable men in the regiment, Fitzgerald was the second to be demobilized and was discharged on February 14, 1919.

As Fitzgerald departed Montgomery, townspeople were preparing to welcome home the local boys from the Rainbow Division of the 167th Infantry. Zelda joined the morning crowd greeting them on May 12 at 10:30 when they paraded down Commerce Street from Union Station through Court Square to the capitol. The papers announced the reception to follow: "From 2:30–6 pm Court Square will be cleared of traffic and refreshments of 'rainbow' ice cream, homemade cake, candy and cigarettes will be served to all in uniform by charming matrons and pretty girls marshalled by Mrs. W. J. Hannah, Chairman." In a newspaper photograph taken that day, a radiant Zelda is clearly visible along the parade route. Fitzgerald realized he had to prove himself, and quickly.

Zelda's sister Tilde had helped Scott locate an apartment in New York City, where he planned to work for a newspaper, write stories at night, and make enough money to persuade Zelda to marry. After the long train ride north, he immediately telegraphed Zelda. "Telda [sic] found knockout little apartment reasonable rates. I have taken it from 26th." When none of the papers wanted him, he wound up writing light verse for the Colliers Street Railway Advertising Company, part of the Baron Collier agency, working alongside John Held Jr., who illustrated his slogans. He created one highly successful line, a trolley car sign promoting an Iowa steam laundry: "We Keep You Clean in Muscatine." But slogan-writing was not one of his strengths and his salary remained a meager twenty dollars a week—enough only to cover food and lodging at 200 Claremont Avenue in Morningside Heights near Columbia

University. Most evenings he stayed in to work on his stories. He finished nineteen and rapidly accumulated a hundred rejection slips that he defiantly pasted on the walls of his room.

While Zelda wrote encouraging letters suggesting things ultimately would work out—"These hot, sticky nights—when the air seems heavy and tropical—and my hair gets damp and my eyes sleepy—Scott, darling, I want you more all the time and I love you with all my heart and soul"—she continued to line up alternate fiancés. Francis Stubbs and Pete Bonner, two star Auburn football players, competed seriously for her attention. Stubbs presented her with his gold football pendant, which she wore on a chain around her neck, and Bonner invited her to Auburn for the weekend of February 22, writing to remind her and warn his college competition: "Have a date with you on Saturday p.m. Look out Stubbs." Zelda was so popular at Auburn that she and Livyre Hart were chosen Auburn sponsors and maids. Five members of the football team even formed a new fraternity in her honor—Zeta Sigma. Induction required a date with Zelda and charter members included Francis Stubbs, Harvey Allen, Clem Cardy, Bob Fields, and George Lumpkin. After seeing her photo or noticing her at a dance, numerous college undergraduates wrote to her—in the same vein as Solomon Tedford: "I sure would like to meet you. I have one of your pictures and it sure does look good to me."

Zelda kept Scott well informed about her dates on college campuses. His mounting anxiety prompted him to ask his mother for her engagement ring so he could present it to Zelda and bind her more tightly. Although she accepted it, neither she nor her family took the proposal seriously. After wearing his ring at one country club dance, she put it away, telling Scott: "I know you love me, Darling, and I love you more than anything in the world, but if it's going to be so much longer we just can't keep up this frantic writing." Her growing impatience and the strain of their long-distance relationship made Zelda unsettled and anxious. She developed the nervous habit of biting the inside of her mouth and lips. "I'd probably aggravate you to death today," she wrote Scott, "there's no skin on my lips, and I have relapsed into a nervous stupor—it feels like going crazy knowing everything you do and being utterly powerless not to do it—and thinking you'll surely scream the next minute."

Although they had promised to write daily, Zelda soon lost interest in maintaining a continual correspondence. "I hate writing when I haven't time, and I just have to scribble a few lines—I'm saying this so you'll understand—hectic affairs of any kind are rather trying, so please let's write calmly and whenever you feel like it." And while Scott saved every letter she wrote, as he had done with Ginevra's, Zelda saved none. Scott grudgingly accepted her decision to stop writing, but remained determined to marry her. He discussed his predicament with John Biggs. "I remember the first time he told me about Zelda. It was prior to their marriage in 1920. . . . I was at home in Wilmington. He said simply that he'd met this girl [Zelda Sayre] in Montgomery, Alabama, while stationed nearby with the Army and that he was going to marry her. I asked him what she was like. 'Oh, she's a blonde,' he said. Then he described her vaguely. I remember him saying that 'She's got a superb figure,' which she did have. I said, 'Scotty, you can't get married without money.' [Growing even more serious, Fitzgerald said,] 'Well, I'm going to marry her regardless. I had a hell of a time getting her away from Bankhead's son [the son of the late Speaker of the U.S. House Bankhead and brother of actress Tallulah Bankhead]. . . . He was crazy to marry her. But I'm going to.' "

Scott knew Biggs was right about the money and he aggressively tried to sell his stories. Edmund Wilson introduced him to George Jean Nathan that June, and he finally got word from H. L. Mencken that "Babes in the Woods" would be published in *The Smart Set*. Elated by this first success, he spent the $30 story fee on a blue ostrich fan for Zelda and a pair of white flannel trousers for himself. But even when Mencken purchased "The Debutante," Fitzgerald realized these initial story sales would not provide enough money to rent a better apartment or lure Zelda to the altar.

Scott was mired in conflicting feelings and confided to Ruth Sturtevant, whom he had casually dated at Princeton, that though he was obsessed with Zelda, he feared marriage to her would distract him from writing. "My mind is firmly made up that I will not, shall not, can not, should not, must not marry—Still, she is remarkable." He also talked things over with Stephen Parrott, his classmate from Newman and Princeton who was now studying architecture at MIT. The two met at the Yale Club (which had temporarily merged with the Princeton Club) on Vanderbilt Avenue across from Grand Central Station where Fitzgerald usually ate dinner. He read Parrott the parts of Zelda's diary he was using to revise his novel. It was a southern custom for women to keep courtship diaries, and during the nineteenth century they often presented them to bridegrooms on their wedding day. But Zelda's diary was something else entirely. It chronicled her personal observations and emotions in a highly original stream of consciousness. Parrott found it fascinating but hard to decipher. He wrote Fitzgerald, "As you say, it is a very human document, but somehow I cannot altogether understand it." After reading all the entries and hearing Scott's description of Zelda, Parrott was intrigued. "I wish I could meet a Zelda just now," he wrote Scott in April 1919. "I feel a horrible desire to fall in love with somebody, I feel so parched and wisely cold like a Babylonian scroll that has been buried for centuries." When he finally met Zelda for the first time, his flirtatiousness with her caused a permanent rift between the two men.

While Fitzgerald ground out slogans and submitted stories to magazines, Zelda continued collecting beaux. In addition to dating Sellers, she was crowned prom queen at three different campuses that season: the University of Alabama, the University of Georgia, and Sewanee. With each week she became less certain about her feelings toward Scott, and told her Sewanee date, John Dearborn, that while she was no longer passionate about Fitzgerald, she felt it her mission to help him become a great writer.

Scott sensed a new coolness but attributed it solely to his poverty. "He had met her when she was seventeen, possessed her young heart all through her first season . . . and then lost her slowly, tragically, uselessly, because he had no money and could make no money. . . ." He would never forget Zelda's reluctance to marry him while poor, because it rekindled painful memories of Ginevra King and reinforced his love-hate feelings about the rich. "The young man with the jingle of money in his pocket who married the girl a year later would always cherish an abiding distrust, an animosity toward the leisure class . . . not the conviction of a revolutionist but the smoldering hatred of a peasant. In the years since, I have never been able to stop wondering once where my friend's money came from, nor to stop thinking that at one time a sort of 'droit de seigneur' might have been exercised to give one of them my girl." From this juncture, he eyed the rich with suspicion, considering them a separate species. Hemingway later mocked these feelings in *The Snows of Kilimanjaro*, writing, "He remembered poor Scott Fitzgerald and his romantic awe of [the rich] and how he had started a story once that began, 'The very rich are different from you and me.' And how someone had said to Scott, 'Yes, they have more money.' But that was not humorous to Scott. He thought they were a special glamorous race and when he found out they weren't, it wrecked him as much as any other thing that wrecked him."

Fitzgerald had no illusions about winning Zelda without a substantial income, and though she sent encouraging letters—"We're swimming all the time, and every dive makes me think of how we're always going—I wish I had done everything on earth with you—all my life. . . . You are the only man on earth who has ever known and loved 'all' of me"—she tempered her encouragement with generous descriptions of her dates at parties and proms. Hoping his presence might persuade her to marry, Scott made three train trips to Montgomery between April and June of 1919. Nevertheless, the courtship remained at a standstill.

In June of 1919, Zelda ended what had always been a trial engagement. She coldly explained that his inability to support her would sour their marriage and inevitably leave them frustrated and miserable. Though the rejection hurt and angered him, he put her parting words to quick use, fusing them into Rosalind's rejection of Amory in *This Side of Paradise*.

ROSALIND: I can't, Amory. I can't be shut away from the trees and flowers, cooped up in a little flat, waiting for you. You'd hate me in a narrow atmosphere. I'd make you hate me. (Again she is blinded by sudden uncontrolled tears.)

AMORY: Rosalind—

ROSALIND: Oh, darling, go—Don't make it harder! I can't stand it—

AMORY: (His face drawn, his voice strained) Do you know what you're saying? Do you mean forever? (There is a difference somehow in the quality of their suffering.)

ROSALIND: Can't you see—

AMORY: I'm afraid I can't if you love me. You're afraid of taking two years' knocks with me.

ROSALIND: I wouldn't be the Rosalind you love.

AMORY: (A little hysterically) I can't give you up! I can't, that's all! I've got to have you!

ROSALIND: (A hard note in her voice) You're being a baby now.
AMORY: (Wildly) I don't care! You're spoiling our lives!
ROSALIND: I'm doing the wise thing, the only thing."

This second rejection was almost unbearable. Somehow, he had to quickly prove himself, so he visited Maxwell Perkins at Scribner's to discuss his novel. Perkins suggested he rewrite it in the third person, and on July 4, 1919, Fitzgerald quit his Collier's job and prepared to leave New York for St. Paul. On his last, bittersweet days in Manhattan, he wandered around 127th Street, envious of those who appeared more successful than he, and, in the cheapest seats he could buy—lost himself for a few hours on Broadway. "I was a failure, mediocre at advertising work and unable to get started as a writer. Hating the city, I got roaring, weeping drunk on my last penny and went home."

Back in his parents' house in St. Paul at 599 Summit Avenue, he stopped drinking and started revising "The Romantic Egoists" according to Perkins's suggestions. He retitled the book *This Side of Paradise* after Rupert Brooke's poem "Tiare Tahiti." The last lines of the poem—"Well this side of Paradise! There's little comfort in the wise"—would appear on his title page, suggesting that mature wisdom provided no more satisfaction than youthful enthusiasm. Set mainly at his alma mater, Princeton, the novel narrated the career hopes and love disappointments of its hero, Amory Blaine—a thinly veiled version of himself.

Scott forced himself not to write Zelda and concentrated solely on revising his manuscript. Throughout the summer he reworked the story, adding portions of Zelda's letters and diaries into the novel's central section to further develop the affair between Amory Blaine and Rosalind Connage. He then restructured the entire narrative to reflect his infatuation with Zelda. In his parent's third-floor guest room, he pinned chapter headings and outlines to window curtains, reworked old material, and wove in new. Writing day and night, he stopped only to eat the food his mother placed outside the door. His windows looked out over the trees lining Summit Avenue, and for a break, he crawled onto the belvedere to enjoy the view. When he finished the draft, he showed it to his boyhood friend Tom Daniels, who found it fascinating. His wife, Frances, however, was of the opposite opinion. Daniels was about to take the train east, and volunteered to carry the completed manuscript to

Scribner's. He knew one of the editors, a former classmate at Yale, and offered to put in a good word. On September 3, 1919, Fitzgerald gave Tom Daniels the completed novel to hand-deliver. Days later, he got word that Daniels inadvertently had left the manuscript in a Manhattan taxicab. Miraculously, Daniels was able to track down the driver, retrieve the package, and deposit it at Scribner's. It was the second time the book had been lost, and Fitzgerald was traumatized by the experience; it took days before he recovered.

While he waited for word from Scribner's, he began dividing sections of "The Demon Lover" into character sketches of debutantes, dandies, and flappers, selling them for $40 apiece to *The Smart Set*. Most evenings, he walked down to Mrs. Porterfield's boardinghouse at 513 Summit Avenue near Mackubin and sat on the veranda discussing books with two of her roomers,—John DeQuedville Briggs, headmaster of St. Paul Academy, and Donald Ogden Stewart, a Yale graduate working for the American Telephone Company. Later, Stewart would become a popular humorist and friend of Ernest Hemingway in Paris. The three often strolled to W. A. Frost's drugstore on Selby Avenue to buy Cokes and cigarettes, and occasionally played golf at St. Paul Seminary with Father Joe Baron, St. Paul's young dean of students.

In Montgomery, Zelda discussed her reservations about marrying Scott with his Princeton classmate Lawton Campbell. He vividly recalled their conversation. "During Scott's courtship, he had told Zelda about me. It was natural when I met her that she should ask what I thought of him. I could honestly give her a glowing account because I was genuinely devoted to Scott and admired him greatly. Then she told me that they were engaged, off and on, but that he wanted her to come to New York to marry him. Frankly, it all seemed such a gamble to her she said, and besides Scott was without the necessary funds. I told her I was sure Scott could make money from his writing and she told me about the interest some publisher had in his book and about his encouraging letters. As nearly as I can remember, my impression from what she said is something like this: 'If Scott sells the book, I'll marry the man, because he is sweet. Don't you think so?' "

At Scribner's, opinions of Fitzgerald's novel continued to be split between young and old editors. The elder Charles Scribner still considered it frivolous, but Maxwell Perkins recognized that

Fitzgerald's distinctive exploration of flappers' attitudes was unlike anything published before. He pushed for approval. On September 16, 1919, news of Scribner's acceptance arrived in St. Paul via special delivery from Perkins. "I am very glad, personally to be able to write you that we are all for publishing your book, "This Side of Paradise." . . . The book is so different that it is hard to prophesy how it will sell, but we are all for taking a chance and supporting it with vigor." Fitzgerald was ecstatic. He stopped cars on the road and people in the street to share the good news, bought a new suit and paid past due bills. He wired Zelda he was on his way to Montgomery and arrived with the manuscript, a bottle of Sazarac—her favorite gin—and an unwavering conviction that the Scribner's contract would change Zelda's mind. It took several days and all his persuasive powers to get her tentative agreement to marry. Still, she insisted on waiting until the novel actually was in bookstores. In a letter written to Scott following his departure for New York, she confessed her past misgivings. "I am very proud of you—I hate to say this, but I don't think I had much confidence in you at first. . . . It's so nice to know that you really can do things—anything—and I love to feel that maybe I can help just a little." Indeed, Fitzgerald knew he had in Zelda an unending source of story material.

To avoid the Minnesota winter he feared would aggravate his bronchitis (probably the result of too many cigarettes), and to be nearer Zelda, Scott headed for New Orleans in January of 1920. He took a room in a boardinghouse at 2900 Prytania Street and began reading the galley proofs Scribner's had sent. He also worked on new stories and managed to send a couple to Harold Ober, his newly acquired agent at the Paul Revere Reynolds Agency in New York. He made two trips from Louisiana to Montgomery, and on the second, resumed his sexual relationship with Zelda. They had slept together early in the courtship, but subsequently Zelda had held back. Fitzgerald referred to this ploy in story notes: "After yielding, she holds Philippe at bay like Zelda and me in the summer 1919." Relieved and emboldened by their renewed physical intimacy, Scott insisted they tell Zelda's parents of their engagement. Hoping Zelda might still change her mind, the Sayres did not place an announcement in the local papers, nor did they tell anyone of the impending wedding. Though her parents never spoke out directly against him, all her sisters did, and until the last moment Zelda wavered. But the massed power of her family's disapproval was, in the end, overpowered by Zelda's determination to escape Alabama.

Most of Fitzgerald's friends also opposed the marriage because of Zelda's insistence on financial security. He dismissed their warnings. From Princeton's Cottage Club on February 26, 1920, he wrote Isabelle Amorous, sister of his Newman friend Martin Amorous, who earlier had congratulated him for good judgment when hearing their engagement was off. "I've always known that any girl who gets stewed in public, who frankly enjoys and tells shocking stories, who smokes constantly and makes the remark that she has 'kissed thousands of men and intends to kiss thousands more,' cannot be considered above reproach even if above it. But, Isabelle, I fell in love with her courage, her sincerity and her flaming self-respect and it's these things I'd believe in even if the whole world indulged in wild suspicions that she wasn't all that she should be. . . . I love her and that's the beginning and end of everything."

An additional complication surfaced when Zelda feared she might be pregnant. Fitzgerald sent pills to induce abortion, but she refused to take them, writing Scott: "I wanted to for your sake, because I know what a mess I'm making and how inconvenient it's all going to be—but I simply can't and won't take those awful pills—so I've thrown them away. I'd rather take carbolic acid. You see as long as I feel that I had the right, I don't mind what happens—and besides, I'd rather have a whole family than sacrifice my self-respect. They just seem to place everything on the wrong basis—and I'd feel like a damned whore if I took even one, so you'll try to understand." It turned out Zelda was not pregnant, but their premarital sexual involvement and the pregnancy scare weighed on Fitzgerald's Catholic psyche. From then on, he continually asked other men whether they had slept with their wives before marrying them.

Awaiting his book's publication, Fitzgerald stayed in New York at various Manhattan hotels: first the Knickerbocker, then the Murray Hill, and finally the Allerton on 39th Street. One evening he ran into Lawton Campbell at the Yale Club and openly expressed his euphoria over the novel's impending release. "As I started up the stairs to the second floor, Scott was coming down, beaming. He had in his hand a color-illustrated jacket cover of a book. On seeing me, with almost childish glee and radiating good news, he said, 'Look what I have here!' He showed me the cover. 'It's all about Princeton,' Scott said in that breathless way he spoke when he was excited.

'You'll probably recognize some of your friends. You might even recognize something of yourself.' . . . Zelda flashed across my mind. I told him I had seen her when I was in Montgomery and had put in a good word for him. He thanked me and then looked at the jacket cover. He knitted his brow a minute as if to indicate that the months of hard labor on the book would be rewarded in more ways than one. He smiled and said, 'I phoned her long distance last night. I guess the Judge is getting tired of my calls. She's still on the fence and I may have to go to Montgomery to get her but I believe this will do the trick.' "

Though the impending publication had moved Zelda closer to marriage, no actual wedding date was set until Harold Ober sold the story "Head and Shoulders" to the *Saturday Evening Post* for $400 plus movie rights at $2,500. Fitzgerald had met Ober in October 1919 through the St. Paul novelist Grace Flandrau. He specialized in placing fiction with high-paying magazines, and became Fitzgerald's most vigorous promoter and close friend. The publication of "Head and Shoulders" in the *Saturday Evening Post* was a major breakthrough for Fitzgerald, since that magazine became his best market. The sale also initiated what would become Scott's continuing dilemma—and pursues authors to this day: the desire to be a serious writer yet earn big money. In addition to selling the movie rights of "Head and Shoulders" to Metro-Goldwyn-Mayer, Ober also persuaded three other film studios to pay $4,500 for film rights to three additional stories to be published in the *Post*. As a result, Fitzgerald's fees escalated to $2,500 a story, having the purchasing power of $25,000 in today's dollars. The lucrative movie sales prompted Fitzgerald to discuss this new market with Ober. "I was talking to Mrs. Flandrau last night and her saying that she'd gotten offers for movie rights to her 'Post' story reminded me of something I wanted to ask you. Is there money in writing movies? Do you sell scenarios?" Ober's affirmative response elated Fitzgerald.

To celebrate his first big success, Fitzgerald visited a Fifth Avenue jewelry store and purchased an extravagant platinum and diamond wristwatch for Zelda. He wanted to be at Princeton holding court when the book came out, so he left for Cottage to attend a prom and waited there for the March 26 publication date. On that day *This Side of Paradise* appeared in Scribner's bookstore on Fifth Avenue. Its window advertised Fitzgerald as "The youngest writer for whom Scribner's has ever published a novel." It was an

overnight best-seller—of the five thousand copies in the first printing, three thousand sold in three days. Fresh and trendy, the glib
book was also formless and superficial, showing little of the power
Fitzgerald would achieve in later works. But it was the novel that
made him famous, and spokesman for the Jazz Age.

News of Fitzgerald's literary success and the arrival of the exquisite watch did the trick. The formal announcement of their engagement appeared on March 28 in the *Montgomery Advertiser*. It read
simply: "Judge and Mrs. A. D. Sayre announce the engagement of
their daughter, Zelda, to Francis Scott Fitzgerald, of New York, the
marriage to take place at an early date." A few days later the paper
elaborated: "Mrs. M. W. Brinson (Marjorie Sayre Brinson) accompanied by her sister Miss Zelda Sayre have gone to New York City,
and while there will be guests of Mrs. J. M. Palmer, formerly Miss
Clothilde Sayre." Still, there was no mention of the date or location
of the wedding. The announcement shocked Montgomerians, including two of Zelda's boyfriends who expected to marry her themselves and refused to believe the story.

Convinced that Scott would not take proper care of his daughter,
Judge Sayre remained opposed to the union. Zelda encouraged
Fitzgerald to write her father and reassure him. "Darling—Mama
knows that we are going to be married some day—but she keeps
leaving stories of young authors, turned out on a dark and stormy
night, on my pillow—I wonder if you hadn't better write to my
daddy just before I leave—I wish I were detached—sorter without
relatives. I'm not exactly scared of 'em, but they could be so unpleasant about what we're going to do." Fitzgerald went ahead with
the wedding plans and wired simply: "I have taken rooms at the
Biltmore and will expect you Friday or Saturday. Wire me exactly
when." On departure day, her sister Marjorie accompanied Zelda to
Montgomery's Victorian train station where they were met by a
crowd of well-wishers. "Zelda's friends, carrying bouquets for her,
went to the station to see her off," recalled Rosalind. "Several years
ago I was introduced to a Montgomery woman and mentioned as
Zelda's sister. 'I did not know Zelda personally,' she said, 'but I happened to see her in the station the morning she was leaving for her
marriage, and I've never forgotten how beautiful she was.'"

Zelda arrived in Manhattan immaculate and rested even after the
long journey. "My husband and I met Zelda and my eldest sister at
the train when they arrived," said Rosalind, "and found Zelda . . .

appropriately dressed in the gray-blue Spring suit which she later wore to the ceremony at St. Patrick's enhanced by a corsage Scott had sent her for the occasion. She was as beautiful then as I had ever seen her and quite fit for Fifth Avenue." Fitzgerald and his best man, Ludlow Fowler, also were at the train station and escorted the two sisters to the Biltmore.

On the eve of the ceremony there were stars in their eyes and the excitement of great expectations. Scott welcomed Zelda's dependency, telling one reporter: "I think just being in love—doing it well, you know—is work enough for a woman. If she keeps her house the way it should be kept, and makes herself look pretty when her husband comes home in the evening, and loves him and helps him with his work and encourages him—oh, I think that's the sort of work that will save her." Zelda agreed. It was not until later that she would develop a very different idea of what women's work should be, one that would take a heavy toll on the marriage.

CHAPTER 2

America's Darlings

On March 26, 1920, Fitzgerald wrote his friend Ruth Sturtevant: "You may laugh when I tell you I am getting married April Fools' Day, but as a matter of fact I think I am. I have no idea where we'll live—we're going to the Biltmore for a week or so, but my pocketbook wouldn't stand that long, so we may take a cottage at Rye or somewhere like that." The ceremony actually took place at noon on Easter Sunday, April 3, in the rectory of St. Patrick's Cathedral on Fifth Avenue. Fitzgerald's cousin Father William B. Martin officiated.

Zelda wore her gray-blue suit and matching hat trimmed with leather ribbons and buckles. She carried the orchid corsage Fitzgerald had sent a week earlier with some swansonia and small white flowers to freshen it up. Neither of their parents attended. Witnessing the nuptials in the nearly empty cathedral were Scott's Princeton classmate Ludlow Fowler as best man, Zelda's sister Marjorie Brinson and Rosalind with her husband, Newman Smith. Her sister Clothilde and husband, John Palmer, were delayed en route from Tarrytown and arrived minutes late. A nervous and overeager Fitzgerald had instructed his cousin to begin the ceremony without them. Zelda was upset by his thoughtlessness. In addition, her sisters were astonished to find he had not arranged for music, a photographer, or even a reception. "There was no luncheon after the wedding because it appeared to us that it was not wanted," Rosalind recalled. "Scott did not communicate with us until the day before the wedding, when he phoned to say that it would take place at St. Patrick's the next morning, which made us feel that plans had been made as he and Zelda wanted them or he would have come to discuss them with us."

Though Rosalind and Newman were not personally offended by the lack of amenities, Clothilde and her husband were, and the relationship between them and the Fitzgeralds was never fully repaired. Scott's rudeness initiated a lasting alienation between himself and most of Zelda's family. "Tilde and her husband were invited, arrived at the hour they were told was appointed, only to find the wedding over," Rosalind remembered. "Scott had become fidgety with waiting for the ceremony to begin, and despite Zelda's and my protesting, had told the priest to go on with it. So we met the Palmers on the sidewalk, chatted for a few minutes, then Scott and Zelda walked away to wherever they were going. They may have lunched at the Fowlers. . . . Scott had done all the planning without consulting me or telling me anything about it, and under those circumstances, I could not offer entertainment. They obviously did not want it after the wedding. Marjorie and the Palmers, and Newman and I lunched together, then Marjorie went home with Tilde for a visit."

The honeymoon commenced immediately in room 2109 of the Biltmore on 43rd Street and Vanderbilt Avenue. Their first wedding present, a chocolate set with a delicate Tiffany urn, remained on the dressing table—beside a fading Easter lily—their entire two-week-long stay. Zelda considered it the most romantic day of her life. "Do you remember," she wrote Scott, "our first meal in the Biltmore when you said 'And now there'll never be just two of us again—from now on we'll be three [you, me, and us].' And it was sort of sad somehow and then it was the saddest thing in the world, but we were safer and closer than ever."

The Biltmore was a hotel favored by Princetonians, and several of Scott's classmates showed up to celebrate. The newlyweds drank Orange Blossom cocktails in their room and entertained Edmund Wilson, John Peale Bishop, Alex McKaig, and Lawton Campbell. The wealthy Ludlow Fowler, model for Fitzgerald's protagonist in

"The Rich Boy," invited them home for dinner. It was the first time Zelda had ever seen an elevator in a private residence. He introduced the couple to Manhattan's best restaurants and nightspots. Feeling her clothes were not chic enough for such places, Zelda went shopping with Marie Hersey, Scott's friend from St. Paul. It was the style to copy the costumes of musical star Justine Johnson, so Zelda purchased a sophisticated Patou suit. "It seemed very odd to be charging things to Scott Fitzgerald," she later said. To complement her new outfit, Scott bought Zelda a corsage on April 20, charging its $2.50 cost to their room.

Over the April 24 weekend they accepted an invitation from Princeton to chaperone a house party at Cottage. Harvey Firestone drove them down in his new robin's-egg-blue car. They arrived determined to shock everyone—and did. Fitzgerald introduced Zelda as his mistress, got roaring drunk, and started a fight. At breakfast, Zelda poured applejack over the club's eggs and ignited them to make omelettes flambés, then invited Cottage members in to watch her bathe. By Sunday, Scott was sporting a black eye, and Zelda had so outraged Cottage members and Princeton's administration that Fitzgerald was temporarily suspended from the club.

Free to do as they pleased, the twenty-four-year-old groom and his bride of twenty acted like teenagers who had just escaped parental authority. Zelda *was* only one year out of her teens, and her sense of liberation would be echoed years later by her heroine in *Save Me the Waltz*. "Alabama lay thinking in room number twenty-one-o-nine of the Biltmore Hotel that her life would be different with her parents so far away. David David Knight Knight Knight, for instance, couldn't possibly make her put out her light till she got good and ready. No power on earth could make her do anything, she thought frightened, any more, except herself."

In early May they were asked to leave the Biltmore. At the Commodore, they made such a disturbance—walking down hallways on their hands, circling continuously in the revolving doors, and hosting all-night parties—its management also asked them to go. Their banishment from these hotels was neither a surprise nor a disappointment. They were eager to leave Manhattan—Fitzgerald couldn't write in hotel rooms and Zelda wanted a place to sun and swim. Ruth Sturtevant suggested Lake Champlain, and with the help of Leon Ruth (one of Zelda's former boyfriends who was studying at Columbia), they purchased a secondhand Marmon sports-coupe touring car and headed north on U.S. 1 for Rye, New York. They found it a dull, unattractive resort, so they continued north to Lake Champlain, which was prettier but too cold for swimming. Turning southeast they finally ended up in Westport, Connecticut, on Long Island Sound.

Westport appealed to them and with the help of a local realtor they found the Burritt Wakeman cottage at 244 South Compo Road. It was a secluded, gray-shingled, two-story saltbox of Revolutionary vintage just outside of town. The cottage faced the road, but Scott and Zelda could see the Sound from their second-floor bedroom window in the back of the house. It was only a five-minute walk to the Sound and Compo Beach. The Fitzgeralds thought it a perfect place to summer and signed a five-month lease on May 14. Scott wrote Ruth Sturtevant, "arrived here at 9 o'clock this morning and immediately found the slickest little cottage on the Sound. We signed the lease on it at noon. There's a beach here and loads of seclusion and just about what we're looking for. We'd just about given up hope so now we're in the most jovial mood imaginable." While the house was being readied, the couple spent a week at a nearby boardinghouse. The place was surrounded by lilacs and quite lovely, but the food was too heavy for Zelda. They took long walks and sat up together several nights to finish one of Scott's stories.

The frenzied pattern of their life together was quickly established during that honeymoon summer. Zelda joined the Longshore Beach and Country Club and swam daily in its pool, while Fitzgerald worked on his second novel, "The Flight of the Rocket" later to be retitled *The Beautiful and Damned*. It was a fictionalization of their life in Westport, loosely based on their first months of marriage, with Anthony Patch and Gloria Gilbert as its main characters. Fitzgerald later told his daughter, Scottie, that "Gloria was a much more trivial and vulgar person than your mother. I can't say there was any resemblance except in the beauty and certain terms of expression she used, and also I naturally used many circumstantial events of our early married life. We had a much better time than Anthony and Gloria had."

The book immortalized the Wakeman cottage, which seemed to possess an almost magical quality with its covered porch off to one side, trellis, and sitting benches by the front door. "It was dark when the real estate agent of Marietta showed them the gray house.

They came upon it just west of the village, where it rested against the sky that was a warm blue cloak buttoned with tiny stars. . . . the house had been bolstered up in a feeble corner, considerably repartitioned and newly plastered inside, amplified by a kitchen and added to by a side porch—but save for where some jovial oaf had roofed the new kitchen with red tin, Colonial it definitely remained." It was a picturesque place, surrounded by farmland, perhaps three or four houses visible in the distance, an area abounding in small wildlife and a great variety of birds: goldfinches, orioles, cardinals, martins, swallows, and sparrows. Zelda and Scott strung a hammock and "close together on the porch they would wait for the moon to stream across the silver acres of farmland, jump a thick wood and tumble waves of radiance at their feet."

However, the Fitzgeralds' appreciation of this pastoral majesty diminished as they began to feel lonely and isolated. Zelda grew especially restless after a Western Union telegram arrived from Montgomery friends on May 17: "Hurry back to Montgomery as town is shot to pieces since you left." "No pep, no fun. No one to give the gossipers a source of conversation. The country club is intending firing their chaperone as there is no further need for her. Knitting parties prevail. Jail converted into sewing room. For the sake of saving dear old Montgomery pep up and hurry back."

To break the monotony, they commuted to parties in Manhattan or eagerly welcomed guests to Westport. These weekend parties became their chief source of entertainment. "More from their fear of solitude than from any desire to go through the fuss and bother of entertaining," Fitzgerald wrote, "they filled the house with guests every week-end, and often on through the week."

Because she had grown up with household help, Zelda expected the same in marriage, so an Asian houseboy named Tanaka was hired through T. M. Fujimori of the Japanese Reliable Employment Agency at 25 W. 42nd Street in New York City. Tanaka's job was to assist with housekeeping and party preparations. As inept as Zelda was with domestic chores, Scott was equally useless at repairing things or taking care of the grounds. So it seemed to them that help was a necessity rather than a luxury. Zelda later wrote, in *Save Me the Waltz*, how "they had tried to do without him till Alabama cut her hand on a can of baked beans and David sprained his painting wrist on the lawn mower." Unfortunately, Tanaka barely spoke

English and soon became the brunt of an elaborate joke fabricated
by George Jean Nathan and H. L. Mencken, who accused him of
being a German spy—Lieutenant Emil Tannenbaum.

The Wakemans had owned the house on Compo Road for over a
hundred years and were a well-respected Westport family. Various
family members had served as town selectmen, one had been a state
representative, and another a probate judge. In the nineteenth century, Henry Wakeman's Shore Road Farm was one of the area's
most impressive—producing large quantities of strawberries, cur-
rants, potatoes, and peas. There was a large strawberry patch behind the Compo Road house, the fruit of which made it to the
Fitzgerald's breakfast table. Historically, Westport had always been
a quiet, rural community. But its proximity to New York City (just
fifty miles from downtown Manhattan) made it the perfect place for
an artists' colony and popular summer retreat. Besides the Fitzgeralds, its residents included the literary critic Van Wyck Brooks,
artist Edward F. Boyd and his wife Marguerite Van Voorhis, and
Dorothy and Lillian Gish. Thomas Wolfe often visited Maxwell
Perkins at his home in nearby New Canaan, and would stop off in
Westport before returning to New York. John Held Jr., with whom
Fitzgerald had worked at the Collier Advertising Agency, lived
nearby in a beach cottage on South Compo Road. There was also a
large colony of theatrical people including Eva Le Gallienne and
the producer John Williams, who continuously entertained young
actresses at his large home on the Sound.

With the Fitzgeralds as renters, the formerly staid Wakeman
cottage took on a whole new character. Zelda began inviting people
up for weekend house parties. Most of her guests were male. Four
or five would arrive on Friday afternoon and inaugurate the weekend with cocktails, followed by dinner, then a ride to Cradle Beach
or Rye Beach Country Club, more drinking, then late-night frol-
icking on the beach and swimming in the Sound. In the morning,
Scott and Zelda often fought about whatever had happened the
night before, but they were still in love and arguments got quickly
resolved. Zelda recalled how they once "quarreled in the gray
morning dew about morals; and made up over a red bathing suit."
Two of their favorite hangouts were the Miramar Club, which featured a gambling casino and big band headliners, and the Compo
Inn, owned by Marion and Jake Levy. In a letter to Ludlow Fowler,

Zelda teased: "Scott's hot in the middle of a new novel and Westport is unendurably dull, but you and I might be able to amuse
ourselves—."

Zelda had no woman friends. She required all female guests to
conform to her criteria of "good" women. As Scott defined it in *The
Beautiful and Damned*, that meant "she must be either simple and
reproachless or, if otherwise, must possess a certain solidity and
strength." Not many qualified, so Zelda allowed few women in the
house. She was also accustomed to being the center of attention.
With Scott capturing the public limelight, Zelda was unwilling to
share the attention of male guests, and would act as outrageously as
necessary to get it. As a result of her mounting boredom, she repeated a Montgomery stunt and called in a false alarm to bring out
the local fire brigade. When they arrived looking for the blaze,
Zelda pointed to her breast. These men were not amused and
hauled Fitzgerald into court. The July 16, 1920, *Westporter-Herald*
placed the story on its front page under the headline: "Person Who
Sent In False Alarm Cannot Be Found; Fitzgeralds, From Whom
Telephone Central Says The Alarm Came, Deny It—Say They
Were Out Of House, But Will Pay The Costs."

With Scott busy working on his novel, Zelda had little to occupy
the long summer days, and eagerly anticipated evenings and weekends. Ever since high school she had kept a daybook noting interesting occurrences—who she was seeing and what she was
feeling—and throughout the summer she maintained in her diary a
running account of their social activities: "There was the road
house where we bought gin, and Kate Hicks and the Maurices and
the bright harness of the Rye Beach Club. We swam in the night
with George before we quarreled with him and went to John
Williams' parties. . . ."

Fitzgerald first saw these diaries during the fall of 1918. He
had already used bits and pieces of them to revise *This Side of
Paradise*, but now he began incorporating whole sections into his
second novel. Scott considered Zelda's diary entries highly original
and evocative, so he had them typed, then sent the manuscript to
Maxwell Perkins at Scribner's. "I'm just enclosing you the typing of
Zelda's diary . . . you'll recognize much of the dialogue. Please
don't show it to anyone else." Perkins thought them extremely
readable and agreed Zelda possessed an original voice and natural
talent. Scott also sent sections to Harold Ober, indicating that he

was using parts of Zelda's diary in "The Flight of the Rocket" for which *Metropolitan Magazine* had advanced $7,000 for serial rights. Describing the novel to Ober, he wrote, "it is a collection of episodes strung together loosely in the manner of 'This Side of Paradise' [that] would include one long thing which might make a novelette for the 'Post' called 'The Diary of a Popular Girl,' and a dozen or so cynical incidents that might work for 'The Smart Set' as well as one or two stories for either 'Harpers' or 'Scribner's magazine.' " Scott's Princeton classmate Alex McKaig later noted in his journal that Fitzgerald openly acknowledged that "Zelda's ideas entirely responsible for 'Jelly Bean' and 'Ice Palace.' Her ideas largely in this new novel 'The Beautiful and Damned.' "

Scott was so impressed with Zelda's verbal ability that he also showed the diaries to George Jean Nathan, who expressed an immediate interest in publishing them under the title *A Young Girl's Diary*. At once, Scott sensed that he had made a mistake, and when Nathan insisted on meeting the diary's author, Scott became intensely jealous. During July 1920, Nathan made frequent visits to the Wakeman cottage, and during one all-night party, after several guests had passed out, he wandered into the cellar and found Zelda's diaries in a storage box. Unconcerned about invading anyone's privacy, he spent half the night reading them, then approached Zelda directly with a proposal to publish. "They interested me so greatly that in my capacity as a magazine editor, I later made her an offer for them." But Scott already had plans for using the material and resented Nathan's intrusion. "Fitzgerald's answer was a resounding no," Nathan recalled. "He said he had gained a lot of inspiration from them and wanted to use parts of them in his own novels and short stories." Still considering it her mission to help Scott realize his writing potential, and knowing that through his fiction they would succeed financially, Zelda agreed they should not be separately published. But she had mixed feelings about Scott cannibalizing her diaries, and it made her think more seriously about her own writing. She was flattered that Nathan had liked her entries and found his arrogant, sophisticated manner attractive.

From 1914 to 1923, Nathan and H. L. Mencken were co-editors of *The Smart Set*. Besides being the first magazine to accept Fitzgerald's stories, *The Smart Set* published writers like Jack London, Aldous Huxley, and Theodore Dreiser. As an experimental and avant-garde publication, it became a market for authors ignored by more conservative magazines like *Scribner's* and *The Atlantic Monthly*, and accepted stories by Fitzgerald that were inappropriate for the *Saturday Evening Post*. Founded in 1900 by William Mann with the slogan "A Magazine of Cleverness," it wasn't until Mencken and Nathan's editorial leadership that *The Smart Set* lived up to that description. Though Mencken primarily wrote book reviews and Nathan drama critiques, both jointly authored "Repetition Generale," dispensing satiric commentary on Manhattan's cultural life. The magazine's best fiction appeared between 1919 and 1922. In addition to Fitzgerald's "Babes in the Woods" (September 1919) and "The Diamond as Big as the Ritz" (June 1922), it also published Sherwood Anderson's soon-to-be famous "I Want to Know Why," Stephen Vincent Benét's "Summer Thunder," and Willa Cather's "Coming, Eden Bower!"

Though Mencken and Nathan started off writing book and drama reviews, as co-editors of *The Smart Set* they soon became major forces in the literary world. Nathan influenced public taste and raised American theater standards more than anyone else in the country; and Walter Lippmann called H. L. Mencken "the most powerful influence on this whole generation of educated people." While Mencken and Nathan could be highly critical of one another, they nevertheless managed to remain close friends. Describing Nathan, Mencken emphasized his colleague's tendency toward hedonism. "He is a man of middle height, straight, slim, dark, with eyes like the middle of August, black hair which he brushes back à la française, and a rather sullen mouth. . . . He smokes from the moment his man turns off the matutinal showerbath until his man turns it on again at bedtime. . . . He has his shoes shined daily, even when it rains. . . . He has never had to work for a living. . . . He owns thirty-eight overcoats of all sorts and descriptions. . . . He hasn't the slightest intention of ever getting married." Mencken shared Nathan's attitude about matrimony until he met Zelda's Montgomery friend Sara Haardt. But during their protracted bachelor years, both men enjoyed a rich social life and dated some of the era's most beautiful and dynamic women.

Henry Lewis Mencken was born in 1880 to a middle-class German-American family in Baltimore, where he lived most of his life. Two years older than Nathan, he was the more famous when he was named literary editor of *The Smart Set*. At eighteen he became a newspaperman, working first at the *Baltimore Morning Herald*, then as editor of the *Evening Herald* and finally as a columnist for the *Baltimore Evening Sun*. He enjoyed wielding his sharp, satiric pen to attack America's politics, educational system, and lack of culture. Mencken became the most influential social critic of the first half of the twentieth century and, as editor of *The Smart Set* (1914–24) and *American Mercury* (1924–33), championed a generation of bold American writers. New York literary society did not appeal to him, so he lived in Baltimore and commuted up to *The Smart Set* offices several days a month. When in New York, he stayed at the Algonquin but took his meals at Luchow's, which served the best German food and beer. Seldom seen without a "Mister Willy" cigar clenched in his teeth, he was, according to Nathan, "very polite to women, particularly if he dislikes them, which is usually. . . . He wears B.V.D.s all the year round, and actually takes a cold bath every day. . . . He drinks all the known alcoholic beverages but prefers Pilsner to any other. . . . He detests cut flowers, carpets, the sea-shore, hotels, zoological gardens, the subway, the Y.M.C.A. and literary women."

At age fifty, much to everyone's surprise, Mencken married one—the thirty-two-year-old writer Sara Haardt. When Zelda was a senior at Sidney Lanier High School, her friend Sara was a sophomore at Goucher, then one of the few women's colleges offering a solid, liberal arts education. In March 1920, when the *Montgomery Advertiser* announced Zelda's engagement, it cited Sara Haardt's election to Phi Beta Kappa on the same page. A history major with concentrations in English, psychology, and philosophy, Haardt edited Goucher's newspaper, yearbook, and literary magazine and won several prestigious short story prizes. After graduation, she returned to Montgomery where she taught at Margaret Booth's School for Females and became active in the local suffrage movement. In 1922, Haardt returned to Goucher as one of the youngest members ever to serve on its faculty. While teaching, she also wrote short vignettes for *College Humor*, literary criticism for *Bookman* and the *North American Review*, and essays for *Scribner's* and *Country Life*. When she joined the Goucher faculty, her Montgomery friend Sara Mayfield was there majoring in English. And in May 1923, Mayfield won a story contest—the prize: a dinner with H. L. Mencken. Professor Harry Baker, formerly a *Smart Set* staffer, had arranged Mencken's visit to campus and asked Haardt to join them for that supper. Despite the difference in their ages and Mencken's professed misogyny, their mutual attraction was obvious by the end of the evening. Haardt was drawn to Mencken's vitality and wit; he to the fact that she was clever, literary, and very feminine. She was a tall woman with soft brown hair, deep brown eyes, and a delicate quality that made her the epitome of the southern lady. That evening commenced a seven-year courtship. They married in 1930.

Born in 1882 in Fort Wayne, Indiana, Nathan remained a die-hard bachelor until he was seventy-nine when, after converting to Roman Catholicism, he wed the actress Julie Haydon. During the twenties he was the most widely read and best-paid drama critic in the world, and though highly opinionated and quick to judge, his knowledge of world drama and standards of excellence were widely respected. He consistently recognized the first-rate and condemned the mediocre. An early supporter of Eugene O'Neill, the theater and personal pleasure were his primary occupations, and like Zelda, he viewed life as a play with himself in the starring role. While he was always impeccably dressed in exquisite, tailor-made suits, Nathan's theater attire was even more remarkable. For performances, he donned an Inverness cape and silk top hat, carried a walking stick, and sported a large amethyst ring. Describing Nathan's character, Ernest Boyd, the Irish-American critic and longtime member of Mencken's circle, said: "His business is the theater, and his business is his pleasure, but of life itself he has made a play in which he is the leading character. George Jean Nathan's 42 years, however, are the supreme triumph of his art in the comedy of life, for he has that air of eternal youth which is the prerogative of theatrical stars. . . . He is slim, dark and dapper, and looks like a preternaturally knowing college boy. . . . His suits are always freshly pressed and although he sits down, the knees of his trousers never bag." A connoisseur of fine food and drink, Nathan dined out nightly—his favorite restaurants being the Colony, "21," and Luchow's.

Nathan knew everybody in the theatrical and literary world, and after their first meeting, Zelda asked him to pass along a letter to James Branch Cabell. He promptly agreed and Cabell was completely charmed by her missive: "For a very young and pretty girl, won't you please do an amazing favor? I simply have got to have a copy of 'Jurgen' and don't you know where I can find one? I want to give it to Mr. F. Scott Fitzgerald for a Xmas present. I've grown weary and musty with ransacking bookstores and I've also tried to steal Mr. George Jean Nathan's copy under pretense of intoxication."

Dapper, urbane, and exceedingly witty, Nathan was unlike any man Zelda had ever encountered. Despite an eighteen-year age difference, they cavorted openly that summer in Westport, teasing one another, exchanging suggestive notes, dancing cheek to cheek, and brazenly expressing their affection. During all-night revelries by the Sound, Zelda and Nathan often disappeared for long swims, and at one of John Williams's parties, they sat at the piano flirting to the tune of "Cuddle Up a Little Closer."

Westport quickly had turned into a wild place, and it was rumored that sixty liquor stills operated in the area. The artist Guy Penè duBois recalled, "In the prohibition period the summers at Westport . . . exceeded the riotousness of New York. There gin and orange juice ruled the days and nights . . . work was an effort made between parties." Mentioned in Zelda's diary as her most vivid memory of summer there was "the beach and dozens of men." Charles Hanson Towne, a senior editor with Edmund Wilson and John Peale Bishop at *Vanity Fair*, was a frequent guest at these beach parties. Wilson remembered how "Charley Towne and George Nathan had been on a visit to them [the Fitzgeralds] which had become so disgracefully debauched that Towne, on his way home, to the great amusement of Nathan, was full of horrified compunction"—and second thoughts—after "reveling nude in the orgies of Westport."

While Zelda and Nathan continued their infatuation, Fitzgerald squired several attractive women around Westport—among them the actress Miriam Hopkins and Tallulah Bankhead's older sister, Eugenia ("Gene"). In perpetual rivalry with her famous little sister, Gene drank heavily, took drugs, smoked a hundred and fifty cigarettes a day, and was unabashedly promiscuous. In retaliation for Zelda's flirtation with Nathan, and because Gene, after all, was a Bankhead, Fitzgerald started a brief affair with her. At the time, Gene was engaged to Morton Hoyt, brother of the poet Elinor Hoyt Wylie, who was dating Fitzgerald's classmate John Peale Bishop. The engagement, however, did not stop Bankhead from having sexual liaisons with others; she craved excitement and passed from one man to another. She would wind up marrying seven times.

Turn around was fair play, and as a result of the dalliance between Scott and Gene, Zelda began taking the train into Manhattan to meet Nathan at his West 44th Street Royalton Hotel suite.
Most likely they were involved sexually; Edmund Wilson recalled
how she "used to say that hotel bedrooms excited her erotically."
Zelda intrigued Nathan because she combined the appearance of
youthful purity with the era's reckless spirit—a combination he
found irresistible. "Most alluring to man," he wrote, "is that woman
whose wickedness has to it a touch of the angelic and whose virtue a
touch of the devil." That was Zelda, and when not seeing her alone,
Nathan frequently suggested the Fitzgeralds join him and *Salamander* star Ruth Findlay for drinks. Though Zelda frequently agreed
to come, she would often not show up. Naturally, this tantalized
Nathan and elicited a prompt reaction. "Sweet Souse: What happened to you? Ruth and I got to the Beaux Arts at eleven and sat
sucking ginger ale until midnight. Were you and Scott arrested? . . .
Fair Zelda—Why didn't you telephone me, as you promised? I
missed your telephone message at the Royalton by half an hour. I
had a table for four at the Century dress rehearsal and Ruth and
I were compelled to occupy it alone. You missed a very good show."

Nathan's Royalton Hotel apartment, while modest, was decorated for dramatic effect. Thick drapery veiled the always closed
windows, and a variety of comfortable divans were strategically
placed to encourage conversation. Nathan owned a startling array
of "various elegant devices for holding, passing around and consuming alcoholic beverages," and his extensive liquor stores contained the makings of a plethora of concoctions, including the
dangerously addictive absinthe cocktails. His parties were fascinating affairs peopled with New York's theatrical and literary elite.

Always delighted to see Zelda alone, Nathan was less hospitable
when Scott arrived with a gaggle of his Princeton buddies. "When
in his cups, it was his drollery to descend upon my working quarters
in company with his friends Edmund (Bunny) Wilson, . . . Donald
Ogden Stewart, Ed Paramore and Edna St. Vincent Millay, all in a
more or less exalted state, and to occupy his talents in applying
matches to the rubber bindings on the pillows on my sofa. Their
howls of glee when the rubber started to stench up the place could
be heard a block away and were matched by my less gleeful ones."

Nathan's apartment was directly across from the Algonquin Hotel, where H. L. Mencken maintained a suite to entertain friends.

On East 44th Street, the Algonquin, owned by Frank Case, catered to the literary and theatrical crowd, its mahogany and brass-decorated lobby and Blue Bar being their unofficial clubhouse. Nathan and Mencken sometimes hosted Saturday-night poker games there, and occasionally lunched with the theater and film people from New York and Hollywood who ate there regularly. The famed Algonquin "Round Table" included Dorothy Parker, George S. Kaufman, Robert Benchley, Heywood Broun, Alexander Woollcott, and the actresses Helen Hayes, Ina Claire, Lynn Fontanne, and Tallulah Bankhead. Bankhead had moved into the Algonquin during 1919 while playing a small role in *A Virtuous Vamp* (a screenplay Anita Loos wrote for Constance Talmadge). At fifteen, she had answered a magazine ad calling for photographs of aspiring actresses and won a trip to New York City. Casting directors were intrigued by her husky voice and quick wit, and she soon became a regular member of the Broadway scene. The Round Table's favorite was Ring Lardner, who seldom came and couldn't understand why his company was so feverishly desired. Fitzgerald, who wanted to meet Ina Claire, whom he had long admired, finally wangled an invitation to the group's table. But Mencken found the group's caustic wit unappealing, and preferred eating with the "Inside Straight Club" on the second floor.

Having transplanted himself from the Midwest to Manhattan, George Jean Nathan had cultivated his sophisticated tastes during childhood summers spent with his father in Europe. He had also developed two other characteristics that he shared with Zelda: a quickness of mind, and a passion for continual excitement and diversion. Though he had been an unexceptional student at Cornell University, he excelled in dramatics and journalism. Before graduating in 1904 he had claimed the editorship of both the college's daily paper, *The Sun*, and its literary magazine, *The Cornell Widow*.

An admitted male chauvinist, Nathan liked women best when they were beautiful but not intellectually threatening, and, at twenty, Zelda was both. Writing of this preference, he claimed: "To a man, the least interesting of women is the successful woman, whether successful in work, or in life, or on the mere general gaudy playground of life. A man wants a woman whose success is touched, however faintly, with failure. The woman who is sure, resolute and successful, he may want for an associate in business, a friend and a confidante, a nurse or a housekeeper, but never for a sweetheart."

Zelda shared her attitude about this with Alex McKaig, who described the discussion in his diary. "Had long talk with her [Zelda] this evening about way fool women can rout intelligent women with the men." Another of his entries summarized their discussion about women's noses: "Zelda, Fitzgerald and I out for dinner. Very heated discussion about reality. If a girl has a crooked nose but sufficient charm to give her face an appearance of beauty—which is truthful?—a photograph showing the girl ugly with the crooked nose or a painting showing her beautiful because of her charm. Fitzgerald and I said painting. Zelda, the photo."

Nathan claimed that his test of a woman's mental agility was to ask directions to Grand Central. If she was half right, she was intelligent enough for him. Of his decision to eschew matrimony, he wrote: "I have never married because, very simply, in the language of a current music-show ditty, I am having too much fun. I can think of nothing that marriage could give me, but I can think of many things it could take away from me." He cherished his freedom to pursue "the slightly more charming woman just around the corner." Nathan was attracted to petite, young women who were shorter than his own five feet seven and a half inches, and had a particular fondness for blond actresses. One of these was Anita Loos, whom both Nathan and Mencken dated. The author of *Gentlemen Prefer Blondes*, believed to have been inspired by Mencken's attitude toward women, Loos worked as a film writer for D. W. Griffith. She lived in Hollywood where she had a laissez-faire marriage to film director John Emerson. As a child, she had appeared on stage with her older sister, Gladys, but her interest in acting waned after her sister's premature death from appendicitis. Zelda admired Anita, who was twelve years her senior. Loos had always loved to write, and when only six had won a limerick contest. By twenty-five, she had sold over thirty-five scripts to various film companies. Nineteen of those were produced by Biograph, which relied on her to provide material for their leading comedienne, Dorothy Gish.

Loos's marriage allowed her considerable freedom, and when in New York she usually stayed at the Algonquin. Though she projected the image of an independent woman who enjoyed a good time, Loos actually was a highly disciplined and conservative writer. Funny and vivacious, she became noticeably subdued around her husband, John, a second-tier director fourteen years her senior who was incapable of being faithful. They had no children and maintained separate suites on different floors of the Algonquin, a necessary arrangement since Emerson always reserved Tuesday nights for other women. Loos spent those evenings with Mencken and his entourage—George Jean Nathan, the novelist Joseph Hergesheimer, and the critic Ernest Boyd. Before making theater rounds, the group often dined at Luchow's on 14th Street, and inevitably capped off the evening at Mencken's favorite German bar, a rathskeller in Union City, New Jersey. Like Lorelei Lee in *Gentlemen Prefer Blondes*, Loos was expert at playing the "dumb blonde," seasoning her performance with vivacity and wit. She had quickly written *Gentlemen Prefer Blondes*, in diary form, on the train from New York to Los Angeles, but only on Mencken's insistence offered the manuscript for publication. Mencken loved her brainless characterization of Lorelei Lee—who insisted sex had more to do with ego than love—and wrote a glowing review, praising Loos for being the first American writer to make fun of sex in literature. Carl Van Vechten agreed, calling the book "a work of art," an evaluation Scott ridiculed. He felt too much of it aped Ring Lardner's work, but his criticism primarily was motivated by competitive jealousy. *Gentlemen* became the year's top best-seller, the European rights sold quickly, and Loos suddenly was rich and famous.

Nathan was attracted to actresses like Loos and Ruth Findlay because they gave the impression of being content to be "playthings." "I have known many women in this life of mine," he wrote, "and among them all, I have never known one who did not, in the lovely heart of her, wish to be, above all the more serious things of the world, a pretty and desirable toy. . . . Every time a woman buys a new dress or puts on a new hat, it is of herself as a plaything that she is thinking. Why is it that the women of the stage are generally more alluring than the women in private life? Because they have about them the plaything air." This was precisely the allure Zelda held for Nathan. Yet, though thoroughly infatuated, Nathan feared Fitzgerald's anger. After Zelda brazenly showed Scott one of Nathan's amorous letters, George reprimanded her: "The calling of a husband's attention to a love letter addressed to his wife is but part of a highly sagacious technique. It completely disarms suspicion. . . . Why didn't you call me up on Friday? Is it possible your love is growing cold?"

By midsummer Zelda was writing Nathan too frequently and showing enough affection to cause angry words between the two men. The argument may have been precipitated by an accident in Nathan's bathroom. Bathing was ritualistic for Zelda, who often asked Scott's friends to help wash her. Comfortable with nudity and proud of her body, she commonly disrobed in front of others before heading for the bath. But one evening at Nathan's, after much drinking, she cut her tailbone on a bottle near his tub and required three stitches. Fitzgerald incorporated the incident into *The Beautiful and Damned*, writing how "one night in June he had quarreled violently with Maury [Nathan] over a matter of utmost triviality. He remembered dimly the next morning that it had been about a broken pint bottle of champagne." Nathan denied arguing with Fitzgerald about the bathroom incident or Zelda. "In his biography on Fitzgerald, Mizener alleges that I once tried to flirt with Zelda and so enraged Scott that he engaged me in a furious fist fight. The facts are far different. While Zelda and I were accustomed to engage publicly in obviously exaggerated endearing terms, which Scott appreciated and which were in the accepted vein of Dixie chivalry, our close friendship was never interrupted."

Others viewed it differently. James Mellow cited Fitzgerald's 1922 letter to Edmund Wilson in which Fitzgerald acknowledged, "Nathan and me [*sic*] have become reconciled by letter." Arthur Mizener always believed the infatuation had evolved into a full-fledged affair. For his Fitzgerald biography, Mizener had written to Nathan in January of 1950, requesting permission to quote from his September 12, 1920, letter to Zelda in which Nathan directed, "I suggest that you hire a post office box for my future confidential communications. This, true enough, is an obvious gesture, but what else can we do—? Through the Ages—George." Nathan adamantly refused Mizener use of that letter, responding, "Under no circumstances can I grant you permission to use the September 12, 1920, letter to Zelda Fitzgerald. This is final." Mizener's research into Nathan's relationship with Zelda convinced him the liaison was sexual, and he noted in his own handwriting on the top of Nathan's response, "He also made love to Zelda. He carried it off with typical high spirits."

For Zelda this was just another flirtation; she had no intention of leaving Scott. And while openly admitting she could sleep with other men without it affecting her feelings, she never let Fitzgerald know precisely how far she had gone. Nathan remained cynical about *all* women's intentions. "The man of ninety, dying," he wrote, "carries with him to the grave, if not the boyhood illusion of one woman's love, the senescent illusion of all women's faithlessness. . . ." Not only did he believe that women were inherently untrustworthy, he also maintained that they were interested primarily in their own survival. "No woman has ever loved a man so truly and deeply that she has not at some time permitted herself the thought of the pleasurable heartache his death would bring her." He considered Zelda typical of her sex.

Throughout the summer, Scott obsessed over Zelda's faithfulness. Nathan was so much on his mind that he drew upon him for two characters in *The Beautiful and Damned*. At first he intended to make Nathan the primary protagonist, but when that didn't work, he characterized him as two minor ones: the brilliant Maury, resembling "a large, slender and imposing cat," and Joseph Bloeckman, the stout but dignified thirty-five-year-old Jew who "assumed the consciously tolerant smile of an intellectual among spoiled and callow youth." As described by Scott (mirroring the expressions of Nathan and himself), Bloeckman's face "combined that of a middle-western farmer appraising his wheat crop and that of an actor wondering whether he is observed." Nathan was disappointed by Scott's dreary characterization of him and later explained, "[Fitz] came to me somewhat apologetically and explained that he had tried, but could not lionize me in his novel. . . . What he started as heroic me resulted in a wholly minor and subsidiary character not distinguished for any perceptible favorable attribute." Nevertheless, Nathan was included on the dedication page along with Shane Leslie and Maxwell Perkins—"In Appreciation of Much Literary Help and Encouragement." In Fitzgerald's novel, Bloeckman, the vice president of "Films Par Excellence," is attracted to Gloria Gilbert, but loses her affections to Anthony Patch. After marrying Anthony, with little to occupy her time, Gloria encourages Bloeckman's attentions. To him, she confides her ambition to become a film star. "I want to be a successful sensation in the movies . . . I hear that Mary Pickford makes a million dollars annually." Eager to help her, an encouraging Bloeckman responds: "You could you know. I think you'd film very well." But Anthony, mirroring Fitzgerald's feelings about Zelda entering the movie business, squelches the idea: "I hate actors . . . a lot of cheap chorus people . . . It's just you craving for excitement." Anthony continually insists marriage should provide Gloria with adequate satisfaction, and dismisses her ambitions with the complaint: "It's such a hell of a career—what am I supposed to do? Chase you all over the country? Live on your money?" Gloria reluctantly relinquishes her dream for three years. Then, just seven days before her twenty-ninth birthday, she contacts Bloeckman and announces: "I'm going into the movies—at last—if I can." Bloeckman, who has since changed his name to Black, is now a successful producer. Glad to see her, unbeknownst to Anthony, he takes Gloria for a daylong car trip through New York State in his "foreign car, large and impressive, crouched like an immense and saturnine bug at the foot of the path." Aware that her youth is fading, Gloria knows she has little time left to succeed. Ignoring Anthony's warnings, she announces, "Bloeckman said he'd put me in, only if I'm ever going to do anything, I'll have to start now." Fitzgerald worked in Zelda's own conflicted feelings about Nathan by having Gloria pose the question. "Was it wrong to make Bloeckman love me? Because I did really make him. He was almost sweetly sad to-night." At the screen test Bloeckman arranges, Gloria auditions poorly, and the film's director decides a younger woman is needed for the part. The novel ends with a veiled reference to Fitzgerald's alleged fight with Nathan, as a drunk Anthony Patch confronts Black at a private party and calls him "a Goddam Jew." The scene ends with Black punching Anthony in the mouth and drawing blood. Anthony swings, misses, and falls down pathetically.

Like Bloeckman, Nathan could easily have propelled Zelda into the cinema or theater. She was envious of Tallulah's overnight success and always talking about going on the stage. His failure to do so suggests Zelda's *own* uncertainty and Fitzgerald's dogged determination to keep her out of the limelight. As a theater critic, Nathan was on close terms with film producers and stage directors, including the influential John D. Williams. The Fitzgeralds' Westport neighbor, he often came to their parties and was photographed on the lawn of the Wakeman cottage sitting with Scott, Zelda, Nathan, and Alex McKaig. Fitzgerald sent that snapshot to McKaig several weeks after their Independence Day party at Westport. An enigmatic and emotionally charged image, it shows Scott and McKaig sitting cross-legged on the grass, McKaig holding a bottle of whiskey. Nathan and Zelda are together on the porch steps, his shoulder touching hers. He peers arrogantly at the photographer with a wry look, as an expressionless Zelda holds the handle of her parasol against her left cheek. Williams, dressed in white pants and shoes, drink in hand, confidently gazes at the camera. On July 19, 1920, McKaig noted the snapshot's arrival in his journal and pasted it above his entry. "Just received . . . photograph from Fitzgerald. Scene—weekend house party. Gentleman lacking half a face—William Mackie [a Princeton friend], next row—left to right—John D. Williams who produced 'Beyond the Horizon,' Zelda F., George Jean Nathan—dramatic critic, lower row—Tana— Jap servant, Fitz and Alex McKaig." An earlier entry—July 4— further detailed that weekend's activities: "Went to Fitzs for the day. George Jean Nathan there. John D. Williams, Al and Mrs. Maurice—Bill Mackie, etc. Drinking, eating, swimming. Fitzgerald spent $43. for liquor in one day. I paid for most of the food for dinner. Nathan and I had great argument—autocracy vs. bureaucracy."

Eager to separate Zelda from Nathan, and thinking a change of scenery might defuse the situation, Scott suggested a car trip to surprise Zelda's parents in Montgomery. Late that July they prepared for the excursion by ordering matching white knickerbocker suits— the newest golf-inspired fashion trend. Called "plus fours," knickers were eye-turning in the North but scandalous enough in the South to get the Fitzgeralds barred from several hotels and restaurants. In Norfolk they stayed at The Monticello, and in Greenville at the O. Henry, where "they thought a man and his wife ought not to be dressed alike in white knickerbockers in 1920 and we thought the water in the tubs ought not to run red." They planned to document their journey in a series of magazine articles, so they purposely ambled along bad roads, state to state, in their 1917 Marmon. Along the thousand-mile journey, they suffered a broken axle and numerous flat tires. When they finally pulled up in front of the Sayres' house, they discovered the place empty; Zelda's parents had gone on a trip to New York! Meanwhile, the Marmon was in such poor shape it had to be junked. To make the best of the situation, Scott and Zelda spent two weeks visiting relatives and friends, playing golf and tennis, and going to the recreational park at Pickett Springs. One night they stayed with Katherine Haxton who later remembered Zelda's search for her toothbrush. "She called, 'Scott, what did you do with the toothbrush?' 'Didn't have but one.' I thought that was the sweetest, most romantic thing I had ever heard of." Relieved of their car, they gladly boarded a train back to

New York. Their account of the disastrous trip was later published in *Motor* magazine under the title "The Cruise of the Rolling Junk."

The Sayres were very sorry to have missed Zelda. Without her, the Montgomery house seemed large and empty. Judge Sayre even found himself peering nostalgically into her old bedroom from time to time. They promised a visit to Westport the following month. When they arrived, however, they were appalled to find two of Scott's drunken friends asleep on the lawn and the cottage a mess. Though Zelda maneuvered Scott's friends to a nearby road-house, they returned at three in the morning to continue drinking. Then Fitzgerald started an argument that led to Zelda getting slammed in the kitchen door hard enough to give her a bloody nose and black eye. The situation was intolerable for the Judge, who vehemently opposed alcohol and detested drunken behavior. The Sayres expressed their disapproval by departing earlier than planned and heading for Zelda's sister Clothilde in Tarrytown. Humiliated and embarrassed, Zelda later incorporated the conversation her father had had with her over the incident into *Save Me the Waltz*. " 'Understand . . . that I am not passing a moral judgment on your personal conduct,' the Judge was saying, 'You are a grown woman and that is your own affair.' 'I understand,' she said. 'You just disapprove, so you're not going to stand it. If I don't accept your way of thinking, you'll leave me to myself. Well, I suppose I have no right to ask you to stay.' 'People who do not subscribe,' answered the Judge, 'have no rights.' "

Rosalind recalled her father's distress over this incident—and others like it—but qualified the severity of his disapproval. "He left it to us to carve our own paths, not financially but in getting along in other ways, this most certainly not from indifference, for in his undemonstrative way he loved us and kept an interested eye on us, but because he considered us old enough to think and decide for ourselves, as he was doing at nineteen, and must surely have trusted that the examples he and mama had set of honorableness in all things, together with the good education we had received would lead us the right way."

As soon as the Sayres left, Scott's friends started showing up. Stephen (Peevie) Parrott, Fitzgerald's classmate from Newman and Princeton, who was infatuated with Zelda, appeared days later, his arrival reported by Scott to Shane Leslie. Each day brought new visitors and more distractions as the house filled with people. Some stayed until midweek, and though most were pleasant, some were not. John Biggs Jr. was among the worst offenders. Grandson of the former governor of Delaware, Biggs was Fitzgerald's junior-year roommate at Princeton. Together they had written Triangle's 1916 production *Safety First!* After graduation, the dyslexic Biggs entered Harvard Law School where he was a poor student. "I got there in April. I never went to any classes," Biggs admitted. "I used to go to [Felix] Frankfurter's classes occasionally, but not very many. I used to go to patent law regularly, but I skipped everything else and worked from everybody else's notebooks. I got a C plus. I couldn't have done any better if I'd worked myself to death." He visited Westport frequently that summer and was drunk much of the time. A hulk of a man with an enormous head and loud voice, Biggs made Zelda feel physically threatened; he was the only one of Scott's friends she avoided. Sometimes he would not leave Westport until Fitzgerald asked him to go. McKaig resented his presence and noted in his diary entry for September 4, 1920: "Biggs is a drunken bum. Noted at college for nothing. Now supposed to be at Harvard Law. [He] went to visit Fitzgeralds at Westport. They had to burn his socks, sheets—everything. Stayed drunk for two weeks straight. Atmosphere of crime, lust, sensuality pervaded the house. Finally, Zelda said either he or she would have to leave house and then ran away herself."

Although Scott was aware of the animosity Zelda and others had toward Biggs, he did little to intervene. In *The Beautiful and Damned*, he fictionalized Biggs as the stocky derelict Joe Hull, who smells bad and has a maudlin laugh. In one scene, Anthony's drunken friends lift Gloria and pass her around the room, ignoring her demands to be put down. She flees to her room and minutes later observes Hull swaying drunk at her door. Fitzgerald's words convey the pervading atmosphere of evil: "Some one had come to the door and was standing regarding her, very quiet except for a slight swaying motion. She could see the outline of his figure distinct against some indistinguishable light. There was no sound anywhere, only a great persuasive silence—even the dripping had ceased . . . only this figure, swaying, swaying in the doorway, an indiscernible and subtly menacing terror, a personality filthy under its varnish, like smallpox spots under a layer of powder." Fleeing from the house to the train station, Gloria is pursued by her husband and his friends. But she refuses to return and boards the train for Manhattan to spend the night with a male friend.

This story was based on an actual incident, and it was probably to Alex McKaig's apartment that Zelda fled. He noted in his diary on September 15, 1920: "In evening, Zelda—drunk—having decided to leave Fitzgerald and having nearly been killed walking down railroad track—blew in. Fitzgerald came shortly after. He had caught same train—with no money or ticket. They threatened to put him off but finally let him stay on—Zelda refusing to give him any money. They continued their fight while here. Helped Zelda bathe and then she went to sleep in my bed. Fitzgerald, John and I talked until 1:00 a.m."

That year Scott's circle of Princeton friends living in Manhattan included McKaig, John Peale Bishop, Edmund Wilson, Lawton Campbell, Ludlow Fowler, Townsend Martin, and Bill Mackie. Fitzgerald was the only married man. Not since Montgomery had Zelda been surrounded by so many attractive men, and, barring the occasional unpleasantry, she thrived on their attention. "There were Townsend's blue eyes and Ludlow's rubbers and a trunk that exuded sachet and the marshmallow odor of the Biltmore," she wistfully recalled. "There was always Ludlow and Townsend and Alex and Bill Mackie and you and me. We did not like women and we were happy."

By October 1920, Carl Van Vechten became the newest addition to the Fitzgeralds' circle. George Jean Nathan, who was trying to put some distance between himself and Zelda, introduced him. At forty, Van Vechten was older than most of their friends and lived comfortably in an apartment at 150 West 55th Street. Born in 1880 in Cedar Rapids, Iowa, he received his B.A. from the University of Chicago in 1903, and thereafter began his writing career as a cub reporter for the *Chicago American*. He became assistant music critic for the *New York Times* in 1906, and, later, America's first serious ballet critic. Zelda and Van Vechten, whom she called "Carlo," liked and admired each other from the start. Besides their mutual interest in dance, each possessed an idiosyncratic way of thinking and talking. Carlo loved Zelda's wit and free association of ideas, and she relished his urbane humor, which was, no doubt, further improved by the numerous Sidecars he imbibed. The Fitzgeralds enjoyed making the rounds of Manhattan's all-night speakeasies and Harlem bars with Van Vechten and his wife, Fania Marinoff, the Russian-born actress who was quickly becoming a celebrated movie figure. Despite his successful marriage to Fania, Van Vechten, who had previously been married to Ann Snyder, also involved himself in homosexual relationships.

Tall, with the lean sturdy physique of a Scandinavian, Van Vechten dressed in exquisite clothes and had a definite preference for the odd, the charming, and the glamorous. Zelda liked to call him an "experimentalist." He was someone with whom she could exchange clever barbs and engage in stimulating conversations. He reminded her of Nathan and, like him, was a dedicated partygoer and giver. There was never a dull evening with Carlo. Van Vechten was equally fond of the Fitzgeralds, and immortalized their evenings out in his novel *Parties*, using Zelda and Scott as the prototypes for his main characters, David and Rilda Westlake. Clearly, he had paid close attention to the nuances of the Fitzgeralds' relationship, for he characterized the Westlakes as a couple who "loved each other . . . desperately, passionately . . . [and] clung to each other like barnacles cling to rocks, but . . . wanted to hurt each other all the time."

It was one thing to socialize with Carlo and other friends in Manhattan, but quite another to entertain people continually at Westport. As Fitzgerald drew closer to completing *The Beautiful and Damned*, he needed absolute quiet, and increasingly he sent Zelda into the city alone so he could write. On these excursions, she might visit Ludlow Fowler, meet Lawton Campbell for lunch at his club, or go to a theater matinee with Alex McKaig. She once threw Campbell into hysterics by arriving in a hat she had made from blotting paper. People never knew what to expect, or whether she was being serious or funny. Campbell recalled how "she passed very quickly from one topic to another and you didn't question her. It wouldn't occur to you to stop her and to ask what she meant."

Like the fictionalized Gloria in *The Beautiful and Damned*, Zelda was predisposed to liking many men, especially those who gave her "frank homage and unfailing entertainment." She flirted openly and felt that sleeping with another man did not make her unfaithful. It was a perturbing thought for Fitzgerald. The mere notion of Zelda having sex with another made him frantic. Whenever she returned from one of her excursions without a full explanation, he became distraught. His anxiety mounted further when she implied she'd been with a man. McKaig commented on the tension: "If she's there, Fitzgerald can't work—she bothers him—; if she's not there, he can't work worried of what she might do." And though Scott was proud that Zelda was attractive to so many, he expected her to have feelings only for him, and resented what he viewed as a lack of commitment. McKaig advised him to bury these thoughts and complete his novel, noting on September 15, 1920 in his diary: "None of the men . . . she now knows would take her for a mistress."

Zelda loved teasing and flirting recklessly with Scott's friends. Edmund Wilson remembered how she played one against the other by proclaiming her sincerity separately to each. "John [Bishop], I like you better than anybody in the world: I never feel safe with you!—I only like men who kiss as means to an end. I never know how to treat the other kind." Gazing passionately at Zelda, Bill Mackie exclaimed, "I've been twirling the thyrsus tonight in Greenwich Village—I can feel my ears getting pointed!" (By this arch bit of indirection he meant he had been drinking and felt like a satyr.) Mackie became so aroused, Wilson recalled, "he withdrew to the bathroom where he was found in a state of collapse murmuring: 'She made provoking gestures to me!' One night he was found weeping outside Townsend's house."

Zelda's high school yearbook had printed, under her picture: "Why should all life be work, when we all can borrow, Let's only think of today and not worry about tomorrow." Now, as Scott's wife, she pushed that credo to its limit. Fitzgerald was awed and dismayed by what he considered her coldhearted selfishness, and infused Gloria with that trait in *The Beautiful and Damned*. "The magnificent attitude of not giving a damn altered overnight; from being a mere tenet of Gloria's, it became the entire solace and justification for what they chose to do and what consequence it brought. Not to be sorry, not to loose one cry of regret, to live according to a clear code of honor toward each other, and to seek the moment's happiness as fervently and persistently as possible. 'No one cares about us but ourselves, Anthony,' she said one day. 'It'd be ridiculous for me to go about pretending I felt any obligations toward the world, and as for worrying what people think about me, I simply don't, that's all.' "

Sometimes when Zelda came into Manhattan she stopped off at the *Vanity Fair* offices of Edmund Wilson and John Peale Bishop. Of the magazines gaining popularity during the twenties, *Vanity Fair* and *The New Yorker* (founded in 1925) were the most widely read. Both chronicled the era's extravagances for sophisticated audiences and attracted the most popular writers. The elegant *Vanity Fair*, first published before World War I, aimed at the elite and boasted as its illustrator John Held Jr., who regularly drew bare-kneed, flat-chested, short-haired flappers for its covers.

Wilson became managing editor of *Vanity Fair* in January 1920 when his friends Dorothy Parker and Robert Benchley resigned after an argument with the magazine's publisher, Condé Nast. With his high-pitched voice and bright red hair, Wilson had been considered eccentric and overly intellectual at Princeton. In New York, he was a perfect fit for the literary crowd. After graduating at the top of his class, he had served with the ambulance corps in Europe, then returned to the States and became a reporter for the *New York Evening Sun*. Upon accepting the *Vanity Fair* post, Wilson hired his classmate John Peale Bishop, who had also just returned from the war. While excellent co-editors, the two men were worlds apart personally—Wilson detached and absentminded; Bishop urbane and refined with a core of sensuality. Like Bishop, Wilson intended to be a novelist and poet, but after becoming a highly successful critic put those aspirations aside. During the twenties he read and reviewed more books than any other journalist. He and Bishop simultaneously dated Elinor Hoyt Wylie and Edna St. Vincent Millay, who occasionally contributed a poem to their magazine. At the time, Millay lived in a cold-water flat and would come over to Wilson's 16th Street apartment to bathe, often parading around naked. Like Zelda, she enjoyed flouting convention and was promiscuous, occasionally engaging in heavy petting with Bishop and Wilson at the same time.

It was Bishop, not Wilson, who became Scott's close friend. "In a sense we were not very close," Wilson recalled. "I was ahead of him at college, and from the time he went to live in Europe, I hardly ever saw him. John was Scott's great friend, I wasn't." Throughout the war, Bishop kept up a prodigious correspondence with Fitzgerald, writing from the trenches: "Oh, Scott—I am hungry for beauty, for poetry, for talk, for kindly mirth, for subtle wit, for quiet hours and peace, for nights and late rising, for tweed knickerbockers and cafe au lait, for all things I have not, for the sight of you and T.M., and Alex and Bunny, for a mistress, for love, for religion, for shirred eggs—." He and Scott had even planned to room together after the war, Bishop writing, "Will you honestly take a garret (it may be a basement but a garret sounds better) with me somewhere near Washington Square?"

When Scott and Zelda unexpectedly married, Bishop was forced to share a small apartment with Alex McKaig. His unhappiness with that situation turned to delight when Townsend Martin's luxurious flat became available. Also a Princeton graduate, Martin was the nephew of the socially prominent philanthropist and author Frederick Townsend Martin. With little money of his own, Townsend seldom stayed long in Manhattan, but circulated among European royalty and the wealthy at their chic resorts. Martin loved to name-drop, which impressed Zelda, and, like McKaig, he intended to become a playwright but never got around to writing anything. His handsome Nordic features and deep blue eyes were attractive to Zelda, and she loved his tastefully decorated apartment, which resembled a stage set. It was, however, his self-absorption that particularly appealed to her, and she told him so. "You and I are really the only ones who are really interested in ourselves." He knew she thought him sophisticated and attractive, but while he encouraged her attentions he also resisted getting involved. One afternoon he brought the flirtation to an abrupt halt when Zelda cornered him in his bathroom and demanded he give her a bath. Before the week was out he announced his departure for Tahiti. Zelda was disappointed to see him leave, and when he sent a photograph from Pago Pago appearing happy and relaxed in a tie-dyed sarong, oxford cloth shirt, and canvas sneakers without socks, she gave it an entire page in her scrapbook.

Whenever Townsend was away, he gave John Peale Bishop the use of his apartment and Bishop immediately treated the residence as his domain. There was a dramatic quality about Martin's rooms that transformed the place into fantasy and Bishop into the epitome of the young lord, as he strutted around in Townsend's silk dressing gowns among the Japanese screens and antique porcelains. It was exactly the lifestyle Bishop wanted, and in appreciation, he dedicated his first book of poetry, *Green Fruit*, to Martin. The expensively furnished apartment soon became a gathering place for Bishop's friends, including the Fitzgeralds, Alex McKaig, George Jean Nathan, Edmund Wilson, and Gilbert Seldes, editor of *The Dial*. Seldes recalled one all-night party there when he had fallen asleep on Townsend's Renaissance bed and awakened to see Scott and Zelda coming toward him. "Suddenly, this double apparition approached me. The two most beautiful people in the world were floating toward me smiling. . . . I thought to myself, 'if there is anything I can do to keep them beautiful—I will do it.' " Unfortunately, there was not.

With Townsend in Tahiti, Zelda turned her attention to Bishop, whose solid intellect, fastidious taste, and eighteenth-century southern manners she found enticing. While Fitzgerald allowed friends one wedding kiss with his new wife, she quipped that kisses were only a means to an end. One evening she rushed into Bishop's room as he was preparing for bed and insisted that she was going to spend the night. It was a ruse the fellow-southerner well understood, but in deference to Fitzgerald, he ignored the declaration.

In addition to working with Wilson at *Vanity Fair*, Bishop also tutored the children of the affluent. But it was for poetry he lived. After working all day at the magazine, he spent most evenings writing, and while shaving in the morning recited his new poems to the bathroom mirror. But he hated the daily grind of a job, and was determined to marry a wealthy woman who could support him. As a young man he had been seriously ill and accustomed to being cared for by women. Late in the summer of 1920 he was involved with the poet Elinor Wylie, who was several years older and whose brother Morton, a freelance writer for *Vanity Fair*, had just married Tallulah Bankhead's sister, Gene. But Elinor was already a well-established poet, and far too involved with her own career to support Bishop. So when the wealthy Chicago socialite Margaret Hutchins came on the scene, his relationship with Elinor ended. Margaret was not only rich, she was controlling, and Bishop gladly turned over the reins of their relationship to her. An agrarian southerner who had never been comfortable in New York City, he agreed to move to France where Margaret eventually purchased the Château de Tressancourt at Orgeval, Seine-et-Oise. Only forty minutes outside Paris, the Château was originally built as a hunting lodge by Henry of Navarre, but had been expanded into a gracious home during the eighteenth century.

By early fall of 1920, Westport was already growing chilly, and even with its two big fireplaces going, the Fitzgeralds' cottage was damp. They moved into a Manhattan brownstone apartment at 38 West 59th Street, adjacent to the Plaza Hotel, which conveniently delivered their meals. That spring they moved several blocks east to larger quarters at 381 East 59th Street. With Townsend still in Tahiti and Bishop occupied with Margaret, Zelda spent increasing amounts time with Alex McKaig, who carefully recorded their activities in his diary. McKaig had also settled in New York City to become a writer, and considered Manhattan the hub of creative activity. He was baby-faced with dark curly hair and a pug nose. Fitzgerald had known McKaig only casually at Princeton, and Alex was not among his closest friends. As Fitzgerald had done one year previously, McKaig was working for an advertising agency, and writing at night and on weekends, when not partygoing or attending the theater. That was seldom, for he loved Manhattan's exciting nightlife and squired the loveliest women he could attract. He took Zelda out whenever Scott was occupied. Describing his social engagements in his naval logbook, McKaig carefully detailed the daily happenings, emotional attachments, and rivalries among his Princeton friends.

After leaving Princeton, McKaig attended Annapolis and began his diary in a small navy logbook while at sea serving as a lieutenant, junior grade. The book, six inches in length and four and a half inches wide, started with a February 10, 1918, entry and, until July 5, 1918, the commentaries mainly covered shipboard activities. Thereafter, the log documents McKaig's struggle to secure a good job. On July 5, 1918, he noted his first day of work at the *Baltimore News*. Because the money was poor, in January of 1919, McKaig moved to New Haven and joined the U.S. Rubber Company, but was soon bored. "Don't think I shall care for New Haven—too little. I want girls. I want to do big things as a writer, preferably." By spring he was in Manhattan working at various jobs and keeping a running account of the activities of Princeton classmates, his worries over money, and his intense dislike of the business world. The bulk of McKaig's time, aside from work, was spent dating women, lunching with celebrities, attending parties, going to the theater, getting drunk, and worrying about his writing career. Gradually his entries begin to focus on his progress as a writer: "Working hard on movie work—adapting foreign plays to make scenarios. Have as a boss old Jew named Max Simon—formerly dramaturger at German State Theatre. He is teaching me something."

McKaig's earliest reference to Fitzgerald appears in his Monday, December 22, 1918, entry. "Wrote and congratulated Fitzgerald on

selling his stories and novel." More detailed entries concerning
Scott and Zelda begin on April 12, 1920, two weeks following their
marriage, and continue until May 5, 1921, two days after their departure for Europe aboard Cunard's *Aquitania*. As an aspiring
writer, McKaig relished associating with his more successful classmates, and pasted photographs of his favorites—John Peale Bishop,
Townsend Martin, Don Lake, Sap Donahoe, Bob Crawford—into
his journal. He saw the Fitzgeralds almost daily, listening to Scott
read manuscript drafts and Zelda complain about the difficulty of
being married to a famous author.

In his April 12, 1920, journal entry, McKaig notes: "Called on
Scott F. and his bride. Latter temperamental small town Southern
belle. Chews gum—shows knees." Before long, however, he was
completely infatuated with Zelda and reversed his initial opinion,
writing on November 27, 1920, that he had "spent evening shaving
Zelda's neck—to make her bobbed hair look better." She was then
wearing the highly fashionable "Ponjola" bob, a hairstyle popularized by Irene Castle, which two years earlier had been radical
enough to keep women out of New York's better restaurants. By
Christmas, McKaig admitted to being in love with her, writing,
"She is without a doubt the most brilliant and most beautiful young
woman I've ever known." Zelda was completely uninterested, but
enjoyed teasing him by offering her mouth up for a kiss in the back
of a cab. It meant nothing to her, but upset McKaig, who felt guilty
about the disloyalty. His December 4, 1920, entry read: "Took
Zelda to lunch. In taxi Zelda asked me to kiss her but I couldn't. I
couldn't forget Scott—he's so damn pitiful."

Most likely, what McKaig meant by "pitiful" was that Zelda
played the field recklessly, and probably was unfaithful to Scott. Yet
it seems unlikely her affairs were any more than flirtations; on the
other hand, McKaig did not understand the extent to which Scott
needed to watch Zelda in action in order to create the women in his
novels. Working the issue into his new novel *The Beautiful and
Damned*, Fitzgerald wrote a scene portraying the newly married
Gloria and Anthony in bed discussing Gloria's previous romantic
life. "I suppose I ought to be furious because you've kissed so many
men. I'm not, though." At that Gloria sits up and says: "It's funny,
but I'm so sure that those kisses left no mark on me—no taint of
promiscuity, I mean—even though a man once told me in all seriousness that he hated to think I'd been a public drinking glass. . . . I

just laughed and told him to think of me rather as a loving cup that goes from hand to hand, but should be valued none the less. . . . *my* kisses were because the man was good-looking, or because there was a slick moon, or even because I've felt vaguely sentimental and a little stirred. But that's all—it's had utterly no effect on me."

While Scott sequestered himself in their apartment to finish the final revision of *The Beautiful and Damned*, McKaig continued escorting Zelda to teas, parties, and theater performances, noting in his diary: "Took Zelda to lunch at Gotham. Townsend, Scott and I then took Zelda to cocktail party at John Coles and then tea in Biltmore." McKaig's life soon turned into an endless round of luncheons, teas, cocktail hours, dinners, theater performances, and parties. His interest in the craft of playwriting, and Zelda's passion for Broadway theater, made them perfect companions. And the 1920 season was full of good shows. Theda Bara was playing in *The Blue Flame*, Ina Claire—McKaig's and Fitzgerald's favorite—was at the Lyceum, and Marilyn Miller, whom Zelda strongly resembled, was starring in the hit show *Sally*. McKaig saw all of them. His journal entry for October 12, 1920, notes taking the Fitzgeralds and others to the Follies: "George Jean Nathan came and then Ludlow. Nathan left. Ludlow and Zelda went to delicatessen store to get a good cold dinner—ate it in apartment. Fitzgerald read me his bookshop story—damn good—a part of his novel—fair. Then I gave a theatre party—to Greenwich Village Follies. Never seen such wealth of beauty."

On October 14: "Dinner with Mackie and thence to theatre— 'Spanish Love,' in spite of my determination to work in evening— what a poor weak wretch I am." October 25: "Went to Follies with Scott and Zelda. Fitz very cuckoo. Lost purse with $50 . . . and then after everyone in place hunted for it—found it. He did not have enough money to pay check, of course. Home 3 am." December 4: "Went to see 'Enter Madame.' Zelda fell off seat. Actors complained of our behavior. Zelda got mad and left—followed by Scott. I stayed." August 16: "Went at 11:30 p.m. to party at Emily Stevens—the actress—have admired her for some time in 'Unchastened Woman' and other plays. Now in Zoe Atkins' 'Foot Loose.'" In an addendum to this entry McKaig tallied the plays he had seen throughout the season: John and Lionel Barrymore in *The Jest*, Ruth Chatterton in *Moonlight and Honeysuckles*, Ethel Barrymore in *Déclassée*, Booth Tarkington in *Clarence*, Emily Stevens in *Footloose* and *The Checkerboard*, and the Theater Guild's presentation of Shaw's *Heartbreak House*.

In the audience of so many Broadway shows, Zelda and Scott soon became Broadway's most recognized couple. New York's most popular pair, everyone wanted them at parties and openings. The papers constantly quoted Zelda, because everyone was eager to read about her. She was quickly becoming as famous as her husband, making Ring Lardner proclaim, "Scott is a novelist and Zelda is a novelty." Wanting them in the audience, critic George Jean Nathan gave them theater passes, and they attended numerous opening nights with him and actress-girlfriend Ruth Findlay, afterward drinking with them at such places as the Jungle Club and Beaux Arts. Three things got etched in Zelda's memory about this time: "Georges apartment, and his absinthe cocktails and Ruth Findley's gold hair in his comb." She was thrilled to be part of the star's social circle, and even may have appropriated Findlay's nickname "Dodo" from *The Salamander* as her own endearment for Scott. Fitzgerald spent a monthly average of $55 on theater tickets, purchasing seats for three to five shows at a time. They attended so frequently that Scott claimed the expenses on his income tax. Scott cleverly incorporated a discussion of the theater season into Muriel and Maury's amusing dialogue in *The Beautiful and Damned*.

MURIEL: Have you seen "Peg o' My Heart"?
MAURY: No, I haven't.
MURIEL: (Eagerly) It's wonderful! You want to see it.
MAURY: Have you seen "Omar, the Tentmaker"?
MURIEL: No, but I hear it's wonderful. I'm very anxious to see it. Have you seen "Fair and Warmer"?
MAURY: (Hopefully) Yes.
MURIEL: I don't think it's very good. It's trashy.
MAURY: (Faintly) Yes, that's true.
MURIEL: But I went to "Within the Law" last night and I thought it was fine. Have you seen "The Little Cafe"?

This continued until they ran out of plays.

The Fitzgeralds enjoyed mixing with the theater crowd and cultivated friendships with Lillian Gish, Helen Hayes and her playwright-suitor Charles MacArthur, Anita Loos, and Lillian Hellman. So omnipresent were they in theater circles, that Reginald Marsh immortalized them on the overture curtain of the 1922 Greenwich Village Follies. His scene showed Zelda diving into the Union Square fountain and Scott—in the company of fellow writers Edmund Wilson, John Peale Bishop, Gilbert Seldes, and John Dos Passos—careening down Seventh Avenue in a truck on the road to success. The fountain dive, which became an emblem for the era, actually occurred after a dinner party at John Williams's apartment off Union Square. Looking to do something outrageous, Zelda surprised guests by stripping off her clothes and running down the street toward the Union Square fountain—Williams and Fitzgerald in hot pursuit. There the three of them were confronted by a dozen policemen ready to arrest Zelda. When one of them mistakenly took Scott for an Irish comedian, she was freed without charges.

With each Broadway performance she saw, Zelda grew increasingly interested in becoming an actress. Women like Ruth Findlay and Anita Loos provided excellent examples of the independent, talented woman she now wanted to become. So when Hollywood offered Scott and her leading roles in the film version of *This Side of Paradise*, Zelda considered it her big break. Her exhilaration was short-lived, for while Scott initially was positive about the idea, he changed his mind on the advice of Maxwell Perkins, who warned that accepting the movie roles would confuse the reading public, damage his career as a writer, and hurt future book sales. It was a crushing disappointment for Zelda, who had long envied Tallulah Bankhead's meteoric rise to fame, and considered herself equally talented. Unsuccessfully, she tried to change Scott's mind, sharing her frustration with Alex McKaig. He told her frankly, she "would have to make up her mind whether she wanted to go into the movies, or get in with the young married set." Meanwhile, Fitzgerald incorporated her disappointment into *The Beautiful and Damned* by having Anthony threaten to leave Gloria if she takes the screen test and enters the movies. Like Gloria, who yields to her husband's wishes, Zelda also reluctantly put aside her ambitions so as to maintain domestic tranquillity.

Breaking into the theater or film business without a ready-made vehicle was a more difficult proposition, and Zelda had no idea how to accomplish it. McKaig doubted she would expend the effort, noting: "Zelda increasingly restless. Says frankly she simply wants to be amused and is only good for useless, pleasure-giving pursuits." His observation was partially correct, but there was another, more serious impediment to her success—her fear of failing. "I hope I'll never get ambitious enough to try anything," she had told Scott during their courtship, prophetically, as it turned out. "I might not be able to if I tried [and] that of course would break my heart."

As icons for the Jazz Age, the Fitzgeralds felt obliged to keep things lively, so they embarked on a new adventure each night. "Spinach and champagne. Going back to the kitchens at the old Waldorf. Dancing on the kitchen tables, wearing the chef's headgear. Finally, a crash and being escorted out by the house detectives." One evening, on their way to a party, Scott rode atop the taxi's roof while Zelda perched on its hood. Another time, in the theater, as they sat in row six of George White's *Scandals*, Scott discarded his coat, vest, and shirt in an effort to outdo the scantily clad chorus and was promptly evicted by ushers. From the first row at *Enter Madame*, they antagonized the cast by telling jokes and laughing in the wrong places. And, of course, there were those jumps into city fountains. Besides the one at Union Square, Zelda plunged into the water fountain at Washington Square and Scott leapt into the Pulitzer fountain outside the Plaza on 59th Street.

To keep reporters interested in their every move, the Fitzgeralds constantly planned new stunts, while remaining doggedly oblivious to what people thought of their actions. Observed McKaig, "She [Zelda] and Fitzgerald like only aristocrats who don't give a damn what the world thinks, or clever bohemians who don't give a damn what the world thinks. That narrows the field." Recalling their first year of marriage, Fitzgerald later wrote, "I remember riding on top of a taxi-cab along deserted Fifth Avenue on a hot Sunday night, and a luncheon in the cool Japanese gardens at the Ritz with wistful Kay Laurel and George Jean Nathan, and writing all night again and again, and paying too much for minute apartments, and buying magnificent but broken down cars. We felt like small children in a great bright unexplored barn."

Friends, however, were becoming increasingly worried about their behavior. "Evening at Fitzgeralds. Fitzgerald and I argued with Zelda about notoriety they are getting through being so publicly and spectacularly drunk," McKaig noted in his diary. "Zelda wants to live life of an 'extravagant'—no thought of what world will think—or for the future. I told them they were headed for catastrophe if they kept up at the present rate." But there was little to interest Zelda outside of theater and parties. Again, McKaig summarized the problem in his journal: "Went to the Fitzgeralds. Usual problem there. What should Zelda do? I think she might do a little housework. Apartment looks like a pigsty. If she's there Fitzgerald can't work—she bothers him—if she's not there he can't work—worried of what she might do. Discussed her relations with other men."

Scott was accustomed to changing his shirts twice daily, and insisted on fresh clothes being available, but Zelda was used to having a laundress and let the dirty clothes pile up in closets. As usual, Fitzgerald put the apartment's disarray to fictional use in his novel-in-progress. "Before they had been two months in the little apartment on Fifty-seventh Street, it had assumed for both of them the same indefinable but almost material taint that had impregnated the gray house in Marietta. There was the odor of tobacco always—both of them smoked incessantly; it was in their clothes, their blankets, the curtains, and the ash-littered carpets. Added to this was the wretched aura of stale wine, with its inevitable suggestion of beauty gone foul and revelry remembered in disgust. About a particular set of glass goblets on the sideboard the odor was particularly noticeable, and in the main room the mahogany table was ringed with white circles where glasses had been set down upon it. There had been many parties—people broke things; people became sick in Gloria's bathroom; people spilled wine, people made unbelievable messes of the kitchenette." Lawton Campbell arrived once for a 1 P.M. lunch and found the apartment, of which Fitzgerald writes, a total wreck, "the room was bedlam. Breakfast dishes were all about, the bed unmade, books and papers scattered here and there, trays filled with cigarette butts, liquor glasses from the night before. Everything was untidy and helter-skelter."

In the midst of this chaos Zelda started hiding money; $500 in June and $100 in November. Initially, it was in order to buy a $700 squirrel coat that Fitzgerald insisted they could not afford, but later because she disliked always having to ask him for money. With no bank account of her own, she was completely dependent on Scott's generosity and the capricious nature of a writer's finances—there was either an abundance of money or none at all. Her sister Rosalind recalled one luncheon at the Plaza when Zelda paid for their meal with a wad of bills as big as a tennis ball. "Why on earth are you carrying that much money around with you?" she asked. "Because," Zelda explained, "Scott gave it to me this morning as I went out the door so what else could I do with it but bring it along." Zelda had no idea how to handle money and, apart from acquiring a few chic clothes, was not all that interested in material possessions. According to Rosalind, "She had little training in money matters, having little to spend as a girl, and Scott as his history proves had little sense about them. Saving and building for security never entered into his thoughts (so he told me), and when he had money, he gave it freely to Zelda to spend as she wished without an accounting. This she did and in that sense she was extravagant, but she never made demands or seemed to me to want 'things.' " She did not really care for clothes as most women do, and as one as beautiful as she might have been expected to do, and she cared little about style and wore her things as long as they lasted. (Scott gave her a squirrel coat once in early 'flush' days after selling a story and she still had remnants of it when she died.) She wore no ornaments, had no jewels, was not the glamor girl type as far as appearance or temperament was concerned, her glamor deriving from her natural beauty, which she kept natural and her scintillating personality."

Although their style of living had taken its toll on their living quarters, it had not yet affected their appearance. Scott still looked like an undergraduate and Zelda, like Gloria in *The Beautiful and Damned*, still captured the attention of anyone who saw her. "Gloria at twenty-six was still the Gloria of twenty," Fitzgerald wrote, "her complexion a fresh damp setting for her candid eyes; her hair still a childish glory, darkening slowly from corn color to a deep russet gold; her slender body suggesting ever a nymph running and dancing through Orphic groves. Masculine eyes, dozens of them, followed her with a fascinated stare when she walked through a hotel lobby or down the aisle of a theatre." Mrs. Sayre recalled Scott's admiration and awe of her daughter's appeal as they waited for Zelda one day in the Biltmore lobby. " 'You couldn't know how beautiful she is, could you,' said Fitzgerald. 'You just watch that elevator, because Zelda will be down in a minute, and then watch all the men here in the lobby. . . . There will be fifty men here who will tell you exactly how beautiful Zelda is . . .' Zelda appeared, and Scott stood there bursting with pride as she walked over to us and I was amazed to see every man seem to watch her as she drew near, and Scott was right, she was a beautiful girl." Zelda, who placed great importance on her youth, since it was, after all, one of her few resources, recalled that they "never could have a room at a hotel at night we looked so young" and that to register once they "filled an empty suitcase with the telephone directory and spoons and a pin cushion at The Manhattan."

With prohibition in full swing, it was a game to know where to drink, and New York's speakeasies were doing a booming business. The liquor served, however, was of questionable origin and content. "Many people made their own liquor at home," recalled Lawton Campbell, "hence the name bath-tub gin. Some liquor was made for medicinal purposes under government supervision and undoubtedly large quantities of this type did get into circulation through unauthorized channels. But the vast amount of liquor consumed in those days was made in stills, and could be dangerous to physical and mental well-being. In fact, thousands of people were poisoned permanently or wrecked mentally, and many more were impaired organically for life by this illegal and non-inspected liquor." The Fitzgeralds thought they knew where to find good liquor. They frequented only the best speakeasies, their favorite being the Jungle Club, popularized by Owen Johnson in *The Salamander*, where couples danced the Shimmy and Charleston. Such places attracted a rough crowd, which made them appealing to Zelda, who enjoyed the excitement and tension. She was always the more courageous one, an attribute Scott envied and incorporated into his working manuscript of *The Beautiful and Damned*. "Gloria knew within a month that her husband was an utter coward toward any one of a million phantasms created by his imagination.... Herself almost completely without physical fear, she was unable to understand, and so she made the most of what she felt to be his fear's redeeming feature, which was that though he was a coward under a shock and a coward under a strain—when his imagination was given play—he had yet a sort of dashing recklessness that moved her on its brief occasions almost to admiration, and a pride that usually steadied him when he thought he was observed. The trait first showed itself in a dozen incidents of little more than nervousness—his warning to a taxi-driver against fast driving ... his refusal to take her to a certain tough cafe she had always wished to visit."

One evening Scott was put to the test at the Jungle Club, where he was supposed to meet Zelda. He arrived first, already drunk, and was refused entry by the bouncer—a hulk of a man weighing over two hundred pounds. Lawton Campbell remembered the ensuing fight and later wrote about it. "Zelda appeared at the door of the bar, looking around for Scott. I went over to her and escorted her to our table but she refused to sit down, because she said Scott had walked out on her. I told her that Scott had had a slight altercation with the bouncer . . . "No so-and-so bouncer can prevent Scott from going anywhere he pleases.' Despite my entreaties, Scott and Zelda with heads high and with the grim determination of young Davids, went to the door of the bar. The bouncer let Zelda by but refused admittance to Scott. Zelda turned in the doorway and spoke to Scott where-with he took a feeble punch at his opponent, which missed its mark. A few other phantom attempts were made and finally the bouncer lost his patience and gave Scott a shove that sent him half-way across the room, crashing into a table. Instead of that being the end of it Zelda then yelled, 'Scott, you're not going to let that so and so get away with that,' marching him back into the bar where he was badly beaten."

Zelda was still the leader, making all the social decisions in their relationship, while Fitzgerald followed. More important, she continued to be an unending source of creative inspiration. "He [Scott] would hang on her words and applaud her actions," remembered Campbell, ". . . often repeating them for future reference, often writing them down as they came from the fountainhead. I have seen Scott jot down Zelda's remarks on odd pieces of paper or on the back of envelopes and stuff them in his pockets. At times his pockets were fairly bulging with her bon-mots and bits of spontaneous observations. She would often make the most unexpected comment on something that had nothing to do with the subject of conversation but segregated by itself was sound and worth remembering." Edmund Wilson agreed that she had an extraordinary ability with language: "She talked with so spontaneous a color and wit—almost exactly in the way she wrote—that I very soon ceased to be troubled by the fact that the conversation was in the nature of free association of ideas and one could never follow up on anything. I have rarely known a woman who expressed herself so delightfully and so freshly; she had no ready-made phrases on the one hand and made no straining for effect on the other."

Her facility with words, particularly non sequiturs, impressed people because, while random, they were somehow uncannily right. She shared this ability with Tallulah, who also employed free association but sparked it with a liberal use of profanity. For Zelda and the Bankhead sisters, the more shocking, the better. Appraising the three women, Fitzgerald exclaimed, "How far they had come, those three, and how quickly! They were clever and lovely and racy, and they would do anything on a dare. Men and women fell in love with them almost without regard to their sex. They charged the air around them with expectation; in their presence it seemed always that something wonderful was just about to happen. They were like superb animals, raging to perform. Whatever they did, it would be as if for the first time and as if without effort, a lightly thrown-away success. Effort and failure were for their imitators."

Zelda also possessed a highly original, off-center humor, frequently couched in provocative questions—"Don't you think Al Jolson is as important as Jesus?" she would query. She posed her Al Jolson query to many, including Gerald and Sara Murphy, John Biggs, and Ernest Hemingway. The Murphys simply ignored the remark, Gerald recalling, "There was someone else there with us at the time who did not know her, and I didn't want to embarrass her by pushing the topic further." Hemingway thought it peculiar and labeled it madness: "Zelda was very beautiful and was tanned a lovely gold color and her hair was a beautiful dark gold and she was very friendly. Her hawk's eyes were clear and calm. I knew everything was all right and was going to turn out well in the end when she leaned forward and said to me, telling me her great secret, 'Ernest, don't you think Al Jolson is greater than Jesus?' Nobody thought anything of it at the time. It was only Zelda's secret that she shared with me, as a hawk might share something with a man. But hawks do not share." Hemingway missed the point entirely. Lillian Gish recalled how Zelda's conversation was always full of novelty, and that "Zelda could do outlandish things—say anything. It was never offensive when Zelda did it, as you felt she couldn't help it, and was not doing it for effect." She relished using questions to shock, taunting John Biggs over dinner one evening by asking, "John, aren't you sorry you weren't killed in the war?"

By January 1921, the Fitzgeralds were growing weary of New York and their own outlandish behavior. Now, evenings frequently ended with an argument—especially when a more accomplished woman came along. McKaig, who then was writing *Dark Victory* for Tallulah Bankhead, recalled one such "terrible battle in evening with Ludlow and Jack Dennison, Fitzgerald, Zelda, Tallulah Bankhead, a harmless and non-paying poet or so, and some wild women." Then everything changed; in February, Zelda discovered she was pregnant. McKaig had discussed that possibility with them four months earlier, noting in his October 21, 1920, entry: "Went up to Fitzgeralds to spend evening. They just recovering from awful party. Much taken with idea of having a baby." But the pregnancy came as a surprise to other friends. Wilson broke the news to Nathan, who quipped that the child "would probably be a cross between the Ziegfield Follies and Moore's restaurant." Expanding on that idea, Scott wrote it into *The Beautiful and Damned*. "To put it briefly, there are two babies we could have, two distinct and logical babies, utterly differentiated. There's the baby that's the combination of the best of both of us. Your body, my eyes, my mind, your intelligence—and then there is the baby which is our worst—my body, your disposition and my irresolution. 'I like that second baby,' she said." Still hopeful of playing herself in the movie version of Scott's second novel, Zelda was ambivalent about impending motherhood and its affect on her life.

Determined to have as much fun for as long as possible, in March, with her figure still intact, she attended Montgomery's annual Les Mysterieuses ball, a masquerade dance marking the end of Mardi Gras and the beginning of Lent. The yearly ball was presented by Montgomery's debutantes, whose escorts were invited by unknown voices over the telephone. Each young woman wore a mask throughout the evening, and joined her date only in the grand march. At the ball's opening there was a show in which members of Les Mysterieuses performed. Of course, Zelda was one of them. She wore red flowers in her hair and a hula costume with a short grass skirt, sash of Roman stripes, a tan blouse, and a black, red, and gold Bolero. Lawton Campbell, who escorted one of the debutantes, vividly remembered her performance. "On this particular occasion, the young ladies were dressed in Hawaiian costumes and among the numbers was a hula dance performed by the entire ensemble. During this number, the audience began to notice that one masker was doing her dance more daring than the others. All eyes were concentrated on her. Finally the dancer in question turned her back to the audience, lifted her grass skirt over her head for a quick view of her pantied posterior and gave it an extra wiggle for good measure. A murmur went out over the auditorium in a wave of excitement and everyone was whispering, 'That's Zelda.' It was Zelda and no mistake! She wanted it known beyond a doubt and she was happy with the recognition. A mere mask could not hide her individuality and no matter what the routine of the dance might be, she was going to give it her own interpretation."

In less than three years, the union of F. Scott Fitzgerald and Zelda Sayre had created a powerful myth that Fitzgerald dubbed the Jazz Age. With parenthood looming, common sense would have dictated that they should settle down to a more domesticated existence. But already they were careening out of control, blinded by the light of instant celebrity and captives of their own creation.

CHAPTER 3

Baby Makes
Three

With just six months of freedom remaining before the birth of their child, the Fitzgeralds headed for Europe. They embarked on Wednesday, May 3, 1921, for Cherbourg and Southhampton, traveling first class aboard Cunard's *Aquitania*. The leisurely voyage took six days, six hours, and ten minutes. Their hasty departure surprised Nathan, who had not fully repaired his friendship with Scott. Edmund Wilson told Fitzgerald that when Nathan dropped by *The Smart Set* offices, he "seemed a little crestfallen and I think he was sorry that you should have gotten off without patching up your quarrel." McKaig was even sorrier to see them leave, and noted in his May 5 journal entry: "Fitzgeralds gone gloriously to Europe on the Aquitania. I miss them dreadfully—used to see them every day."

This was their first European trip, and they behaved like children on summer holiday. In London they stayed briefly at the Hotel Cecil and received an invitation on May 13 from John Galsworthy for dinner with the St. John Ervines and Lennox Robinson that evening at eight. Tallulah Bankhead, who was in London appearing in a play, and would remain in England until the end of the decade, went out drinking with the Fitzgeralds and introduced them to the Marchioness of Milford Haven. Zelda later recalled the time for her daughter, Scottie. "We went to London to see a fog and saw Tallulah Bankhead, which was, perhaps, about the same effect. Then the fog blew up and we reconstituted Arnold Bennett's 'Pretty Lady' and the works of Compton McKenzie which Daddy loved so, and we had a curious nocturnal bottle of champagne with members of the British polo team. We dined with Galsworthy and lunched with Lady Randolph Churchill and had tea in the mellow remembrances of Shane Leslie's house, who later took us to see the pickpockets pick in Wapping. They did." Wapping was the dangerous wharf area in East London where Leslie did social work, and their all-night experience there became a high point of their stay. Zelda dressed like a boy in loose clothes, and she and Scott wandered with Leslie through the slums, shipyards, and streets where Jack the Ripper had murdered his victims.

Shane Leslie (born John Randolph Shane Leslie) lived in London at 46 Great Cumberland Place. The son of an Anglo-Irish baronet and American mother, during his American travels he had taught briefly at Fitzgerald's prep school, Newman. Author of the popular novel *The Skull of Swift*, he was better known as a biographer. As a Scribner's author, he helped place Fitzgerald's first novel and labeled him "an American Rupert Brooke." Leslie had known Brooke at Cambridge where, as an avid walker, he invented the idea of "hiking," and during a 1907 trip to Russia had become friendly with Tolstoy. A first cousin to Winston Churchill and related to Joseph Parnell, Leslie was socially well connected. He introduced the Fitzgeralds to Lady Randolph Churchill, Winston's mother, with whom they had tea at 8 Westbourne Street near Hyde Park, ate "strawberries as big as tomatoes," and attended a cricket game with her son Jack.

The Fitzgeralds took trips to Grantchester and Oxford, which Fitzgerald called "the most beautiful spot in the world," and visited Windsor where Zelda was photographed in her gray squirrel coat and Scott was snapped sporting his elegant walking stick. After touring Eton, Trinity College at Cambridge, and the Houses of Parliament, they marveled at the White Cliffs of Dover as they crossed the English Channel on May 20. A day later they were happily ensconced in Paris and attending the Folies-Bergère. They had a wonderful time at performances of the Sunshine Tiller's Girls of London and New York, "Les Chevaliers de L'Au-Dela," and a sketch by M. A. Couturet called "Le Crise du Logement." After going on a shopping spree, they took a day trip to Versailles, where Zelda was caught by the camera sitting on "Josephine's Bench." She was also photographed at Malmaison, where in nine years she would be a patient. When it was time for them to leave Paris, the management of their Right Bank hotel was delighted. Zelda had continually secured the elevator cage to their floor with Fitzgerald's leather belts!

From France they traveled south by train to Italy, stopping first in Venice, where they stayed at the Royal Danieli and gambled at their card tables. In the harbor they discovered the American destroyer *Sturtevant*, named for Ruth Sturtevant's brother Albert, and, after touring the vessel, wrote Ruth about the remarkable experience. They strolled in Piazza San Marco, where Zelda, in a beautiful pin-striped dress with a wide collar and scalloped hem, had her photo taken beside the Doges Palace with Lieutenant Robbins from the American ship. Kay Laurell, star of the Ziegfield Follies, whom they had met with George Jean Nathan, telegraphed from Paris: "How long will you remain Venice? Might come. Reply." But they were ready to leave and proceeded on to Florence. They visited Fiesole, wandered through the city's quaint streets and attended a piano recital at the Hotel d'Italie. In Rome, they checked into the Grand Hotel, which turned out to be flea-ridden, toured the Roman Forum and the Colosseum, and took a buggy ride along the Via Appia on June 10.

On the whole, they found Italy disappointing because neither spoke the language or cared for the Italian temperament. They returned to Paris early, hoping to locate Edmund Wilson and Edna St. Vincent Millay, both of whom had recently arrived. After checking into the Hotel St. James et d'Albany, they found Edna on assignment for *Vanity Fair* but could not track down Wilson, who had come two days earlier but neglected to leave his address with American Express. He had followed Millay, who was now involved with someone else, in hopes of winning back her affection, and was staying nearby at the Hotel Mont-Thabor. But only after they departed did he learn they had been looking for him.

Back in London, the Fitzgeralds checked into Claridge's, where they were given a drab inside room, away from the hotel's important guests, with the waiter their only contact. Wilson tried convincing them to return to Paris, but Scott was sick of Europe and Zelda was tired from her pregnancy, so both wanted to return home. Though they had intended to remain in London longer, on July 9 they boarded the White Star Line's S.S. *Celtic* in Liverpool for the return trip to New York. Before leaving, Fitzgerald wrote Wilson in Paris: "God damn the continent of Europe. It is merely of antiquarian interest. Rome is only a few years behind Tyre and Babylon ... France makes me sick. Its silly pose as the thing the world has to save. I think it's a shame that England and America didn't let the Germans conquer Europe. It's the only thing that would have saved the fleet of tottering old wrecks." Zelda, who had been ill with morning sickness and tired much of the time, agreed and was delighted to see England's fair isle fade into the distance.

Because they wanted their child to be born in Montgomery, the Fitzgeralds headed for Alabama, where Zelda hoped they might buy a house and settle for a while. But with prohibition still law and Judge Sayre insisting on no drinking, the atmosphere proved too confining. Montgomery was in the grip of a heat wave when they arrived. To cope with the unbearable humidity, Zelda promptly headed for the city pool. In those days, however, pregnant women did not swim in public, and her appearance there caused a scandal. Lawton Campbell was visiting home at the time and recalled that "Zelda had no secret pain to conceal, either she accepted her condition as a natural state of beauty or she felt that public exhibitions helped startle the populace into a more formidable appreciation of her independence. At any rate, while well advanced with child, she stepped into a bathing suit, a more matronly size than she would ordinarily wear and rode out to the municipal swimming pool. With no cloak or cape to conceal her figure, she paraded her pre-maternal glory before a wide-eyed audience. If she had remained on the edge of the pool, perhaps there would have only been whispers but that was not enough for Zelda. She plunged head-long into the sunny waters that came from Montgomery's famous and pure artesian wells and the on-lookers with one accord shouted 'That's Zelda!' " After being ordered from the pool, Zelda and Scott fled Montgomery's heat and conservatism by boarding the train for Fitzgerald's more temperate Minnesota home.

Once resettled in St. Paul, Zelda continued shocking people by standing and smoking in the back of trolleys and using unvarnished language. At the movies, she spoke in a loud voice, declaring, "I think Gilda Gray is the most beautiful girl in the world, don't you? If I were a man I'd give a year of my life to live with her for a week."

She particularly enjoyed unsettling the young men she danced with at parties by saying things like, "My hips are going wild; you don't mind, do you?" Seemingly overnight the Fitzgeralds became the focus of St. Paul's social life, attending dinners and Saturday night dances at the University Club and organizing the Junior League's musical review. They rented a house at Dellwood, the resort on White Bear Lake, where Minneapolis society retreated until fall. Later, Zelda wrote of the hordes of people who fled there in her story "The Girl the Prince Liked." "When summer came, all the people who liked summer time moved out to the large clear lake not far from town, and lived there in long, flat cottages surrounded with dank shrubbery and pine trees, and so covered by screened verandas that they made you think of small pieces of cheese under large meat-safes. All the people came who liked to play golf or sail on the lake, or who had children to shelter from the heat. All the young people came whose parents had given them for wedding presents white bungalows hid in the green—and all the old people who liked the flapping sound of the water at the end of their hollyhock walks. All the bachelors who liked living over the cheerful clatter of plates and clinking locker doors in the Yacht Club basement came, and a great many sun-dried women of forty or fifty with big families and smart crisp linen costumes that stuck to the seats of their roadsters when they went to meet their husbands escaping from town in the five o'clock heat."

Scott and Zelda stayed at White Bear Lake until October, when they moved back to St. Paul and checked into the Hotel Commodore until Scott's friends, Xandra and Oscar Kalman, arranged for them to lease Mrs. Arnold Kalman's home at 626 Goodrich Avenue. The month before the birth, Zelda occupied herself with procuring necessities—buying a bassinet and baby bed, and making arrangements for the doctor, nurse, and hospital room. The Kalmans were a tremendous help, since Scott spent most of his day revising *The Beautiful and Damned* in the small office he had rented downtown. On his way home, he often stopped by the Kilmarnock Book Shop on Fourth and Minnesota Avenues to chat with its owner. One day he ran into Mencken's novelist friend Joseph Hergesheimer there, and had an animated discussion with him about the solitary life of a writer. Lucy Norvell, a friend of Hergesheimer who was visiting St. Paul and staying at the Hotel Radisson, entertained the Fitzgeralds one evening, and Grace

Warner gave a bob-ride party in their honor. Writing from his *American Mercury* offices, Mencken jokingly told Scott he had recently visited the South and instructed him to "tell her [Zelda] I dropped into her ancient stronghold, Montgomery, a couple of months ago. They showed me the place where she once jumped a horse over five hay wagons, and also the grave of the colored clergyman on whom the horse landed. Please give her my affectionate devotion."

Zelda eagerly anticipated the end of her pregnancy. She'd felt wretched during the final weeks and was upset over all the weight she had gained. She and Scott were both nervous and excited when their baby was born on October 26, 1921. With pen and notebook ready, Scott scribbled down Zelda's first words out of anesthesia. "Goofo, I'm drunk. Mark Twain. Isn't she smart—she has the hiccups. I hope it's beautiful and a fool—a beautiful little fool." He tucked the sentence away for future use. Years later in *The Great Gatsby*, Daisy would say almost the same thing. "I woke up out of the ether with an utterly abandoned feeling and asked the nurse right away if it was a boy or a girl. She told me it was a girl, and so I turned my head away and wept. 'All right,' I said. 'I'm glad it's a girl. And I hope she'll be a fool—that's the best thing a girl can be in this world, a beautiful little fool.' "

Zelda had chosen the name Patricia for their daughter. But the day after the baby was born, Scott insisted she be called Frances Scott Key Fitzgerald. Though she was nicknamed "Scottie," Zelda still called her "Pat" five years later. A large frosted cake arrived from Ramaley's on Grand Avenue with "Welcome Sweetest Baboo" inscribed in its frosting. Telegrams came from Zelda's parents and Scott's friends: Townsend Martin, John Biggs, Alex McKaig, and John Peale Bishop. Ludlow Fowler wired: "Congratulations. Feared twins. Have you bobbed her hair; love from all."

Fitzgerald had really wanted a son and Zelda, who also preferred a boy, told Ludow Fowler, "She is awfully cute, and I am very devoted to her, but quite disappointed over the sex." However, it was not long before Scott was sending telegrams announcing "a second Mary Pickford has arrived." Mencken received one and responded: "I am delighted to know that your posterity is viable and active. One of my friends says that babies should never bawl. Simply clout them over the head, and they will cease. No narcotics! Scaring them is enough." When Nathan received photographs of Zelda with the baby, he wrote back cryptically: "The pictures prove to me that you are getting more beautiful every day, but whose baby is it? It looks very much like Mencken." It reminded her how much she missed his biting humor and the sophistication of New York City.

That year the St. Paul winter was particularly bitter and Zelda complained to Fowler, "This damned place is 18 below zero and I go around thanking God, anatomically and proverbially speaking, I am safe from the fate of the monkey." It snowed continuously. In a photograph of Zelda taken on her way to the Cotillion Club dance on January 13, 1922, she appears miserable and half frozen in her gray squirrel coat. By March, she and Scott were eager to return east for the publication of *The Beautiful and Damned*—the most autobiographical but least known of Fitzgerald's novels. Focusing on a young woman who craves self-fulfillment through economic and emotional independence, but is married to an insecure man who undermines her ambition and threatens divorce if she pursues a career, it made Gloria Patch the prototype for all women yearning for self-actualization. It also closely foretold what would be Zelda's life story.

Securing a $5,600 royalty advance, the Fitzgeralds left Scottie with a nanny and headed for New York. They checked into room 644 at the Plaza Hotel and began a monthlong celebration. One night they toured the Greenwich Village nightclubs and new speakeasies, and another evening attended a party at Nathan's, with whom Fitzgerald had reconciled. There were numerous luncheons with Edmund Wilson, Donald Ogden Stewart, and John Peale Bishop. Stewart, who had recently been fired from his bank job, was floundering and Fitzgerald introduced him to Edmund Wilson, who provided entry to the publishing business. Stewart never forgot the favor, acknowledging "that is how I became a writer instead of a banker." He would later repay the debt by introducing Fitzgerald to Hemingway in Paris. There was one person Zelda and Scott avoided—Alex McKaig. After their return from Europe he had gotten into a fight with Scott—perhaps over Zelda—and it would be years before they would be reconciled.

Wilson was surprised at how much the couple had changed in one year. Scott appeared tired and Zelda looked matronly and fat. She was sensitive about her appearance and worried that her figure would be permanently ruined. Then, less than five months after the birth of Scottie, Zelda was aghast to find she was pregnant again.

They did not want a second child so soon, and arranged for an abortion. Fitzgerald referred to this arrangement in his ledger during March of 1922 as "Zelda and her abortionist" and "Pills and Dr. Lackin." Though Scott was a Catholic, he seems not to have objected to the abortion at this time. Only later did he feel guilt, anger, and revulsion at what he termed the "chill-mindedness of his wife," writing in his notebook that "His son went down the toilet of the xxxx Hotel after Dr. X—pills."

In the midst of publication and serialization parties for *The Beautiful and Damned*, Burton Rascoe, literary editor of the *New York Herald Tribune*, asked Zelda to write a satiric review of Scott's new novel. "Will you please write a review for me of 'The Beautiful and Damned,' say about 800 or 1,000 words? I think that if you could view it, or pretend to view it, objectively and get in a rub here and there it would cause a great deal of comment. It would help the book immensely and it would help (in the way of sparkle) this new book department I am running in the Tribune. I can pay you a little—not much, but a little." Zelda was excited to be doing the review and also designed an alternative book jacket. Fitzgerald wanted something to replace the illustration W. E. Hill had done, but her crayon drawing of a naked flapper splashing in a champagne glass went unused. As she carefully read Scott's novel for her review, she was amazed to see how much of her own writing had been utilized, and commented on this in the piece for Rascoe. "It seems to me that on one page I recognized a portion of an old diary of mine which mysteriously disappeared shortly after my marriage, and also scraps of letters which, though considerably edited, sound to me vaguely familiar. In fact, Mr. Fitzgerald—I believe that is how he spells his name—seems to believe that plagiarism begins at home." In certain parts, her words appeared verbatim, particularly in the diary section, where, under the April 24 entry, she recognized whole sentences had been used. "What grubworms women are to crawl on their bellies through colorless marriages. Marriage was created not to be a background but to need one. Mine is going to be outstanding. It can't, shan't be the setting—it's going to be the performance, the live, lovely glamorous performance, and the world shall be the scenery."

Zelda's review of Scott's novel appeared on April 2, 1922, under the title "Mrs. F. Scott Fitzgerald Reviews 'The Beautiful and Damned,' Friend Husband's Latest," and its ironic tone drew amused nods. "Where could you get a better example of how not to behave than from the adventures of Gloria? It is a wonderful book to have around in case of emergency. . . . For this book tells exactly, and with compelling lucidity, just what to do when cast off by a grandfather or when sitting around a station at 4 a.m., or when spilling champagne in a fashionable restaurant, or when told that one is too old for the movies. Any of these things might come into anyone's life at any minute. . . . To begin with everyone must buy this book for the following aesthetic reasons: first because I know where there is the cutest cloth-of-gold dress for only three hundred dollars in a store on Forty-second Street, and also if enough people buy it, where there is a platinum ring with a complete circlet. . . ." Rascoe loved the piece but withheld payment until Fitzgerald hounded, "I'm writing you at the behest of the famous author, my wife, to tell you that the great paper which you serve is withholding from her the first money she has ever earned. Whatever it be, from a rouble [*sic*] to a talent, prick your clerk into satisfying her avarice—for she has become as one mad." After additional prodding, Zelda finally received a check for $15 and an apology. It was her first professional writing fee and the job had been so easy that she considered doing more essays and stories. *McCalls* was so pleased with the review, they asked Zelda to write a 2,500 word article entitled "Where Do Flappers Go?" At ten cents a word, she was paid $300 even though the piece was never published. She was so proud of her efforts that she pasted the *Herald Tribune* check stub into her scrapbook along with Rascoe's apologetic note: "You fled New York without giving me your St. Paul address. The check will go out today."

Although Zelda was repeatedly interviewed about flapper attitudes, she still seemed content to play the supporting role. "I think a woman gets more happiness out of being gay, light-hearted, unconventional, mistress of her own fate, than out of a career that calls for hard work, intellectual pessimism and loneliness." But something in her already was beginning to rebel against being solely the wife of a famous writer. Initially, she had been flattered to have Scott appropriate her ideas for his fiction, and agreed that he, as the breadwinner, had earned the exclusive use of all creative materials. But that notion was gradually changing, and a reservoir of hostility mounting as she saw all elements of their life together being used as raw material for his fiction. She especially disliked Scott using her "originalities" to impress other women, and later in her novel *Save Me the Waltz* wrote of how David had flattered the attractive Gabrielle by saying, " 'I imagine you wear something startling and boyish underneath your clothes . . .' He'd stolen the idea from her. She'd worn silk BVD's herself all last summer."

After celebrating their second anniversary at the Biltmore, they returned to St. Paul during the first week of April 1922 for the Junior League Frolic on April 17—in which Zelda played the part of a southern flapper—and the Post-Lenten Cotillion at the University Club on the twenty-eighth.

Zelda's career hopes again were raised when several producers expressed interest in casting the couple in a film version of *The Beautiful and Damned*, but Scott was still opposed to the idea. Hearing of the possibility, H. L. Mencken wrote on May 18 offering his services for a bit part. "Are you going to act in 'The Beautiful and Damned'? If so, I bespeak the part of the taxi-driver." Warner Brothers ultimately cast Marie Prevost in the role Zelda wanted, and while the studio also owned rights to *This Side of Paradise*, did not move forward on that project.

On June 17, 1922, the Fitzgeralds wired congratulations to John Peale Bishop on his marriage to Margaret Hutchins, even though they considered it a bad match and the end of John's creative life. Edmund Wilson agreed: "I regard it as more or less a calamity, but I suppose it is inevitable. She will supply him with infinite money and leisure but, I fear, chloroform his intellect in the meantime."

Again, they spent the first part of summer at White Bear Yacht Club where Zelda improved her water-skiing and competed in a golf tournament with Xandra Kalman, winning two games to one. Zelda loved White Bear and would have stayed the entire season, but their all-night parties disturbed other guests and they were asked to leave. They rented a house on the lake near the club, and settled in to enjoy the rest of summer. Scott spent most of every day revising *The Vegetable*, a play he intended on bringing to Atlantic City for tryouts, and would only emerge from his study late in the afternoon for a swim before dressing for dinner and the evening. Zelda seemed content to participate in water sports and play with her baby daughter. But while one photo showed her lifting Scottie with carefree ease and pride, another revealed her nervously twisting back her left hand in an oddly strange way—a mannerism often seen in schizophrenics. She is dressed in the style of the day, her summer dress accentuated by symbolic designs on the sleeve and pocket, and John Held Jr. would later portray that same dress on his flapper adorning the March 18, 1926, cover of *Life* magazine.

In September, this time leaving Scottie with Fitzgerald's parents, they returned to New York for the publication of *Tales of the Jazz Age*, Scott's first collection of short stories. They wanted to find a suitable home in the New York area, and planned to stay at the Plaza Hotel only until they found one. With the aid of a realtor they began to search for a place on Long Island. While at Princeton, Fitzgerald had accompanied Shane Leslie to some of the great Long Island estates, and since then the area had become a mecca for theater people and millionaires. On the day Zelda and Scott began house-hunting, they had arranged a luncheon for John Dos Passos and Sherwood Anderson at the Plaza; afterward they convinced Dos Passos to join them on their excursion.

Introspective and shy, Dos Passos was the illegitimate son of a wealthy New York lawyer and grandson of an immigrant shoemaker from Portuguese Madeira. He was born in Chicago in 1896 and educated at Choate, then Harvard. During World War I, he drove ambulances in Italy and France and had fictionalized those wartime experiences in his 1921 novel *Three Soldiers*, which Fitzgerald reviewed favorably.

With Dos Passos in tow, Zelda and Scott explored Long Island with their realtor in a chauffeured red touring car, but seeing nothing of interest, dropped off their agent and stopped at the Lardners'. Because Ring was too drunk to socialize, the three continued on to Manhattan, stopping at a carnival, where Zelda and Dos Passos got out to ride the Ferris wheel while Scott remained in the car drinking. Zelda loved the excitement of these rides and insisted on continuing long after John suggested stopping. When Dos Passos insisted they get off the wheel and Zelda refused, he became highly agitated. It was a game she played with great skill. But her behavior was new to Dos Passos, and he would later characterize it as "off-track," saying, "The gulf that opened between Zelda and me, sitting up on the rickety Ferris wheel, was something I couldn't explain. It was only looking back at it years later that it occurred to me that, even the first day we knew each other, I had come up against that basic fissure in her mental processes that was to have such tragic consequences. Though she was so very lovely, I had come upon something that frightened and repelled me, even physically." If Zelda was beginning to show signs of madness, nobody else noticed.

The house Zelda and Scott finally leased on Long Island was close to Ring Lardner's in the incorporated village of Great Neck Estates at 6 Gateway Drive. Their neighbors included other newspapermen, theater people, artists, and writers, all of whom would provide character material for Fitzgerald's next novel, *The Great Gatsby*. At that time, the film industry was still located on the East Coast, and show business celebrities occupied many of the larger estates. Among the most famous were Eddie Cantor, Leslie Howard, Groucho Marx, and Basil Rathbone. The area was also home to rich bootleggers who entertained lavishly. One of their close neighbors was the sportsman-journalist Herbert Bayard Swope, executive editor of the *New York World*, whose frequent and extravagant parties became Fitzgerald's inspiration for Jay Gatsby's. George M. Cohan and his partner, Sam Harris, lived nearby, as did Ernest Truex, who would star in Fitzgerald's play *The Vegetable*. These entertainers knew how to give parties, and Ring told the Fitzgeralds about one July 4 celebration at Ed Wynn's house where, following a fireworks display, "All the Great Neck professionals did their stuff, the former chorus girls danced, Blanche Ring kissed me and sang, etc. The party lasted through the next day and wound up next evening at Tom Meighan's where the principal entertainment was provided by Lila Lee and another dame, who did some very funny imitations (really funny) in the moonlight on the tennis court." Esther Murphy, who lived on her father's estate farther out on the Island at Southampton, was introduced to the Fitzgeralds by Edmund Wilson and Alex McKaig. Esther and McKaig dated for a time and Wilson thought they might marry, but Esther had more interesting beaux. Her father, Patrick Murphy, had built the Mark Cross leather goods store into a thriving business, and her brother Gerald, who was disinclined to follow the family trade, had recently left for Paris to become a painter.

After signing a two-year lease on the Gateway Drive house at $300 a month, the Fitzgeralds hired a staff that included a live-in couple at $160 a month, a nurse at $90, and a part-time laundress at $36. Zelda then went to St. Paul to retrieve Scottie. When they returned, Fitzgerald met mother and daughter at the train station in his newly purchased Rolls-Royce. Now feeling overshadowed by husband and daughter, Zelda exhibited little maternal warmth during their time in Great Neck, and Fitzgerald utilized that coolness to build his characterization of Daisy in *The Great Gatsby*. One Great Neck houseguest recalled that when the nanny brought Scottie in for a greeting, Zelda ordered, "Kiss mother, dear," only to have the child shake her head. Unaffected, Zelda quipped to the guest, "You see! She loathes me but she hates Scott." Fitzgerald did not come more naturally to parenting than Zelda. In his 1925 story "The Baby Party," his character John Andros's sentiments about his daughter reflected his own attitude. "He liked to take her on his lap. . . . Having paid this homage, John was content that the nurse should take her away. After ten minutes the very vitality of the child irritated him. . . . His feelings about his little girl were qualified. She had interrupted his rather intense love affair with his wife, and she was the reason for their living in a suburban town. . . ."

The Fitzgeralds' Gateway Drive house was small in comparison to the huge "Gold Coast" mansions of Florenz Ziegfeld, Lillian Russell, and George M. Cohan. Still, it had adequate room for entertaining friends. The songwriter Gene Buck, an assistant to Flo Ziegfeld, lived nearby and was a frequent guest. He and his wife, Helen, accompanied the Fitzgeralds to Princeton football games and played golf with Zelda at Great Neck's Soundview Golf Club. Though Buck liked the Fitzgeralds' company and enjoyed attending their parties, he warned others: "If you want to get your furniture antiqued up, you want to get the Fitzgeralds in—they'll antique it up in a single night—why, they'll put their own wormholes in the furniture with cigarette ends!"

Just thirty minutes by Long Island Railroad to Broadway's theater district, the Fitzgeralds' Great Neck house attracted Manhattan friends who took advantage of their hospitality as an inexpensive way of fleeing the city on weekends. Although they put up a sign reading "Weekend guests are respectfully notified that invitations to stay over Monday, issued by the host and hostess during the small hours of Sunday morning, must not be taken seriously," guests often refused to leave. They kept Scottie awake all night, and left the place a mess on Monday morning. Things got so chaotic that when Zelda's sister Tilde and husband, John, came for a planned luncheon, they arrived to find the Fitzgeralds completely unprepared. It was the second slight. Rosalind recalled that "Tilde and John did not forget Scott's rudeness to them at the wedding, which is understandable, nevertheless they accepted an invitation to lunch at the Fitzgeralds in Great Neck, and that too proved a fiasco, what with the hosts in bed when the guests arrived, and the wet diapers staining the borrowed suitcase, and no further effort was made by either side to reestablish peace." Fitzgerald's ledger for July 1923 summarized the month's distractions: "Tootsie [Rosalind] arrived. Intermittent work on novel [*The Great Gatsby*] Constant drinking. Some golf. Baby begins to talk. Parties at Allen Dawns. Gloria Swanson and the movie crowd. Our party for Tootsie, the Perkins arrive. I drive into the lake." Zelda also remembered Long Island as a time of constant disruptions. "In Great Neck there was always disorder and quarrels. . . . We gave lots of parties: the biggest one for Rebecca West. We drank Bass Ale and went always to the Bucks or the Lardners or the Swopes when they weren't at our house." They attended so many parties, they felt obliged to give their own, and these turned into exhausting and expensive affairs. During their first year at Great Neck, between normal household expenses, entertaining costs, and weekly excursions into Manhattan, they spent more than $29,000 with little to show for it but constant hangovers.

Fitzgerald's first novel had generated nine printings and his stories about flappers' attitudes resonated with the public and brought incredible celebrity. His story fee with the *Saturday Evening Post* climbed to $4,000 (equal today to $40,000), and throughout 1923, the Fitzgeralds remained Manhattan's most popular couple and tireless leaders of its nightlife. Gloria Swanson invited them for supper and dancing at the Ritz Carlton on Thursday, March 27, and they were celebrity guests at the 1923 championship boxing matches and World Championship baseball games. However, when their photograph, taken for the signing of Fitzgerald's exclusive contract with Hearst Syndicate, appeared on the cover of *Hearst's International*, and was picked up by most American newspapers, their celebrity status became official. While the caption somewhat exaggerated Zelda's position by stating, "Mrs. Scott Fitzgerald started the flapper movement in this country—so says her husband," Zelda certainly had evolved into the era's most famous flapper. She called that Hearst photograph her "Elizabeth Arden" shot, and it does look as though she had just come from the beauty parlor (Arden's salon being noted in her address book). Uncommonly, her hair is parted down the middle and tightly waved. Holding her hand lightly, Scott leans toward her protectively. Her white, ermine-lined dress and pearls imply royalty, suggesting the couple have reached the pinnacle of celebrity. Asked by one reporter what it was like being the original flapper, Zelda enthusiastically replied, "Three or four years ago girls of her type were pioneers. They did what they wanted to, were unconventional, perhaps, just because they wanted to fight for self-expression. Now they do it because it's the thing everyone does." Queried about her own ambitions, she eerily foreshadowed her future by answering, "I've studied ballet. I'd try to get a place in the Follies. Or the movies. If I wasn't successful, I'd try to write."

Although their house was constantly filled with people, their only real friends were the Lardners. Ring, nine years Scott's senior, also was a midwesterner, born in Michigan. He was already an advanced alcoholic when he and Scott met, and resembled Buster Keaton in his solemn and melancholy ways. But Ring was also a kind man whom Fitzgerald came to admire and to whom he dedicated *All the Sad Young Men*, his third collection of short stories. Lardner, a successful sportswriter who sold baseball stories to *The Saturday Evening Post*, had also achieved some renown as a lyricist and writer of satiric poetry. His primary income derived from the quick journalistic pieces he wrote between alcoholic binges. He and Fitzgerald were on the same drinking path, but Scott was still young and resilient enough to go on a binge without exhibiting the debilitating symptoms Lardner suffered. Each man saw himself reflected in the other, and Ring expressed more affection for Scott and Zelda than for anyone outside his immediate family. Lardner's son, Ring Jr., rightly observed that what "fascinated Scott in the Great Neck days was the image he saw of his own future. He probably felt satisfaction that he could sleep off a drunk and get back to work with much more ease than his older friend, but he must have known he was heading in the same direction. Even the pattern he came to of setting a specific beginning and ending date for going on the wagon was Ring's."

Fitzgerald's house was directly across the drive from Lardner's and they often shouted back and forth across their lawns. The *Westporter-Herald* quoted a New York paper that documented the activity. "F. Scott Fitzgerald and Ring Lardner are neighbors in Great Neck, L.I. In the morning, when the young author who glorified the flapper springs out of bed, he sings through an open window. 'O, the great Fitzgerald is just out of bed. Oh, the great Fitzgerald.' And soon across the space booms the voice of Lardner: 'The Mighty Lardner prepareth to shave. Soapsuds and lather! O the beautiful, sylph-like Lardner.' Neighbors have been trying to mitigate the annoyance but to no avail. For Fitzgerald and Lardner continue their rhyming fooleries at intervals all during the day."

This was the gestation period for *The Great Gatsby*, and Lardner's friendship provided access to personalities who would inform the book's characters. Ring's son recalled that "there was a porch on the side of our house facing the Swopes' and Ring and Scott sat there many a weekend afternoon, drinking ale or whisky and watching what Ring described as 'an almost continuous house-party' next door. Though their entertaining fell a whit short of Gatsby's, the location of the Swopes' house was just right for the view of Daisy's pier across the bay. And while there is no other significant similarity between Herbert Swope and Jay Gatsby, Swope's friend Arnold Rothstein was reputed, like Gatsby's friend Meyer Wolfsheim, to have fixed the 1919 World Series."

The two authors became confidants, sharing their interest in books, sports, and theater, and after sitting up half the night over a case of Canadian ale, they occasionally would go on a spree. In May 1923 they danced across Nelson Doubleday's lawn at Oyster Bay to attract the attention of houseguest Joseph Conrad, whom they greatly admired. Fitzgerald and Conrad were both poetic writers more interested in feelings than facts, and Conrad the only author Scott wanted to meet. But even though Scott and Ring were celebrities themselves, their intrusion was unwelcome. They were cited for trespassing and thrown off the property.

Scott was closer to Ring and his wife, Ellis, than Zelda was. She was outwardly pleasant but considered Ring a drunkard and Ellis ordinary. "He is a typical newspaperman whom I don't find very amusing," she wrote Rosalind. "His wife is common but I like her. He is six feet tall and goes on periodical sprees lasting from one to X weeks. He is on one now which is probably the reason he calls on us. He plays the saxophone and takes us to Mr. Gene Buck's house—Mr. Gene Buck originated Ziegfeld's Follies and lives in a house designed by Joseph Urban. It looks like a lot of old scenery glued together."

Fitzgerald was intrigued with Zelda's feelings about Ellis and funneled them into his characterization of Mrs. Markey in "The Baby Party": "She did not care for Mrs. Markey; she considered her both snippy and common," but "the two women kept up an elaborate pretense of warm amity." Describing the Markeys as next-door neighbors in suburbia (Great Neck), "where they paid for country air with endless servant troubles and the weary merry-go-round of the commuting train," Fitzgerald narrated a situation in which two wives argue during a children's party. "Your wife comes in here and begins shouting about how common we are! Well, if we're so common, you'd better stay away."

It is doubtful that Ellis knew Zelda's true feelings. She considered her beautiful and fascinating, and her children, particularly Ring Jr., adored her. "Zelda was twenty-two years old when we first knew her and Ellis already thirty-five. She didn't pay as much attention to us as Scott did, but we were used to that from visiting children, and that was how we thought of her, as another child, free and impulsive in saying or doing whatever she felt like. I have never known another adult, except my Aunt Anne, who seemed to say exactly what came into her head as it came, without any apparent exercise of judgment. I watched and listened to her in total fascination until the time came when grown-ups and children went their separate ways and she was unfairly borne off with the former."

For her part, Zelda considered Ring a bad influence on Scott, particularly when he began following Lardner's habit of disappearing into Manhattan for days, returning home on the odd morning to fall asleep on the lawn. John Biggs recalled one of those hard-drinking episodes: "During prohibition Scott Fitzgerald and I were at the Biltmore in New York and Scott got some liquor from a bellboy. It was full of ether. We drank some and got so bemused that we each leaned out of a window and talked to each other from window to window. I used to wear cordovan leather shoes of which I was very proud, and I spilled some of the liquor on the shoes. My God, when I woke up in the morning I found the leather on my good cordovan shoes was absolutely eaten out. Our stomachs must be utterly remarkable to have stood that stuff."

But the liquor was taking its toll. Once, when Zelda and her

Montgomery friend Eleanor Browder went into Manhattan to meet Scott at the Plaza, they found him being escorted out of the Palm Court after staggering in with a champagne bottle under one arm and Anita Loos on the other. Another time, when Fitzgerald recognized Loos on Fifth Avenue and pulled over, he convinced her to come home with him for dinner. On a whim, she accepted, but was soon sorry when she observed him swigging champagne from a bottle positioned between his knees. When they arrived in Great Neck, Scott served martinis before dinner and became so drunk he started a fight with Zelda, dumped the dishes on the floor, and sent Loos and Zelda racing across the lawn to the Lardners', where they stayed until Fitzgerald passed out. Loos never forgot the experience.

With passing months, Fitzgerald's drunkenness grew increasingly obnoxious. At dinner parties, after falling into a stupor, he would often crawl under a table and babble incoherently, or try to eat his soup with a fork. When one party ended with him dropping a whole orange peel down his throat and gagging, Zelda told Rosalind she felt powerless to change things and regretted marrying him. As to why Fitzgerald behaved this way, Edmund Wilson agreed with John Dos Passos that it was an act of protection. He "suggested to me once that Scott was by no means always so drunk as he pretended to be, but merely put on disorderly drunken acts, which gave him an excuse for clowning, and outrageous behavior, because he had never learned to practice the first principles of civilized behavior." That is, of course, a possibility. But in the twenties everybody drank like fish—it was a mark of sophistication. The fact was, and remained, that Scott, as Hemingway later noted, could not handle even one drink, but felt he had to drink to maintain his mythical presence, and, later, even to be able to write.

In the midst of these disruptions, Fitzgerald was still trying to finish *The Vegetable*, his satiric play about a newsboy who becomes president. After two additional revisions—making a total of six—it was published in April 1923 and garnered a favorable review from Edmund Wilson. In his pursuit of a financial backer to produce it on stage, Fitzgerald first approached fellow Princetonian John Williams, who immediately declined. He then asked Alex McKaig to introduce him to film producer Max Simon, and Gilbert Miller at the Frohman Literary Agency, but McKaig, who was still estranged from the Fitzgeralds, resisted. It was George Jean Nathan who finally convinced Sam Harris to produce it. Fitzgerald's Princeton hero Walker Ellis auditioned for the main part but was rejected by Harris. Instead, Ernest Truex, their Long Island neighbor and a popular actor, was cast in the lead role of Jerry Frost. He was a friend of Anita Loos and had co-starred with Louise Huff in *Oh, You Women*, for which Loos had written the screenplay. But it would take more than his thespian talent to make *The Vegetable* successful. The play went into New York rehearsals during October 1923, and in November the Fitzgeralds and Lardners left for the Atlantic City tryouts at Nixon's Apollo Theater. Opening night, November 10, 1923, told the sad story: most of the audience departed by the second act. Though Fitzgerald attempted extensive rewrites before tryouts ended, and improved the action and dialogue, the play closed after a week and never made it to New York. Zelda wrote Xandra Kalman in St. Paul: "In brief, the show flopped as flat as one of Aunt Jemima's famous pancakes—Scott and Truex and Harris were terribly disappointed. . . . The first act went fine, but Ernest says he has never had an experience on the stage like the second . . . people were so obviously bored! "

The failure of *The Vegetable* left the Fitzgeralds in dire financial straits, since Scott had spent months writing the play to the exclusion of everything else. To get out of debt, he sequestered himself in a room above the garage and during four months wrote eleven stories that netted $17,000. He also completed a humorous essay for the *Saturday Evening Post* entitled "How to Live on $36,000 a Year," which explored why the more he earned the more he sank into debt. The financial crisis made them realize they could neither financially nor emotionally remain in Great Neck, and they hastily decided to go abroad. Both agreed it had been a wasted year with too much alcohol and too many visitors. Scott told Edmund Wilson they would stay abroad until he had accomplished something important. Their impending departure was the second of four European trips they would make during the twenties. Their first, in May of 1921, had included the obligatory stops in Paris, Venice, Florence, and Rome. This second one would extend from May 1924 through December 1926. The third would be shorter—April through September 1928—and after the last sojourn from March 1929 until September of 1931, they would remain permanently in the United States.

The past year had been very unsettling. Besides doing too much drinking and socializing, they had essentially ignored their child; Zelda had had an abortion (with whatever psychological and physical effects that might entail); and Scott's drunken antics had turned ugly and sometimes dangerous. With the failure of his play, Scott had suffered his first real setback as a writer, and they were chronically short of money. Yet despite the excesses, they were still young— Zelda twenty-four and Scott twenty-eight—and resilient. Their flight to Europe was an obvious attempt to start over again. Only was it too late?

They told only Wilson, Maxwell Perkins, and the Lardners of their plans, packed their belongings and asked Ring to sublet their house, on which six months remained of their two-year lease. On May 3 they left aboard the S. S. *Minnewaska*, their departure evoking a poetic farewell from Ring. "Zelda 'fair queen of Alabam', Across the waves I kiss you! You think that I don't care a damn, but God how I will miss you! For months and months you've meant to me what Mario meant to Tosca. You've gone, and I am all at sea just like the Minnewaska. So dearie, when your tender heart of all his coarseness tires, just cable me and I will start immediately for Hyeres." Following the poem he sent a sardonic telegram: "When are you coming back and why, please answer." But Zelda didn't; she was relieved to be leaving Great Neck and told a friend, "Ring is drinking himself to an embalmed state so he'll be all ready for the grim reaper. I don't think he'll have long to wait if he keeps on. His wife is worried sick." Whether aware of it or not, she was referring to herself as much as Ellis.

CHAPTER 4

Expatriates Abroad

In 1921, when Fitzgerald wrote Edmund Wilson that Europe was only of antiquarian interest, his disappointment stemmed from isolation; he did not speak a foreign language and there was nobody to show him around. Three years later that situation had significantly changed when the Fitzgeralds became part of the great exodus of creative people leaving America for European cities. The 1913 Armory show inspired many to go abroad, with Stuart Davis and Julian Levi, two rising artists, leading the way. By 1924, Paris was inundated with American writers, journalists, and artists searching for inspiration and personal freedom. Scott and Zelda found many of their friends living in tiny hotel rooms pursuing varied interests: John Dos Passos was staying near the Pantheon studying anthropology at the Sorbonne, Malcolm Cowley was learning French on a fellowship, e. e. cummings was working on a book of poetry, and Ramon Guthrie, the poet and anthologist, was researching Provencal verse. John Peale Bishop was now living there with his wife, Margaret, and soon to arrive were Archibald MacLeish, Gilbert Seldes, Donald Ogden Stewart, the poet Glenway Westcott, and Matthew Josephson. Also in Paris was Stephen

Parrott, but Fitzgerald was still angry about his flirtation with Zelda in New York earlier that winter and avoided him.

During the Fitzgeralds' first European trip there were only six thousand Americans living in Paris. By 1924 more than thirty thousand resided there. What made the French capital so attractive to those artists and writers whom Gertrude Stein called "the lost generation" was the freedom it offered. Foreigners generally could do as they pleased and news of such latitude spread quickly. When Ernest Hemingway returned to Paris from Toronto in 1924, he was surprised by the number of writers, painters, and composers crowding the second-class boat train to Cherbourg. This mass exodus from the United States was due in part to Prohibition laws that reflected an America where middle-class values held full sway. "All of our friends from New York arrive," wrote Zelda to her friend Madeline Boyd, "with tales of such horror and self-sacrifice that all my waking hours are spent in commiseration." Paris offered the opportunity to deny the demands of mortgage payments, boring jobs, and, often, family obligations. "The lost generation" was more responsibility-free than mislaid. The epigram "You are all a lost generation," which Hemingway used as an inscription for *The Sun Also Rises*, was popularized by Gertrude Stein after she had heard it from a hotel proprietor in Belley who conjectured that the men of eighteen who left for World War I had missed being "civilized" in the normal manner. Hemingway extended the concept to include spiritual loss, transforming his protagonists into folk heroes.

The primary reason for the Fitzgeralds' move to Paris was economic; everyone talked about how inexpensive Europe had become since the war. Germany was the best bargain. The mark was almost worthless against the dollar, so a week with meals at a German hotel cost less than two dollars per person. France was nearly as inexpensive. The franc hovered at nineteen to the dollar and a meal with wine cost as little as three franc—about sixteen cents. The seriously frugal could get by on twenty-five dollars a month, which covered a small room, modest meals, and occasional drinks at streetside cafés. Some of the Fitzgeralds' friends, like Malcolm Cowley, managed to live even more cheaply by renting unheated rooms in the Latin Quarter and eating lunches at Montparnasse creameries, where an omelette, wine, and strawberries cost only twenty-five cents, and suppers in the international students' pension slightly more. The dollar was worth about ten times its value today, and much more in Europe where many of the currencies were being devalued. To give some idea of its purchasing power, in 1924 a doorman in New York started working at $27.50 a week. With that, he could buy a quart of milk for 14 cents, a Coke or candy bar for 5 cents, an electric iron for $3.96, a man's 14K gold wedding ring for $2.98, or, if he was out to impress someone, a Hudson Coach with a four-cylinder engine for $1,250. During the twenties, Fitzgerald's income averaged $25,000 a year—good money, but no fortune. Considering their living expenses included expensive restaurants, nightclubs, and cabarets, Paris was still infinitely cheaper than Manhattan. Besides its economic advantages, the French city also was the undisputed artistic capital of the world. A new ballet or play premiered weekly and there were always new exhibitions and recitals. At any corner, one might happen upon a Dadaist manifestation, then engage in all-night conversation at one of the numerous cafés lining the boulevards.

It took the Fitzgeralds ten days to cross the Atlantic on the *Minnewaska*. With the anticipation of two explorers heading for great adventure, they proceeded by train to Gare St. Lazare with seventeen pieces of luggage and Scott's set of the *Encyclopaedia Britannica*. They intended to head for the Riviera, where they could live cheaply, Zelda could swim, and Scott work on *The Great Gatsby*. After checking into the Hotel des Deux Mondes on avenue de l'Opera, they started interviewing English nannies and lunched with the Bishops at Armenonville in the Bois de Boulogne. Bishop recalled the late and confused meal: "His wife and child were with him, and it was very hard to order satisfactorily for a little girl [Scottie was three] in so expensive a restaurant. Fitzgerald, to quiet her, took out his shoestring and gave it to her with a handful of French coins to play with on the gravel under the tables." While their Château de Tressancourt was being renovated outside Paris at Orgeval, Seine-et-Oise, the Bishops were staying at the Hotel Campbell on avenue de Friedland. Two years earlier Bishop and Edmund Wilson had co-authored *The Undertaker's Garland* and both seemed destined for literary fame. But after Bishop's departure for France, Wilson had confided to Fitzgerald that he considered Bishop's writing career over. The poet Alan Tate agreed: "John is like a man lying in a warm bath who faintly hears the telephone ringing downstairs, but is too comfortable to really do anything about it." Both Fitzgeralds were fond of Bishop and intended to see him often, but they disliked Margaret and tried to avoid her whenever possible.

Two individuals they specifically set out to find were Esther Murphy and her brother Fred. Fred was a stranger to them, but they had entertained Esther at Great Neck and found her fascinating. Called "Tess," she was elegant and authoritative and possessed a remarkable mind. An expert on the work of Edith Wharton, about whom she intended to write, Esther was also highly knowledgeable about the essayist Madame de Maintenon, the second wife of Louis XIV. Somewhat mannish in appearance and a chain smoker, after a brief relationship with Alex McKaig she married and divorced British writer and theorist John Strachey. She then married Chester A. Arthur III, grandson of the twenty-first American president. Esther was delighted to see the Fitzgeralds again, and invited them to her home at 23 quai de Grand Augustins, where she introduced them to her other brother, Gerald, three years younger than Fred. They never did meet Fred, who was badly injured during World War I serving as a tank officer with the American Expeditionary Force, and had been cited for heroism and decorated for gallantry with the Croix de Guerre and Division citation. According to Edmund Wilson, Fred Murphy had been pieced together by surgeons, and continued to live in constant pain and danger of collapse. He was a highly intelligent and impressive man, Wilson recalled, even though their first meeting had led Wilson to think him supercilious because he kept contracting his eyebrows as if in pain. "He was," Wilson added, "but I didn't know it." By the time the Fitzgeralds arranged a meeting, Fred lay in a Parisian hospital with complications from his war injuries and was in no condition to see them. He died that May from a perforated intestine.

Through Tess's introduction, the Fitzgeralds established a warm friendship with Gerald and Sara Murphy, who were established figures at the center of Paris's artistic scene. Both were studying stage design with Natalia Gontcharova, the first woman set designer to work at the Ballets Russes, from whom Gerald was also taking painting lessons. Gontcharova had trained at the Moscow School of Painting, Sculpture and Architecture and was a sculptress as well as painter. Through their association with her and her lifelong companion, Mikhail Larionov, the Murphys became friendly with many of the talented artists involved with the Ballets Russes, including its director Sergei Diaghilev, composer Igor Stravinsky, and poet and artist Jean Cocteau, who wrote libretti and designed programs and playbills for the company. Of all the Americans then living in Paris, only the Murphys enjoyed close access to the Russian ballet circle. Not only did they attend most of the Ballets Russes performances, they also went to rehearsals, helped paint Gontcharova's sets, and socialized with many of the company's members. Through her friendship with them, Zelda met the most talented dancers and choreographers in Paris, and her involvement with the ballet became a pivotal event in her creative life.

In 1909, Alexander Benois first suggested taking the Russian ballet to Europe, and Diaghilev responded enthusiastically by engaging Anna Pavlova, Vaslav Nijinsky, Sofia Fedorova, and other principal dancers from St. Petersburg's Maryinsky Theatre and Moscow's Bolshoi Ballet. With Michel Fokine as its choreographer, the company debuted in Paris at the Theatre du Chatelet in the spring of 1909 and continued to perform under Diaghilev's directorship until his death in 1929. A theatrical pioneer with unerring judgment and flawless taste, Diaghilev was also a great organizer and discoverer of new talent. He drew out the best in people and inspired artists to develop their gifts to the fullest. His broad knowledge of art, music, and dance enabled him to explore new methods of expression and to integrate the greatest achievements of painting, music, and poetry into ballet. Diaghilev was most interested in a new and unique blend of artistic styles, and his collaborations attracted brilliant painters including Pablo Picasso, whose first wife, Olga, was deuxieme ballerina with the company; Georges Braque; Giorgio de Chirico; André Derain; Max Ernst; Juan Gris; Henri Matisse; Joan Miró; Maurice Utrillo; and Georges Rouault. To provide the ballet with original scores, he hired the most talented composers—Prokofiev, Debussy, Stravinsky, and Ravel—and employed the century's most gifted choreographers—Nijinsky, Fokine, Massine, Nijinska, and Balanchine. Everyone worked as a member of the team. When a fire destroyed numerous Ballets Russes sets, the "team" went into action helping to create new background scenery. Gerald Murphy and John Dos Passos volunteered to repaint the drop curtains, backdrops, and flats for "Scheherazade" and "Pulcinella." They met Braque and Derain, who were also helping, along with Picasso, who had originally created the scenery and costumes for the premiere of "Pulcinella" in 1920.

Upon the Fitzgeralds' arrival in Paris, the Ballets Russes was at its most popular and its performances the high point of every artistic season. Each production was the result of an elaborate amalgam of composers, choreographers, dancers, and artists. Synthesizing music, choreography, and art, and striving for perfection with new forms of expression, Diaghilev created daring ballet spectacles filled with brilliant costumes and scenery. Zelda was awestruck by the post-Cubist sets of Mikhail Larionov and Léon Bakst's imaginative costume designs, which garnered as much press as the ballets. Bakst would die in December of that year, but his influence lingered and was noticeable in everything from furniture manufacture to carpet and textile design. A decade earlier, his costumes for "Scheherazade" precipitated the rage for orientalia, and many of Paris's top couturiers had based their designs on his creations. Bakst possessed a unique understanding of the role of costume in theatrics and became renowned for capturing "the frozen moment," a concept Zelda later incorporated into her artistic work. As Diaghilev's leading set and costume designer, Bakst epitomized the company's amazing creativity with his extraordinary visions of the exotic. Through his bold use of color and sadoerotic themes, he evoked a fantastic world of opium-induced sensations and sensual pleasures. Interpreting the body as a kinetic force, he emphasized dancers' movements by attaching feathers and veils to their garments and used intricate patterns and decorations in his costumes. To create these, he executed meticulous drawings, many of them actual portraits of the company's dancers in characteristic poses. Revealing a mastery of color and line, these sketches were appreciated and collected by members of the troupe and others who knew great art when they saw it.

The Ballets Russes' artists considered Gerald Murphy a highly talented painter who took his work seriously. He maintained a studio in the rue Froidevaux where he worked daily, and struck up a friendship with Fernand Léger, who believed "Murphy's paintings were the only truly American response to the Cubist fervors that had swept across the easels of Paris." Admiring his talent and hoping to interest some of Murphy's wealthy friends, Léger commis-

sioned Gerald, in autumn of 1923, to create an American ballet for
the Ballet Suedois, a Swedish dance company performing in Paris.
For the project, Murphy tracked down his college friend Cole
Porter and together they created "Within the Quota," a half-hour
musical satire. Murphy provided the story and stage sets; Porter
composed the music. It opened in the Theatre des Champs-Elysees
to rave reviews. Even Picasso went out of his way to pay the two
Americans enthusiastic compliments.

Gerald had married his wife, Sara, in December 1915. One of
the popular and attractive Wiborg sisters of Cincinnati and daughter of a wealthy ink manufacturer, Sara was five years older than
Gerald, whom she had known since childhood. Their families vaca-
tioned on neighboring estates in East Hampton, Long Island. A
1912 Yale graduate, Gerald was the son of Patrick Francis Murphy,
the owner of Mark Cross, the Manhattan leather goods store catering to the carriage trade. The elder Murphy had started as a clerk
when the fashionable shop was still in Boston. A keen businessman,
he soon became the store's owner and moved the shop to New York
City, where it became extraordinarily successful. To his father's disappointment, Gerald showed no interest in business, and after Yale
enrolled in a two-year landscape architecture program at Harvard.
Following its completion and to avoid joining Mark Cross, he left
for France in 1920 with Sara and their three small children: Honoria born in 1917, Baoth in 1919, and Patrick Francis II in 1920.
While giving the appearance of great wealth, the Murphys actually
were not affluent; they simply took full advantage of the French exchange rate against the dollar to maintain a comfortable lifestyle.
To live well, Gerald constantly dipped into his capital and Sara
tapped her annual stipend of $7,000. Their daughter Honoria later
emphasized that their living expenses never matched those of the
Fitzgeralds—"Scott and Zelda spent lavishly . . . far more than my
father and mother ever dreamed of spending."

In 1924, when they and the Fitzgeralds became friends, the Murphys had just renovated their rented apartment at 1 rue Git-le-
Coeur at St. Cloud in the quai des Grand Augustins. It was a
sixteenth-century building overlooking Paris, with two floors of
rooms that once belonged to the composer Gounod, and still remained in his family. Soon, it was not unusual for Scott and Zelda
to appear under their windows after an evening of drinking to shout
they were leaving the next day on the *Lusitania*. The Murphys

initially found this amusing, but soon put a stop to their infantile behavior. Then, after swearing the Fitzgeralds to a higher standard of decorum, they invited them to visit Antibes where they were renovating their Villa America.

Gerald and Sara, who had adopted the Spanish adage "living well is the best revenge" as their family motto, had discovered the summer Riviera only one year earlier. It was actually Cole Porter's find. Always curious and innovative, Porter came upon the Riviera almost deserted during the summer of 1922 when he and his bride, Linda, along with their traveling companion Howard Sturges, nephew of the philosopher George Santayana, rented a château at Cap d'Antibes. The French considered it a winter resort and, thinking it unhealthy during summer months, normally departed after May for Deauville on the Atlantic coast.

Murphy and Porter had been at Yale together—Porter the class of 1913, Murphy 1912—and Porter owed much of his college success to Murphy's friendship. Tall and handsome with a keen intelligence and perfect manners, Gerald was in the college's top fraternity, DKE. In his senior year he was also elected to Skull and Bones, Yale's prestigious secret society, which was housed in a huge, windowless brownstone on High Street in downtown New Haven. Election to Skull and Bones was regarded as the highest social distinction at Yale. Fifteen undergraduates were chosen annually for membership at a ritual called "tap day," and it was a particular honor to be the fifteenth man tapped. But Murphy never spoke of his Skull and Bones experience, even to his friend Archibald MacLeish, who was elected into the society a few years later. Monty Wooley, who graduated the year before Gerald, believed some misfortune had befallen Murphy and a clubmate there. Voted the best-dressed in his class, Gerald possessed a sophistication Porter did not yet have, and he helped get Porter into DKE and selected for Scroll and Key, second in importance only to Skull and Bones. Murphy's style remained legendary at Yale long after he graduated, and when MacLeish left for Paris he was told to find Gerald if he wanted to experience the European avant-garde firsthand.

After they visited Cole Porter in Antibes during the summer of 1922, the Murphys became enthusiastic about the area's dry, hot days and cool nights, and began searching for a moderately priced villa of their own. What they found was an unpretentious chalet below the Antibes lighthouse. They named it Villa America and began a two-year renovation to expand its structure by replacing the peaked chalet roof with a second story for extra bedrooms. The modest house was turned into a beige, Moorish-style villa with yellow shutters and an outside terrace of gray and white tiles. Gerald used his knowledge of landscape gardening to beautify the grounds, planting a variety of olive trees and lemon and tangerine orchards. He transformed the gardens, buttressed by terraces overlooking the Mediterranean, into a horticultural marvel. Adding her own creative touches, Sara placed wicker garden furniture indoors and out and hung Japanese lanterns throughout the palm garden and eucalyptus groves. Fitzgerald later described that garden patio in *Tender Is the Night* with its "lanterns asleep in the fig trees and a big table and wicker chairs and a great market umbrella from Siena."

When renovations were completed, Villa America would include a fourteen-room villa on seven acres, a guest house called the Bastide, a small farm named La Ferme des Oranges, Gerald's painting studio, a playhouse for the children, a gardener's cottage, chauffeur's quarters, donkey stable, and storehouse. But from June of 1923 until June of 1925, while renovations were still in progress, the Murphys stayed at the Hotel du Cap in Antibes during the summer and their St. Cloud apartment the rest of the year. Occasionally, Gerald remained in Paris alone at his painting studio on 69 rue Froidevaux.

Eager to deepen their friendship with the Murphys, and assured that Antibes would provide Scott a distraction-free environment, the Fitzgeralds departed for the Riveria in June of 1924. En route, they stopped first at Grimm's Park Hotel in Hyeres, which was suffering through a heat wave. Zelda hated the place. She found the food inedible and was convinced they were being served goat meat nightly for dinner. To avoid other hotel guests and combat the heat, she and Scott cooled themselves late into the night at Café L'Universe in the town's plaza. They departed Hyeres soon after Fitzgerald saw a twelve-year-old child afflicted with congenital syphilis wandering around the streets, its face looking like a huge scab with tiny slits for eyes.

Arriving in St. Raphael, they checked into the Hotel Continental until they could locate a house to lease. They felt lucky to find the Villa Marie only two and a half miles above St. Raphael at Valescure. The two-bedroom villa and guest cottage were secluded by a terraced rock garden and set amid a grove of olive trees and umbrella pines. Its $79 monthly rent included a gardener and its only disadvantage was that it was thirty miles east of the Murphy's hotel at Cap D'Antibes. Fitzgerald purchased a Renault for $750 that Sara dubbed "Rat Renault," and with things seemingly under control—his daughter supervised by her English nanny, Lillian Maddock, and Zelda with outdoor activities to occupy her time—Scott grew a mustache and settled down to work on *The Great Gatsby*.

It was the first time since cloistering himself in Westport to write *The Beautiful and Damned* that he managed to eliminate distractions, and Scott relished the solitude. Besides taking a brief swim late every afternoon—running into the water, diving under, and immediately coming out—and evening meals with Zelda, Scottie, and Miss Maddock, he eschewed all distractions.

Meanwhile, Zelda was developing a warm friendship with the Murphys and daily improving her French by plowing through French novels. During her first week at St. Raphael, with the aid of a French/English dictionary, she read the year's best-seller, *Le Bal du Comte*, and before long was speaking French with Gerald and Sara. Whereas Fitzgerald was uninterested in studying the language—satisfied with learning how to ask for the bill—Zelda's facility with words made her conversational mastery of French easy. In the mornings, while Miss Maddock played with Scottie or knitted in the shade, Zelda dove, swam, and browned her body to a rich, even tan. She had worked hard to regain her lithe figure, and once more had complete confidence in her appearance. At the beach she enjoyed the attention of onlookers and flirted with men who stopped to exchange pleasantries. Photos of her that summer in espadrilles and casual dresses capture her fresh good looks and vitality.

Honoria Murphy remembered how lovely Zelda appeared that summer: "tanned and beautiful, often wearing her favorite color, salmon pink . . . a strikingly beautiful woman—blonde and soft and tanned by the sun who usually dressed in pink and wore a peony in her hair or pinned to her dress." Pink was that year's fashionable color, with shades ranging from flesh color to coral, French pink to orchid to cyclamen. The huge pink peonies in the Murphys' garden were Zelda's favorites, and she often brought one back to St. Raphael to wear at dinner. She told Sara Mayfield, who was studying at the Sorbonne that year, that her hairdresser Antoine had styled a "peony cut" just for her. "I love peonies—my favorite flowers. . . .

Violets and muguets and lilacs are so tame and self-satisfied." The bright peonies in her shining hair accentuated her healthy, well-scrubbed look. The starched cotton dresses she was fond of wearing, unknown in France during those days and considered strictly "Americaine," contributed to what Gerald Murphy later recalled as her "individuality, her flair. She might dress like a flapper when it was appropriate to do so, but always with a difference. Actually her taste was never what one would speak of as à la mode—it was better, it was her own."

Joining the Murphys daily on the little beach they had cleared, Zelda built sand castles with Scottie and read Edith Wharton and Henry James. The days soon blended into one another, punctuated only at noon by the two-car train passing near the beach on its way to Menton. That signaled lunchtime, and they would all wave at it and head home. Afternoons were quiet, with the children playing on the beach. Calm prevailed.

But contentment was elusive even in the idyllic setting of Antibes. Scott, who was concentrating on his novel, absolutely forbade interruptions, which left Zelda to her own devices. There was, generally, as Scott had previously written in *The Beautiful and Damned*, "A great rush of preparation, and 'quiet, I'm working now, and . . . don't sing . . . and I won't be through for a long time . . . so don't stay up for me,' and a tremendous consumption of tea or coffee. And that's all." With little to occupy herself, Zelda became increasingly restless. To allay her boredom, Scott suggested an all-day beach party for Scottie, the Murphy children, and their friends. In addition to planning the guest list and arranging for food, Zelda spent days building a castle from papier-mâché—complete with elaborate battlements, peaked towers, and an intricate series of moats filled with ducks. It was a great success. She delighted the children and amazed their parents by providing sound effects for an evil witch and beautiful princess, and Scott lent his army of toy soldiers to besiege the castle and rescue the damsel from her tower.

But the party was a fleeting diversion and Zelda increasingly resented the long hours alone while Fitzgerald wrote. She saw no distinction between writing short stories for the popular market and writing a novel, and could not understand why Scott struggled so with *Gatsby* when magazine stories earned the same amount of money. So when Fitzgerald made it clear that writing was his top priority, and suggested Zelda spend more time with others, she obliged. Zelda's jealousy of Fitzgerald's total immersion in productive work, and perhaps her determination to recapture his attention—or any attention—once again led her to seek the attention of other men. Ellen Barry, wife of the playwright Philip Barry, who was vacationing in Antibes that summer, witnessed Zelda's flirtations and overheard the Fitzgeralds' persistent teasing of each other—"Are you jealous of me? I'm jealous of you."

The affair began simply enough. After a morning swim, Zelda usually started her afternoons by sipping Cinzano or porto on the outdoor patio of the Café de la Flotte, and practicing her language skills with the French air force officers from a nearby base. As it happened, the villa adjacent to the Fitzgeralds' was being rented to some French naval pilots who had made it available to their friends: René Silvy, son of a Cannes notary public; Bobbé Croirer, the oldest of the group, who had fought at Verdun; and a twenty-five-year-old lieutenant named Edouard Jozan, son of a middle-class family from Nîmes with a long military tradition. The three officers quickly became part of the Fitzgeralds' social circle, attending casual dinners where Zelda would experiment with making bouillabaisse, or appearing in their starched white uniforms at more formal, catered affairs. It was to Jozan that Zelda was attracted. Dark and handsome, Jozan was athletic and muscular, a born military leader who carried himself with an air of assurance. Zelda was drawn to his strength and sensuality, though their initial contacts were innocent enough as all four played tennis, swam, or lounged on the beach. On some afternoons, they would all pile into Zelda's Renault and drive off for a seaside picnic, explore the countryside, or visit an amusement park where Zelda and the men would ride the Ferris wheel and join the children on the merry-go-round.

But soon it was Zelda and Edouard alone on the beach, dancing at one of the waterside bistros, or visiting a casino. An entry card with Zelda's name showed her in the Salon Privé of the Casino de Monte Carlo on June 10, 1924. Everyone except Scott noticed that they had paired off and suspected they were having an affair. Jozan showered Zelda with the attention she craved, and she began the liaison with no fear of the consequences. "You took what you wanted from life if you could get it, and you did without the rest," says Zelda's protagonist, Alabama, about her affair in *Save Me the Waltz*. The sensuality of Alabama's romantic liaison is fully described in the novel. "The music stopped. He drew her body against him till she felt the blades of his bones carving her own. He was bronze and smelled of the sand and the sun; she felt him naked underneath the starched linen. She didn't think of David. She hoped he hadn't seen; she didn't care."

Going on to a distinguished naval career as vice admiral commanding France's Far Eastern Fleet and recipient of the Legion d'Honneur, Jozan steadfastly denied adultery with Zelda. In interviews with Nancy Milford and Sara Mayfield, he characterized his relationship with Zelda only as a summer flirtation, claiming her account in *Save Me the Waltz* was close to what had occurred. In the novel, Jacques Chevre-Feuille, sweet as his surname "honeysuckle" suggests, is introduced to Alabama by her husband, who encourages her to pass time with the pilot to improve her French. Zelda never makes absolutely clear in her novel if the affair is sexual; the aviator wants a mistress but does not encourage the woman to leave her husband. And since she never discussed the affair with Fitzgerald, either to confirm or deny unfaithfulness, he remained uncertain about its nature. Though she ultimately regretted keeping him in the dark, she never revealed details to Scott about any of her flirtations—either with John Sellers, Stephen Parrott, Nathan, or Jozan—and just how far she allowed those entanglements to go only Zelda knew. However, while Jozan continually denied a physical relationship with Zelda, that is unlikely. When attracted, Zelda was sexually aggressive and Jozan had ample opportunity to respond.

Years later Scott would explain, "I liked [Jozan] and was glad he was willing to pass the hours with Zelda. It gave me time to write. It never occurred to me that the friendship could turn into an affair." Only after Zelda confessed she had fallen in love with the handsome officer and wanted a divorce, did Scott put *Gatsby* aside and confront the seriousness of the situation. There are several versions as to how he responded. Fitzgerald told Sheilah Graham that after learning of the affair on July 13, 1924, he became so incensed that he bought a pistol and challenged Jozan to a duel, each man firing a shot but missing. To others he confided he had demanded both declare their love to him but that the confrontation never took place. In another version, Scott claimed that he tried to "wring the aviator's neck," but that Jozan refused to confront him. Scott also bragged to Zelda's doctor, Robert Carroll, that he could have beaten Jozan in a fight, asserting that "at the time of my quarrel . . . with her French friend I could have annihilated him in two minutes. I boxed for some months with Tommy and Mike Gibbons as a young man and this kid didn't know his left hand from his right." But Fitzgerald was actually a poor boxer and the French naval pilot, who was far stronger and in much better shape, could easily have protected himself or seriously hurt Scott.

Whatever else he may have done, Scott forbade Zelda to leave the Villa Marie from mid-July of 1924 to mid-August. During her enforced isolation, she had ample time to ponder the situation with Jozan and her limited options. She had been more physically attracted to the Frenchman than to anyone previously and had experienced real passion. Her physical relationship with Scott had never been overwhelmingly sexual. Among former girlfriends, Fitzgerald had acquired the reputation of not being "a very lively male animal." And his Minnesota friend Oscar Kalman always believed that he basically considered sex dirty and sinful; "Scott liked the idea of sex, for its romance and daring, but was not strongly sexed [and] was inclined to feel the actual act of sex was messy."

As she had done two years earlier with Nathan, Zelda succeeded in recapturing Fitzgerald's attention, but underestimated the toll her flirtation would take on the marriage. Whatever the Jozan relationship entailed, it generated a deep distrust and left an indelible scar. While locked in the Villa Marie, Zelda realized she was also locked into her marriage and, relinquishing her southern belle role, determined to have no further romantic liaisons. Deeply troubled that she might never again be happy with Fitzgerald, yet aware of her inability to survive on her own, she recognized a power shift in their relationship and the reality struck her painfully. To ease the situation, Jozan requested a transfer from the nearby base at Frejus to Hyeres. Later he wrote Zelda, enclosing a photo, but she tore up the picture and would not read his letter.

The affair's aftermath also resonated with Scott, who used it in *Gatsby*, and later acknowledged he may even have encouraged the affair to add verisimilitude to his work. He certainly regretted allowing it to happen, "knowing how she would pay." Whatever damage the affair did to their marriage, both incorporated it into the myth they continually created of themselves. Hadley Hemingway recalled how the Fitzgeralds used to narrate the Jozan episode like a Chinese opera. "It was one of their acts together. I remember Zelda's beautiful face becoming very, very solemn, and she would say how he had loved her and how hopeless it had been and then how he had committed suicide. Scott would stand next to her looking very pale, adding comments now and then to flesh out the story." Equally dramatic was Fitzgerald's relish of Zelda's confusion and contrition. Hemingway recalled walking with Fitzgerald a year later through the Luxembourg gardens, and Scott telling him with satisfaction that Zelda "had fallen in love with the French navy pilot and . . . had never made him jealous with another man since."

Even though the Jozan affair permanently damaged their marriage, Scott wrote in his notebook that "September 1924 . . . I knew something had happened that could never be repaired." The couple never told anyone at the time what was happening. Incredibly, they appeared relaxed and happy to Gilbert Seldes and his new wife, who arrived in St. Raphael on their European honeymoon early that August. But two weeks later in Antibes, when the Fitzgeralds were visiting the Murphys at the Hotel du Cap, Zelda attempted suicide by taking an overdose of sleeping pills. The Murphys recalled how Scott, green-faced and trembling, rushed to their room at three in the morning saying Zelda had overdosed on barbiturates. Returning to their room with him, they induced Zelda to vomit and walked her back and forth all night to keep her from falling asleep. With her sense of humor still intact, Zelda resisted Sara's efforts to make her swallow olive oil and quipped: "No, if you drink too much olive oil you turn into a Jew."

When their five-month lease on Villa Marie expired in November 1924, the Fitzgeralds moved back into the Hotel Continental until mid-November, when they drove their Renault down to Rome. They checked into the Hotel des Princes at the foot of the Spanish Steps in the Piazza di Spagna, where full board for three with wine and service was $525 monthly, and where they planned to spend the winter. Zelda recalled the place vividly: "In the Hotel des Princes . . . we lived on Bel Paese cheese and Corvo wine and made friends with a delicate spinster who intended to stop there until she finished a three-volume history of the Borgias. The sheets were damp and the nights were perforated by the snores of the people next door, but we didn't mind because we could always come home down the stairs to the Via Sistina. . . ."

Zelda had been sick from the time they arrived in Italy and entered a Rome hospital to determine the cause. The Italian doctors recommended a surgical procedure, but instead of helping, the operation precipitated a lingering ovarian infection. It is unclear exactly what the problem was, though it may have had something to do with her earlier abortion. It may also have been aggravated by Zelda's repression of her emotions and distress over the Jozan affair. It is not unusual for inflammation to seek out the weakest part of the body, and Zelda's female organs may have been adversely affected by the turmoil the Jozan affair created. Whatever the actual problem, she recovered slowly and with great difficulty, not what one would expect of a normally healthy, twenty-four-year-old woman.

During her recuperation they spent most of their time watching the filming of *Ben Hur*, starring Carmel Myers, the attractive and highly intelligent daughter of a San Francisco rabbi. Both Fitzgeralds were impressed by her. Scott told a friend: "She is the most exquisite thing I have met yet, and is just as nice as she is beautiful." Myers showed them around Rome, where they found unlimited things to do. But even with the distractions, they continued to argue over the Jozan affair. The only thing Zelda recalled about that Christmas was "drinking under the gold statue of Victor Emmanuel in Rome, lost in time and space and the majestic prettiness of that square before the cavernously echoing Piazza Colonna." The *Ben Hur* cast invited them to a holiday party, but when Zelda refrained from going, Fitzgerald asked Howard Cox to drive her home and went alone. In the car, either she made up to him or he to her, since she refers to the incident in a letter, calling Howard "Hungry Cox."

Edmund Wilson, who kept a journal during the twenties, recalled the evening Howard Cox went out drinking with Fitzgerald and announced: "I could sleep with Zelda anytime I wanted to." He may have been referring to the Rome incident. Cox would later accuse Fitzgerald of retaliating for the remark by portraying him as the unattractive Collis Clay in *Tender Is the Night*, which Fitzgerald denied, assuring Cox by letter, "The character was not intended to be any possible portrait of my impression of you." Cox had graduated from Princeton in 1920, and was the author of *Passage to the*

Sky, a novel set in Florence. He was a minor writer compared to Fitzgerald, and was intensely jealous of Scott, who was then earning more money than most other writers of his generation. Wilson suspected that Cox envied the couple's notoriety and that "Zelda was not so loose nor Howard so dangerous as this implied."

January's continuing damp weather made Rome increasingly unpleasant. Scott caught the flu and their disillusionment with the city accelerated after Fitzgerald picked a fight with a taxi driver and was badly beaten. Scott tucked the incident away to be later used in *Tender Is the Night* as an indicator of Dick Diver's fall from grace. But the ugly altercation convinced them to leave Rome.

By mid-February 1925, the revised *Gatsby* proofs were in New York City and the Fitzgeralds off to Capri for a two-month stay. They rented a suite with an airy balcony on the top floor of the Tiberio Palace, "a high white hotel scalloped about the base by the rounded roofs of Capri, cupped to catch rain which never falls. We climbed to it through devious dark alleys that house the island's Rembrandt butcher shops and bakeries; then we climbed down again to the dark, pagan hysteria of Capri's Easter." As Zelda rested on the balcony, still recuperating, she distracted herself by taking painting lessons that reawakened her interest in art. After five weeks she had learned color theory, but was still not entirely well. The diagnosis was an ovarian inflammation complicated by colitis brought on by anxiety, but she derived little benefit from the injections prescribed by doctors. Her lingering illness distressed Fitzgerald, who wrote John Peale Bishop: "Zelda's been sick in bed for five weeks and is only now looking up." But Scott was unable or unwilling to make any connection between her ailments and her desperate unhappiness.

Late that February, the couple finally got around to looking up Compton Mackenzie. He represented an older generation of writers and had been Scott's literary idol at Princeton. As Capri's major literary figure, Mackenzie had resided on the island since 1913 and was a celebrity among its expatriate community, which lived primarily on trust funds and family allowances. Scott and Zelda visited Compton and his wife, Faith, at their Villa Solitaria perched high on a cliff above the Tyrrhenian Sea. The genial Scottish novelist was the son of theatrical parents and a good-looking man who dressed in dramatic clothes. Mackenzie was also known for his extravagant tastes, which included owning two stunning villas on the island. He was an immensely successful author; his first novel, *Sinister Street*, had greatly impressed Fitzgerald, and his second, *Carnival*, drew high praise from critics. By the mid-twenties, however, financial obligations had compelled the forty-two-year-old Mackenzie to produce a steady stream of popular novels that Scott considered uneven and amateurish. Particularly sensitive to this issue, Fitzgerald feared similar circumstances for himself. One evening he actually asked Mackenzie "why he had petered out and never written anything that was any good since 'Sinister Street' and those early novels." Even so, Mackenzie was pleased the Fitzgeralds had sought him out and introduced them to other visiting authors who enjoyed talking all night around the table once owned by Maxim Gorky. While Scott seemed to enjoy these conversations, he confided to Edmund Wilson that he found Mackenzie "pleasantly mundane."

Capri, tolerant of outsiders during the twenties, was a haven for British lesbians and homosexuals fleeing the restrictions of lingering Victorianism in England. It particularly attracted literary figures, including Norman Douglas, Edward Frederick Benson, Somerset Maugham, and his friend John Ellingham Brooks. In particular, Axel Munthe and Francis Brett Young popularized the island. Gossip and parties were the main pastimes, and a steady availability of sensual delights—cocktails, wine, cocaine, ether, opium—were set against the irresistible backdrop of a blue sea, white sand, and ragtime. Fitzgerald was simultaneously repelled and fascinated by Capri's homosexual milieu and complained to Maxwell Perkins that the place was "full of fairies." Zelda was more comfortable in the sexually free environment and eager to meet the lesbians depicted in Mackenzie's novel *Extraordinary Women*, which detailed the island's lesbian liaisons. She enjoyed meeting the artist Romaine Brooks, who had recently ended her affair with concert pianist Renatta Borgatti, a tall, striking woman with gray eyes, pale skin, and lush black hair who resembled Franz Liszt. The daughter of a celebrated Italian tenor with whom she had toured as a child, Borgatti was an admired musician herself, and before ending their relationship Brooks captured Borgatti's passion for music in a stunning portrait of Renatta at the piano.

The Fitzgeralds lingered on Capri longer than intended. On April 10, 1925, they finally boarded a ferry for Naples, planning to drive the Renault to Paris. But Zelda did not feel up to the journey, so they booked passage on the S.S. *President Garfield* and departed Naples for Marseilles. In a letter to Roger Burlingame on April 19, 1925, Fitzgerald explained: "Zelda has been too sick for the long overland trip to Paris in our French Ford so we had to catch a boat on a day's notice to get the car back to France within the 6 mos. period of the International touring arrangement." While their car was being loaded aboard the *Garfield* its roof got damaged. At Zelda's suggestion, a mechanic in Marseilles removed it rather than attempt the costly repair. It was now irrevocably a convertible, and as they headed for Paris torrential rains forced them to stop in Lyon where they stored the car in a garage and continued on to Paris by train. It would be two months before Scott and his new friend Ernest Hemingway retrieved it. The episode got propelled into literary history when it became part of Hemingway's *A Movable Feast*.

Finally back in Paris after a brief pass-through the year before, they stayed at the Hotel Florida while they hunted for a suitable place to live. On May 12, 1925, they moved to a furnished, fifth-floor apartment at 14 rue de Tilsitt in the district of l'Etoile near l'Arc de Triomphe. It was a gloomy flat—walls badly in need of paint, heavy drapes blocking the light—that always smelled musty and was impossible to heat or ventilate. They leapt upon any reason to leave. In Fitzgerald's ledger for that year he documents their excuses to go places and see people. They spent time with the Murphys, Gerald's sister Esther, Cole Porter and his wife, Linda, the Kalmans visiting from St. Paul, and John and Margaret Bishop, who, though now living in their newly renovated country estate at Orgeval, also kept a fashionable Etoile apartment and frequently invited the Fitzgeralds to dinners and parties. On one occasion, the poet Allen Tate and his novelist-wife, Caroline Gordon, were at the Bishops', and Zelda marveled how the two writers seemed to have established a mutually supportive relationship. She had never seen a marriage in which husband and wife were creative equals.

Fitzgerald and Hemingway met in late April 1925 when Donald Ogden Stewart introduced the two writers at the Dingo, a Montparnasse café that soon became the Fitzgeralds' favorite. Stewart, who was born in Ohio in 1896, had been advised by John Peale

Bishop to find Hemingway in Paris, and on his first evening there accidentally ran into Hemingway at the Rendezvous des Mariners. Stewart became friendly with the younger author and joined Ernest and Hadley in July 1924 for a week at the Feria de San Fermin bull ring in Pamplona, later fishing with Ernest in Burguete, a mountain village near the French border.

At the time, Hemingway was twenty-five and married to Elizabeth Hadley Richardson, a strong midwesterner eight years his senior. She dressed simply, never flirted, and was not as popular as Zelda. Hadley backed Ernest in whatever he did, required little attention, had no personal ambitions, and supported his writing efforts wholeheartedly. They had come from Chicago on the advice of Sherwood Anderson, who thought the European experience would broaden Ernest's vision, even though Hemingway already had a formidable reputation among authors. The Hemingways had been in Paris for only a year when the Fitzgeralds arrived.

Hemingway and Scott could not have been in more divergent circumstances. Fitzgerald was a commercial success with three published books, and had earned more than $28,000 in 1923, but was determined to write serious novels. Hemingway was poor but appreciated by intellectual readers of the new fiction, and was struggling for broader recognition. Writing articles for the *Toronto Star* at a penny a word, and contributing to the *Transatlantic Review*, Ernest claimed in 1924 that he had earned only $80 from his writing. Chicago's *Cooperative Commonwealth*, where he was earning $52 a week, recently had let him go, and he had arrived in Paris without a job. After some effort, he finally convinced the *Toronto Star* to let him freelance.

His first impression of Fitzgerald was negative. He recalled that Fitzgerald repeatedly asked if he had slept with Hadley before marriage, then ordered champagne and passed out after one glass. His initial response to Zelda was more positive. He told Gertrude Stein and Alice B. Toklas that she had really impressed him. "Dear Friends: Fitzgerald was around yesterday afternoon with his wife and she's worth seeing so I'll bring them around Friday afternoon unless you warn me not to." Scott found Stein fascinating, but Zelda detested being relegated to a tea table at the back of the room with Toklas, and recalled the atmosphere as so smoky and mysterious that "a young poet vomited out of sheer emotion." *The Great*

Gatsby had been published and was bringing Fitzgerald critical ac-
claim, further elevating his reputation within literary circles. Stein
was impressed by Scott's talent and considered him and Hemingway
among America's most promising young writers. But Hemingway admired Stein more than Fitzgerald did, and heeded her advice about
the importance of self-discipline. She warned both men that alcohol
would dull their minds, and emphasized the folly of seeking excitement in the bohemian life—an admonition Scott ignored.

Before World War I, Gertrude and her brother Leo had held
regular Saturday night gatherings at their apartment. These were
rather formal soirees for which they sent invitations and required
introductions. But after Leon moved out and Toklas in, Stein continued this tradition only at irregular intervals. On occasional
Saturday nights, with a less restrictive guest list and without introductions, the Stein apartment welcomed Montparnasse intelli-
gentsia. One of her favorite guests was Zelda's friend Carl Van
Vechten, who became Stein's close ally and located her first and last
American publisher. She had also befriended Van Vechten's first
wife, Ann, who had visited with Gertrude's English friend Miss
Gordon Caine and spent the entire evening lamenting over her
marriage to Carl. Most visitors found Stein's apartment a comfortable place to talk and relax. The sitting room, heated by a cast-iron
stove, was a mass of furnishings bordered by sideboards, chests, and
buffets on which guests found a variety of refreshments. The walls
were covered floor to ceiling with impressive works of art.

But it was not the visitors to Stein's salon whom the Fitzgeralds
wound up befriending. They preferred the regulars at the Montparnasse bars: Harold Stearns, Duff Twysden, Robert McAlmon,
and Harry and Caresse Crosby. And Stearns, more than the others,
epitomized the lost young men of his generation. A Harvard graduate, he arrived in Paris after the death of his wife in childbirth and
stayed on as Paris representative for Horace Liveright Publishers.
Then, as correspondent and reporter on the horse racing scene, he
wrote the "Peter Pickem" column in the Paris edition of the
Chicago Tribune, the favorite paper of expatriates. When Americans
arrived in the French capital and registered at the information office, their names got printed in the *Tribune* the following day. Besides Stearns, other *Tribune* writers at the time included Henry
Miller, James Thurber, Morrill Cody, and Virgil Geddes. Stearns

lived in a hotel on the rue Vavin next to Café Le Select and could usually be found there drinking. He considered himself a spokesman for American intellectuals, and in 1921 edited *Civilization in the United States*, a compilation of the opinions of America's foremost thinkers. But he was on the road to permanent drunkenness and never reached his full intellectual potential. Scott was drawn to him (as to Ring Lardner) and went out of his way to help him. He promised that if Stearns would write about Paris, he would get Scribner's to publish the piece. But Stearns considered it too much work and preferred borrowing money from Scott instead. When he finally convinced Stearns to write something, Maxwell Perkins agreed to publish it and Fitzgerald wrote, thanking him for the assignment: "I think Stearns will be delighted and hereby accept for him. Send me a check made out to him—he hasn't had that much money since I gave him $50." Fitzgerald also interceded on Stearns's behalf with Alexander Woollcott, inquiring of the critic whether there was some animosity toward Stearns at the *World* or *New York Herald*. "He has been helped by various people (for the last month his typewriter has been in pawn in Feauville), but he is terribly depressed by what he imagines is a sort of universal blackball against him. The favor I want to ask you is to find out if there is stuff of his lying unused and unpaid for in the 'World' office. He says he's written and written and can't get an answer." For a time the wealthy American divorcée Josephine Bennett became Stearns's mistress and included him in her social activities. But that only aggravated his alcoholism, and he was portrayed as a lost cause by several twenties writers—as Wiltshire Tobin in Kay Boyle's *Monday Night*, and Harvey Stone in Hemingway's *The Sun Also Rises*.

Josephine Bennett often brought expatriate writers together at her parties. Scott and Zelda frequently attended, and met the writer/publisher Harold Loeb there one evening along with Hadley Hemingway and Mina Loy. During 1922, Loeb had briefly known them in New York City where he located Scott an out-of-print book through his Manhattan bookshop the Sunwise Turn. A member of the wealthy Guggenheim family, Loeb wore round tortoise-shell glasses that made him look owlishly intelligent and dressed in casual but expensive clothing—pastel Fair Isle sweaters and white duck pants being his trademark. He was legally separated from his wife, who lived back in the States with their two children, and was one of several Americans publishing avant-garde magazines. His was called *Broom*, being that it aimed to sweep away old ideas. It was inexpensive to print these publications at German or Austrian presses where the favorable exchange rate meant five hundred copies of a small magazine could be produced for as little as twenty dollars. These low costs spawned numerous other publishing ventures: Robert McAlmon's *Contacts Editions*, William Bird's *Three Mountain Press*, Samuel Putnam's *The New Review*, Eugene Jolas's *Transition*, Ford Madox Ford's *Transatlantic Review*, and Harry and Caresse Crosby's *Black Sun Press*, which published Ezra Pound, James Joyce, Gertrude Stein, and Djuna Barnes.

The Crosbys' hedonistic life fascinated the Fitzgeralds, who were occasional guests at their rue de Lille apartment in the Faubourg St. Germaine. Like Loeb, the Crosbys had founded their publishing house with inherited wealth (Harry Crosby's mother was a sister of Mrs. J. P. Morgan). Their *Black Sun Press* also published Ernest Hemingway and Archibald MacLeish. Like Hemingway, Crosby had been an ambulance driver in World War I. Both men had volunteered with other American writers, like John Dos Passos, e. e. cummings, and Malcolm Cowley, for the American Ambulance Corps dispatched as Red Cross or Norton-Harjes drivers. Both MacLeish and Hemingway were closer to the Crosbys than the Fitzgeralds were, and spent weekends at their country retreat, a renovated mill on land once owned by Count Armand de la Rochefoucauld. The two writers had met the Crosbys during a ski holiday at St. Moritz, became friendly on the slopes, and renewed their acquaintance at Ada MacLeish's concert at the Paris Conservatoire. Crosby introduced Hemingway to the Spanish circus, which was temporarily housed in Paris, and took him backstage to drink with the lion tamers and freaks. To return the favor, Hemingway gave Crosby inside tips on horses that he got from Harold Stearns. These were not always accurate and one afternoon Harry lost three thousand francs at Auteuil, famous for its steeplechasing. Ernest and Hadley were also avid fans of the races at Auteuil, but Hadley was luckier than Crosby and frequently picked winners from the racing form by matching them with Stearns's tips.

The Crosbys were even more notorious than the Fitzgeralds throughout Paris for the wild parties they held in their three-story eighteenth-century town house. It was an impressive residence w high ceilings, open fireplaces, and crystal chandeliers. Ha brary, with its massive doors and tall windows, spanne length of the third floor. The house had a formal drawing room and a "Sicilian" dining room with sandstone columns and inlaid wooden paneling. Its most talked about feature was the sunken marble tub in a huge bathroom decorated with inlaid wood and black and white tiles. Guests often bathed there—unaware that others were watching through a concealed peephole in the wall. Evenings were often all-night affairs, with the Crosbys and guests occasionally gathering in the huge tub. Harry wrote of the "great drinking of cocktails in our bathroom—it was too cold in the other rooms— and there were eleven of us all drinking and shrieking and we went to eat oysters, and then to the Jungle where there was a great drinking of whiskey and mad music, and life is exciting nowadays with all the pederasts and the lesbians—no one knows who is flirting with who."

Paris was a drug center during the twenties, with hashish, opium, and cocaine inexpensive and easy to obtain. Drugs were abundant at the Crosbys' gatherings, as they were at most of the parties attended by the Fitzgeralds. Cocaine, called "a deck of snow," cost only a dime, and locals could buy hashish joints for twenty cents; tourists paid a dollar. Drugs were freely available at most cabarets, the most notorious being a narrow bar called the Hole in the Wall on rue des Italiens. It was a hangout for young writers from newspaper offices around L'Opera and was rumored to have a secret escape passage into the Parisian sewers. Robert McAlmon recalled how "poverty stricken boys and girls of good German families sold and took hashish as they congregated in the dreary nightclubs for warmth not available on the streets or in their homes—if they had homes." These young Germans had fled to Paris after the war to escape the disillusionment and poverty rampant throughout Germany, especially in Berlin where, Djuna Barnes observed, "People were for sale at bargain prices, and all sorts of sexuality and dress could be seen any evening along the Unter den Linden." In Berlin the dollar had twenty times the purchasing power it had elsewhere and drugs were cheap and easy to obtain. Though more expensive in France, a greater variety was available along with the best absinthe, whiskey, passiflorine (a vehicle for drugs), champagne, and brandy in Europe.

The Crosbys, like the Fitzgeralds, were always looking for novel entertainments. When barge parties became the newest diversion, they borrowed *Le Vert-Galant* (owned by a young Dutch couple, Frans and Mai de Geetere), which was moored at the base of Ile de la Cité near Pont Neuf, and invited people for chowder and corn bread (or Gouda cheese, wine, and fruit) and a night of revelry. Scott and Zelda also liked the novelty of barge parties and gave a large one about which the journalist Janet Flanner commented: "Their famous dinner on the houseboat anchored in the Seine was the only social American event that achieved a kind of historical importance, as if it had been French." Her remark was something of an exaggeration given that the Murphys' 1923 barge party, which followed the Ballets Russes' opening of "Les Noces," was already legendary. It had been planned for the Sunday following the ballet's premier and was held in a restaurant on a renovated barge near the Chambre des Deputes. Forty musicians, artists, writers, dancers, and ballet patrons attended, including Cocteau, Diaghilev, Picasso, Léger, Stravinsky, and Tristan Tzara. It was impossible to purchase fresh flowers on a Sunday, so the Murphys bought bags of toys from a Montparnasse bazaar and arranged the small fire engines, cars, animals, and dolls in pyramids along the banquet table. Picasso got a kick out of arranging the toys in a fantastic "accident" and topped it off with a cow perched on a fireman's ladder. The dinner ended with Igor Stravinsky leaping through the center of an enormous laurel wreath. The party came off with such flair and style that it became the talk of Paris and made the Murphys famous for their entertaining.

When the Fitzgeralds weren't at one party or another, they frequented the cafés, which they came to regard as an extension of their apartment. By 1925, Parisian cafés had replaced salons as meeting places for artists and writers, and were where information got shared and magazine editors went looking for contributors. Because they were neither bars nor restaurants, cafés were where friends met, exchanged gossip, and stayed warm or cooled off. Anyone sitting at an outside table on a warm night might see a parade of the famous: Harold Loeb walking by with Hemingway after a boxing match or a night at the races, Stein and Toklas parking their Model T Ford Coupe, or Scott and Zelda arriving by cab after dinner at Mitchell's or Florence's. So popular were these cafés that one observer noted, "Paris has only 17,000 bakers, 14,500 butchers, but 33,000 drinksellers." Americans did little at-home entertaining since it was cheaper and more relaxing to meet at a café. People usually bought their own drinks and socializing continued until the establishment closed. Most shut at three in the morning, but some, like the Dingo, stayed open all night, which was an added benefit since French law forbade excessive noise in residences after 10 P.M.

Zelda and Scott's favorite cafés were located on the Right Bank, where the Fitzgeralds became permanent fixtures in the nightclubs and bars of the grand hotels clustered around l'Arc de Triomphe. The Seine divided Paris's Left and Right Bank. The Right was the playground of the rich and extended from Place de l'Etoile east to the Louvre. The Left Bank, defining a small part of the city, was home to struggling artists and writers, and the American colony, which congregated in the sixth arrondissement from the Seine to boulevard du Montparnasse, and spilled over into sections south of the boulevard. Marking the hub of the colony were the three adjacent cafés at the corner of boulevard du Montparnasse and boulevard Raspail—the Dome, Rotonde, and Select bars. The Rotonde attracted painters, the Dome drew American writers, and the Select claimed a diverse international clientele. The Dingo's famous bartender Jimmie Charters remembered: "Montparnasse was little more than a gray and dull street holding a broken double row of cafés, but in spirit it was stronger than home or religion, the ultimate of the social reaction to the war. Whoever had troubles with his parents or his wife, whoever was bored with the conventions of stability, begged or borrowed the money to come to Montparnasse, led on by a promise of complete escape. Never has there been such an international gathering of more or less brainy excitement eaters."

Americans arriving in Paris usually headed for the Dome to look for old friends or make new ones. "In the normal course of events," Charters recalled, "you went there in the morning, or whenever you got up, for a breakfast of croissants and coffee, to read the morning papers, and to rehash with your friends the events of the night before. That finished, you wandered off to your occupation of the day. . . . But by afternoon you would be back again on the terrace of the Dome drinking your aperitif, and by nine or ten o'clock back again at the Dome terrace."

While expatriate writers preferred the Dome or Rotonde, other popular gathering places included the Select, Deux Magots, and Le Jockey. The Jockey was decorated inside and out with large painted figures and an image of an Indian riding an Appaloosa at its entrance. Its bartender was an American Indian who had remained in Paris after Buffalo Bill's Wild West Show departed. But the Jockey's greatest drawing card was the model Kiki, Man Ray's mistress, who sang and danced while passing the hat. Hemingway's favorite bar was Closerie des Lilas, which had been the choice of poets and writers since Baudelaire's days. At Closerie, French patrons never intruded on anyone's privacy. Hemingway considered it the best drinking establishment in Paris. "It was warm inside in the winter and in the spring and fall it was very fine outside with the tables under the shade of the trees." The Fitzgeralds preferred the Dingo, "the Crazy One," which featured Jimmie Charters as its bartender and catered to Englishmen and Americans by serving corned beef and cabbage, chicken-fried steak, and American soups. The Irishman Charters had an impish grin and was a sympathetic listener and friend to loyal customers. He had previously served drinks at many other famous Montparnasse bars: the Parnasse, Falstaff, Hole-in-the-Wall, Jockey, Jungle, Bar de L'Opera, and Trois et As.

The Fitzgeralds only used the bars as a place to commence their evening. Gerald Murphy explained: "I don't think it was parties that started Scott and Zelda on their adventures. . . . Their idea was that they never depended upon parties. I don't think they cared very much for parties, so called, and I don't think they stayed at them very long. They were all out, always searching for some kind of adventure outside of the party." In a 1974 interview with Winzola McLendon, their daughter, Scottie, recalled that time. "It was a constant merry-go-round for them. [My father] devoted six or seven years of his life, from about 1924 to 1931, to having a good time in Paris. He wrote a few short stories just to keep the family alive—some of them good, some not so good—and he kept talking about the novel he was writing without doing much writing. . . . His greatest problem was all the distractions in Paris."

Zelda's Parisian address book provides some insight into their activities. It lists bootleggers' names, dressmakers, fur repairers, rental agencies, hat and corset shops, shoe stores, and cleaning establishments. It identifies the best places to buy sweaters, where to purchase dancing shoes, and what specialty shops stocked the finest perfume. Second only to the large number of doctors listed under "D" (twenty-five) are lingerie stores, numbering eight, including a separate entry for Elizabeth Arden. Stephen Parrott's address at 120 rue du Bac is listed even though the Fitzgeralds had not yet renewed their friendship with him. Also included is the recent Yale graduate and aspiring poet Cary Ross, who admired Fitzgerald's writing and was thrilled to be included in their circle. There are also addresses for other writers—Edith Wharton, James Joyce, John Dos Passos, Ford Madox Ford, Michael Arlen, and Ernest Hemingway. It is amusing that Zelda spells Hemingway's name incorrectly, including it first as "Hemminway" but correcting it in a later entry.

In August 1925, Fitzgerald wrote John Peale Bishop, "I am beginning a new novel next month on the Riviera. I understand that MacLeish is there, among other people (at Antibes where we are going). Paris has been a mad-house . . . as you can imagine, we were in the thick of it. I don't know when we're coming back—maybe never."

The summer of 1925 was Gerald and Sara Murphy's first in their newly renovated Villa America and they invited friends to see it. The MacLeishes arrived first and, renting a nearby villa, shared milk from the Murphy's two cows. Archibald, who was also a Yale graduate and Skull and Bones member, had looked up the Murphys immediately after arriving in Europe in the summer of 1923. Born in 1892 in Glencoe, Illinois, MacLeish attended Hotchkiss before Yale, where he earned his Phi Beta Kappa key. He continued on to Harvard Law, three years ahead of John Biggs, and finished first in his 1919 class. Following graduation, he joined one of Boston's best law firms—Charles F. Choate Jr.—and also lectured at Harvard Law School. But in 1923, MacLeish left the legal profession to write poetry. "I date the beginning of my life from that year," he affirmed. Accompanied by his two young children and wife, Ada, an accomplished soprano whose operatic singing was promoted by the legendary musician Nadia Boulanger, he came to Paris. Then in his thirties, he quickly became good friends with Gerald Murphy, who also had come to artistic endeavors late in life.

Arriving in August, the Fitzeralds stayed at the Hotel du Cap, making the drive out to Villa America daily. Pleased to be included in the Murphy's social group, they nonetheless sensed something had changed from the year before. Some guests were at the hotel with the Fitzgeralds, but others were housed at the Murphys' Bastide or Ferme des Oranges, a donkey stable converted into a housekeeping cottage across the road from the main house. Fitzgerald made note of who was lodged where. The attire was informal but stylish—French workmen's pants and jockey caps for men, linen trousers with striped shirts for women. A typical day started at eleven with a late-morning swim on the Murphys' tiny beach called the *garoupe*. Just forty yards long, it had been raked entirely free of seaweed and transformed into a perfect place to sunbathe and swim. For most of the day, the three Murphy children and Scottie swam or played on straw mats shaded by huge striped umbrellas while the adults sat chatting nearby. There were lots of extra umbrellas, blankets, and mats for the guests, who, at midmorning, were offered Gerald's favorite sweet biscuits and sherry from various wicker baskets. By noon, the group had returned to the Villa America for lunch or to their own lodgings. Everyone reconvened late in the afternoon at Eden Rock, where all the children took diving lessons. Zelda, easily the best swimmer in the group, was taking it somewhat easy after her operation. Even so, she joined MacLeish in diving from the high cliffs, and they became good friends during those lazy afternoons. Evenings commenced with cocktails for six or eight of the Murphys' friends. Gerald usually mixed a special concoction of brandy, liqueur, and lemon juice and served it in long-stemmed glasses that had been rimmed with lemon and dipped in coarse sugar. After cocktails there was a sit-down dinner, good conversation, and a song or dance by the children. An evening filled with music and laughter generally followed. In August 1925, Fitzgerald facetiously wrote John Peale Bishop: "I went to Antibes and liked Archie MacLeish enormously. . . . There was no one at Antibes this summer except me, Zelda, the Valentinos, the Murphys, Mistinguet, Rex Ingram, Dos Passos, Alice Terry, the MacLeishes, Charlie Brackett, Maude Kahn, Esther Murphy, Marguerite Namara, E. Phillips Oppenheim, Mannes the Violinist, Floyd Dell, Max and Crystal Eastman, ex-premier Orlando, Etienne de Beaumont—just a real place to rough it, an escape from the world." The Fitzgeralds, who had worried that the previous summer's crisis might have spoiled Antibes for them, were relieved it had gone so well and planned to return the following year and remain until January.

On the *garoupe* that summer Zelda got to know Picasso's wife, Olga Koklova, deuxieme ballerina with the Ballets Russes. She was fascinated by Olga's stories of behind-the-scenes ballet intrigues. When she and Scott returned to Paris that fall, Zelda decided to renew the ballet training she had begun in Montgomery. Everyone she knew was involved in the Parisian avant-garde. She asked Scott to contact the Murphys and find out who taught dance to their daughter Honoria. It seemed harmless enough, so Scott immediately wrote Gerald. Replying on September 19, 1925, from Antibes, Gerald explained, "Honoria's teacher is Madame Egorova (Princess Troubetzkoy), top floor over the Olympia Music Hall on the Boulevard. The stage entrance is on the side street, 8 or 10 Rue Caumartin. You walk up thro' the wings while the performance is going on, and her studio!! A big, bare room just for learning to dance in." To Fitzgerald, it seemed a good way for Zelda to occupy her time. She wholeheartedly plunged into studying classical Russian ballet—the most difficult, influential dance aesthetic of the twentieth century. So enthusiastic was she about beginning her lessons that she took Hadley Hemingway along to watch her practice.

Lubov Egorova, director of the ballet school for Diaghilev's Ballets Russes, had trained at the Maryinsky Imperial Theatre in St. Petersburg, a boarding school that educated young dancers at the czar's expense. Maryinsky students studied for eight years under strict discipline. Their parents relinquished control, and visitors were allowed only during certain rehearsals. Only after years of intense training did pupils finally get the opportunity to perform. Egorova debuted as principal dancer in "Francesca Da Rimini," with music by Tchaikovsky on November 28, 1915. Six years later, she danced the title role of Aurora, alternating with four other exiled Russian ballerinas, in Diaghilev's first full-length Marius Petipa ballet *The Sleeping Beauty* at a London production in the Princes' Theatre. A talented dancer and gifted teacher, Egorova was considered the most demanding of the Russian dance coaches in Paris. She offered Zelda the discipline she craved and an escape from aimlessness; she would also unknowingly precipitate her mental collapse.

When the Murphys returned to Paris, Zelda enthusiastically joined them for theater performances, abstract painting exhibitions, French poetry readings, and most important, ballet. She accompanied them to Etienne de Beaumont's fantastic "Soirees de Paris" in

Montmartre and numerous Ballets Russes performances, going backstage afterward to meet the dancers and choreographers. Two new Massine ballets and one by Balanchine premiered during 1925: "Zephire and Flore" for which Georges Braque did the costumes and decor, and "Les Matelots" and "Barabau," with set designs by Maurice Utrillo. Zelda relished all of these activities, and her exposure to the abundance of creativity in Paris influenced all her future creative pursuits.

After a dance opening, there would often be an all-night discussion of the debut at the Dingo. In 1924, the Dingo had been purchased by Lou Wilson, an American whose Dutch wife, Jopie, befriended many Montparnasse women. Jopie enjoyed Zelda's company as well as that of Zelda's primary rival for attention among the expatriates, Lady Duff Twysden. Both women spent ample time at Jopie's bar sharing confidences. The Fitzgeralds became friendly with Twysden during the winter of 1925, and saw a great deal of her at the Dingo, where she and her companion, Patrick Guthrie, spent most evenings. Duff was a great drinker on whom alcohol had little effect. Her distant cousin, Guthrie, on the other hand, was not only addicted to drugs but, like Fitzgerald, became drunk after one or two drinks. At thirty-two, Duff was eight years older than Zelda and infinitely more sophisticated. She had been educated in Paris, spoke French well, and cursed broadly in it and English. She shared Zelda's desire for adventure, flirted often and indiscriminately, and confessed her real feelings to no one. Even though Hemingway labeled her an "alcoholic nymphomaniac," he found her sexy and exciting, as did Harold Loeb, who, during their brief affair, encouraged her to utilize her artistic talents. Once, after seeing her drawings, Loeb asked if she planned an artistic career. She quickly dismissed that notion, telling him she considered work the concern of others. "Different people need different things. The grasshopper has always managed or some of us wouldn't be here. . . . I have nothing against work—for those who like it." Five years earlier, Zelda had expressed similar sentiments to Scott. "I hope I'll never get ambitious to try anything," she'd told him. "It's so much nicer to be damned sure I could do it better than other people."

Lady Duff stood just under six feet and was poised, elegant, and sure of herself. She sported bobbed, light brown hair brushed back like a boy's, often topped with a man's slouch hat worn at a rakish angle. Fond of dressing casually, she usually wore a jersey over a simple Eton-collared blouse and a Scottish tweed skirt. Independent and aloof, Duff drew much of her confidence from the title acquired through her second husband who was a baronet. The daughter of a wine merchant, she was born Dorothy Smurthwaite in 1892 in Yorkshire, England. Following her parents' divorce, she left for Paris, where she became fluent in the language and an accomplished pen-and-ink artist. After a return to England and brief World War I marriage to naval officer Luttrell Byrom, followed by a second to Baronet Roger Twysden, with whom she had a child, she left her son and husband behind and returned to France with Patrick Guthrie. Duff and Guthrie, who lived hand-to-mouth on family money, resided in seedy Parisian hotels, and whenever Patrick was too drunk to make bar rounds, she joined his homosexual friends, who served as protection. Duff was the most talked-about, controversial foreign woman in Montparnasse. She slept with whomever she pleased, but probably had fewer lovers than her reputation implies. At first, Zelda was the more popular and better known, though Duff was liked and despised equally by the same people. Robert McAlmon disliked Duff, considering her "the most copied, the least witty or amusing [who] could turn to 'acting her ladyship' at most dangerous moments." In contrast, Edward Fisher praised her naturalness and unpretentiousness, saying, "She was truly real, intuitive, gentle and of course—doomed." At first, both Fitzgeralds were taken with Duff's vivacity and charm. They spent many evenings with her and sometimes brought along the Hemingways. Ernest quickly became infatuated and flirted openly. He took Duff out to bars alone and then back to his apartment, but either because of Duff's loyalty to Hadley or her own lack of interest, she did not go to bed with him. Instead, she began an affair with his sparring partner, Harold Loeb. Hadley Hemingway, appreciating her integrity and determination to shun affairs with married men, admired Duff and referred to her as "a very lovely and a very fine lady, very popular and very nice to women, fair and square."

Although the Fitzgeralds had fled Great Neck specifically to avoid distractions, once again they found themselves immersed in a nonstop gala, where a party begun on Wednesday might continue through the weekend. More than once, Scott found himself sobering up in Brussels without a clue as to how he'd gotten there. American and English expatriates accustomed to low-alcohol French

wine were now consuming cognac, absinthe, and Pernod—a favorite among women—all high in alcohol content. Drunkenness,
and its accompanying stomach disorders, were common. Sweet
Pernod proved the greatest offender. Most parties were delirious,
all-night affairs that culminated at sophisticated spots like Maxim's
or Coupole, which attracted the most charming people, who by
night's end had lost much of their appeal. Fictionalizing the period
in *Save Me the Waltz*, Zelda wrote how "nobody knew whose party
it was. It had been going on for weeks. When you felt you couldn't
survive another night, you went home and slept and when you got
back a new set of people had consecrated themselves to keeping it
alive. . . . There were Americans at night and day Americans, and
we all had Americans in the bank to buy things with. The marble
lobbies were full of them." Fitzgerald would later describe the same
environment in "Babylon Revisited": "The memory of those days
swept over him like a nightmare—the people they had met traveling, the people who couldn't add a row of numbers or speak a
coherent sentence . . . the women and girls carried screaming with
drink or drugs out of public places. . . ."

Sleeping off hangovers from the previous night, by lunch the
Fitzgeralds might head for Trianon, James Joyce's favorite, or stop
at Ciro's, Foyot, or La Reine Pedauque. As big spenders and good
tippers who ordered extravagantly, they were favored customers
who commanded good tables and got excellent service. To avoid
their grim apartment, after dressing for a full evening, they would
often spend all night out. The Dingo was their customary starting
place. There, they talked with Charters at the bar, where they usually found Duff Twysden, Pat Guthrie, and other regulars sitting.
As the evening progressed, they dropped by the Select, Dome, or
Lipp's, then an intimate place with eight tables and only two waiters, where Zelda often entered into long conversations with other
patrons about ballet. After making obligatory appearances at the
Montparnasse bars, they would head for dinner on the Right Bank,
which Zelda preferred, and Prunier's, where they often ordered
Pouilly-Fuisse and bouillabaisse. An institution by the twenties,
Prunier's had opened as an oyster shop in 1872 after its owner had
planted Cape Cod clams and Blue Point oysters in Brittany and advertised them in the *Paris Herald*. The restaurant quickly attracted
American and British patrons and became a favorite of writers and

journalists. After dinner, the Fitzgeralds might Charleston at Claridge's on the Champs-Elysees or stop at the Ritz or Crillon bars, which were packed with Americans, including many of Scott's Princeton classmates. The Ritz, in the Place Vendôme, Paris's most expensive hotel, had two bars: a tiny area reserved for women where champagne cocktails were the favorite, and a larger bar with its main entrance on rue Cambon. The Fitzgeralds frequented both, but by eleven at night were often back in Montmartre on the rue Fontaine at Joe Zelli's, a cabaret that had outgrown its unpretentious roots to become an expensive nightclub, its window plastered with photos of entertainers and topless bar girls.

Also on the rue Fontaine was Le Boeuf sur le Toit, a business venture of Louis Moyses and Jean Cocteau, specializing in jazz and "foie gras de Strasbourg." Catering to celebrities like Igor Stravinsky, Raymond Radiguet, and Constantin Brancusi, it was often filled with South American playboys doused in that year's popular cologne, Carnaval de Venise. Stopping off at either Le Boeuf sur le Toit or Le Perroquet was the Fitzgeralds' favorite way to end the evening, and Zelda did a Cubistic drawing of a woman piano player at Le Boeuf and pasted it into her scrapbook. Determined to maintain her slim figure, she seldom ate full meals, but Fitzgerald could often be found eating a late supper at Lipp's, which served until midnight and made excellent sauerkraut, potato salad, and cervelas, a wide sausage split in two and covered with a special mustard sauce. It was Hemingway's favorite dish there.

In 1925, black cabarets like Mitchell's and Florence's, owned by African Americans, were becoming all the rage. They were always crowded with Parisian women dancing with Antillean and Sudanese men. Bricktop's at 53 rue Pigalle was among the most famous of these nightspots, opened by Ada Smith du Conge, a black woman who dyed her hair orange—hence the name Bricktop. Ada knew her customers by name and watched over them protectively. But even Mme du Conge was not quick enough to stop Zelda the night she gave her pearls away. Sylvia Beach recalled how Zelda impulsively gave the pearls to her black female dance partner, even though they had been a gift Scott had purchased with a $1,700 story advance. Fitzgerald later used the backdrop of these clubs to create a sense of nostalgic regret in his story "Babylon Revisited": "He passed a lighted door from which issued music, and stopped with the sense of familiarity; it was Bricktop's, where he had parted with so many hours and so much money. . . . Zelli's was closed, the bleak and sinister cheap hotels surrounding it were dark."

Zelda had grown up in the segregated South and was fascinated by the black American performers entertaining at Parisian clubs. She occupied a front seat to see Snakehips, Whispering Jack Smith, and Josephine Baker with her snake Kiki and pet leopard Chiquita. In October of 1925, Baker was a smash in the hit revue at the Champs-Elysees Theatre, for which John Dos Passos helped paint the sets designed by Mexican artist and caricaturist Miguel Covarrubias. Naked from the waist up, Baker wore a tutu of bananas and exuded sensuality as she descended from a mirrored ball to a stage filled with cornucopias of hams and watermelons. Backing her was a troupe of twenty-five black performers called the Negro Revue, which had been organized by Caroline Dudley, wife of the surrealist Joseph Delteil. The show was the hit of the season, and the following year, while still performing at the Casino de Paris and other theaters, Baker opened her own club on the rue Fontaine. She was followed by numerous other black singers and dancers. The French passion for Negro performers reached its peak with the arrival of the American Negro Dance Company. Black clubs, including the Cabane Cubaine, Boule Blanche, and Bal Negre in the rue Blomet, across from the building where the surrealists met, suddenly sprang up throughout Paris. Overnight, so many Parisians wanted to learn the Negro-originated Black Bottom that by 1926, Orrea Waskae of the American Negro Dance Company was advertising herself as the "colored American danseuse" and instructing sixty French dance teachers. Zelda loved the new dances and level of excitement filling these black cabarets. Patrons of Florence's, Zelli's, and Mitchell's rubbed shoulders with criminals, and Florence's was the site of a shoot-out between jazz saxophonist Sidney Bechet and musician Mike McKendrick. Though neither was wounded, a passing woman was accidentally struck by a stray bullet. After the incident, attitudes changed rapidly. Until then, Paris police had given black performers considerable latitude, but afterward opportunities for Negro musicians narrowed as French authorities, reacting to black monopolization of nightclubs, imposed measures dictating that fifty percent of any band had to be composed of French nationals. The French courts sentenced Bechet to eleven months in prison and, after he had served only part of that sentence, expelled him from France.

Along with the altering black nightclub scene, Scott's drinking habits were changing. Sara Mayfield recalled that when she "ran into two friends of the Fitzgeralds who had been to Ciro's with them the night before [they] were frank to say that if you got involved with them these days you did so at your own peril." Zelda was often embarrassed by Scott's behavior at these black clubs, where, with increasing frequency, he got into scuffles. Morley Callaghan, a young Canadian reporter, was with him when "his wallet had been stolen. He had accused a Negro, the wrong Negro, and the police had come; there had been a humiliating scene, then long hours of police interrogation as he tried to undo his false accusation yet prove his wallet had actually been stolen. The accused man and his friends had turned ugly." Fictionalizing the incident for "The World's Fair," a novel he worked on for several years but ultimately abandoned, Fitzgerald drew a grim picture of the clubs' antagonistic undercurrent, highlighting the tensions between American blacks and whites. "In the corner a huge American Negro, with his arms around a lovely French tart, roared a song to her in a rich beautiful voice and suddenly Melarky's Tennessee instincts remembered and were aroused . . . he began looking at everyone disagreeably and truculently. Dinah glanced at him and then suddenly got up to go. She was a minute too late. As we were going, another colored man was coming in—he had just finished playing in some night club orchestra for he carried a horn case, and was coming to meet his friends—the case swung against Francis' knee. 'God damn it, get out of my way!' said Francis savagely. 'Or I'll push your black face in.' 'You're not behaving like a gentleman should behave,' said the colored man indignantly, 'I cern'ly intended—' Then, before we could intervene, it had happened— Francis hit him a smashing blow in the jaw and he crashed up against the door and down into the cafe—his legs disappearing slowly down [the] steps." Zelda usually could control such situations and maneuver Fitzgerald through their evenings at the black clubs without incident, but it was becoming harder.

By fall of 1926 the French capital was dazzled by all things African, and the Fitzgeralds occasionally accompanied Nancy Cunard, heiress to the shipping line fortune, and her black boyfriend Harry Crowder to the newest "in" place, The Plantation, with its trademark Mississippi steamboat mural. Harry played jazz piano there. Cunard epitomized the era's uninhibited woman. Dressing in boyish fashions like Duff Twysden, her shingled hair bobbed, Cunard spent most of her time in nightclubs and could drink more than most men. The poet William Carlos Williams observed, "I never saw her drunk; I can imagine she was never quite sober." She had undergone an elective hysterectomy in 1920 to avoid pregnancies, and was sexually promiscuous. In playing the liberated role, she pursued affairs with black and white men while also engaging in various lesbian relationships. Fitzgerald had ambivalent feelings about her, as did Zelda, who simultaneously was attracted and repelled. Initially intending to give her a copy of *The Great Gatsby*, endorsing its flyleaf to her, he later crossed out her name and substituted Sylvia Beach's.

The Fitzgeralds were brought into Cunard's circle by Michael Arlen, whom they met and socialized with during the winter of 1926. Arlen's novel *The Green Hat* was a 1924 best-seller, and Arlen was as talked about as Hemingway. Fitzgerald was keenly aware of the competition between the two authors. As Arlen gained money and literary fame from his book's enormous popularity, he was viewed jealously by other expatriate artists who considered him a commercial writer. He remained oblivious to their sneering, saying, "I'm a disease, an international disease. Nobody likes me. Most of the people who read me say: 'How horrid, or how silly, or how tiresome,' And yet they all read me." The relationship between Arlen and Fitzgerald soon soured over their divergent views on Hemingway, who had become Scott's literary hero and masculine ideal. Six inches taller and forty pounds heavier, Hemingway was the man Fitzgerald wanted to be—avid sportsman, war hero, and foreign correspondent. Arlen shared Zelda's view that Ernest was overrated, and expressed those feelings to Scott, who in turn called Arlen, "a finished second rate writer that's jealous of a coming firstrate writer." In print, Arlen retaliated: "Scott F. came by one evening, hours late for dinner, striped blazer, white flannels, full of booze from one of Gerald Murphy's parties, embarrassed, garrulous, then silent, leaned his head down on the table top (hair halfway in the soup). . . . 'This is how I want to live. . . . This is how I want to live,' he said, and fell asleep."

In the early years of the decade, Arlen and Nancy Cunard had been lovers and Cunard surfaced as Iris March in *The Green Hat* with some characteristics of Duff Twysden added. Nancy's mother, like Duff Twysden, had acquired her title ("Lady Cunard") through marriage with millionaire Sir Bache Cunard of the shipping line. Nancy was much written about during the twenties. Besides appearing in Arlen's best-seller, she was also featured in three Aldous Huxley novels, including *Antic Hay* and *Point Counter Point*. Huxley actually used an incident from Nancy's unconventional life for *Eyeless in Gaza* in which a dead dog falls from an airplane onto a couple making love outdoors. Nancy always insisted this actually happened. (The laws of physics suggest even a small dog would have caused severe injury.) Cunard's life also became raw material for Louis Aragon's *Blanche ou l'Oubli*. She was painted by Oskar Kokoschka, John Banting, and Eugene McCown, and her face inspired Brancusi's famous wood sculpture *Jeune Fille Sophistique*.

The black clubs were too expensive for the Hemingways, who often went out with the Fitzgeralds but frequented inexpensive dance halls, called *bals-musettes*, on the boulevard de Sebastopol or rue de Lappe. The rue de Lappe was a particularly sordid street near Les Halles, the all-night city market where the best onion soup was available around four in the morning at Pere Tranquille. Each *bal musette* attracted its own unique clientele: on rue de Valence, members of street gangs congregated, homosexuals frequented Bal de la Montagne Sante-Genevieve, Arab pimps could be found at Rue Fagon and Bal de la Marine, and Au Clair de Lune drew sailors and serving girls. There was a standard dress at these dancehalls, and foreigners copied local styles: girls wore satin blouses and skirts with suspenders, and men, striped shirts and caps. Zelda and Hadley dressed as for a masquerade on those evenings when they mingled with the working class who congregated around imitation-leather banquettes. To prevent brawl damage, tables were generally nailed to the floor. Colored streamers hung from ceiling corners to the center, where a revolving, prismed ball cast fragmented light below.

Like the Fitzgeralds, the Hemingways were heavy drinkers who normally consumed a bottle of wine at lunch, aperitifs before dinner, and two bottles of wine with the evening meal. Drinking was liberating and Hadley recalled, "We drank like fishes. We'd get so tight—we'd throw up together." *Bal musettes* appealed to Hemingway because they had a rough-and-tough atmosphere where everybody played by the same rules. No woman had the right to reject a stranger's invitation to dance even if she was with an escort or new to the place. "An invitation to dance was made at long distance. In places like this, no man got up and bowed to a woman. He gave her a hard stare from across the room and emitted a loud, sonorous psst! The sounds—Psst! Psst! shot from table to table in every direction before every dance like an orchestra of crickets. Yet, no sooner would these couples take a few turns on the floor . . . then the band would grind to a halt and the owner's voice would ring forth: 'Shell out! Shell out!' And each dancer would dig into his pocket and pull out twenty-five centimes, five sous, the price per dance. Only the men paid."

Zelda loved the raw environment. The crowd reminded her of enlisted men's dances in Montgomery where the ratio of women to men had been lopsided and competition for women's attention fierce—no sooner would one dancer cut in than another would be waiting to interrupt. Early on, Scott had recognized the appeal such places held for Zelda. And in *The Beautiful and Damned* he had Gloria claim: "I'm like they are—like Japanese lanterns and crape paper, and the music of that orchestra. . . . I've got a streak of what you'd call cheapness. I don't know where I get it but it's—oh things like this and bright colors and gaudy vulgarity. I seem to belong here."

Increasingly, however, the Fitzgeralds' nonstop carousing was causing friends to turn away, including Hemingway, who had begun to heed Stein's advice about becoming more disciplined. Scott's inability to concentrate on work made a continued friendship with Ernest dubious. Hemingway was now serious about his writing, and no author in Paris at the time worked harder or wanted more desperately to succeed. He was becoming a celebrity on the Left Bank, and already by 1926 attention was directed toward him. But his confidence and bravado masked the insecurity he felt for not being college-educated and lacking the intellectual foundation a higher education would have given him. While outwardly he gave the impression of toughness, inwardly he was old-fashioned and exactly what his named implied—earnest. He was, however, unwilling to share this vulnerability and instead accentuated his physical interests. Hemingway's swagger so irritated Zelda that she always referred to him as a "professional he-man" and "pansy with hair on his chest," declaring suggestively to friends: "nobody is all that male." Honoria Murphy recalled how those taunts infuriated Ernest, but believed Zelda had "just nailed it down." Hemingway's exploits, particularly his heroics on the Italian front, were much exaggerated. And he was not above embellishing his background. He told one *Chicago Tribune* reporter he had graduated from Princeton, later admitting he had lied because he envied Fitzgerald's education there. While others talked literature, Hemingway was more likely to sing the praises of boxers and bullfighters, and his determination to excel at sports and project toughness covered deep-seated feelings of inadequacy. Boxing was his particular passion and he picked up extra money sparring at the American Gym. He also frequented the Cirque de Paris and Cirque d'Hiver-Bouglione off the boulevard des Filles-du-Calvaire where he usually got Harold Loeb to pay for his ticket or used one of the free passes his friend Guy Hickok, who worked for the *Brooklyn Daily Eagle*, gave him to watch the bicycle races.

Hemingway had never seen a live bullfight, so in 1924, on Gertrude Stein's suggestion, he journeyed down to Pamplona, getting Robert McAlmon to pay the way. The Pamplona trip was undertaken while Hadley was pregnant because Ernest thought observing the bullfights might have a positive effect on their unborn child. Joining their party was Bill Bird, owner of Three Mountains Press and European manager of the Consolidated Press, a news service he co-founded. The Hemingways, Bird, and McAlmon stayed at a bullfighters' pension before proceeding to the Corpus Christi bullfights in Seville. Ernest made careful notes of all he saw. As he watched the gored horses drag their entrails across the ring, he was so impressed with the courage of bullfighters Manual Garcia and Nicanor Villata that he decided to name his unborn child, if a son, John Hadley Nicanor Hemingway; it was.

But the Pamplona trip was not entirely pleasant; as the weather became ugly so did Hemingway's mood. A disturbing aspect of his personality was that he could quickly turn against those who helped him. Now Robert McAlmon suffered the brunt of his sarcasm. The two had met in 1923 at the Hotel Splendide in Rapallo, Italy. A writer whose best work was a short story collection called *Distinguished Air*, McAlmon was also a publisher. His initial offerings included Hemingway's first book, *Three Stories and Ten Poems*. Printed in a limited edition of three hundred copies, the book generated little interest outside Paris's English-speaking colony. McAlmon's publishing house, Contact Editions, shared office space and secretarial help with Bill Bird's Three Mountains Press at 29 quai d'Anjou. Besides Hemingway, McAlmon published the work of other expatriate writers, including William Carlos Williams, Mina Loy, Gertrude Stein, Djuna Barnes, Kay Boyle, and Marsden Hartley, printing their books on Bird's antique press in Paris and in Lyon with Maurice Darantiere.

As leader of "the crowd," McAlmon was followed from café to café by a group of expatriates who expected him to pick up the tab. Famous for being able to hold his liquor, in contrast to Scott, he could drink six whiskeys in thirty minutes with little effect. He came to Paris from Manhattan, where, as a nude model for Cooper Union art classes, he met Winifred Ellerman, better known as Bryher, the name she used to sign her poetry. The daughter of Sir John Ellerman, of the British shipping fortune, Winifred, according to terms of a will, needed a husband in order to receive her inheritance. In exchange for an annual stipend, McAlmon agreed to a marriage of convenience. Although legally his wife, she would continue to live independently while he pursued his own interests on the substantial monthly allowance her parents gave him. He and Bryher never consummated their marriage or lived together. She pursued a lesbian relationship with the writer Hilda Dolittle, and he, though inclined toward homosexuality, also had sexual relationships with women.

At first, Hemingway was impressed by the slender, thin-lipped writer/publisher. Only later did he label McAlmon "Robert McAlimony," claiming he had a mind like an ingrown toenail and had wasted his talent being lazy and self-indulgent. On entering the Dome bar, Ernest would often hurl insults at McAlmon's table— "How is the North American McAlmon, the unfinished poem?" McAlmon would then fling some derisive comment back at Hemingway, whom he called "the original Limelight Kid," warning people, "Just you watch him for a few months. Wherever the limelight is, you'll find Ernest with his big lovable boyish grin, making hay." Hemingway was friendly toward McAlmon long enough to get published and to Pamplona, then dropped him. He had convinced McAlmon to pay for his Spanish trip in the same manner he maneuvered Scott into picking up dinner tabs. Zelda agreed with McAlmon's observations about Ernest, and insisted that Scott stop lending him money since there was always a hundred dollars out that never got repaid.

Hemingway enjoyed playing the starving artist and relying on the generosity of friends. He dressed in a torn fisherman's shirt, baggy tweed coat patched at the elbows, and ragged workingman's pants. In the dead of winter with his butt showing, he would tease affluent friends, "Some of you rich guys ought to buy the old man a pair of pants so he wouldn't have to freeze his ass in this weather." The act usually worked. One of Harold Loeb's girlfriends, Kitty Cannell, recalled how Hemingway's plea sent Loeb home to retrieve his new white flannel pants. Cannell, a journalist, also considered Ernest an opportunist who established friendships chiefly to benefit his career, and helped only those who could return the consideration. She resented his flirtations with other women in full view of Hadley, and deplored the conditions in which he insisted they live. In contrast to the Fitzgeralds' comfortable style of life, the Hemingways in 1925 were existing on interest from the $8,000 trust fund Hadley had inherited from her maternal uncle. That money, combined with Ernest's salary, netted them only $5,000 a year. In Paris, their first apartment was a damp, two-room flat in a working-class neighborhood at 74 rue du Cardinal Lemoine next to Bal du Printemps, a dancehall for prostitutes, sailors, and French gangs. It was a dark place four flights up with rancid hallways and no running water. They slept on a mattress covering the floor. The only good thing about the place was their neighbors across the hall, a bicycle racer and his wife, who introduced them to the six-day races.

The Hemingways wanted their baby to be born in North America, so before Hadley delivered they vacated this apartment and left for Toronto. When they returned to Paris, their new apartment was only slightly better. However, it was much more conveniently located at 113 rue Notre Dame des Champs, near a metro stop and only a short distance from the Rotonde, Select, and Dome cafés; Sylvia Beach's bookstore; Gertrude Stein's apartment; and the Luxembourg Gardens, where Ernest liked to walk and where he occasionally met Fitzgerald. At thirty dollars a month it was a bargain, but had no electricity or hot water. There was a narrow kitchen with a stone sink and two-ring gas burner, a tiny bedroom for the baby and a bigger one for them, and a dining room large enough to hold their massive table and chairs. With a sawmill continually screeching next door, it was a noisy as well as cramped place. Such limitations no doubt accounted for Closerie de Lilas becoming Ernest's second home. Like the Fitzgeralds, Hadley and Ernest avoided their apartment as much as possible and ate out often, but for the Hemingways, dinners at Tour d'Argent were out of the question unless Scott paid the bill, which he often did, making Zelda furious. Alone, the Hemingways took meals at the inexpensive Negre de Toulouse on boulevard Montparnasse (also a favorite of Kitty Cannell's). Here, the daily menu was mimeographed on paper in purple ink and the specialty was a cassoulet accompanied by Cahors wine diluted with water. Ernest and Hadley ate there so often, they were permitted to mix their own salad dressing and to leave their red-and-white-checked napkins on a wall hook.

At first Zelda charmed Hemingway as she did all men, and his early notes to Scott usually included greetings and inquiries about her health. Though Ernest considered her frivolous and spoiled, he was physically attracted to her and noticed her lovely legs, hair, and skin. Recalling their first meeting, he wrote: "I did not like her but that night I had an erotic enough dream about her. The next time I saw her I told her that and she was pleased."

Zelda initially impressed Ernest enough to warrant his introducing the Fitzgeralds to Gertrude Stein. But that opinion soon changed, and he warned Scott about Zelda's jealousy of his talent and determination to keep him from writing. "Of all the people," he told Fitzgerald, "you need discipline in your work and instead you marry someone who is jealous of your work, wants to compete with you and ruins you . . . and you complicate it even more by being in love with her." Insisting she had a "festival conception of life" that could only bring him harm, Ernest encouraged Fitzgerald to leave her. But Scott ignored those admonitions and simply reported his comments back to Zelda. Hemingway honestly believed that Zelda intentionally thwarted Fitzgerald's work by making him drink beyond his capacity. He despised seeing any man manipulated or controlled by his wife, and hated what he considered Zelda's dominance over his friend. Actually, he harbored animosity toward any woman he considered unworthy of her man, because it reignited sour feelings about his own mother's dominance over his father. Zelda particularly reminded him of his mother because she hated to

cook and always expected others to arrange meals. That circumstance brought back Ernest's memories of his own father returning
home from a medical practice and having to prepare dinner.

The relationship became so strained that whenever Hemingway
stopped by, Zelda either sniped mercilessly or left the room. For his
part, Ernest was capable of being hostile to her face or behind her
back. He wrote Maxwell Perkins that Fitzgerald could be saved by
only two things: Zelda's death or a stomach ailment that would
make it impossible for him to drink. From her stance, Zelda blamed
Hemingway for Scott's drinking excesses, since Ernest could drink
with little effect, whereas Fitzgerald became drunk after two drinks.
Both were convinced that the other was the catalyst for Scott's
downfall, and equally blind to the reality that Fitzgerald was congenitally alcoholic. For a while, Scott and Ernest saw each other
daily. But the relationship cooled when Ernest was reprimanded by
his concierge after Scott tried to break down his apartment door at
3 A.M., unraveled a roll of toilet paper down the stairwell, and uri-
nated on his front porch. Hemingway, who was following the strict
discipline of going to bed at nine and getting up at six, now deplored Scott's banging at the sawmill gate on his way home after a
night out. Having finally understood that writing was hard labor, he
was determined to avoid distractions. He began the slow process of
distancing himself from Fitzgerald.

Writing Madeline Boyd, Zelda confessed obliquely that hers and
Scott's drinking was a big problem: "We have been passing the winter agreeably among plagiarists who are always delightful and have
spent a good deal of time in taxis, if you know what I mean. After
we saw you we went to Antibes to recuperate and all we recouped
was drinking hours. Wow, once again the straight and narrow path
goes winding and wobbling before us and Scott is working." Meanwhile, Fitzgerald told Maxwell Perkins, "My work is the only thing
that makes me happy—except to be a little tight."

Zelda and Scott were both falling into the old pattern of too
much socializing, too many parties, and too much booze. Though
neither mentions the state of their marriage, we can read something about it into Fitzgerald's comment to Perkins that Zelda was
no longer making him happy. On her part, Zelda found the contrast between Caroline Gordon and Hadley Hemingway something
to ponder: the one an independent artist on equal footing with her
husband, the other a self-effacing helpmeet to her famous spouse.

Whatever was running through her mind, she continued her strenuous ballet lessons with Egorova.

The Fitzgeralds celebrated Christmas eve with the MacLeishes and Bromfields around a tinseled tree decorated with glass balls, snowy houses, and spun-glass birds of paradise. Scott shopped for his daughter at the Nain Bleu (Blue Dwarf) toy store, which displayed the most exquisite dolls, stuffed animals, and toys, and returned with a doll named Monique that came with her own wardrobe trunk filled with outfits for various seasons. They ignored their nanny's admonishment concerning the French custom of giving New Year's gifts rather than Christmas presents and set out scores of parcels under their Christmas tree. In front of it, Zelda and Scott posed with their daughter for a holiday photo, Zelda wearing a corsage of Christmas greenery across the front of her dress. There they stand—the three of them, legs kicked up in chorus line fashion, arms intertwined. A happy family picture, it was Scottie's favorite. "There are dozens of pictures of my mother, my father and me, because my father, had he not become a writer, would have made a splendid archivist. But of them all, my favorite is the one of us dancing in front of the heavily-tinseled tree in Paris. Not only was I, at the age of 4, at my most photogenic, but Christmas was the time I was at my most useful. That is when I allowed my parents to give full vent to their romantic imaginations and throw themselves wholeheartedly into fantasy."

After New Year's celebrations, the three of them left for Salies-de-Bearn, a spa at the foot of the Pyrenees. It had been recommended by Zelda's gynecologist, Dr. Gros, who believed its medicinal waters could help her lingering ovarian infection, which had been further aggravated by Paris's damp winter. Because it was off-season, the only place open was the Hotel Bellevue, with just seven other registered guests. The almost vacant hotel, where Henry IV's mother was born, and empty town became etched in Zelda's memory. "In Salies-de-Bearn . . . we took a cure . . . and rested in a white pine room . . . flushed with thin sun rolled down from the Pyrenees. There was a bronze statue of Henry IV on the mantle in our room. . . . The casino was closed. The boarded windows were splotched with bird droppings and Salies awaited the return of its own special season. Idling along the smoky streets we bought canes with spears on the end and authentic beret Basques and whatever there was in the souvenir shops."

They stayed until March. Scott worked on his stories while Zelda painted. A scrapbook photograph shows her with a paintbrush in one hand and a watercolor portrait of Scott in the other; her handwritten caption underneath read: "Portrait of the Artist with Portrait of the Artist." (Perhaps this was her wry allusion to the equality she noted between Alan Tate and Caroline Gordon.) With little to do, they picnicked in the countryside and took carriage rides to nearby towns and excursions to Biarritz, Lourdes, and San Sebastian. Annoyed at being stuck there and eager to leave, Scott wrote Harold Ober, "We have come to a lost little village called Salies-de-Bearn in the Pyrenees where my wife is to take a special treatment of baths for eleven months for an illness that has run now for almost a year. Here they have the strongest salt springs in the world—and out of season nothing much else—." When they were finally ready to go, they hired a limousine to take them "careening around the gray block of Carcassonne and through the long unpopulated planes of the Cote d'Argent" to Toulouse, where they stayed at the Hotel Tivollier before returning to Paris via Nice.

Back in the Parisian capital, Hemingway took time away from his work to introduce them to Sylvia Beach, whose Shakespeare and Company English-language bookstore at 12 rue de l'Odeon was becoming the best-known expatriate address and popular gathering place for writers. It was directly across from Adrienne Monnier's La Maison des Amis des Livres (The House of the Friends of Books). Beach's shop quickly evolved into a salon where writers came for intellectual stimulation. The Fitzgeralds frequented both stores and borrowed books from their lending libraries. Beach had heard rumors about the Fitzgeralds' extravagance, but even so, when she was invited to their apartment for dinner, she was surprised to see the large amount of money set on a plate in their foyer so that people arriving with deliveries could be tipped.

The daughter of a conservative New Jersey minister, Beach first visited Paris at fourteen with her family. In 1917 she returned to settle there permanently. She initially started Shakespeare and Company as a lending library and mail-drop service, but after entering into a relationship with Monnier, expanded its services, selling little journals and reviews, providing free mailing services, sponsoring readings, and occasionally even lending authors money. Monnier's Les Amis des Livres offered similar services to its French clients. Moving into Adrienne Monnier's fifth-floor apartment a few doors away from the stores, Beach began promoting expatriate books and the experimental fiction of authors like James Joyce, Ernest Hemingway, and Djuna Barnes. Her shop was a cheerful place with books piled high on the tables, a big stove going in winter, and walls covered with framed photographs of authors. Hemingway and Fitzgerald occasionally met there—that is, until the publication of *The Sun Also Rises*.

The extraordinary success of that novel in 1926 irrevocably transformed Scott and Ernest's friendship by thrusting Hemingway permanently into the limelight. Following the book's publication, the novel's characters achieved star status. Jake Barnes, modeled after Hemingway, became the decade's best-known antihero. Duff Twysden, the template for Lady Brett Ashley, became a cult figure and role model for free-thinking women. And Zelda, the quintessential American "flapper," who had previously held that position, summarily was replaced. With dizzying alacrity, both Zelda and Scott were eclipsed by Hemingway's fame.

Everyone now wanted to meet Ernest; everyone was talking about Duff. Hemingway had created the novel from events surrounding the 1925 Pamplona festival, and filled it with Montparnasse personalities. Simultaneously drawn to and repelled by the quarter's denizens, he wanted to write a popular novel about them with the bullfights as backdrop. In June 1925 he and Hadley had left Paris by train for the bullfights to meet Duff Twysden, Patrick Guthrie, Bill Smith (Hemingway's boyhood pal from Oak Park), and Harold Loeb, who had just come from a two-week affair with Duff. Given that Ernest was also attracted to Duff, the atmosphere seethed with tension. Loeb got transformed into Robert Cohn in the book, Lady Duff into Lady Brett, Bill Smith into Bill Groton (with some of Donald Ogden Stewart's characteristics), and Ernest became Jake Barnes. Hemingway also included some other recognizable Montparnassians: Loeb's former girlfriend Kitty Cannell became Frances Clyne, Harold Stearns became Harvey Stone, Ford Madox Ford was Braddocks, and Glenway Westcott emerged as Robert Prentice. Hadley was omitted, suggesting what was about to transpire in the marriage. Hopeful of reaping big money and gaining recognition, Hemingway began writing the highly charged drama in Madrid, continued working on it in Hendaye, and completed the manuscript in Paris. It took only six weeks to finish, and while it was still in draft form, he showed it to Fitzgerald, who liked it but made numerous suggestions for change. He recommended that Ernest eliminate the first two chapters, cautioning that "to pursue these perverse and willful non-essentials, you've done a lot of writing that honestly reminded me of Michael Arlen." Zelda, who considered Hemingway's passion for bullfighting just another example of his pathological emphasis on masculinity, reacted less favorably. As far as she was concerned, the novel was about "bull-fighting, bullslinging and bull." Everyone in Paris was curious about the book, especially after Hemingway told Kitty Cannell: "I'm tearing those bastards apart. I'm putting everyone in it and that kike Loeb is the villain."

Each person portrayed in the book reacted differently to his sudden fame. Depicted as an unappealing, weak character, Loeb was angry, and rumors circulated that he aimed to shoot Hemingway. Loeb successfully avoided Ernest until they ran into each other at Lipp's, where Hemingway sat with his back to Loeb, who "watched his neck go red" with embarrassment. At first, Duff was unconcerned, saying "he was writing a novel, and he had the right to do anything with the characters that he wished." But after seeing herself characterized as an alcoholic nymphomaniac, she became increasingly angry. Already notorious before the novel's publication, afterward she became legendary as Vassar and Smith undergraduates emulated Lady Brett's actions and adopted her opinions. Duff had frequently socialized with the Fitzgeralds before Hemingway's book was published, but following it, their relationship abruptly ended. Scott acknowledged that his dislike for Duff affected his reaction to the book. He told Maxwell Perkins, "As to Ernest's book, I like it but with certain qualifications. The fiesta, the fishing trip, the minor characters are fine. The lady I don't like because I don't like the original."

Hemingway, now more famous than Fitzgerald, was completely caught up in the excitement surrounding his wildly popular novel. Scott reacted by staying drunk and entering into "a time of 1,000 parties and no work." The Fitzgeralds had re-created the frenetic squalor they had come to France to escape. Under the circumstances, it seemed a good idea to accept the Murphys' repeat invitation to Antibes, where Zelda might recuperate on the beach and Scott refocus on his writing.

In March 1926, Zelda and Scottie left with Fitzgerald for the

Riviera, where they rented the Villa Paquita at Juan-les-Pins. They were hoping for a repeat of the two previous summers with the Murphys and their friends but found the Riviera greatly changed. It was no longer a tranquil place, and Zelda sensed a pervasive atmosphere of "carnival and impending disaster." She later wrote, "We went to Antibes and I was sick always and took too much Dial," a sedative containing alcohol. Three years earlier there had been only one restaurant and cinema in town, but new establishments were now opening daily, and the place was overrun with Americans. There were celebrities on the shoreline, celebrities at the recently constructed hotels, celebrities—Rebecca West, Gilbert Seldes, Isadora Duncan, Charles MacArthur, Alexander Woollcott—everywhere.

The competition for the Murphys' attention was also fiercer, especially from the Hemingways, who had been invited to stay at the Murphys' guest cottage. After the incredible success of *The Sun Also Rises*, everyone wanted to meet Ernest, and this brought out the worst in Scott. Nonetheless, Scott was sympathetic to Hadley when she arrived before Ernest with their young son Bumby, who had contracted whooping cough. The Murphys' English doctor immediately ordered the two into quarantine. Concerned for their own children's health, Gerald and Sara asked Hadley to find accommodations elsewhere. Having recently vacated the Villa Paquita, on which a three-month lease still remained, Scott and Zelda offered Hadley their house. The Murphys had rented it for the Fitzgeralds before they arrived, but it proved a damp, uncomfortable place, so they had moved into the more accommodating Villa St. Louis on the shoreline a hundred yards from the casino. It proved an excellent remedy. Hadley stayed with Bumby at Villa Paquita until June, when Ernest finally arrived. And Zelda, Scott, the MacLeishes, and the Murphys visited her daily at cocktail time, talking with Hadley from a distance through the iron gate rimming the property.

It was a difficult time for Hadley, who, like Zelda, had been the overprotected baby in her family and youngest of six. Briefly invalided by a childhood accident, she was raised believing she was fragile, and found Hemingway's robustness powerfully appealing. Her father, an executive in the family's pharmaceutical business, had committed suicide when Hadley was twelve. She was then sent to boarding school at Mary Institute, where she befriended Katy Smith, who would later marry John Dos Passos. After finishing at the institute, she spent a year at Bryn Mawr. Tall and attractive in a natural way, Hadley was more handsome than beautiful and an excellent tennis player and pianist. Throughout their courtship, she always insisted Hemingway's writing would be her primary concern. Like Zelda, who had told Scott, "I want to be your helpmate," Hadley assured Ernest, "I want to be your helper—not your hinderer." And she was. When Zelda argued that she was *too* accommodating, complaining, "Ernest makes all the decisions in your house and you just go along," Hadley explained that was exactly how she wanted it. She had also suffered a power shift in her marriage, similar to Zelda's after the Jozan affair, though the cause was not unfaithfulness.

The situation occurred over Hemingway's manuscripts. In December of 1922, Ernest asked Hadley to hand-carry three folders of his writing to Lausanne, where he was covering the territorial negotiations between Greece and Turkey for the *Toronto Star*. Lincoln Steffens, the famous muckraker, was also in Lausanne. He had read Hemingway's writing and wanted to see more. Hadley responded quickly. She packed all of Ernest's manuscripts—handwritten originals, typescripts, and carbon copies representing a year's work, including the novel about his war experiences, along with poems, short stories, and Paris sketches—into a valise and boarded a train for Switzerland. After placing the valise in an overhead rack, she momentarily left to buy water and returned to find the valise gone. According to another version of what happened, Hadley entrusted the valise to a porter who left with it. In Hemingway's mind, however, the loss was connected with infidelity. He felt Hadley should have better understood the importance of his work and cared enough to safeguard its value. He never forgave her or forgot the incident, and she felt guilty for it the rest of her life. Like Scott, who held fast to his anger over the Jozan affair, Ernest always deeply resented Hadley's supposed carelessness. It provided him with an excuse for retribution and infidelity.

Zelda sympathized with Hadley's predicament but was fighting her own demons. On her return to Paris, she began to notice that even a little alcohol made her terribly agitated, and a lot triggered hysteria. She later described such an incident in *Save Me the Waltz*: "They went to Bourget and hired an aeroplane. David drank so much brandy before they left that by the time they were over the Porte St. Denis he was trying to get the pilot to take them to Marseilles. When they got back to Paris he urged Alabama to get out with him at the Cafe Lila's. 'We'll find somebody and have dinner,' he said. 'David, I can't honestly. I get so sick when I drink. I'll have to have morphine if I do—like the last time.' " The episode alludes to an incident at the Villa St. Louis, when Zelda drank too much, became hysterical, and Scott had to call a doctor who sedated her with a shot of morphine. Becoming hysterical as a result of drinking alcohol is now recognized as an early symptom of the onset of schizophrenia; at the time, though, no one recognized it as a hint of Zelda's deteriorating mental state.

In June, Zelda underwent another surgical procedure, this time at the American Hospital at Neuilly, outside Paris. It may have been an appendectomy, or an attempt to cure her lingering ovarian difficulties. Much later, in 1930, on her admittance to the Valmont Clinic in Switzerland, one of her doctors would note: "At twenty-four in Europe has a near peritonitis caused by an inflammation of the right ovary and is practically disabled for a year. The matter is cleared up by an operation for appendix. (Dr. Gross and Dr. Martell) Dr. Martell finds appendix in bad shape but ovary fundamentally healthy."

Worried about her sister's health and Neuilly confinement, Rosalind wrote the hospital inquiring why Zelda had been admitted. She received no response. "What it was all about I cannot say, however her stay in the hospital I recall as being not long enough for a serious operation. I sent her flowers from Brussels that she acknowledged promptly by a cheerful note, saying also that she and Scott were going to provincial France, I've forgotten just where, for her recuperation, but not mentioning what her illness had been. Feeling uneasy about her, as I always did after seeing what her life had become, I wrote the head of American hospital, after she had left, in an effort to learn what her trouble was. Naturally I got no reply, which would have been a violation of ethics with Zelda a married woman no longer in the care of her family. I once thought it may have been an abortion, but remembering that Scott was a Catholic, no longer practicing but still Catholic enough to have wanted to be married in the Church, and to have Scottie baptized in it, I dismissed that idea." Whatever the procedure was for, its resulting stitches temporarily restricted her from strenuous activity.

While Zelda was in the hospital, Scott enjoyed himself in typical fashion. One night he was out drinking alone at the Ritz bar when he encountered a group of Princeton graduates and young women from Westport. Herding them all into a hearse with ebony draperies and black plumes, he ordered the driver to take them to Les Halles, the city market behind the Louvre. There they loaded the hearse with vegetables and took off for the Ritz. His fictionalization of the episode was probably close to the truth: "Six of us, oh the best and noblest relics of the evening . . . were riding on top of thousands of carrots in a market wagon, the carrots smelling fragrant and sweet with earth in their beards—riding through the darkness to the Ritz Hotel and in and through the lobby—no, that couldn't have happened, but we were in the lobby and the bought concierge had gone for a waiter for breakfast and champagne."

When the heat descended on Paris in July, they headed back to the Riviera. Because of Zelda's animosity toward Ernest, and her feelings about their marriage, she and Hadley did not see much of each other that summer. But there was another, more noticeable change taking place in Zelda, a growing self-possession and distancing from all the Murphys' guests. Ada MacLeish recalled she spent less time on the beach, partly because she was still recuperating from the Neuilly operation, but also because she did not feel like socializing. Zelda remembered the summer as one of unhappiness and isolation: "I wanted you to swim with me at Juan-les-Pins, but you liked it better where it was gayer at the Garoupe with Marise Hamilton and the Murphys and MacLeishes. . . . You left me lots alone."

When she regained her strength, she hired a ballet teacher in nearby Switzerland to continue the dance lessons begun the previous winter with Egorova in Paris. Archibald MacLeish vividly recalled her Herculean efforts to become a dancer. "Zelda was a very extraordinary woman; she had an intense urge to create, to do something, and it was that summer she decided to take up ballet dancing. She would drive for two hours into Switzerland, practice for seven hours, then drive back every night. At this time she was twenty-eight, I believe [she was twenty-six], and you must know for a woman of that age to seriously try to take up ballet, to work that hard on all that strenuous exercise, well it was just ridiculous. But she had convinced herself that she could be great at ballet, and she had always wanted to do it, so that was what she set out to do, and the physical strain to which she subjected herself, and her inability to conquer the art were what greatly contributed to the nervous breakdown that ruined her."

As weeks progressed, Zelda became increasingly reclusive, and when Gerald and Sara organized a celebration in Hemingway's honor, she was reluctant to go. The Murphys were eager to introduce their famous friend, and hosted a welcoming party in the Casino at Juan-les-Pins. Jealous of all the attention being accorded Hemingway, and disappointed over his own treatment, Scott realized that he and Zelda were just two more names on a list of illustrious guests that included Charles and Elizabeth Brackett; Philip and Ellen Barr; Donald Ogden Stewart and his bride, Beatrice, the Princesse de Poix; and Princess Caraman-Chimay. Zelda finally agreed to attend the celebration, but regretted her decision when Scott stared rudely at guests, criticized the champagne and caviar as "affected," and tossed ashtrays from table to table. The final straw came when he flung a fig at the back of the Princesse de Poix, who picked it off casually as if nothing had happened. Zelda got up to leave, but not before a noticeably upset Gerald had already excused himself. "He [Scott] really had the most appalling sense of humor," Murphy said, recalling the incident, "sophomoric and— well, trashy."

Frustrated at being relegated to the sidelines, Fitzgerald took to uttering shocking remarks and taking dangerous risks. Introduced to new people, he would frequently say something offensive about their appearance, or bluntly declare, "I'm an alcoholic." At first the Murphys ignored his behavior, as did his family, who even made excuses for it. "Good writers," Scottie later attempted to explain, "are essentially muckrakers, exposing the scandalous condition of the human soul. It is their job to strip veneers from situations and personalities. The rest of us accept our fellow beings at face value, and swallow what we can't accept. Writers can't: They have to prod, poke, question, test, doubt, and challenge, which requires a constant flow of fresh victims and fresh experience."

Scott seemed determined to beat Ernest at his own game, and Archibald MacLeish recalled one incident that placed their lives in direct danger. "We were swimming at the beach in front of the villa, Ada and I, Scott and Zelda and Ernest Hemingway. The villa lay above the beach on the cliff and in front of it was a circular section of gravel, not really very large, I suppose fifty feet or so across, so that a large car could just barely turn around in it. Scott got out of the water and went over to his car, and beckoned for Ernest and me to come over and get in with him. We couldn't understand what

he could possibly want, but he stayed there waving at us and insisting we come, until finally we got up and went over to him. His car
was a small one (and I don't know whether you've ever seen a rumble seat, which is a very small affair in the back), but this is what his
car had. And Ernest and I got into the back though it was a very
tight squeeze. Scott drove up the road to the villa and as he approached it he began to put on speed; when he reached the circle he
turned the car around very suddenly so that we were afraid in that
small area it would overturn, and then headed it for the cliff with as
much speed as he could get. He ran as fast as he could towards the
edge of that cliff, and applied the brake at the very last minute, the
last second—I was sure he had done it too late—so that we came to
rest on the very edge of the cliff. Then he jumped out of the car and
looked round at us; his face was very flushed and red, and he
laughed like a mad-man, almost uncontrollably, for several minutes.
I was petrified; I still couldn't believe that it had happened; it had
all taken place so quickly, and Ernest, beside me, was white as a
sheet. Ernest was a very brave man, but he hated stupid risks such
as Scott had taken, and it was probably well for Scott that he was so
shocked and pale; he said nothing and did not get out of the car for
a while. . . . When Zelda found out about it (she knew because she
had seen it from below), when she saw him, she was very angry with
him for doing something so ridiculous and let him know it."

Nevertheless, Scott was pleased to have made Hemingway trem-
ble. Another childish prank perpetrated by Fitzgerald that summer was the making of a provocative film with Charlie MacArthur
and Ben Finney. MacArthur was the boyfriend (later husband) of
actress Helen Hayes, and a playwright. He would co-author *The
Front Page* with Ben Hecht in 1928. For their elaborate prank, the
three men planned a silent film about the "wickedest woman of Europe"—a composite portrait of Duff Twysden and Nancy Cunard—
using the Hotel du Cap as backdrop. With a borrowed camera, they
shot footage to accompany a blatantly suggestive script, capturing
surprised hotel guests in comic poses on film. Drunk, the three at
one point chased the actress Grace Moore through the lobby, then
compounded their offensive behavior by appropriating the white
walls surrounding her villa for their obscene subtitles. At first,
Moore found their antics amusing, but quickly tired of repainting
her fence line and ordered them off the property.

Eventually, Fitzgerald's penchant for shocking people so offended the Murphys that they banned Scott and Zelda from Villa America for three weeks. This occurred after a particularly nasty evening during which Scott broke several of Sara's favorite Venetian wineglasses. Sara wrote him a stern reprimand, pointing out that she and Gerald were past the age to appreciate such immaturity, and warned him that if things didn't change, they could not remain friends. Humiliated by her husband's behavior, Zelda added her own admonition to Sara's, locking Scott out of their villa several times, packing his trunk and leaving it outside the door, or packing her trunk and moving it into the street. But nothing got resolved. Sara Mayfield recalled, "Whenever they fought, Zelda threatened to pack up and leave. She threw everything she owned into her trunk and dragged it out to the street. There she would wait—one never knew what for. When she got sleepy she'd go back to bed, but the trunk was left behind." Where *was* she to go?

Fitzgerald's behavior so exacerbated Zelda's nervousness that she either became moody and quiet or provoked Scott with her own dangerous stunts. Once she dared Scott to dive alongside her from the highest cliffs at Eden Rock. Sara Murphy recalled the challenge: "One had to be a superb diver in order to make it. There were notches cut in the rock at five, ten, up to thirty feet. Now, that's a high dive at any time, but especially at night; one had to have a perfect sense of timing or one would have been smashed on the rocks below. Zelda would strip to her slip and very quietly ask Scott if he cared for a swim. I remember one evening when I was with them that he was absolutely trembling when she challenged him, but he followed her. They took each dive, returning from the sea all shivering and white, until the last, the one at thirty feet. Scott hesitated and watched Zelda until she surfaced; I didn't think he could go through with it, but he did." Then, on the same curved driveway where Scott had frightened Hemingway and MacLeish, the Fitzgeralds took Gilbert Seldes on a nerve-racking ride. "The road from their villa had been built for carriage traffic and there was one point at which it dangerously narrowed and curved," Seldes remembered. "Every time, just at this point, Zelda would turn to Scott, who was driving and say, 'Give me a cigarette, Goofo.' Somehow, Scott would manage simultaneously to give Zelda a cigarette and straighten the car, but it was very dangerous and very frightening."

Archibald MacLeish recalled another dangerous incident. "One particular night we had driven over through the mountains and spent an evening there at sort of a Swiss nightclub, and Scott and Zelda, who were particularly gay, had finished off the evening dancing on one of the tables, which the proprietor seemed to think was very gay and very romantic, but which was the sort of thing they were always doing. As we were driving home that night, Ada and I were riding with the Murphys, and Scott and Zelda were driving ahead. About halfway home, there was a place where the road veered off to the left and we were all surprised to see Scott drive straight ahead into a little dirt road which went on, and as we went around the curve, we looked back to see that he had driven out on to a large railroad trestle which crossed a pass in the mountains there, and it must have been two or three hundred feet down from where he stopped his car right in the middle of it. Ada and I were worried and thought we should go back for them, but Gerald Murphy laughed and said that Scott had probably found out that the trains did not run at night or something, and was trying to give us all a scare, and that we would probably see them in the morning. The next morning, while we were at breakfast, Scott and Zelda came in and told us that they had spent the night on the trestle, and upon waking in the morning had driven home. I really have no reason to doubt it, because it seemed like just the kind of thing Scott would do."

When Sara warned against doing such things, Zelda laughed it off, saying, "But Sara, didn't you know? We don't believe in conservation." Through it all, Zelda steadfastly maintained her dignity, Sara Murphy recalling her natural reserve: "She was so self-possessed. . . . Somehow she was incapable of doing anything unladylike." Even when she pulled up her skirts and stepped onto the casino table at Juan-les-Pins to dance among the glasses and bottles, she so impressed the orchestra, they provided accompaniment for her improvised ballet. One evening, at a dinner given by Grace Moore on the outdoor terrace of the Eden Rock Hotel, in honor of her fiancé Chato Elizaga and drama critic Alexander Woollcott, Zelda grew bored with the toasts being made to honored guests. She suddenly announced, "I have been deeply touched by all these kind words, but what are words? Nobody has offered our departing heroes any gifts to take with them. I'll start off." With that, she slipped out of her black lace panties and threw them to Chato

Elizaga, who, in a gesture of gratitude, dove into the water from the rocks fronting the terrace. Not to be outdone, Woollcott took off all his clothes, saluted Zelda, and marched naked through the lobby to his room.

Another time, when the Fitzgeralds and Murphys were dining on the terrace of Colombe d'Or at St. Paul de Vence, Gerald had directed Fitzgerald's attention to Isadora Duncan, seated with three men at a nearby table. Scott went over to introduce himself and, kneeling at her feet, saluted Duncan as a revolutionary artist. Having received an advance to write her memoirs, she was being pressured by publishers for the manuscript, and asked for Scott's help. When he seemed open to the idea, she gave him the name of her hotel and room number, then proceeded to run her fingers through his hair and call him her "centurion." Zelda, who overheard only this part of the conversation, became highly agitated. She scaled the low wall bordering the terrace and threw herself down the stone steps of the restaurant's entrance. Though her intention was probably to recapture Scott's attention, she could easily have killed herself. When Sara reached her at the bottom of the stairs, luckily she had only bloodied her knees. Since childhood, Zelda had dreamed of dancing like Pavlova, and was struggling to become as renowned as Isadora. Did she interpret Scott's kneeling at Isadora's feet as a sign that she had failed by comparison? After the incident, she became more withdrawn, and though there were days when she swam with the Murphys on their beach, she increasingly distanced herself from the world around her. "She wasn't of it anyhow, not really," Sara Murphy later observed. "She had an inward life and feeling that I don't suppose anyone ever touched."

As summer ended, so did the Hemingways' marriage. Ernest and Hadley made a special trip to Antibes to tell the Murphys they were separating. During fall of 1924, Hemingway had begun an affair with Pauline Pfeiffer, fashion correspondent for *Paris Vogue*, and now he wanted to be free. Pfeiffer's father owned a drugstore chain and huge tracts of rich Arkansas farmland; her uncle held controlling stock in Warner Pharmaceuticals and the Richard Hudnut Company. Though Hadley attributed the breakup in part to her loss of Ernest's manuscripts, she openly admitted that she could not compete with Pfeiffer's wealth, sophistication, and determination to steal her husband. Pleased to have two women in love with him,

Ernest was still guilt-ridden over the situation and asked the Murphys for advice. They supported his decision to leave Hadley, whose self-effacing, passive manner seemed provincial to them. They loaned Ernest $400 and gave him the keys to Gerald's Paris studio. Though he was grateful at the time, he later would castigate the Murphys for supporting his decision to abandon Hadley and his young son. "They collected people then as some collect pictures and others breed horses and they only backed me in every ruthless and evil decision that I made. . . . I hated these rich because they had backed me and encouraged me when I was doing wrong. . . . It was only their fault for coming into other peoples' lives. They were bad luck for people." Back in Paris, Hadley maintained an outward appearance of composure but felt deeply betrayed. When Donald Ogden Stewart took her home from a party, she cried all the way back to her apartment. "Our life has gone to hell," Hemingway complained to Fitzgerald in September of 1926, "which seems to be the one thing you can count on a good life to do."

Scott was experiencing similar feelings. The summer had ended badly all around. He and Zelda were estranged from the Murphys, the Hemingways had broken up, and Scott had little to show for his writing efforts. On his thirtieth birthday in September—for him commencing middle age—he told Ernest that he had celebrated by getting tight for a week. He decided it was time to go home. After two and a half years abroad, the Fitzgeralds bid farewell to Paris and their acquaintances. On December 10, 1926, with Scottie and her governess, Miss Maddock, they boarded the *Conte Biancamano* and, traveling first class, headed back to New York.

They could not know it, but their lives would never again be the same. Published in April of 1924, *The Great Gatsby* had earned respectful reviews but did not sell well. In contrast, Hemingway's *The Sun Also Rises* had become a runaway best-seller. Overnight, Ernest had usurped Scott's place as the latest, brightest, new young writer. Since *Gatsby*, Scott had written nothing of consequence, but instead wasted his time socializing. The Fitzgeralds' behavior no longer could be written off as youthful hijinks, but had become something uglier. Scott was now a confirmed alcoholic, who, before passing out each night, might be intolerably rude to someone (even close friends) or do something malevolently destructive—like break Sara Murphy's Venetian wineglasses. At the same time, while trying to develop a life of her own, Zelda was beginning to display symptoms of schizophrenia. Even in the tolerant, Bohemian world in which they traveled, Scott had become a bore. Their friends and acquaintances recognized something was very wrong. But Scott and Zelda were oblivious to the reality that their life together had reached its peak two years earlier, and would now spiral downward. By fleeing the past, they seemed to think they could find a brighter future. At the beginning of their European trip, Zelda had boasted of escaping "all the things that almost got us but couldn't quite because we were too smart for them." She did not understand that they carried those "things" with them wherever they went.

CHAPTER 5

Ascent to Madness

After the Fitzgeralds arrived back in Manhattan, they spent a week visiting friends before heading for Washington to see Scott's parents, who were living at the Hotel Roosevelt. They continued on to Montgomery and spent Christmas with the Sayres, intending to return to Manhattan for the winter. But their plans suddenly changed when Fitzgerald heard from John Considine Jr., president of Feature Productions, that he had a three-month contract to write a flapper comedy for Constance Talmadge. United Artists was offering $3,500 with an additional $12,500 if the script was accepted. Since they needed the money and going to Hollywood appealed to them, they deposited Scottie and her English governess with Fitzgerald's parents and boarded the Twentieth Century Limited for Los Angeles.

They checked into suite 17 at the Hotel Ambassador, one of a series of luxurious apartment bungalows nestled among palm groves on Wilshire Boulevard, "where white roses swung luminous in the midst from a trellis outside the window of their suite of rooms." Their neighbors included the actress Carmel Myers, whom they had met in Rome, John Barrymore, Pola Negri, and Carl Van Vechten. Zelda was glad to see "Carlo" again and the three went out together every night. Zelda told *Motion Picture* reporter Margaret Reid that Van Vechten "came for a little peace and rest and disrupted the entire colony." Writing his wife, Fania, on January 19, 1927, Carl described his living arrangements: "This hotel is extraordinary. It is like living in London. You need a guide. I am in one of the cottages on the grounds and Scott Fitzgerald is in another just opposite me. The Fitzgeralds are here because he is writing a scenario for Constance Talmadge. I had great fun with them yesterday afternoon." All was not harmonious, however, for when Carl invited Zelda to join him and actress Betty Compson for dinner, Fitzgerald made a scene and would not let her go. Once again she was alone much of the time.

Scott and other United Artists scriptwriters were obliged to keep strict hours. But other than passing them in the hallways, Fitzgerald had little to do with fellow colleagues, who, like his childhood playmates, considered him a snob and took an immediate dislike to him. Sara Haardt was in Hollywood at the time and defended him, saying, "Scott's basically a sweet, nice person. . . . His arrogance is a kind of defense mechanism with him. He's trying to cover up a feeling of social inferiority he's always had. Underneath it, he's really a generous, sensitive man who wants people to like him." At least one screenwriter remained unconvinced, saying, "underneath it, as you and I both know, Scott's really a son of a bitch."

By the end of their first week in California, the Fitzgeralds were being courted by Hollywood notables. Introduced to well-known producers, directors, and stars, they were repeatedly interviewed by celebrity columnists and invited to numerous parties. The best gatherings occurred on Sundays when actors and actresses had the entire day off. To parody actors arriving from the set still in costume, the Fitzgeralds appeared at one of these affairs in nightgown and pajamas. They socialized with John Barrymore, went to high tea at Ronald Coleman's, visited Mary Pickford and Douglas Fairbanks at Pickfair, and attended a cocktail party at the home of Norma Shearer and Irving Thalberg, who would become the central figure in Fitzgerald's last novel.

During one of these social events, Scott was introduced to the blond, blue-eyed Lois Moran, a seventeen-year-old protégée of Samuel Goldwyn. Described by Henry Pringle in the December 1932 issue of *Colliers* magazine as "small and just a shade too sweet in appearance," she was a younger version of Ruth Findlay. Zelda saw in her another example of the successful woman she now yearned to be, and mockingly characterized Moran as being "like a breakfast food that so many men identified with whatever they missed from life." Surprisingly refined and cultured for her age, Lois was chaperoned and managed by her twice-widowed mother, with whom she had moved to Paris at the age of eleven. She had joined the Paris Opera as a ballerina when she was only fourteen and acted in her first French film the following year. In 1925, she made her American debut as the daughter in Samuel Goldwyn's film *Stella Dallas*.

Scott admired Lois's determination to succeed in Hollywood and spent much of his limited free time with her. Her Irish beauty and manner appealed to him, and they began a serious flirtation that did not go unnoticed by Zelda. Flattered by Scott's interest, Lois repaid the compliment in a newspaper interview by naming him, along with Rupert Brooke and Romain Rolland, as one of her favorite authors. She even suggested that Fitzgerald play the leading man in her next picture, and went so far as to arrange a screen test. Studio bosses, however, were unimpressed by his acting abilities.

However, following the failed screen test, Famous Players Studio renewed their interest in having Fitzgerald play Amory and Zelda portray Rosalind in *This Side of Paradise*. Scott again heeded the advice of Maxwell Perkins, who remained convinced it would diminish his literary reputation. For the second time he rejected their offer. Scott's continued involvement with Moran and his interest in co-starring with her while refusing to act in the film adaptation of *Paradise* frustrated and angered Zelda. Bored and unhappy in Hollywood, she wrote six-year-old Scottie how desperately she missed France. "The weather here makes me think of Paris in the spring and I am very homesick for the pink lights and the gay streets . . . for the wine and the little cafes on the sidewalk." To help pass the time, she spent hours swimming in the hotel's pool and learned to dance the Black Bottom. Though she continued to seek out a movie role, Zelda felt insecure when she compared herself to other actresses whom she considered more beautiful and talented. "Everybody here is very clever and can nearly all dance and sing and play and I feel very stupid," she told Scottie. "If we ever get out of here I will never go near another moving picture theatre or actor again."

The abundance of beauty and talent in Hollywood also impressed Scott. "This is a tragic city of beautiful girls," he wrote his cousin Ceci. "The girls who mop the floor are beautiful, the waitresses, the shop ladies. You never want to see any more beauty." Scott antagonized Zelda by admiring not only their beauty but their commitment to work and determination to do whatever was necessary to succeed. He saw Moran as a person who fully utilized her potential, and praised the actress by contrasting her with Zelda. Such comparisons kept Zelda constantly off-balance. On one hand, Scott held her back, and on the other, he criticized her for lack of ambition. The manipulation hurt deeply and kept the power on Fitzgerald's side. With cool interest he now observed that "there was a side of Zelda that he could no longer reach—a brooding—a vast doubt." As tormenting as Fitzgerald's involvement with Moran was, Zelda felt she was being punished for the Jozan incident and accepted there was little she could do. Only years later did she reproach Scott: "In California, though you would not allow me to go anywhere without you, you yourself engaged in flagrantly sentimental relations with a child." At first she suppressed her anger at being so often left behind while Fitzgerald took Lois and her mother out. Then, one evening after Scott had gone off to dinner with them, her rage exploded. She gathered all the clothes she had designed and made, heaped them in the bathtub and set the lot afire. It was probably an unconscious attempt to show Scott what she could not articulate, that she had worked hard to create something, and that, by ignoring her *success*, Scott, in essence, was destroying it. The message was as lost on Scott as it was obscure to Zelda.

The fire marked the start of a general downturn in the Fitzgeralds' fortunes. After eight weeks, United Artists flatly rejected Scott's "Lipstick" script. Though the studio complained about the story's weak premise, Fitzgerald had not helped matters by arguing with Constance Talmadge about the plot. In March of 1927, with their advance spent and the $12,500 of Scott's fee withdrawn, the Fitzgeralds headed back East. Shortly after boarding the train, a violent quarrel erupted when Scott announced that Moran would be visiting them. Zelda, who had assured Scott that she "would never get ambitious enough to try anything," was now being criticized for lack of ambition and compared to a woman who was more focused and career-driven than she ever was allowed or encouraged to be. In fury, Zelda opened their compartment window and hurled the diamond and platinum wristwatch Fitzgerald had given her as an engagement present out onto the tracks.

Moran's telegram, sent from Los Angeles on March 14 at 11:40 A.M., followed them east. "Hollywood completely disrupted since you left. Bootleggers gone out of business. Cotton Club closed. All flags at half mast. Love to you both, Lois." Moran followed up with letters addressed only to Scott. "Darling Scott—I miss you enormously—life is exceedingly dull out here now. Have just been bumming around the studios and seeing people I am not the least interested in." Another letter hinted at the extent of their involvement: "Darling, dumbbell, upsetting adorable Scott—I keep remembering and forgetting, remembering and thinking you are forgetting—then forgetting again, then a word from you—. You're outrageously upsetting." Equally disturbing to Zelda was Moran's impending arrival, but, exhibiting a calm exterior to Scott's parents, they retrieved Scottie in Washington and began searching for a house in Delaware.

Zelda was eager to establish a real home and told Scottie, "I am crazy to own a house . . . but Daddy said we must rent a house first . . . to see if we are going to like America." They settled on Wilmington since Fitzgerald wanted to be close to George Lorimer's *Saturday Evening Post* offices in Philadelphia, and Maxwell Perkins had suggested the locale as a quiet place where Scott could work on his next novel. Glad to have them back East, Mencken wrote, inviting them to Baltimore for a visit. "Thank God you escaped alive! I was full of fears for you. If Los Angeles is not the one authentic rectum of civilization, then I am no anatomist. Any time you want to go out again and burn it down, count me in. Can you and Zelda come to lunch on Sat. of this week? I'll ask Sara Haardt to come along; she will be eager to hear the latest Montgomery scandals."

The only person they knew well in the Wilmington area was John Biggs, descended from an influential Delaware family and, having apparently matured a great deal, now a practicing attorney there. He offered to help the Fitzgeralds find a suitable home. In 1925, Biggs had married Anna Rupert, a childhood neighbor and the daughter of a successful manufacturer. They found the Fitzgeralds a beautiful estate called Ellerslie on the west bank of the Delaware River in the village of Edgemoor, several miles north of

Wilmington. Built in 1843, the Greek Revival mansion, with its imposing two-story Doric columns, looked out over a spacious lawn that sloped gently down to the river. From 1890 to 1901 it had been occupied by managers of the Edgemoor Iron Company, and for many summers was used as a vacation house by the Wilmington families of William F. Sellers and Henry B. Bradford. The Bradfords lived there year round from 1901 to 1922. In March 1927 the Fitzgeralds signed a two-year lease on the house for $150 a month.

In conjunction with the Calvert School in Baltimore, Scottie was tutored at home under the supervision of her English governess. In her memoir, she recalled: "My earliest formal education took place at 'Ellerslie,' the house my parents rented outside Wilmington, Delaware, now torn down to make way for a Dupont paint factory, where every week a packet would arrive from the Calvert School in Baltimore, complete with wonderful stickers to be pasted in workbooks and red and gold stars to be dispensed when a poem was memorized or a dictation properly taken down." Geography became her favorite subject and inspired Scottie to visit the places she had studied. "I wanted to go everywhere that Calvert took me, and many years later when I walked into a Nigerian village to find the women naked and the men carrying spears, I felt like Marcel Proust with his Madeleine. I was six years old and pasting a picture of this same village in my workbook."

Their closest neighbors were fishing families up the road who considered the Fitzgeralds odd and whispered about the all-night drunken parties and croquet games played with plow horses on their lawn. With its high ceilings, broad windows, and thirty rooms, Ellerslie was much too large for the three of them, but a splendid place to entertain Manhattan friends who caught the train down from New York. As Zelda recalled, "The rooms were high and full of the immensity of beautiful proportions. The house was so perfect that the doors grew smaller at the top like the columns of a Greek temple. A circular stair-well plumbed its depth." Violets grew amid yellow roses in the yard between a white pine and a chestnut tree, and along the riverbank adjacent to a nearby boiler factory, bounded by a hedge of white roses, a government buoy station stood—its red roof jutting out above the sandbars.

Six weeks after moving in, they welcomed their first guests. It was May 21, 1927, the weekend Lindbergh landed at Le Bourget in Paris, and their visitors included Lois Moran and her mother, the critic Ernest Boyd, Helen Hayes and Charlie MacArthur, Ben Hecht, Carl Van Vechten, and the dancer Catherine Littlefield and her male partner. John Biggs was also there and described the evening. "We used to have riotious parties at Ellerslie. We used to do all kinds of crazy things like playing polo using croquet mallets and balls on huge Percherons borrowed from the nearby Edgemoor Iron Works. It was a bright moonlit night. I was feeling very cocky, I remember, because my first son had just been born. Lois Moran, to show how strong she was, picked up her stage mother; Charlie MacArthur then picked up the mothers of both Helen Hayes and Lois Moran, and I, to show how strong I was, picked all of them up, but I couldn't hold them and dropped one of them into the river. Catherine Littlefield was doing jetés and her partner dropped her and she nearly broke her neck." One photo of that weekend shows a very Irish-looking Lois smiling directly at the camera, her right arm slipped through Scott's, while another catches her affectionately looking up at Scott as Carl Van Vechten glances at them critically.

Zelda maintained a superficial cordiality to both Biggses and Moran, whom she derided as having "no definite characteristics of her own save a slight ebullient hysteria about romance," as she played the gracious hostess at an afternoon picnic on the shaded, sloping lawn. But as the weekend progressed, Zelda became increasingly angry over Scott's attentions to the young actress. Finally, after much drink, Zelda's rage at Scott, not only for taking up with Moran but also for flaunting her before their guests in her presence, bubbled forth to produce a nasty scene that left her guests only slightly less embarrassed than she would be upon sober reflection. A week later, an apologetic Zelda wrote Van Vechten, "From the depths of my polluted soul, I am sorry that the weekend was such a mess. Do forgive my iniquities and my putrid drunkenness. This was such a nice place, and it should have been a good party if I had not explored my abysses in public. Anyhow, please realize that I am sorry and contrite and thoroughly miserable with the knowledge that it would be just the same again if I got so drunk." Zelda admired Van Vechten and enjoyed his company. She appreciated his uniqueness and considered him an experimentalist and a connoisseur. "Carl is divine," she wrote later, "he spent six months in prison rather than pay his wife alimony."

Van Vechten came frequently to Ellerslie that summer, and Zelda recalled how, on each visit, "He brought suppressed Nigger records and a cocktail shaker." The weekend following her outburst over Moran, he returned and had a much better time, writing his wife, Fania, on May 27, "Dearest Babykins, We had a wonderful time at the Fitzgeralds. They have a marvelous yellow plaster house on the Delaware with iron balconies and endless space—about fifteen bedrooms and a drawing room nearly a hundred feet long. Chestnut trees bloom on the lawn. Negro bands came in the evening and the numerous retainers danced." Zelda considered Carlo a good friend, and that summer and fall she wrote him numerous letters that he considered important enough to keep. They clearly indicate her dogged determination to find something in which to excel: "I am painting again and will have to work if I am to turn two apples and a stick of gum into an affair of pyramids and angles and cosmic beauty before fall" (September 6, 1927).

Fitzgerald's infatuation with Moran, and his criticism of Zelda's aimlessness, fueled her determination to pursue a career. Seemingly overnight she became incapable of living vicariously through Scott's reputation, though her standoffishness the previous summer was clearly the beginning of an effort to feel her way to a separate "identity." "I think that Zelda saw the handwriting on the wall with Scott going downhill a mile a minute," her sister Rosalind postulated, "and wanted to prepare herself for a career whereby she could make her own living." She felt increasingly separated from Scott's world by her own lack of accomplishment, just as her alter ego would in her later novel, *Save Me the Waltz*. "David's success was his own—he had earned his right to be critical—Alabama felt she had nothing to give to the world and no way to dispose of what she took away." Likening her own life to that of a parasite fish living off sharks, Zelda would later remind Scott: "I have often told you that I am like that little fish who swims about under a shark and, I believe, lives indelicately on its offal. Anyway, that is the way I am. Life moves over me in a vast, black shadow and I swallow whatever it drops with relish, having learned in a very hard school that one cannot be both a parasite and enjoy self-nourishment without moving in worlds too fatalistic for even my disordered imagination to people with meaning."

John Biggs's sister-in-law Amy Rupert Thomas visited Ellerslie that summer and noticed that Zelda had placed "at her dressing table gold and silver stars leading up to the ceiling, ten feet high like a milky way." She was photographed wearing a necklace of these same stars; they were a symbol of her newfound ambitions to excel on her own. But while attracted to the independence a career could offer, Zelda still lacked confidence and harbored a deep fear that ambition might consume her. As weeks passed, she grew increasingly isolated and angry. Scott repeatedly traveled to New York City for dates with Moran, but absolutely forbade Zelda to entertain male friends at the house while he was gone. Dick Knight, who had attended their party for Paul Morand, was specifically off limits after he had infuriated Fitzgerald by initiating an intimate correspondence with Zelda. Nonetheless, she confided in Knight, a lawyer with a magnetic voice and outgoing personality, and they frequently talked on the phone. (His last name later would surface as the hero's in her novel.) In an autobiographical statement written for her psychiatrist in 1932 that is probably more reliable about the emotions it describes than about the facts, Zelda said that she had appeared at Knight's New York apartment in a black lace dress and spent one lost afternoon with him. They had cocktails and "afterwards she sat a long time on the stairway, oblivious with a kind of happy desperation." The phrasing "afterwards" suggests "after sex." But did she? As always, Zelda was not telling. Scott, however, saw the potential for problems and, as with Jozan, forbade Zelda to see Knight again or invite him to Ellerslie.

In September, Ludlow Fowler and Townsend Martin visited and stayed on for several days. They participated in a polo match and danced to the gay music of a band hired for the occasion. Zelda's attraction to Townsend was now muted, and rather than playing the outgoing, flirtatious southern belle, she appeared serious and withdrawn. The young writer Tom Wolfe for a while came by nightly—bottle in hand. After supper he and Scott usually adjourned to the deck chairs on the open terrace where they drank and talked through the night. It was similar to the relationship Scott had shared with Lardner in Great Neck except that now Scott was the more advanced alcoholic.

Though Fitzgerald's admiration of Moran's abilities is what initially motivated Zelda to seriously pursue a career, in her mind the value of work quickly escalated until she considered it her sole path to survival. This attitude was in stark contrast to her earlier beliefs when she had told her young daughter, "I am so outrageously clever that I believe I could be a whole world to myself—if I didn't like living in daddy's better." Now she interpreted success in terms of what she could achieve on her own. Her first inclination was to try painting. She had taken lessons on Capri and liked working with colors, so she began attending classes in Philadelphia three days a week. After a month at the easel, however, she found the strain hurt her congenitally weak eyes. Unwilling to wear glasses and uncertain in what direction to proceed, she temporarily redirected her energies toward sewing outfits for herself and Scottie, and redecorating the house. In Philadelphia, she purchased oversized furniture to complement the scale of the large rooms and designed other pieces for special areas. She made a multitude of playthings for Scottie, including an elaborate dollhouse with period furniture that she secretly created in a third-floor attic room for Christmas. "Though it was my father who had the most fun playing with my Christmas toys," recalled Scottie in a 1974 interview, "it was my mother who had the most fun making them. One year it was a dollhouse, which was an almost exact copy of the house we lived in, including the curtains, paintings, and slipcovers on the sofas." Zelda also painted a series of lamp shades in meticulous detail with fairy tales and animals as subjects—one with Alice-in-Wonderland characters and another depicting a merry-go-round of their friends against a background of former residences. She had learned this lamp shade technique from Mina Loy in Paris. On one shade, rendered as backdrop, were images of their favorite places: the Westport cottage, Plaza Hotel, White Bear Yacht Club, Spanish Steps, Capri, the Villa Marie at St. Raphael, Juan-les-Pins, the Villa St. Louis, and Ellerslie. In the foreground was a merry-go-round of people they knew—Scottie was on the horse, nanny on a mouse, George Jean Nathan on a lion, Tana the Westport butler on a turtle, their Negro maid on the kangaroo, Amy Rupert Thomas on the goose, and Scott on an elephant. Zelda painted herself on the rooster. One of Scott's relatives visiting that fall also remembered seeing a handpainted screen of seashore scenes, and the backs of old-fashioned lawn chairs illustrated by Zelda with maps of their travels. She also created an elaborate set of paper dolls for Scottie. Years before, in Montgomery, she had designed and made paper dolls for herself

and her childhood friend Eugenia McGugh Tuttle, but she now returned to making them in a more sophisticated way. Using as inspiration the French design book *L'Histoire du Costume Féminine
Français de l'an 1037 a l'an 1870*, she carefully researched women's
clothing and created elaborate costumes for her figures. It was a
perfect medium for her fanciful imagination and an avenue of communication between herself and her daughter. Scottie always trea-
sured the "cardboard coach of Louis XIV containing paper dolls
of the king and such dashing members of his court as the three
musketeers, complete with ruffled and lacy dress-up costumes."

When news came late that summer of Isadora Duncan's accidental death, Zelda's aspirations shifted toward dance. She was invigo-
rated by the idea that she might replace Duncan as America's
premiere dancer. Recalling the accolades her dancing had received
in Montgomery, and the progress she had made taking ballet lessons
in France and Switzerland the previous year, she took the money
she had saved and applied it toward ballet training in Philadelphia.

She shared her new hopes with Sara Haardt, who had witnessed
her early ballet successes in Montgomery and was interviewing
Zelda at Ellerslie for a *Good Housekeeping* article on wives of famous
authors. During their conversation, Zelda acknowledged that she
had lost precious time, but she still believed she could become a
great dancer. Haardt recalled her words. " 'Of course, it requires
youth, especially the resilience of youth—but I feel much younger
than I did at sixteen, or any other age.' She paused and looked past
the windows to where the Delaware River glistened palely between
the trees. 'I'll always think of myself as belonging to the generation
of the war,' she continued softly. 'It was strange what the war did to
us. . . . Of course, I suppose it goes back further than that, but it
was as if everything in the air, in life, sort of led up to it.' . . . She
broke off sharply, and a faint smile edged her lips. The next moment she was laughingly reciting some of the incredible happenings
of those glamorous days, and yet in her charming voice there was
always a note of mingled gaiety and sadness."

Inquiring about good teachers, she settled on Catherine Littlefield, whom she had met socially. Littlefield headed the Philadelphia Opera's Corps de Ballet and had studied in Paris under Lubov
Egorova, with whom Zelda briefly trained the previous year. On
October 10, she wrote Van Vechten, "I joined the Philadelphia

opera ballet, and guests came, and everybody has been so drunk in
this country lately that I am just finding enough chaos to pursue my
own ends in, undisturbed again. . . . I hope I will never again feel attractive." As startling as this last assertion may seem, what Zelda
was expressing was her hope to be judged, and to judge herself, according to her accomplishments, and not her ability to attract men.
Three days a week, she and Scottie commuted by train from Wilmington to Philadelphia for lessons. Six-year-old Scottie was only
moderately interested, but Zelda would often take four lessons a
day, then practice routines for hours in the living room. She had
partially converted it into a dance studio, complete with ballet barre
and a gigantic, gilt-framed mirror that had once been the property
of a brothel. In his ledger, Fitzgerald referred to it as "the whorehouse mirror." John Biggs's wife, Anna, who occasionally went
shopping with Zelda in Philadelphia, recalled the day Zelda found
it in an antique store. "One of the objects that caught her fancy was
a gigantic gilt mirror, nineteenth century, I think. It was surrounded by scrollwork and cherubs and wreaths in the best heavily
decorated style. She loved it. At Ellerslie when I next saw it, it was
hung in the front room beside her Victrola. She had run a ballet bar
in front of it and practiced there all day. She would sometimes
dance the entire time that we were there—whether it was for dinner, for a long afternoon's talk, whatever. She would perhaps stop
for a few minutes for a drink or something, but then continue."
John Biggs remembered how she would "start at six or seven
o'clock in the morning and . . . had one tune she used to play constantly, 'The Parade of the Wooden Soldiers.' She would keep it up
until ten o'clock at night when she would drop from sheer exhaustion." So often had he heard the tune played there that he said the
melody was "engraved on every organ he possessed." The repeti-
tious music and Zelda's practicing disturbed Scott enough to make
him move his writing desk from the main part of the house into the
library. His own frustration and unhappiness during this period got
expressed in a story called "The Ring" in which a Broadway producer watches his wife attain ballet success while his life disinte-
grates and he becomes ill with TB. It was an obvious psychological
parallel to what he feared.

At twenty-seven, Zelda was old for a novice ballerina and
Fitzgerald did not take her ambition seriously. He knew she had

enjoyed early acknowledgment in Montgomery, but he categorized
her dancing, along with her writing and painting efforts, as amateurish, underestimating her desperate resolve to build an independent identity. As the weeks progressed, her commitment became
increasingly evident. Fitzgerald soon resented Zelda's repeated trips
to Philadelphia and what he considered her total disregard for the
running of the house. He once became furious when, after spending the afternoon writing a story in the Philadelphia library, she
had gone to an Italian restaurant with several fellow students and
came home drunk. Such behavior, which was typical for Scott, was
in his view totally unacceptable for his wife, and he complained that
there was no one supervising the household or planning family
meals. The refrigerator was almost always empty. On Zelda's small
frame extra pounds showed immediately, so she was compelled to
diet stringently. She drank to maintain energy, but ate practically
nothing. Viewing Zelda's balletic endeavor as pathetic, Scott took it
upon himself to make sure Scottie was overseen by a governess and
began spending more time in Wilmington and New York bars. It
seemed that whenever he and Zelda did get together, they argued.
On one occasion, after they had spent the evening drinking and
quarreling, Zelda became so hysterical a doctor once again was
called to give her an injection of morphine.

But Zelda was not to be deterred. Focused on becoming an accomplished dancer, she was determined to pay for the lessons herself. During a visit to Ellerslie, H. L. Swanson, the editor of *College
Humor*, had suggested she write a series of stories about female
types—young marrieds, debutantes, and southern belles. Swanson
expected Scott to edit these pieces and he planned to publish them
under both their names. Zelda worked on the six stories throughout
the winter. But though they were written by her, with only a cur-
sory polishing by Scott, five appeared as written "by F. Scott and
Zelda Fitzgerald" and the sixth, "A Millionaire's Girl," published in
the *Saturday Evening Post* for a fee of five thousand dollars, appeared under only Scott's name. Harold Ober felt uncomfortable
about the situation. "I really felt a little guilty about dropping
Zelda's name from that story," he told Scott, "but I think she understands that using the two names would have tied the story up with
the 'College Humor' series and might have gotten us into trouble."
With Scott and Zelda listed as co-authors, Ober could command a
thousand dollars a story, but when only Zelda's name appeared, the

fee dropped to five hundred. She was compelled to rely on Fitzgerald's fame as entrée for publication. Realizing that without his reputation, her pieces would not garner high fees, and eager to earn as much as possible, Zelda allowed them to be published under Scott's name. No doubt it hurt her pride. But writing the pieces was cathartic, because the stories all dealt with fashionable girls leading empty lives and suffering from an inability to overcome lethargy and produce something of value. "She wanted to get her hands on something tangible," says one of Zelda's heroines, "to be able to say, 'That is real, that is part of my experience, that goes into this or that category, this that happened to me is part of my memories.' " In several of the stories, Zelda's heroines weigh the instability of the single, professional life against the security of home and family— the same dilemma Zelda was facing in her pursuit of a dance career.

It came as a welcome respite when Canadian Railways, anticipating they would write about the experience, offered the Fitzgeralds a free trip to Quebec and Montreal. In January of 1928, they left Wilmington for Canada and stayed in Quebec City at the Chateau Frontenac, which Zelda described as "built of toy stone arches, a tin soldier's castle." Following several unsuccessful attempts at skiing, they eschewed the chilly weather and holed up in their room playing cards and eating fancy salads from the hotel's menu. The two Zelda liked best were the "Belvedere" (chicory, escarole, sliced apples, beets, and mayonnaise over chili sauce) and the "Cendrillon" (lettuce, diced knob of celery, potato, apple, asparagus tips, and vinaigrette). As they looked out their windows on the gray bleakness of the Canadian winter, they composed amusing postcards for their daughter. From Quebec, Scott and Zelda sent Scottie a barrage of them, documenting the activities of "the man with three noses." On one card the man is drawn passively walking the promenade at Mt. Royale, but in another he is about to attack the Fitzgeralds' surrey driver with an ax. On a postcard sent from Sous-le-Cap, the Fitzgeralds finally hung him from a street overpass. On January 25, Scott wrote Scottie: "We'll be back Fri. night late or Sat. morning early. I have been elected President of Canada but am too busy as King of the World to take the job."

They had enjoyed their Quebec stay but were anything but rested after the long train ride back to Delaware. A parade of new visitors came almost immediately. After John Biggs introduced them into Wilmington society, people were always dropping by, and Fitzgerald wanted all his friends to see Ellerslie, with its impressive portico and river view. But when John Peale Bishop and Edmund Wilson arrived for one party, both were disturbed by the raucous delirium that had overtaken the guests—Charlie MacArthur and others shooting up the dinner service, using plates for target practice on the front lawn, and ruining the flower beds by playing polo with plow horses. John Dos Passos complained that there was never any food at these parties. "Those delirious parties of theirs; one dreaded going. At Wilmington, for instance, dinner was never served. Oh, a complete mess. I remember going into Wilmington—they lived some miles out, trying to find a sandwich, something to eat."

Edmund Wilson was a return house guest in February of 1928, along with Zelda's sister Rosalind and her husband, Newman Smith. During her sister's visit, Scott started a violent argument with Zelda after she made a derogatory comment about his father. In his rage, Scott knocked over some chairs, smashed Zelda's favorite vase, and slapped her hard enough to cause a nosebleed. Newman Smith attempted to intervene, and an indignant Rosalind tried to convince Zelda to leave the house. Fitzgerald remembered the incident somewhat differently. He recalled that he had returned from Princeton to find Zelda drunk. "You were throwing yourself into your brother-in-law's arms, making dives, and he was pretending to catch you. And every time you would fall on the floor. They went up to bed. I told you to go to bed. You made a rush at me and I hit you on the nose and you had a nose-bleed." Nevertheless, Scott felt guilty afterward, asking friends: "Is there any man present who can honestly say he has never hit his wife in anger?"

Rosalind encouraged Zelda to file for divorce. She would never forget the incident or forgive Fitzgerald. Scottie, who had witnessed her parents' marriage deteriorate over the years, continued distancing herself. "I knew there was only one way for me to survive [my parents'] tragedy and that was to ignore it." At an early age, she had managed to develop a selective amnesia, the ability to ignore unpleasant episodes and bury painful feelings. Zelda sensed this and fictionalized those feelings through the character of Bonnie in *Save Me the Waltz*: "Life at home was simply an existence of individuals in proximity; it had no basis of common interest. Bonnie thought of her parents as something pleasant and incalculable as Santa Claus that had no real bearing on her life outside the imprecations of Mademoiselle."

The escalating domestic tension began to show. When Maxwell Perkins visited, he found both Fitzgeralds on the verge of nervous exhaustion. Fitzgerald was always drinking and Zelda confined to bed on orders from the family physician, Lefty Flynn. Fleeing Delaware seemed the only solution, and Zelda wrote Van Vechten toward the end of March that they were planning a return to Europe. "We want to go in May because Wilmington has turned out to be the black hole of Calcutta, and I simply must have some Chablis and curry and fraises du bois with peaches in champagne for dessert. Also I want to feel a sense of intrigue which is only in Paris." The truth is that Zelda was eager to continue ballet lessons with Egorova, and Fitzgerald, who had spent too much time in Wilmington and New York speakeasies, was hopeful the change would reduce tensions and help focus his writing. In April 1928, with time still remaining on their lease, Fitzgerald temporarily closed "Ellerslie" and purchased three tickets aboard the S.S. *Paris*. Sara Mayfield would follow two months later with her brother on the S.S. *Corinthia*, registering for courses at the Sorbonne and becoming Zelda's confidante.

They wanted to find an apartment close to Gerald and Sara so that Scottie could play with the young Murphys, but their choices were limited because of the tourist explosion in Paris. They finally found a flat at 58 rue de Vaugirard on the corner of rue Bonaparte, adjacent to the Luxembourg Gardens and just minutes away from the Murphys. It was an expensive but dismal place that they nicknamed "Hotel de la Morgue." The atmosphere in Paris had greatly changed. So many foreigners now flooded Montparnasse bars that the bohemian ambience of those establishments was lost. "With each new shipment of Americans spewed up by the boom," Fitzgerald wrote, "the quality fell off, until toward the end there was something sinister about the crazy boatloads." Paris was filled to capacity with Americans.

That year Alan Tate was there on a Guggenheim Fellowship, along with his novelist wife, Caroline Gordon, and he remembered Zelda as "not a beautiful woman but immensely attractive, with the Southern woman's gift for conversation that made people feel that she had known them for years." Townsend Martin and Teddy

Chanler, a young musician whose mother knew Edith Wharton, and who had been among the visitors to Ellerslie, also had come over, along with Esther Murphy, e. e. cummings, and Oscar and Xandra Kalman. Fitzgerald's ledger book lists social engagements with the Bishops, meetings with Janet Flanner, known to readers for her "Letter From Paris," Margaret Anderson, founder of the *Little Review*, and theatrical agent, Caroline Dudley. At one of Dudley's parties, Scott and Zelda met the artist Jules Pascin, a legendary figure in Montparnasse who would soon commit suicide. Zelda recognized Pascin's melancholy, and commented that he was "already enveloped in tragedy and pursued by a doom so powerful that he could well afford the nonchalance in which lay his sober charm."

Scott was eager to track down old friends and visit favorite haunts before settling down to work. He spent the first three weeks attending a round of parties, generally alone because now Zelda was now committed to becoming a premiere danseuse. As her alter ego in *Save Me the Waltz* explained, "reaching her goal, she would drive the devils that had driven her . . . in proving herself, she would achieve that peace which she imagined went only in surety of one's self—that she would be able, through the medium of the dance to command her emotions, to summon love or pity or happiness at will, having provided a channel through which they might flow." To summon emotions at will—as Zelda says, "having provided a channel through which they might flow"—is Freud's definition of sublimation and a sign of growing emotional maturity. Without realizing how closely she was in accord with Freud's ideas, Zelda was saying she was finally ready to grow up.

Zelda's address book from this period shows Madame Egorova's dance studio changing locations from 10 rue de Caumartin, to number 8, and finally to 27 rue des Petits-Hotels in the tenth arrondissement. Egorova taught Zelda both in the morning and afternoon, charging three hundred dollars a month—a high fee in those days, which Fitzgerald paid with reluctance. It was twice what it cost to rent Ellerslie. She was the oldest of Egorova's students and shared her lessons with other determined dancers, later vividly described in *Save Me the Waltz*. "There was Marguerite, who came in white, and Fania in her dirty rubber undergarments, and Anise and Anna who lived with millionaires and dressed in velvet tunics, and Céza in gray and scarlet—they said she was a Jew—and somebody else in blue organdie, and thin girls in apricot draperies like folds of skin, and three Tanyas like all the other Russian Tanyas. . . ."

Continually denigrating Zelda's efforts, Fitzgerald characterized her goal as unrealistic, emphasizing she was too old, short, and awkward to become a prima ballerina. He constantly reminded her that ballet was the most difficult of all the arts, and that she was competing with dancers who had trained all their lives. "There's no use killing yourself," David tells Alabama in *Save Me the Waltz*. "I hope you realize that the biggest difference in the world is between the amateur and the professional in the arts"—Scott's view exactly.

After the 1919 Russian Revolution made refugees of the Russian nobility and Imperial Ballet, Paris blossomed as the dance capital of the world. Between 1926 and 1928, Balanchine alone mounted seven new ballets, including "La Chatte," with Naum Gabo providing set and costume design, and "The Gods Go A-Begging," for which Juan Gris designed the costumes. With the ruble nearly worthless, aristocratic men were forced to work as taxi drivers and waiters, and formerly wealthy women became seamstresses for the couturier houses and governesses. Many renowned ballet dancers opened studios, and Lubov Egorova became one of the most sought after, because of her rigorous approach and the fact that she had danced with Nijinsky in the Russian Imperial Ballet's production of *Sleeping Beauty*. Born in St. Petersburg in 1880, she had acquired the title of Princess Nikita Trubetzkoy by marrying Prince Trubetzkoy. In 1917 she left Russia and, in 1923, on the suggestion of Diaghilev, opened a ballet school in Paris to train replacements for his corps de ballet. She also taught ballet to the children of the wealthy, including Gerald and Sara Murphy's daughter, Honoria.

Now Zelda resumed training in earnest, spending hours each day in concentrated practice to mold her body into one capable of professional dancing. Her efforts quickly grew obsessive. She took group classes in the morning, private lessons in the afternoon, and practiced four hours every evening. At night, Scott usually wanted to go out drinking, but Zelda had outgrown that need, and instead took to walking the Paris streets alone, spending "blank recuperative hours over books and prints in the dank Allee Bonaparte." She was too physically exhausted to do anything else, later capturing the pain of a dancer's life in her novel. "Alabama rubbed her legs with Elizabeth Arden muscle oil night after night," Zelda wrote in *Save Me the Waltz*. "There were blue bruises inside above the knee where the muscles were torn. Her throat was so dry that at first she thought she had fever and was disappointed to find that she had none. . . . She was always stiff, and she clutched the gilt flowers in pain. She fastened her feet through the bars of the iron bed and slept with her toes glued outwards for weeks. Her lessons were agony." There was constant competition between Zelda and the younger dancers in Egorova's classes, and they would be vividly described in her novel: "girls in the starkness of white who looked like boys in swimming, and girls in black who looked like women, a superstitious girl in mauve, and one dressed by her mother who wore cerise to blind them all in that pulsating gyroscope, and the thin pathetic femininity of Marte, who danced at the Opéra Comique and swept off belligerently after classes with her husband."

While she made slow but steady progress in Egorova's studio above Olympia Hall, Scott had come to an impasse in his writing. For distraction, he began frequenting a gym on rue de Vaugirard near their apartment, run by a questionable character named Georges and his helper Phillipe. Hemingway occasionally went there to box with Morley Callaghan, a twenty-six-year-old Canadian reporter, or anyone willing to get into the ring. Seeing it as a way to repair their relationship, Fitzgerald served as timekeeper for several matches, as did the Catalan painter Joan Miró. Hemingway had met Miró at Gertrude Stein's apartment, and visited him in Montroig. Having been advised by Maxwell Perkins to look up Fitzgerald in Paris, Callaghan started drinking with Scott in the afternoons at the oak-paneled Falstaff bar. Once, when he stopped at the Fitzgeralds' to get Scott, he found both of them in bad shape. "Zelda came to the door. As soon as I saw her I knew I shouldn't have come. Pale, haggard, dark patches under her eyes, she stared at me vaguely, then tried to smile and failed. She and Scott had had no sleep for twenty-four hours. Some trouble over the theft of Scott's wallet in a night club. She had a deep perplexed frown. Her obvious anguish made me hesitate to sit down."

The Fitzgeralds' marital situation had deteriorated further since Ellerslie. They had stopped talking when alone, and had not been intimate since arriving in Paris—mainly because of Fitzgerald's drinking. One doctor told Scott that his alcoholism and poor physical condition had weakened his sexual drive, and that he might never again father a child. "You were constantly drunk," Zelda later told him accusingly. "You didn't work and you were dragged home at night by taxi drivers when you came home at all. You said it was my fault for dancing all day. What was I to do? You made no advances toward me and complained that I was unresponsive. You were literally eternally drunk the whole summer. I got so I couldn't sleep and I had asthma again. You were angry when I wouldn't go with you to Mont Matre. You brought drunken undergraduates in to meals when you came home for them, and it made you angry that I didn't care anymore. I began to like Egorova."

Zelda confided to Sara Mayfield, who was at the Sorbonne, that their marriage was a sham. "Scott and I had a row last week, and I haven't spoken to him since—not even at the table to say 'Pass the butter, please.' When we meet in the hall, we walk around each other like a pair of stiff-legged terriers spoiling for a fight." Fitzgerald documented their disintegrating relationship in his ledger, and during June and July of 1928 mentions two trips to jail, "being carried home from the Ritz," "drinking and general unpleasantness," and "general aimlessness and boredom."

The strain of the domestic situation showed on Zelda, who found it increasingly difficult to engage in even the most mundane conversations. Distracted and edgy, she retreated into impenetrable silences, her facial grimacing and nervous rubbing of hands noticeable to those around her. At fifteen pounds below normal weight she looked painfully thin. Gone was the sparkle from her eyes and luster from her hair. One afternoon, Zelda and Sara Mayfield met at Prunier's for lunch, and though Zelda wore a fashionable blue Patou outfit, she appeared unkempt and haggard. After quickly downing a martini, she ate only a few shrimp and some salade niçoise. She was probably anorexic, as many dancers are. As she gazed into her compact mirror, she told Sara wistfully, "I'm twenty-eight years old and I've already got sweetbreads under my eyes and calipers around my mouth. Look at me!" Sara reassured her that she only looked like a "femme du monde." "Don't try to be so damn tactful," Zelda responded. "I look like hell, feel like hell, and act like hell. All I do is dance and sweat—and drink to keep from getting dehydrated."

Gone with her looks was any hope of saving her marriage. Years earlier she had harbored reservations about their life together, warning Ludlow Fowler not to drink if he wanted his marriage to succeed. Now she admitted that Scott's alcoholism irredeemably had ruined their relationship. In the beginning, the Fitzgeralds drank to flout convention. Alcohol provided an excuse to behave outrageously, and it was sophisticated for Scott to arrive in Montgomery with Zelda's favorite gin. In the early twenties, their drinking seemed benign; after two drinks, Scott passed out, and Zelda, after three or four, curled up and fell asleep. They often fell asleep together. Hemingway recalled how "becoming unconscious when they drank had always been their great defense. They went to sleep on an amount of liquor or champagne that would have little effect on a person accustomed to drinking, and they would go to sleep like children. I have seen them become unconscious not as though they were drunk, but as though they had been anesthetized, and their friends, or sometimes a taxi driver, would get them to bed, and when they woke they would be fresh and happy, not having taken enough alcohol to damage their bodies before it made them unconscious."

But now Fitzgerald's drinking pattern was noticeably different. And Malcolm Cowley observed that change in many of Scott's contemporaries. "There seemed to be more drinking than before, in literary and business circles; at least it was noisier and more public. It appeared to be a different sort of drinking, with more desperation in the mood behind it. People no longer drank to have a good time or as an excuse for doing silly and amusing things that they could talk about afterward; they drank from habit, or to get away from boredom, or because they had a psychological need for alcohol. There was as much horseplay and laughter as before, but it seemed strained and even hysterical." Fitzgerald recognized the difference, but was powerless to change, describing in his story "A New Leaf" the exact circumstances in which he found *himself*. "Just when somebody's taken him up and is making a big fuss over him, he pours the soup down his hostess's back, kisses the serving maid, and passes out in the dog kennel. But he's done it too often. He's run through about everybody." Sara Murphy chastised him, but to little avail. "Why—for instance should you trample on other people's feelings continually with things you permit yourself to say and do—owing partly to the self-indulgence of drinking too much and becoming someone else (uninvited) instead of the Scott we know and love and more—unless from the greatest egotism and sureness that you are righter than anyone else. I called it 'manners' but it is more serious—it is that you are only thinking of yourself."

Zelda also sensed a weakening of her natural defenses. Having observed Fitzgerald's increasing loss of control, she formulated a plan for moderating her daily alcohol and cigarette consumption. In her spiral notebook, she planned a rationing schedule: "10 cigarettes a day, 1 aperitif before breakfast, white wine, champagne, an aperitif before lunch, two water glasses of red wine [here she had crossed out one and substituted two] and a cocktail before supper and white wine." Those used to the kind of social drinking currently fashionable will be startled by what Zelda suggested *as a regimen to cut down.* Any normal person today, unaccustomed to the type of heavy drinking that used to prove you belonged to the right socioeconomic class, would be reeling before lunch on that kind of "moderate" drinking. By contrast, Scott's daily consumption could reach thirty beers and a quart of gin. Zelda described such a night of drinking to Mayfield: "We've been on a party. Nobody knows where it started, when it'll end, or whose party it is. All of the people were white, I think. But one of the women had slept with a Negro, a six-day bicycle racer, and a prizefighter that sniffs cocaine. Mere peccadilloes, ma cherie. Another one says she sleeps with men for money and women for fun. And she looked like such a nice, simple, home-loving type. Just some of the swell friends Scott's picked up at the Dingo Bar. All they talk about is sex plain, striped, mixed and fancy."

Ignoring others' advice, Scott refused to moderate his alcohol consumption. If Zelda complained, he drank more, and when she ignored the situation, it simply persisted. Her frustration with the worsening situation was later expressed through her protagonist, Alabama, in *Save Me the Waltz.* "She wished she could help David to seem more legitimate. She wished she could do something to keep everything from being so undignified. Life seemed so uselessly extravagant."

Fitzgerald's disappointment over the poor sales of *The Great Gatsby*, well shy of the estimated eighty-thousand copies, further aggravated the problem. He was proud of his novel and had counted on its commercial success to bring in substantial revenue and irrefutable recognition as a major American writer. Its relative failure left him uncertain about what to do next. John Biggs recalled his despondency over his faltering reputation: "I asked him to please try and tell me why he had to drink so heavily . . . often

pure gin. 'I drink because I'm the top of the second rates.' . . .
Fitzgerald wanted to be the greatest writer of his generation. It was
like a demon within him. But he didn't feel he was accomplishing
this."

In "A New Leaf," published by the *Saturday Evening Post* during
July of 1931, Fitzgerald has his protagonist, Dick Ragland, explain
the cause of his alcohol addiction, and it is probably close to the
truth of Scott's own dependency. "About the time I came into
money I found that with a few drinks I got expansive and somehow
had the ability to please people, and the idea turned my head. Then
I began to take a whole lot of drinks to keep going and have everybody think I was wonderful." But ever-increasing amounts of alcohol were now required for Scott to feel good, and only a few drinks
had the opposite effect. Early in the twenties, it had been different,
Scott remembered: "There was a kindliness about intoxication—
there was that indescribable gloss and glamour it gave, like the
memories of ephemeral and faded evenings." Now, "Two drinks
puts him in a manic state, absolutely manic," Zelda told Sara Mayfield, "he wants to fight everybody, including me. He's drinking
himself to death." Ring Lardner had been Fitzgerald's alcoholic in
Great Neck; now the tables had turned. "Am going on the water-
wagon from the first of February to the first of April," he wrote
Maxwell Perkins, copying Lardner's habit of dating, "but don't tell
Ernest because he has long convinced himself that I am an incurable alcoholic due to the fact that we almost always meet at parties.
I am his alcoholic just like Ring is mine and do not want to disillu-
sion him." If he did go on the wagon, it appears to have done no
good. He simply picked up where he had left off.

Scott continued accepting invitations to everyone's parties, occasionally dragging Zelda along. "Nice life," she told Sara Mayfield,
"sitting in a café all day and a *bal musette* all night. You have to drink
yourself blotto to keep from being bored to death. It's no fun here
anymore; if we go out at night Scott gets pie-eyed, and if we stay at
home we have a row." Robert Penn Warren observed their incessant arguing, over their rotten apartment or servants' unbearable
body odor—"frightful hissing quarrels, well-laced with obsceni-
ties." For the most part, however, they argued about Zelda's dance
obsession. Every evening, Zelda practiced before retiring early to
prepare for the next day, and Scott often went out alone to Closerie

des Lilas, where he would strike up a conversation with strangers and reminisce about happier days. He often spent days sitting in front of Deux Magots, just watching people walk by. Their friends, such as they were now, avoided them, and Scott's ledger for that year suggests why: "First trip to jail, and dive in Lido," then "second trip to jail."

When Scott accompanied Gerald Murphy on a visit to his son's school in Germany, Gerald became very concerned over Scott's drinking behavior. He told his daughter, Honoria, that "Scott had disappeared periodically from their compartment on the train, and each time he returned, he was in a condition decidedly more altered by alcohol. Finally, my father went to the washroom, and he found a dirty public cup next to the basin. Scott, who was carrying a flask of gin, was chasing the gin with water from that cup." He had a grab bag of excuses: to stimulate creativity, assuage self-doubt when he couldn't write, mollify his loneliness and bolster self-confidence. His absolute dependence on alcohol had become as overwhelming as his protagonist Anthony's in *The Beautiful and Damned*: "He hated to be sober. It made him conscious of the people around him, of that air of struggle, of greedy ambition, of hope more sordid than despair, of incessant passage up or down."

As alarming as Scott's dependency on drink was, Zelda's obsession with ballet was equally disturbing. When the Murphys stopped by Egorova's studio to attend one of Zelda's recitals, they were embarrassed by what they saw. "There was a grotesque intensity about her movements that made one nervous watching her. It was really terrible. One held ones breath until it was over. Thank God she couldn't see what she looked like." But Zelda was oblivious to this. "I was determined to find an impersonal escape," she explained, "a world in which I could express myself and walk without the help of somebody who was always far from me." Dance was everything to her now. The sense of purpose it gave her, and the emotional release generated by her lessons, were heightened by a growing infatuation with the teacher she idolized.

Because all their things were at Ellerslie, and just five months remained on their lease, they decided to return to the United States. On October 1, 1928, the Fitzgeralds boarded the S.S. *Carmania* bound for New York. They were accompanied by Scottie's French nanny and Phillipe, a former taxi driver and boxer, whom Fitzgerald had met at the rue de Vaugirard gym. He was hired as chauffeur, general handyman, and drinking companion. It was an unsettling voyage during which Zelda confided she was in love with her ballet teacher. Fitzgerald made light of the confession, but in his note-book commented: "I've seen that every time Zelda sees Egorova and me in contact, Egorova becomes gross to her. Apart, the opposite happens."

On October 7, 1928, the *Carmania* docked in New York harbor. Immediately, Fitzgerald ran into difficulty with U.S. Immigration because Phillipe had arrived without a passport. After an emergency call to John Biggs and days of negotiations, the problem was on its way to being resolved. In the meantime, they checked into a Manhattan hotel. When Phillipe's papers were finally in order, the group headed south to Ellerslie. But the question now arose of what to do when the lease expired. Zelda wanted to settle in "a house with a room to paint and write" with "Mondays that were different from Sundays," where Scottie could experience a normal childhood. Life at Ellerslie was as unreal as their superficial friend-ships with rich neighbors. She told her daughter, "I want you to have a lovely little Japanese room with pink cherry blossoms and a ducky little tea table and screen." But with no guarantee that he could earn an income sufficient to pay the mortgage, Scott was un-willing to make the commitment. They remained at Ellerslie.

Owning her own home had special significance for Zelda. Ironi-cally, her father's reasons for never wanting a mortgage were not dissimilar from Fitzgerald's. But she had married Scott believing life would be different from that in Montgomery. It was, but not in the way expected. Accepting that the purchase of a home was not possible, Zelda again redirected her efforts toward dance, resum-ing lessons in Philadelphia with almost a religious fervor. Her teacher was the thirty-six-year-old Alexandre Gavrilov, a Nijinsky protégé who was the lead dancer at the Ballet Moderne in New York City. Gavrilov had graduated from the Maryinsky School in 1911. He left the Imperial Ballet that same year to join Diaghilev's Ballets Russes, where he understudied Nijinsky and alternated with him in several roles. Zelda's intensity and agitated state excited him. One afternoon Gavrilov took Zelda to Reuben's for lunch, then back to the apartment he shared with his mistress at 5-20 Chestnut Street. It was an icy day and Zelda never forgot the strange tension she felt. "There was nothing in the commercial flat except the white spitz of his mistress and a beautiful collection of Léon Bakst. It was a cold afternoon. He asked me if I wanted him to kill me and said I would cry and left me there. I ran to my lesson through the cold streets." Gavrilov spoke French and Zelda understood it. Instead of implying murder, the words. "If I wanted him to kill me" might well refer to the French expression "the little death" meaning orgasm.

Zelda's focus on ballet, to the exclusion of everything else, masked the desperate unhappiness she felt being emotionally and physically estranged from Scott. Recalling that year, she wrote, "He [Scott] left me so much alone that I was very ashamed of wanting him once." Fitzgerald spent most of his time drinking with Phillipe, whom, Zelda recalled, "had an air of being always startled, perhaps in his uncertainty of his present role." The two men often wound up in barroom brawls and were frequently arrested. John Biggs, who had emerged as a successful and influential lawyer, regularly bailed them out. After his appointment to the federal court by Franklin Roosevelt, Biggs resented having to rescue Fitzgerald repeatedly from trouble. "I'm a Federal Court Judge," he later complained, "I know Presidents etc., but all people want to ask me is what my drunken roommate was like."

To worsen matters, there were ongoing problems with the Fitzgeralds' household staff. Scottie's governess had become infatuated with Phillipe and walked around the house weeping; their cook, Ella, constantly sang spirituals at the top of her voice from the kitchen, and their high-spirited maid was forever laughing uncontrollably. "I do not know what Scott was doing during that year," Zelda recalled of those discordant days at Ellerslie. "He went to New York. I didn't want to go. He worked a little, we lived in the cinders and the wind from the river and sometimes, rarely, we did things together." On November 17, Pauline and Ernest Hemingway came for an overnight stay after attending the Princeton-Yale game with the Fitzgeralds. They met Scott and Zelda on campus at Cottage, and after the game at Palmer Stadium (Princeton won 10-2) took the train down with them to Wilmington, where they were picked up by Phillipe in Fitzgerald's Buick. Nervous at dinner, Fitzgerald uncorked too many wine bottles, and tastelessly baited the black maid; "Marie, Tell Mr. Hemingway what a grand piece of pussy you are." (Ten years later, he would do the same thing to Sheilah Graham, declaring "what a great lay she was" to fellow passengers on a flight from Los Angeles to Chicago.) The evening's unpleasantness precipitated a hasty departure by the Hemingways the following day. Ernest later apologized for their retreat: "I am sorry I made, shall we say, a nuisance of myself about getting to the train on time—We were there far too early."

The Fitzgeralds breathed a sigh of relief when their two-year lease finally expired in March 1929. Glad at the time to be leaving Delaware, Zelda always nostalgically recalled their time there, albeit with sadness. She particularly regretted it had not been a happier time for Scottie. "There was the lone and lovely child knocking a croquet ball through the arches of summer under the horse-chestnut trees and singing alone in her bed at night," Zelda wrote in an autobiographical sketch. "She was a beautiful child who loved her mother. At first there had been Nanny, but Nanny and I quarreled and we sent her back to France, and the baby had only its mother after that, and a series of people who straightened its shoes. I worried. The child was unhappy and thought of little besides how rich people were and little touching, childish things. The money obsession was because of the big house and going to play with the Wanamakers and the Dupont children. The house was too immense for a child and too dignified."

Freed from their lease on Ellerslie, the Fitzgeralds immediately made preparations to return to Europe—this time to Italy. As they said their farewells, John Biggs was struck by Zelda's agitation and nervous distraction. Her condition seemed serious and a chilling reminder of the night she had questioned, "John, aren't you sorry you weren't killed in the war?" He knew she didn't like him, but could never figure out what she meant by that remark. He finally attributed it to jealousy over his loyalty to Fitzgerald. "Zelda never got along with anybody—male or female—who liked Fitzgerald," Biggs postulated. "She was wildly jealous of both men and women who liked Scotty. I don't think she liked me."

Their vessel, the *Conte Biancamano*, docked in Genova late that March of 1929. Immediately, the Fitzgeralds headed for the French Riviera, where they remained through April. At the time, Nice was suffering a "mistral" wind that Zelda described as "brittly cold." The weather kept them indoors much of the time. Scott drank and played baccarat and chemin de fer at the Palais de la Mediterranee

Casino, while Zelda attended ballet performances she considered mediocre in the Casino on the Jeteé, and took lessons with a Russian ballet coach named Nevalskaya. She was a skilled instructor but her studio was damp and unaccommodating. They were happy to be back in France, and the tension between them eased, as they sipped aperitifs at the Blue Café in front of the Jeteé, walked along the promenade observing the parade of people, or watched the frog swallowers on the boardwalk. Occasionally, they attended comedies at the Casino, making fun of the amateurish performers, or drove out to Villefranche for salade niçoise or a bouillabaisse seasoned with saffron. Zelda enjoyed the dish enough to ask for the recipe, and made some notes to herself about it. "A bouillabaisse, to be served under perfect conditions according to the regular custom of Marseilles, demands at least seven or eight convivial people. Here is the reason; as one uses in preparing it, a great variety of so-called rock-fish, it is a good thing to make it in large quantities in order to put in as many kinds as possible. Observe above all that the cooking is done quickly, that is one of the essential points, this way the oil is perfectly blended with the bouillon, otherwise it separates and floats on the top, which is hardly appetizing."

By May, they were eager to return to Paris, where Zelda enthusiastically renewed dance lessons with Egorova. She took group sessions each morning and individual ones in the afternoon. To defray a small portion of the high cost of her lessons, she wrote several stories, hoping to sell them. "I hated taking his money for my lessons; I wanted my dancing to belong to me, so I wrote to pay for them." Because Egorova's studio on rue Caumartin was often hot and humid, Zelda brought fresh lemonade for her teacher. She also brought her a bouquet of flowers daily: poppies, narcissus, white lilacs, pink tulips, lemon carnations, red roses, and gardenias—purchased from the stalls near the Madeleine. Still infatuated with her teacher, Zelda wrote that "she [Egorova] seemed to me like a gardenia, so I gave her gardenias and found some Oriental gardenia perfume for her. She was reticent and I don't know what she thought."

Egorova took Zelda's ambitions seriously and worked hard with her. "She was very good and kind and always gave me lessons; the famous dancers clamored for her hours." Lessons became her obsession. She worried about the weather and how it might aggravate her asthma and force her to miss a class. The first student to arrive,

she was the last to leave. Any disapproval by Egorova made her terribly anxious. Once, when she was asked to practice with a less capable student, she took it as a sign of Egorova's displeasure and
became inconsolable. She tried to help Egorova in any way possible, persuading Scott to find Egorova's son a job. Accustomed in
Russia to the trappings of nobility, Egorova now lived modestly
in Paris. So Zelda frequently invited Egorova and her husband
to dinner at expensive restaurants like George V. Fitzgerald once
bitterly complained that Zelda had spoiled a story he was working on by insisting they entertain the couple that particular night.
These social occasions sometimes went smoothly, but not always.
Once, when the four dined at Egorova's studio, Scott humiliated
Zelda by getting drunk and passing out. The incident unsettled her
for days.

With June upon them and Paris steaming hot, they headed for
Cannes, where they rented the Villa Fleur des Bois for the summer.
Eight-year-old Scottie took swimming and gymnastics lessons on
the beach each morning, while Zelda resumed her daily ballet practice and lessons in Nice. She danced in several recitals and also created her own ballet, titled "Evolution," for which she made the
scenery and costumes.

Then came Zelda's big opportunity. On Egorova's recommendation, Julia Sedova, director of the San Carlo Opera Ballet Company
in Naples, invited Zelda to join her Italian troupe. As a debut piece,
Sedova offered Zelda the solo in *Aïda*, emphasizing how professionally important the role could be. She promised that if Zelda remained the entire season, she would receive other important roles
and an adequate monthly salary. When Zelda did not immediately
respond, a second offer, handwritten in French, was sent, arriving
on September 29, 1929. It encouraged Zelda to accept, pointing
out that food and lodging in Naples were very inexpensive. *"Notre
théâtre est magnifique et il vous serait très utile de danser sur la scène.
La vie de Naples n'est past très chere et on peut avoir le pension complet a
35 lires par personne par jour."*

Both Sedova and Egorova had trained with the Maryinsky Ballet
Theatre in St. Petersburg. In 1909, Sedova had been premiere dancer
with the Imperial Ballet, performing with Pavlova in "Chopiniana."
At that time she was married to Boris Schidlovsky, the ballet critic
for a small St. Petersburg newspaper. Two years later, while dancing

in a "Saison Russe" with an Italian company at the Sarah Bernhardt Theatre in Paris, Sedova became embroiled in controversy. Several French theatrical unions threatened a strike to protest the engagement of some Italian musicians. Perhaps because of her affection for the Italian troupe, Sedova afterward went to Naples to assume the directorship of the San Carlo Opera Ballet Company.

After Zelda's arduous struggle to acquire the skill that would warrant such an offer, she agonized over whether to accept. If she went to Naples, it was going to be alone. Fitzgerald hated Italians and would never follow. Her sister Rosalind remembered Scott's disapproval and Zelda's own ambivalence. "I have always felt that this frantic effort on Zelda's part, towards a professional career in the thing she did best, was motivated by the uncertainty of their situation at this time, perhaps also by unhappiness, which she refused to admit, but which nevertheless I thought I saw beneath an always brave front, and by her desire to put herself on her own. She told me that she received an offer from one of the Italian Opera companies as a premiere ballerina, but that Scott would not allow her to accept it."

Other factors weighed in Zelda's decision. She didn't care for Italians herself and considered the San Carlo Opera a step down from ballet companies in London and Paris. She was also uncomfortable with the idea of living alone in Naples, and leaving Scottie in Fitzgerald's care. Accepting the offer would mean relinquishing the comforts she had come to expect and reversing a pattern of dependent behavior followed since childhood. She was torn with doubt—was she self-sufficient enough to live on a meager salary and trained well enough to succeed? Ultimately, Zelda's decision to reject Sedova's offer was based on her fear of going it alone. But what she could not do in life, her heroine accomplished in fiction. In *Save Me the Waltz*, Alabama ignores her husband's disapproval, accepts the Naples offer, and becomes a huge success. Her ballet roles reap rave reviews from the Italian critics: "She had promise and should be given a bigger role, the papers said. Italians like blondes; they said Alabama was as ethereal as a Fra Angelico angel because she was thinner than the others."

Hopeful of other offers, Zelda realized that by rejecting a full season of performances, she had jeopardized future prospects. Her disappointment turned to deep remorse when she heard that Sergei

Diaghilev had died in Venice. Her dreams of someday dancing with the Ballets Russes were over. "Diaghilev died." Zelda wrote. "The stuff of the great movement of the Ballets Russes lay rotting in a French law court . . . some of his dancers performed around the swimming pool of the Lido to please the drunk Americans in summer, some of them worked in music-hall ballets; the English went back to England. What's the use?"

Brooding silently, Zelda distanced herself from almost everyone. Fitzgerald paid for a month's pass to the Casino in Juan-les-Pins, but Zelda had no interest in going. "We went [to] sophisticated places with charming people but I was grubby and didn't care." Suddenly, things looked very odd to her. Tallulah Bankhead saw her that summer and recalled her strange behavior. "I was there in the south of France when Zelda, poor darling, went off her head. She had gone into a flower shop and suddenly for her all the flowers had faces." In unguarded moments her odd nervousness was readily apparent. Her speech patterns altered and there was a mixture of wild delight and terror in her laugh. One evening at a cinema near Antibes, as the Fitzgeralds and Murphys watched a documentary about underwater life, Zelda became hysterical. "There were all sorts and varieties of strange fish swimming by the camera," recalled Murphy. ". . . Quite nonchalantly an octopus, using his tentacles to propel himself moved diagonally across the screen [and] Zelda, who had been sitting on my right, shrieked and threw herself all the way across my lap on to my left shoulder and burying her head against my neck and chest, screamed, 'What is it? What is it?' Now, we had all seen it and it moved very slowly—it was perfectly obvious that it was an octopus—but it nevertheless frightened her to death." Sara Murphy warned Fitzgerald not to ignore the situation: "You don't even know what Zelda and Scottie are like—in spite of your love for them. It seemed to us the other night, [Gerald too] that all you thought and felt about them was in terms of yourself. . . . I feel obliged in honesty of a friend to write you that the ability to know what another person feels in a given situation will make—or ruin lives."

Scott, however, remained oblivious to Zelda's worsening condition throughout that summer. In October of 1929 they began their return trip to Paris by car through Aix, Arles, Pont du Gard, Vichy, and the château country. They argued much of the way. Scottie curled up with a book in the back and ignored them. As Scott wove their car through the mountainous Grande Corniche, Zelda suddenly seized the wheel, shouted "God's will," and tried to steer the automobile over a cliff. Grabbing the wheel from her hands, Fitzgerald brought the car to a stop at the lip of the drop-off. All three sat stone still, in terrified shock; Zelda could not explain why she had done it.

A spontaneous explosion of Zelda's suppressed feelings, the episode commenced a dark period culminating in her total mental collapse. A decade earlier she had told Scott about a wild streak inside her that made her do crazy things. He had fused that unpredictability into Eleanor's character in *This Side of Paradise*, and one of his scenes bore an uncanny similarity to the Grande Corniche incident. "Eleanor drew her horse up sharply and he reined in beside her. 'Will I?' she said in a queer voice that scared him. 'Will I? *Watch! I'm going over the cliff!*' And before he could intervene she had turned and was riding breakneck for the end of the plateau. He wheeled and started after her, his body like ice, his nerves in a vast clangor. There was no chance of stopping her. The moon was under a cloud and her horse would step blindly over. Then some ten feet from the edge of the cliff she gave a sudden shriek and flung herself sideways—plunged from her horse, and, rolling over twice, landed in a pile of brush five feet from the edge. The horse went over with a frantic whinny. '. . . I've got a crazy streak,' she faltered. 'Twice before I've done things like that. When I was eleven mother went—went mad—stark raving crazy.' " Incredibly, the same thing was about to happen to Zelda.

Back in Paris, they resettled on rue Pergolese in yet another musty apartment. Within days, Zelda had returned to Egorova's studio with an intensity bordering on mania. Despite all her indecision, the Naples offer had reinforced her conviction that she was a professional. Starving to stay thin, she drank to keep up her energy. She installed a practice barre and mirrors in the living room of their flat, and wore theatrical greasepaint to class. "I worked constantly and was terribly superstitious and moody about my work, full of presentiments. . . . I lived in a quiet, ghostly, hypersensitized world of my own." Whatever free time she allowed herself was spent with Scottie; any communication with Scott was perfunctory. He continued to consider her ballet ambitions a neurotic obsession, and grew more bitter and obstructive. "I found myself saying hateful things to her," he recalled. "I couldn't stop. I was at war with myself. We quarreled, poked in the ashes of the past, and flung words that raised a wall of indifference between us. We became hostile strangers and went our separate ways while living a hell under the same roof."

Fitzgerald resented her commitment to the dance, forgetting he had been similarly obsessed with writing, and complained that "she no longer read or thought or knew anything or liked anyone except dancers and their cheap satellites ... she was becoming more and more an egotist and a bore." He laughingly wrote Harold Ober about some visitors to Egorova's studio, who Zelda thought were ballet scouts, but were really Folies-Bergère agents. Later, he regretted making the comment, admitting his cruelty had driven them farther apart, and caused Zelda to take refuge in her teacher. "It was probably my fault. I shouldn't have taunted her. I can be a bastard when it comes to taunting and accusing people." In another, Fitzgerald's statement might be viewed as contrition, but it may have been a form of self-aggrandizement. Was he seeing things in such a way as they centered on him?

Eating practically nothing, Zelda had grown so thin, she seemed to be wasting away. Fitzgerald finally perceived the seriousness of the situation. Thinking a vacation might help, he followed up on an idea the Murphys had suggested years earlier. In 1925, Gerald had written, "We might all four take that Compagnie General trip to Tunisia. Just three weeks. Very cheap. High-powered cars with Arab chauffeurs meet you at the boat, and you course through the country staying as long as you want in each town. More like being a guest than a tourist, they say. Wonderful hotels even in the desert. Beaumont told us about it." Instead of Tunisia, however, Fitzgerald signed on for a Compagnie Transatlantique tour of Algeria. Their ship sailed from Port-Vendres on February 7, 1930, with scheduled stops in Biskra, Constantine, and Algiers. It was a poor decision, given Zelda had been ill with fever for two weeks and in no condition to travel. She had missed several ballet lessons, and could not put Egorova from her mind. No sooner had they arrived in Algiers than she begged to return. When Scott forbade it, Zelda set about buying her teacher presents—a bandanna filled with perfumes, green silk for a dress, and amber chips from Central Africa. She spent hours writing Egorova letters and then scouted for places to mail them. "Altogether it was an unsuccessful attempt at relaxing," Zelda remembered. "In Algiers I thought of my teacher always and wrote many letters from Biskra and Bou Saad, and was miserable in the gorge of Constantine and unhappy at Tungaad and nervous in the big, tearing bus."

She was on the brink of collapse. Scrapbook photographs taken of their trip show the extent of her distress. Throughout the journey she objected to having her picture taken, but in the desert oasis of Biskra, visiting the studio of sculptor Claire Sheridan, Scott caught her perched awkwardly on a camel. He photographed her again at the Gorge of Constantine appearing muted and depressed. "It was a trying winter," she later remembered, "and to forget the bad times we went to Algiers. The Hotel du l'Oasis was laced together by Moorish grills; and the bar was an outpost of civilization with people accentuating their eccentricities. Beggars in white sheets were propped against the walls, and the dash of colonial uniforms gave the cafes a desperate swashbuckling air." As the journey continued, the world became increasingly bizarre to Zelda, who visualized "the Arabs fermenting in the vastness; the curious quality of their eyes and the smell of ants; a detachment as if I was on the other side of a black gauze—a fearless small feeling. . . . The world crumbled to pieces in Biskra; the streets crept through the town like streams of hot white lava. Arabs sold nougat and cakes of poisonous pink under the flare of open gas jets. . . . In the steep cobbled alleys we flinched at the brightness of mutton carcasses swung from butchers' booths." She could not wait to leave, later admitting that the experience was tainted by her "impatience to get back, my jealousy of Scott's ability to amuse himself, and an implacable sense of desperation that haunted me constantly like a person crossing a dangerous stream, not daring to look further ahead than the next stone." She chewed the inside of her lip so badly that she had to extend it to avoid pain. On the return voyage to France, the sea was so turbulent that she was convinced the ship would sink. Too nauseated to move from bed, she stayed in her cabin for the entire trip.

Zelda felt she had barely escaped disaster. Her only comfort was to be near Egorova. "I wanted to dance so well," she wrote, "that she would be proud of me and have another instrument for the symbols of beauty that passed in her head that I understood, though apparently could not execute. I wanted to be first in the studio, so that it would be me that she could count on to understand what she gave out in words, and perhaps it is depraved, but I wanted to be near her because she was cool and white and beautiful." Describing her behavior at this time—from August 1928 to February 1930—Fitzgerald later told Zelda's doctors that her "first indications of lesbianism [were] directed towards Egorova . . . and her utterly uncharacteristic tendencies toward lesbianism [manifested] usually with liquor."

As uncharacteristic as lesbianism had been earlier in her life, Zelda now turned in that direction and befriended several members of Paris's lesbian community. These women brought a semblance of stability to her life. She had met some of them four years earlier on Capri; others were new acquaintances. "In Paris again, I saw a great deal of Nemtchinova after classes, and my friend at the Opera. I worked constantly, and was terribly superstitious and moody about my work, full of presentiments about the sun and the rain and the wind. I lived in a quiet, ghostly, hypersensitized world of my own. . . . I had grown to resent the people we knew who did not work, no matter how attractive they were, and to feel contemptuous of them." Her emphasis on work, and revulsion for people who did not, is pivotal. Until this point, she seems to have believed Scott's taunts that she was not a professional. Because of her efforts to become a skilled dancer, and feeling estranged from Fitzgerald, she now no longer cared what he thought.

Zelda was initially introduced to Paris's lesbian subculture by Esther Murphy, who took the Fitzgeralds to Romaine Brooks's studio at 74 rue Raynouard on the Right Bank in the affluent sixteenth arrondissement. Described by Zelda as "a glass-enclosed square of heaven swung high above Paris," its walls were lined with paintings of women dressed as men, and men attired in women's clothes: Jean Cocteau, Reynaldo Hahn, and Robert de Montesquieu, Lily de Clermont-Tonnerre, Renée Vivien, and Lady Una Troubridge. In 1925, Brooks had designed the building's sparsely decorated, top-floor apartment to suit her own needs. Serving as living quarters, studio, and salon, it contained ten rooms with ceilings rising one and a half stories—a bright open space looking down on the rooftops of Paris. Brooks's lover Natalie Barney, who had left the Princesse de Polignac to begin a long-term relationship with Romaine, was often there. Zelda had met Brooks while taking art lessons on Capri, when Romaine was still the lover of Renatta Borgatti, and had encountered the Princesse de Polignac, sister of sewing machine magnate Paris Singer, at one of the Murphys' parties in Antibes.

She met other lesbians at the Swedish restaurant Stryx, and at sapphic bars like the Monocle on boulevard Edgar-Quinet, where women dressed in tuxedos and slicked back their bobbed hair. Another popular lesbian club was the Bal de la Montagne Saint-Genevieve, which had booths lining the walls and a space in the middle for dancing. It was opposite the Ecole Polytechnique on a hill behind the Pantheon. Lesbian bars could often turn dangerous; Bernice Abbott and Gwen Le Gallienne were arrested during a police raid on one of them. Zelda liked the excitement of these places, but Fitzgerald was apprehensive when she went to these clubs alone. In typical Hemingway style, Ernest wrote of Scott's distress. "At this time Zelda could drink more than Scott could and Scott was afraid for her to pass out in the company they kept that spring and the places they went to. Scott did not like the places nor the people and he had to drink more than he could drink and be in any control of himself, to stand the people and the places."

In 1929, Zelda established a close relationship with Dolly Wilde and Emily Vanderbilt, both of whom were bisexual. "In all that horror, Dolly Wilde was the only one who really made sense," she told Scott, and Emily Vanderbilt, whom they had accompanied to Natalie Barney's salon, "suddenly seemed to represent order and independence." Zelda's love of women, untinged by guilt or remorse, brought her a measure of emotional and sexual fulfillment. It seems no accident that, as Zelda's madness became more manifest, she not only felt more equal to Fitzgerald but freer to express her sexuality as she wished. Four years later, with her madness at its peak, she would attempt to explain exactly how she felt. In a long and confusing letter to Scott, written from the mental hospital where she was being treated, she told him: "Since Eden man has been endowed with a double sexual impulse. Complete sexual fulfillment between man and wife is homosexuality. . . . Man's promise to God is to breed, and to, in love and warmth, in devotion and in mutual support and in the happiness of his circumstance, to keep the race alive. God's promise to man is emotional fulfillment, surcease for the impersonal appreciation of the beauty of God which haunts us. That is sucking the genital organs of your mate, and its requitement is the fulfillment of man's desire to cherish and to serve, and of man's necessity for emotional surrender. God wants that we should accept this added sexual blessing with reverence and with gratitude. . . . Acknowledging the beauty of homosexuality as our marital relationship, as God wills, we may acknowledge in honor and without the necessity to conceal or repress the second of our sexual functions. And homosexuality between members of the same sex, which is aberrantory and the justification for which is the emotional integrity of the impulse, may disappear. Thus there will no longer be any necessity for the use of catatonic and homosexual controls which have sold too many of us into bondage—."

Zelda now considered lesbian love a natural act, and an extension of masculine-feminine sexuality. Her attitude was similar to Gertrude Stein's, who had told Hemingway: "Women do nothing that they are disgusted by, and nothing that is repulsive, and afterwards they are happy and can lead healthy lives together." Neither Ernest nor Scott was convinced. And Fitzgerald noted in his ledger, angrily, that Dolly Wilde had made a pass at Zelda when she was drunk during a party.

Morley Callaghan, who had continued seeing the Fitzgeralds, observed how Zelda became agitated over the simplest things. "I became aware that Scott kept his eye on her. He let her talk on, saying little himself, just listening; then, abruptly to our surprise he told her that she was tired. When she indicated she was not Scott's tone grew peremptory as he took her by the wrist and put her in a taxi. 'You go home now and go to bed.' Zelda's face was half-hidden yet her whole manner changed; it was as if she knew he had command over her; she agreed meekly."

As Easter, 1930, approached, Zelda felt danger at every turn. She wanted to buy Scottie a holiday present, but was afraid to shop alone, and needed the housekeeper to accompany her. She said things that made no sense, smiled inappropriately, and expelled bursts of nervous laughter. Suddenly, she would become dazed, and while apparently understanding what people said to her, often could not make out what they meant. When Scott told her that he had dismissed their housekeeper Lucienne, Zelda knew something was wrong, but could not understand what. In the open market, she heard flowers talking. Disturbing dreams woke her at night, leaving her confused and incoherent the next morning. For days, she went without sleeping or eating. She heard threatening voices in her head—their tone so menacing she took refuge in barbiturates. She believed there was a conspiracy to keep her from being a great dancer. So sure was she that people were talking against her, that when John Peale Bishop came for lunch, she tried to catch him at it. Once, when Bishop came for dinner and they all went to a fairgrounds afterward, Zelda hallucinated and became hysterical. Again, morphine was required to calm her. To quiet the voices in her head, she jumped higher at dance class, but the next morning she would have terrible headaches and feel sick all day. She danced so hard at lessons that by nightfall she had no energy left. "For six months now she has been so exhausted Saturday night," Fitzgerald wrote, "that she sleeps all through Sunday till dinner time and then all night." She became sensitive to sunlight, and began experiencing strange visual hallucinations—first everything would be brightly colored, and then have no color at all. Solid objects appeared vaporous. These spells generally were preceded by a "buzzy" feeling so intense that she could predict when they would occur. "In Paris, before I realized I was sick, there was a new significance to everything: stations and streets and facades of buildings—colors were infinite, part of the air, and not restricted by the lines that encompassed them, and lines were free of the masses they held. There was music that beat behind my forehead, and other music that fell into my stomach from a high parabola and there was some of Schumann that was still and tender, and the sadness of Chopin mazurkas. Some of them sounded as if he thought that he couldn't compose them—and there was the madness of turning, turning, turning." At Egorova's studio, Zelda resisted looking through the windows because people outside began to look like ants in a bottle.

Frightened, Zelda asked Scott to explain what was happening. He had no answer. Later, she would accuse him of retreating from her and hiding himself in a locked bathroom. "When you saw in Paris that I was sick, sinking—when you knew that I went for days without eating, incapable of supporting contact with even the servants—you sat in the bathroom and sang . . . if you had explained to me what was happening the night we had dinner with John Bishop and went to the fair afterwards which left me in hysterics. The obligation is, after all, with the people who understand, and the blind, of necessity, must be led." That she thought Scott understood indicates her delusion that he could remedy what was now an impossible situation.

As it became more difficult for her to talk with people, or function in any normal way, Rosalind and Newman Smith became very concerned. Since 1922 they had lived in Brussels, where Newman worked for Guaranty Trust. They had kept in close touch, but there was little they could do to avert the oncoming crisis. "We saw him and Zelda fairly often at this period, through our visits to Paris, and felt uneasy about the whole worsening situation."

Finally, at the Fitzgeralds' apartment in April, during a luncheon with Xandra and Oscar Kalman, Zelda had her breakdown. Midway through the meal, she suddenly became anxious over being late for her ballet lesson, and called a cab to take her to Egorova's studio. Oscar sensed that something was wrong and accompanied her. When the cab got caught in traffic, Zelda jumped out and started running between the cars in the direction of the studio. Kalman telephoned Scott and described Zelda's strange behavior, stressing that she was in no condition to find her way home. Fitzgerald promptly retrieved her. To explain the situation to Egorova, Zelda persuaded her teacher to come to their apartment. When she arrived, however, Zelda became so overwrought that she threw herself at her teacher's feet; Egorova made a hasty retreat.

Clearly, Zelda needed to be hospitalized. Egorova recommended La Sanitarium de la Malmaison as the most reputable psychiatric facility near Paris. It was a private hospital just ten kilometers from the city in a park surrounded by iron gates. Zelda was admitted in a highly agitated, intoxicated state on April 23, 1930. Pacing the room, she flirted with doctors. She told them she was in love with her dance teacher, and had previously loved a friend in the Paris Opera. Insisting her husband was a homosexual, she told them he was in love with a man named Hemingway. Worried that the medical staff might believe her, Fitzgerald argued that Zelda's hallucinations had been precipitated by a dissolute life and a family history of mental instability. He explained there were nervous disorders on both sides of her family, and proceeded to recite a disturbing inventory: her maternal grandmother had committed suicide, so had her mother's sister; there were several unbalanced uncles, her sister Marjorie had spent two years recovering from a nervous breakdown, and her father had once been so depressed that he had had to leave the judicial bench for nine months. Malmaison's diagnosis was "anxiety." The medical report, written by attending physician Professor Claude, theorized that "it is a question of a *petite anxieuse* worn out by her work in a milieu of professional dancers. Violent reactions, several suicidal attempts never pushed to the limit." The evaluation and her confinement were of little help, so Zelda discharged herself on May 2, telling Scott, "I went of my own free will to the clinic in Paris to cure myself. You also know that I left [with the consent of Professor Claude], knowing that I was not entirely well because I could see no use in jumping out of the frying pan into the fire, which is what was about to happen, or so I thought."

After her brief stay at Malmaison, Zelda left the hospital and returned to Paris alone. She found their apartment empty. Fitzgerald had moved into the Murphys' untenanted quarters on rue Pergolese, and Zelda arrived there to find the flat a disordered mess and filled with left-over party guests. There is no indication where Scottie was. Hung over from the night before, Scott was surprised to see her. After several days of rest, she tried resuming dance lessons, but her condition was compounded by asthma and psychosomatic eczema. Within a week she experienced hallucinations and attempted suicide by taking an overdose of barbiturates.

On May 22, following the recommendation of friends, Fitzgerald drove Zelda to Valmont Clinic in nearby Glion, Switzerland. Complaining of noises in her ears, dizziness, and vibrations from the people around her, she was placed under medical observation. Her doctors ultimately uncovered no neurological or organic disorders. During her confinement, one of Valmont's nurses reported having to repulse Zelda's "overly affectionate" behavior. She then became infatuated with a second nurse. In a semicoherent letter to Fitzgerald she tried to explain her behavior: "I also went, practically voluntarily, but under enormous pressure to Valmont with the sole idea of getting back enough strength and health to continue my work in America as you had promised me. There, my head began to go wrong and the pristine nurse whom you accused me of attacking played almost constantly on the thing that I assumed I was there to get over. Finally my constant references to Feol and plantanes and other pronounced and vulgar symbolism, I at least began to believe that there was but one cure for me; the one I had refused three times in Paris." The remainder of the letter trailed off incoherently, but suggests she made advances toward other female patients and nurses. Fitzgerald described Zelda's condition at Valmont as one of "violent psychosis, wild homosexuality towards nurses, suicide threats, attempts to escape and delusions." The official report from Valmont's physicians summarized Zelda's psychological history and its relevance to her collapse.

PATIENT: ZELDA SAYRE FITZGERALD

Two sisters have nervous breakdowns, a third suffers from a nervous affliction of the neck.

At twenty-four [actually, twenty-six] in Europe has a near peritonitis caused by inflammation of the right ovary and is practically disabled for a year. The matter is cleared up by an operation for appendix. (Dr. Gross and Dr. Martell) Dr. Martell finds appendix in bad shape but ovary fundamentally healthy. Morphine taken for two weeks during peritonitis attack.

Becomes depressed in Hollywood by the fact that younger girls than herself have attained a position of their own and a relative importance.

At twenty-seven takes up an old ambition, ballet dancing—her first really serious effort. Three hours a day, six days a week. Stops drinking.

Till the time of taking up ballet work, she has been a heavy but intermittent drinker and inclined to hysteria when drunk. Violent hysteria—occasionally even suicidal, occurred perhaps four to seven times a year, when she could only be calmed by a minimum dose of morphine. Capacity to hold liquor diminishing.

While dancing, drinks half a pint of wine at meals and either an aperitif or a nightcap.

—during times of enforced idleness on shipboard, it becomes more and more obvious that all capacity to use liquor has departed. Hysteria almost sure after two days of what would usually be considered the most moderate drink. Never in danger of dipsomania because after two days she collapses. Understands this herself and avoids alcohol except when circumstances force it on her.

Previously a heavy smoker, but has reduced consumption to a minimum. Drinks 4–5 cups of coffee a day.

Last Autumn made enormous progress. Two substantial offers to appear as ballet dancer, La Scala in Naples and as premiere dancer at Folies-Bergères.

Writing only with a fixed obsession to pay, quite unnecessarily, for her dancing lessons herself and make her own career.

Writing has never been a pleasure because one eye is practically blind and the other strained and she pays for it in agonizing headaches. Once a great reader, has given up reading.

Sequence of symptoms: no appetite, depression, quarrelsome, rude to old friends in curious ways, quarrels with Egorova and quits school, then on Egorova's urgent request returns to school, drinks heavily and collapses, develops a curious horror of people— this produces a violent timidity in her, a horror and shrinking away from people, becomes silent with friends, pale and shaken in stores, becomes abnormally quiet with sudden outbursts of despair, hums to herself all the time, wants to be alone, music her only pleasure, resents African trip husband forces on her, hysteria lasting 6 days, hears voices, imagines people are criticizing her and makes scenes about it, unable to face shopkeepers, servants etc., seems to live in some horrible, subconscious dream, more real to her than the real world, sleeps a good deal, honestly wants to die, hysteria breaks out without warning, can't let Scott out of her sight, complete lack of control—picking at fingers."

END OF REPORT

Since Valmont was known primarily for treating gastrointestinal problems, not nervous disorders, Fitzgerald retained the specialist Dr. Oscar Forel to aid in diagnosing Zelda's condition. Forel quickly ran into difficulty and consulted with Swiss psychiatrist Eugen Bleuler. Bleuler was director of a Zurich hospital and professor of psychiatry at the University of Zurich. In 1911 he had introduced the term *schizophrenia* as a substitute for "dementia praecox," and was a leading authority on psychoses. Interested in schizophrenics' regressive behavior, he theorized that the discrepancy between high aspiration and moderate achievement precipitated delusions, but remained uncertain as to whether mental disorders were organic or psychogenic. Bleuler's consultation fee was five hundred dollars, which Zelda thought an exorbitant waste of money. He suspected she had acute schizophrenia and recommended confinement in Dr. Forel's newly opened, private sanitarium in Switzerland at Les Rives de Prangins near Nyon on Lake Geneva. Both Forel and Bleuler identified three reoccurring states in Zelda's condition: a depressed but calm attitude during which there was hope for recovery; wild hysteria during which others were blamed for everything; and a state of lesser hysteria during which her difficulties seemed insoluble and she wanted to die.

Zelda initially agreed to become Forel's patient, but after quarreling violently with Scott in Lausanne, and calling Bleuler "a great imbecile," she changed her mind and refused to go. Only after Newman Smith arrived from Brussels and had a long talk with her did she agree to enter the sanitarium. The three of them left Valmont on June 4, 1930, and headed for Prangins. The building had once been the château of Joseph Bonaparte, and stood on a one-hundred-acre park between Geneva and Lausanne.

Zelda arrived disheartened and exhausted. Her Herculean effort to become her own person, to identify and do valuable work, love whom and how she pleased, and escape from being F. Scott Fitzgerald's wife and model for his heroines had ended in madness. "Our ride to Switzerland was very sad," she wrote. "It seemed to me that we did not have each other or anything else, and it half killed me to give up all the work I had done. I was completely insane and made a decision: to abandon the ballet and live quietly with my husband. I had wanted to destroy the picture of Egorova I had lived with for four years, and give away my tous-tous and the suitcase full of shoes and free my mind from the things." However, once she succumbed to the madness—which most probably had always been in her genes, fully potentiated by the terrible strain she put on herself—there was no turning back.

Prangins had been open for less than a year, but already it was considered the best psychiatric clinic in Europe. James Joyce's daughter Lucia, who shared Zelda's obsession with ballet and studied under both Egorova and Isadora Duncan's brother Raymond, also became a patient there under Forel's care. At a thousand dollars a month, it was extraordinarily expensive. During 1930–31, Zelda's treatment there cost 70,561 Swiss francs, the equivalent of $13,000. The place looked more like a resort than a hospital, offering, in addition to occupational therapy and the newest medical treatments, golf, riding, skiing, tennis, a bathing beach, and billiard and music rooms.

In spite of all these amenities, the place quickly proved unbearable for Zelda. Isolating herself from doctors and other patients because they frightened her and seemed alien, she feared anyone who offered help and refused to speak about herself. During the first month, she had to be forcibly restrained after becoming violent and attempting escape. Control methods included two-point restraints—wrists tied to the bed—and four-point restraints—both wrists and ankles bound. Whenever she hallucinated she was given tranquilizing shots of chloral hydrate and placed in solitary confinement at E'glantine, the building at Prangins for patients who might do harm to themselves. Her condition worsened. "Now I see odd things" she wrote Scott, "peoples' arms too long, or their faces as if they were stuffed, and they look tiny and far away, or suddenly out of proportion. . . . I seem awfully queer to myself, but I know I used to have integrity even if it's gone now. You've got to come to me and tell me how I was."

Fitzgerald made arrangements for a move to Switzerland. He entrusted full-time care of Scottie to an Alsatian governess in Paris, where both lived at 21 rue Marionniers. Scottie attended private school there, and the most serious thing she had to think about was passing her courses. "My first school was the Cours Dieterlen in Paris," she recalled in her memoir, "where I went for the equivalent of third and fourth grade. . . . You went two days a week and the rest of the time you did your lessons with your 'institutrice,' in my case a Mlle. Serze to whom I was devoted. . . . Education for privileged French girls at that time was no joke. . . . It consisted mainly of memorizing whole scenes from plays by Corneille or Racine or else the names of not only the French kings but their wives and principal ministers." Scottie generally saw her father four or five days a month, occasionally visited Rosalind in Brussels, and took weekend trips to Mlle. Serze's family home. She was told nothing about her mother's condition: "I knew she was ill because she was in a hospital, but I didn't know why." Fitzgerald commuted between Paris and Nyon and stayed in nearby Lausanne or Geneva. In his story "One Trip Abroad," more truth than fiction, he described this difficult period as a routine of "daily visits of their two doctors, the arrival of the mail and newspapers from Paris, the little walk into the hillside village or occasionally the descent by funicular to the pale resort on the lake, with its Kursaal, its grass beach, its tennis clubs and sight-seeing buses." Scott wanted to renew sexual relations with Zelda, but Forel insisted they wait until a specific course of treatment could be established.

Writing Scott on June 16, 1930, from Brussels, Rosalind interrogated Fitzgerald to determine precisely when Zelda's problems had started. "You say you place the beginning of the change in her at about ten months before our visit to Ellerslie. That would be just about three years ago. . . . You think the change began at

Hollywood. Did anything happen out there to particularly disturb her? . . . were there any unhappy incidents? I seem to remember also having heard something about Zelda throwing from the window of the train, en route to Hollywood, a wristwatch that you had given her as her Christmas present. Is that true, and if so, why did she do it, and wouldn't it signify the trouble had already begun?" Rosalind places the wristwatch incident out of sequence, but recognized something had altered in Zelda after her return from California, and blamed Fitzgerald for whatever that was. Like John Biggs, she had also noticed Zelda's strained behavior at Ellerslie. "What I saw in her then was a great irritation which had not been part of her normal character . . . a lack of patience with, and less affection for Scottie than she had previously displayed, a general resentment towards all the circumstances of her then existence, and a decided morbid tendency that was not entirely subjective. Her nature and her appearance had entirely changed, even then, and she already needed serious medical attention."

Rosalind held Scott responsible for Zelda's condition. "I would almost rather she die now," she told him, "than escape only to go back to the mad world you and she have created for yourself." She insisted that Fitzgerald was in no condition to oversee Scottie's needs, and that it would be better for the child to live with Newman and herself. "It was at this point," Scottie wrote, "that [Rosalind's] smoldering quarrel with my father broke out into the open, because she deemed him too unreliable to be in charge of me while my mother was in the hospital and demanded that he let her adopt me. This he refused to do, and one of his most famous short stories 'Babylon Revisited' is based on this controversy." In the story, Marion and Lincoln Peters, drawn from the personalities of Rosalind and Newman Smith, have guardianship over Charlie Wales's daughter, Honoria. (The name of the Murphys' daughter.) Charlie's wife, Helen, is dead, and after three years of separation, he has returned to Paris to convince her sister, Marion, that he can now take care of Honoria. "Marion shuddered suddenly; part of her saw that Charlie's feet were planted on the earth now. And her own maternal feeling recognized the naturalness of his desire; but she had lived for a long time with a prejudice—a prejudice founded on a curious disbelief in her sister's happiness, and which in the shock of one terrible night, had turned to hatred for him." Making the decision to give Honoria to him, Marion changes her mind when two of Charlie's drunken friends show up at the Peters' apartment. "He would come back some day," Charlie muses, "they couldn't make him pay forever. But he wanted his child, and nothing was much good now, besides that fact." Interestingly, Fitzgerald sent Rosalind a copy of the story while still in manuscript. "Scott sent me the transcript of his 'Babylon Revisited,' " said Rosalind, "which he said was inspired by my feeling that the child should be in better hands, and my suggestion that she live with us in Brussels. We saw him and Zelda fairly often at this period, and felt uneasy about the whole worsening situation."

Under tremendous emotional and financial strain, Fitzgerald vehemently rejected Rosalind's accusations and intimations. "I know your ineradicable impression of the life that Zelda and I led, and evidently your dismissal of any of the effort, struggle and success or happiness in it: and I understand also your real feeling for her—but I have got Zelda and Scotty to take care of now as ever and I simply cannot be upset and harrowed still further." Later he composed a harsher response, but did not mail it: "Do me a single favor. Never communicate with me again in any form and I will try to resist the temptation to pass you down to posterity for what you are." Though outwardly he discounted Rosalind's assessment of his culpability for Zelda's breakdown, inwardly he agonized over the part he had played, and shared his feelings of guilt with Zelda. But she would have none of it, and dismissed all questions of blame. "Please don't write to me about blame. Blame doesn't matter. The thing that counts is to apply the few resources available to turning life into a tenable, orderly affair."

Fitzgerald then turned to friends for support. "Scotty fell ill and I left at midnight by plane for Paris to decide about an immediate appendix operation," he wrote Harold Ober. "In short it's been one of those periods that come to all men I suppose, when life is so complicated that with the best will in the world, work is hard as hell to do. Things are better, but no end in sight yet. I figure I've written about 40,000 words to Forel (the psychiatrist) on the subject of Zelda, trying to get to the root of things and keeping worried families tranquil in their old age and trying to be a nice thoughtful female mother to Scotty."

Zelda was also writing to Dr. Forel, who had asked her to summarize the important emotional moments in her life. In part, she wrote of her love for Egorova and obsession with dance.

I had begun dancing in Paris, with a great ballet dancer, but I was obliged to leave her because of my illness. . . . When I returned to Paris I went again to the same school. I have worked four hours a day and in the evening, and Sundays, during the holidays, on the boat when I was traveling. I began to understand it.

Suddenly last spring I began to see all red while I worked or I saw no colors. I could not bear to look out windows, for sometimes I saw humanity as a bottle of ants. Then we left for Cannes where I worked on technique and where after the lessons I had the impression that I was an old person living very quietly in winter. I loved my ballet teacher in Paris more than anything else in the world. But I did not know how. She had everything of beauty in her head, the brightness of a Greek temple, the frustration of a mind searching for a place, the glory of cannon bullets; all that I saw in her steps. From Christmas on I was not able to work correctly anymore, but she helped me to learn more, to go further. She always told me to look after myself. I tried to, but I was worse. I was in a real mess. One day the world between me and the others stopped—I was dragged like by a magnet—I had headaches and I could jump higher than ever, but the day after I was sick. Madame came to encourage me. Enough to give me the strength to go to Malmaison. There the doctors told me that I was well and I came back to the studio, unable to walk in the streets, full of medicine, trying to work in an atmosphere which was becoming more and more strange. . . . My husband forced me to go to Valmont—and now I am here, with you, in a situation where I cannot be anybody, full of vertigo, with an increasing noise in my ears, fearing the vibrations of everyone I meet. Broken down.

When Rosalind suggested discussing Zelda's condition with her parents, Fitzgerald pleaded against it, knowing they would be consumed with worry. "I beg you to think twice before you say more to them than I have said. That is your business of course, but our interests in this matter should be the same. Zelda at this moment is in no immediate danger. And I have promised to let you know if anything crucial is in the air." Aware that the Sayres also held him responsible for Zelda's condition, he defended himself in another *unsent* letter, this time to Zelda. "I'd like to discover the faintest basis for your family's accusation that I drove you crazy . . . you were 'crazy' in the ordinary sense before I met you. I rationalized your eccentricities and made a sort of creation of you." In retrospect, it was an easy accusation; Zelda's behavior had always raised eyebrows. It was all point-of-view. Carl Van Vechten thought she was a true original; Rebecca West was certain she was mad. Meeting her in Great Neck, she wrote: "I was terrified not exactly of, but for, his wife." In one conversation with Scott, West recalled Fitzgerald talking about something odd Zelda had done, and how she had censored the words on her mind, "But surely you realize she's insane?"

By midsummer, Zelda's condition had settled into a deep depression. "The panic seems to have settled into a persistent gloom punctuated by moments of bombastic hysteria," she wrote Scott, "the crises of the sinking bed and the hydraulic heart have been more or less mastered." Her life had pared down to simple pleasures. "The radio is a god-send," she told Fitzgerald. "It is my constant guide and companion and I put it in bed at night to warm the sheets. Waffles can also be cooked on its sleek, shiny top." Zelda's sense of humor or insane delusion? Depositing money into her hospital account, Fitzgerald told doctors to give her whatever she desired. "I gave word in Switzerland for her to have every luxury in the line of Paris clothes and so forth that she wanted, because I felt she needed cheering up after her long ascetic effort in the ballet." Zelda appreciated the gesture, and whenever lucid, composed loving letters to Scott. She always wrote in pencil on her personalized green stationary—"Zelda" embossed across its top, identical to her mother's letterhead with its simple, embossed heading, "Mama." Like those from Montgomery a decade earlier, the letters are beautifully written, only wiser and more poignant. They show the depth of feeling that Zelda felt for Scott when he was sober. One, describing a hike in the mountains near the hospital, overflowed with tenderness. "Dear Sweetheart—Walking along up so high there were white stones with black moss spots like the backs of ponies grazing, and there were stones that menaced and pierced the earth like broken bones, and there were stones that the earth caught on like a garment in the wind, and there were meadows spread out to dry and the clouds moved so fast as if they could crush you and the sky was like a rippling beach and we stood on the horizon. There we were in the highest place—with the whole world rolling away like a lot of sculptors clay about our feet and we the memorial to some forgotten lyric poet. There were yards and yards of fraises du bois like an old-fashioned print, red dots hanging on a preponderance of grace and there were calves depressed like bad boys who've just had their faces washed and there was love everyplace for you. Darling, Wednesday usually comes in the middle of the week, so I won't see you for another half of a whole. It's unbearable. Dear, I love you so much that loving is like being one of those cheeses that drip through a cloth, which is you, of course—and darling and love and dear—good night."

Incredibly, she still believed her best hope for recovery rested in her own independent accomplishment. She implored Scott to ask Egorova whether she had enough talent to become a first-rate dancer. Forel warned against this because he felt Zelda's strenuous ballet training had contributed to her mental collapse, and he advised her to abandon the effort. But in late June, Zelda again implored Scott. "You have always had so much sympathy for people forced to start over later in life that I should think you could find the generosity to help me amongst your many others, not as you would a child but as an equal."

He finally agreed and wrote to Egorova on July 9, 1930, having the letter translated into French. Her response was more positive than he expected. In her assessment of Zelda's abilities, Egorova explained that because Zelda began training so late, she would never be a dancer of the very first rank, but emphasized that she could master important roles in repertory companies and smaller ballet groups as well as secondary roles with larger companies. Egorova twice emphasized that Zelda could become a very good dancer. Her only caveat was that she would never attain the excellence of a Nemtchinova, Nikitina, or Danilova. The three were superb Russian prima ballerinas. Vera Nemtchinova, three years younger than Zelda, had started dancing as a child and been recruited by Serge Grigoriev for Diaghilev's Ballets Russes in 1923, beginning in his corps de ballet, then advancing to ballerina. In 1929 she toured Europe with her own company and Zelda may have seen her in performances with Colonel de Basil's ballet company in Monte Carlo. Alice Nikitina, who was also Egorova's student, performed with the Ballets Russes from 1923 to 1929. She was nine years Zelda's junior, and had made her debut with the Ljubljana Opera Ballet in Yugoslavia, and later danced with the romantic theater of Boris Romanoff. Although Maria Danilova died prematurely at seventeen, she was considered the greatest Russian dancer of the nineteenth century. Beautiful, graceful, and technically strong, she had entered the St. Petersburg Imperial School of Ballet at the age of eight. All three were extraordinary ballerinas and Egorova's comparison was not meant to belittle Zelda's ability.

While Egorova's comments were primarily positive, her evaluation came as a disappointment to Zelda, whose sole ambition was to become a prima ballerina in a company at the level of the Ballets Russes. She abhorred the thought of becoming a secondary dancer in a repertory company like Leonide Massine's, Diaghilev's leading male dancer from 1914 to 1921, who became director of Colonel de Basil's Ballets Russes in Monte Carlo. Bitterly disappointed, Zelda saw no alternative but to give up her dream. With despairing finality, she packed up all her ballet paraphernalia and put it in a trunk. "Without hope or youth or money I sit constantly wishing I were dead," she wrote Scott. "I want to get well but I can't it seems to me, and if I should what's going to take away the thing in my head that sees so clearly into the past—into dozens of things that I can never forget."

She yearned for the familiarity of Montgomery and wanted to go home. While not legally committed to Prangins, each time she tried to leave, she was forcibly brought back and confined to E'glantine, where she was kept in a dark room and given bromides and morphine. Referred to as the "Swiss sleeping cure," these drugs induced a prolonged narcosis during which patients slept for one or two weeks, awakened only to eat and relieve bladder and bowel functions. Nurses controlled each patient's fluid intake and administered enemas every two days. Widely used throughout Europe during the 1920s and 1930s, the method had evolved from nineteenth-century "rest cures" aimed at restoring exhausted nervous systems. In theory, rest cured the sick mind in the same way that inactivity cured the sick lung in a tuberculosis victim. The oldest therapy known to psychiatry, sleep treatments were effective in reducing anxiety, and provided temporary relief from depression and hysteria. The most common formula for inducing narcosis was called "Cloetta's Mixture," containing paraldehyde, amylene hydrate, chloral hydrate, alcohol, barbituric acid, digitalin, and ephedrine hydrochloride, diluted with water and made into a clear solution. Preceded by an enema, "Cloetta's Mixture" was administered rectally and induced narcosis within twenty minutes. After the long artificial sleep, patients generally awoke relaxed and rested.

The procedure was not always without side effects. On July 15,

1930, when Zelda returned to Prangins's main house, she was calmer but covered with eczema and in excruciating pain. Her neck and head felt as if they were on fire. Starch compresses, Flemings solution–soaked bandages, and applications of grease and powder provided little relief. She believed she was being tortured by God and graphically described her agony to Scott. "What I have, however, is not eczema but a visitation. It is something that rotted for centuries in the catacombs and poisoned the cellars of classic ruins; it is a foul plague that I hope is on the wane. At any rate I slept last night. It runs and makes sores and fills up all the cavities back of the eyes with fire, and looks rather like those heads in your pictures of the war. Sheer putrification [sic]." Throughout the summer her eczema persisted, and when Scott visited it worsened. She was experiencing severe mood swings, and vacillating from warmth to bitterness and back in the space of an hour, and Fitzgerald recalled how one day, "after lunch she returned to the affectionate tender mood, utterly normal, so that with pressure I could have maneuvered her into intercourse, but the eczema was almost visibly increasing so I left early. Toward the end she was back in schizophrenia."

In August for four days, Fitzgerald brought Scottie with him to Prangins. Their visit so aggravated Zelda's skin condition that Dr. Forel suggested Fitzgerald stay away for the rest of the summer. When he visited next in September, her eczema again flared up so severely that Zelda implored him not to return until the condition was under control. Late that September, Forel placed Zelda in a thirteen-hour hypnotic trance. Upon wakening the eczema was almost gone, and when it reappeared, it was in a much milder form. But while her skin condition improved, the unmotivated smile on her lips and inclinations toward lesbianism remained unchanged. Scott commented on how Zelda, "in spite of tenderness toward him still makes irrational erotic remarks," and that in early fall she became so infatuated with a red-haired girl at the clinic that Prangins was forced to change her living quarters. In his ledger Scott noted, "They change the house of one girl after whom she tags."

Still uncomfortable about making a final diagnosis, Forel again consulted Bleuler. "The more I saw Zelda," he stated, "the more I thought at the time: she is neither a pure neurosis nor a real psychosis—I considered her a constitutional, emotionally unbalanced psychopath—she may improve, never recover. It was a great help to discuss this difficult patient with Bleuler." On November 22, 1930, the two doctors finally agreed on a diagnosis of "schizo-phrenie," defined by them as an organic brain disease impairing various functions and causing bizarre and dangerous behavior.

Just two years earlier, the American Psychiatric Association had completed its standard nomenclature of diseases, with schizophre-nia accounting for 22 percent of all first-time psychiatric hospital admissions. Resulting from problems with brain chemistry and structure, the disease included abnormalities potentially induced by childhood viral infections of the brain. Schizophrenia tended to run in families, with certain individuals predisposed. Bleuler considered schizophrenia to be the reaction of an inadequate personality to his or her environment. It frequently manifested in individuals who suppressed their emotions, or felt angry at their inability to control life situations. "The simple schizophrenics," Bleuler wrote, "vege-tate as day laborers, peddlers, even as servants. They are also vagabonds and hoboes. . . . On the higher levels of society," he added with unconscious sexism, "the most common type is the wife who is unbearable, constantly scolding, nagging, always making de-mands, but never recognizing duties."

According to Bleuler, the most prevalent symptom of schizo-phrenia was blunted emotion. Patients were not only unresponsive to stimuli, but uncooperative in following the simplest, most rea-sonable requests. There were also perceptual disturbances involv-ing illusions, hallucinations, and confused thinking. Schizophrenics were often sensitive to light, colors, and sounds, and commonly ex-perienced frightening distortions, saw nonexistent objects, and heard terrifying voices that, doctors conjectured, erupted from a suppressed subconscious. The prognosis for recovery was bleak; most physicians believed the illness progressively undermined a pa-tient's cognitive capabilities. Bleuler actually considered recovery from schizophrenia improbable. "Let us openly say to ourselves and to others," he told fellow doctors, "that at present we know of no measures which will cure the disease, as such, or even bring it to a halt."

Zelda experienced most of the perceptual manifestations associ-ated with schizophrenia, including the propensity toward homo-sexuality, which Forel noted was common in female schizophrenics. Commenting on this aspect of her case, Dr. Forel explained: *"L'ho-mosexualité est un symptome de la maladie—tout comme Madame Egorova a été la première passion lesbienne apres le debut de la maladie."*

(Homosexuality is a symptom of the disease—just as Madame Egorova was the first lesbian passion after the onset of the disease.) Menstrual cycle disturbances and lesbianism often were concomitant in female schizophrenics, suggesting endocrine or chemical imbalances. And endocrine treatments, utilizing powders of dried thyroid glands and ovarian extracts, were frequently recommended. In an attempt to alleviate other symptoms, some patients were injected with their own blood, given potassium bromide or administered "cerebrotoxin," a serum made from the brain substance of a mentally sound person. Forel gave Zelda injections of Calcium Sandoz to counteract bone calcification (Sandoz being the name of a large Swiss pharmaceutical firm then and now) and Morphone (morphine) to relieve pain and induce sleep. He also administered Belladenal (belladonna) for pain and prescribed l'Emge Lumiere (phenobarbital), commonly known as luminal, a barbituric sedative. Hydrotherapy treatments and purges of sedlitz water also were recommended.

In 1930 the standard treatment for schizophrenics included seclusion, sedatives, wet packs, and hydrotherapy, all of which had only temporary therapeutic effects. The drugs used made patients feel restless, lethargic, and alternately agitated and depressed. Antipsychotic medications to correct chemical imbalances in the brain were not yet available. The disease had first been recognized by the ancient Egyptians, who thought it was caused by a disturbance of blood and gas in the ventricles, and had been redefined at the beginning of the twentieth century by Eugen Bleuler and Emil Kraepelin to literally mean "split mind." Generally, it began with symptoms of listlessness, vacancy, and withdrawal; progressed to include hallucinations, disturbed associations, and delusions; and ultimately ended in dementia. As was true of most psychiatrists of his era, Kraepelin was convinced that psychoses had biological causes, often genetic in origin, making them essentially incurable. He identified twenty psychoses, the two most common being manic-depression and dementia praecox, and divided them into four classifications: hebephrenic schizophrenia, in which patients experience language disorders and smile inappropriately or make grotesque gestures; catatonic, in which the patient is mute and rigid; simple-schizoid, in which the withdrawing patient shows lack of interest or drive; and paranoiac, characterized by delusions. While Kraepelin and Bleuler both felt the disease ran in families and that a predisposition to it could be inherited, they also believed that environmental factors exerted a strong influence, and that certain life events or persistent situations could precipitate the illness. Individuals at risk were especially sensitive to particular stressors, intrusive experiences, and demoralizing or threatening environments.

Fitzgerald acknowledged that Zelda might have avoided those stressors had she married someone else, and agreed with Kraepelin's theories about schizophrenia evolving from physical causes. "I can't help clinging to the idea that some essential physical thing like salt or iron or semen or some unguessed-at holy water is either missing or is present in too great quantity." But even with Bleuler's expert diagnosis, Forel was not absolutely certain that Zelda was schizophrenic rather than severely depressed. Taking into consideration the relatively late onset of her illness, her passionate involvement in life, and alternation between psychosis and normality, her symptoms suggested a mood disorder as much as they did schizophrenia.

However, if not initially schizophrenic, the medicines and interventions prescribed for that disease certainly accelerated the hallucinations, stupor, and delusions characteristic of it. Separated from her home environment and language, Zelda was in a precarious position at the Swiss hospital. Her southern accent and manner of speaking made communication with her European doctors very difficult. Most spoke little English and held the sexist belief, common to the time, that Zelda's recovery depended on the continuation of her marriage to Fitzgerald. Instead of encouraging her to take responsibility for her own recovery and develop her skills, they discouraged those objectives and advised her to stop antagonizing Fitzgerald. Since alcohol triggered Zelda's psychotic episodes, Dr. Forel warned her against drinking even the smallest amount. And since he considered Fitzgerald's alcoholism a precipitating factor in Zelda's breakdown, he strongly advised Scott to stop drinking. Fitzgerald countered that without liquor he could not write. He did, however, promise to drink only wine, and late that summer Zelda asked him if he had stuck to his resolve. "Dr. Forel told me to ask you if you had stopped drinking—so I ask." There is no evidence, written or otherwise, of his response.

Early that September, Fitzgerald moved to Lausanne, where he stayed first at the Beau Rivage Hotel, then at the Grand Hotel de la

Paix. In Montreux and Vevey he spent time with Thomas Wolfe, who was summering there. He was still not allowed to see Zelda, so he communicated with her through telephone calls and letters. Lonely, Scott began an affair with a titled Englishwoman named Bijou O'Connor whom he met at his hotel. Maybe Zelda had some indication of what was going on, because during the month Scott and Bijou were together, she was confined to E'glantine for "refractoriness," as Scott called it in his ledger.

Desperate to establish a link with the outside world and to understand what was happening to her, Zelda questioned Forel about the disintegration of her personality and slowness of her recovery. "Can't you please explain to me why I should spend five months of my life in sickness and suffering, seeing nothing but optical illusions, to devitalize something in me that you yourself have found indispensable, and that my husband has found so agreeable as to neglect shamefully his wife during the last four years. When this sort of thing happens to you, there is usually the other person to teach you the game, but since it happened to me in pursuit of the unattainable, alone and unenlightened, I am forced to bear the hopeless months of the past, and God knows what is the future. Exalted sophistries are not much of a prop. Why do I have to go backwards when everyone else, who can, goes on? Why does my husband and other people find that, what was so satisfactory for them, is not the thing for me—and if you do cure me, what's going to happen to all the bitterness and unhappiness in my heart—it seems to me a sort of castration, but since I am powerless, I suppose I will have to submit, though I am neither young enough to think that you can manufacture out of nothing something to replace the song I had."

Surrounded by vacant-eyed patients who muttered and paced the corridors, Zelda was aware she was losing her "self" at Prangins, and begged Fitzgerald for release: "Please, please let me out now . . . granted that in another six months, the Teutonic sophistries of Dr. Forel, could render inactive the element in me which so many others have not found undesirable. . . . I want to leave here. I have spent as much time as I intend to—unable to step into the corridor alone." When her initial request were ignored, she turned belligerent. "I have not the slightest indication of what your intentions are towards me. After five months of suffering and misery and isolation, at least the pathological side of my illness has disappeared. For the rest, I am a woman of thirty and, it seems to me, entitled to some voice in decisions covering me. I have had enough and it is simply wasting my time and ruining my health keeping up the absurd pretense that a lesion in the head is curable. Will you make the necessary arrangements that I leave here and seek some satisfactory life for myself." Believing he was acting in her best interests, and frustrated by her insinuations, Scott ripped her letter once down the center and refused to answer. Zelda warned him that she was going to write her parents and ask them to intervene. "Shall I write to daddy that he should come over? They know what's the matter with me so do not think that I feel the slightest hesitancy in communicating with them. I believe three months is the usual limit of these sort of struggles, and I have no intention of any longer internment. . . . If I have to stand much more to take away the thing in me that all the rest of you find so invaluable and superior, when I get out I'm going to have Scottie at least."

When threats did not work, she again pleaded, "Of course I realize that you have done all in your power to help me and of that I am exceedingly grateful, but you must try to understand how dreary and drastic is my present position—far away from all my friends and all my family across the Atlantic, and alone in a strange part of Switzerland, with hardly a soul to speak English with. It's heart-rending and sometimes I feel like crying . . . for a month and two weeks I have been three times outside my room, and for five months I have lived with my sole desire that of death. If you are coming here under the illusion that I am well, or even better, you will have to wait another year or so, since I can see no possibility of escape from here." Another letter suggests her bitter awareness of Fitzgerald's freedom in contrast to her own incarceration. "If you want an idea of what it's like, you might pass up your next tennis game . . . you might even come here. I would always be more than glad to see you, and will always be devoted to you—but the farcical element of this situation is too apparent for even a person as hopeless and debilitated as I am."

Zelda's condition was further aggravated when Fitzgerald mentioned that he had taken Emily Vanderbilt out in Paris. "You know I was much stronger mentally and physically and sensitively than Emily," Zelda angrily reminded him, "but you said that she was too

big a poisson for me. Why? She couldn't dance a Brahm's waltz or
write a story—she can only gossip and ride in the Bois and have
pretty hair curling up instead of thinking." Rebecca West had seen
Fitzgerald and Vanderbilt at Armenonville. She observed Emily
telling Scott a long, sad story and going over it repeatedly. "He was
leaning towards her, sometimes caressing her hands. . . . Finally, he
stood up and seemed to be saying, 'You mustn't go over this any
more.' " Emily Vanderbilt later committed suicide.

As fall progressed, Zelda insisted she be released or transferred
to another hospital. "You've got to make Dr. Forel arrange what
can't happen, because I am too feeble to go into the world," she
wrote Scott. "If there's nobody in all this barred brothel who will
look after me, I demand that I be allowed to go immediately to a
hospital in France where there is enough human kindness to prevent the present slow butchery. Scott, if you knew what this is like,
you would not dare in the eyes of God leave a person in it. Please
help me." When he implored her to have patience, she countered,
writing, "What are you going to do? Or would you prefer that I
wrote Newman. If you are under the least doubt as to my mental
capabilities, I will more than gladly welcome any alienist you may
suggest."

In the midst of her struggle to get released, she received an encouraging letter from Edmund Wilson, who had suffered a breakdown the previous year. He confided that he had barely survived
the experience of hydrotherapy and had nearly become addicted to
paraldehyde at a New York sanitarium in Clifton Springs. He urged
Zelda to be strong and maintain faith in her recovery. Since she was
also undergoing hydrotherapy treatments, it was reassuring to hear
from someone who had undergone the same ordeal and survived.

As early as 1890, hydrotherapy had been used in French hospitals by Jacques Charcot, who introduced spinal douches for certain
forms of hysteria. Called "Charcot's Douche," the treatment was
fairly simple and involved applying a cold-water jet to the spine in
order to agitate the neurovascular structure and stimulate nerve
centers. Though the water struck the skin so violently it often
caused tissue damage, the invigoration of the circulation had a tonic
effect on some patients and reestablished equilibrium. By the early
thirties, application of water at various temperatures, or "hydrotherapy" as it came to be called, became a medical specialty for

the treatment of neurasthenia. Since body functions rely on nerve action, and nervous system abnormalities influence the entire system, a variety of water therapies became popular for the treatment of nervous disorders. The most common included: continuous tub immersions, douches, spritzers and hoses, irrigations and affusions, sitz baths, wet and dry packs, rubdowns and salt rubs, vapor and hot-air baths, steam and electric light cabinets, and needle showers at varying temperatures. One of the simplest, but most effective treatments, was the hot bath, in which water of 90 to 100 degrees F flowed around a patient for an extended period of time. Promoting tranquility, these baths regulated cardiac activity by dilating peripheral vessels and inducing an increase in cerebral circulation. Cold-water baths were also employed to stimulate nerve centers, revive organic functions, and restore an equilibrium of circulation. Wet-sheet packs, in which patients were tightly wrapped in cold, wet sheets and then overwrapped with a blanket to reduce loss of body heat, were used to calm agitated or uncooperative patients. Zelda underwent this treatment several times while confined in E'glantine. In 1927, two major advancements in treating schizophrenia were made when Julius Wagner von Jauregg, chief of the psychiatric clinic in Vienna, won the Nobel Prize for Medicine and Physiology for his malarial treatments, and concurrently it was discovered that fever produced improvement in schizophrenics. As this approach became widely adopted in Europe, special devices, like electric mummy bags, were developed to artificially heat patients. Hot baths, hot air, radiothermy, diathermy, and infrared lightbulb cabinets were also employed to induce high fevers.

By December 1930, various medications and therapies had improved Zelda's condition to the point where Fitzgerald and Scottie could visit. They arrived early during Christmas week to help trim her tree, but the excitement of seeing them overstimulated Zelda and she began to break the ornaments. Fitzgerald quickly departed and took Scottie skiing at Gstaad. He did not see Zelda again until after his father's funeral. When Scott learned of his father's death in January 1931, of a heart attack, he crossed the Atlantic on the S.S. *New York*. After the funeral in Rockville, Maryland, he took a side trip to Montgomery to see the Sayres. The Judge was ill with influenza, and Mrs. Sayre received Scott coolly, but they were glad for the opportunity to discuss Zelda's condition.

Returning to Switzerland, Scott found Zelda noticeably improved to the point where she could go skiing, and was interacting more normally with other patients. Her masklike smile had almost disappeared and she seemed to be emerging from her shell. "I have been to a dance, or dance as they were called in my day and I had a very nice time," she wrote Scott. "It was not quite as good as the war between men and women, but I got myself stepped on a sufficient number of times to make it quite worthwhile. There is a long tall man such as they used to have in Montgomery, who roams the banquet halls as a spectre-like echo of my past. He is a nice man; he is sort of a mechanical man who would be very nice made of tin." But Zelda was still a long way from recovery, and as the first anniversary of her hospital confinement approached, she lamented, "Ages have passed since your last visit and conditions do not seem to improve any with time. I have quite lost my mind and roam all over the place in a half daze that is exceedingly unpleasant to bear. . . . It's most depressing being closed in what appears to me to be a semi-insane asylum since what will soon be a year's time now."

By summer 1931 she was feeling somewhat more optimistic, involved in occupational therapy and making clothes for Scottie and herself, as well as fashioning a series of paper dolls. "I've made Scottie some wonderful paper dolls, you and me and her, but they have no clothes yet," she wrote Scott. "I had such fun imagining you as I drew. I remember every single spot of light that ever gouged a shadow beside your bones, so you were easy to make— and I gave you some very doggy green socks to match your eyes." Fitzgerald could now visit and take her on short outings: lunch at a café, a visit to a nearby museum, or sightseeing excursions into the surrounding towns. One evening they went to Montreux to watch a performance by Serge Lifar, who had danced with the Ballets Russes. For her thirty-first birthday in July, Fitzgerald took Zelda and Scottie to the lakeside resort of Annecy in Haute-Savoie, where they spent an idyllic two weeks sailing, swimming in the lake, playing tennis, and picnicking in the gardens of the Hotel Palace. They explored the countryside in an open car, and Zelda sent a postcard of Annecy's canal to her father, writing, "Annecy is so blue that it tints the air and makes you feel as if you were living in an aquarium. It is as peaceful inside its scalloped mountains as a soup-ladle full of the sky and reminds me of North Carolina." For once, the couple eschewed recriminations and they all enjoyed being together as a real family. Zelda remembered every moment. "First we lived at the Beau Rivage, a rambler rose-covered hotel, with a diving platform wedged beneath our window between the sky and the lake, but there were enormous flies on the raft so we moved across the lake to Menthon. The water was greener there and the shadows long and cool and the scraggly gardens staggered up the shelved precipice to the Hotel Palace. We played tennis on the baked clay courts and fished tentatively from a low brick wall. The heat of summer seethed in the resin of the white pine bathhouses. We walked at night toward a cafe blooming with Japanese lanterns, white shoes gleaming like radium in the damp darkness." In the evenings, they danced in the hotel's ballroom, circling to the same Viennese waltzes they had once heard in Montgomery. It reminded Zelda of "the good gone times when we still believed in summer hotels and the philosophies of popular songs."

Forel's approach was to wean patients gradually from Prangins by allowing them short trips of around ten miles, first with a nurse and then with other patients or family members. If the patient did satisfactorily, he or she could go to dinner in Geneva, take longer trips, and visit with family members in a hotel. After that, if all went well, the patient was allowed an extended holiday. Zelda's Annecy trip was followed by an excursion to Vienna, trips to Munich and Caux, and a visit to Gerald and Sara Murphy's mountain retreat in the Austrian Tyrol. From the Restaurant du Parc des Raux-Vives in Geneva, Zelda wrote her mother an optimistic postcard: "Here is where Scott and I lunched yesterday in the soft Spring air—and I thought you would be proud to know: without a nurse—much progress." During their next holiday at Vevey, Zelda nursed Scottie through a bad cold and found it very difficult to say good-bye. With her health improving, it became increasingly hard to return to Prangins. She wrote Scott: "the other day when I kissed her [Scottie] goodbye, the little school child scent of her neck and her funny little hesitant smile broke my heart." She yearned to have her family under one roof; she missed Paris. "Was the Madeleine pink at five o'clock and did the fountains fall with hollow delicacy into the framing of space in the Place de la Concorde," she asked Scott, "and did the blue creep out from behind the Colonnades in the rue de Rivoli through the Tuileries and was the Louvre gray and metallic in the sun and did the trees hang brooding over the cafes and were there lights at night and the clicks of saucers and auto horns that play de Bussey . . . ?"

There had been so many farewells at the Swiss train stations that whenever Fitzgerald's face wasn't on the platform Zelda visualized it there. While traveling through Bern on a day trip with another patient, she wrote Scott: "I went to Geneva all by myself with a fellow maniac and the city was thick and heavy before the rain . . . on the way back from Bern, I searched each person in your station when we passed. It seemed incredible that anything so dear as your shining face should not be where I last saw it." What kept her going was the hope of being with her family again; she told Scott that more than anything—along with getting well—she wanted to have another child.

On September 15, 1931, fifteen months after entering Prangins, Zelda was finally released. According to psychiatrists, her illness was precipitated by deceptive ambitions invented as a compensation for feelings of inferiority. They were optimistic about her recovery if conflicts between the couple could be avoided.

Zelda was determined to recover and remain well. She warned Scott to stop feeling sorry for himself by agonizing over fault, and preparing to leave the hospital, admonished: "Can't you possibly be just a little bit glad that we are alive, and that all the year that's coming we can be together and work and love and get some peace for all the things we've paid so much for learning. Stop looking for solace: there isn't any. . . ." Once again, it was an extraordinarily astute declaration for one who had just spent two years in a mental institution. After saying farewell to Zelda's doctors and nurses, the Fitzgeralds headed back to France. They stopped for a few days on Lake Geneva, then checked into Paris's Majestic Hotel before booking passage to New York on the *Aquitania*.

The new photo in Zelda's reissued passport shows the physical toll her illness had taken. Eyes expressionless, her nose more pronounced on her angular face, the softness of her expression has been replaced by severity and coarseness. A simple barrette holds back unstylish hair. Only remnants remain of her youthful beauty. As they crossed the Atlantic, she reread the life summary she had written for Dr. Forel, in which she listed the probable causes of her collapse, and realistically assessed future difficulties. *I am dependent on my husband and he told me I must get cured. I accept, but as I am lost about anything with him, with his life in which there is nothing for me except the physical comfort, when I get out of your clinic it will be with an idea: to arrange myself in any condition to be able to breathe freely.* It was a summary without recriminations, and leaving Europe, to which they would never return, both Fitzgeralds seemed, once again, determined to put the past behind them.

CHAPTER 6

I Believed I Was
a Salamander

After fifteen months of treatment, Zelda returned home more determined to become self-reliant and independent. Though the breakdown had taken a huge physical toll, it had also given her a new maturity. In a photo taken aboard the *Aquitania*, the same vessel that had taken them on their first European trip in 1921, her expression appears optimistic as she sits with a sketch pad on her lap and squints at the camera. The ship held many memories for the Fitzgeralds, who grew nostalgic walking the decks and peering out at the vast ocean. After docking in Manhattan, they checked into the New Yorker for ten days to look up old friends. They saw Ludlow Fowler, Townsend Martin, Alex McKaig, and John and Margaret Bishop; Fitzgerald met alone with Maxwell Perkins and Harold Ober, and shared a quick lunch with Ernest Hemingway.

With the new decade had come economic depression, and the atmosphere in New York was noticeably different from what it had been two years earlier. "It was a year when a new mood became perceptible," Malcolm Cowley recalled, "a mood of doubt and even defeat. People began to wonder whether it wasn't possible that not only their ideas but their whole lives had been set in the wrong direction." That question certainly crossed the Fitzgeralds' minds.

Needing a quiet place for Zelda to recuperate, the family headed south for Montgomery. Scott braced himself for a tense visit, but on arriving they found the Sayre house bustling with nurses taking care of Judge Sayre, who had contracted influenza the previous spring. They stayed downtown at the Jefferson Davis Hotel, where three rooms and four baths cost them only $9 a day. Eager to find a place to settle, Zelda started house hunting. She was still intent on buying a place of their own, but in the interim they signed a six-month lease on a home at 819 Felder Avenue, across from the brick-paved streets surrounding Cloverdale Park. Most houses in the Cloverdale section, one of Montgomery's nicest neighborhoods, sat on picturesque winding streets under blooming camellia trees. As usual, theirs was an exception; it was too big for them and not particularly comfortable. Real estate was far more affordable than in Wilmington, and the thought that they might actually buy a home energized Zelda, and she began looking for ways to contribute financially to the purchase. She reread Scott's stories to analyze their construction, made some preliminary notes for a novel, and in short order completed seven stories, including "A Couple of Nuts," which *Scribner's Magazine* purchased for publication the following year. Zelda swam, played tennis, visited old friends, and did some painting and sculpting. Occasionally she joined Scott for golf at the country club. The clubhouse brought back many happy memories since it was the place where they had met a decade before. Scottie entered Margaret Booth's School for Females and was privately tutored by the French governess who had accompanied them from Europe. A black couple was hired to cook and clean.

Determined to make Zelda's and Scott's transition easier, the Sayres were very supportive. But the proximity to Zelda's parents forced Fitzgerald to modify his drinking habits and that always put him on edge. Though he was hard at work on a series of stories, when a contract from Metro-Goldwyn-Mayer arrived late in October, Scott jumped at it. The studio offered him $1,200 a week to revise the screenplay of Katherine Brush's 1931 best-selling novel *Red-Headed Woman* for Jean Harlow. It was a two-month commitment with completion expected by Christmas. He was excited to be working under Hollywood's creative genius Irving Thalberg, who would become his model for Monroe Stahr in *The Last Tycoon*. When he boarded his train early in November 1931, Scott was in high spirits, Zelda less so. This time there was no question about her accompanying him. Her father remained in serious condition, and Zelda's mental state was too fragile.

MGM's contract stipulated at least six weeks of work, but things got off to a bad start when Fitzgerald and Dwight Taylor, another MGM scriptwriter, were invited to Thalberg's home, and Scott got drunk and began reciting "Dog," a sophomoric Princeton party song. Thalberg despised drunks, and observing Fitzgerald from the side of the room, made a mental note to get rid of him. Scott sensed his disapproval and realized he had ruined an important opportunity. As usual, he later made excuses: "While all was serene on top, with [Zelda] apparently recovered in Montgomery, I was jittery underneath and beginning to drink more than I ought to. . . . I wanted to get east . . . to see how [Zelda] was. This was later interpreted as 'running out on them' and held against me."

Scott had accepted MGM's offer and departed Montgomery so quickly that Zelda was left feeling unnerved. Not only was she unhappy at being left behind, she was also insecure about Scott being in Hollywood with glamorous movie people, and she dreaded another Lois Moran–type affair. After quarreling with him at the train station, she telegraphed apologies and made a point of sending him daily letters full of warm sentiment. "The little mossy place on the back of your neck is the sweetest place and I can rub my nose in it like a pony in his feed bag when you come home."

Zelda had convinced Scott to let her take ballet lessons during his absence, but soon fell out with her teacher. "I have stopped my dancing lessons since I had a violent quarrel with Amalia this morning," she wrote Fitzgerald. "She called me a cow because I told her I couldn't do steps that neither fit the time nor the spirit of the music. I even bought a book of Shubert waltzes and took them up there thinking that she could conceive them, but she evidently has impedimented hearing—so that's off your mind." Instead of dancing, she played with Scottie, wrote Fitzgerald thirty-two letters during his eight-week absence, worked in her mother's garden, and played tennis with her sister Marjorie's daughter, Noonie. To keep creatively productive, she wrote a one-act play for Scottie and her friends, composed a Bach-like fugue, a nocturne à la Chopin, and a gay bit of Schumann-esque music. As a holiday surprise for Scott, Zelda rented Montgomery's Little Theatre for Christmas week, where she intended to perform Dalcroze rounds with the children costumed, and serve eggnog and cake. Looking forward to his return, she began present shopping early. When she momentarily lost Scottie in a holiday crowd, she panicked, as any parent would. "I lost Scottie in a store today for 1/2 hour and it was ghastly," she wrote Fitzgerald, "like being whirled through endless rotating hypotheses of life and being in some chaotic functioning of the unconsciousness without the mind. I let her shop alone and she went to the car after instead of meeting me where she said."

Zelda had expected Montgomery to provide security and comfort, but instead it felt oppressive and unsettling. She realized how much her contentment depended on Scott, writing him, "When you are not here everything presents itself only in terms of your impressions and I have no independent self, save the one that lives in you—so I'm never thoroughly conscious except when you're near." Her father had been ill almost a year and was now dying. Zelda daily visited her parents, going for morning walks with her mother and sitting by the Judge's bed throughout the afternoons. During November, their conversations about Zelda's marriage became candid and she and her father discussed divorce. But Zelda was aware that her uncertain mental health and dependence on Fitzgerald's financial support and celebrity (to bolster her own sense of self-worth) precluded that possibility. She acknowledged as much in one of her many letters to Hollywood: "It's so nice to have important men and I'm glad you are one."

On November 17, Zelda telegraphed Scott that her father had died. But Scott did not come east and she steeled herself to face the funeral alone. The flag atop Montgomery's capitol was flown at half-mast and the entryway to his supreme court chambers draped with black crepe. Zelda accompanied her mother to the Judge's office and helped gather personal belongings. During the memorial service, she placed roses on his casket. Relatives from throughout the South converged on Montgomery and the house filled with people. Rosalind arrived from Brussels with her husband. "Newman and I were in Europe when Papa died in November, 1931. I came to Montgomery as soon as I could to help with the problem of where Mama now would live. She did not want to leave the old house but I persuaded her that it was an impractical idea, and to buy the cottage that fortunately was for sale next door to Marjorie on Sayre Street."

After a week of mourning, Zelda's eyes ached and patches of eczema appeared on her neck. Then her asthma was aggravated by two weeks of rain. She wrote Scott that she was inconsolable over her father's death and felt light-headed and unstable. "I feel like a person lost in some Gregorian but feminine service here—I have come in on the middle and did not get the beginning and cannot stay for the end, but must somehow seize the meaning. It's awful to think that daddy isn't here anymore. . . . I miss my daddy terribly. I am losing my identity here without men. I would not live two weeks again where there are none, since the first thing that goes is concision, and they give you something to butt your vitality against so it isn't scattered all over the air like sprays of dynamite."

Finding it increasingly difficult to sleep, Zelda thought the Florida sunshine and salt air might help. She wrote Scott that she was going south for a few days. When he suggested she wait until he returned, she objected. Tired of hearing about the exciting things he was doing and the interesting people who crossed his path—including Carmel Myers, who now lived on Maybery Road in Santa Monica—she wrote, "If you mention one more time . . . Lily Dalmita or Constance [Talmadge], I will go off to Florida for a week and spend our money and make you jealous of my legs a la Creole when you get home." That was precisely what she did, though only for a long weekend. She reassured Scott, however, by taking along a nurse. "I found myself almost desperate to get away into the sun alone," she explained upon her return. "I have not had a quiet moment since you left. First two sleepless weeks with asthma and then touches of eczema which I could not trace since I have done my best to lead as healthy a life as possible so you would find me fresh and cheerful when you get back. Having no resources at my command to distract myself without my eyes, I dreaded that you arrive fine and vital and I should be harassed and half sick." She returned home tanned and rested with ambitious ideas about writing a novel based on their marriage. Using psychological terms to describe their experiences during the twenties, she began making notes for a thinly veiled narrative about their life abroad. Her intention was to write a best-seller, achieve fame, and gain some financial independence. She had been forced to abandon ballet, felt she had insufficient control of painting technique, so writing seemed the next best creative outlet. With dogged determination she sequestered herself in the bedroom of the Cloverdale house, and though weak eyesight jeopardized her work, in three weeks she produced the outline of her novel.

Fitzgerald was having less success writing in Hollywood. Five weeks into the *Red Headed Woman* assignment, MGM's story editor Sam Marx still could not make Fitzgerald understand that Thalberg wanted the audience to laugh *with* the heroine, not at her. Thalberg finally ordered Scott off the script, but before he was officially informed, the film's director Marcel De Santo bluntly told Fitzgerald that the script had been given to Anita Loos for a rewrite. Fitzgerald was humiliated. Loos knew the formula for these movies and her revision received immediate approval from Thalberg. The film adaptation of Katharine Brush's novel, about a secretary who becomes the wife of a French aristocrat, was a smash hit. It made Jean Harlow a star and placed Loos at the top of the screenwriting ranks.

Unaware how badly things were going in Hollywood, Zelda eagerly awaited Scott's return. Following her father's death, she had canceled most of her Christmas plans, including the extravaganza at the Little Theatre. She rather giddily admitted how excited she was about Scott coming home. "It's fun thinking of Christmas and the night you will get home and how you will look as you come out of the gate. I will be surprised at your modernity and very amazed that you are so powerful and I will be very happy that you are so handsome and when I see how handsome you are my stomach will fall with many unpleasant emotions like a cake with too many raisins, and I will want to shut you up in a closet like a dress too beautiful to wear."

Fitzgerald arrived in time to celebrate Christmas, but his failure at MGM put him in a terrible frame of mind. When he learned that Zelda was working on a psychological novel about their joint experiences, he became indignant—after all, he intended to use that material for his own novel. Scott insisted she stop. But Zelda thought she had as much right to their story as he did. "The . . . material which I will elect [to write about] is nevertheless legitimate stuff which has cost me a pretty emotional penny to amass and which I intend to use." She was surprised and angered by Fitzgerald's insistence that their life together was off limits, and his directive that she stop writing became a running argument. Pressuring Zelda until she finally relented, Scott remained suspicious, interrogating her whenever she spent excessive time in her study. She grew increasingly nervous and frustrated by the whole situation. Her asthma flared up. Fitzgerald suggested that another trip to Florida might alleviate the symptoms, so in January of 1932 they drove down the

Gulf coast to St. Petersburg where they checked into the Don Ce-Sar Hotel on the beach. Zelda remembered how the hotel "stretched lazily over the snubbed wilderness, surrendering its shape to the blinding brightness of the Gulf. Opalescent shells cupped the twilight on the beach and a stray dog's footprints in the wet sand staked out his claim to a free path round the ocean." One day they went deep-sea fishing but were "sorry for the deep-sea bass and the amber jacks—they seemed such easy game and no sport at all."

The hotel was almost empty and there were so many waiters milling about that the Fitzgeralds dreaded meals in the dining room. They spent much of their time reading under an umbrella or browning themselves on the deserted beach. It wasn't long before they were arguing again over Zelda's proposed novel. The tension reactivated Zelda's symptoms, and by week's end her asthma had returned and she was unable to sleep. Against Dr. Forel's warnings, she began drinking and immediately suffered an outbreak of eczema—a warning sign of emotional turmoil. Then, on the first night of their trip back to Montgomery, as Fitzgerald slept in their hotel room, Zelda began to hear voices in her head. She found Scott's whiskey flask in his suitcase, drank the contents, and was seized by terrifying hallucinations of people doing terrible things to her. By the time they arrived in Montgomery, Zelda had to be hospitalized. There were four prolonged psychotic episodes within the following three weeks.

On February 1, Scott wrote Dr. Forel for advice. He recommended Zelda return at once to Prangins; when that was ruled impractical he suggested Dr. C. Jonathan Slocum's private sanitarium, Craig House, in Beacon, New York. Because his letter was delayed in reaching Fitzgerald, by the time it arrived Zelda had already been admitted to the Henry Phipps Psychiatric Clinic of Johns Hopkins University in Baltimore, Maryland. On February 12, Scott took Zelda to Phipps and placed her under the care of clinic director Dr. Adolf Meyer and Dr. Mildred Squires, one of its residents. Zelda arrived looking haggard and actively hallucinating, her mouth twisted in an uncontrollable smile of amusement. After talking with her doctors and satisfying himself that she would be in competent hands, Fitzgerald returned to Montgomery. He had left Scottie with Zelda's relatives and rather than interrupt her school year, determined they should stay out the lease on their Cloverdale house.

Repeatedly making the exhausting train trip from Montgomery to Baltimore, Fitzgerald had plenty of time to ponder his situation. He usually stayed at the Rennert Hotel, only a short walk from Mencken and Sara Haardt's house on Cathedral Avenue, and often stopped by to discuss Zelda's condition. Again the single parent, Fitzgerald made all decisions about Scottie's care. Zelda dealt with her hospitalization as best she could, writing Scott, "I am glad you and Scottie are getting some time with each other. She feels very alone when you and I are together. Being so close, we must move ectoplasmicly [*sic*] across a great many peoples' visions like visitations from another world." The relapse frightened Zelda, who suddenly understood the extent and seriousness of her illness. Trying to regain her equilibrium, she asked Scott to keep a distance while doctors did their work. "I do not seem to be strong enough to stand much strain at present and rather than have another string of unhappy times behind us, I'd rather just stay here until I'm quite well. Your role is not to be that of a doctor and in my present condition you have to mother me and bear with a lot of unpleasantness which is not part of how I feel towards you at all but the result of my health—simply." Again, despite her fragile mental state, she perceived her own condition clearly.

Dr. Meyer, who was in charge of her case, had also been highly recommended by Oscar Forel. Born in Zurich, Meyer had trained as a neurologist and pathologist with Oscar Forel's father Auguste, professor of psychiatry at the University of Zurich. In 1892, when Meyer arrived in the United States, he worked first as a pathologist at the Kankakee Hospital in Illinois while teaching at the University of Chicago. He then moved to Worcester Hospital in Massachusetts during 1895 and taught at Clark University. From 1902 to 1909, Meyer directed the Psychiatric Institute of New York State Hospital, where he worked with Dr. Abraham Brill, who had studied in Zurich with Carl Jung in 1908 and had visited Freud during that summer. When the Phipps Clinic of Johns Hopkins Medical School opened in 1910, Meyer was named its chief, and from 1930 to 1950 was the generally acknowledged dean of American psychiatry. Though his treatment of mental illness included the consideration of psychological and social factors along with biological determinants, Meyer had not really developed any theory about the cause of mental illness or a practical therapeutic program. His psychobiological approach, however, was broad enough to accommodate various somatic treatments. He favored occupational therapy and the use of psychiatric social workers, utilizing play and work therapy to strengthen elements of a patient's personality. Since Freud did not consider psychoanalysis effective in treating schizophrenia, most psychiatrists had adopted the same attitude toward psychotherapy. But Meyer still employed therapy, because without an explanation of the cause of mental illness, he believed that all available treatments should be offered patients regardless of diagnosis or results.

Meyer was considered an authority on the treatment of schizophrenia, and after reviewing Zelda's case, determined that hers was a "joint problem." He called his diagnosis *une folie a deux*," in which two closely associated people develop similar obsessions, the weaker and more submissive yielding to the stronger. In many of these cases, the disturbed person relinquishes their delusions when separated from the other. Fitzgerald found the diagnosis fascinating, acknowledging that he and Zelda were intricately bound to each other: "Liquor on my mouth is sweet to her; I cherish her most extravagant hallucinations." But theirs was a highly complex interaction of unconscious denial, cross-identification, and alcohol-escapism. While Meyer recognized the Fitzgeralds' interdependency, he understood that Scott was able to function in the world while Zelda was not. He infuriated Scott by insisting that he also required treatment if Zelda was ever to improve. The two men never communicated effectively, and Zelda found it impossible to establish a good rapport with Meyer, whom she considered too rigid, Germanic, and humorless.

It was Mildred Taylor Squires, the assistant resident psychiatrist at Phipps, who earned Zelda's trust and established an effective therapeutic relationship. Only four years older than Zelda, Dr. Squires had received her medical training at the University of Pennsylvania, and while not a specialist in psychiatry, was personally interested in Zelda's case and proved very helpful. On February 17, just five days after Zelda's arrival at Phipps, Dr. Squires wrote Fitzgerald about her condition, saying she seemed preoccupied, had scattered thoughts, and often stopped speaking in the middle of sentences. Indirect and vague in her responses, Zelda refused to discuss her feelings or symptoms. Appearing extremely tense, she had delayed responses and exhibited restless fidgeting and jerky body movements. Squires emphasized the difficulty of effectively treating someone who did not wish to be treated. "At no time have I been able to get any statement of the suspicious, paranoid ideas which apparently led up to her coming to the clinic," Squires admitted to Fitzgerald. ". . . She has told both Dr. Meyer and me that she will not talk about any of her illness, and of course we cannot force her to do so." Furthermore, Squires related, "Mrs. Fitzgerald does not accept any of the nurse's suggestions unless they are labeled as my orders. These she has accepted but in a reluctant, though very friendly spirit, trying to avoid them but usually giving in rather gracefully."

To clarify information Zelda may have shared with her, Squires requested that Fitzgerald write a detailed letter about their sexual compatibility. He agreed, responding: "Our sexual relations have been good or less good from time to time but they have always been normal. She had her first orgasm about ten days after we were married, and from that time to this there haven't been a dozen times in twelve years, when she hasn't had an orgasm. . . . The difficulty in 1928–30 was temperamental—it led to long periods of complete lack of desire. During 1929 we were probably together only two dozen times and always it was purely physical, but in so far as the purely physical goes it was mutually satisfactory. I have had experience and read all available literature, including that book by the Dutchman I saw on your shelves and I know whereof I speak." To enhance his knowledge of sexuality, Fitzgerald, in fact, had secured *The Scented Garden* by Dr. Bernhard Stern, a 450-page treatise on love in the Levant, touted as one of the most complete and authentic works on erotic life in the Orient. Extensively illustrated with photographs, and sold only by subscription to physicians, lawyers, and adult students of sexual anthropology, the text was advertised as unexpurgated with rare facts about love charms and aphrodisiacs, Turkish sexual orgies and erotic perversions. However, while Fitzgerald characterized his sexual relations with Zelda in a positive light to Squires, he admitted to others that since the Jozan affair in 1924 he could not satisfy her. And later he confided to Squires's colleague Dr. Thomas Rennie, "In the last analysis she is a stronger person than I am. I have creative fire, but I am a weak individual. She knows this and really looks upon me as a woman.

All our lives, since the days of our engagement, we have spent hunting for some man Zelda considers strong enough to lean upon. I am not."

In a gesture to cheer Zelda and provide her something to do, Fitzgerald sent their chess set. Unfortunately, it produced a rather sad nostalgia. "Thanks for the chess. It made me very lonely for you seeing our scores on the back. However, we are both such triumphant victors and such ignominious losers that it's just as well we abandoned the emotional upheaval of our tournaments." And while she complained about the hospital's environment—"I have got so fetid and constantly smell of rubbery things about here—it's ghastly, really. I do not know to what depths the human soul can sink in bondage"—inwardly she was grateful for the clinic's protection.

In 1931, American mental hospitals were still widely separated from the mainstream of American medicine. Their staffs rarely received specialized training since medical schools offered no regular instruction in psychiatry. Young, untrained physicians were often in charge of a ward and their selections of treatments largely a matter of personal preference and convenience. Zelda was fortunate to have Dr. Squires on her case since female doctors were a rarity in psychiatric hospitals. Though a powerless minority, woman doctors were often perceived as kinder, more intuitive, and more interested than their male colleagues, who were frequently described as patronizing and hurried. This was certainly Zelda's impression. "I do not see how Dr. Squires can remain a sprig of old English lilac in this seething witches' cauldron," she told Scott. Through extensive therapy sessions with Squires, Zelda was able to gain an understanding of the dynamic between Fitzgerald and herself. To show her appreciation for these valuable insights, she designed Christmas cards for her doctor, printing them in black ink and adding white gouache by hand. Blending a manneristic and Cubist style, Zelda's card depicted a solitary female figure holding a lighted candle and wreath above her knees. (The muse of enlightenment.) In hand-lettering on the gray card was the greeting "Mildred Squires Wishes You A Merry Christmas." Squires made the mistake of sending one to a consulting physician on Zelda's case, Dr. Frederic Wertham. He questioned the appropriateness of using a patient's design and sent it to another doctor with the comment, "This card was designed and printed by Mrs. Fitzgerald. I knew nothing of them until they arrived. I thought you might be interested in seeing them."

Uninterested in playing chess, or participating in any of the hospital's other recreational activities, Zelda returned to work on her novel. Squires supported her efforts and allowed Zelda two hours daily to write. During February and March she worked furiously, and by her sixth week of hospitalization the book was completed. After Dr. Squires had read it and offered suggestions, Zelda secretly sent the manuscript to Maxwell Perkins at Scribner's. Fitzgerald had been kept informed of Zelda's progress by Squires, and expected to read the novel before it was submitted. When Perkins called to say he was reading the manuscript, Fitzgerald was furious and telegraphed him on March 16, 1932: "Please do not judge, or if not already done, even consider Zelda's book until you get revised version, letter follows." Perkins, however, was already impressed by the novel's originality, and though it needed substantial revisions, was considering it for publication. When Fitzgerald confronted Zelda about sending the manuscript behind his back, she explained that she had changed the mailing address only at the last moment to avoid his negative comments. "I did not want a scathing criticism such as you have mercilessly—if for my own good, given my last stories." Several Phipps psychiatrists apologized for allowing Zelda to send the novel without Fitzgerald's permission. He was incensed that *Save Me the Waltz* had been written on time paid for by money he had been forced to earn writing magazine stories rather than his own novel. Surprised by the bitterness of his resentment, Squires initiated a discussion about the possibility of a legal separation. Fitzgerald rejected the idea outright, saying, "It would be throwing her broken upon a world which she despises; I would be a ruined man for years." Was he referring to guilt or some more arcane emotion?

Scott railed at the prospect of letting Zelda tell the story he intended to write. Considering her an amateur in a professional's game, he insisted on major revisions before allowing Perkins to consider the book, including the elimination of its central section and the change of the protagonist's name ("Amory Blaine," identical to his hero in *This Side of Paradise*). Zelda's new choice of name, David Knight, was her ironic reference to Dick Knight. During late spring and summer of 1932, Scott supervised Zelda's revision of the manuscript, cutting it drastically and forcing her to suppress almost a third of the book, including the entire middle section, which he considered an unfair portrayal of himself as an alcoholic. These sections were replaced with passages Fitzgerald liked, but which rendered the book far less coherent. Only after the manuscript met with his approval did Fitzgerald finally give the go-ahead for publication. But it was a vastly different book from the one Zelda had written, and badly disjointed because of the cuts. A member of Scribner's promotion department, who had seen the original version, confided to Tony Buttita, proprietor of the Intimate Book Shop in Asheville, North Carolina, that Zelda's version had been very provocative, including vindictive attacks on Scott as writer and husband and scandalous material about their private life.

Regardless of its deletions and changes, the novel remains the most important record we have of Zelda's impressions about growing up in Montgomery, life in France, and the difficulties of being married to a famous writer. Almost entirely autobiographical, the book's details are drawn from fact: the room David and Alabama occupy during their Biltmore honeymoon is the same as the one in which the Fitzgeralds stayed, the incident of the aviator falling from his plane occurred just as Zelda describes it (Scott used the same event in "The Last of the Belles"), and Bonnie's blue ski suit is identical to Scottie's (shown in scrapbook photographs of her in the Swiss Alps with her parents). Rosalind wholeheartedly agreed with this assessment. "The figures in her story whom I knew, are drawn with keen perception, particularly those of our parents. To be with them again I have only to read the book." As the novel traces the development of a woman who marries young and fails to find fulfillment, it also recounts the unsettled growth of an impulsive and free-thinking girl, born and raised in a small southern town. Escaping from her restrictive family by marrying an artist, the girl (Alabama) finds that living a glamorous, whirlwind existence through another's accomplishments offers little fulfillment. As Alabama travels to wherever David's success takes them, she discovers Europe's exciting cities to be as empty and tiresome as America's small towns. Boredom sets in and the couple drifts apart, until a dancing accident and the death of Alabama's father reunites the couple. Because the story so closely matches Zelda's experiences, there are also numerous similarities between the heroine's and Zelda's feelings, as when Alabama professes early in the narrative, "I am so outrageously clever that I believe I could be a whole world to myself if I didn't like living in daddy's better." The opening words of the novel could very well be said (and probably were) of Zelda: " 'Those girls,' people said, 'think they can do anything and get away with it.' " As the youngest child of older parents who neither understand her nor empower her with a sense of self, Alabama "wants to be told what she is like, being too young to know that she is like nothing at all." She has three elder sisters and envies her more sophisticated sister Dixie, who represents the excitement of the outside world and who is involved in an affair with a married man. When their father prohibits the continuation of Dixie's liaison, Alabama's interest turns to her other sister Joan. Though Joan is less worldly than Dixie, she is more practical and better organized. But when Joan rejects her devoted but poor suitor Harlan, in favor of a wealthier beau, Alabama deems that choice a mistake. "I'm not glad," Alabama complains. "Harlan's hair goes up like a Spanish King. I'd rather Joey [Joan] marry *him*." Her father's pragmatic response—"People can't live off the hair of Spanish Kings"— doesn't change her opinion. Alabama flouts convention and though her wild behavior raises eyebrows, she suffers no public disdain. "She's the wildest one of the Beggs' but she's a thoroughbred." With the advent of World War I, a reactivated army post nearby brings young men from around the country, and Alabama's life changes overnight. Suddenly, officers replace local boys on the pages of her date book. David Knight is one of them, his blue eyes and Olympian features typifying the hero of her dreams. Within months they are in love, and by year's end married. Bored with "just sitting on the porch and having dates and watching things rot," Alabama follows David north to the glamorous life she has always imagined for herself. Marriage is the route to security and freedom.

Although she enjoys the luxury of doing exactly as she pleases, Alabama still wants to feel quiet and secure, a dichotomy that leads to her question: "Why am I this way, why am I that? Why do myself and I constantly spat? Which is the reasonable, logical me? Which is the one who must will it to be?" Evidence of this duality occurs during her parents' visit to the Knights' Connecticut home, which matches the actual occurrence in Westport. Attempting to impress them with a well-organized household, Alabama fails miserably when two of David's drunken friends disrupt the proceedings. The scene quickly turns into burlesque after Alabama's face is slammed into the kitchen's swinging door, causing a nosebleed. Unable to condone her lifestyle, her parents leave early, but not before Judge Beggs delivers a forbidding admonition: "People who do not subscribe have no rights."

Determined to put recklessness behind them, the Knights leave for France. Outwardly, they seemed to have changed little: "The girl still looked all day long as if she'd just got up; the man's face was still as full of unexpected lilts and jolts as riding the amusements of the Million-Dollar Pier." Inwardly, however, they are beginning to deteriorate. Alabama's declaration "Oh, we are going to be so happy away from all the things that almost got us but couldn't quite" has an ominous ring.

As in the Fitzgeralds' marriage, the novel's turning point comes when the husband's emotional neglect precipitates his wife's infidelity. Alone much of the time, Alabama grows frustrated with David's disregard of her needs, and begins an affair with a French aviator named Jacques Chevre-Feuille. After putting a quick end to it, in retaliation David spends the night with another woman, and thereafter freely engages in extramarital affairs while continuing to demand total fidelity from his wife. (An exact mirroring of Scott's response after the Jozan affair.) Finding herself excluded in all meaningful ways from David's life, Alabama realizes she will never find contentment until she accomplishes something on her own. When she teases David about wanting to enter his world—"I wish I could live in your pocket"—he responds dismissively: "There'd be a hole you'd forgotten to darn and you'd slip through and be brought home by the village barber." With surprising determination Alabama takes up ballet and masters even the most difficult steps. Initially supportive, David professes to understand her needs. "Poor girl. I understand. It must be awful just waiting around eternally." Her fellow dancers are less sympathetic and eye her with suspicion, uncertain as to why a married woman would voluntarily undergo such difficult training. The climax in the narrative comes when an invitation arrives from an Italian ballet company in Naples. David, in contrast to the way Scott responded, encourages Alabama to seize the opportunity. She joins the company and pursues her goal, leaving her daughter and husband behind in Paris. Though Alabama is more competent than other members of the ballet company and draws favorable reviews from Italian critics, she still does not feel fulfilled. When her daughter, Bonnie, comes to visit, Alabama is too preoccupied to pay her much attention. And on her return to Paris, the child confides to her father: "It is better here than with Mummy's success in Italy."

The novel's denouement occurs shortly after Bonnie's visit, when Alabama's father dies of a heart attack and David sends word to her in Naples. The news reaches her as she is undergoing her own crisis in the hospital, recovering from a serious infection caused by toe-shoe glue seeping into a blister. So badly damaged are her tendons and arteries that she can never dance again. David arrives to comfort her and offers the soothing comment "but it has brought us together again." Alabama's cynical response is "Yes—what's left." With the dream of becoming a great ballerina over, Alabama ponders the impact of destiny on life. "Always, she thought, we will have to seek some perspective on ourselves, some link between ourselves and all the values more permanent than us, of which we have felt the existence, by placing ourselves in our father's setting." Any illusion of the marriage being amicable is shattered when David reprimands Alabama for dumping guests' ashtrays before they have departed: "We would be happier if Alabama refrained from doing things like that." Her response closes this chapter of her life and the novel. "It's very expressive of myself. I just lump everything in a great heap which I have labeled 'the past' and having just emptied this deep reservoir that was once myself, I am ready to continue." Writing *Save Me the Waltz* was a cathartic experience for Zelda because her protagonist, Alabama, emerges as a new breed of female protagonist who establishes her identity by taking responsibility for her life, and who searches for happiness outside the confines of traditional marriage.

Scott had warned Scribner's not to overdo publicity on *Save Me the Waltz* so that Zelda would not assume "delusions of grandeur" (his words). Therefore, the book was printed on cheap paper rather than Scribner's high-quality stock, and had no accompanying publicity or distribution plan. Dedicated to Mildred Squires, and arriving in bookstores on October 7, 1932, it sold only 1,392 copies from a printing of 3,010, earning Zelda a meager $120.73. The figure was this low because Fitzgerald had not arranged for proofreading, as he always did for himself, and much of Zelda's royalty had gone toward corrections in page proofs. Incredibly, the remainder of Zelda's profits was held back to repay Fitzgerald's outstanding debts to Scribner's. Even with last-minute corrections, the *New*

York Times complained, "It is a pity that the publisher could not have had a more accurate proofreading for it is inconceivable that the author should have undertaken to use as much of the French language as appears in this book, if she knew so little of it as this book indicates—almost every single French word (and there are many) as well as many foreign names and a good many plain English words are misspelled." Zelda could speak French but not write it, and she needed someone—other than Scott—to scrutinize the manuscript for errors.

Fitzgerald continued to view the novel as a personal attack that compromised both of them. He had no compunction about sharing those feelings with anyone who would listen. "Turning up in a novel signed by my wife as a somewhat anemic portrait painter with a few ideas lifted from Clive Bell, Léger, etc., puts me in an absurd position and Zelda in a ridiculous position. This mixture of fact and fiction is calculated to ruin us both, or what is left of us, and I can't let it stand. Using the name of a character I invented to put intimate facts in the hands of friends and enemies we have accumulated en route—My God, my books made her a legend and her single intention in this somewhat thin portrait is to make me a non-entity."

Reviews of the book were mixed. Some criticized it for its strained imagery and abstract language, as when Zelda describes her sisters as "incubated in the mystic pungence of Negro mammies," or one of their suitors: "Randolph's hair [was] like nacre cornucopias pouring forth those globes of light that make his face." Clearly, Zelda had been influenced by the French surrealists and post-Cubists and was writing in an expressionistic mode—transcending the limits of physical reality to capture the inexpressible. And the book's poetic imagery and free association of ideas captured several critics' attention. There were good reviews in some of the smaller journals, including one by Gilbert Seldes in *The Dial*. He praised the novel, calling it "a gallery of unforgettable pictures which Mrs. Fitzgerald, out of a series of images and metaphors, distills the actual spirit of the age." The *Philadelphia Public Ledger* thought it extremely clever, "a book constructive in thought, clever in execution, individual, fascinating and brisk." Critic Frank Daniels agreed, saying, "*Save Me the Waltz* is written in lively fashion, sprightly with conversations and adventure among the gay young post-war cynics of America and Europe." However, after a few feature articles and interviews, the novel quickly dropped from sight.

Frustrated at having her work drastically altered by Scott, and deflated over the novel's poor sales, she expressed her disappointment to Maxwell Perkins and wrote Scribner's suggesting they place an advertisement on the dance page of either the *New York Times* or *Herald Tribune*. Nothing happened. The book fell into obscurity, and Zelda was forced to accept the fact that it was a financial failure. Perkins cautioned her not to be overly disappointed about poor sales on a first novel, especially one published in the midst of the depression. He urged her to continue, citing both her talent and her unique style. "You should go on writing because everything you do has an individual quality that comes from yourself, and no one else can duplicate it. And each thing you do, it seems, shows a growing skill in expression."

However, the book's failure was a powerful blow to Zelda's psyche, and Perkins's encouragement did not ease the pain. The progress of her recovery at Phipps was slowed, and by late spring of 1932 she showed only modest improvement. Her letters to Fitzgerald barely camouflage the despair and disappointment she was feeling. "We had a mad-man's ball today. You would imagine that 'les Neuroses' would be capable of projecting themselves into any role convincingly, but no. It was as restrained as a Hollywood reception. We were dressed as George Washington and Independence Hall and the Fall of Ticonderoga. Only I went as a Manet courtesan. The blue ice cream we had at the party was made of old New England blood, furnished to the insane asylum by the pressure of modern life on old American stock like my own."

By May she was finally nearing the stage when she would be allowed to leave Phipps on day trips. With Scottie out of school, and the lease on the Cloverdale house expired, Scott enlisted the aid of Princeton classmate Edgar Allan Poe Jr.—a descendant of the famous writer—to locate a suitable residence for them near the hospital. What Poe found was a rambling, fifteen-room, Victorian country-house, complete with gables, porches, and balconies, on the Bayard Turnbull estate near Towson, Maryland. Called La Paix because of its peaceful setting, the house was situated on twenty acres with a tennis court and small lake for swimming. It had been built in the nineteenth century by Turnbull's father as an expansive summer cottage. After visiting the place, Zelda described it to John Peale Bishop: "We have black-gums over the tennis court and pink dog-wood trees over the pond and the place looks as if it was constructed to hide bits of Italian marble from the public. Scott likes it better than France and I like it fine. We are more alone than ever before while the psychiatres [*sic*] patch up my nervous system." At first, Zelda was allowed only day trips, and spent her time swimming and horseback riding. Edmund Wilson was visiting Scott during one of these days, and commented on how well she looked in her blue sweater and light tan riding breeches.

Meanwhile, Fitzgerald hired a new secretary, Mrs. Isabel Owens, whose job was to type manuscripts and supervise Scottie, and over the years she became an important influence on her. Father and daughter made frequent trips to Phipps hoping to find Zelda improved. "We went to see her often," recalled Scottie. "It was a strain, and so sad because she began to look different—as most people with mental illness do. I suppose you are under such a strain that you begin to show the intense fatigue in your face. Mother was not pretty anymore. Sometimes she would seem very normal, but her mind would drift away into some world of her own and we'd all feel the tension. I felt sorry about it, but I had lots of friends and loved school and Daddy took good care of me. A nice person named Mrs. Owens, his secretary, was sort of a substitute mother—so it wasn't terrible at all. I think I was too self-centered to worry much."

The Turnbull family lived adjacent to La Paix in a new house they had designed for themselves. Fitzgerald established a warm relationship with Mrs. Turnbull, who enjoyed their conversations and found him charming. But he was only tolerated by Bayard Turnbull, a Baltimore architect who disapproved of his drinking habits. The Turnbulls' three children—Eleanor, Frances, and eleven-year-old Andrew—were delighted to find a new playmate in Scottie. Scottie also became good friends with Margaret "Peaches" Finney, who lived nearby. She was the daughter of Fitzgerald's Princeton classmate Eben Finney. When Scottie left the Calvert School after sixth grade, she and Peaches became day students at Bryn Mawr, and whenever things grew tense at home, Scottie went to stay with the Finneys. Writing her Paris playmate Fanny Myers Brennan, Scottie described La Paix: "We are living near Baltimore now, on a big estate of 32 acres. This is a photograph of our house.

Minnie Sayre, Zelda's mother

Judge Anthony Sayre, Zelda's father

Anthony Sayre, Zelda's brother

Marjorie Sayre, Zelda's sister

Clothilde Sayre (called Tilde),
Zelda's sister and the model for
Joan in *Save Me the Waltz*

Zelda in costume for "Folly" in
Les Mystérieuses Ball, 1919

Montgomery's young women
welcoming the 4th Alabama
167th Infantry Regiment back
from France after the end of
World War I. Zelda is the
second girl on the right.

Zelda at the time she met
Scott Fitzgerald in Montgomery

Swimming at
Compo Beach,
Westport, July 1920

Zelda and Scott in the front yard of the Sayre house in Montgomery, March 1921

Zelda relaxing on the grass

Drawings of Zelda
and Scott done by
Gordon Bryant for
Metropolitan Magazine,
June 1922

Cover of *The Smart Set*, June 1922, announcing the
publication of Scott's novelette "The Diamond as Big as the Ritz."
Zelda and Scott were the prototypes for the dancers.

Zelda, in knickers,
on the Fitzgeralds' auto
trip south to Montgomery

The Fitzgeralds on
their auto trip south

Photo from Alex McKaig's naval logbook showing Scott and Zelda with friends,
July 4, 1920, Westport, Connecticut. McKaig is sitting to the right of Scott.

Alex McKaig

John Peale Bishop

Sap Donahoe

Actress Ruth Findlay portraying Dore Baxter in the film version of Owen Johnson's 1914 novel, *The Salamander*

Zelda in front of the White Bear Yacht Club at White Bear Lake, Minnesota, during the summer of 1922. She appears relaxed, except for the tortured position of her hands.

top left: The Pulitzer fountain, in front of the Plaza Hotel at Fifth Avenue and 59th Street, New York City. While Zelda is often reputed to have jumped into this fountain, it was actually Scott who did so.

middle left: The Washington Square fountain. Zelda jumped into the fountain at Washington Square after a party at the Greenwich Village apartment of theater producer John Williams. The fountain's rim is all that remains.

bottom left: The site of the Union Square fountain into which Zelda jumped. That leap was depicted on the overture curtain of the 1922 *Greenwich Village Follies* by Reginald Marsh. Nothing remains of the fountain today.

Zelda holding Scottie, summer 1922

Original cover of *The Beautiful and Damned*, modeled after Zelda and Scott, is shown as it exists in Zelda's scrapbook.

Original cover of *The Great Gatsby*

The Fitzgeralds on the grass with Scottie in Great Neck, Long Island

Zelda, Scott, and Scottie with Scottie's nanny, Lillian Maddock, San Raphael, France, 1924

The Fitzgeralds kicking up their heels in front of the Christmas tree, Paris, December 1925 (Scottie's favorite picture of her family)

Zelda, Scott, and Scottie on the beach in France

The Fitzgeralds with Scottie out for a walk in Paris

The Fitzgeralds, arms linked, in the South of France

Zelda and Scott with Scottie on the
steps of Villa St. Marie, France

The Fitzgerald family aboard ship heading for Europe

Photo from Scott's
French identity card, 1929

Photo from Zelda's
French identity card, 1929

Ballerinas by Zelda Fitzgerald, oil painting, 1941

Harold Ober, Scott and Zelda's literary agent,
April 30, 1944

SAVE ME THE WALTZ

ZELDA FITZGERALD

Dust jacket for *Save Me the Waltz*

Zelda in her ballet costume, 1931

Female Patient by Zelda Fitzgerald, oil on canvas, a fellow patient at Highland Hospital

Magnolia by Zelda Fitzgerald, watercolor

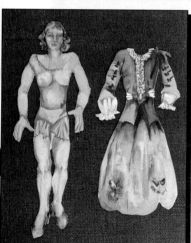

Self-portrait as a paper doll with costume by Zelda Fitzgerald

Zelda, her face showing the effects of the treatments for her illness, wearing the necklace of stars she had made at Ellerslie

Scott and Zelda assessing damage after the fire at La Paix

Candler, North Carolina by Zelda Fitzgerald, gouache on paper, 1947

Deposition by Zelda Fitzgerald, oil painting, 1938

below: Postcard of the F. Scott and Zelda Fitzgerald Museum, Montgomery, Alabama. Zelda and Scott lived in this house at 919 Felder Avenue from October 1931 to April 1932.

top: The author in front of the Alabama Historical Commission plaque commemorating the Fitzgeralds' house in Montgomery as a historic site.

Do-Do in Guatemala, drawing of Scott by Zelda

below: Jack Lanahan and Scottie Fitzgerald (center) at their wedding on February 13, 1943. Harold Ober gave away the bride. His son, Nat (right), then attending Exeter, is shown carrying Scottie's suitcase. Her Vassar roommate (left) was bridesmaid.

right: Scottie at Zelda's retrospective exhibition

The fire at Highland Hospital, March 11, 1948. Zelda's locked room was on the third floor of this building. She died in the blaze

On the same place, but in another house live a boy and a girl. So it is like as if I had a brother and sister (I wish I had). I now go to Calvert School but take French outside with a French lady who lives in Baltimore so as not to forget it. I have a beautiful white Persian cat now, with great big yellow eyes and a tail as long as me."

Fitzgerald established a close relationship with Andrew Turnbull, whom he treated like a son. On a section of lawn encircled by a gravel driveway in front of La Paix, Scott constructed a boxing ring where he and Andrew would spar and toss the football. Scott also took Andrew to Princeton for athletic events. They had long conversations about books, and as an adult, Turnbull would become one of Fitzgerald's biographers. "There was always something of the magician in Fitzgerald," recalled Turnbull. "He was the inventor, the creator, the timeless impresario who brightened our days and made other adult company seem dull and profitless. It wasn't so much any particular skill of his, as a quality of caring, of believing, of pouring his whole soul and imagination into whatever he did with us." He had less interaction with Zelda, remembering her as a wraith of a woman in sleeveless summer dresses and ballet slippers, who kept to herself and talked to no one. On the days she visited La Paix, Andrew would sometimes see her sitting nervously under an oak tree or down "at the deep, cool quarry in the country where we used to swim. She wore a two-piece maroon bathing suit and her short, tawny hair would be water-slicked and her skin very brown, as she sat on the raft smoking and glorying in the sun."

As time drew closer to Zelda's partial release from Phipps, Scott became increasingly apprehensive. Between overseeing Scottie and being responsible for Zelda, he doubted there would be much time to write. On May 17, 1932, he wrote Dr. Austin Fox Riggs at Stockbridge Sanitarium in Stockbridge, Massachusetts, to ask if Zelda could spend part of the summer there. Before he would respond, Riggs informed Scott that he required an evaluation of Zelda's condition from Dr. Meyer. His final decision is not known, but he may have denied Fitzgerald's request since there was no further correspondence between them on the matter.

Early in June, Scott took Zelda on an extended outing to Virginia Beach, where they stayed at the Cavalier Hotel and Zelda swam and tanned on the beach in the warm sun. She was feeling healthy and refreshed when she returned to Phipps to hear the good news—that she could spend mornings at La Paix and return to the clinic in the afternoon for psychiatric appointments. Though therapy sessions could not cure schizophrenia, they provided Zelda important emotional support and helped her deal with its terrifying symptoms. The interior voices still remained, but now she recognized them as signs of distress and sought help before they became overwhelming.

After four and a half months of confinement, Zelda's partial release from Phipps finally took place on June 26, with her medical record reading "condition unimproved." She would remain in the same "unimproved" state for the next year and a half. But on that summer morning, she was elated to be leaving the hospital and going to La Paix. "Do go into my room," she teased Scott, "then it would be nicer when I get back. I've always tried to make you use things first and get into strange beds before me because any place you've been is a good place and anything you've touched is desirable."

Scott still held some hope for her recovery. Since doctors warned she could relapse into madness if she worked at anything too strenuously, he insisted on a strict schedule of work and play. Emphasizing moderation—at least for her—he developed a regimen that alternated exercise and rest. There was time allotted for swimming, tennis, horseback riding, ballet and painting. Zelda's spiral notebook from that year reveals the careful structure of her days. In her handwriting she scheduled: "Six hours study, six hours work, six hours play and six hours sleep." Under "work" she listed, "1 hour dance technique, 1 hour dance, 2 hours design–stage costume, 2 hour music composition"; under "study" she wrote "architecture, chemistry, medicine and literary composition," and under "play," "1 requisite sport—5 hours a week: swimming, tennis, skating."

But keeping Zelda within these limits was not easy, for she often wanted to paint and write into the night. Fearing another breakdown, Fitzgerald implored Dr. Meyer to allow him the option of readmitting Zelda to Phipps if she became unmanageable. Meyer would never agree. Fitzgerald felt the doctor disregarded his suggestions because he considered him an alcoholic and "never believed I worked very hard, had a serious reputation or made money."

To lighten the household mood, tennis became the family recreation. Scott hired a former professional player named Crosley to give everyone lessons and play with Zelda, Scottie, and Andrew. But Zelda would quickly became frustrated and often end sessions by throwing her racket at Crosley. She illustrated such a scene in a watercolor over graphite titled "Le Sport," in which she depicts two tennis rackets flying over the head of a man. On the reverse of the drawing she wrote in French, *"Il Etait un jeune American qui n'avait besoin de rien!"* (He was a young American who didn't need anything.) The watercolor found its way into the collection of Dr. Frederick Wertham, whom Adolf Meyer had called in as a consultant on Zelda's case to examine her art for diagnostic clues.

Because of her vulnerability to Scott's criticism, Zelda's doctors cautioned her about competing with Fitzgerald in his field. Since the novel form required intense concentration, they considered it an unsuitable vehicle of expression for her. In part influenced by Scott, who was paying the bills, they suggested she give up writing fiction. Scott was still furious with Mildred Squires for encouraging Zelda to infringe on what he considered his literary rights, and tried to have another physician put in charge. He did get Dr. Thomas A. C. Rennie assigned, but Zelda insisted on keeping Squires, and for a time both doctors worked on her case.

To familiarize himself with Zelda's history, Rennie asked the Fitzgeralds each to share personal perceptions of their marriage. On October 10, 1932, Zelda wrote seven numbered paragraphs describing her emotional attitude toward herself, Scottie, and her husband. It was a devastating account that showed how void of love the marriage had become for her. "I consider myself driven to a dry shallow shell of myself with no life of my own and reactions infinitely inferior to any that I have ever experienced when normal. My interest in any good literature, music, ideas or social contacts is colored, distorted and debased continually and without exception by ideas so inane, cheap and preposterous that these things are losing all stimulus for me. . . . I am incapacitated for helping her [Scottie] by the constant ill humor in which I find myself in her presence. . . . My relations with my husband are being robbed of all significance or happiness by intrusive and unprovoked irrelative thoughts—all marital relations are strained by the intrusion of ideas so vulgar and offensive and meaningless that they will not bear repeating."

From his viewpoint, Fitzgerald characterized Zelda's illness as resulting from a struggle between their egos. He wrote Dr. Rennie a series of letters linking her recent breakdown to his novel-in-progress. "It is significant that last February her breakdown was associated with my outlining to her a frame for what was then a new approach to my work which was a story of our eight years in Europe. In her subconscious there is a deathly terror that I may make something very fine in the use of this material of 'ours,' that I may preclude her making something very fine. The conflict is bothering her. The nearer I come to completion, that is to artistic satisfaction, and announce it to her—the more restless she becomes, though outwardly rejoicing. The conflict is at the root of it. She feels that my success has got to be, otherwise we all collapse—she feels also that it is a menace to her, '—why should it be him—why shouldn't it be me? I'm as good or better than he is.' " A patently disingenuous assessment. The fact is that Scott hectored Zelda about utilizing their life story in her writing until she broke down. Because of her need for a strong male presence, she was particularly vulnerable. With her father now gone, Scott was all she had left. She did not feel threatened by anything but his disapproval, while he felt threatened not only by his material being preempted but also by how Zelda might make him appear to the public. Regardless of his protestations of love, he balked when she insisted that she had as much right as he did to use her own life in her writing. (Actually, she had more.) For Fitzgerald, it was better that Zelda relapse than poach on his territory. The zeal with which he tried to control *Save Me the Waltz*, and succeeded, was only one evidence of this.

Rennie shared Scott's letters with Dr. Meyer, who acknowledged Fitzgerald's apparent understanding of the case but saw no positive prognosis for Zelda unless Scott relinquished alcohol and participated in the therapeutic process. Meyer also told Rosalind Smith that "he considered Scott as much in need of treatment as she, and had suggested this to him. But Scott scorned the idea. He could not give up alcohol and was afraid that having treatment might get publicized and impact unfavorably on his career." Actually, in December 1932, while drinking heavily and taking Luminal, Fitzgerald did begin treatment with one of Dr. Meyer's colleagues, but he did not continue and later was unwilling to resume.

Rather than write, Fitzgerald told Zelda to focus her creative efforts on painting. But already she was making notes for a second novel called "Caesar's Things," which she planned to begin when she achieved "the tranquillity of spirit necessary to write the story of myself versus myself." Using the highly charged world of ballet and the insane as her backdrop, the novel was to focus on the life of

Vasily Nijinsky, primary male dancer with the Ballets Russes and lover of its director, Sergei Diaghilev. Nijinsky had gone mad and been diagnosed as schizophrenic. Since Fitzgerald was using similar psychological material for his novel *Tender Is the Night*, he was determined to prevent Zelda from tapping that resource. Constantly dissuading her from writing, he encouraged Zelda to prepare oil and watercolor paintings for a New York City exhibition. She was resolved to continue work on her book. Fitzgerald wrote her doctors, "The fundamental struggle continues, shown indirectly by her unwillingness to let me help her with her stories, coupled with a study of my books so profound that she is saturated with them, whole fragments of my scenes and cadences come out in her work which she admits. . . . The fact that her undertaking a long piece of work of a deeply personal order would be a serious menace to her health is apparent to her. And it is an equal menace—this subconscious competing with me." Still, she persisted.

To avoid conflict, Zelda wrote in private moments and painted in her upstairs studio. She also continued to practice her ballet routines in the living room. Andrew Turnbull remembered the Victrola repeatedly playing "Valencia" as she danced, the music carrying across the two yards. One night Malcolm Cowley came for dinner and had a long discussion with Zelda about ballet, later describing the atmosphere of the house: "On the afternoon of my arrival, the brown lodge seemed a cheerful place in which the Fitzgeralds had decided to camp for a week or two before moving into permanent quarters. There was not much furniture downstairs and all of it was shabby; there were no carpets and the only pictures on the walls were two or three framed reproductions out of 'The Dial Portfolio,' which ten years before had introduced modern art to the American middle classes. Still, the house was full of comfortable noises: four or five Negroes laughing in the kitchen, Zelda upstairs talking to her nurse or rustling about her improvised studio as she painted furiously, and little Scottie, home from school, playing with the Turnbull children on the big front porch. . . . Zelda didn't come down for dinner, which was served in style, but afterward Scott took me upstairs to meet her and look at her drawings. They were mostly of ballet dancers and were better than I expected; they had freshness, imagination, rhythm, and a rather grotesque vigor, but they were flawed, exactly as her writing had been, by the lack of proportion and craftsmanship. Zelda herself dismayed me.

'She curled up and went to sleep like a beautiful silky kitten,' Van Wyck Brooks had said of her after a dinner party ten years earlier, but now there was hardly a trace of beauty or silkiness. Her face was emaciated and twitched as she talked. Her mouth, with deep lines above it, fell into unhappy shapes. Her skin in the lamplight looked brown and weatherbeaten, except that on the left cheek there were four parallel red streaks where she had raked it with her fingernails, so that she made me think of a starved Indian in war paint."

She seemed particularly unwell to Cowley that evening. Her mouth continually was twisted in an inappropriate smile of amusement, but camouflaged to suggest she was thinking of something else. Because of her bouts with eczema, she had developed the habit of picking her face, and this had spoiled her complexion. She had also taken to biting her inside lower lip, and distending it for comfort, so her speech had an odd ring to it. The following morning Zelda, who had written Maxwell Perkins that she had taken up horseback riding "as non-committally as possible so as not to annoy the horse," convinced Cowley to go riding and it was the most enjoyable part of his visit. "Zelda, looking vastly younger by daylight, took me for my first horseback ride in twenty years and tried to teach me how to post; then we let the horses walk side by side and chatted amiably."

With Zelda's moods fluctuating daily, Fitzgerald's ability to cope was coming to an end. On April 10, 1933, he wrote Dr. Meyer a ten-point letter of clarification about her condition, in point five again asking permission to return Zelda to Phipps at will. "(1) Is Zelda more worth 'saving' than I am? (2) Zelda is struggling to learn how to write and to paint—while I make myself iller with drink as I try to finish up the work, [my novel] of four years. (3) I began to compromise my own case—by loss of self control and outbreaks of temper. (4) I will probably be carried off eventually by four strong guards shrieking manicly [sic] that after all I was right and she was wrong, while Zelda is followed home by an adoring crowd in an automobile flanked with flowers and offered a vaudeville contract. (5) Since I have to take care of Zelda, will you [Dr. Meyer] give me the authority to ask Zelda when she is persistently refactory [sic] to pack her bag and spend a week under people who can take care of her such as in the clinic? (6) . . . this idea of 'mutual duty' was, from Zelda's youth, the thing most lacking in her personality, much more lacking than in the average spoiled American girl. So that it shocked other women, even gay society women and theatrical women, again and again. (7) Zelda played the baby with me always except when an important thing came up, when she was like a fire-hose in her determination. (8) She cannot work in moderation. Creatively she does not seem able to keep herself around that line. A healthful approach with all that implies and a limited work time never to be exceeded, gives the best results, but seems to be impossible outside of the discipline of a clinic. (9) Possibly she would have been a genius if we had never met. In actuality she is now hurting me and through me hurting all of us. (10) Her 'illusion' is—that her work's success will give her some sort of divine irresponsibility backed by unlimited gold." He further added, "She is working under a greenhouse which is my money and my name and my love. This is my fault—years ago I reproached her for doing nothing and she never got over it. So she is mixed up—she is willing to use the greenhouse to protect her in every way, to nourish every sprout of talent and to exhibit it—and at the same time she feels no responsibility about the greenhouse and feels she can reach up and knock a piece of glass out of the roof at any moment, yet she is shrewd to cringe when I open the door of the greenhouse and tell her to behave or go." While it is true Zelda had not outgrown her need to feel protected by a man, that Fitzgerald largely blames his inability to write on her is a measure of his own desperation. The rest is the fulmination of an alcoholic in denial—a point not lost on Dr. Meyer.

A week later, on April 18, Dr. Meyer responded. He again emphasized the necessity for Fitzgerald to give up alcohol, and specifically rejected Scott's fifth point; he would not allow Fitzgerald, on his own initiative, to return Zelda to Phipps. "Your complaint of the futility of our conversation is as much my own as it is yours. It is a question of both of you and not only one; you also figure as a potential but unwilling patient. Since you refuse a closer understanding between ourselves, as if it would be a psychoanalytic or I don't know what kind of surrender of yourself, I simply should say, I am sorry for the misunderstanding, avoiding any futilities. I wish I could reach a practical plan free of uncertainties. We can get on safer grounds I am sure; but it is difficult without a conjoint surrender of the alcohol."

Again things were deadlocked. Zelda continued to undergo psychotherapy at Phipps, but in May 1933 was very distressed to learn that Mildred Squires was leaving the hospital. Her case was now entirely in the hands of Dr. Thomas Alexander Cumming Rennie. Known as A. C. Rennie, the Scottish born, Nordic-looking bachelor had emigrated to America in 1911 and received his medical degree from Harvard in 1928. Zelda had begun weekly sessions with him in October of 1932, and they had fortunately established good rapport. She confided to Rennie her absolute determination to fight for personal expression. Fitzgerald was adamant that Zelda not continue her novel employing psychological material until he had completed *Tender Is the Night*. But she was ready to start writing about Nijinsky, who, like her, had been diagnosed schizophrenic by Eugen Bleuler, and suffered violent spells, hallucinations, and periodic loss of speech. She intended to infuse the book with knowledge acquired from her own experience in a mental institution.

The argument came down to one of money: Fitzgerald, as financial provider, believed their mutual history belonged to him, claiming he had earned that right by writing stories instead of novels to pay for Zelda's medical bills. His demand for creative control over their lives further alienated Zelda, who felt trapped and powerless. "I wish I had a whole lot of money," she wrote him bitterly. "I would give you every nickel you ever spent on me."

In an attempt to mediate the disagreement, Rennie facilitated a three-way dialogue between the Fitzgeralds and himself in the living room of La Paix on May 28, 1933, at 2:30 P.M. The session, which concerned the issues, conflicts, and grievances of their marriage, was recorded by Isabel Owens on a Dictaphone, and when later transcribed filled 114 pages.

Fitzgerald opened the discussion by describing what he considered the unbearable situation at La Paix. "The evenings are so terrible. Zelda will sit at the table, and stand over by Scottie, and draw her mouth together and make a little noise. She cannot stand it downstairs, and won't take a walk. Nothing for anybody else, nothing. This whole household has got to be for her. She is used to that life in the clinics, where she feels that things are revolving around her."

Zelda then gave her version of life with Scott and the circumstances that had brought them to this point. "He made it impossible for me to communicate with my child by refusing, first, to take any of my judgments or opinions of people who were in charge of her, or anything else, and there was nothing in my life except my work, nothing. I was trying to achieve some kind of orderly life when Scott was being brought in night after night by taxi drivers, at six o'clock in the morning. I just spent sleepless nights until I convinced myself that I did not give a damn and did not care."

Fitzgerald responded that his behavior was a reaction to her mental state. "Zelda—had almost a hundred doctors, I figure, who gave her bromides, morphine . . . I can count six in St. Raphael. . . . I can think of five in New York." When she objected to his arithmetic, Scott reduced the number slightly. "I can think of—well, say fifty. Maybe I have exaggerated, fifty doctors who had to give you morphine injections. Do you remember that?"

Once they got by that point, the discussion centered on what Zelda should, or should not, be allowed to write. Fitzgerald wanted to approve all her ideas and insisted she not write fiction, and if she wrote a play that it not be on a psychological subject, or take place on the Riviera or in Switzerland. He claimed their life as his exclusive literary property and demanded she neither use the novel form nor write about her mental illness until *Tender Is the Night* was completed. Instead, he suggested she go to art school, study commercial design, become a cartoonist, or perhaps write "a series of short observations on things & facts, 'observed things' which she can sell & make money." But Zelda did not consider these valid options, and when Rennie asked what so fueled her ambition, she cited the one crucial issue of her life she had not surmounted. "It is the great humiliation of my life that I cannot support myself. . . . I don't want to be dependent just in every way, that is all. I just don't want to be dependent on him. . . . Here is the truth of the matter, that I have always felt some necessity for us to be on a more equal footing than we are now, because I cannot possibly—I cannot live in a world that is completely dependent on Scott."

At present, however, she was totally dependent on him, and Fitzgerald made that painfully clear. "Why do you think you met Léger? Why do you think you were in the Russian ballet? Why do you think the Johns Hopkins Clinic got us? And why do you think Dr. Forel kept you there? Do you think they did it because you have a pretty face? They did it for commercial reasons. It was part of their advertising and the money that was being paid for it." Accusing Zelda of being reared as a useless society woman, Scott suggested that her ambition for ballet had commenced only after he became interested in Lois Moran, "because the girl seemed to be more honest and direct than Zelda."

After listening to the Fitzgeralds argue all afternoon, Rennie decided that Zelda would have to either abandon her literary ambitions or leave the marriage. It was at this juncture that Zelda suggested divorce. "As far as destroying you is concerned," she told Scott, "I have considered you first in everything I have tried to do in my life. . . . You said I had ruined your life and you did not love me and you were sick of me and wished you could get away. . . . It is impossible to live with you. I would rather be in an insane asylum where you would like to put me. . . . Dr. Rennie, I am perfectly willing to put aside the novel, but I will not have any agreement or agreements, because I will not submit to Scott's neurasthenic condition and be subjected to these tortures all the time. I cannot live in this world, and I would rather live in an insane asylum. . . . I don't want to live with you because I want to live someplace that I can be my own self. I think honestly the only thing is to get a divorce because there is nothing except ill will on your part and suspicion."

Nothing further about this was said, and no immediate steps were taken toward divorce, but Fitzgerald later contacted Edgar Allan Poe Jr., a partner in the Baltimore law firm of Bartlett, Poe and Claggett, to inquire which states permitted divorce on grounds of insanity. In a two-page letter dated June 1, 1933, Poe indicated that sixteen states permitted it under certain conditions. He listed the criteria in great detail. Fitzgerald filed Poe's response among his papers but pursued it no further. However, in his notebook, he outlined a strategy for divorce, calculating a plan of attack if Zelda insisted on continuing with her novel. "Attack on all grounds: Play (suppress), novel (delay), pictures (suppress), character (showers), child (detach), schedule (disorient to cause trouble), no typing. Probable result—new breakdown."

Ultimately, Zelda conceded to putting "Caesar's Things" aside until Fitzgerald completed *Tender Is the Night*. But when she could, she stole away to work on it in secret. "I want to write and I am going to write; I am going to be a writer, but I am not going to do it at Scott's expense if I can possibly avoid it. So I agree not to do anything that he doesn't want, a complete negation of myself, until the book is out of the way, because the thing is driving me crazy the way it is." Despite Rennie's honest efforts to negotiate a compromise, the situation remained unresolved. "So far as my own mood is concerned," Scott told her doctor, "I am absolutely desperate and determined to finish it [my novel] without interference from Zelda sane or insane. . . . The situation has reduced itself in my mind to a rather clear-cut struggle of egos between Zelda and myself. Last night, after a most affectionate day, a day in which at home, at the theatre, in the car she would literally not move an inch from me, nor talk of anything save how she loved me and admired me—a situation which I dread for it almost always proceeds a reaction of some kind—after such a day she suddenly announced in the evening what sounded to me like an ultimatum, a threat to go crazy. She wrote out some notes to Dr. Meyer, which as you will see are all aimed at rather vague persecuting forces and in which I am not named but am suggested."

The conflict remained at an impasse. Scott threatened to destroy any pages of "Caesar's Things" that he found. Zelda realized, after installing a double lock on her study door, that absolute secrecy was impossible. Putting the manuscript aside, and making the best of a bad situation, she redirected her energies toward art. In May of 1933 she participated in the American Art Association's Spring Salon, and exhibited a manneristic oil titled "Ballet Figures" at the Anderson Galleries.

Because she wanted to keep writing, Zelda began working on a play called *Scandalabra*. Her approach to learning dramatic technique was to read every play in the local library. In just a few weeks' time, she produced a complicated farce about a decent farm boy promised millions if he agrees to adopt a life of dissipation. The play was produced by the Vagabond Junior Players, a local university group showcasing talent from college and high school dramatic associations. They had been formed the year before to give Baltimore a summer season of stage productions. Zelda involved herself in every aspect of the production, from painting the curtain to designing the sets and stage screens. Fitzgerald initially saw the play at dress rehearsal. It ran almost five hours, and he immediately realized it needed revising; he rewrote the script in one all-night session. Even so, the play bored audiences and Baltimore critics found the pace too slow and story line disjointed. It was a terrible flop and closed after one week. The failure only reinforced Zelda's fears that she might never succeed at anything.

That the play ever opened was astounding, considering Zelda had set fire to La Paix the week before while burning papers and old clothes in a second-floor fireplace. The roof and upper-floor bedrooms—one that Zelda used for a studio and another in which Scott stored his papers—were most affected. Though all of Fitzgerald's manuscripts escaped unharmed, his war books and photo albums of mutilated soldiers were badly damaged, and a number of Zelda's paintings were destroyed. The headline in the Baltimore paper read: "Art Treasures Destroyed By Fire At Fitzgeralds." A staff photographer caught the scene: Andrew Turnbull, hands in pockets, starring quizzically at the camera and Zelda, seated on a box, sheepishly looking up at Scott. (Was this a repeat of what she had done in Hollywood?) Strewn on the lawn around them are clothes hastily thrown into cartons, the gilt mirror Zelda had brought from Ellerslie, lamps, wicker, and piles of books. A topcoat over his pajamas, Scott eyes the photographer with a tentativeness betraying his fragile state. Though the exact circumstances of the blaze were uncertain, Scott was furious with Zelda for her carelessness. And while the entire structure suffered smoke damage and waterstained walls, Scott begged the Turnbulls to postpone repairs until *Tender Is the Night* was finished. Andrew Turnbull remembered how "the next day, he came up to make his formal apologies for the fire, and to request that repairs on the old house be postponed. With his novel nearly finished, he did not want to be disturbed by the din of workmen." Bayard Turnbull was seething over the incident, but since the damage was contained and covered by insurance, restrained his anger and agreed to wait until Scott's manuscript was completed.

The following month, Zelda had to face a far worse catastrophe when her mother sent news that her brother, Anthony, depressed over the loss of his job, had suffered a nervous breakdown. First, he was sent to a sanitarium in Charleston, South Carolina, for a rest cure; then, after showing little improvement, he was taken to a nerve specialist in Asheville, North Carolina. On August 6, 1933, the Sayres' family physician Dr. Chilton Thorington interceded and took him to another specialist in Mobile, where he was admitted to the hospital. After Zelda spoke to him by phone, Anthony asked to be transferred to Phipps Clinic, but his family resisted, explaining they could not afford it. Fitzgerald wrote Dr. Thorington and inquired about Anthony's diagnosis and condition. Thorington responded on August 11: "Anthony's trouble has been diagnosed as neuro-psychosis—possibly familial, however there are cases of pronounced neurasthenia that defy early recognition, especially among females. His symptoms are of the melancholic type, with obsessions of suicidal and homicidal inclination, however, I do not believe that he would actually do acts of violence, but all patients require constant attendants, until they are pronounced well."

In 1880 the American neurologist George Beard had defined "neurasthenia" as a form of nervous exhaustion related to a variety of complaints associated with depression. Describing it as a functional disease of the nervous system, Beard recommended stimulation as a logical treatment and pioneered early forms of electroshock therapy. But Anthony did not live long enough to undergo such treatment. He leaped to his death from the window of his hospital room. Dr. Thorington had warned of such a possibility. The obituaries in the Mobile and Montgomery papers gave no details, and the Sayres maintained that he died as a result of malaria contracted while working as a civil engineer surveying a swamp near Mobile. They said that Anthony was in a state of fever-induced delirium when he got out of bed for an imaginary football scrimmage and accidentally fell through the open window.

Truth be told, Anthony, who had been as wild as Zelda, was notorious for his behavior at Auburn, from which he never graduated, and for his inability to earn a living. He was always in debt and borrowing money from his mother. Depressed over his job loss and financial problems, he suffered recurrent nightmares and fears that he would murder his mother, confiding to doctors that he would kill himself first. But there may also have been another reason for his strange hospital behavior. Anthony's doctors could have employed Wagner-Jauregg's malarial fever treatments for his neurasthenia in an attempt to eliminate what was then called "toxic poisoning." Anthony, while in unattended delirium, may indeed have accidentally fallen from his hospital window—a liability lawyer's dream case.

Deeply affected by her brother's illness and death, Zelda turned entirely inward. She was now consumed by the belief that her entire family was doomed. That concerned Fitzgerald and while he initially told Mrs. Turnbull, with some sense of vindication, "You see, it's not my fault—it's inherited," he soon abandoned questions of fault. Understanding the impact Anthony's suicide would have on Zelda, he reexamined Anthony's medical history and arrived at a new diagnosis. In a highly perceptive letter, he shared his ideas with Dr. Rex Blankenship: "I have just fully realized that her brother was not a schizophrenic but a manic-depressive, that in fact the hospital in which he died simply characterized his condition as 'depressed,' though he had touches of suicidal and homicidal mania. If at any time it comes naturally to disassociate in my wife's mind her own tendency to schizophrenia from her brother's case, I think it would be invaluable if you could do so. That is to say, there is a new defeatism in her arising from the fact that she believes the whole case to be familial and the whole family doomed. The only actual resemblance between the various sisters and the brother is that they are all unstable." It was Scott at his best.

The following month there was another unexpected death. At the age of forty-eight, Ring Lardner died of a heart attack brought on by alcoholism and tuberculosis—precisely the way Scott would die seven years later. Fitzgerald was deeply saddened and published a tender recollection of his friend and fellow writer in *The New Republic*. "At no time did I feel that I had known him long enough or that anyone knew him; it was not the feeling that there was more stuff in him and that it should come out, it was rather a qualitative difference, it was rather as though, due to some inadequacy in one's self, one had not penetrated to something unsolved, new and unsaid. That is why one wishes that Ring had written down a larger proportion of what was in his mind and heart. It would have saved him longer for us, and that in itself would have been something. But I would like to know what it was, and now I will go on wishing—what did Ring want, how did he want things to be, how did he think things were?"

Like Ring, Fitzgerald counted on alcohol to empower his creative juices and make him relax. But drinking also turned Scott mean, which is why he often compensated for his cruelty with acts of generosity. His live-in secretary Isabel Owens remembered his terrible mood swings and controlling nature. He was "a man who never listened to anyone but constantly told Zelda daily how to live her life." Owens had ample opportunity to observe their household. She remembered Zelda as a sensitive, generous woman who "was just beaten down . . . so polite it hurt . . . Every day I thought that I wanted to leave, but in would walk Scottie and so I'd stay." In the fall of 1933, Owens was there to welcome Scottie back from Camp

Ken-Jockette, seven hours north of Manhattan in South Strafford, Vermont. She returned to school at Bryn Mawr in Baltimore, well aware of her parents' difficulties but determined to ignore the situation by spending as much time as possible with "Peaches" Finney and her family. In November, much to the Turnbulls' surprise, Fitzgerald announced they were leaving La Paix. According to Andrew, "He must have realized that this phase of his life was over, that it was time to go, and giving as his pretext the fact that he wanted Zelda to be near her art school in Baltimore, where she was now studying painting, he moved into town."

It was really financial concerns that compelled Scott to rent the redbrick row house at 1307 Park Avenue on the corner of Lanvale in downtown Baltimore. A narrow, three-story affair with shuttered windows and white marble steps, the house was adjacent to the Fine Arts School. Zelda took painting lessons to improve her oil technique and became friendly with some of the art students. She had already met several of them when she exhibited a still-life in the 4th Annual Society of Independent Artists unjuried show at the Baltimore Museum of Art during the first two weeks of October 1933. The lessons gave her confidence to make the shift from writing to painting. Since she was still considered a minor celebrity, the local paper did a publicity photo of Zelda at the easel with her exhibition submission *Tiger Lilies*. Her artistic endeavors were further encouraged in therapy sessions with Dr. Fredric Wertham, a consulting physician on her case since 1932. Wertham was one of the pioneers in using art therapy for diagnostic purposes. He had come from Europe in 1922 to work with Dr. Meyer at Johns Hopkins, and had developed a mosaic test in which patients manipulated multicolored pieces of wood in a freely chosen design as a means of evaluating ego organization. Expanding this method to evaluate personality disorders, he had Zelda do artistic renderings for her therapy sessions. She painted numerous watercolors for him.

The Fitzgeralds' new residence was only six blocks away from the Menckens' home and the proximity enabled Zelda and Sara to visit frequently. They had renewed their friendship in 1929 when Sara interviewed Zelda at Ellerslie for a piece she was writing on the wives of famous authors. The series was to include Mrs. Ring Lardner and Mrs. James Branch Cabell. The Zelda interview was submitted to W. F. Bigelow, editor of *Good Housekeeping*, and scheduled to be published. But after hearing negative comments about

Zelda, Bigelow decided not to print the interview. Sara and Zelda were closer than Mencken and Fitzgerald. They shared much in common, including their hometown of Montgomery—both had married famous writers and became writers themselves. By 1930, Sara was a well-established freelancer whose chief markets were the women's magazines, and Zelda had great admiration for her. They had a particularly pleasant time whenever Sara's sister Ida came up from the South and they could chatter blissfully about old times.

Fitzgerald was still in awe of Mencken's intelligence, and diffidently read portions of *Tender Is the Night* to the couple on several occasions and noted their criticisms. While the four initially got along, Henry started to have reservations about the relationship when Fitzgerald began stopping by at odd hours with companions he had met on the street. Although the Menckens were sympathetic toward Fitzgerald because of his situation with Zelda, they soon tired of Scott's unannounced calls and eventually stopped answering the door (the same tack Hemingway had taken six years earlier). Mencken finally convinced Scott to see his personal physician, Dr. Benjamin Baker. It was Baker who admitted Scott into Johns Hopkins hospital eight times between 1933 and 1937 to dry out after alcoholic binges and to treat him for recurrences of tuberculosis. Despite these confinements, Fitzgerald could not control his drinking and his behavior became increasingly erratic. The final rift with Mencken occurred in the fall of 1933 after an evening they all spent at the West Chester, Pennsylvania, home of his novelist friend Joseph Hergesheimer. Fitzgerald got very drunk and, in a bid for attention, suddenly arose from the dinner table and dropped his pants. After that, Mencken instructed Sara to have nothing more to do with either of the Fitzgeralds.

To escape the situation at home, Fitzgerald often took the train to New York to visit Helen Hayes and Charlie MacArthur. Hayes recalled how worn out and sad he looked. "Scott stayed with us at our Manhattan flat for a few nights to ease his depression. I can still see his lovely face when he told me that he had sentimentally given Zelda a bouquet which she promptly lifted to her ear. 'Do you hear what they're whispering, Scottie?' she had asked. That was how he knew, once and for all, that it was hopeless."

Zelda's condition remained basically unchanged, and Fitzgerald drank continuously to get through each day. Both Edmund Wilson and Ernest Hemingway witnessed terrible incidents during this time. Wilson recorded one in his journal: "Scott with his head down on the table between us like the dormouse at the Mad Tea Party—lay down on the floor, went to the can and puked—alternately made us hold his hand and asked us whether we liked him and insulted us." Scott apologized afterward, writing Wilson: "I assume full responsibility for all unpleasantness—with Ernest I seem to have reached a state where when we drink together I half bait, half truckle to him." Hemingway had lost patience with Scott and said as much to Malcolm Cowley. "How could he know people except on the surface when he never fucked anybody, nobody told him anything except as an answer to a question, and he was always too drunk late at night to remember what anybody really said."

To make amends for his behavior and in an effort to cheer their holidays, Fitzgerald proposed a trip to Bermuda for Christmas. The weather in Baltimore had been dismal and they had always wanted to visit the island, so, in late December, they left for St. Georges. There, they rode bicycles along the causeway and relaxed on St. Catherine's Beach. Zelda took along a sketch pad and completed twelve drawings. She was always her best at places like this, and on a postcard to her mother, wrote: "We are cooking ourselves and feeling very happy and lethargic. It's so blue and blistered in Bermuda only the mournful cedars make feeble protest that it's real." She later wrote a more detailed description in "Show Mr. and Mrs. F to Number—," published in 1934 under both their names in the May-June issue of *Esquire*. "For years we had wanted to go to Bermuda. We went. The Elbow Beach Hotel was full of honeymooners, who scintillated so persistently in each other's eyes that we cynically moved. The Hotel St. George was nice. Bougainvillea cascaded down the tree trunks and long stairs passed by deep mysteries taking place behind native windows. Cats slept along the balustrade and lovely children grew. We rode bicycles along the windswept causeways and stared in a dreamy daze at such phenomena as roosters scratching amidst the sweet alyssum. We drank sherry on a veranda above the bony backs of horses tethered in the public square. We had traveled a lot, we thought. Maybe this would be the last trip for a long while. We thought Bermuda was a nice place to be the last one of so many years of traveling." As it turned out, it was one of their last trips together, and cut short when the rain persisted and Scott caught a cold that turned into pleurisy and forced them back early.

They returned to an even more modest address in Baltimore—the Cambridge Arms apartment hotel, whose windows overlooked Johns Hopkins University. Almost immediately, *Scribner's Magazine* began serializing *Tender Is the Night* in four installments. It had taken almost eight years to write, and would be Fitzgerald's last completed novel. His friends were thrilled to see it and wired and wrote congratulations. John Peale Bishop's letter was bursting with admiration: "The first installment of the novel confirms what I have long thought, that your gifts as a novelist surpass those of any of us. It is so skillful, so subtle, so right that I have only praise for it."

The knowledge Fitzgerald had acquired about psychiatric illnesses, treatments, and interactions between psychiatrists and patients so informed the characterization of his primary female character, Nicole, that the *Journal of Nervous and Mental Diseases* called the novel "an achievement which no student of the psychobiological sources of human behavior, and of its particular social correlates extant today, can afford not to read."

When Zelda saw it, she relapsed. She had not seen any part of the manuscript and was shocked at how extensively Scott had exploited her psychological trauma and medical history as a catalyst for the story and in his portrayal of the female protagonist. Particularly dismaying to her was the inclusion of entire sections of the letters she had written to Scott during the first weeks of her hospitalization at Prangins. He had used her letters before in novels, but this time he usurped material she considered highly private.

Seeing personal details of her illness in print distressed her so greatly that weekly sessions at Phipps could not keep her stabilized. At the time, she was still mourning Anthony's death as well as struggling with her own alternating states of hysteria and apathy. In early February of 1934 she suffered a breakdown in Baltimore at the Cambridge Arms apartment. And on February 12, two years after her initial entry, she was readmitted to Phipps Clinic and again placed under the care of Drs. Rennie and Meyer.

To Rennie she openly expressed her anger and frustration over Scott's characterization of her in the novel. "What made me so mad was that he made the girl so awful and kept reiterating how she had ruined his life and I couldn't help identifying myself with her because she had so many of my experiences." After being compelled to stop writing her own novel about the experience of madness, seeing herself portrayed in hostile terms by Scott pushed her to the brink of suicide. She was sedated and kept under constant observation, but after three and a half weeks would still not respond to questions and showed no improvement. Requesting she be transferred elsewhere, Zelda wrote Dr. Meyer: "Would you be kind enough to recommend to me another hospital of this clinical standing where I could be just as comfortable for approximately the same amount of money. My reason for wanting to change is that I feel an environment in which I have not suffered so much unhappiness would be beneficial."

Fitzgerald recalled that Dr. Forel had previously suggested Craig House in Beacon, New York, a luxurious clinic on a large estate resembling Prangins. Forel's friend Dr. Clarence Jonathan Slocum, born in Rhode Island in 1873 and trained at Albany, was physician in charge and Dr. Charles M. Gilmore the medical director. He had previously written Dr. Slocum on May 16, 1932: "When the first signs of a relapse appeared last winter I wrote Dr. Forel for advice. He replied sending your name and strongly recommending you. But by the time his letter reached me my wife had already entered Hopkins. If you have accommodations for such a patient for a month or two I should be so much obliged if you would write me telling me of your sanitarium, location, plant, prices etc." The sanitarium at Beacon offered treatments of hydrotherapy, physiotherapy, and massage and utilized the cottage system in which patients lived with their own nurse and doors remained unlocked. Zelda was taken there on March 8, 1934. Dr. Slocum initially seemed perplexed by her symptoms, noting in his admissions report that she suffered from "fatigue," and was "mildly confused and mentally retarded with a degree of emotional instability." Zelda was insane, but mentally retarded she was not.

Founded in 1915, Craig House was one of the most expensive private sanitariums in the United States and possessed all the amenities of a country club. Located two hours north of New York City on the Hudson River above West Point, it occupied 350 acres and offered a private nurse and cottage for each patient. There were indoor and outdoor swimming pools—a fact that at one time would have appealed to Zelda, but was of little interest to her now—a golf course, tennis courts, and varied activities including bowling, backgammon, bridge, and Ping-Pong. The sanitarium's main emphasis was on occupational therapy and recreational activities, so with certain limitations, patients could do as they pleased. At first, Zelda appreciated the atmosphere. "It's so pretty here. The ground is shivering with snow-drops and gentians," she wrote Scott. "The curtains are like those in John Bishop's poem to Elsperth and beyond the lawn never ends. Of course, you can walk to where the young men in bear-cat roadsters are speeding to whatever Ginevra Mitchell's dominate the day—but mostly we walk the other way where tumbling villages prop themselves on the beams of the afternoon sun." Viewing Craig House as a refuge from a world of disappointment, she bided her time and waited for the publication of *Tender Is the Night* in book form so she could resume working on "Caesar's Things."

The sanitarium's schedule encouraged relaxation and rest, and was reminiscent of a summer camp more than of a hospital.

7:30 A.M.	rise, bath
8:00 A.M.	breakfast
9:00–10:00 A.M.	writing
10:30 A.M.–1:00 P.M.	craft
1:00–1:30 P.M.	lunch
1:30–5:30 P.M.	outdoor activities
5:30–6:00 P.M.	preparation for dinner
6:00–6:30 P.M.	dinner
6:30–7:00 P.M.	rest
7:00–9:30 P.M.	reading, bridge
9:30–10:00 P.M.	to room and bed

On March 19, Slocum wrote Fitzgerald that Zelda seemed extremely fatigued, and they recommended a rest cure. "It has been our observation that she tires easily and the matter of fatigue must be watched and cared for. I talked with her yesterday about the possibility of her having a week's rest in bed, getting up between three and four for outdoor exercise and going back to bed." A week later, the director wrote again. "We try to have her rest as much as possible; in this direction we insisted that she have her breakfast served in bed and have her relax following it. She has massage at 11:00 o'clock, and in this way, she rests for a half hour after. She thinks this is not the way to make good, because she wants to be as active as possible in her work. However, I assured her that she requires this amount of rest and she looks much better."

Understanding Zelda's high energy level and need for physical activity, Fitzgerald questioned Slocum's approach and requested a more precise diagnosis. But Slocum was hesitant to respond, telling Scott: "I would not like to make even a tentative diagnosis at this time. . . . I think that therapy would be wrong at this particular time . . . many of her thoughts and feelings are simply a matter of fatigue." Scott had doubts about the approach, and was not surprised when Slocum informed him: "She [Zelda] wished to give up the massage which had been given to her at eleven in the morning and her thought in the matter was that the massage was so relaxing that she was not of much use for the rest of the day. Therefore, we have changed her hour of massage to the hour preceding her bedtime."

In an effort to make the best of her situation, Zelda learned to knit, sarcastically writing Scott about her new skill: "I am knitting myself some wearing apparel and am indeed becoming such an accomplished knitter that I can easily include old chair bottoms, coca-cola straws and even twigs and grasses in my pattern. I feel rather like Betsy Ross." As weeks passed, however, she became increasingly concerned about how much the treatment was costing. "Roaming nostalgically among the clinic's grounds, I wish I were well," she wrote him, "and that you could get something more out of life for all you put into it than bills and more bills." It occurred to her that she might sell some of the art she was making in her occupational therapy. She asked Scott to have Mrs. Owens send her a $2 pointed camel's hair brush from Webers, a pound can of Weber's permalba, and two unfinished canvases she had started at Phipps.

Diligently working to amass a body of artwork for exhibition, she created oils, watercolors, and pastels, employing bright hues in a maelstrom of organic form. In Paris she had been influenced by the Ballets Russes set designers. Now she incorporated elements of Mikhail Larionov's neoprimitivism into her work, using a Cubist perspective to heighten energy. Recalling Diaghilev's theory that successful art shocked the emotions, she exaggerated forms to achieve dramatic characterization, and experimented with line, color, and composition, fracturing pictorial space so that objects were seen from varying viewpoints and planes. Since she still had unresolved feelings about failing to become a ballerina, dancers were a favorite subject. They were depicted with swollen joints and deformed legs in torturous training, bodies so distorted they lacked gender. When questioned as to why she painted them in such tormented poses, she echoed Léon Bakst's response of two decades earlier: "That's how a ballet dancer feels after dancing. I painted them that way to express the pure quality of what it was they were dancing. It wasn't the dancers but the step itself that I wanted to paint." Tirelessly, she worked at getting the essence of dancers' movements into her art so that others might experience it.

Late that March, Fitzgerald arranged for Cary Ross, a Yale graduate and young poet they had met in Europe, to mount an exhibition of Zelda's work. For some time, Ross had been trying to interest New York dealers in Zelda's art, and had even contacted Alfred Stieglitz and Georgia O'Keeffe. Receiving only negative responses, he put together a private showing of thirteen paintings and fifteen drawings in his Manhattan studio at 525 East 86th Street. Some additional pieces were exhibited in the Algonquin Hotel lobby. Both of these exhibitions were psychologically critical for Zelda, who yearned for one success, hoping it would propel her out of illness. Scott also believed that artistic recognition might prove recuperative as well as steer her away from writing. He was determined to have the showings go smoothly. But when he took control of the show, Zelda, remembering how Scott had manipulated the publication of *Save Me the Waltz*, got angry and, after arguing over some details, refused to deal with any of the preparations.

James Thurber ran into Fitzgerald at a Manhattan bar before the opening, and remembered his agitated frenzy. "Zelda was having a show of her paintings in New York. Scott was going on forty then, and my first glimpse of him was when he stepped up to the bar in Tony's famous kitchen on Fifty-second street and ordered a drink. He had in his pockets that night at Tony's at least three dozen of the catalogs of Zelda's show, whose most arresting canvas, I found out later, was a sharp, warm, ironic study of her husband's handsome and sensitive profile, which she called 'Scott in Thorns.' By midnight, I must have had a dozen of these in my pockets because he kept handing them to me." Apparently, Fitzgerald gave them to everyone he met because the next day Thurber ran into a girl who also had a pile. "I have about ten catalogs of his wife's show," she said. "He kept handing them to me all the time."

The exhibition, which ran from March 29 through April 30, was accompanied by a checklist that Zelda had designed. It bore the image of a swan and the words *"Parfois la Folie est la Sagesse"*—"Sometimes madness is wisdom." Scott wanted the title changed, but Ross assured him that the general public would not know that Zelda's work had been completed in a sanitarium, and that her choice of words would be interpreted as symbolic.

Accompanied by a Craig House nurse, she came down to Manhattan for the opening and stayed with Scott at the Algonquin. While in New York, she made a point of seeing the Georgia O'Keeffe show at An American Place. She felt a strong kinship with the artist in style and subject matter, recognizing in O'Keeffe's flower paintings an echo of her own work, particularly those in which organic flower forms were magnified from various angles. O'Keeffe's exhibition viscerally stirred her emotions and she wrote Dr. Rennie about her impressions: "They are so lonely and magnificent and heart-breaking, and they inspire a desire to communicate which is perhaps the highest function of anything creative." She also sent a letter to the *New York Post*: "I went to see the O'Keeffes. They are magnificent and excited me so that I felt quite sick afterwards. I loved the rhythmic white trees winding in visceral choreography about the deeper green ones, and I loved the voluptuous columnar tree trunk with a very pathetic blue flame-shaped flower growing arbitrary beneath it. And there was a swell rhythmic abstraction done in blue and green and heart-breaking aspiration in the little room. It was a grand show. To me she is the most moving and comprehensible painter I've ever seen. Diaghilev had a theory that the purpose of successful art was to shock the emotions. A person certainly could not walk about that exhibition and maintain any dormant feelings."

Maxwell Perkins held a celebration luncheon in Zelda's honor, and several of Scott's friends came to see the exhibition. John Biggs drove up from Wilmington, and Ernest Hemingway, who was in New York, briefly dropped by. Ring Lardner Jr. came up from Princeton, where he was a sophomore, to join his mother, Ellis, for opening night. If Zelda was nervous, she did not show it and greeted everyone warmly. A number of drawings were bought by friends including Richard Myers, Murial Draper, and Robert Lovett. Only the Murphys and Gilbert Seldes bought oils. The Murphys paid $200 for a painting of a gnarled mass of performers called *Chinese Theater Acrobats*, and Gilbert Seldes bought two oils and a

drawing called *Swimmer on a Ladder*. Other drawings were purchased by Adele Lovett, who took *Ferns*; Maxwell Perkins, who
chose *The Plaid Shirt* and *Spring in the Country*; and Tommy Hitch-
cock, who selected *Au Claire de la Lune*. Tom Daniels, who had
hand-carried the manuscript of *This Side of Paradise* from St. Paul to
New York and then lost it, purchased *La Nature*. Zelda's two most
accomplished works—a portrait of Lubov Egorova and one of Scott
entitled *Portrait in Thorns*—were not for sale, but drew enthusiastic
interest and several offers. Mabel Dodge Luhan wrote from New
Mexico to bid on Fitzgerald's portrait, and when her offer was
turned down she purchased a drawing called *Red Death*. John Biggs
vividly recalled Scott's portrait. "Yes, it was good. The eyelashes
were feathers; it was astounding really—looked like him, and then
those mad, lovely, long feathery eyelashes. Portrayed wearing a
piercing crown of thorns which dug into his forehead, Zelda had
caught perfectly the cold blue, almost green color of his eyes as cold
as the Irish Sea someone said. . . ."

After Zelda returned to Craig House with her nurse, Scott
stayed at the Algonquin until the April 12 publication of *Tender Is
the Night*. Zelda was barely out the door before Fitzgerald entered
into a brief, casual affair with Dorothy Parker. The Algonquin was
Parker's favorite haunt, where she was a regular at its Round Table
luncheons. Idolized for her biting wit, Parker was also an alcoholic
and prone to depression. She and Scott had first met in 1926 at the
Murphys in Juan-les-Pins, and she admired his talent and felt com-
passion for him.When he suggested she see Zelda's exhibition, she
gladly went. Before the exhibition closed, she bought a portrait of
Scott entitled *The Cornet Player* and *Etude Arabesque*, depicting a
dancer who resembled Zelda working out at the barre. It wasn't until years later that she admitted she had never displayed them. "I
couldn't have stood having them hang in the house. There was that
blood red color she used and the painful, miserable quality of emotion behind the paintings."

As for the press's reaction to Zelda's work, both *The New Yorker*
and *New York Post* ran complimentary articles, although they devoted more space to discussing Zelda as an icon of the Jazz Age
than a serious artist. Only *Time* seriously discussed her art, calling it
"The work of a brilliant introvert . . . vividly painted, intensely
rhythmic. A pinkish reminiscence of her ballet days showed figures

with enlarged legs and feet—a trick she may have learned from Picasso." Unfortunately, the magazine also ran a particularly unflattering photo of Zelda in an unattractive housedress. Dr. Slocum wrote Scott inquiring how the opening had gone, and Scott promptly answered on April 2. "The exhibition, as she may have told you, was a weird affair of sizable and enthusiastic clusters of people, and of long blanks where Zelda and the curator sat alone in the studio waiting for someone to appear. Whether or not this is the normal condition of art exhibitions I am not familiar enough to know. Nor is she—and I can't guess at her reaction, except she seemed sunk. Unfortunately her backer himself has been a mental patient and seems to react to reverses in a melancholy way instead of being stimulated by them." Fitzgerald obviously had forgotten his own disappointment over the poor sales of *The Great Gatsby* and subsequent retreat into alcoholism.

Overall, critics considered Zelda an inspired amateur, and did not take her exhibition seriously. But despite that judgment, with which he probably agreed, Fitzgerald wrote Zelda at Craig House on April 26, assuring her that the show was well received and the future rich with possibilities. "Your pictures have been a success, your health has been very much better, according to the doctors— and the only sadness is the living without you, without hearing the notes of your voice with its particular intimacies of inflection. You and I have been happy; we haven't been happy just once, we've been happy a thousand times. The chances that the spring, that's for everyone, like in the popular songs, may belong to us too—the chances are pretty bright at this time because as usual, I can carry most of contemporary literary opinion, liquidated, in the hollow of my hand—and when I do, I see the swan floating on it and—I find it to be you and you only." Alluding to the image on Zelda's exhibition checklist, he implored: "But, Swan, float lightly because you are a swan, because by the exquisite curve of your neck the gods gave you some special flavor, and even though you fractured it running against some man-made bridge, it healed and you sailed onward. Forget the past—what you can of it, and turn about and swim back home to me, to your haven forever and ever—even though it may seem like a dark cave at times and lit with torches of fury; it is the best refuge for you—turn gently in the waters through which you move and sail back."

It is one of the most poignant love letters Scott ever wrote Zelda. But what prompted his declaration of love and devotion? Maybe it was a sense of relief at seeing her exhibition take place, or the fact that *Tender Is the Night* was finally in bookstores. Perhaps he recognized, consciously or unconsciously, the need to win Zelda back as his muse. Or he may have wished to establish himself again as protector—her safe harbor, the one who knew best, since once more he was about to control her writing efforts.

Zelda saw the publication of Fitzgerald's novel as a green light to renew work on "Caesar's Things." She was eager to return home and begin, reminding Scott of their agreement. Fitzgerald evaded the issue until Zelda forced the subject. "Aristotle: he said that all emotions and all experience were common property—that the transposition of these into form was individual and art . . . it seems to me the artist's business is to take a willing mind and guide it to hope or despair, contributing not his interpretations, but a glimpse of his honestly earned scars of battle and his rewards. . . . About my book: you and the doctors agreed that I might work on it. If you now prefer that I put it aside for the present I wish you would be clear about saying so. The short story is a form demanding too concentrated an effort for me at present. . . . Please say what you want done, as I really do not know."

Fitzgerald did not respond to her, but cautioned the doctors at Craig House to prevent Zelda from undertaking such an ambitious project. Characterizing her writing as amateurish and unprofessional, he compared it to the work of an inexperienced lumberman. "She will never be able to build a house," he wrote them. "She hops herself up on crazy arrogance at intervals and wanders around in the woods chopping down everything that looks like a tree (vide: sixteen or twenty short stories in the last year—all of them about as interesting as the average high-school product and yet all of them 'talented'). When she comes near to making a clearing, it looks too much to her like all the other clearings she's ever seen, so she fills it up with rubbish and debris and is ashamed to even speak of it afterwards. She can write in the sense that all non-professionals who have a gift for words can write. Somebody once said that every intelligent American thought that they could always sell a plot of land, make a good speech and write a play. Her equipment is better than that, but it does boil down to the slang phrase that she can't take it. She can't stand criticism; she hasn't the patience to revise; she has no conception of how fast the world slips from under ones feet." Fitzgerald's directive worked. The doctors acquiesced and once again Zelda was restricted from working on her novel.

Once it was evident she would not be allowed to resume writing "Caesar's Things," Zelda filled with a peculiar energy. She began experiencing hallucinations in which she was tormented by menacing voices. As she covered her ears to resist the commands of this inner cacophony, a veil dropped between herself and the world. She responded neither to her doctors nor to her surroundings, and the private sanitarium seemed a pointless extravagance. She did not want to remain where Scott paid the bills. "I cannot see why I should sit in luxury," she told Scott, "when you are having such a struggle. Since there seems to be no way in which I can hasten my recovery, maybe it would be wise to try a cheaper place. I promise you I will not be discouraged by any such change you might make, and of course will do the best I can, anywhere. . . . All the beauty of this place must cost an awful lot of money and maybe it would be advisable to go somewhere more compatible with our present means. . . . I am not headstrong and do not like existing entirely at other people's expense, and being a constant care to others any better than you like my being in such a situation." When he ignored her plea, she became insistent. "You must realize that to one as ill as I am, one place is not very different from another and that I would appreciate you making whatever adjustments would render your life less difficult." She suggested a transfer to a state hospital, and told Scott early in May: "I do not feel as you do about state institutions. Dr. Meyers, and I suppose, many excellent doctors did their early training there." Then, with a surprising reference to the writer who had been Zelda's nemesis, she admonished, "in the words of Ernest Hemingway, *save yourself*. That is what I want you to do. You have had a terrible financial struggle lately and if there were any way that I could relieve you of any part of the burden, you know how gladly I would contribute my cooperation which seems like all I have to offer." Was this a form of ironic capitulation, or a self-martyrdom that would give her life a meaning she did not otherwise see in it?

Fitzgerald was aware of the abhorrent conditions at state mental hospitals; he had read contemporary exposes that described them as so overcrowded that patients often slept in basements and hallways; the most severely ill inhabiting dark, padded cells where they were restrained at night in straitjackets. Many were oppressive places filled with chronic schizophrenics who were warehoused more often than treated. Long hours and low salaries often discouraged well-trained professionals from working at state institutions, and there was high turnover among support staff. The hospital director rarely met patients, and the assistant director and staff physicians saw them only briefly. Generally, it was the least educated, poorest paid attendants who interacted with patients—making sure they followed the rules, ate and observed personal hygiene. While these realities kept Fitzgerald from seriously considering a state facility, he researched less expensive private sanitariums by reading the *Directory for Private Institutions* published by the Neuropsychiatric Institute of the Hartford Retreat and discussed options with Zelda's doctors.

Meanwhile, Dr. Slocum was communicating with Mrs. Sayre about Zelda's lack of improvement at Craig House, summarizing her symptoms in a May 7, 1934, letter. "During the period of her residence here, your daughter has shown periods of depression, a certain amount of restlessness, psychomotor activity, and at times there have been slight manifestations of a schizoid nature." Days later, these abnormalities became more severe when Zelda grew listless and began hearing more voices. She told doctors it was Fitzgerald's voice she now heard coming out of the walls and drain pipes. Moving in and out of hysteria, she fell into a semicatatonic state. When she was finally stabilized, it was decided she be transferred to the Sheppard Pratt Hospital in Baltimore, Maryland. On Friday, May 18, she left Beacon, New York, by train with a nurse and when they arrived by noon at Manhattan's Grand Central Station, Fitzgerald met them at the information desk. From there Scott and Zelda continued on alone to Sheppard Pratt, whose grounds ironically bordered La Paix. Acknowledging that Zelda's nine weeks at Craig House had been largely unproductive, Dr. Slocum wrote Fitzgerald the following day: "I hope Mrs. Fitzgerald reached Baltimore safely and comfortably and that Chapman will be able to influence her in the right direction with reference to her progress and career. This, I very much regret to say, our group was quite unable to do." He also wrote Mrs. Sayre on June 4, reassuring her about the move, and underplaying the seriousness of

Zelda's mental state: "I think that the transfer was made largely on account of the economic situation, and does not mean in any way that her condition was worse."

It may have been Dr. Adolf Meyer who encouraged Fitzgerald to bring Zelda to Sheppard Pratt, since he lectured there and three of Pratt's doctors spent one day each week working in Phipps's outpatient clinic. One of America's oldest mental hospitals, Sheppard Pratt originally had two wings, one for women and another for men, each initially housing seventy-five patients. By the time Zelda arrived in 1934, that figure had climbed to over five hundred. Though private, it was much less expensive than Craig House; in 1931, 6 percent of its patients were hospitalized free, and in 1932, 198 of its 271 patients paid less than cost. The largest number of patients paying the full fee, then averaging $38 per week, like Zelda, came from the South, where there were few private mental institutions. Founded as Sheppard Asylum in 1853 by the Quaker merchant Moses Sheppard, the hospital had been open only five years when Enoch Pratt, a wealthy railroad and steamship owner, made it the chief beneficiary in his will. The name then changed from Sheppard Asylum to the Sheppard and Enoch Pratt Hospital. In 1896, several new buildings were added to its western division, including a hydrotherapy unit with a pool, steam cabinets, showers, and continuous tubs. Specially trained nurses were hired to operate this equipment.

Had Zelda been well enough to observe her surroundings, she might have appreciated them. The hospital was designed in high Victorian style and its extensive property, including numerous walkways, drives, and a pergola, had the appearance of a beautiful park. A landscape architect was employed to oversee the grounds and patients assisted with gardening tasks. Each patient's daily schedule included time to enjoy the outdoors; on the north lawn there was even a putting green. Sheppard Pratt also promoted occupational therapy, believing that hard work helped patients attain better mental health, and it conducted daily classes in handicrafts. There was also a program of light gymnastics, team sports, tennis, folk dancing, concerts, and dramatic performances in which patients acted, often in their own productions. Assistant physicians regularly visited the wards in the morning and at night—more often if necessary—to keep track of each patient's mental state, cleanliness, and diet, then reported back to supervisors. A typical

day, encouraging rest and relaxation, began at 7 A.M. and followed a
strict schedule.

7:00 A.M.	clinical observation by hall nurse
7:00–7:30 A.M.	bath
7:30–8:00 A.M.	dressing
8:00–8:30 A.M.	breakfast
8:30–10:00 A.M.	reading, letter writing
10:00–10:45 A.M.	calisthenics, volleyball, games
10:45 A.M.–12:00 P.M.	handicrafts
12:00–1:00 P.M.	any diversion, conversation with patients
1:00–1:30 P.M.	lunch
2:00 P.M.	bath
2:30–3:30 P.M.	tonic baths
3:30–4:30 P.M.	rest
4:30–5:00 P.M.	outdoor time on lawn (including gardening)
4:00–6:00 P.M.	rest, conversation, puzzles, cards, games
6:00–6:30 P.M.	supper
6:30 P.M.	clinical observation
6:45–7:45 P.M.	on the lawn
7:45–8:00 P.M.	on the ward

What made the hospital desirable in Zelda's case was that
Dr. Ross McClure Chapman, who directed Sheppard Pratt from
1920 to 1948, was particularly interested in schizophrenia. Considering it a negative response to anxiety, evolving from difficulties in
adaptation and stress, Chapman believed there was usually a difficult situation to which the schizophrenic could not adjust or some
continuous emotional pressure. These were certainly the circumstances in Zelda's case. While employing different treatments for
various cases, Chapman generally prescribed a well-ordered daily
regimen, including a balanced diet and plenty of sleep. Patients
drank whole milk from dairy cows that grazed on the hospital
grounds and ate eggs laid in the hospital's henhouses. Unlike other
mental hospitals, Pratt utilized restraints only when absolutely necessary. And while seclusion rooms, straitjackets, and wet-sheet packs
were still used, new drug therapies, appearing yearly, were also
administered. In the drug inventory of the day, morphine and its
derivatives were regarded as useful sedatives. Stramonium was prescribed in cases of mania, and digitalis or conium for depression.

The first synthetic sedative, chloral hydrate, and the newly discovered barbiturate sodium amytal, as well as other tranquilizers, were also commonly employed. At various times, Zelda had them all prescribed. Doctors also performed lumbar punctures on some schizophrenics, injecting various substances—one of the most effective being the blood of epileptics in seizure.

During Zelda's confinement from May 19, 1934, through April 7, 1936, Sheppard Pratt was also experimenting with insulin shock therapy and Metrazol as a convulsive treatment for schizophrenics. Dr. Oscar Schwoerer had been hired to supervise the process. He had trained at the University of Vienna with Manfred Joshua Sakel, who had utilized insulin coma therapy for the more serious, schizophrenic twilight states, believing the brain's defective cell connections could be separated during hypoglycemic coma and its malfunctioning ganglion cells destroyed. Incredibly, Sakel had claimed improvement in 88 percent of his patients. Between 1934 and 1935 he published thirteen reports on the therapeutic benefit of provoking epileptic seizures with insulin and cardiazol/Metrazol. Ironically, one of his most prominent patients was the dancer Nijinsky, who improved slightly after undergoing Sakel's therapy, and Zelda may have known of the treatments because of her interest in the dancer's life.

The use of cardiazol/Metrazol for shock therapy initially had been used in 1933 by the Hungarian physician Joseph Ladislas von Meduna, who discovered an antagonism between epilepsy and mental illness and took the next logical step—using induced epileptic convulsions as a treatment for schizophrenia. Twice a week at Sheppard Pratt, certain schizophrenic patients, and Zelda may have been in this group, were injected with a 10 percent aqueous solution of Metrazol (cardiazol in Europe) that caused convulsions. Following the injection, they experienced an explosiveness in their heads and were given an intravenous injection of sodium Pentothal to counteract frightening sensory auras. Within seconds, their mouths opened wide and seizures followed for thirty to sixty seconds, causing severe muscular contractions. These were often violent. Patients had to be held down to defray fractures of the jaw, spine, or hipbone. For many patients, shock therapy produced positive results, but some doctors hesitated using it because they were uncertain why it worked. It was never, for example, used to treat young people during their first attack, or if the prognosis indicated that symptoms would be of short duration. Most commonly, it was reserved for schizophrenics with a long history of the disorder or in a hysterical or catatonic state. It was used at Sheppard Pratt until 1940, when newly produced, electroconvulsive equipment was purchased, making the treatment easier to administer and producing fewer unpleasant side effects.

Like hundreds of other mentally ill female patients in the hospital's towered red brick building, Zelda was confined to an austere ward under the supervision of twenty-nine-year-old Dr. William Worcester Elgin, chief of the hospital's Women's Service from 1934 to 1946. Elgin had graduated from Washington and Lee University and received his medical degree from Johns Hopkins. Described by Sheppard Pratt's director, Chapman was "an excellent physician and able psychiatrist with a pleasing personality," though he did not impress Zelda that way. She took an instant dislike to him. In turn, Elgin found her expressionless and inaccessible. She avoided contact with him and other doctors, ignored other patients, and vacillated between violent outbursts and seclusiveness. Until she exhibited some improvement, Elgin forbade visits from Fitzgerald or anyone else. To survive, Zelda riveted her attention on the scriptures, reading the Bible for hours. "It's my only strength—my only strength," she wrote Sara Mayfield. "And I have to pray to live." Her hallucinations returned, but now Scott's voice cried out the message that her spirit had died. Feeling abandoned and without hope, she made the incredibly courageous determination to leave the marriage, and wrote Scott a highly coherent letter for one so out of her mind: "I have done nothing but turn over cause and effect in my mind for some time. Also your presentation of the situation is poetic, even if it has no bearing on the truth; your working to preserve the family and my getting away from it. . . . I envy you the mental processes which can so distort conditions into a rectitude of attitude for you. You have always told me that I had no right to complain as long as I was materially cared for, so take whatever comfort you may find in whatever self-justification you can construct. . . . I am here, and since I have no choice, I will try to muster the grace to rest peacefully as I should, but our divergence is too great as you must realize for us ever to be anything except a hash together and since we have neither found help or satisfaction in each other the best thing is to seek it separately. You might as well start whatever you start for a divorce immediately."

Again, he did not take her up on the suggestion, though one year earlier he had identified sixteen states permitting divorce on grounds of insanity—Nevada being the most lenient, requiring only a six-week residency with the patient needing only a two-year confinement. Instead, he wrote her poignant letters recalling happier times: "The sadness of the past is with me always. The things that we have done together and the awful splits that have broken us into war survivors in the past stay like a sort of atmosphere around any house I inhabit. The good things and the first years together, and the good months that we had two years ago in Montgomery will stay with me forever, and you should feel like I do that they can be renewed, if not in a new spring, then in a new summer."

Oblivious to the passing of seasons and fearing she would never recover, Zelda confided to Dr. Harry M. Murdoch, a young physician who had gained her confidence, that she intended doing away with herself. Although she was carefully watched and permitted only occasional, closely monitored outings, she once attempted suicide by self-strangulation. And on a visit to La Paix with Scott, she pulled away from him and threw herself in front of the train that ran between the Turnbull estate and the hospital boundary. Only seconds before the engine passed, Fitzgerald grabbed her wrists and dragged her from the tracks. Until she improved, she was permitted no further excursions and transferred to an area of the hospital with round-the-clock observation.

Harry Murdoch had joined Sheppard Pratt's staff in June of 1930, eventually becoming its third director. A graduate of the University of Nebraska Medical School and a Commonwealth Fellow in Psychiatry at the Colorado Psychopathic Hospital, he also taught psychiatry at the University of Maryland. Under the guise of providing background information on Zelda's condition, but really to ingratiate himself with the doctor, Fitzgerald composed a three-page letter to Murdoch detailing Dr. Meyer's previous unproductive treatment. The letter, dated August 28, 1934, in six points summarized Meyer's attitude toward Zelda and himself: "He gave back to me both times a woman not one whit better than when she went in. (1) I could never get an idea of his point of view about Zelda—except for one letter. (2) He seemed to believe Zelda should not get too hospital-minded—he feared her becoming 'hospitalized,' that I drank too much—which complicated the case, that I was a work horse with the nervous system of a swiss peasant.

(3) Largely unprofitable consultations with him—great sheaves of notes taken by Rennie—with no follow-through. (4) He would not permit her to enter and leave his clinic for short stays. (5) He encouraged Zelda's desire to express herself—knowing she had broken down over that twice before! (6) Once he had done what he could with Zelda he shoved her back on me and refused to take her back."

Once again, his fifth point is not entirely ingenuous. Zelda broke down not *from* writing (indeed she had gotten much better when Dr. Squires encouraged her to write), but from *his opposition to* her writing.

Actually, Meyer always disapproved of long-term institutional care for Zelda, believing it would render more harm than good. Recognizing her need for freedom, he warned that continual confinement might further disintegrate her personality and make her passive and unmotivated. Shock therapies had already accounted for a loss of memory and the dulling of her personality. In principle, Fitzgerald agreed with Meyer about this. When her suicidal inclinations passed, Fitzgerald again began taking Zelda away for short excursions. But he could endure the strain for only short periods, and was not always on best behavior. John O'Hara recalled one Sunday afternoon when he visited Scott in Baltimore and accompanied the Fitzgeralds back to Sheppard Pratt. "I had Scott and Zelda in my car and I wanted to kill him. *Kill.* We were taking her back to her Institution, and he kept making passes at her that could not possibly be consummated. . . . I wanted to kill him for what he was doing to that crazy woman who kept telling me she had to be locked up before the moon came up."

Supervising Zelda was an exhausting process. If she worked too hard at anything, she risked a resurgence of hallucinations. And she could not tolerate the ordinary setbacks of life. On the days she felt well, she played tennis on hospital courts, and when she lost—it was common to see her tennis racket go flying across the court. It was a practice she had started years earlier at Ellerslie. Once, after a doctor had soundly beaten her, she took her racket and hit him over the head. Another partner remembered her breaking her racket in half when he won. And when Zelda and Scott were supposed to play, and Scott foisted her off on Bill Warren, a friend from Baltimore's Junior Vagabonds, Zelda openly rebelled. "The wife acted as if her husband were backing out of the honeymoon," Warren re-called, "but Scott ignored her, climbing up into the high judge's chair to referee the match. The two reluctant players took their places and began to rally. After the first point, Zelda took off her sweater. The judge high up over her head said nothing. After the second point, she reached behind her back, unhooked her bra and tossed it away. Still Scott remained silent. After the third point, Zelda's short white tennis skirt dropped like a hoop at her feet. Af-ter the fourth she freed herself from her panties. I was playing with a stark naked woman. She had a gorgeous body—it was the first time I noticed that a woman could be brown all over. But when you're playing tennis with a naked woman whose husband is watch-ing, you try not to look. I was having a terrible time returning her shots." The game ended with Zelda screaming hysterically as hos-pital attendants arrived to wrap her in a cold wet-pack and carry her to her room. Was Scott again collecting material?

Cold wet-packs were routinely used at Sheppard Pratt to sedate agitated patients. The intervention, which took two hours, pro-duced powerful circulatory changes. After a patient's hands and feet were restrained, attendants placed an ice pack under the head, a hot water bag at the feet, then wrapped the patient first in a rubber blanket, followed by a cold, wet sheet, another wool blanket, and a second iced, wet sheet. This produced a contraction of the small ar-teries, capillaries, and veins. Five to twenty minutes after the sheets were applied, the thermic reaction started as capillaries dilated and the patient stopped fighting the restraints. Becoming drowsy and falling into a deep sleep, they usually awoke groggy but calm.

By December of 1934, Zelda had shown enough improvement to spend Christmas week in Baltimore with Fitzgerald and Scottie. On the afternoon of the twenty-fourth, Gertrude Stein, visiting Mary-land on her first trip to America in thirty years, came to have tea. Scott asked Zelda to show Gertrude her paintings and offer any she liked. When Stein chose two already promised to Zelda's doctor, she selected two others—an oil called *The Tulips* and a drawing enti-tled *Crossing Roses*. Scott later wrote Gertrude a letter of apprecia-tion that was an obsequious overstatement of Zelda's sentiments. "It meant so much to Zelda, giving her a tangible sense of her own existence for you to have liked two of her pictures enough to want to own them." Zelda had never liked Gertrude, and Stein actually was more impressed by the teenaged Scottie, to whom she wrote warmly from France: "I did like being with you all in Baltimore and here we have Zelda's picture and it is a very beautiful picture and it gives us a lot of pleasure. I wonder where you are and what you are doing, and I hope you are doing it well whatever it is. You know that I am very fond of you—."

The stress of being in Baltimore for the holidays and entertaining Scott's friends set Zelda back, and when she returned to Sheppard Pratt for the New Year her condition worsened. To prevent potential suicide attempts, she was placed in seclusion. The situation aggravated Fitzgerald's lung condition, and to avoid a TB flare-up, he took Scottie out of school in February for two weeks and headed south to Tryon, North Carolina. A year-round health resort in the Blue Ridge Mountains, Tryon had seven hotels, a live theater, the Lanier Library, and pleasant weather year-round. There was also a tuberculosis treatment center at St. Luke's Hospital, which Fitzgerald intended to enter. Shortly after arriving, he was introduced to Nora and Maurice Flynn, who reminded him of the Murphys. Maurice had been an all-American football hero at Yale and cowboy actor in silent films. Nora came from a wealthy family and had two famous sisters. One was Irene, prototype for illustrator Charles Dana Gibson's upper-class American female—the "Gibson Girl," usually portrayed in a white, puff-sleeved shirt and long skirt, watching a tennis match or hitting a golf ball. The other was Nancy, better known as Lady Astor, the first woman elected to a seat in the British House of Commons. At forty, Nora was two years older than Scott. She was also a Christian Scientist and experienced in rehabilitating alcoholics; she had helped her husband, Maurice ("Lefty"), stop drinking. Like the Murphys, the couple enjoyed creative people, especially writers, actors, and musicians; they immediately took to Fitzgerald and brought him into their social circle. Nora may even have initiated a brief affair with Scott. When Scottie returned to school, Fitzgerald moved into a top-floor room at the Oak Hall Hotel and spent most of March resting, occasionally socializing with the Flynns. Despite efforts to relax, on his return to Baltimore in April, additional X-rays revealed his tuberculosis was still active and that he had considerable lung damage.

With his own health severely compromised, there was little reserve left for Zelda. While he had abandoned hope long before for her total recovery, he had remained emotionally tied to her. Now he tried to distance himself, but it was a lonely existence and he told Margaret Turnbull, "Living alone leaves so many loopholes for brooding, and when I do face the whole tragedy of Zelda, it is simply a day lost. I think I feel it more now than at any time since its inception. She seems so helpless and pitiful." Sensing their life together was over, Zelda encouraged Scott to go on with his life, writing during spring of 1935: "There is no way to ask you to forgive me for the misery and pain which I have caused you. I can only ask you to believe that I have done the best I could and that since we first met I have loved you with whatever I had to love you with. Please get well and love Scottie and find something to fill up your life."

Still, she remained on his mind. He expressed concerns to Dr. Rennie at Phipps about how slowly her recovery was going, and inquired whether Zelda should be transfered to yet another hospital. Rennie responded on May 27, 1935: "It is Dr. Meyer's feeling that this present condition is a true depressive reaction from which she will recover, but the course may be protracted and in her present state of suicidal intent, she needs the constant supervision that she is getting at Sheppard." Rennie had been researching improvement rates among schizophrenics for an article in the *Archives of Neurology and Psychiatry*, and he shared his findings with Fitzgerald. Emphasizing that patients often faced unexpected and unpredictable changes in the course of recovery, he maintained that long-term contact with a trusted physician or hospital was helpful, but the most critical element influencing recovery was the removal of those stressors precipitating psychotic episodes. What Rennie particularly emphasized in his article was that "patients were capable of accepting guidance and of resolving personal conflicts with the help of the psychiatrist," but equally important was "the presence of a favorable and understanding environment to which the patient can be returned, and the help to be obtained from cooperative families in carrying out recommendations." Most critical he concluded was "the removal of the precipitating strains and the person's own ability to utilize advice for resynthesis of the personality." For Zelda's well-being and his own, Scott made the determination at this juncture to remove himself as much as possible from Zelda's life.

Scottie left for summer camp when school ended, and planned to stay with the Obers when she returned. That left Fitzgerald free to go back to Asheville for the summer, where he put himself under the care of lung specialist Dr. Paul Ringer. But instead of hospitalizing him, Ringer allowed Scott to stay at the Grove Park Inn overlooking the Asheville Golf Club on the mountainside near the Vanderbilt estate. The luxurious hotel had extensive grounds and a majestic view of the Blue Ridge Mountains from its upper floors. To save money, however, Fitzgerald took two lower-priced adjoining rooms facing the courtyard; he did not, however, consider economizing on liquor bills.

From Baltimore, Mrs. Owens kept Scott informed about Scottie's activities and Zelda's condition: "Mrs. Fitzgerald has been moved to a closed ward and has a special nurse. She is very confused again and rather depressed but offers no reason. . . . I first noticed the beginning of a change two weeks before you left. . . . Scottie is being well looked after. It's like five mother hens and one chick, but she doesn't seem to resent it." Scott wrote Zelda to ask if she needed anything and she replied cryptically, "I don't need anything at all except hope, which I can't find by working either backwards or forwards, so I suppose the thing is to shut my eyes."

Rosalind became increasingly concerned over her sister's condition. On her way to New York from Montgomery at the end of May, she stopped in Baltimore to see Zelda. After only half an hour she could see how desperate she was. The doctors told her that "Scott had interfered so persistently with their care of Zelda that it had been impossible to do anything for her." From New York she wrote Fitzgerald, "Her present condition was a great shock to me, and I feel discouraged about her. . . . Zelda seemed to me to be very ill. . . . She begged all during the visit for me to take her to ride. . . . She smoked a cigarette and ate a chocolate bar. . . . Most of the time, however, she was reproaching herself for having wrecked your life and having brought Scottie into the world."

On the heels of Rosalind's upsetting letter came another from H. L. Mencken, who wrote on May 30 that Sara Haardt was in critical condition. "My dear Scott, Poor Sara, I fear, is now gravely ill—in fact, the chances that she will recover seem to be very remote. After all her long and gallant struggles she has developed meningitis, and the doctors tell me that the outlook is virtually hopeless. You can imagine my state of mind."

Death and illness hovered over Scott's world. As summer progressed, he grew increasingly depressed and entered into several abortive relationships. He befriended Tony Buttita, proprietor of the Intimate Book Shop in the arcade of Asheville's George Van-derbilt Hotel, and was introduced to Lottie Stephens, a high-priced prostitute who offered her services to hotel guests. Buttita wrote of that liaison in his narrative about Scott's summer in Asheville, in-cluding Stephens's disappointment over Scott's virility. "He was nervous and I thought maybe that was why he was so quick about it," she said. "I asked him if that was his usual way and he said 'yes.' I remember him telling me that he only made love to help him write."

Another woman he met at the Hotel was Laura Guthrie Hearne, a Columbia Journalism School graduate and amateur psychic who supplemented her income by telling fortunes for hotel guests. Hearne was starstruck by Fitzgerald and became his part-time secretary, confidante, and go-between in his affair with Beatrice Dance, a wealthy Texan who was also staying at the Grove Park Inn. On the evenings he was not with Beatrice, Scott often sat up all night drinking with Hearne, who detailed their conversations in her jour-nal and later wrote of the encounter. When he abruptly ended the relationship with Dance that August, Fitzgerald was emotionally drained, but certain the affair would make excellent story fodder. He wrote James Boyd, "I have just emerged not totally unscathed, I'm afraid, from a short violent love affair which will account for the somewhat sentimental cadence of this letter and for the lack of ink in the vicinity. It's no one I ever mentioned to you but it was in the bag when I came to Southern Pines and I had done much better to let it alone because this is scarcely a time in my life for one more emotion. Still it's done now and tied up in cellophane and—and maybe someday I'll get a chapter out of it. God, what a hell of a profession to be a writer."

So emotionally distraught was the rejected Beatrice that she had to be hospitalized—like Zelda! Guilt-ridden, Fitzgerald went on his characteristic drinking spree that proved so debilitating, Dr. Ringer was compelled to admit him into the alcoholics' ward of St. Luke's Hospital. Recalling Scott's pathetic condition that summer and Hearne's later characterization of him, Rosalind Smith acknowl-edged, "The fortune teller did a good job on Scott as he was in his Asheville days. I saw him there at the time of which she writes and remember him as the floundering wreck she describes. Poor devil! I always was sorry for him even while detesting him."

Each day brought additional bad news, the saddest being the

death of Gerald and Sara Murphy's fifteen-year-old child, Baoth. A student at St. George's School in Middletown, Rhode Island, outside Newport, the Murphys' son had caught cold and been placed in the school's infirmary. There he developed measles with ear complications that turned into a double mastoid infection. His uncle Fred had suffered two painful operations for mastoiditis in 1913, and the family was very concerned. They had reason to be; as a result of the operation on his infected ear, bacteria invaded Baoth's spinal fluid, causing meningitis. Transferred to Massachusetts General Hospital, he died there on March 17, 1935. Unlike his fourteen-year-old younger brother Patrick, who had contracted tuberculosis in 1929 and entered Doctors' Hospital late in 1934 with both lungs infected, Baoth always had been the healthier boy, which made his death seem even more tragic. Following his memorial service at St. Bartholomew's in Manhattan, Sara exited the church cursing God. She never fully recovered, telling Scott, "I don't think the world is a very nice place."

Mourning one son, the Murphys now turned their attention to the health of their younger child, Patrick. In previous years, they had taken him to Austria for the fresh-air cure. Hoping he would benefit again from a mountain climate, Sara brought him in July of 1935 to Saranac Lake in the Adirondacks, famous for its cure cottages and "outdoor life" therapy. Besides providing cottages where the intimacy of a home could be preserved, the village offered tubercular patients various activities to combat boredom and provide a sense of the outside world. The Murphys spared no expense for Patrick's care; when the diagnosis of a cavity in one lung was complicated by anemia, three doctors and four nurses assisted with his case. But without antibiotics, pulmonary TB could be cured only by helping the body's immune system fight the disease, and this necessitated great patience and discipline.

The fresh-air cure required patients to rest twenty-four hours a day. During the mandatory eight hours spent outdoors, patients sat in cure chairs on covered verandas breathing fresh air. At night they slept on well-ventilated, unheated porches. Under Sara's supervision, Patrick worked hard to get well and earned everyone's respect, including that of Hemingway, who came to visit him at Saranac. Ernest was one of the few people with whom the Murphys shared their intense grief over Baoth's death and apprehension about Patrick's lingering illness. Fitzgerald was another. "It occurs to me that you alone knew how we felt these days—still feel," Gerald wrote Scott. "You are the only person to whom I can ever tell the bleak truth of what I feel. Sara's courage and the amazing job which she is doing for Patrick make unbearably poignant the tragedy of what has happened—what life has tried to do to her. I know that what you said in 'Tender Is the Night' is true. Only the invented part of our life, the unreal part—has had any scheme of beauty. Life itself has stepped in now and blundered, scarred and destroyed. In my heart I dreaded the moment when our youth and invention would be attacked in our only vulnerable spot—the children, their growth, their health, their future. How ugly and blasting it can be, and how idly ruthless. . . . It has occurred to me in all this that you alone have always—known shall I say?—or felt—that Sara was—that there was about Sara—something infinitely touching—something infinitely sad. Life begins to mark her for a kind of cumulus tragedy." Gerald considered Scott a soul-mate, not only because of the pain he had experienced with Zelda's illness, but because he considered himself and Scott to be "fragile Irish"; "I suppose that we are two blatherskites living in stone huts in some distant Irish valley," he wrote Fitzgerald. "You and I, I mean . . . I guess we are Irish."

Scott kept in close contact with the Murphys throughout the summer. After he was discharged from Asheville's hospital, he drove back to the Cambridge Arms in Baltimore where Scottie had returned and was being cared for by Mrs. Owens. Finances soon required they move to even cheaper accommodations two blocks away at 3300 St. Paul Avenue. Debt-ridden and despondent, Fitzgerald found it increasingly difficult to work, and the manuscripts he sent Ober often arrived illegible and incoherent. The short story market had virtually dried up in the stagnant economy, and nothing was selling. Moreover, Fitzgerald could no longer write what the magazines wanted. To worsen matters, critical praise for *Tender Is the Night* was only lukewarm. A modest success at best, the novel quickly dropped from attention. Scott wrote Mabel Dodge Luhan a cavalier letter meant to cover his disappointment: "I get a pretty highly developed delirium tremens at the professional reviewers: the light men who bubble at the mouth with enthusiasm because they see other bubbles floating around, the dumb men who regularly mistake your worst stuff for your best and your best for your worst, and most of all the cowards who straddle and the leeches who review your books in terms they have cribbed out of the book itself, like scholars under some extraordinary disposition which allows them to heckle the teacher."

By November of 1935 he had hit bottom. Borrowing money from the Kalmans, he gave Scottie ten dollars and informed Mrs. Owens he was leaving. Driving out of Baltimore without luggage, he wound up south of Asheville in Hendersonville, North Carolina, where he rented a cheap room at the Skylands Hotel. Only days before his fortieth birthday, he sat there and wrote three confessional essays in a tone of self-deprecating honesty. The twenty pages were published by Arnold Gingrich in *Esquire*'s February and April issues. For Scott, the three pieces, "The Crack Up," "Pasting It Together," and "Handle With Care," were authentic examinations of his spiritual and emotional bankruptcy; to Maxwell Perkins they were a degrading exercise in self-pity. He admonished Scott that they should never have been published and would undermine his reputation. Understanding the depths of his misery, Sara Murphy offered encouragement and reached out to bolster his spirits. "You have been cheated, as we all have been in one way or another, but to have Zelda's wisdom taken away—which would have meant everything to you, is crueler even than death. She would have felt all the right things through the bad times—and found the right words to help. For you, and for her real friends—I miss her too—you have had a horrible time—worse than any of us, I think—and it has gone on for so long, that is what gets us, saps our vitality—your spirit and courage are an example to us all."

Zelda knew Scott was in trouble but, as Sara had written, was in no condition to help. Her illness had worsened during spring 1936 as her absorption with God expanded into religious mania. Dressed in white, she prayed by her bed for days, and believing the end of the world was near, and that her duty was to spread God's word, she wrote, mimeographed, and distributed religious tracts to friends. She was at a dangerously low point when Rosalind insisted she be transferred to Highland Hospital in Asheville, North Carolina. "Scott first took Zelda to Highland on my insistence," Rosalind explained, "after I found her at Sheppard Pratt weighing only 89 pounds and fast going downhill instead of improving." Experiencing hallucinations in which she claimed she could talk to God and was in direct communication with Jesus Christ, William the Conqueror, and Apollo, Zelda was admitted to the Highland Hospital of Nervous Diseases on April 8, 1936. Rosalind had been asked to gather some of Zelda's things to take to Asheville, and later recalled how few items of value remained among her sister's possessions. "One of the saddest memories I have is of going through her trunk in Baltimore, at Scott's request, before her departure for Dr. Carroll's to see what there was that she might want to take with her. What I found was a bit of old clothing, a brass candlestick, and a musical powderbox with a Pierrot on top that turned with the tune."

There was also little remaining for Scott. All of his books were out of print or going out, and he was $40,000 in debt. He wrote Harold Ober in May that he was being sued by Zelda's last sanitarium for nonpayment and that it was impossible to write under such circumstances. "I realize that I am at the end of my resources physically + financially. After getting rid of this house next month + storing furniture I am cutting expenses to the bone, taking Scotty to Carolina instead of camp + going to a boarding house for the summer. I have got to do that and get a sense of proportion and give her one. The doctors tell me at this rate of work I won't last two years." They were wrong; he lasted four.

CHAPTER 7

The End
of the Story

Near the banks of the French Broad and Swannanoa Rivers, in a residential area just outside Asheville, North Carolina, stood Zelda's sanitarium, Highland. Encircled by the Blue Ridge and Great Smoky Mountains, the hospital occupied fifty acres with an additional four hundred acres of mountain woodland five miles away. It was an inviting place resembling a college campus more than a mental institution, with tennis courts and a swimming pool. Founded in 1904 by the well-known psychiatrist Robert S. Carroll and his wife, Highland was an efficiently managed, modestly priced institution. The quarterly fee was $1,200, but Fitzgerald, pleading financial exigencies, negotiated an even lower rate of $240 a month. Added to that was an additional $100 he supplied each month for Zelda's personal expenses, which included toilet articles, occasional dental work, clothing, dry cleaning, fruit, chewing gum, flowers, and telegrams. There were also the added costs of day trips, concerts, movies, dinners, dancing lessons, and various art supplies.

At the time, Highland was pioneering new treatments for schizophrenia, including Dr. Carroll's controversial injections of horse blood into patients' cerebrospinal fluid. The inactivated horse serum, injected through lumbar punctures, caused aseptic meningitis, which produced fever, headaches, and vomiting but also rendered patients lucid for long periods. The hospital was also experimenting with injections of placental blood, honey, and hypo- or hypertonic solutions. Insulin and electroshock therapy were now in standard use, and Zelda received extensive treatments in both, which resulted in a gradual improvement of her symptoms.

Highland's director, Dr. Robert Carroll, born in Cooperstown, Pennsylvania, in 1869, had taken his medical degree at Marion Sims College of Medicine, and completed psychiatric training at Chicago's Rush Medical College, where Hemingway's father had studied. He was friendly with Adolf Meyer at Phipps, who occasionally sent him patients and may even have recommended Highland to Rosalind. Carroll began his medical career as a pharmacist, and theorized that mental disorders resulted from toxic substances in the body. By restricting the diet to specific foods and requiring extensive exercise, he believed a patient could expel enough toxins to keep nervous disorders under control. The diet included natural juices, plenty of starch, and lots of vegetables, but forbade meat, milk, and eggs; sweets were kept to a minimum. Alcohol, tobacco, and drugs were strictly forbidden. The hospital emphasized good diet, plenty of water, and a reasonable balance of rest and work. Female patients were not permitted to wear makeup, nor were mirrors allowed in their rooms. Moderation in all aspects of life was the underlying guideline.

Critical to Highland's philosophy was the regimentation of exercise. Patients were required to walk five miles a day in the hills surrounding the hospital. At the top of each hill was a pegboard where patients indicated their progress by crossing off a personal number. Each patient was prescribed a specific exercise goal and was expected to work toward it every day. The intention of the exercise program was to get the body into shape and teach perseverance. Additional exercise was prescribed for aggressive patients on the theory that punishment of the body replaced punishment of the mind. Besides the daily walking program, patients also participated in a number of outdoor activities. It was a perfect regimen for someone as athletically inclined as Zelda.

Recreation and occupational therapy were also part of the weekly schedule since Carroll believed such pursuits instilled self-sufficiency. Patients were also encouraged to communicate regularly with family and friends through letter writing. Rosalind recalled how

Zelda's "faithful weekly letters continued to be couched in words drawn from what one of her doctors described to me as one of the most extraordinary and beautiful vocabularies he ever had encountered." To better understand his new patient, Dr. Carroll analyzed Zelda's handwriting and prepared a detailed, amazingly accurate graphological analysis of it for Zelda's mother. It described her as "an enthusiastic person with an active mind and with great firmness and determination of character and the will to have her way recognized or there will be trouble; but all in an amiable and quiet and even-tempered manner." The analysis precisely captured the essence of her personality as well as her approach to life. "While having a scientific mind, her ideas are often inspirational, her intuition even amounting to psychic power. Is earnest and conscientious. Has social gift which makes her companionable, but she is bored by too much concentration on any subject. She has very little reasoning power and does not think connectedly or logically. Has decided creative ability and is interested in life in general, but does not attach herself deeply to any one love, and does not demonstrate affection, her head ruling her emotions. She is capable of great efficiency in any work she undertakes. She has a variety of interests and some gift as a teacher and can transfer her impressions and knowledge with ease, and acts impulsively and hastily on occasions. Has little talent for the waiting game. Most contradictory nature. In almost every trait she has touches of the opposite. One thing the matter is that she cannot concentrate on anything very long. Has scattered her energies in every direction and has unsettled her gifts." What the analysis did not take into consideration is why this had been so.

Zelda found Highland peaceful and liked its strict schedule of daily activities. She had gym class in the morning followed by a snack, then an occupational therapy session, and a five-mile walk on the grounds in the afternoon. When she was finally allowed weekend excursions, she visited her mother, who was vacationing in Saluda, North Carolina, where Zelda had spent childhood summers, and then went up to Manhattan to see Rosalind, who was astonished by her sister's improvement. "At Asheville, where much of the institutional atmosphere was lost in pleasant lodgings, but where uncompromising strictness was the rule, and cooperation of the patient was demanded, Zelda bloomed again, and on several visits to me in New York during that period was almost like her old self, beautiful once more, still interested in music, the theatre and art, but toned down to an almost normal rhythm."

Zelda's favorite outings were still the excursions she took with Scott, when they would drive through the nearby mountains or off to a lake where they could swim. For her birthday in July 1936, Fitzgerald planned such an excursion, but the day was ruined after Scott injured his shoulder that morning in the Grove Park Inn pool. He had been showing off his diving for the young nurse hired to monitor his drinking. There were several versions of what happened. Fitzgerald told his friend Xandra Kalman and Scottie that, while "trying to show off for Zelda he ventured to dive from a 15-foot board, and while still in mid-air tore the muscles of his shoulder so badly he ended up with his arm dangling an inch or two out of the socket." Yet he told Beatrice Dance, with whom he was still in correspondence, that it had happened right before he hit the water during a swan dive, and that he had been alone. When he wrote apologetically to Zelda, he also made no mention of the nurse. "It was too bad on your birthday that everything went so badly. I left the hotel for the hospital that morning fully intending to be back here in time to lunch with you as it looked at first like merely severe strain that could be cured with hot applications and rest and a sling, but the x-ray showed that there was a fracture in the joint of the shoulder and a dislocation of the ball and socket arrangement of the shoulder. . . . They sent for a bone specialist and he said it would have to be set immediately or else I would never be able to raise my arm as high as my shoulder again so they gave me gas like when they pulled your tooth and I fell asleep thinking you were in the room and saying, 'Yes, I *am* going to stay; after all he is my husband.' " He also wrote of the incident to Gerald Murphy, who sent a grim reply that indicated that Patrick's health had not improved at Saranac Lake. "As for life (as they call it) I find it turning out to be the very thing I'd always suspected it to be. A very badly schemed and wasteful process. Having felt it to be such, I find I don't mind it as much."

For his shoulder to heal properly, Fitzgerald was required to wear an awkward plaster cast that kept his right arm over his head. One night, he tripped over the raised platform in his bathroom and lay helpless on the floor for an hour. As a result he developed myotosis, a form of arthritis that laid him up for ten weeks. Another nurse—Pauline Brownell, called "Phil"—was hired to provide assistance. Always the insomniac, Fitzgerald sat up talking with Pauline many of the nights he couldn't sleep. During September 1936, Pauline and her husband, George, drove Fitzgerald to visit Zelda at Highland, and took them for long rides in the North Carolina mountains. Zelda eagerly anticipated these outings and was often well enough to enjoy them, but by day's end she was ready to be dropped off at the sanitarium.

The Brownells also drove Scott to Tom Wolfe's home in Asheville, where they joined the author and his mother for afternoon tea. And they took Scott on a visit to Pauline's family farm near Spruce Pine in Avery County; afterward he inscribed two of his early books to Pauline, writing in *Taps at Reveille*: "In memory of another amusing and unforgettable trip, Asheville-Spruce Pine 1936." On the flyleaf of *This Side of Paradise*, he wrote: "For Pauline—I could see her today as a child, bare-headed, bare-footed—and on bareback, and it was touching to think of her so." Scott also inscribed several books to George, including a copy of Joseph Conrad's *Victory*, in which he had written: "To George Brownell—From His Friend F. Scott Fitzgerald—In Memory of Pleasant Days On The Road, Autumn, 1936," and inside *Tales of the Jazz Age* the inscription read: "For two people who lived after the Jazz Age and had neither its wild pleasures nor its terrible hangover—in hopes they never will." Scott became quite fond of Pauline. When she suffered a bout with depression during the winter of 1936, he paid for her to stay at a rest clinic, and as a parting gesture, gave her an oriental rug, noting the gift in his ledger: "The rug and the books for Pauline."

To express her appreciation, Zelda gave Pauline a watercolor depicting lilies. On her wedding day, there had been an Easter lily on the dresser at the Biltmore, and they were Zelda's sentimental favorite. Now they also held a religious significance. During this period she painted many watercolors of lilies in a religious motif, including one showing a close-up of two flower heads under the title "Easter." Generally there was a lily plant cheering Zelda's Highland room, and in her two-ring binder of thoughts and reflections, she wrote about one dying. "My lilies died; they just plain died and so I can only maybe paint the memory of white desirability—of so much beauty. So perfect. I used to gather them in Alabama under the pines and from the ooze of a dried lake bed and they were always so spiritually splendid." That memory of youth was the lost dream of her own desirability.

As the months passed, Zelda's religious mania gradually subsided and there were no further suicide attempts. To many at the sanitarium, she seemed natural, easy to get along with, and, except for occasional lapses into fantasy, showed only sporadic signs of schizophrenia. When the weather was good, she would lie outside in the sun, coming in only when called. During this first confinement, she exhibited a zest for life, an interest in things around her, and still talked of the book she hoped to write. Occasionally, she even spoke about Scott, their life in Europe, and her regrets for having given up ballet. Her love for dance remained strong, and she found great pleasure choreographing ballets for special events. For Highland's 1936 New Year's Costume Ball, she even performed a short ballet in which she portrayed an angel. But she had to be carefully watched. If the nurses forgot to monitor her, she would practice dance routines to the point of exhaustion and suffer a terrible sense of instability the entire next day.

When Zelda wasn't practicing ballet or participating in the hospital's activities, she often would take the outdoor easel a fellow patient had made for her and march off to paint the Asheville countryside. She found the vista more appealing than the Swiss Alps, and relished painting the lush greens and browns of the North Carolina landscape along with the hollyhocks, magnolias, and rhododendrons that grew profusely around the grounds. Using both oil and watercolor, she portrayed these flowers abstractly, eschewing realistic representation in favor of a highly charged symbolic representation. She had acquired her interest in flowers from her mother, who was an accomplished gardener. During her long walks she collected flowers, and there were always fresh blossoms in her room—lilies, peonies, and angel's trumpets that only bloomed at night. Familar with most flower varieties, Zelda painted them with ease and fluidity.

Scott was relieved to know Zelda was being well cared for, but the cost of Highland, though modest compared to Craig House, combined with Scottie's school tuition and his own monthly expenses in Tryon, were a heavy burden. Only when his mother died suddenly of a cerebral hemorrhage in September 1936 did the money from her estate bring temporary relief from his financial problems. Now, when he visited Zelda once or twice a month, he could bring Scottie and spend the day shopping in Asheville, taking everyone out to dinner afterward. When he came alone, hopeful of finding Zelda improved, there were lucid moments when she still spoke of the house in which they would all live. But her descriptions were increasingly dreamlike. "I wish you had a little house with hollyhocks and a sycamore tree and the afternoon sun imbedding itself in a silver teapot," she told Scott. "Scottie would be running around somewhere in white, in Renoir, and you will be writing books in dozens of volumes. And there will be honey for tea, though the house should not be in Granchester. There are so many houses I'd like to live in with you. I don't know how you get one but I think if we saved a great many things—stamps and cigar bands, soap wrappers and box-tops we could have it some way." The fantasy sustained Zelda's hope about life beyond Highland, away from its restrictions and regulations. She described the hospital's stifling atmosphere to Scott. "Friendship, conviviality, the right of choice, the right of resentment, anger, impetuosities; all these are as much a part of life as obedience, submission, obligation and necessity. In a hospital, or Highland Hospital, these manifestations of the human temperament are subject to reprimand and regarded as illness. Knowing this, patients (mostly) suppress themselves as much as possible, endure, and hope to get out." It was, perhaps, the first time in her life when she submitted to discipline, and, despite her complaint, it had a positive effect on her mental state.

While Scott empathized with Zelda's desire to lead a normal life, that likelihood seemed increasingly unlikely. Though she was allowed excursions whenever her symptoms subsided, the attention she required during those outings exhausted Scott. Sometimes he would drive them back to the Grove Park Inn for lunch. They would sit in the formal dining room away from other guests while Zelda ate a cucumber salad. The strain was enormous on Fitzgerald, and occasionally he turned eccentric, as if a certain amount of craziness was required—and if Zelda did not produce it, he would. Even though it was important for her to remain calm, Fitzgerald would often precipitate a stressful situation. In October 1936, with Zelda by his side, he approached a group of librarians who were meeting at the inn and introduced himself as the author of an Ernest Hemingway novel. When one of the librarians expressed doubts, Fitzgerald responded: "You don't believe me, do you? I'm Scott Fitzgerald. I wrote 'Of Time and the River.' " The absurdity of this statement made one librarian laugh. "I assured him that either he wasn't Fitzgerald or he hadn't written 'Of Time and the River.' This effrontery on my part only increased his indignation. It was unthinkable that a mere snippet of a librarian should doubt the word of a celebrated author. Meanwhile, the woman at his elbow kept muttering impatiently, 'Come on, Scott! Come, on Scott!' 'I'll *prove* to you that I'm Scott Fitzgerald. Come with me!' He was quite excited now, and my companion and I followed him through the crowd to the hotel registration desk. A dark-haired little clerk on duty there saw us coming. The alleged Mr. Fitzgerald said to him indignantly: 'You tell this young lady who I am!' The clerk took in the situation at a glance. In a quiet, even voice and looking directly at me, he said: 'This is Mr. Scott Fitzgerald. He wrote "Of Time and the River." ' We walked over to the elevator after this and the Fitzgeralds, as they proved to be, got out before we did. Mr. Fitzgerald turned and looking me straight in the eye, delivered his parting shot. 'Any time you read a book about a river, remember I wrote it !' "

In the spring of 1936, Scottie had been accepted as a boarding student into Ethel Walker's School in Simsbury, Connecticut, at a reduced tuition of $2,200 a year. Gerald Murphy had recommended it as one of the best girls' schools in the country and to pay its fees Fitzgerald borrowed money from Harold Ober and Maxwell Perkins. He owed both men thousands and was hoping to repay them by securing a position as a Hollywood screenwriter. Scottie later conjectured in her memoir about why her father insisted on sending her to such an exclusive school. "The choosing of what was then one of the five or six best-known rich girls' schools in the country illustrates once again that curious conflict of attitudes he had about money and Society with a capital 'S.' In one sense, I think he would have hated it if I hadn't been at a 'chic' school, but no sooner was I there than he started worrying about its bad influence on me. Of course no young person nowadays could understand the closed upper strata of Eastern Seaboard Society in those days. Either you went to the right school and made your debut, or in the case of a boy, went to an Ivy League college, or you couldn't be in what was in effect a club to which you belonged all your life . . . so I think Daddy was torn between trying to make up for my lack of stability at home with the sense of belonging that comes from being a member of a club and his own instinctive lack of respect for the values of that club." Yet she *was* the daughter of a famous author, and Fitzgerald kept that in mind, both in choosing his daughter's school and wife's sanitarium.

Because Ethel Walker's was so close to Harold and Anne Ober's home in Scarsdale, they assumed additional responsibility for Scottie by visiting her at school, taking her on ski trips, and making their home available to her. The Obers had two sons and lived in a big, comfortable house that was often filled with interesting people. Interested in gardening and music, Ober was a man of great integrity and character whom Scottie admired. He and Anne treated her like the daughter they never had—buying her clothes, listening to her problems, and serving as surrogate parents. Ober had graduated from Harvard in 1905; he joined the Paul Reynolds Literary Agency in 1907, became a partner in 1919, and then opened his own agency in 1929. He had been Scott's agent from the start of his writing career, and represented a broad range of famous authors.

The Obers loaned Fitzgerald money to send Scottie to Camp Red-Wing for Girls in Brackney, Pennsylvania, for the first part of summer 1936. The camp's director wrote Fitzgerald that his daughter was a continual source of fun and mental stimulation, full of inventiveness and natural drive. Her only criticisms were that Scottie never planned ahead, had poor posture, and needed to cultivate more poise and gentleness. After she returned from Pennsylvania, Fitzgerald attempted to bring the whole family together during July in the kind of house Zelda fantasized about. He rented a cottage in the North Carolina countryside that seemed a wonderful place for them to vacation. Scott hoped the experience would be positive, but Zelda's moods fluctuated so rapidly that she required constant attention, making it impossible for him to concentrate on anything else. He explained the situation to Dr. Carroll: "There would be episodes of great gravity that seemed to have no build-up, outbursts of temper, violence, rashness, etc. that could neither be foreseen nor forestalled." To help modify the problem, Scott and Zelda met with a psychiatrist, but after they discussed their difficulties, he was struck by the intimacy they still shared. They understood each other so well that they shifted in tandem, from anger to amusement in seconds. In an attempt to convince Zelda that she was "just an old schizophrenic," Scott told of an episode that had occurred when they were out riding. When Zelda denied the incident, Fitzgerald shrugged it off by saying, "Maybe it was a schizophrenic horse," at which Zelda broke into laughter, declaring, "Oh, Scott, that's really good, that's priceless."

By September 1936, Zelda was back at Highland, Scottie in school at Miss Walker's, and Fitzgerald at the Oak Hall Hotel in Tryon, where he planned to spend the fall. He took Zelda for an outing to Saluda, North Carolina, in late October, and in December left for Baltimore to host an afternoon tea dance for Scottie in celebration of her homecoming for the Christmas holidays. It was to be her coming-out party. He hired an orchestra, invited sixty guests, and with the help of Margaret Turnbull and Peaches Finney made elaborate plans for the December 22 dance at the Hotel Belvedere. The event began well enough, but unraveled quickly when Fitzgerald, after repeated trips to the bar, insisted on dancing with Scottie's friends. He was too drunk to understand their reluctance. When he finally realized how awkward and embarrassed the girls felt, he abruptly ordered everyone to leave and instructed the musicians to continue playing as he sat alone in the ballroom drinking gin. Scott's Princeton classmate Eben Finney took Peaches and Scottie home. "I was busy surviving and what I couldn't ignore . . . I would put in the emotional attic as soon as possible," Scottie later wrote in an introduction to her father's letters. She was mortified by her father's behavior and remembered how "after the ghastly tea dance . . . my friend Peaches Finney and I went back to her house in a state of semi-hysteria. Her parents who were about the nicest and most considerate people I've ever known, fed us eggs and consolation. Within two hours we were dressed and curled, and deposited by them at the door of the next Christmas party." The pathetic nature of the incident did not escape Fitzgerald, who damned himself and drowned in alcohol, spending the holidays holed up in the Cambridge Arms apartment. By New Year's he had checked into Johns Hopkins Hospital to dry out. Scottie celebrated Christmas day with her mother at Highland and Zelda later wrote Scott about how well the visit had gone, commenting on their daughter's growing maturity and ability to accept things as they were. "Scottie writes me vague notes sometimes. I am so sorry for her. She has always been so brave and made her effort in spite of an inevitable sense that all is not as it might have been."

When he got out of the hospital and returned to the apartment, he took to remaining in his bathrobe all day. Emotional outbursts became common. It was not unusual for Scottie to see an inkwell go flying by, and once he appeared in the living room with a shotgun, shouting he was going to kill the cockroaches. Dealing with his erratic behavior by focusing on other things, and trying to maintain self-control, Scottie later recalled her attitude toward the increasingly difficult situation: In the introduction to her father's letters, she admitted, "Self-preservation being the strongest instinct any of us have, especially when we are young, I also knew that there was only one way for me to survive his tragedy, and that was to ignore it. . . . If I'd allowed myself to care I couldn't have stood it."

On January 30, 1937, Fitzgerald, back in Tryon, received a telegram from the Murphys in Saranac Lake telling him that their second son, Patrick, had passed away. It read simply: "Patrick died peacefully this morning." Scott responded immediately. "The telegram came today and the whole afternoon was sad with thoughts of you and the past and the happy times we had once. Another link binding you to life is broken and with such insensate cruelty that it is hard to say which of the two blows was conceived with more malice. I can see the silence in which you hover now after this seven years of struggle, and it would take words like Lincoln's in his letter to the mother who had lost four sons in the war to write you anything fitting at the moment. The golden bowl is broken indeed but it *was* golden; nothing can ever take those boys away from you now."

The tragic fate of those young boys, despite the advantages of wealth and position, occupied Scott's mind, and he pondered the fortune of his own daughter's good health. That spring Scottie would graduate from Ethel Walker's School, like her mother voted the "most popular" in her class. Fitzgerald dreaded attending the ceremony, but wrote Anne Ober, "We will have to make a mass pilgrimage to her graduation this June. I am hoping her mother can come too, and we will watch all the other little girls get diamond bracelets and Cord roadsters. I am going to a costumer's in New York and will buy Scotty some phony jewelry so she can pretend they are graduation presents. Otherwise she will have to suffer the shame of being a poor girl in a rich girl's school. That was always my experience—a poor boy in a rich town; a poor boy in a rich boy's school; a poor boy in a rich man's club at Princeton. So I guess I can stand it. However, I have never been able to forgive the rich for being rich, and it has colored my entire life and work."

As it turned out, he never attended the ceremony. (Perhaps he was drying out again.) Instead, he arranged for Rosalind to accompany Zelda. Anne Ober drove them up to Connecticut from New York. Zelda appeared poised and looked smart at graduation, where she spoke graciously with Scottie's teachers, classmates, and their parents. Scottie, however, was uncomfortable having her there. "I didn't want my mother at graduation because it wasn't the big deal that Daddy was trying to make it, and she *was* crazy. . . . I just didn't see any point in a big production being made of a relatively minor event." But it was a treat for Zelda, who enjoyed staying in Hartford in her own hotel room, and accompanying Rosalind later to New York. They attended two Broadway shows and saw Margaret Sullivan in Scott's film *Three Comrades*, which the *New York Times* had called one of the year's best movies. Zelda felt very nostalgic to be back in Manhattan. It brought back a flood of memories—of Scott's Princeton classmates, the *Vanity Fair* group, George Jean Nathan and Townsend Martin; she went for a carriage ride through Central Park, and stopped by the fountain in front of the Plaza Hotel that she and Scott had made famous.

While Scottie's graduation came off without any problems, a major crisis erupted the following week. Scottie had remained on Ethel Walker's campus to study for Vassar's entrance exams, but had left to meet some boys at Yale. She recalled the episode in her memoir. "A friend . . . asked me to bum a ride with her over to New Haven to have dinner one afternoon in June. This sounded like a splendid idea so we slipped out of our uniforms in the woods below the school, changed into our civilian clothes, and walked up to the main road by a devious route." After joining the two Yale boys, being shown around the campus, and eating dinner in one of the dining halls, they were driven back at twilight to the school's driveway, where they were confronted on the front porch by the entire staff and faculty. The girls were told to pack their bags and directed to leave school grounds first thing in the morning. "It seems that the dreaded Latin teacher had seen us on the road with our thumbs up (in those days this was not as dangerous as it would be now) and instead of picking us up had waited until we got into a car, and rushed back to school to report us." Scottie was suspended and her acceptance into Vassar delayed until Fitzgerald could intercede with the dean of the college. On the strength of his reputation and persistence, he managed to get her admitted the following spring.

The Obers were delighted that Scottie was coming to Vassar. "It

is going to be great fun for me having Scottie so near," Anne wrote
Scott. "It only takes an hour and a half to drive up by the parkways
which makes it an easy as well as short drive—and I am going to try
to keep in close enough touch with her to know what is happening.
I know you think Harold and I spoil her, but so far Scottie trusts me
and I *think* I have at least part of her confidence. It is an important
relationship to me and while she may not realize it, I think it is to
Scottie too. PLEASE let me know what I can do and WHEN to expect my child."

In May 1937, Fitzgerald again had to ask Harold Ober for
money. "What I need is a substantial sum 1st to pay a percentage on
the bills, 2nd for a full month's security + 3rd to take Zelda for a
three-day trip to Myrtle Beach which I've been promising for two
months and which the sanitarium wants her to take. She hasn't
been out of hospital for 3 1/2 years + they feel that she's well enough
for the trip." Ober had just arranged a six-month writing assignment for Scott at MGM beginning in July. He agreed to the loan,
hoping the Hollywood assignment would enable Scott to pay some
of the thousands he was owed. Before leaving for California, Scott
and Ober met in Manhattan while attending the second American
Writers' Congress (over which Donald Ogden Stewart was presid-
ing). Fitzgerald enjoyed seeing many old friends, but after Hemingway presented a riveting anti-Fascist speech on June 4 before the
audience of 3,500 writers, he grew despondent. Afterward, everyone was talking about the speech, and the contrast between Ernest's
reputation and his own stalled career was painful. The next day,
Carl Van Vechten ran into Scott at the Algonquin, and was shocked
at how sad and defeated he looked. "I was to have lunch with Edmund Wilson," Van Vechten recalled. "We were to meet at the Algonquin. As I came into the room my eyes had to readjust to the
darkness and I noticed a man with Wilson. I didn't recognize him
and went forward to be introduced. It was a terrible moment; Scott
had completely changed. He looked pale and haggard. I was awfully
embarrassed."

Scott arrived in Hollywood during July 1937. He was grateful for
the lucrative MGM contract Ober had negotiated—a thousand dollars a week for six months, with an extension in January 1938, if all
went well, for a second year at $1,250 weekly. He judiciously bud-
geted a monthly allowance for Scottie and thirty dollars a week for
Zelda, but sent more whenever he could. Aware he had to be care-

ful about studio politics, he wrote Scottie: "I must be very tactful, but keep my hand on the wheel from the start—find out the key man among bosses and the most malleable among the collaborators, then fight the rest tooth and nail until, in fact or in effect, I'm alone on the picture. That's the only way I can do my best work. Given a break I can make them double this contract in less than two years."

He was determined to avoid alcohol and shunned heavy drinkers. When he ran into Dorothy Parker and Robert Benchley at the studio, they were dumbfounded by his refusal to roam the bars with them. As Scott took on the mantle of a reformed drunk, he became almost evangelistic in his determination to remain sober. To save on expenses, he moved into Hollywood's Garden of Allah at 8152 Sunset Boulevard—a compound of two-story stucco bungalows catering to movie people and writers—where, for $300 a month, he shared a unit with screenwriter Eddie Mayer. He bought an old Ford coupe so he could easily commute to MGM.

When he reported for his first full day of work, he was asked to polish the script of *A Yank at Oxford* starring Robert Taylor, an easy assignment given the volume of material he had written about Princeton. Even so, he had difficulty getting down to work. Trying to avoid distractions, he ignored most of the other writers in his building, talking only to those he already knew—Anita Loos, Dorothy Parker, and Ogden Nash. He rarely ate in the commissary, preferring to sit alone at his desk, drinking Cokes and chain-smoking filtered Raleighs. If anyone entered his office uninvited, he complained of the interruption. Such unsociability was interpreted as arrogance, provoking other writers to undermine him and talk behind his back.

He became even more reclusive after seeing Hemingway again at the home of Frederic March and Florence Eldridge. Scott had been invited there for a screening of *Spanish Earth*, which Ernest had written with Lillian Hellman, Archibald MacLeish, and Joris Ivens. Afterward, Hemingway made an impassioned plea for donations to buy ambulances for Spain, and the highly successful fund-raiser took in $17,000. But when the party moved on to Dorothy Parker's place, Fitzgerald declined to attend until Lillian Hellman changed his mind. He knew he might have to speak with Ernest there and was embarrassed. Fitzgerald still considered Hemingway the best living writer of the English language, and knew Ernest condemned him for betraying his writing gift and had said so to Maxwell Perkins. "Scott has so lousy much talent and he has suffered so without knowing why, has destroyed himself so, and destroyed Zelda, though never as much as she has tried to destroy him." He also remained sensitive about Hemingway's disdain for Zelda. Always convinced that Scott's downfall was Zelda's fault, Ernest had written Perkins, "Scott should have traded Zelda in five or six years ago before she was certifiably crazy." Arriving at Parker's house, he avoided Ernest the whole evening by staying in the kitchen and talking with the hostess, Lillian Hellman, and Dashiell Hammet. The next morning he telegraphed Ernest: "The picture was beyond praise and so was your attitude." But in his notebook, he admitted their friendship was finally over, writing, "I talk with the authority of failure—Ernest with the authority of success. We could never sit across the table again."

Less than two weeks later, at a Screen Writers' Guild dance on July 22 at the Ambassador Hotel, Scott's luck changed when he met celebrity columnist Sheilah Graham. He had noticed her the week before at a party given by Robert Benchley at the Garden of Allah, and had been struck by her resemblance to the youthful Zelda. He did not introduce himself then, but made a mental note of her features. He later recalled the incident for use in *The Last Tycoon*, describing Stahr's meeting with Kathleen Moore and her uncanny resemblance to his dead wife, Minna Davis. "Smiling faintly at him from not four feet away was the face of his dead wife, identical even to the expression. Across the four feet of moonlight, the eyes he knew looked back at him, a curl blew a little on a familiar forehead, the smile lingered—changed a little according to pattern, the lips parted—the same." There is some irony in the fact that—just as Sheilah Graham reminded Fitzgerald of the young Zelda, some twenty years earlier, *she* had reminded Scott of the Chicago debutante Ginevra King.

Struggling to keep sober and fighting TB, Fitzgerald was grateful for Graham's attention and entered the affair quickly. For the first time, he felt strong enough to pursue a relationship apart from Zelda. "I've become hard here," he wrote Sara Murphy, "and I don't feel the grief I did once—except at nite or when I catch myself in some spiritual betrayal of the past." Still, he would not consider divorcing Zelda, and when someone suggested he reduce expenses by sending Scottie to a less expensive school and putting

Zelda in a state hospital, he rejected the idea outright. Whatever the circumstances, he considered Zelda and Scottie his primary responsibilities, and made that clear to Graham from the start. "Life ended for me when Zelda and I crashed. If she could get well, I would be happy again. Otherwise, never." Graham was naive about the complexity of Scott and Zelda's relationship and the nature of their emotional dependence on one another. "I now realize that during the time I knew Scott, he was leading a sort of double life," she later admitted. "I knew he looked after Zelda, and I understood that he must. But I didn't know that he was still—certainly in the first couple of years of our association—writing her love letters."

He hadn't been in California more than a month when Scottie paid her first visit. She made the train trip accompanied by Helen Hayes, the two boarding in New York City on August 2. Rather than stay at the Garden of Allah with her father, Scottie checked into the Beverly Hills Hotel, where Helen Hayes and Charlie MacArthur occupied one of the luxurious bungalows. "The first Hollywood visit was fabulous," Scottie later wrote. "Daddy was on the wagon and he took me everywhere with him. I had a room at the Beverly Hills Hotel and Helen Hayes was supposed to be my 'chaperone.' Even then, Daddy put a fly in the ointment by making me take a streetcar halfway across Los Angeles to study tap-dancing every day (he was so hell bent on improving everybody), but it was a very pleasant time." Scottie was introduced to numerous Hollywood celebrities, including her dance idol Fred Astaire. She attended dinners at the homes of Norma Shearer, Marion Davies, and Zoe Akins, and went to the Coconut Grove at the Ambassador Hotel with David McQuillan, Scott's cousin from St. Paul. As he had done with Zelda's work, Fitzgerald revised a story Scottie had written, which was later published in *College Bazaar*. He was pleased by how well the visit was going, and wrote Maxwell Perkins: "So far Scottie is having the time of her young life dining with Crawford, Shearer, etc., talking to Fred Astaire and her other heroes."

Graham had been working as a Hollywood columnist for just over a year when she met Fitzgerald, and while earning only a modest salary, had achieved some notoriety writing a gossip column. Accentuating her British accent, and presenting herself as English aristocracy, she carefully hid the truth—that she was poor, Jewish, and the daughter of an alcoholic father. She felt flattered to be with

Fitzgerald, still considered a famous author. When he took her East to meet the Murphys, Maxwell Perkins, and Harold Ober, reviews on her were mixed. Some friends found her materialistic and self-serving, while others considered her a good influence on Scott and genuinely caring. Certainly, she was initially able to keep him sober. After meeting Graham, Edmund Wilson told his Princeton professor Christian Gauss that Scott seemed to be in better shape with his "new girl," but he was mild, less interesting, "rather unsure of himself, and at times almost banal."

Fitzgerald himself had mixed emotions about Graham; he cared, but considered her ignorant and shallow. Helen Hayes believed he stayed with her because he needed emotional support, and treated her badly because "she represented . . . the second-rate he had fallen into." As months passed they grew more involved, and Sheilah ingratiated herself with Scottie by sending her the fur coat she seldom wore in southern California.

Perhaps to relieve his conscience about the affair with Graham, Scott visited Zelda at Highland during the first week in September. He returned three months later at Christmas to take Scottie and her mother to Charleston, Myrtle Beach, Palm Beach, and Miami. Then he and Zelda flew to Montgomery for a brief visit with her family. The trip went well, but when Zelda suggested she return to Hollywood with him, Scott dismissed the idea, explaining that they would have to live apart as long as she needed treatment. Weary from the long trip, Fitzgerald told Scottie: "Your mother was better than ever I expected and our trip would have been fun except that I was tired."

Being with Zelda was equally difficult for Scottie, who usually limited her visits to three days. "The pattern was always repeated," she told Winzola McLendon, "The first day she would seem so well you couldn't believe she was a mental patient," Scottie recalled. "She would have all the old charm about her and was as witty and gay and fun to be with as I remembered. Then the second day she would begin to be nervous and somewhat absent-minded, and by the third day you knew she was under a strain. It was almost like watching a watch run down." Scottie also had difficulty corresponding with her mother, and her reluctance to write incurred the criticism of Aunt Rosalind. "I think your chief trouble is a lack of sympathy and not much ability to put yourself in another person's place," she scolded. ". . . When you fail to write as you do quite often, she gets very unhappy. You owe it to Mama to do all you can to keep your mother in a good frame of mind." Rosalind had found someone besides Scott at whom to shake her finger.

Their last vacation as a family took place during Easter, 1938, when Fitzgerald took Zelda and Scottie to Virginia Beach and then to visit cousins in Norfolk. This time it was Zelda who started an argument. They were having lessons on the golf course when Zelda picked a fight with Scottie, and Fitzgerald proceeded to get drunk and react so violently that she reported him to the Cavalier Hotel's manager. At the precise same moment, both had reached the end of their ability to tolerate one another. The episode sent a distraught Zelda back to Highland and crying into Dr. Carroll's office. Scott later admitted to the doctor: "Each time that I see her, something happens to me that makes me the worst person for her rather than the best." For the sake of his own mental health and hers, Scott told Dr. Carroll that it would be better if he stayed away. "The outworn pretense that we can ever come together is better for being shed. There is simply too much of the past between us. When that mist falls, at a dinner table, or between two pillows, no knight errant can traverse its immense distance. The mainsprings are gone."

The incident was a setback for both of them. Back in Los Angeles, Scott found it increasingly difficult to stay sober. Then, completely unexpectedly, he received a telegram from Ginevra King. He had not seen her in two decades, and had spoken to her only once in 1933, when he had telephoned to ask if she would entertain Zelda at the World's Fair, which she did; aside from that, there had been no contact. Ginevra was now a recent divorcée, and since she was planning to visit Santa Barbara, suggested their meeting. But Fitzgerald was anxious about seeing her again and expressed his reservations to Scottie. "She was the first girl I ever loved and I faithfully avoided seeing her up to this moment to keep that illusion perfect, because she ended up by throwing me over with the most supreme boredom and indifference. I don't know whether I should go or not. It would be very, very strange." In the end, he decided to see her and they met in Hollywood for lunch. Fitzgerald arrived nervous and quickly ordered a series of double Tom Collinses. Though the reunion was obscured by an alcoholic haze, Scott still found Ginevra attractive and called her repeatedly over the next several days. Then, as suddenly as she had dumped him years before, he abruptly let it drop.

The consequences of the reunion were disastrous; seeing Ginevra again unsettled Fitzgerald and threw him violently off the wagon. After getting drunk in a bar on Santa Monica Boulevard, he picked a fight and wound up at the Georgia Street Receiving Hospital in downtown Los Angeles. This first incident was followed by numerous others, including several abusive encounters with Graham in which Scott humiliated her in front of people, hit her, and threatened to kill himself. When she temporarily ended their relationship, Fitzgerald claimed it was for the best, acknowledging he was in no condition for an emotional involvement. "People are either good for each other or not, and obviously I am horrible for you. I loved you with everything I had but something was terribly wrong. You don't have to look far for the reason—I was it. Not fit for any human relation."

His professional life was also coming apart. The intrigues of Hollywood politics confused Scott, who was a novice at studio games. "I don't know how this job is going," he wrote Zelda. ". . . Things depend on such hairlines here—one must not only do a thing well but do it as a compromise, sometime between utterly opposed ideas of two differing executives. The diplomatic part in business is my weak spot."

In the midst of this turmoil, Scottie wrote that she wanted to repeat the experience of the previous summer, and suggested she spend her entire vacation in Los Angeles. Fitzgerald's response was disappointing. "I really don't want you out here for the whole summer because there is no Helen Hayes and really nothing much to do that would interest you except a repetition of last summer—only less interesting." Settling on a two-week stay, Scottie and Peaches Finney flew to Los Angeles in April 1938. But she and her father, who was now renting a bungalow on Malibu Beach, quarreled much of the time. Things became so tense one evening that the girls fled the house for the beach. In her memoir, Scottie remembered that summer as "the first of several distressing reunions with my father, because he had entered a phase in his drinking in which his personality changed from Jekyll to Hyde, unexpectedly and frighteningly. His drinking seldom affected his personality for long, and I remember being very relieved that Peaches was along to provide a buffer."

The two made up during the last few days of their visit, when Scottie and Peaches toured the studios where Fitzgerald worked,

and were introduced to film stars Maureen O'Sullivan, Beatrice
Lillie, and Errol Flynn. Fitzgerald also arranged a brief meeting
with Sheilah Graham, downplaying the relationship and insisting it
not be discussed with Zelda. Scottie had no romantic illusions
about their affair, and considered her father's romance with Graham totally separate from his relationship with her mother. "He
had a wife who couldn't live with him. It was an unbelievable emotional and financial drain. . . . More than anything, I think my father needed someone who was eminently practical, someone with
her feet on the ground, someone with an inner calm and stability—
someone perhaps like Sheilah Graham." Scottie's candid feelings
are hinted at in the word *perhaps*. She kept the affair a secret, believing knowledge of it could seriously harm her mother. Nonetheless,
Zelda suspected the liaison, and after publication of *The Last Tycoon*
she wrote Margaret Turnbull about her dislike for Kathleen Moore,
the female protagonist modeled after Graham. "I confess I didn't
like the heroine; she seemed the sort of person who knows too well
how to capitalize on the unwelcome advances of the iceman and
who smells a little of the rubber shields in her dress." However,
Kathleen symbolized the economically and intellectually independent woman who had emerged following World War II, and when
Fitzgerald summarized her appeal for Monroe Stahr, based on
Hollywood producer Irving Thalberg, he was also speaking for
himself. "This girl had a life—it was very seldom he met anyone
whose life did not depend in some way on him or hope to depend
on him." Ironically, in a direct reversal of the way he had felt two
decades earlier, he was drawn again to a woman who had succeeded
where Zelda failed.

After returning from her two weeks in California, Scottie left for
a tour of Europe with Sara Murphy's close friend Alice Lee Myers.
Alice and her husband, Dick, a wine broker for M. Lehmann in
New York, had befriended the Fitzgeralds when the couple were
guests at the Murphys' Ferme des Oranges in Antibes. Alice and her
daughter Fanny, a good friend of Scottie's, were taking a small
group of girls on a moderately priced, station wagon tour of
France, Belgium, and Holland. Since the Murphys were leaving for
France at the same time, Scottie joined them for the crossing. Sara
and Gerald telegraphed Scott at MGM: "Alice Lee arranged to
have Scottie sail with us. Delighted to know her better."

Scottie returned to Vassar that fall, and, like her parents, was more interested in socializing and the theater than in her classwork. Worried she would repeat his Princeton failure, Fitzgerald continually badgered her to study math and science, for which Scottie had little interest, and warned her against frivolous activities that could threaten future success. In a July 1938 letter he was particularly critical: "What you have done to please me or make me proud is practically negligible since the time you made yourself a good diver at camp (and now you are softer than you have ever been). In your career as a 'wild society girl' vintage of 1925, I'm not interested, I don't want any of it—it would bore me like dining with the Ritz Brothers. When I do not feel you are 'going somewhere,' your company tends to depress me for the silly waste and triviality involved. On the other hand, when occasionally I see signs of life and intention in you, there is no company in the world I prefer. For there is no doubt that you have something in your belly, some real gusto for life—a real dream of your own—and my idea was to wed it to something solid before it was too late—as it was too late for your mother." Scottie, however, was determined to find her own way and resented his overbearing, advice-laden letters. "He didn't want me to have the fun of making my own mistakes—" she wrote. "He wanted to make them for me, but gave up in despair trying to nag and bully me into a worthwhile character."

From a safe distance of three thousand miles, Fitzgerald tried to make Zelda's life at Highland more tolerable by sending extra money for day trips and special excursions. "Dr. Carroll is taking a car load of people to Sarasota, Florida, tomorrow and I am at last a privileged character," she wrote Scott in November 1938. "It's five days en route and I can roll contentedly recapitulating through the Georgian clay-banks, and through the stark and lovely pines; and over long abandoned roads—the way I love to." For three weeks, she happily took life drawing classes at the Ringling School of Art along with a course in clothes designing, for which Fitzgerald paid. Relishing the stimulation and sunny weather, she wrote Scott: "I'm tanning myself and exploiting my soul to my private delectation, and am rapt and happy in such fine heaven. In this part of Florida, life seems to have nothing further to worry about than to open its shutters to a bright and new bazaar or newly acquired aspiration. It's such a good place and I am most deeply grateful to you for sending me here." A postcard followed on November 19: "Thanks for the trip. Fairy tale foliage and a gentle breeze echo the soft lap of the surf. Devotedly, Zelda." Fitzgerald responded that he was happy she had been able to get away from the hospital for so long, but his words had a distant ring. He was focusing on his own survival.

Zelda sensed the subtle change in Scott's communication, and became increasingly curious about details of his life in California. Though he had given her a post office box and several addresses where he could be reached, he never told her precisely where he lived. Now she wanted to know. "Meanwhile: what is your actual address? S'pose I wanted to phone you—or do something unprecedented like that?" In another letter, she complained: "I lost your address: Please send it again. What would I do if I should have a bad dream, or an inspiration? It's much more conventional to know where your husband is when you've got one—besides I might have something to tell you." But it was exactly this kind of intimacy he was trying to avoid.

Highland had arranged an excursion to Cuba for selected patients, but because of Fitzgerald's tardy approval—the letter had taken time to be forwarded from one address to another—Zelda was forced to remain behind. Disappointed but philosophical, she told Scott: "Havana is probably a substantial sort of place and may well be there till next time. Anyway, it's all very expensive, and we are so well adapted to spending money together. When you come East there will be that much more justification for buying things. I am as grateful to you as if I were on board. Come on! Let me see you fly East! We can go to Cuba ourselves, as far as that goes." Scott promised they would make the trip together, and that gave Zelda something to look forward to and write about. "I wish we were astride the tops of New York taxis and a little hilarious in parcs [sic] and public places, and younger than young people. But we will be when our trip is over and we are brown and briny and the world is completely secondary to the twilight breeze." When Zelda's sister Rosalind learned of the impending trip, she wrote to Dr. Carroll and questioned the wisdom of such a far-off excursion. But Zelda was determined to go and continued to tease Scott about their southbound vacation. She completed a drawing of him, entitled *Do-Do in Guatemala*, and wrote that she would "cook and so forth, and maybe discover gold if you will take me to Guatemala—or are you too busy?"

The Havana trip finally took place in April 1939, after Paramount canceled the script of "Air Raid," on which Scott was working. He left Los Angeles in a foul mood. Driving to the airport, he and Sheilah had quarreled and he arrived in Asheville exhausted, drunk, and running a fever. Zelda was nervous about departing with him in this condition but, desperate to leave Highland, decided to go. In Cuba, they checked into the Club Kawama at Varadero, which had charming beachfront cottages and a private tennis court. They took little advantage of either; Fitzgerald drank at Club Kawama's bar, built in the form of a ship's hull, while Zelda remained in their room praying. She realized the serious mistake she had made when Fitzgerald, after wandering off and trying to stop a cockfight, returned badly beaten. She was forced to get them both back to New York City. She planned to take him to the Obers', but Scott started a fight with the cabdriver on the way in from the airport, and they ended up at the Algonquin, where he collapsed from exhaustion. Trying to remain calm, Zelda called her sister Clothilde in Larchmont, and they got Scott admitted to Doctors' Hospital on East End Avenue. There, in room 403, from April 24 to April 27 he recuperated, accumulating a bill of $115.23. Against doctors' orders, after three days, he left for Los Angeles. The whole affair embarrassed Zelda; fearful that the incident might threaten future privileges, she took the train back to Asheville alone and told nobody what happened. Unstable as she was, in a crisis Zelda was still capable of being the sane one. Now she was fully cognizant of how badly things had deteriorated for Scott. "I wish things had been so that we were going on together somewhere," Zelda wrote regretfully in late April. "There are lots of happy places: it says so in the time tables."

When Scott arrived back in California, he immediately went to bed and remained in an alcoholic stupor for days. Guilty over what had happened and with genuine affection, he wrote Zelda apologetically: "You were a peach throughout the whole trip and there isn't a minute of it when I don't think of you with all the old tenderness and with a consideration that I never understood that you had before. . . . You are the finest, loveliest, tenderest, most beautiful person I have ever known, but even that is an understatement because the length that you went to there at the end would have tried anybody beyond endurance."

Archibald MacLeish had long agreed with that assessment. "Zelda was a finer wife to Scott than anyone else could have been. I can't say, I don't know, whether they were really in love then, or why she had married him; of course there was always that dashing boyish charm and recklessness about Scott that attracted women. But whether she loved him then or not, I don't think there was anyone else in the world, no other woman I have known, who could have put up with Scott the way he was, and with such understanding and kindness."

Paradoxically, the Cuban fiasco brought the couple closer than they had been in years, and even made Scott consider bringing Zelda to California. But after reconciling with Sheilah he decided against it, reminding Scottie to maintain silence about the relationship. Zelda continued writing letters expressing how much she wanted to be with him. She was well enough now to do artwork and produced enough for two exhibitions—the first in the spring at Maude King's Art School Sketch Club, and the second in the summer at the 1939 Asheville Artists' Guild Rhododendron Festival. Both received favorable reviews from the *The Asheville Citizen*, which commented on the supercharged, expressive nature of Zelda's work. "There is an arresting and imaginative quality about the painter's use of vivid color and abstract circular design to portray pure emotion that sticks in the observer's mind long after he had left the gallery. And there is a velvety effect about her handling of oil paint, which suggests the visions one conjures up by pressing the palms of the hands over the eyeballs in a dark room." When Dr. Carroll suggested that Zelda paint floral scenes on window screens in the new assembly building, she was exhilarated at the prospect. But excitement turned to anger when the screens wound up in patients' bedrooms. "To waste a professional talent," she wrote Scott bitterly, "the cumulate result of years of effort, aspiration and heartbreak on a venture which will never see the light of day but most probably will be maltreated by every manifestation of psychosis is, to me, an abuse of the soul, human faith, and metier that is almost beyond my capacity to envisage."

Sympathetic, Scott was too distracted by his own precarious circumstances to offer much solace. Hollywood had branded Fitzgerald an unsuccessful screenwriter and unreliable drunk, and he was now unable to find screen work. He also faced the dilemma of finding a new agent. Ober, who had represented him since the early twenties and was accustomed to providing royalty advances, no longer was willing to do so. In July 1939 they severed their long relationship. Scott told Harold sorrowfully, "The shock wasn't so much at your refusal to lend me a specific sum . . . it was rather 'the matter of the doing.' " He went on to thank Ober for his help over the years. "My unwritten debt to you is terribly large and I shall always be terribly aware of it." On July 19, Scott wrote Maxwell Perkins to confide his deep disappointment about the breakup. "Harold Ober and I are parting company. . . . I think something to do with it is the fact that almost every time I have come to New York lately I have just taken Zelda somewhere and have gone on more or less of a binge, and he has formed the idea that I am back in the mess of three years ago. . . . It is impossible to continue a relation which has become so strained and difficult. . . . There is a new fashion of discussing my stories as if he was a rather dissatisfied and cranky editor and of answering telegrams with delayed airmails and most of all, changing his old policy of backing me up to the limit of what the next story will probably be sold for."

For Scottie, the changed situation between Ober and her father was a terrible strain. She considered Harold and Anne surrogate parents, and her awkward position temporarily made continuing that relationship difficult. Scott further poisoned the waters even when he told Perkins: "Mrs. Ober and I had a run-in in which she told Scottie that she merely used her house as a convenience. The truth of the matter is one of those sad facts of life that for the past two years Scottie has only gone to the Obers on orders from me because I did not want to hurt her feelings. Mrs. Ober is, to say the least, an extremely difficult person."

Unable to borrow advance money from Ober, Scott was in desperate financial straits. At the end of May, to economize on monthly warehouse bills, Scott wrote Mrs. Owens in Baltimore, asking her to go through what they had in storage and reduce the space required. "I want to keep the lampshades Zelda made, three pairs of ballet slippers and throw out the rest, the lead soldiers, war slides, small china ornaments Zelda was fond of, all pictures, and all of Zelda's work."

With no further writing assignments coming from Universal or any other studio, Fitzgerald had little choice but to concentrate on his own work. Since no one was hiring him, he turned his attention to completing *The Last Tycoon*, a novel about the movie industry and Irving Thalberg, who had died three years earlier at thirty-seven. Hollywood's boy wonder, Thalberg's successes from the period included *Mutiny on the Bounty* and *Grand Hotel*. Scott had met the famous director in 1927 and greatly admired his intelligence and talent. Inspired to write about him, Fitzgerald contacted *Collier's Magazine* to ascertain their interests in a novel about Hollywood with Thalberg as the fictionalized main character. Their initial response was positive. They agreed to pay up to thirty thousand dollars if the first fifteen thousand words were approved. That was enough to make Fitzgerald concentrate almost full-time on the project. Given his low energy, that amounted to a few hours a day, generally propped up in bed against a pillow. Fitzgerald strongly identified with Stahr, modeled entirely on Thalberg, whose total mastery of the technical and artistic elements of filmmaking mirrored Scott's own talent in writing. Having completed the first chapter, he sent six thousand words to *Collier's*, who were unwilling to base their decision on the limited submission. Angrily, Scott broke off negotiations and went on an alcoholic binge that culminated in a nasty fight with Sheilah. In the ensuing months, he struggled to finish the first half of the novel and outline the rest.

Without money, he quickly fell behind in payments to Highland. On September 27, 1939, he wrote asking Dr. Carroll's associate, Dr. R. H. Suitt, for an extension. "I hope you will find it possible to let things go on as they are for another month trusting me as you did before. I hope that this does not mean Zelda will be deprived of ordinary necessities. As you know I tried to give Zelda every luxury permissible when I could afford it (the trip to Florida, etc.), but it is simply impossible to pay anything even on installments when one drives in a mortgaged Ford and tries to get over the habit of looking into a handkerchief for blood when talking to a producer."

Aware of the debt she was incurring, Zelda discussed the situation with her sister Marjorie, and suggested leaving Highland to live with her mother in Montgomery. When Marjorie received a telegram from Scott on October 20 saying that he was broke except for $100 in the bank, she questioned why he still insisted that Zelda remain at Highland. "If you can't pay her board, where is she to go? Or is Dr. Carroll to keep her free of charge? Zelda only wants to come home because she also is worried about you and thinks she could quit being such a financial drain on you."

Zelda continually wrote Scott asking to be released so she could live with her mother in Montgomery. Dr. Carroll discussed the situation with her, but felt it was still too soon for her to leave the hospital. He wrote to Mrs. Sayre on October 15 explaining the situation: "The facts remain unchanged—that she has been mentally injured, that the central nervous system is peculiarly susceptible, and that she should be protected with the same intelligence that any family would expect to give a member who has suffered from a damaging tuberculosis. Our suggestions have been carefully thought out and include her having short vacations of ten days to three weeks about once in two months during the year. She is not prepared to live comfortably with any of the members of her family."

Scott refused to be held responsible for another mental collapse, so was firmly set against Zelda going home. On the same day he had telegraphed Marjorie, he pleaded with Dr. Carroll to persuade Zelda to stop demanding her release. "I think if there is any way to stop this continual nagging through Zelda it will be a help. I had every intention of sending her to Montgomery with a nurse this October but there was no money. Of course, at present I am not in any mood to give her anything, even if I could afford it. After a few weeks in Montgomery, her first attempt would be to beg or borrow enough to get out here and hang herself around my neck—in which case a California State Asylum would be the last stop on this tragic journey. *All pretty black, isn't it? Please try and persuade her not to send me any more of those letters.*"

But Zelda had the support of her sisters, and her continued pressuring of Fitzgerald precipitated a bitter exchange of letters among Rosalind, Marjorie, and Scott. They accused Fitzgerald of warehousing Zelda at Highland so as not to be inconvenienced. Scott shot back, reminding Rosalind of how poorly Mrs. Sayre had supervised Zelda as a girl, angrily writing Marjorie, "I have taken this whole thing pretty well from Roz's first accusation in 1930 that I 'drove Zelda crazy' through your mother's accusations that I sent her to Johns Hopkins in 1932 for ulterior motives. I am sick of all this God damn hypocrisy. The preposterous idea that Zelda's sanity can be bought with a one-way ticket to Montgomery is in line with everything you've thought about the case as a family from 1930 on. You all lie on your backs shaking your fists, mistaking your cowardice for an aristocratic attitude. You have nothing to offer. Why don't you for God's sake, shut up!" Scott had the good sense, however, not to send the letter.

Instead, he continued to communicate civilly with Mrs. Sayre. In a lengthy analysis of Zelda's shattered psyche, he had written her the previous January, exhibiting a deep sensitivity and an understanding of her illness. Because of his own inability to care for Zelda in California, and an awareness of her condition, he stressed the necessity for a safe and protected environment. "There is no favorable prognosis for dementia praecox. In certain diseases the body builds new cells, drawing on its own inner vitality. When there has been destruction in the patterns of the mind only the very tiniest shell can be formed over them—so to speak—so that Zelda is always living in a house of thinly spun glass. Most of the time she functions perfectly within this house because the hospital protects her from any of life's accidental stones or from any damage that she might carelessly or absentmindedly do herself. Carroll believes that this is the only way that she will be able to function."

To be certain Scottie understood the actual circumstances, Fitzgerald asked Dr. Suitt to write her about Zelda's condition. "I would like her [Scottie] to know from a medical source the simple facts that her mother, no matter how well she may hold up for short periods, will almost certainly never be able to hold her own in the world again without some strong guiding and directing hand. Secondly, I think she should know that the onset of menopause is most likely to cause sudden and unpredictable derangement. Thirdly, that any prolonged strain might cause a sudden outbreak with very little warning which would be dangerous and possibly disastrous to everyone around her."

But while Scott outwardly continued to refuse Zelda's release, he quietly began discussing that possibility with Dr. Carroll. However, he insisted that Carroll provide a letter absolving him of any responsibility in the event of relapse, and demanded the doctor's guarantee that Zelda could reenter Highland whenever necessary. He had taken the same stand with Dr. Meyer at Phipps, but Meyer would never agree to allow Zelda to reenter at will. Now, Fitzgerald remained firm on this point. He wrote Scottie: "I'm having a controversy with Highland Hospital. They want to keep your mother there with only 6 weeks out a year and a few trips with Dr. and Mrs. Carroll. I can't see it—. I think she should be out from one fourth to one half the time, using the hospital only as a base."

At the end of the month, Zelda's future was finally settled when Carroll wrote Scott: "What do you think of letting her go home, say about the lst of April—giving the mother an outline of certain danger signs which, should they appear, indicate a tendency to re-lapse. Thus we let the family share the responsibilities as long as all is well. *She can return to the hospital from Montgomery at any time need should develop.*" Scott immediately wrote Mrs. Sayre. "This morning I have a letter from Dr. Carroll in which he suggests for the first time that Zelda try life in Montgomery. This is a complete about-face for him, but I do not think that his suggestion comes from any but the most sincere grounds." He simultaneously shared the good news with Zelda. "It is wonderful to be able to write you this. Dr. Carroll has for the first time and at long last agreed that per-haps you shall try to make a place for yourself in the world. In other words, that you can go to Montgomery the first of April and remain there indefinitely or as long as you seem able to carry on under your own esteem. [*sic*] . . . I share your joy—."

Knowing the Highland bills would stop took some financial pressure off Scott, but to further economize, he considered moving into Hollywood. He had vacated his Malibu cottage in October of 1938, and had been renting a guest house called Belly Acres on the Encino estate of Edward Everett Horton. It was a pleasant enough place where pink roses climbed the garden gate, but out in the San Fernando Valley. The decision was accelerated when he experi-enced his first heart spasm in January 1940 while opening a jammed window at the Encino cottage. The sharp pain took his breath away and he immediately called his physician, Dr. Clarence Nelson, who warned him to be cautious if he wanted to avert a more serious at-tack. It scared him. To eliminate the long drive into town and be nearer to Sheilah, with whom he had reconciled, he rented a fur-nished apartment on North Laurel Avenue in West Hollywood, just one block from hers. In March, he moved into an upper floor of the two-story, L-shaped garden complex set back from the street. It had a living room, dining room, small kitchen, and bedroom, and was a sterile place containing few personal items except his books.

Scott wrote Zelda's mother that he had moved, still keeping the exact address secret. "I am moving into town to be nearer my work, but have not yet an address. For the present will you or Zelda write me care of my new agent (Phil Berg, 9484 Wilshire Boulevard, Beverly Hills) or else 'General Delivery, Encino, Calif.,' as they will forward it."

As she assumed full responsibility for Zelda's care, Mrs. Sayre was informed that her daughter's condition was cyclic and that ma-

nia could recur at any time. Scott made sure the family understood
that Zelda would probably remain an invalid for the rest of her life.
On April 15, 1940, four years and one week after she was admitted
to Highland, Zelda boarded an early morning bus for Montgomery.
She carried a letter from Scott that wished her well, but one written
with unfamiliar coolness. "I do hope this goes well. I wish you were
going to brighter surroundings but this is certainly not the time to
come to me and I can think of nowhere else for you to go in this
dark and bloody world. I suppose a place is what you make it but I
have grown to hate California and would give my life for three
years in France. So Bon Voyage and Stay well." Writing the Murphys of her release, the side effects of her electroshock therapy are
evident in his description of her altered personality. "Zelda is home
since this week Tuesday—at her mother's in Montgomery. She has
a poor pitiful life, reading the Bible in the old-fashioned manner
walking tight lipped and correct through a world she can no longer
understand—playing with the pieces of old things as if a man a
thousand years hence tried to reconstruct our civilization from a
Baroque cornice, a figurine from Trajan's columns, an aeroplane
wing and a page of Petrarch all picked up in the Roman forum. Part
of her mind is washed clean + she is no one I ever knew."

As Scott had feared, Zelda's readjustment to life in Montgomery
was easy for neither herself nor her family. Within eight weeks she
experienced her first setback. On June 6, Fitzgerald wrote Scottie:
"Dear, I have had a very depressed letter from your mother and another from your grandmother—the second told me in cautious language that your mother had had a 'toxic attack.' I know what this
means, only I had expected her to hold out at least two months. She
seems to be recovered from that, but her own letter shows a great
deal of despair, and your grandmother has a defeatism in her letter
that I have never seen before." Mrs. Sayre, who had never witnessed Zelda's illness firsthand, was shocked by its severity. She had
her daughter back, albeit a greatly changed one, but caring for her
proved an exhausting, full-time job. It was a situation Scott knew
well. Fitzgerald urged Scottie to sacrifice part of her summer and
visit Zelda in Montgomery. "I don't know what is going to happen,"
he wrote, "but as this may be the last time you have a chance to see
your mother in a sane period, *I want you to find ten days to spend with
her in June.*"

Zelda telegraphed Scott in California on the morning of June 18:

"I won't be able to stick this out. Will you wire money immediately that I may return Friday to Asheville. Will see Scottie there. Devotedly Regretfully Gratefully—Zelda." That same afternoon she wired again: "Disregard telegram am fine again. Happy to see Scottie. Devotedly, Zelda." Whatever the crisis had been, it passed, and Scottie arrived on June 20—determined to make their visit pleasant. "I have been an angel with mama," she wrote her father, "and we have really gotten along rather well. I even went so far as to discuss marriage with her so as she'd feel she had some ideas to contribute." But their relationship had seldom been of a mother-and-daughter nature, and the visit was a burden for Scottie, who recognized how circumscribed and artificial Zelda's life had become. "I always forget how people can dull their desire for an energetic life. She is nevertheless like a fish out of water. Her ideas are too elaborately worded to be even faintly comprehensible to anyone in the town, and yet too basically wrong to be of real interest to people who really know anything. . . ." What Scottie failed to take into consideration, and what Fitzgerald had long hid from her, was that Zelda's changed personality was the result of the insulin and electroshock therapies she had undergone for almost a decade.

Though he had not seen Zelda since the episode in Cuba a year earlier, Fitzgerald remained the faithful correspondent. It had been twenty years since Westport and *This Side of Paradise*, and he had written wistfully on June 14: "Ten years ago Paris was having almost its last great American season but we had quit the gay parade and you were gone to Switzerland. Five years ago I had my first bad stroke of illness and went to Asheville. Cards began falling badly for us much too early." Clearly feeling elegiac, he wrote Scottie the same day: "What little I've accomplished has been by the most laborious and uphill work, and I wish now I'd never relaxed or looked back—but said at the end of 'The Great Gatsby' 'I've found my line—from now on this comes first. This is my immediate duty—without this I am nothing.' "

The summer dragged on. Scott's energy was at a low ebb and the theft of his Ford by a teenager made matters worse. Yet he ultimately saw the humor in it and wrote Scottie: "The police have just called telling me they've recovered my car. The thief ran out of gas and abandoned it in the middle of Hollywood Boulevard. The poor lad was evidently afraid to call anybody to help him push it to the curb. I hope next time he gets a nice, big producer's car with plenty of gas in it and a loaded revolver in each side pocket and he can embark on a career of crime in earnest. I don't like to see any education left hanging in the air."

The impossibility of meeting even reduced expenses was a constant worry. He was unable to sleep, consumed vast amounts of gin, and developed a hacking cough from too many cigarettes. And though Sara Murphy recognized a streak of hypochrondria in Scott, she grew worried. "I do not like to feel that you consider yourself ill. I can't believe you are," she wrote him in August. "Your account of your condition for some reason recalled to me my own surprise the day you came to see us in New York wearing rubbers— which you removed and remembered to put on again when you left. It seemed so unlike my idea of you. It still is." Fitzgerald appreciated her concern and wished she was right.

By September, he was forced to ask the Murphys for a loan, telling them, "You saved me—Scottie and me—in spite of our small deserts. I don't think I could have asked anyone else and kept what pride it is necessary to keep." Fitzgerald happily confided to Gerald that he and Scottie were much closer now: "She is nicer now than she has been since she was a little girl. I haven't seen her for a year but she writes long letters and I feel closer to her than I have since she was little." About life in Los Angeles, he added, "I find, after a long time out here—It is—such a slack soft place—even its pleasure lacking the fierceness or excitement of Provence—that withdrawal is practically a condition of safety. The sin is to upset anyone else, and much of what is known as 'progress' is attained by more or less delicately poking and prodding other people. . . . Everywhere there is, after a moment, either corruption or indifference." Gerald and Sara agreed, writing, "We share in retrospect your feelings about Hollywood. We stood alone in a community made of tight little sets, all of whom distrusted each other." Scott carefully apportioned the Murphys' money, sending some to Scottie at Vassar and applying the rest toward outstanding bills.

The realization he could no longer make a living took a devastating physical toll. At a cocktail party at Dorothy Parker's home that September, Clifford Odets noted that Scott looked "pale, unhealthy, as if the tension of life had been wrenched out of him." Initially, Zelda did not take his condition seriously. "I'm sorry you can't sleep; and sorry that you don't like to get up," she wrote Scott. "Maybe you ought to complain to the management. Or take a reconstituting week such as I have been nagging about for the last twenty years; of sunshine, of relaxation, of letting events take place in the papers. . . ." But as weeks passed, she sensed the seriousness of his circumstances and became increasingly concerned. "Take care of yourself," she warned. "Though you say the doctors say you're far better than they think, I know you're not given to very accurate estimates of your condition." She suggested a different climate. "This part of the world is far more conducive to good health; also it is cheaper. Why don't you consider it again? . . . Maybe you would be better off in this climate where the mountains might help you find more resistance again. Why don't you move to Arizona, or come back to Tryon? Don't just stay there and drift away. Besides, it must not be happy to be sick alone. If you come East, Scottie and I could see you more often."

Two months later, on November 28, he suffered his first serious cardiac spasm at Schwab's drugstore and was ordered to bed rest. Determined to finish his novel, he kept writing *The Last Tycoon* propped up against pillows. "The doctor after seeing my cardiogram has confined me to the house," he wrote Scottie. "So at this moment I couldn't go to the studios if I wanted to." Then, in what would be his last letter to his daughter, Fitzgerald advised: "You have two beautiful bad examples for parents. Just do everything we didn't do and you will be perfectly safe. But be sweet to your mother at Xmas despite her early Chadean rune-worship which she will undoubtedly inflict on you. Her letters are tragically brilliant in all matters except those of central importance. How strange to have failed as a social creature—even criminals do not fail that way— they are the law's 'Loyal Opposition' so to speak. But the insane are always mere guests on earth, eternal strangers carrying around broken decalogues that they cannot read." Feeling fragile, he put his will in order and specifically directed his executor to keep any sensitive material about Zelda away from Scottie. "All correspondence in a file that is devoted exclusively to my wife's illness shall be destroyed, or else, in case she should prove to still be unwell, that the salient documents should be handed over in packet to the responsible doctor and the others destroyed. *I do not want these to reach my daughter.* To recapitulate in this important regard: such documents as are medically necessary would be preserved and all else destroyed."

In December, after experiencing recurrent dizzy spells, Fitz-

THE END OF THE STORY

gerald vacated his second-floor apartment on North Laurel and moved into Sheilah Graham's nearby ground-floor flat on North Hayworth. So as not to worry Zelda, he minimized his condition. "No news except that the novel progresses and I am angry that this little illness has slowed me up. I've had trouble with my heart before but never anything organic. This is not a major attack, but seems to have come on gradually and luckily a cardiogram showed it up in time. I may have to move from the third- to the first-floor apartment but I'm quite able to work, etc., if I do not overtire myself."

In an effort to bolster his deteriorating health, he stopped drinking entirely and ate dinner—usually a simple meal of chicken or steak prepared by the part-time maid—with Sheilah every night. He had completed almost 45,000 words of his novel, when, after seeing a movie with Graham on December 20, he suffered a second more serious heart attack. The next day he had a third attack and at 3:00 P.M. on Saturday, December 21, 1940, Fitzgerald died. The cause of death was alcoholic cardiomyopathy—enlargement of the heart chambers—a condition common in alcoholics, often leading to heart failure.

Harold Ober called Zelda in Montgomery to inform her of Scott's death, but she was taking a long afternoon walk with her friend Julia Garland. When she got home, her mother told her the sad news. Scottie, who was staying with the Obers in Scarsdale over the Christmas holidays, had gone to a dance in Poughkeepsie, so Harold sent his son Dick to tell her. At John Biggs's request, Frances Kroll, Fitzgerald's secretary, called a Los Angeles mortician and arranged for Fitzgerald's body to be taken to the Pierce Brothers Mortuary on West Washington Boulevard, where it was put on view in the William Wordsworth Room. Fitzgerald had made few friends in California. Dorothy Parker was among the small number of mourners in a room of empty chairs and one lone bouquet. Scottie immediately left the Obers to be with her mother.

In an attempt to make his passing seem more real, Zelda telephoned Frances Kroll on Christmas Eve to learn the details of Scott's death. It upset her that she had not had the chance to say good-bye, and she deeply regretted that Scott had been alone and so far from his family at the end. However, Zelda did not inquire about anyone else in his life, and after writing Kroll to express her gratitude, wrote a second letter to ask for Scott's notebooks and his well-worn thesaurus. In Fitzgerald's first will, composed in June

1937, he had named John Biggs and Harold Ober as co-executors. But after severing relations with Ober—on November 10, 1940, just one month before his death—he had crossed out Ober's name and replaced it with Maxwell Perkins's. Biggs actually served two functions: executor of the estate, and overseer of Zelda and Scottie's trust after the estate was settled.

Initially, Zelda seemed confused and gave strange orders for the disposition of Scott's body. After regaining her composure, she directed Biggs to have the coffin shipped to Maryland; Biggs then asked Frances Kroll to have Fitzgerald's casket transported east by train. When it arrived in Baltimore, it was brought to the William J. Tichnor and Sons Mortuary. Too distraught to attend the funeral, Zelda remained in Montgomery under the careful watch of her mother, and asked her brother-in-law, Newman Smith, to serve in her place. He arrived from Atlanta to oversee the arrangements and followed the directives Zelda sent by letter. Fitzgerald had always hoped to be buried beside his Maryland ancestors in his family's plot at St. Mary's Catholic Cemetery in Rockville, Maryland; "I belong here where everything is civilized, gay, rotted and polite." But when Zelda tried to arrange this, an official with the Baltimore Diocese refused to grant him a Catholic burial because Fitzgerald was not a practicing Catholic at the time of death and had not received last rites. John Biggs, who was then the youngest judge sitting on the Third U.S. Circuit Court of Appeals, questioned that decision with Baltimore's bishop, but was unable to reverse the opinion of the Baltimore Diocese. "I made repeated requests to the office of the Bishop of Baltimore that Fitzgerald be given a Catholic funeral and buried beside his father. In so far as I can recall, I was finally informed that Fitzgerald had not made his 'Easter duty' and that his writings were undesirable." So they held a memorial service at the Pumphrey Funeral Home with a eulogy by Reverend Raymond Black, an Episcopalian minister. This time the room overflowed with flowers—the Princeton Class of 1917 sent yellow roses, the Turnbulls a wreath of white ones, Honoria Murphy mixed roses, and John and Margaret Bishop white chryanthemums. Ludlow Fowler sent a spray of pink gladioli, John and Anna Biggs red roses, lilies, and snapdragons; the Sayre family red roses; and Zelda a basket of pink gladioli.

The burial took place at dusk on December 27, 1940, at the Union Cemetery in Rockville, Maryland, with approximately twenty-five of Fitzgerald's friends and relatives attending. Standing in the rain at Fitzgerald's grave were nineteen-year-old Scottie and several of her friends, Newman Smith (Rosalind did not come, nor did Sheilah Graham, who was asked to stay away), Scott's cousin Cecilia Taylor and her four daughters from Norfolk, Maxwell and Louise Perkins, Harold and Anne Ober, the Murphys, Turnbulls, Biggses, and Ludlow Fowler. "About everybody," surmised the absent Rosalind, "who could have been reasonably expected for a funeral in a Maryland village on a winter day, for one who had been away for years. And from New York came an old playmate from the 'cuckoo days,' the man who stood on his head at the Metropolitan Opera, whose name I have forgotten and who has since died [Dick Knight]." People commented on Zelda's absence and Scottie's stoicism. But she had always been a private person and hated public displays of emotion. "Of course I was upset that my father was dead," she later wrote: "And of course my friends were concerned and supportive of me or they wouldn't have gone to the trouble to go with me." But she also admitted being "sort of ashamed of him because he was far more famous as a drunk fallen on hard times than as a brilliant writer."

Following the funeral, Zelda wrote Harold Ober a letter about her life with Scott. "In retrospect, it seems as if he was always planning happiness for Scottie and me. Books to read—places to go. Life seemed so promissory when he was around, and I always believed that he could take care of anything. It seems so useless and purposeless that I won't be able to tell him about all this. Although we were not close anymore, Scott was the best friend a person could have been to me." Convinced that he would ultimately be judged a major American writer, and sensing Scottie's ambivalence toward his reputation, Zelda wrote her daughter, "I always feel that daddy was the key-note and prophet of his generation and deserves remembrance as such since he dramatized the last post-war era and gave the real significance to those gala and so-tragically fated days. He tabulated and greatly envied football players and famous athletes and liked girls from the popular songs; he loved gorging on canned voluptes [sensuous pleasures] at curious hours and, as you have had many controversial run-ins with, was the longest and most exhaustive conversationalist I ever met."

In 1940, Fitzgerald's entire estate amounted to less than $35,000, out of which Biggs was challenged to provide a monthly income for

Zelda and Scottie. He purchased an annuity that brought Zelda fifty dollars a month, and also secured, after substantiating details of Fitzgerald's army enlistment, a monthly veteran widow's pension for an additional $35. To further enhance their financial situation, he consolidated whatever cash he could—principally life insurance proceeds—and invested that money in El Paso Natural Gas and Panhandle Eastern Pipe line. But the biggest financial benefit came from royalties he astutely collected from Fitzgerald's writing by having unpublished material printed, and by licensing the literary rights to *The Great Gatsby* and *Tender Is the Night* for film projects and television.

With loans from Ober, Perkins, and Murphy, Biggs also paid Scottie's Vassar bills, which enabled her to remain at the expensive school. Scottie helped by pawning the fur coat Sheilah Graham had sent her. During some school holidays, she stayed with the Biggses at their Woodale, Delaware, home and confided to John: "If it weren't for you nothing could have gone so smoothly and we would undoubtedly all be floating around in space tearing our hair out." And Zelda, as a way of expressing her own appreciation to Biggs for his efforts, gave John the oil painting of calla lilies that he had long admired. He promptly hung it on the center wall of his study. But being executor of Fitzgerald's estate left such an indelible mark on Biggs's identity that even after forty years of distinguished judicial service, he was still occasionally introduced as Fitzgerald's executor and Princeton roommate—a representation he came to resent.

On Fitzgerald's death, the unfinished draft of *The Last Tycoon* consisted of sixty thousand words, accompanied by a sheaf of notes, bringing the story approximately halfway to conclusion. Edited by Edmund Wilson, it appeared posthumously in October of 1941, and even in truncated form, made for absorbing reading. A behind-the-scenes look at the movie business and the men who control it, Fitzgerald's intuitive perceptions are evident throughout. As Scott had successfully done in *Gatsby*, a narrator is used to advance the story—the daughter of another Hollywood producer who looks back on events from the distance of several years. Fitzgerald had gotten it just right and the reviews were glowing. The *New York Times* called it an ambitious book showing a firm grasp of the material, which, if finished, would have been Fitzgerald's best work. And critics from the *Chicago Tribune* and *The New Yorker* gave it high praise. In 1971 the novel still garnered enough interest to be adapted for the movies by Harold Pinter. Co-directing the film were Jack Nicholson and Elia Kazan; actors included Robert De Niro, Anjelica Houston, Robert Mitchum, and Tony Curtis.

Scott's death and the cyclical nature of her illness put Zelda at constant risk for relapse. Fitzgerald's foresight proved critical, for during the next eight years, she voluntarily reentered Highland three times: the first, from August 1943 until February 1944, then for eight months beginning in early 1946 until late summer, and from November 2, 1947, until March 10, 1948. But during this second round of Highland stays following Fitzgerald's death, Zelda's symptoms were more pronounced, and the interventions to relieve them more dramatic. These primarily involved repeated insulin and electroshock therapies. Zelda had probably undergone these treatments at Sheppard Pratt when they were in experimental stages; now they were standard procedure.

In January of 1937, Dr. Manfred Sakel had presented a paper at the New York Academy of Medicine documenting several case histories with successful outcomes after utilizing insulin therapy. While it still remained unclear why insulin shock shortened the course of schizophrenia, Sakel was absolutely convinced that it was the most effective method for providing symptomatic relief. *Time* magazine in April of 1939 reported that "Sakel frankly declared he does not know how and why his cure works, but that it indubitably works." Dr. Sakel had received an honorary degree from Colgate University and was offered a professorship in the Midwest, but preferred to live in New York City. There he attracted private funding through the Gimbel Foundation and established the Sakel Foundation, which trained physicians in the methods of insulin therapy. On the January day that Sakel presented his paper at the Academy of Medicine, Adolf Meyer was in the audience, and he was impressed enough with Sakel's results that he shortly thereafter introduced insulin treatments at Phipps Clinic. He also recommended its use to other physicians, including Dr. Carroll at Highland, and soon insulin therapy was universally touted as the best treatment available for schizophrenia.

By 1941, insulin, Metrazol, and electroshock therapies were

extensively being used in most American psychiatric hospitals. Administered in a separate ward where patients could be closely monitored, insulin treatments required a precise and systematic application to obtain a series of hypoglycemic comas of specific length and frequency. The deeper the coma, the greater the destruction of the sick neurons in the brain. However, since insulin also created an acute disorganization of the carbohydrate metabolism in the brain's ganglion cells, finding the appropriate dose was of critical importance. Doctors had to be extremely careful because patients kept too long in coma risked brain damage or death. Patients were given insulin injections to reduce their blood sugar levels and induce hypoglycemic shock. The goal was to precipitate between fifty and one hundred deep, prolonged comas with an average treatment lasting three months. During the period of treatment, patients remained in a daze and experienced weight gains of twenty to sixty pounds because of the insulin combined with a high-sugar and starch diet. A more serious side effect was memory loss. Insulin treatments were sometimes enhanced with electric or cardiazol shock, a procedure that produced epileptic seizure. Believing grand-mal epileptic convulsions to be biologically antagonistic to schizophrenia, doctors theorized that the disorder might be cured by introducing symptoms of epilepsy. Used in Italy since 1937, when it was discovered by Ugo Cerletti in collaboration with Lucio Bini, electroshock initially was used exclusively for schizophrenia, but then was found to be effective in treating depression. The standard treatment required twenty consecutive shocks to be given three times a week. A frightening experience, causing both temporary and permanent memory loss, it often accelerated a patient's motivation to improve—in many cases simply to avoid further treatments.

As terrifying as they were, these interventions were effective in reducing symptoms. By artificially lowering a patient's level of consciousness, making it easier for them to cope, regained memories often returned without the accompanying anxiety. However, while insulin and electroshock therapy could calm patients for substantial periods of time, they could not eradicate the cause of mental illness, and ultimately symptoms of the underlying abnormality returned. Nevertheless, both of these interventions enabled Zelda to live away from Highland for long periods of time. For most of the eight years following Scott's death, she was able to remain in Montgomery with her mother in the little white bungalow at 322 Sayre Street, which the family had nicknamed Rabbit Run.

Zelda made the most of those years. She took long daily walks, bicycled, worked in the garden, sewed her own clothes and kept in touch with friends. "Down here, the little garden blows remotely poetic under the voluptes of late spring skies," she wrote Ludlow Fowler. "I have a cage of doves who sing and woo the elements and die. My mother is 85 but still able and extremely interesting. This little house looks like something out of the three bears; it would be fun were life less tempestuous. Being decorous and dutiful is beyond my immediate capacity, but I still read faithfully my Bible and ask God for justice."

Her sister Rosalind refuted the notion that during this time Zelda was an invalid. "I find the description of her as 'frail' unfitting. She had great physical endurance and energy. And even in her last years at our mother's here, she walked miles every day and worked the garden she kept. She was too vital to appear delicate." The living room at Rabbit Run was a cozy place with wide-armed rockers, a chintz-covered sofa, and numerous pictures and mementos adorning both the mantel and Zelda's old upright piano. In the afternoons, Zelda read on the outdoor patio as the doves cooed in their cage. She played casino games with her mother on the front porch and had frequent conversations with her sister Marjorie, who lived next door. She also befriended a young spastic girl with whom she deeply emphathized—highly intelligent but painfully shy because of her facial contortions.

In support of the war effort, Zelda folded bandages at the local Red Cross twice a week. But this time she had no military suitors among those assigned to local depots. Dance still interested her and she took occasional lessons from Amelia Harper Rosenberg, who had been a pupil of George Balanchine. Zelda practiced her ballet steps on the outdoor patio adjacent to the kitchen and also painted there. In August 1941, she exhibited a collection of paper dolls in the Children's Room of the Montgomery Museum of Fine Arts. The *Montgomery Advertiser* reviewed the collection favorably, saying, "They are in no way ordinary paper dolls, but paintings after the manner of the modern French painters, which Mrs. Fitzgerald believes is the best way to introduce children to the trends in contemporary painting." The positive response encouraged her to contact Maxwell Perkins about the possibility of publishing them. "I have painted . . . King Arthur's roundtable, Louis XIV and court, Robin Hood are under way. The dolls are charming. . . . Would you be kind enough to advise me what publishers handle such 'literature,' and how to approach?" Perkins thought they were very good and encouraged Zelda to continue making them. But they would not see publication until the 1960s when *Esquire* initially published some, and 1996 when Abrams brought all of them out in book form.

Throughout 1942, she continued to paint and donated a number of canvases to Herndon Smith for the Federal Artists' Project at Maxwell Field Army Base, as well as exhibiting oils and drawings in two shows. The first opened in May and ran through Christmas at the galleries of the Montgomery Museum of Fine Arts and the other was held in December at the Women's Club. Among the most discussed of her works was a portrait of Fitzgerald with a cat on his shoulder done in varying hues of green, and a self-portrait in which her intense eyes dominate the entire composition.

Two years after Fitzgerald's death, Scottie graduated from Vassar. She had evolved into a capable journalist and weeks after commencement in June 1942 began her reporting career as a temporary staffer at *The New Yorker*. Her assignment: to find interesting tidbits for the eclectic column "Talk of the Town." Following that, she took a full-time publicist's job at Radio City Music Hall, but found the position uninspiring and left after ten weeks. She then moved to the sports department of *Time*, which was replacing reporters who had been called to wartime service. But Scottie knew little about athletics, and did a poor job reporting on baseball, harness racing, boxing, tennis, and golf. She was quickly transferred to the magazine's fifteen-minute radio program "Time Views the News," and later to *Fortune*.

She had been dating a naval officer, and Zelda was delighted when Scottie decided to marry Ensign Samuel Jackson Lanahan, called Jack, a Baltimore native who was serving in the Atlantic as assistant navigator aboard the U.S.S. *Card*. He was the son of a wealthy stockbroker and a 1937 graduate from Saint Paul's. He had entered Princeton as an English major, and during Christmas holidays of his junior year had met Scottie. Jack was not only handsome, he also represented the stability she craved. Fitzgerald had known of him and in April of 1940 had written Scottie: "I am glad you are going to Princeton with whom you are going. I feel you have now jumped a class. Boys like Kilduff and Lanahan are on a guess more 'full of direction' than most of the happy-go-luckies in Cap and Gown."

When he was granted a leave from his ship—on which he served twenty-seven months—the wedding was hastily planned by the Obers. Anne purchased the dress and Harold gave Scottie away. The short ceremony took place on February 13, 1943, at 3:00 P.M. in Manhattan's Church of St. Ignatius Loyola. The Biggses were among the guests at a reception in the Barclay Hotel. Sadly, Zelda did not attend or assist with preparations. "I felt guilty about having left notifying my mother until it was too late for her to plan to come," Scottie later wrote, "but she was not well enough at the time and I feared that if she was in one of her eccentric phases it would cast a pall over the affair."

Instead, early the following summer, Zelda went north to see Scottie in Scarsdale and stopped at the Biggses' Woodale house on her way back to Montgomery. During their brief visit, they observed how tense Zelda appeared. She was; in August, she readmitted herself to Highland for six months. This time she refused to interact with anybody. One of the few hospital employees able to penetrate her self-imposed isolation was Landon Ray. He had directed outdoor activities at Highland since February of 1938, and knew Zelda from previous admissions. More than others, Ray was able to communicate with Zelda during this period, and could calm her bouts of emotional turmoil. Tall and attractive, he was eight years Zelda's junior, full of energy and the kind of individual Zelda liked. They often took walks to gather wood for camping excursions. Ray recalled one such hike across Sunset Mountain near the Grove Park Inn when it began to rain and Zelda marched off into the wet briar to hunt for dry kindling. She and Ray got along well when alone, but if another female patient diverted his attention, she became jealous. "She once became so envious," Ray remembered, "that she slapped a cup of coffee out of the hand of another woman who approached us in conversation."

In February 1944, Zelda was released from Highland and returned home to continue living nostalgically in the past. On the rear wall of her mother's cottage she painted a mural about her life with Scott, and to supplement her income decorated wooden bowls and metal trays with scenes of Paris and New York. She painted a series of these for Scottie depicting all the places they had lived during her childhood.

She also continued working on "Caesar's Things," which had greatly changed from her initial idea and become a collage of fantasy, autobiography, and religious doctrine. Her writing, however, was hampered by recurring messianic delusions. With her father, brother, and Scott now gone, there were no men in her life, and her reliance on God filled her need for the male strength upon which she had always depended. For a time she considered becoming a Catholic, as George Jean Nathan later would do. Mimeographing essays to express her religious fervor, she sent them to friends to save their souls. Edmund Wilson received one, as did Carl Van Vechten, and she warned John Biggs—whose efforts on her behalf she appreciated, but whose behavior toward women she abhorred—that he would die in a year and should conduct himself accordingly. In contrast, she assured Maxwell Perkins, whom she had always admired, that the Lord watched over him. Regularly on Sundays she attended mass at the Episcopal Church of the Holy Comforter, but also went on weekdays to avail herself of the serenity she could not find elsewhere. "There's no place else to go and think," she told Sara Mayfield, "unless I take a streetcar and ride to the end of the line and back." Though a quiet life, it was not altogether an unhappy one. Rosalind recalled that "she became a person of the utmost rectitude who spent her time at her art and in trying bravely to rehabilitate herself and in doing good for others. She remained a highly nervous person and occasionally had to return to the hospital to get herself under control, but she also had many long good periods when she was able to follow her interests, keep up with her friends, and live a fairly normal life. She had a warm friendliness that attracted people to her even when she was ill, and in Montgomery up to the last, there were many who admired her and were devoted to her."

In February 1944, Zelda was excited to hear that Scottie had been offered another reporting job at *The New Yorker*. Her success in competing for the highly coveted position was due both to her pedigree—she was after all Fitzgerald's daughter—and the fact that a fair number of reporters were still serving in the military. But she was also a good writer. At eighteen, Scottie had sold her first story, "A Wonderful Time," to *The New Yorker*, and Harold Ross, the magazine's founder and editor, liked her keen intelligence, honesty, and energetic good nature. Brendan Gill was on the editorial staff at the time and considered her a valuable asset. He remembered seeing the watercolors and drawings she regularly received from her mother, and from time to time tried to persuade the art editor to publish them. "The pictures consisted of non-representational diagonal slashes," Gill recalled, "triangles and other geometric forms, in which one saw, or given the circumstances, convinced oneself that one had seen, the expression of a violent, undischarged rage." Scottie remembered the happy times at the magazine, writing, "There was a great collection of eccentrics and everyone was encouraged to do his or her own thing." In her spare time she managed to write a story for the *Saturday Review of Literature* called "New Yorker Story 1945," and another for *Colliers* entitled "The Importance of Being Kissed."

During January 1945 she took time away from *The New Yorker* to follow Jack's new ship, the U.S.S. *Osage*—a landing ship, vehicle, or LSV—from Tampa to Galveston. A long separation for the newly married couple followed in February as the *Osage* sailed to New Orleans and then off to the Pacific theater. After the surrender of Japan, Jack was back, and in November 1945 discharged. The couple took an apartment above the Woman's Exchange on Madison Avenue. Just as Jack entered Columbia Law School, Scottie discovered she was pregnant. But she continued working at *The New Yorker* until six weeks before delivery. Born on April 26, 1946, the 7 1/2-pound boy was officially named Thomas Addison Lanahan, after Jack's eighteen-year-old half-brother killed at the Battle of the Bulge, but was always called Tim. (He would later commit suicide.) For her first grandchild, Zelda immediately commenced making a collection of historical paper dolls just as she had done for Scottie. And she proudly announced his arrival to Ludlow Fowler, reminding him of Scottie's birth and "the telegrams which we exchanged when she greeted the dim light of a St. Paul autumn, I know you will be interested." Less than two months after Tim's birth, Scottie returned to *The New Yorker*, both as book reviewer for their "Briefly Noted" section and to cover the nightclub circuit for "Tables for Two." She remained at the magazine until the birth of her second child, Eleanor, two years later, on January 25, 1948. Jack was not entirely happy with her working, but she was uninterested in staying home with the baby and promptly hired a nanny and a housekeeper. "This work-or-not issue drives me crazy," she protested. "I know Jack would rather I'd take care of Bébé but I have no patience and calm to do it—. He is so cute but Miss M. is better for him."

That summer, Zelda went north to see her grandson. She took the train up by herself, but did not feel well enough to return home alone. Anne Ober accompanied her back to Montgomery, and they stopped in Wilmington to see the Biggses. Anna Biggs recalled Zelda's strange departure. It was getting close to train time, and John Biggs suggested they leave for the station. "Zelda said we didn't need to worry, the train wouldn't be on time anyway. We laughed and said, perhaps, but it was a risk we didn't intend to take. 'Oh no,' she said, 'it will be all right. Scott has told me. Can't you see him sitting here beside me?' When they got to the station, the train was running thirty minutes late." In October, Zelda again took the train up, this time for Tim's christening. In her engagement book, Scottie documented Zelda's tense, weeklong stay. "To Larchmont—gruesome day with Mama nervous at the beginning but very sweet at Palmers . . . [Tim] furious when woken up but eyes like saucers on drive home—Mama loved it too. Made formula at night—Mama to beb [*sic*]—'Those 2 fingers look so good I'm going to have some myself as soon as I get home.' " The comment may have referred to the baby, but could also have been her wry observation on Scottie's drink.

In the fall of 1946, Jack was required, as an ensign in the Naval Reserve, to report for temporary duty, so Scottie left Tim with his nanny and accompanied Jack to California. Afterward, she spent a weekend with Zelda in Montgomery. It was a stressful experience that stirred up painful childhood memories. "Mother got quite drunk and while in this condition raved like a madwoman," she wrote John Biggs. "I mean real nonsense of an Orphelia [*sic*] kind which scared me, since she was physically perfectly in control and not so drunk as to be passed off as alcoholic insensibility." Scottie was unaware that alcohol precipitated schizophrenic symptoms in Zelda and that she was forbidden to drink. Zelda's sister Marjorie tried to warn others and became incensed whenever people made liquor available to her. She complained to her friend Helen Blackshear: "They know that she simply cannot drink, yet they insist on inviting her to parties where they know liquor will be served. Zelda was always the center of all the fun when she was young, and they still expect her to be witty and sparkling. They can't seem to realize those times are over and that she needs help. . . . They aren't interested in anything but themselves. Zelda was a big name for a while and it gives them some reflected glory to entertain for her. Then they say, 'Oh, a little sherry won't hurt you!' and one thing leads to another. It ends up that we get a phone call in the middle of the night and find her in such a state that we have to get a nurse and a hypodermic to calm her down! Some friends! They're doing everything possible to put Zelda back in the hospital." When she first returned to Montgomery, people were eager to see Zelda and everyone invited her to their parties. "I remember one she came to," recalled one of Zelda's friends. "Everyone was standing in the garden with drinks in their hands and when Zelda saw them she dropped to her knees in prayer. You can imagine how that ripped Montgomery."

Zelda was embarrassed about these incidents and therefore preferred seeing only a few close friends. The oppressiveness of that life was occasionally relieved when someone came to interview her about Fitzgerald or to discuss literature. In the early forties, a University of Alabama student named Paul McLendon became a regular visitor. And for two days in March 1947 a Princeton undergraduate named Henry Dan Piper, who wanted to write about Fitzgerald, conducted a lengthy interview. Zelda showed him her manuscript of "Caesar's Things," and discussed the four major disappointments in her life—the end of her relationship with Lubov Egorova, her brother Anthony's death, her own suicide attempts at Sheppard Pratt, and the end of her marriage to Scott. Before Piper left Montgomery to return to Princeton, she took him to see her paintings stored at the Montgomery Museum of Fine Art and surprised him with the farewell gift of a self-portrait. (Later, her sister Rosalind would repeat the gesture by offering me Zelda's paperdoll watercolor portrait.)

While Zelda always spoke of Scott with appreciation, he came up less and less in her conversation as she withdrew further into herself. The severity of her symptoms fluctuated from day to day. During bad periods, her speech would become unintelligible and she would refuse to bathe or get dressed. She had promised Dr. Carroll to walk five miles a day and kept to that regimen. But since distance walking was uncommon in Montgomery at the time, neighbors did not know what to make of her constant wandering through town.

"Zelda returned to Montgomery. She had been released from the mental institution. She stayed at the old home but roamed the streets all day," Mrs. H. L. Weatherby recalled. "Before I saw her, some of my friends told me that she looked like the old beggar she had impersonated in our high school days. Then, I saw her several times on the streets in town. She looked old, haggard, unkept and listless. The last time I saw her was one day when I boarded the bus and seeing her, sat with her. After I began talking, she recognized me and talked rationally all the way into town. She asked about my family, other friends of our teenage days, and told me about Scottie. There was nothing to recall for me the Zelda I had known. It wasn't too long afterward that she had to be carried away again."

Scott's Princeton classmate Lawton Campbell also remembered her walking by his aunt's home on Sayre Street. "While I was conversing with them on topics of the day, I looked up Sayre Street and saw coming down the hill a forlorn figure. 'There's something familiar about that woman coming down the street,' I said. 'Who is it?' My aunts turned to answer my question and said in unison, 'that's Zelda.' But it was a different 'that's Zelda' than they would have said in the old days. It had no overtone of shock or surprise. It had only the undertone of pity. As she moved down the street, I could get a good picture of her. She wore a crewman's cap, a dingy sweater, a nondescript skirt and tennis shoes. Her hair was straggly and had lost its burnished gold. I walked down the steps to meet her as she approached the house. She greeted me with kind recognition but no spark of even feigned excitement. It almost seemed as if I were talking to a lifeless, faded, wax image. 'The doctor has ordered me to walk five miles a day,' Zelda announced to me. We talked for a few minutes but she did not mention Scott. So of course I did not refer to him either."

Late in the fall of 1947 her mental condition had deteriorated to the point where even the smallest incidents brought her to tears. As the situation worsened, Mrs. Sayre encouraged Zelda to take longer walks, and when all else failed, the two women knelt by Zelda's bed as they had done when she was a child. But prayers afforded little relief. "I have tried so hard and prayed so earnestly and faithfully asking God to help me," Zelda told her sister. "I cannot understand why he leaves me in suffering." On November 2, 1947, she again boarded the train for Asheville to voluntarily reenter Highland.

Dr. Carroll had retired two years earlier and Dr. Basil Bennett was now in charge. To the staff, who remembered her from earlier stays, Zelda was noticeably changed—her skin showed the long-term effects of illness and her personality had a hard, cynical edge. The surroundings were of little interest to her; she avoided others and was given to long periods of solitude.

In January 1948, two months after arriving, she began a three-month series of combined insulin and electric shock treatments, but her attending physician, Dr. Irving Pine, noted only a modest improvement. Impatient with the slow pace of recovery, Zelda shared her concern with her mother, who wrote Scottie on January 17: "I'm distressed Zelda does not improve. Her letters to me are cheerful and she seems interested in the activities of the hospital. She also gives directions about her garden as if she expected to return. She is now in the hands of professionals and I must not make suggestions. The electric treatment is now being used in all hospitals for mental trouble. It may do her good. At least we can hope so. I miss her more than I care to say."

Zelda was upset over her lack of progress and considerable weight gain. Because of the insulin, she had put on twenty pounds, bringing her up to 130—the heaviest she had ever been. Time passed slowly and Zelda wrote thoughtful letters to family and friends, and worked on Bible illustrations for eighteen-month-old Tim. On March 9, she told Scottie: "To-day there is promise of spring in the air and an aura of sunshine over the mountains; the mountains seem to hold more weather than elsewhere and time and retrospect flood roseatre [sic] down the long hill-sides." Six weeks earlier, Scottie had delivered her second child—a daughter, Eleanor, and Zelda wished she could travel north. "I long to see the new baby," she wrote Scottie. "Tim must be phenomenal by this time." With this new generation came increased consciousness of her own mortality. She again contacted Ludlow Fowler, "There is hardly time to live at all anymore, save within the most inexorable of regimentations. I am glad of it since the doctrine of free will has got to be mostly free, and so little will of recent years, that the aboriginal patterns of life were hardly discernible and I often mistook myself for some other kind of person." The shock treatments had further damaged her memory. She knew she had forgotton something, but was not sure what.

For the duration of her insulin treatments, she was moved to the top floor of Highland's main building. There, away from others, insulin patients recovered and were carefully monitored for delayed shocks. Zelda wrote her mother that she was finally seeing some improvement and hoped to be home by spring. Increasingly, she was able to interact with others, and she described life at the hospital: bridge games twice a week, a sewing class, time for reading, and her daily five-mile walk.

She had been at Highland for nearly four months when an electrical fire broke out around midnight on March 11, 1948. It started in the first-floor kitchen of the main building, and quickly spread up the small dumbwaiter shaft leading to the roof, spewing flames onto each landing. With no automatic fire alarm or sprinkler system, the stairways were instantly cut off as the blaze engulfed the interior of the structure. The alarm was not turned in until thirty minutes after the fire began, and by the time the firemen arrived the building had been burning for forty-five minutes. They doused the flames with water but the heat was so intense it had little effect. Corridors and stairwells were filled with smoke as firemen and volunteers hacked with fire axes through locked doors, chains, and barred windows. They carried some of the women patients to safety while hospital attendants struggled to unlock doors and lead others through the dark, smoke-filled halls.

By 4:00 A.M., the blaze was out of control—floors and ceilings, from the roof to the basement, collapsed, outside walls toppled, and the central building's three-story structure was reduced to rubble. There were twenty-nine patients in that central building when the fire broke out. Most of those housed on the lower floors were saved. But at the height of the blaze, Zelda's third-floor room was unreachable. Her room was adjacent to an open porch and hospital doctors conjectured that, had she been conscious, she might have escaped. Of the nine patients who died on the top floor, most were overcome not by flames but by thick smoke and fumes.

During one of his many attempts to rescue patients, Dr. Bennett recalled seeing one smoke-filled room in which a patient lay unconscious on an unburned bed. The bedsheets were undisturbed and there was no sign that the victim had made any attempt to escape though an open window that lead to a porch. Bennett believed that long before the flames reached her, Zelda had been asphyxiated by noxious fumes rising from the ground level. Dr. Pine agreed, saying, "Had she not been asleep, Zelda ought to have been well enough to have escaped and walked away from the top floor where she was trapped." The *New York Herald Tribune*, however, reported a different story in its March 12 issue. They postulated that her escape was impossible because all the patients on Zelda's floor had been locked in their rooms, and the windows, shackled with heavy chains and padlocks, could not be opened far enough for patients to escape. Of the ten women housed in the top-floor rooms, only one was able to break a window and jump to safety; Zelda and eight others perished. People rushing to the scene heard the harrowing screams of those inside. The townspeople retrieved several women who had wandered off into the nearby woods.

Zelda's remains could be identified by only their location, dental records, and a single burned slipper found beneath her charred body. The victims' families were each awarded $3,000 in compensatory damages for the disaster, and Highland's director, Dr. Basil Bennett, was forced to resign. He was replaced by Dr. Carroll's adopted daughter Charmian, a former nurse who had become a psychiatrist. She would serve as director of Highland until 1963 and oversee the bequest of the hospital to Duke University.

Zelda's remains were sent to the same Bethesda mortician who had supervised Scott's funeral, and the same Episcopalian minister, Raymond P. Black, was called on to officiate at her memorial. Mrs. Sayre did not feel well enough to come, but all of Zelda's sisters attended. "There were many floral remembrances and the little chapel was fairly well filled with friends, most of them unknown to me," Rosalind recalled. "The few I recognized were Judge Biggs, the Obers, Mrs. Turnbull, the Stanley Woodwards and Peaches Finney." On a warm, sunny St. Patrick's Day in Rockville, Maryland, Zelda was buried beside Scott on the slope of a shaded hill in Union Cemetery. It required an additional expenditure to alter the original burial plot, but Judge Biggs, in consultation with Zelda's mother, made the decision to do it. "Scott loved Zelda with his last breath and spent a fortune trying to restore her health . . . ," he wrote Mrs. Sayre. "As I told Scottie, Zelda's place was with Scott even though it meant a double vault. They were together twenty years, their blood was mingled in their lovely child and they should rest together." Two days later, after considering what to say, Scottie wrote her grandmother a tender, consoling letter.

"Dearest Grandma—I am sure by now everyone has written you

to tell you how very charming, simple and moving the service and the burial were. I had forgotten, it was so cold and blustery when daddy died, how very beautiful the little cemetery is, so sunny and hilly and remote it gives one a real sense of the past and of the significance of life. I was so glad you decided she should stay with daddy, as seeing them buried there together gave the tragedy of their lives a sort of classic unity and it was very touching and reassuring to think of their two high-flying and generous spirits being at peace together at last. I have simply put out of my mind all their troubles and sorrows and think of them only as they must have been when they were young. I do think that in the years when they were happy they had a more intense enjoyment and experience than the majority of people can hope to have in all their lives, so that in a sense, the quality of their two lives atones for their brevity. It is hard for me now to think of them as my parents, they were such very extraordinary people and I have reverted so entirely to the uneventful mediocrity which is the fate of 99% of human beings. For that reason I felt the impersonal loss much more strongly than the personal. But all through the service in Bethesda and the drive out to Rockville I kept thinking of you, Grandma, and of how unjust it seems that you should have to bear this pain when you have always done so much for others and helped them to carry on themselves. I hope it is a consolation to you to know that you were always there to give Mama a sense of security and belonging whatever else her troubles were. If it had not been for you she would certainly have been far more unhappy than she was. I hope that should it be necessary I will be equally able to help my own children; for to have done in all conscience the *best you can* for any human being is a rare and great achievement. Please try and keep as much as possible from being sad: Mama was such an extraordinary person that had things continued as perfect and romantic as they began, the story of her life would have been more like a fairy-tale than a reality. I am certainly far from occult and have never understood or sympathized with mysticism but I have such a strong sense of destiny about her death that I cannot help but feel it was part of a pattern and as inevitable as day and night. Anything inevitable is surely right and therefore good. I have thought about it all so much and this is the only conclusion I can reach."

POSTLUDE

In the fall of 1949, after graduating from Columbia Law School, Jack Lanahan accepted a position with the Treasury Department in Washington, D.C., and moved the family to Chevy Chase, Maryland. "Jack decided to become a specialist in tax law, which meant he needed experience with the government," Scottie wrote in her memoir. "He found a job in Washington with what was then called the Bureau of Internal Revenue, and I remember the great excitement we both felt about moving to a new and mysterious city. I had always assumed we would one day go to live in Baltimore, but since I was already a little hooked on politics, Washington seemed by far the more exciting alternative." In preparation for the move, Scottie loaned Princeton University fifty-six boxes of Fitzgerald material, including her father's manuscripts and proofs, her parents' letters, and miscellaneous records. She kept the family scrapbooks and photo albums, Fitzgerald's personal library, and the ledger book containing his diary. In Washington, the Lanahans had a third child, a boy, Jack Jr. (called Jacky), born on April 29, 1950, and in October 1951 a fourth child called Cecilia Scott. From the Treasury Department, Lanahan went on to work in the Department of Justice, and then joined the staff of the Joint Committee on Internal Revenue Taxation. In the summer of 1955, the family moved from their Chevy Chase residence to a bigger house—the former quarters of the Indian embassy—in Georgetown, then in 1958, to an even larger home at 2211 King Place.

Scottie, who had become involved in Democratic politics, accepted a volunteer position with the *Democratic Digest*, a publication patterned after *The New Yorker* but with a *Reader's Digest* format. During 1956 she worked on Adlai Stevenson's presidential campaign, which brought her into contact with his press secretary, Clayton Fritchey. He was twenty years older than Scottie, separated from his wife, and living in an apartment in the Fairfax Hotel. Fritchey and Scottie began an affair that would continue through the next decade. In 1957, Scottie became a political correspondent for the *Northern Virginia Sun*, which was run by Fritchey. She stayed there until March 1960, when she took a temporary job at the *Washington Post* while she worked as a volunteer press aide for Stuart Symington of Missouri, who was running for the Democratic nomination against Kennedy, Johnson, and Humphrey. Though Scottie and Lanahan remained married, they lived separate lives—Scottie with Clayton Fritchey who was neither interested in marriage nor in becoming encumbered with her four children; Jack with several women whom he occasionally invited aboard his boat the *Amanda*.

The emotional stress of her failing marriage and obligations of motherhood made life difficult for Scottie. With no maternal role model, parenting did not come easy, and spending time with her four children exhausted her. "I don't like putting them to bed at night if they make a lot of demands," she wrote in her diary, "or dawdle, or cry. I don't like crying or quarreling in any form, and I don't like trying to fix lunch or supper or breakfast while somebody spills things all over the floor or interrupts me all the time." What she did enjoy was taking them to interesting places and buying them fabulous gifts. The day-to-day caregiving she found a wearying bore—and after four or five hours, usually had had enough. To reduce her family responsibilities—mirroring what Zelda had done—she hired a nurse, cook, laundress, and part-time gardener. "My mother sent us to camps, bought us nice clothes, and gave us festive birthday parties," her daughter Eleanor recalled, "but in between she wished we'd just be happy and leave her alone and stop being spoiled and use our imaginations." Like her parents, Scottie was also incapable of properly supervising household help, and they often took advantage of her good nature. "Her management strategy was to be nice," recalled one daughter. "She never asked her employees to do too much, and turned a blind eye to moderate drinking. There was a certain extravagance in the atmosphere and she made allowances for a spillage of household funds between the gas station, market and home."

Jack, who had disengaged himself from life at home, was fond of saying that "anyone who works for Scottie is unemployable by the time they leave." But he chose not to interfere and that placed responsibility for the household solely on Scottie's shoulders. The couple was incapable of confronting their problems face-to-face, so Scottie resorted to leaving letters for Jack on the kitchen counter. "I'm not trying to rationalize or gloss over everything. I do think our family life leaves a hell of a lot to be desired, and that I as the presumably central figure of it have done only a C job, with occasional B's but even more often D's and F's. But I do wish on the other side of the ledger you'd be more understanding of the fact that I'm both by training and temperament incapable of being consistently B or even A, any more than I could be a concert pianist, and that hostility, coldness and resentment are scarcely the proper encouragement. . . ."

Scottie was as generous and extravagant as her father, and, like him, was also capable of an over-the-top concern for others. Fritchey described her as someone who would give you *more* than the shirt off her back—"She would give you the skin off her back. She had enormous generosity and an enormous interest and care for her friends. And she had great integrity." Through the years, Scottie habitually picked up the tab for meals and regularly overdrew her bank account buying things for others. She was more circumspect about sharing her feelings; years of being uprooted and supervised by others had taught her that keeping an emotional distance was the key to personal survival. Scottie's characteristic coolness prevailed throughout her life, and she seldom seemed vulnerable, even to her family. Her daughter Eleanor, in a bid for reassurance, once asked her mother if she was happy with her four children. "I am especially lucky to have two boys and two girls," Scottie replied. "What could be better?" This, of course, was not the response Eleanor craved, and all four children were bitter about not being a more integral part of her life. Eleanor often attempted to unsettle Scottie's reserve by saying cruel things. "I kept my feelings aloof from my mother and harbored a submerged resentment that I wasn't more important to her. And I was indignant that she couldn't read my mind on this matter. She seemed to have a sort of highly evolved, adult, emotional armor and was never wounded by anything I said."

But Scottie was well aware of her emotional deficiencies with her children. Writing in her diary, she admitted, "I can't seem to give them anything except the things that money will buy. I hope they're absorbing through their pores some of the inspiration of this countryside, so that if they grow up like me, to put a screen of smoke and cocktails between themselves and the natural world, they will know where beauty lies in art and nature."

Scottie, who attributed most of her psychological problems to an unstable upbringing, remained firmly against giving interviews about her parents or childhood experiences. But in an introduction

to her father's letters, she admitted, "I can remember nothing except the troubles of the 30's which were reflected in our relations:
my mother's hopeless illness, daddy's own bad health and lack of
money, and hardest of all I think, his literary eclipse. . . . In my next
incarnation, I may not choose again to be the daughter of a famous
author. People who live entirely by the fertility of their imagination
are fascinating, brilliant and often charming but they should be sat
next to at dinner parties, not lived with." Once, while Scottie was a
college student, she expressed an interest in writing about her parents. Her father was appalled by the idea. "You once made the astounding statement that you were immediately going to write our
biographies. . . . I would never write anything about my own
mother or father till they had been at least ten years dead." In a
May 1940 letter, Fitzgerald implored her to remain closemouthed
about her personal life. "You will be interviewed again, and once
more I ask you please do not discuss your mother or myself even
faintly with them."

Scottie followed her father's directive for twenty years. Then, in
1963, when Nancy Milford offered to catalog Zelda's letters and
put them in chronological order, Scottie lifted her own rule of privacy and agreed to discuss her childhood with Milford. She also entrusted her with Zelda's scrapbooks and correspondence. "I lent her
the letters, mostly written in pencil and undated, with the [belief]
that she would make it her project to sort them out, get them typed
and xeroxed." But when Milford's book was completed in 1970,
Scottie found she had done much more. The book's approach was
so disturbing that Scottie was determined to keep parts of it from
being published. Her daughter Eleanor recalled, "My mother was
so distressed by the book's focus on Zelda's mental illness that she
refused to deal directly with Milford. Instead she asked Matt [Bruc-
coli] to be her representative. It was he who persuaded Milford to
show him a complete transcript of the book before it was published,
and he who read it. Matt discovered that Zelda's aged psychiatrist
in Switzerland had released confidential records to Milford, which
she used in the book along with her own conjectures about Zelda's
sexuality. . . . Matt succeeded in persuading Milford to cut her
sexual speculations, which he said is all they were. He also got her
to return all the material she had borrowed from Scottie, which she
didn't want to give up until the book was published."

The book caused great turmoil in the Lanahan household. "If I had no daughters and no Aunt Rosalind, I honestly don't think I would give much of a damn," Scottie asserted. "I have developed a rather thick layer of tough skin over the years which enables me to hear about my drunken father and my crazy mother with enough equanimity to collect the royalty checks and try to ignore it. But it will kill Aunt Rosalind for sure, and I really can't bear the children suffering through this at just the age when they are most vulnerable. It just makes me physically ill, that's all." The book had a devastating effect on Rosalind Smith in Montgomery. Scottie told one Washington *Sunday Star* reporter that she was rushing down to Alabama to see her aunt. "She is eighty years old now and this book has given her a heart attack. She went to the hospital three days ago and is desperately ill." Scottie also hired a lawyer to discover how Milford had obtained Zelda's medical records from Dr. Forel at Prangins—a breach of Swiss confidentiality laws. She was determined to fight Milford "on every level which won't bring her a lot of publicity." But the book achieved immediate popularity—it made the best-seller list and stayed there for months.

Since Scott and Zelda both seemed genetically disposed to serious illnesses—Fitzgerald to alcoholism and Zelda to schizophrenia—Scottie worried about similar problems in her own children. Her firstborn son, Tim, had, from childhood, manifested psychological problems and she was convinced he had inherited a genetic predisposition to mental illness through her. The CIA had a personnel file on Tim, collected when he applied for a position, that characterized him as an odd character who imagined terrible things about himself and others. After he graduated from Princeton he had experimented with LSD and other drugs while serving in Vietnam. Tim ultimately shot and killed himself on October 18, 1973, at Diamond Head Park in Honolulu. He was about the same age Zelda's brother, Anthony, had been when he took his life. Scottie's three other children fared better: Cecilia is married and lives in Pennsylvania; Jack Jr. resides in Oregon; and Eleanor, who wrote a biography of Scottie in 1995, is an artist with three children and lives in Burlington, Vermont.

Scottie's marriage to Jack Lanahan finally ended in divorce after more than twenty years. Her children blamed her for pursuing her own interests to the detriment of family life. But she saw it differently, explaining her version of the split-up to one of her daughters: "We got married in a great big rush during World War II and we both knew not too long afterwards that we just weren't made to live together. I can't describe exactly what was wrong, but to over-simplify we each needed more reassurance from the other. . . . This is what I felt with Daddy: inadequate. I couldn't bring him the single-minded devotion he needed . . . because while I'm feminine in some ways, I have to do 'my own thing.' " With Jack, Scottie's explanation was more pointed: "I just think that we were mis-mated," she admitted in her memoir. "I'm still not sure what kind of a woman you need, but I know for myself what I needed: some-body who would love me, not quarrel with me. Yours and my life have been one long argument, often fun and definitely challenging, but dry. So little love, so little plain affection. A sort of rivalry, al-ways—a competition. I have never felt as if I could do with you what I want to so badly, and hope I'll do before I die, which is crawl into someone's arms and feel there solace." From Jack's viewpoint, he may always have felt like the son-in-law of F. Scott Fitzgerald.

Scottie hoped to find the comfort she craved with Clayton Fritchey, but that relationship came to an abortive end. Instead, in 1967, she married C. Grove Smith. Though supportive, Smith was a heavy drinker and after they married, he quit his job as marketing adviser for the Department of Commerce and took to relaxing at home with a glass of Scotch. According to Eleanor Lanahan, he ex-acerbated Scottie's drinking habits, which had worsened during the sixties. Eleanor recalled mornings of wandering "through the smoky twilight of the living rooms, like an archeologist perusing hastily abandoned chambers. Clusters of stale drinks sat on the end tables. Ashtrays burgeoned with butts, some ringed by lipstick and others stubbed out after one or two extravagant puffs. By noon the maid would open the curtains, vacuum, dust tables, plump cushions and restore order." Ironically, Fitzgerald had described almost identically the Manhattan apartment he and Zelda rented in 1920: "There was the odor of tobacco always . . . ash-littered carpets. Added to this was the aura of stale wine, with its inevitable sugges-tion of beauty gone foul." What Scottie so long resisted she seems to have attracted.

In 1973, to escape her deteriorating second marriage, Scottie moved to Montgomery—ostensibly to care for her aunt Rosalind. She arrived just as the old Sayre house was to be demolished and purchased many of its architectural remains. "I do wish the house could be saved as people constantly ask me about it," she wrote, "but as it has no architectural value whatsoever (it was built about 1900) it doesn't come under the Landmarks Foundation sphere of interest, & I am not about to spend $30,000 or so restoring it when it's in the worst slum neighborhood in town." While in Montgomery, she became active in many volunteer organizations and closely involved herself with the Montgomery Museum of Fine Arts. Following Mrs. Sayre's death in 1958, Zelda's sister Marjorie had directed the yardman to burn all the paintings stored in Zelda's makeshift studio behind the old house, but Scottie was able to acquire a number of others for a bequest to the museum.

Since Fitzgerald always considered Maryland his ancestral home, and had even prophesied, "Zelda and I will snuggle up together under a stone in some old graveyard there," Scottie was determined to have her parents reburied in consecrated ground. Not until 1975, however, did Catholic authorities finally agree that Scott could be reinterred in the Fitzgerald family plot. Scottie then transferred her parent's caskets from Union Cemetery to St. Mary's Church in downtown Rockville, where they were both buried next to Scott's father, grandfather, and cousins. At the reinterment, Matthew Bruccoli read from Fitzgerald's work, and a new stone, inscribed with the last lines of *The Great Gatsby*—"So we beat on, boats against the current, borne back ceaselessly into the past"—was placed above the double vault.

Scottie enjoyed the years she spent in her mother's hometown, where she was a celebrity, but after divorcing C. Grove Smith in 1980, intended returning to Washington to be nearer political activity and her family. Those plans changed after she was diagnosed with esophageal cancer. Resolute, she told her family, "It's my own fault. I smoked and drank and those are common causes of esophageal cancer." Years before, her father had written to her warning against both addictions. "I didn't begin to be a heavy smoker until I was a sophomore but it took just one year to send me into TB and cast a shadow that has been extremely long. . . . Like me you were subject to colds when young—deep chest colds near pneumonia. . . . I wish there was something that would make you cut it out."

Sadly, when Scottie looked back over her life, she found little of which to be proud. Like her mother, she admitted that she had neither taken herself seriously nor focused her energies. Her ex-husband Jack agreed. "What a shame that someone with such incredible talent wasted her valuable energy on social events in Washington." In her will, she designated Lanahan as executor. Writing her own obituary, Scottie left instructions for its delivery to the Associated Press. But even after so many years, she still denied (or could not face) the realities of her early years. "My parents were always very circumspect around me," she wrote. "I was unaware of all the drinking that was going on. I was very well taken care of and I was never neglected. I didn't consider it a difficult childhood at all. In fact it was a wonderful childhood." In an earlier observation, however, included in an introduction to her father's letters, she was somewhat more candid about her parents' decline and her own feelings. "The fact that my father became a difficult parent does not surprise or offend me. He gave me a golden childhood, which is as much as any of us can ask for. I can remember nothing but happiness and delight in his company until the world began to be too much for him, when I was about eleven years old." But after that, she added, "I can remember almost nothing but the troubles which were reflected in our relations—my mother's hopeless illness, his own bad health and lack of money, and hardest of all I think, his literary eclipse." Scottie died in Montgomery on June 15, 1986. Two days later, at St. Mary's Church in Rockville, Maryland, she was laid to rest at the feet of her parents.

Scottie's disappointment in life and interpretation of her parents as tragic figures echoed Fitzgerald's own beliefs about the insidious nature of his era. He had characterized Zelda's madness as endemic to the period, telling Dr. Carroll at Highland: "I know scarcely a beautiful woman of Zelda's generation who has come up to 1938 unscathed." During the twenties, Fitzgerald had received a letter in Antibes from a friend urging them to return home, and they considered leaving until they noticed it was posted from a Pennsylvania sanitarium for nervous disorders. Mental problems incapacitated many of their friends. Sara Mayfield was confined to Sheppard Pratt in Baltimore (the same hospital Zelda entered in 1932), and then transferred to Bryce Mental Hospital in Tuscaloosa, Alabama. Only after questions surfaced as to whether her sixteen-year commitment was justified did President John F. Kennedy intervene (at the request of Governor George Wallace) and secure Sara's release in 1963. The men fared little better. Alex McKaig died in his mid-forties at a Middletown, New York, mental hospital. After visiting him there, John Peale Bishop wrote of his appalling condition to Edmund Wilson, who himself was manic-depressive. "He [McKaig] is hopelessly and completely insane. It sounds like paresis. He is unable to receive any communication and only sporadically and uncertainly receives visitors." Fitzgerald's college friend Stanley Dell was treated by Carl Jung, and even Hemingway grew paranoid and ultimately committed suicide.

Malcolm Cowley, writing about the twenties from the distance of one decade, tallied the price it had exacted from participants: "In New York the year was one of nervous breakdowns; the psychiatrists were busy when every other profession except that of social service was losing its clients. One friend who was being psychoanalyzed told me that the doctor's office was crowded with people he knew; it was like a publisher's tea. Many of the letters one received would be dated from sanitariums in Pennsylvania or Massachusetts. It was a year of suicides, not only among stockbrokers but also among wealthy dilettantes. It was a year of insomnia and sleeping tablets. It was a year when classmates and former friends became involved in speakeasy brawls, divorces, defalcations and even murders."

Like Cowley, Fitzgerald also reflected in print on what happened to people he knew—contemporaries of his who had met untimely deaths. "A classmate killed his wife and himself on Long Island, another tumbled 'accidently' from a skyscraper in Philadelphia, another purposely from a skyscraper in New York. These are not catastrophes that I went out of my way to look for—these were my friends." Even John Dos Passos experienced tragedy. The soft-spoken writer had married Katy Smith, a friend of Hadley and Ernest Hemingway. After Smith and Dos Passos met at Ernest's Key West Home in 1929, they married and remained so until 1947, when she died in a car crash. Dos Passos was driving when, blinded by the sun, he smashed into a parked truck—slashing off the top of Katy's head. She was killed instantly; Dos Passos lost an eye.

Fitzgerald believed that Zelda's conservative southern upbringing had left her ill-prepared to survive their years together. "She didn't have the strength for the big stage—sometimes she pretended and pretended beautifully, but she didn't have it. She was soft when she should have been hard and hard where she should have been yielding. She never knew how to use her energy." Raised in a society that conditioned women to expect protection, Zelda was conscious of her inclination to lean on men, having once described herself as "the girl who was a law unto herself, and the other who wanted a normal life and someone to protect her." After her father died, she had written Scott: "I miss my daddy terribly. I am losing my identity here without men. I would not live two weeks again where there are none." And when she had the chance to become a professional dancer in Naples, she could not take the decisive step that would lead to self-sufficiency and independence. After much confusion she finally chose to stay with Fitzgerald, though it may have been the deciding strain that brought on her madness. "She realized too late," Scott wrote, "that work was dignity and the only true dignity, and tried to atone for it by working, but it was too late." Again, he is half-right. He leaves two things out: that he often thwarted her efforts to find fulfilling work, and, what Zelda never seems to have fully realized, that without her, Fitzgerald could never have written the fiction he wrote. He did not just base his heroines on Zelda. He copied from her letters and diaries, watched her intently, continually wrote down her comments, and endlessly analyzed and dissected what she said. Scott's female protagonists *were* Zelda. Even for someone born with a robust mental constitution, such treatment would cause unbearable stress. In effect Zelda was Scott's co-author. Without her there would have been no Rosalind Connage, Daisy Buchanan, or Nicole Diver.

But it was the Jozan affair that became the turning point for Zelda. The turmoil it created led to her first emotional crisis and initial suicide attempt. From this juncture, Fitzgerald controlled their relationship and never relinquished that power. The second blow to Zelda's psyche came when Fitzgerald, in retribution for the Jozan incident, entered into an affair with Lois Moran and openly compared her abilities with his wife's. Zelda accepted the challenge and immersed herself in ballet until it became an obsession. Her potential success so threatened Fitzgerald that he placed numerous obstacles in her path, including perhaps the most effective one—his contempt. As she attempted to establish herself first as a dancer, then as a writer, she was continually undermined, not only by her own ambivalence, but also by Fitzgerald's harsh criticism. After her first breakdown, every aspect of her creative life—how long she might practice ballet, what she could write, how long she could spend painting—was strictly regulated by Fitzgerald or her doctors. Ultimately, she lost the sense of herself as an individual and withdrew into a private world.

Once thought to be the result of poor communication within families, schizophrenia is now recognized as a disease of the brain, caused by a dysfunction of its neuronal transmitter system in which there are impaired dopamine channels. Dramatic advances in our understanding of the disease occur daily, with neuroscientists conjecturing that the seeds of the disorder are sown during fetal brain development. Autopsies of schizophrenics' brains offer new evidence that certain nerve cells may have migrated to the wrong area while the brain was taking shape, leaving small regions of the brain miswired or out of place. There is even speculation that misconnections may develop after a woman contracts a particular virus early in her pregnancy. While the onset of symptoms, as in Zelda's case, generally occur when people are in their late twenties, subtle signs of the disorder are evident early in life. For example, schizophrenics often display odd hand movements, reminding us of Zelda's photograph at White Bear Lake in the summer of 1922. Malnutrition also seems to play a key role. Scottie always believed that her mother's illness was caused both by diet deficiencies and a chemical imbalance. And considering Zelda's peculiar eating habits, which got much worse when she was dancing, she may well have been right.

Whatever was amiss in Zelda's brain worsened that Sunday afternoon in May of 1933, when Dr. Rennie attempted to get the Fitzgeralds to discuss their marriage, and Scott made it clear, once and for all, that because he paid the bills, he had the primary right to use their joint life as material for his fiction. Baldly stated, it is obvious nonsense that Dr. Rennie seems to have perceived—given he recommended they divorce. Zelda was willing to do that, at times preferring life in an insane asylum to the life Fitzgerald imposed on her. But Scott was determined to remain in the marriage. He would not relinquish his source of inspiration, though she was failing mentally and he was losing his ability to transcribe her life. Having won his point, he could wax sentimental and optimistically suggest that their life together might be renewed—"if not in a new spring, then in a new summer."

That summer never arrived for the emblematic couple of the Jazz Age. Scott died young, and Zelda never saw any of her talents brought to fruition. As Scottie reflected on her parents' all too short life together, she could not herself avoid becoming sentimental when she tried to answer the question of why interest in their story endures. "It was my mother's misfortune to be born with the ability to write, to dance and to paint and then never to have acquired the discipline to make her talent work for rather than against her. . . . My father was on the scene when we started to lose our way, during Gatsby's time, and he recorded it all—the generosity, the greed, the innocence and the cynicism, the magnificence and the waste that was America between the two world wars—with sensitivity and with love, but also with a growing sense of disillusionment and alarm. In his way he was a prophet. And the rebellion of his generation, which he helped create, was the herald of the larger, deeper one taking place today." Once again, Scott receives the credit and Zelda is dismissed as lacking discipline.

Perhaps, if Zelda had survived through the fifties, when enormous advances in psychopharmacology were made, she might have been successfully treated with the newly discovered neuroleptics. After 1952 there was an explosion of antipsychotic and antidepressant drugs that often alleviated symptoms of psychosis for long periods of time. Mood stabilizers like lithium blunted emotional swings, Thorazine and Haldol controlled hallucinations, Mellaril was effective as a tranquilizer, and Clozapine and Risperidal subdued interior voices. But no such remedies were available to Zelda—and even had they been, perhaps it was already too late. Away from the hospital, she was largely dependent on her own strength, of which she had much. "In the last analysis she is a stronger person than I am," Scott confessed to Dr. Rennie. Recognizing the *folie a deux* that bound them together, he admitted, "We ruined ourselves. I have never honestly thought we ruined each other." Zelda was in agreement, adding, "Nothing could have survived our life." Yet she did survive longer than he, and with a certain degree of quietude and contentment between outbreaks of schizophrenia. She had used up her life providing material for a writer who to this day is considered one of America's greatest, yet

who as a man and husband was cunningly controlling. When she finally tried to make a life for herself, apart from the marriage, it was
too late. She had scant resources left. The only way out was through
the insanity to which her family was prone. In writing the epigram
"sometimes madness is wisdom" she was revealing the paradigm of
her life.

NOTES

PREFACE

xv. "I knew there was only one way": Interview with Scottie Fitzgerald by the author, January 24–28, 1964.

xv. "If you come to Washington": Letter from Scottie Fitzgerald to the author, September 23, 1963. Collection of the author.

xv. "Kendall Taylor has asked me to": Letter from Scottie Fitzgerald to the author, January 27, 1964. Collection of the author.

xvi. "I went to bed for two days after I saw you": Ibid.

xviii. "exposes, bleeds, mourns, whines": Eleanor Lanahan, quoted in Eleanor Lanahan, *Scottie, the Daughter of . . .* (New York: HarperCollins, 1995), p. 5.

xviii. "I don't think that any woman really affects the kinds of things a man writes": Interview with Archibald MacLeish by the author, April 16, 1964, Uphill Farm, Conway, Massachusetts.

INTRODUCTION: EMBLEM AND ERA

1. "There was the little major": Zelda Fitzgerald, *Save Me the Waltz*, in *The Collected Writings*, ed. Matthew J. Bruccoli (New York: Charles Scribner's Son's, 1991), p. 37.

2. "Before 1905 or 1906, there was scarcely a ripple": Sara Haardt, "Zelda Fitzgerald," unpublished interview with Zelda Fitzgerald, initially submitted to *Good Housekeeping* magazine, p. 2, Enoch Pratt Free Library, Special Collections, Baltimore, Maryland.

2. "As long as I can remember and long before that": C. Lawton Campbell, "The Fitzgeralds Were My Friends," unpublished essay, p. 11. Collection of the author.

3. "men from Princeton and Yale who smelled of Russian Leather": Zelda Fitzgerald, *Save Me the Waltz*, in Bruccoli, *Collected Writings*, p. 37.

3. "Through the summer Alabama collected soldiers' insignia": Ibid., p. 37.

3. "Montgomery friends yield most reluctantly this beautiful": *Montgomery Advertiser*, newspaper clipping from Zelda Fitzgerald Scrapbook, Fitzgerald Collection, Princeton University Library, Princeton, New Jersey.

4. "My marriage, after which I was in another world": Nancy Milford, *Zelda, a Biography* (New York: Harper & Row, 1970), pp. 175–176.

5. "Darling, I nearly sat my seat off in the Strand Theatre today": Zelda Fitzgerald, letter to F. Scott Fitzgerald, quoted by Milford in *Zelda*, p. 39.

5. "I am in the world to do something unusual": Owen Johnson, *The Salamander* (Indianapolis: Bobbs-Merrill Company, 1914), p. 385.

5. "was too permissible and lacked the element of danger, of the forbidden": Ibid., p. 388.

6. "It had a large and brazenly well-stocked bar": Campbell, "The Fitzgeralds Were My Friends," p. 19.

6. "She comes from somewhere out of the immense reaches": Johnson, *The Salamander*, p. 2.

6. "She can meet what men she wishes": Ibid., p. 2.

6. "The man I marry has got to be able to": Ibid., p. 451.

7. "A prop is a youth": Ibid., p. 15.

7. "she had met a few real men": Ibid., p. 56.

7. "It was not simply three or four intrigues": Ibid., p. 399.

7. "She went through her wintertime beaux": Zelda Fitzgerald, "The Girl the Prince Liked," in Bruccoli, *Collected Writings*, pp. 310–311.

8. "What grubworms women are to crawl on their bellies": F. Scott Fitzgerald, *The Beautiful and Damned* (New York: Charles Scribner's Sons, 1950), p. 147.

8. "She was again keeping half a dozen dates a day": F. Scott Fitzgerald, *The Great Gatsby* (New York: Charles Scribner's Sons, 1969), p. 151.

8. "Rotten, rotten old world": F. Scott Fitzgerald, *This Side of Paradise* (New York: Charles Scribner's Sons, 1970), p. 216.

8. "discovery and sensational exploits": Campbell, "The Fitzgeralds Were My Friends," p. 19.

9. "They were having the bread line at the Ritz that year": Zelda Fitzgerald, *Save Me the Waltz*, in Bruccoli, *Collected Writings*, p. 48.

9. "Brilliant men, beautiful jazz babies, champagne baths": *Motoplay Magazine*, August 21, 1923, p. 18.

9. "None of the Victorian mothers": F. Scott Fitzgerald, *This Side of Paradise*, p. 60.

10. "The basement was bedlam": Jack Shuttleworth, "John Held, Jr., and His World," *American Heritage* 16, no. 5 (August 1965): 29.

10. "Oh, just one person in fifty has any glimmer of what sex is": F. Scott Fitzgerald, *This Side of Paradise*, p. 216.

11. "the flapper awoke from her lethargy of sub-deb-ism": Zelda Fitzgerald, "Eulogy on the Flapper," in Bruccoli, *Collected Writings*, p. 391.

11. "could play golf all day, dance all night": Dorothy Dix quoted in Shelly Armitage, *John Held Jr.: Illustrator of the Jazz Age* (Syracuse, N.Y.: Syracuse University Press, 1987), p. 72.

11. "took all the things of life for hers to choose from": F. Scott Fitzgerald, *The Beautiful and Damned*, p. 62.

11. "Aren't you interested in anything except yourself": Ibid., p. 112.

11. "I love Scott's books and heroines": Zelda Fitzgerald, interview with the Louisville *Courier-Journal*, September 30, 1923, quoted in Matthew J. Bruccoli, ed. *The Romantic Egoists* (New York: Charles Scribner's Sons, 1974), p. 112.

12. "If you could afford to take her out, she was yours for the evening": Zelda Fitzgerald, "The Girl the Prince Liked," in Bruccoli, *Collected Writings*, p. 316.

12. "You know I'm old in some ways": F. Scott Fitzgerald, *This Side of Paradise*, p. 180.

12. "The most enormous influence on me in the four and a half years": Letter from F. Scott Fitzgerald to Edmund Wilson, January 1922, quoted in *The Letters of F. Scott Fitzgerald*, ed. Andrew Turnbull (New York: Charles Scribner's Sons, 1963), p. 331.

CHAPTER 1: MONTGOMERY AND ALL THAT JAZZ

14. "Zelda's heart was of July, but her tears were of April": Robert Edward Francillon, *Zelda's Fortune* (Boston: James R. Osgood and Company, 1874), p. 224.

16. "the door was always open": Rosalind Smith, unpublished documentation on Zelda Fitzgerald, W. S. Hoole Special Collections Library, University of Alabama, Tuscaloosa.

16. "He was considered a great Judge": Scottie Fitzgerald, quoted by Eleanor Lanahan in *Scottie, the Daughter of . . .* (New York: HarperCollins Publisher, 1995), pp. 19–20.

17. "Already she is in the crowd": Article in the *Montgomery Advertiser*, quoted in Nancy Milford, *Zelda, a Biography* (New York: Harper & Row, 1970), p. 15.

17. "I never considered Zelda especially spoiled": Rosalind Smith, unpublished documentation on Zelda, Mayfield Collection, University of Alabama.

18. "There was, for example, her stomach": F. Scott Fitzgerald, *The Beautiful and Damned* (New York: Charles Scribner's Sons, 1950), p. 161.

18. "She had . . . a great deal more than the audacity": Sara Haardt, "Zelda Fitzgerald," unpublished interview with Zelda Fitzgerald, pp. 1–2, Enoch Pratt Free Library, Special Collections, Baltimore, Maryland.

19. "I was very active as a child and never tired": Zelda Fitzgerald, quoted in Milford, *Zelda*, p. 8.

19. "During those days, she cared very little for clothes": Letter from Mrs. H. L. Weatherby to the author, April 1963. Collection of the author.

20. "The Gentiles thought he was Gentile": Interview with Rosalind Smith by the author, August 4, 1963.

20. "A feature of the evening was the exquisite solo": Clipping from the *Montgomery Advertiser*, in Zelda Fitzgerald Scrapbook, Fitzgerald Collection, Princeton University Library (hereafterward P.U.L.).

20. "in a resplendent costume of crimson and white": Haardt, "Zelda Fitzgerald," p. 5.

21. "Dear Miss Sayre, I saw your picture": Zelda Fitzgerald Scrapbook, P.U.L.

21. "In the afternoons, after we snatched a mouthful": Ibid., p. 3.

21. "I do not believe that he [Judge Sayre]": Rosalind Smith, unpublished material on Zelda Fitzgerald, Mayfield Collection, University of Alabama, p. 3.

22. "she swam and dove as well as most of the boys": Eleanor Addison, "Why Follow the Same Pattern," *Columbus Dispatch*, October 27, 1963, p. 4C.

22. "I remember playing tag and police": Sara Haardt, "Zelda Fitzgerald," p. 2.

22. "Listen, you'll break your neck": Sara Mayfield, *Exiles from Paradise: Zelda and Scott Fitzgerald* (New York: Dell Publishing Co., 1971), p. 13.

23. "When we were in our teens, Zelda dived": Addison, "Why Follow the Same Pattern?" p. 4C.

23. "Zelda lived just around the corner": Letter from Mrs. H. L. Weatherby to the author, April 1963. Collection of the author.

24. "Even in those days": Mayfield, *Exiles from Paradise*, p. 18.

25. "We played hooky almost every day": Haardt, "Zelda Fitzgerald," p. 3.

26. "I have never seen a photograph": Ring Lardner Jr., *The Lardners: My Family Remembered* (New York: Harper Colophon Books, 1976), p. 161.

26. "She was not a legitimate beauty": Gerald Murphy, quoted in Honoria Murphy Donnelly, *Sara and Gerald: Villa America and After* (New York: Times Books, 1982), p. 151.

26. "The specialist to whom Mama took her": Rosalind Smith, unpublished documentation on Zelda, Mayfield Collection, University of Alabama.

27. "I saw her as she had looked at that last Christmas dance": Sara Haardt, "Zelda Fitzgerald," p. 1.

28. "Some of the girls who were heads of the committees": Ibid., p. 4.

28. "I danced every night . . . through the late spring": Ibid.

29. "The ones I enjoyed the most were the privates' dances": Ibid.

30. "Every Saturday at 1 o'clock": F. Scott Fitzgerald, quoted in "The Man Who Discovered Fitzgerald," A. Scott Berg, *Princeton Alumni Weekly*, October 23, 1979, pp. 15–20.

30. "In spite of its disguises": Letter from Shane Leslie to Charles Scribner II, Ibid.

31. "The story does not culminate in anything": Ibid.

31. "When are you coming": Letter from John Peale Bishop to F. Scott Fitzgerald, Fitzgerald Papers, Box 39, Folder 20, P.U.L.

31. "He smelled like new goods": Zelda Fitzgerald, *Save Me the Waltz*, in *The Collected Writings*, ed. Matthew J. Bruccoli (New York: Charles Scribner's Sons, 1991), p. 39.

31. "girls too tall or too prim": Zelda Fitzgerald, "Southern Girl," in Bruccoli, *Collected Writings*, p. 302.

32. "I didn't have the two top things": F. Scott Fitzgerald, quoted in Matthew J. Bruccoli, *Some Sort of Epic Grandeur* (New York: Harcourt Brace Jovanovich, 1981), p. 55.

33. "Her voice . . . was full of money": F. Scott Fitzgerald, *The Great Gatsby* (New York: Charles Scribner's Sons, 1925), p. 120.

33. "Let me tell you about the very rich": F. Scott Fitzgerald, "The Rich Boy," in *The Stories of F. Scott Fitzgerald*, ed. Malcolm Cowley (New York: Charles Scribner's Sons, 1951), p. 177.

33. "Never before in his life had Amory considered": F. Scott Fitzgerald, *This Side of Paradise* (New York: Charles Scribner's Sons, 1948), p. 232.

33. "One day, a lady who was on the committee": Haardt, "Zelda Fitzgerald," p. 4.

34. "Remember there were three pines": Letter from Zelda Fitzgerald to F. Scott Fitzgerald, Zelda Fitzgerald Papers, Box 45, Folder 6, P.U.L.

34. "We were more closely supervised": Letter from Mrs. H. L. Weatherby to the author, April 1963. Collection of the author.

35. "some heavenly support beneath his shoulder blades": Zelda Fitzgerald, *Save Me the Waltz*, in Bruccoli, *Collected Writings*, p. 37.

35. "I don't believe she liked many people": Sara Murphy, quoted in Donnelly, *Sara and Gerald: Villa America and After*, p. 150.

35. "devastating wit—yet not so much": Haardt, "Zelda Fitzgerald," p. 5.

36. "Mrs. Francesca—who never heard of you": Letter from Zelda Fitzgerald to F. Scott Fitzgerald, 1919, Fitzgerald Papers, P.U.L.

36. "We're twins": F. Scott Fitzgerald, *The Beautiful and Damned*, p. 131.

36. "So much she loved the man": Zelda Fitzgerald, *Save Me the Waltz* (New York: Charles Scribner's Sons, 1932), p. 40.

37. "Always intensely skeptical of her sex": F. Scott Fitzgerald, *The Beautiful and Damned*, pp. 234–235.

37. "You like men better": Ibid., p. 134.

37. "Don't you ever intend to see": Ibid.

37. "Because you're so clean": Ibid., p. 131.

37. "During his undergraduate days": George Jean Nathan, "Memories of Fitzgerald, Lewis and Dreiser," *Esquire* 50 (October 1958): 148–149.

38. "Three months before I was born": F. Scott Fitzgerald, quoted in Andrew Turnbull, *Scott Fitzgerald* (New York: Charles Scribner's Sons, 1962), p. 7.

39. "His father had gone out a comparatively young man": F. Scott Fitzgerald as quoted in Andrew Mellow, *Invented Lives* (New York: Houghton Mifflin, 1984), p. 18.

39. "his father used to drink too much": F. Scott Fitzgerald, Facsimile of Ledger Book, Fitzgerald Collection, P.U.L., August 1906, p. 160.

39. "this time to a flat on East Willow Street": Ibid., p. 157.

39. "I knew I was 'fresh' and not popular": F. Scott Fitzgerald, quoted in Scott Donaldson, *Fool for Love* (New York: Congdon & Weed, 1983), p. 178.

43. "Long afterwards, I complained to him": John Peale Bishop, "The Missing All," *Collected Essays of John Peale Bishop* (London: Scribner's, 1948), p. 67.

44. "I was a sophomore at Princeton": Alice Anders, "Fitzgerald in Wilmington," *Delaware Today* 6 (October-November 1967): 25–26.

46. "The fun in those first years": Haardt, "Zelda Fitzgerald," p. 2.

46. "Many of those older people": Ibid.

46. "Last night a small crowd of practical jokers": Letter from Zelda Fitzgerald to F. Scott Fitzgerald, 1919, Zelda Fitzgerald Papers, P.U.L.

47. "I have always been inclined towards masculinity": Letter from Zelda Fitzgerald to F. Scott Fitzgerald, quoted in Mellow, *Invented Lives*, p. 67.

47. "Yesterday Bill Le Grande and I drove his car": Letter from Zelda Fitzgerald to F. Scott Fitzgerald, April 1919, Zelda Fitzgerald Papers, Folder 11, Box 42, P.U.L.

47. "Zelda was interesting, attractive": Letter from Mrs. H. L. Weatherby to the author, April 1963. Collection of the author.

48. "yesterday, when the university boys": Letter from Zelda Fitzgerald to F. Scott Fitzgerald, Zelda Fitzgerald Papers, Folder 10, Box 42, P.U.L.

48. "She introduced him to us": Mayfield, *Exiles from Paradise*, p. 27.

50. "Peyton wired Sara [Haardt] that he was coming to Baltimore": Ibid, p. 127.

50. "Here is the mentioned chapter": Letter from F. Scott Fitzgerald to Zelda Fitzgerald, July 1918, *The Correspondence of F. Scott Fitzgerald*, ed. Matthew Bruccoli and Margaret Duggan (New York: Random House, 1980), p. 32.

51. "It isn't really a cemetery, you know": Letter from Zelda Fitzgerald to F. Scott Fitzgerald, quoted in Milford, *Zelda*, p. 45.

52. "Alabama and the lieutenant lingered": Zelda Fitzgerald, *Save Me the Waltz*, in Bruccoli, *Collected Writings*, pp. 38–39.

52. "She was not perfectly sure—except for the sexual recklessness": Letter from F. Scott Fitzgerald, quoted in Arthur Mizener, *The Far Side of Paradise* (New York: Houghton Mifflin, 1949), p. 78.

52. "When she saw him leave the dance floor": Zelda Fitzgerald, *Save Me the Waltz*, p. 39.

53. "The assumption is that you were": Letter from F. Scott Fitzgerald to Zelda Fitzgerald, fall 1939, quoted in Bruccoli and Duggan, *Correspondence of F. Scott Fitzgerald*, p. 559.

53. "Your mother took such rotten care of Zelda": Unsent letter from F. Scott Fitzgerald to Marjorie Brinson, December 1938, quoted in Donaldson, *Fool for Love*, p. 63.

53. "pretended to be drunk and fell down on the floor": Mayfield, *Exiles from Paradise*, p. 24.

54. "You invited me to dine and I had never": Letter from Zelda Fitzgerald to F. Scott Fitzgerald, (no date), Zelda Fitzgerald Papers, P.U.L., also quoted in Mellow, *Invented Lives*, p. 8.

54. "From 2:30–6 pm Court Square will be cleared of traffic": *Montgomery Advertiser*, clipping in Zelda Fitzgerald Scrapbook, P.U.L.

54. "Telda [*sic*] found knockout little apartment": Telegram in Zelda Fitzgerald Scrapbook, P.U.L.

55. "These hot, sticky nights": Letter from Zelda Fitzgerald to F. Scott Fitzgerald, late spring/summer 1919, Zelda Fitzgerald Papers, Box 42, Folder 6, P.U.L.

55. "Have a date with you on Saturday": Note from Pete Bonner in Zelda Fitzgerald Scrapbook, P.U.L.

55. "I sure would like to meet you": Note from Solomon Tedford, March 12, 1920, pasted in Zelda Fitzgerald Scrapbook, P.U.L.

55. "I know you love me, Darling": Letter from Zelda Fitzgerald to F. Scott Fitzgerald, quoted in Mellow, *Invented Lives*, p. 68.

55. "I'd probably aggravate you": Letter from Zelda Fitzgerald to F. Scott Fitzgerald, April 1919, quoted in Bruccoli and Duggan, *Correspondence of F. Scott Fitzgerald*, p. 43.

55. "I hate writing when I haven't time": Letter from Zelda Fitzgerald to F. Scott Fitzgerald, quoted in Milford, *Zelda*, p. 50.

56. "I remember the first time he told me about Zelda": John Biggs quoted by Rex Polier, "Fitzgerald in Wilmington: The Great Gatsby at Bay," *Philadelphia Sunday Bulletin*, January 6, 1974, Sec. 4.

56. "My mind is firmly made up": Letter from F. Scott Fitzgerald to Ruth Sturtevant, December 4, 1918, quoted in Mellow, *Invented Lives*, p. 58.

57. "As you say, it is a very human document": Letter from Stephen Parrott to F. Scott Fitzgerald, quoted in Mellow, *Invented Lives*, p. 64.

57. "He had met her when she was seventeen": F. Scott Fitzgerald quoted in Mizener, *The Far Side of Paradise*, p. 83.

57. "The young man with the jingle of money": F. Scott Fitzgerald, "Pasting

It Together," in *The Crack-Up*, ed. Edmund Wilson (New York: New Directions, 1956), p. 77.

57. "He remembered poor Scott Fitzgerald": Ernest Hemingway, *The Snows of Kilimanjaro* (New York: Charles Scribner's Sons, 1955), p. 23. Scott's name changed to "Julian" in 1955 edition.

58. "We're swimming all the time": Letter from Zelda Sayre to F. Scott Fitzgerald, Fitzgerald Papers, P.U.L.

58. "Rosalind: I can't, Amory": F. Scott Fitzgerald, *This Side of Paradise*, pp. 179–180.

59. "I was a failure": F. Scott Fitzgerald, "My Lost City," in *The Crack-Up*, p. 26.

60. "During Scott's courtship": C. Lawton Campbell, "The Fitzgeralds Were My Friends," unpublished essay, pp. 12–13. Collection of the author.

61. "I am very glad, personally to be able": Letter from Maxwell Perkins to F. Scott Fitzgerald, quoted in Matthew J. Bruccoli, ed., *The Romantic Egoists* (New York: Charles Scribner's Sons, 1974), p. 53.

61. "I am very proud of you": Letter from Zelda Fitzgerald to F. Scott Fitzgerald, quoted in Mellow, *Invented Lives*, p. 79.

62. "I've always known that any girl": Letter from F. Scott Fitzgerald to Isabelle Amorous, February 26, 1920, in Bruccoli and Duggan, *Correspondence of F. Scott Fitzgerald*, p. 53.

62. "I wanted to for your sake": Letter from Zelda Fitzgerald to F. Scott Fitzgerald, February 1920, in Bruccoli, *Collected Writings*, p. 447.

62. "As I started up the stairs": Campbell, "The Fitzgeralds Were My Friends," pp. 13–14.

64. "Judge and Mrs. A. D. Sayre announce": Newsclipping in Zelda Fitzgerald Scrapbook, P.U.L.

64. "Darling—Mama knows that we are going to be married": Letter from Zelda Fitzgerald to F. Scott Fitzgerald, April 1920, Folder 12, Box 42, P.U.L.

64. "I have taken rooms at the Biltmore": Telegram from F. Scott Fitzgerald to Zelda Fitzgerald, March 28, 1920, Zelda Fitzgerald Scrapbook, P.U.L.

64. "Zelda's friends, carrying bouquets for her": Rosalind Smith, unpublished documentation about Zelda Fitzgerald, Mayfield Collection, University of Alabama.

64. "My husband and I met Zelda and my eldest sister": Ibid.

65. "I think just being in love": Zelda Fitzgerald, quoted in Bruccoli, *Some Sort of Epic Grandeur*, p. 166.

Chapter 2: America's Darlings

66. "You may laugh": Letter from F. Scott Fitzgerald to Ruth Sturtevant, March 26, 1920, quoted in Andrew Turnbull, *The Letters of F. Scott Fitzgerald* (New York: Charles Scribner's Sons, 1963), pp. 458–459.

67. "There was no luncheon after the wedding": Rosalind Smith, unpublished documentation on Zelda Fitzgerald, W. S. Hoole Special Collections Library, University of Alabama, Tuscaloosa.

67. "Tilde and her husband were invited": Ibid.

67. "Do you remember our first meal in the Biltmore": Letter from Zelda Fitzgerald to F. Scott Fitzgerald, no date, Zelda Fitzgerald Papers, P.U.L.

68. "Alabama lay thinking": Zelda Fitzgerald, *Save Me the Waltz*, quoted in *The*

Collected Writings of Zelda Fitzgerald, ed. Matthew J. Bruccoli and Margaret Duggan (New York: Charles Scribner's Sons, 1991), pp. 43–44.

69. "arrived here at 9 o'clock": Letter from F. Scott Fitzgerald to Ruth Sturtevant, May 14, 1920, quoted in Turnbull, *Letters*, p. 461.

69. "Gloria was a much more trivial": Letter from F. Scott Fitzgerald to Scottie Fitzgerald, quoted in Andrew Mellow's *Invented Lives* (New York: Houghton Mifflin, 1984), p. 134.

69. "It was dark when the real estate agent": F. Scott Fitzgerald, *The Beautiful and Damned* (New York: Charles Scribner's Sons, 1950), p. 177.

70. "close together on the porch": Ibid., p. 179.

70. "Hurry back to Montgomery": Western Union telegram to Zelda Fitzgerald, May 17, 1920, Zelda Fitzgerald Scrapbook, P.U.L.

70. "More from their fear of solitude": F. Scott Fitzgerald, *The Beautiful and Damned*, p. 235.

70. "they had tried to do without him": Zelda Fitzgerald, *Save Me the Waltz*, in Bruccoli, *Collected Writings*, p. 52.

72. "Scott's hot in the middle of a new novel": Zelda Fitzgerald to Ludlow Fowler, quoted in Scott Donaldson, *Fool for Love* (New York: Congdon & Weed, 1983), p. 68.

72. "she must be either simple and reproachless": F. Scott Fitzgerald, *The Beautiful and Damned*, pp. 234–235.

72. "Person Who Sent In False Alarm Cannot Be Found": *Westporter-Herald*, July 16, 1920, Westport, Connecticut, Historical Society.

72. "There was the road house": Zelda Fitzgerald, summary of her marriage (Prangins 1930), quoted in Matthew J. Bruccoli, *Some Sort of Epic Grandeur* (New York: Harcourt Brace Jovanovich, 1981), p. 300.

72. "I'm just enclosing": Letter from F. Scott Fitzgerald to Maxwell Perkins, February 1920, quoted in Bruccoli, *Some Sort of Epic Grandeur*, p. 166.

73. "it is a collection of episodes": Letter from F. Scott Fitzgerald to Harold Ober, November 1919, quoted in Henry Dan Piper, *F. Scott Fitzgerald: A Critical Portrait* (New York: Holt, Rinehart and Winston, 1965), p. 83.

73. "Zelda's ideas entirely responsible": Alexander McKaig Diary, April 17, 1920. Collection of Robert Haft, New Peterborough, New Hampshire.

73. "They interested me so greatly": George Jean Nathan, quoted in Nancy Milford, *Zelda, a Biography* (New York: Harper & Row, 1970), p. 71

73. "Fitzgerald's answer was a resounding no": Ibid.

74. "He is a man of middle height": Carl Bode, *Mencken* (Carbondale, Ill.: Southern Illinois University Press, 1969), p. 62.

75. "very polite to women": Ibid., p. 64.

76. "His business is the theater": Ernest Boyd, *Portraits: Real and Imaginary* (New York: George Donan Company, 1920), pp. 199, 201.

76. "For a very young and pretty girl": Letter from Zelda Fitzgerald to James Branch Cabell, December 1921, Zelda Fitzgerald Papers, Box 5, Folder 2, P.U.L.

77. "In the prohibition period": Guy Pene du Bois, as quoted by Barbara Probst Solomon in "Westport Wildlife," *The New Yorker*, September 9, 1996, p. 82.

77. "Charley Towne and George Nathan had been on a visit to them": Edmund Wilson, "After the War," in *The Twenties*, ed. Leon Edel (New York: Farrar, Straus, & Giroux, 1975), p. 59.

78. "Most alluring to man": George Jean Nathan, "On Women," in *The World of George Jean Nathan*, ed. Charles Angoff (New York: Knopf, 1952), p. 139.

78. "Sweet Souse: What happened": Letter from George Jean Nathan to Zelda Fitzgerald, no date, Zelda Fitzgerald Papers, Col. 187, Box 5, File 18, P.U.L.

78. "When in his cups": George Jean Nathan, "Memories of Fitzgerald, Lewis and Dreiser," *Esquire*, October 1958, p. 148.

79. "To a man, the least interesting of women": Nathan, "On Women," in *The World of George Jean Nathan*, p. 131.

80. "Had long talk with her": McKaig Diary, April 17, 1920.

80. "Zelda, Fitzgerald and I out": Ibid., February 5, 1920.

80. "I have never married because": Nathan, "On Women," in *The World of George Jean Nathan*, p. 137.

81. "I have known many women": Ibid.

81. "The calling of a husband's attention": Letter from George Jean Nathan to Zelda Fitzgerald, September 12, 1920, quoted in Donaldson, *Fool for Love*, p. 68.

82. "one night in June he had quarreled violently": F. Scott Fitzgerald, *The Beautiful and Damned*, p. 388.

82. "In his biography on Fitzgerald": Nathan, "Memories of Fitzgerald, Lewis and Dreiser," p. 148.

82. "Nathan and me [*sic*] have become reconciled by letter": Letter from F. Scott Fitzgerald to Edmund Wilson, 1922, cited in Mellow, *Invented Lives*, p. 151.

82. "I suggest that you hire a post office box": Letter from George Jean Nathan to Zelda Fitzgerald, September 12, 1920, Zelda Fitzgerald Papers, P.U.L.

82. "Under no circumstances": Letter from George Jean Nathan to Arthur Mizener, January 10, 1950, interview with Arthur Mizener, Cornell University.

82. "He also made love to Zelda": Arthur Mizener, handwritten note on Nathan's response to Mizener's letter of January 10, 1950, interview with Arthur Mizener, Cornell University.

82. "The man of ninety, dying": Nathan, "On Women," in *The World of George Jean Nathan*, p., 139.

83. "No woman has ever loved a man so truly": Ibid., p. 131.

83. [Fitz] came to me somewhat apologetically": Nathan, "Memories of Fitzgerald, Lewis and Dreiser," pp. 148–149.

83. "I want to be a successful sensation": F. Scott Fitzgerald, *The Beautiful and Damned*, p. 213.

84. "It's such a hell of a career": Ibid., p. 306.

84. "Was it wrong": Ibid., p. 146.

85. "Just received . . . photograph": McKaig Diary, July 19, 1920.

85. "Went to Fitzs for the day": Ibid., July 4, 1920.

85. "they thought a man and his wife": Zelda Fitzgerald, "Show Mr. and Mrs. F. to ___," in Bruccoli, *Collected Writings*, p. 419.

86. " 'Understand . . . that I am not' ": Zelda Fitzgerald, *Save Me the Waltz*, in Bruccoli, *Collected Writings*, p. 56.

86. "He left it to us to carve": Rosalind Smith, unpublished documentation on Zelda Fitzgerald, W. S. Hoole Special Collections Library, University of Alabama, Tuscaloosa.

87. "I got there in April": John Biggs, quoted in Seymour A. Toll, *A Judge Uncommon: A Life of John Biggs, Jr.* (Philadelphia: Legal Communications, Ltd., 1993), p. 46.

87. "Biggs is a drunken bum": McKaig Diary, September 4, 1920.

87. "Some one had come to the door": F. Scott Fitzgerald, *The Beautiful and Damned*, p. 243.

88. "In evening, Zelda—drunk": McKaig Diary, September 15, 1920.

88. There were Townsend's blue eyes": Zelda Fitzgerald, summary of her marriage, (Prangins, 1930), quoted in Bruccoli, *Some Sort of Epic Grandeur*, p. 300.

89. "loved each other ... desperately, passionately": Carl Van Vechten, *Parties: Scenes from Contemporary New York Life* (Freeport, N.Y.: Books for Libraries Press, 1971), p. 90.

89. "she passed very quickly": C. Lawton Campbell, "The Fitzgeralds Were My Friends," unpublished essay, p. 20. Collection of the author.

89. "If she's there Fitzgerald can't work—": McKaig Diary, October 11, 1920.

90. "None of the men": Ibid., September 15, 1920.

90. "John [Bishop], I like you better": Edmund Wilson, in *The Twenties*, p. 55.

90. "I've been twirling the thyrsus tonight": Ibid.

90. "The magnificent attitude": F. Scott Fitzgerald, *The Beautiful and Damned*, pp. 226–227.

91. "Oh Scott—I am hungry for beauty": Letter from John Peale Bishop to F. Scott Fitzgerald, November 11, 1918, quoted in Arthur Mizener, *The Far Side of Paradise* (New York: Houghton Mifflin, 1949), p. 79.

91. "Will you honestly take a garret": Letter from John Peale Bishop to F. Scott Fitzgerald, November 11, 1918, ibid.

93. "Suddenly, this double apparition": Gilbert Seldes quoted in Milford, *Zelda*, p. 97.

94. "Don't think I shall care for New Haven—too little. I want girls": McKaig Diary, January 1919.

94. "Working hard on movie work": Ibid., March 31, 1920.

94. "Wrote and congratulated Fitzgerald": Ibid., December 22, 1918.

95. "Called on Scott F. and his bride": Ibid., April 12, 1920.

95. "spent evening shaving Zelda's neck": Ibid., November 27, 1920.

95. "She is without a doubt": Ibid., April 17, 1921.

95. "Took Zelda to lunch": Ibid., December 4, 1920.

95. "I suppose I ought to be furious": F. Scott Fitzgerald, *The Beautiful and Damned*, p. 181.

96. "Took Zelda to lunch at Gotham": McKaig Diary, December 4, 1920.

96. "George Jean Nathan came and then Ludlow": Ibid., October 12, 1920.

96. "Dinner with Mackie and thence": Ibid., October 14, 1920.

96. "Went to Follies with Scott and Zelda": Ibid., October 25, 1920.

96. "Went to see 'Enter Madame' ": Ibid., December 4, 1920.

96. "Went at 11:30 p.m. to party": Ibid., August 16, 1920.

97. "Scott is a novelist and Zelda is a novelty": Ring Lardner Jr., as quoted by Edmund Wilson, in *The Twenties*, p. 278.

97. "Georges apartment, and his": Letter from Zelda Fitzgerald to F. Scott Fitzgerald, late summer/early fall 1930, written from Prangins, in Bruccoli, *Collected Writings*, p. 451.

97. "Muriel: Have you seen 'Peg o' My Heart'?": F. Scott Fitzgerald, *The Beautiful and Damned*, p. 96.

98. "would have to make up her mind": McKaig Diary, October 11, 1920.

98. "Zelda increasingly restless": Ibid., October 15, 1920.

99. "I hope I'll never get ambitious enough to try anything": Letter from Zelda Fitzgerald to F. Scott Fitzgerald, quoted in Milford, *Zelda*, p. 57.

99. "Spinach and champagne": Campbell, "The Fitzgeralds Were My Friends," p. 18.

99. "She [Zelda] and Fitzgerald like only aristocrats": McKaig Diary, October 12, 1920.

99. "I remember riding on top of a taxi-cab along deserted Fifth Avenue": F. Scott Fitzgerald, *The Crack-Up*, ed. Edmund Wilson (New York: New Directions, 1945), pp. 27–28.

99. "Evening at Fitzgeralds": McKaig Diary, December 11, 1920.

99. "Zelda wants to live life of an 'extravagant' ": Ibid.

100. "Went to the Fitzgeralds": Ibid., October 11, 1920.

100. "Before they had been two months in the little apartment": F. Scott Fitzgerald, *The Beautiful and Damned*, pp. 295–296.

100. "the room was bedlam": Campbell, "The Fitzgeralds Were My Friends," p. 17.

101. "Why on earth are you carrying": Rosalind Smith as quoted in Sara Mayfield, *Exiles from Paradise: Zelda and Scott Fitzgerald* (New York: Dell Publishing Co., 1971), p. 65, also in Rosalind Smith, unpublished documentation on Zelda, W. S. Hoole Special Collections Library, University of Alabama, Tuscaloosa.

101. "She had little training": Rosalind Smith, unpublished documentation on Zelda, W. S. Hoole Special Collections Library, University of Alabama, Tuscaloosa.

101. "Gloria at twenty-six": F. Scott Fitzgerald, *The Beautiful and Damned*, pp. 296–297.

101. " 'You couldn't know how beautiful' ": F. Scott Fitzgerald quoted in Milford, *Zelda*, pp. 73–74.

102. "Many people made their own liquor at home": Campbell, "The Fitzgeralds Were My Friends," p. 19.

102. "Gloria knew within a month": F. Scott Fitzgerald, *The Beautiful and Damned*, p. 157.

103. "Zelda appeared at the door": Campbell, "The Fitzgeralds Were My Friends," p. 20.

103. "He [Scott] would hang on her words": Campbell, "The Fitzgeralds Were My Friends," p. 20.

103. "She talked with so spontaneous a color and wit": Edmund Wilson, quoted in Jeffrey Meyers, *Edmund Wilson: A Biography* (Boston: Houghton Mifflin, 1995), p. 109.

104. "How far they had come": F. Scott Fitzgerald, notes for *The Great Gatsby*, in Zelda Fitzgerald Scrapbook, P.U.L.

104. "Zelda was very beautiful and was tanned": Ernest Hemingway, "Hawks Do Not Share," in *A Moveable Feast* (New York: Bantam Books, 1965), pp. 183–184.

104. "Zelda could do outlandish things": Lillian Gish, quoted in Mayfield, *Exiles from Paradise*, p. 60.

104. "John, aren't you sorry you weren't killed in the war?": Zelda Fitzgerald, quoted in Mizener, *The Far Side of Paradise*, p. 234.

105. "terrible battle in evening": McKaig Diary, October 3, 1920.

105. "Went up to Fitzgerald's to spend evening": Ibid., October 21, 1920.

105. "To put it briefly": F. Scott Fitzgerald, *The Beautiful and Damned*, p. 184.

105. "On this particular occasion": Campbell, "The Fitzgeralds Were My Friends," p. 12.

CHAPTER 3: BABY MAKES THREE

107. "seemed a little crestfallen": Letter from Edmund Wilson to F. Scott Fitzgerald, June 22, 1921, in Edmund Wilson, *Letters on Literature and Politics*, ed. Elena Wilson (New York: Farrar, Straus & Giroux, 1977), p. 63.

107. "Fitzgeralds gone gloriously": Alexander McKaig Diary, May 5, 1921. Collection of Robert Haft, New Peterborough, New Hampshire.

108. "We went to London to see a fog": Letter from Zelda Fitzgerald to Scottie Fitzgerald, c. 1944, in *The Romantic Egoists*, ed. Matthew J. Bruccoli (New York: Charles Scribner's Sons, 1974), p. 84.

110. "God damn the continent": Letter from F. Scott Fitzgerald to Edmund Wilson, misdated by Andrew Turnbull as May 1921, in his *The Letters of F. Scott Fitzgerald* (New York: Charles Scribner's Sons, 1963), p. 326.

110. "Zelda had no secret pain to conceal": C. Lawton Campbell, "The Fitzgeralds Were My Friends," unpublished essay, p. 24. Collection of the author.

110. "I think Gilda Gray is the most": Zelda Fitzgerald quoted in Arthur Mizener, *The Far Side of Paradise* (New York: Houghton Mifflin, 1949), p. 137.

111. "When summer came, all the people": Zelda Fitzgerald, "The Girl the Prince Liked," in *The Collected Writings*, ed. Matthew J. Bruccoli (New York: Charles Scribner's Sons, 1991), p. 311.

112. "tell her [Zelda] I dropped into": Letter from H. L. Mencken to F. Scott Fitzgerald, January 4 (no year), Fitzgerald Papers, Col. 187, Box 51, Folder 9, P.U.L.

112. "Goofo, I'm drunk": F. Scott Fitzgerald, Facsimile of Ledger Book, October 1921, P.U.L.

112. "I woke up out of the ether": F. Scott Fitzgerald, *The Great Gatsby* (New York: Charles Scribner's Sons, 1969), p. 17.

112. "Congratulations. Feared twins": Telegram from Ludlow Fowler to Zelda and Scott Fitzgerald, reprinted in Bruccoli, *The Romantic Egoists*, p. 87.

112. "She is awfully cute": Letter from Zelda Fitzgerald to Ludlow Fowler, December 22, 1921, quoted in Nancy Milford, *Zelda, a Biography* (New York: Harper & Row, 1970), p. 114.

112. "I am delighted to know": Letter from H. L. Mencken to F. Scott Fitzgerald, Fitzgerald Papers, P.U.L.

113. "The pictures prove to me": Letter from George Jean Nathan to Zelda Fitzgerald, May 29, 1922, Zelda Fitzgerald Papers, P.U.L., also quoted in Andrew Mellow, *Invented Lives* (New York: Houghton Mifflin, 1984), p. 151.

113. "This damned place is 18 below zero": Letter from Zelda Fitzgerald to Ludlow Fowler, November 1921, quoted in Milford, *Zelda*, p. 85.

114. "His son went down the toilet": F. Scott Fitzgerald, *Notebooks*, No. 1564, F. Scott Fitzgerald Papers, P.U.L.

114. "Will you please write a review": Letter from Burton Rascoe to Zelda Fitzgerald, March 27, 1922, Zelda Fitzgerald Papers, P.U.L.

114. "It seems to me that on one page": Zelda Fitzgerald, "Mrs. F. Scott Fitzgerald Reviews *The Beautiful and Damned Friend Husband's Latest*," *New York Herald Tribune*, April 2, 1922, reprinted in Bruccoli, *The Collected Writings*, p. 388.

114. "What grubworms women are to crawl": F. Scott Fitzgerald, *The Beautiful and Damned* (New York: Charles Scribner's Sons, 1950), p. 147.

115. "Where could you get a better example": Zelda Fitzgerald, "Mrs. F. Scott Fitzgerald Reviews *The Beautiful and Damned*," in Bruccoli, *Collected Writings*, p. 387.

115. "To begin with everyone must buy this book": Ibid.

115. "I'm writing you at the behest of the famous author": Letter from F. Scott Fitzgerald to Burton Rascoe, April 1922, F. Scott Fitzgerald Papers, P.U.L., also quoted in *Correspondence of F. Scott Fitzgerald*, ed. Matthew J. Bruccoli and Margaret Duggan (New York: Random House, 1980), p. 100.

115. "You fled New York without": Note from Burton Rascoe to Zelda Fitzgerald, April 17, 1922, Zelda Fitzgerald Scrapbook, P.U.L.

115. "I think a woman gets more happiness": Interview with Zelda Fitzgerald by the Louisville *Courier-Journal*, September 30, 1923, "What a Flapper Novelist Thinks of His Wife," reprinted in Bruccoli, *The Romantic Egoists*, pp. 112–113.

116. "I imagine you wear something": Zelda Fitzgerald, *Save Me the Waltz* (New York: Charles Scribner's Sons, 1932), p. 147.

116. "Are you going to act in": Letter from H. L. Mencken to F. Scott Fitzgerald, May 18 (no year), Fitzgerald Papers, Col. 187, Box 51, Folder 9, P.U.L.

117. "The gulf that opened between Zelda and me": John Dos Passos, *The Best Times* (New York: New American Library, 1966), p. 130.

118. "All the Great Neck professionals": Letter from Ring Lardner to Zelda and Scott Fitzgerald, August 8, 1925, in Bruccoli, *Correspondence of F. Scott Fitzgerald*, p. 177.

119. "He liked to take her on his lap": F. Scott Fitzgerald, "The Baby Party," in *Fathers and Daughters: Portraits in Fiction*, ed. Terry Eicher and Jesse Geller (New York: Plume Book, The Penguin Group, 1991), pp. 29–30.

119. "Weekend guests are respectfully notified": House rules of Zelda and F. Scott Fitzgerald, quoted in Mellow, *Invented Lives*, p. 186.

119. "Tilde and John did not forget Scott's rudeness": Rosalind Smith, unpublished documentation on Zelda Fitzgerald, W. S. Hoole Special Collections Library, University of Alabama, Tuscaloosa.

120. "Tootsie (Rosalind) arrived": F. Scott Fitzgerald, Facsimile of Ledger Book, July 1923, P.U.L.

120. "In Great Neck there was always disorder": Letter from Zelda Fitzgerald to F. Scott Fitzgerald, late summer/early fall 1930, from Prangins Clinic, in *F. Scott Fitzgerald: A Life in Letters*, ed. Matthew J. Bruccoli (New York: Simon & Schuster, 1995), p. 191.

120. "Mrs. Scott Fitzgerald started the flapper movement": Caption of article on the Fitzgeralds in *Hearst's International*, May 1923, reprinted in Bruccoli, *The Romantic Egoists*, p. 105.

121. "Three or four years ago girls of her type were pioneers": Interview of Zelda Fitzgerald with the Louisville *Courier-Journal*, September 30, 1923, reprinted in Bruccoli, *The Romantic Egoists*, p. 112.

121. "I've studied ballet": Ibid., p. 113.

121. "fascinated Scott in the Great Neck days": Ring Lardner Jr., *The Lardners: My Family Remembered* (New York: Harper Colophon Books, 1976), p. 164.

122. "F. Scott Fitzgerald and Ring Lardner are neighbors in Great Neck": "About Scott Fitzgerald; Famous Author who Spent Summer Here in Public Print," *Westporter-Herald*, April 20, 1923.

122. "there was a porch": Lardner, *The Lardners: My Family Remembered*, p. 163.

122. "He is a typical newspaperman": Letter from Zelda Fitzgerald to Rosalind Smith, quoted in Lane Yorke, "Zelda: A Worksheet," *Paris Review*, Fall 1983, p. 219.

123. "She did not care for Mrs. Markey": F. Scott Fitzgerald, "The Baby Party," in Eicher and Geller, *Fathers and Daughters, Portraits in Fiction*, p. 32.

123. "where they paid for country air with endless servant troubles": Ibid., p. 31.

123. "Your wife comes in here and begins shouting about how common we are": Ibid., p. 38.

123. "Zelda was twenty-two years old": Lardner, *The Lardners: My Family Remembered*, pp. 161–162.

123. "During prohibition Scott Fitzgerald and I": John Biggs, as quoted by Seymour Toll in *A Judge Uncommon: A Life of John Biggs, Jr.* (Philadelphia: Legal Communications, Ltd., 1993), pp. 61–62, originally quoted in Lee Reese, *The House on Rodney Square* (Wilmington, Del.: The New Journal Co., 1977), p. 174.

124. "suggested to me once that Scott": Edmund Wilson, *The Twenties*, ed. Leon Edel (New York: Farrar, Straus, & Giroux, 1975), p. 95.

125. "In brief, the show flopped as flat as one of Aunt Jemima's famous pancakes": Letter from Zelda Fitzgerald to Xandra Kalman, quoted in Mellow, *Invented Lives*, p. 199.

126. "Zelda, 'fair queen of Alabam,' Across the waves I kiss you!": Ring Lardner, quoted in Milford, *Zelda*, p. 103.

126. "When are you coming back and why, please answer": Telegram from Ring Lardner to Zelda Fitzgerald, in Zelda Fitzgerald Scrapbook, P.U.L.

126. "Ring is drinking himself to an embalmed state": Letter from Zelda Fitzgerald to a friend, quoted by Mellow, *Invented Lives*, p. 193.

CHAPTER 4: EXPATRIATES ABROAD

128. "All of our friends from New York arrive": Letter from Zelda Fitzgerald to Madeline Boyd, December 18, 1925, Zelda Fitzgerald Papers, Box 5, File 1, P.U.L.

129. "His wife and child were with him": John Peale Bishop, "The Missing All," *Virginia Quarterly Review*, Winter 1937, p. 110.

129. "John is like a man lying in a warm bath": Alan Tate, *Memoirs and Opinions, 1926–1974* (Chicago: Swallow Press, 1975), p. 72.

133. "Scott and Zelda spent lavishly": Gerald Murphy as quoted in Honoria Murphy Donnelly, *Sara and Gerald: Villa America and After* (New York: Times Books, 1982), p. 107.

136. "tanned and beautiful": Ibid., p. 148.

136. "I love peonies—my favorite flowers": Sara Mayfield, *Exiles from Paradise: Zelda and Scott Fitzgerald* (New York: Dell Publishing Co., 1971), p. 139.

137. "individuality, her flair": Gerald Murphy, quoted by Nancy Milford in *Zelda, a Biography* (New York: Harper & Row, 1970), p. 107.

137. "A great rush of preparation": F. Scott Fitzgerald, *The Beautiful and Damned* (New York: Charles Scribner's Sons, 1950), pp. 211–212.

138. "You took what you wanted": Zelda Fitzgerald, *Save Me the Waltz*, p. 98.

139. "The music stopped. He drew her body": Ibid., p. 86.

139. "I liked [Jozan] and was glad": F. Scott Fitzgerald, quoted in Sheilah Graham, *The Real F. Scott Fitzgerald: Thirty-Five Years Later* (New York: Grosset & Dunlap, 1976), p. 61.

140. "at the time of my quarrel": Letter from F. Scott Fitzgerald to Dr. Robert Carroll, quoted in Matthew J. Bruccoli, *Some Sort of Epic Grandeur* (New York: Harcourt Brace Jovanovich, 1981), p. 408.

140. "Scott liked the idea of sex": Oscar Kalman, quoted in Jeffrey Meyers, *Scott Fitzgerald* (New York: HarperCollins, 1994), pp. 151–152.

141. "It was one of their acts together": Hadley Hemingway, quoted in Milford, *Zelda*, p. 114.

141. "had fallen in love with the French navy pilot": Ernest Hemingway, *A Moveable Feast* (New York: Bantam Books, 1965), p. 179.

141. "September 1924": F. Scott Fitzgerald, quoted in Bruccoli, *Some Sort of Epic Grandeur*, p. 199.

141. "In the Hotel des Princes": Zelda Fitzgerald, "Show Mr. and Mrs. F. to Number ___," in *The Collected Writings*, ed. Matthew J. Bruccoli (New York: Charles Scribner's Sons, 1991), p. 422.

142. "She is the most exquisite thing": F. Scott Fitzgerald, quoted in Meyers, *Scott Fitzgerald*, p. 119.

142. "drinking under the gold statue": Letter from Zelda Fitzgerald to F. Scott Fitzgerald, late summer/early fall 1930, Zelda Fitzgerald Papers, P.U.L.

142. "I could sleep with Zelda anytime I wanted to": Edmund Wilson, *The Twenties*, ed. Leon Edel (New York: Farrar, Straus, & Giroux, 1975), p. 297.

142. "The character was not intended to be any possible": Letter from F. Scott Fitzgerald to Howard Cox, April 15, 1934, *Correspondence of F. Scott Fitzgerald*, ed. Matthew J. Bruccoli and Margaret Duggan (New York: Random House, 1980), p. 350.

143. "Zelda was not so loose": Edmund Wilson, *The Twenties*, p. 298.

143. "a high white hotel scalloped about the base": Zelda Fitzgerald, "Show Mr. and Mrs. F. to Number ___," in Bruccoli, *Collected Writings*, p. 422.

143. "Zelda's been sick in bed for five weeks": Letter from F. Scott Fitzgerald to John Peale Bishop, March 1925, in Andrew Turnbull, *The Letters of F. Scott Fitzgerald* (New York: Charles Scribner's Sons, 1963), p. 355.

145. "Zelda has been too sick": Letter from F. Scott Fitzgerald to Roger Burlingame, April 19, 1925, quoted in Bruccoli and Duggan, *Correspondence of F. Scott Fitzgerald*, p. 160.

146. "Dear Friends: Fitzgerald was around": Note from Ernest Hemingway to Gertrude Stein and Alice B. Toklas, quoted in James Mellow, *Hemingway: A Life Without Consequences* (Reading, Mass.: Addison-Wesley Publishing Co., 1992), p. 291.

148. "I think Stearns will be delighted": Letter from F. Scott Fitzgerald to Maxwell Perkins, October/November 1928, quoted in Bruccoli and Duggan, *Correspondence of F. Scott Fitzgerald*, p. 222.

148. "He has been helped by various people": Letter from F. Scott Fitzgerald to Alexander Woollcott, Fall 1925, in Turnbull, *The Letters of F. Scott Fitzgerald*, p. 486.

150. "great drinking of cocktails in our bathroom": Harry Crosby as quoted in Barnaby Conrad, III, *Absinthe: History in a Bottle* (San Francisco: Chronicle Books, 1988), p. 142.

150. "poverty stricken boys and girls": Robert McAlmon, *Being Geniuses Together*, (Garden City, N.Y.: Doubleday, 1968), p. 110.

150. "People were for sale at bargain prices": Djuna Barnes as quoted in Andrew Field, *Djuna: The Formidable Miss Barnes* (Austin: University of Texas Press, 1985), p. 118.

151. "Their famous dinner on the houseboat": Janet Flanner, *Paris Was Yesterday* (New York: Viking Press, 1972), Introduction, pp. xviii–xix.

152. "Montparnasse was little more than a gray and dull street": Jimmie Charters, *This Must Be the Place*, ed. Morrill Cody (London: Herbert Joseph, 1934), p. 111.

152. "In the normal course of events": Ibid., p. 12.

153. "It was warm inside in the winter": Ernest Hemingway, quoted in Arlen J. Hansen, *Expatriate Paris: A Cultural and Literary Guide to Paris of the 1920's* (New York: Arcade Publishing, 1990), p. 142.

153. "I don't think it was parties": Gerald Murphy, quoted in Bruccoli, *Some Sort of Epic Grandeur*, p. 254.

153. "It was a constant merry-go-round": Scottie Fitzgerald, as quoted in Eleanor Lanahan, *Scottie, The Daughter of . . .* (New York: HarperCollins, 1995), p. 39.

154. "I am beginning a new novel next month": Letter from F. Scott Fitzgerald to John Peale Bishop, August 9, 1925, quoted in Malcolm Cowley, *Fitzgerald and the Jazz Age* (New York: Scribner Research Anthologies, Charles Scribner's Sons, 1966), p. 102.

155. "I went to Antibes and liked Archie MacLeish enormously": Letter from F. Scott Fitzgerald to John Peale Bishop, probably September 1925, in Turnbull, *The Letters of F. Scott Fitzgerald*, p. 359.

156. "Honoria's teacher is Madame Egorova": Letter from Gerald Murphy to F. Scott Fitzgerald, September 19, 1925, quoted in Bruccoli and Duggan, *Correspondence of F. Scott Fitzgerald*, p. 179.

157. "Different people need different things": Duff Twysden as quoted in Harold Loeb, *The Way It Was* (New York: Criterion, 1959), p. 272.

157. "I hope I'll never get ambitious": Zelda Fitzgerald, quoted in Milford, *Zelda*, p. 57.

159. "nobody knew whose party it was": Zelda Fitzgerald, *Save Me the Waltz*, p. 95.

162. "ran into two friends of the Fitzgeralds": Mayfield, *Exiles from Paradise*, p. 135.

162. "his wallet had been stolen": Morley Callaghan, *That Summer in Paris: Memories of Tangled Friendships with Hemingway, Fitzgerald, and Some Others* (New York: Coward-McCann, 1963), p. 192.

162. "In the corner a huge American Negro": F. Scott Fitzgerald, "The World's Fair," quoted in Arthur Mizener, *The Far Side of Paradise* (New York: Houghton Mifflin, 1949), p. 182.

163. "Scott F. came by one evening": Michael Arlen, *Exiles* (New York: Farrar, Strauss & Giroux, 1970), p. 174.

165. "An invitation to dance was made": Brassai, *The Secret Paris of the 30's*, trans. Richard Miller (New York: Pantheon Books, 1976), p. 11.

165. "I'm like they are—like Japanese lanterns": F. Scott Fitzgerald, *The Beautiful and Damned*, p. 73.

168. "Some of you rich guys": Ernest Hemingway, quoted by Kathleen Cannell, *Connecticut Review* 2, no. 1 (1968).

169. "I did not like her but that night": Ernest Hemingway, quoted in Mellow, *Hemingway: A Life Without Consequences*, p. 291.

169. "Of all the people, you need discipline": Letter from Ernest Hemingway to F. Scott Fitzgerald, quoted in Mellow, *Hemingway: A Life Without Consequences*, p. 436.

170. "We have been passing the winter": Letter from Zelda Fitzgerald to Madeline Boyd, Winter 1925–26, Zelda Fitzgerald Papers, Box 5, File 1, P.U.L.

171. "There are dozens of pictures": Scottie Fitzgerald, in Lanahan, *Scottie, the Daughter of . . .* , p. 28.

171. "In Salies-de-Bearn . . . we took a cure": Zelda Fitzgerald, originally published in Zelda Fitzgerald's "Show Mr. and Mrs. F. to Number ___," in Bruccoli, *Collected Writings*, p. 423, as quoted in Bruccoli, *Some Sort of Epic Grandeur*, p. 389.

172. "We have come to a lost little village": Letter from F. Scott Fitzgerald to Harold Ober, January 1926, quoted in Jeffrey Meyers, *Scott Fitzgerald* (New York: HarperCollins, 1994), p. 160.

174. "to pursue these perverse": Letter from F. Scott Fitzgerald to Ernest Hemingway, quoted in Andrew Mellow, *Invented Lives* (New York: Houghton Mifflin, 1984), p. 270.

174. "I'm tearing those bastards apart": Ernest Hemingway, as quoted in Mellow, *Hemingway: A Life Without Consequences*, p. 305.

174. "As to Ernest's book": Letter from F. Scott Fitzgerald to Maxwell Perkins, quoted in Matthew J. Bruccoli, *Scott and Ernest: The Authority of Failure and the Authority of Success* (New York: Random House, 1978), p. 50.

175. "We went to Antibes": Zelda Fitzgerald (Prangins, 1930), quoted in Bruccoli, *Some Sort of Epic Grandeur*, p. 304.

176. "I want to be your helpmate": Hadley Hemingway, quoted in Gioia Diliberto, *Hadley* (New York: Ticknor & Fields, 1992), p. 92.

176. "They went to Bourget and hired an aeroplane": Zelda Fitzgerald, *Save Me the Waltz* (New York: Charles Scribner's Sons, 1932), p. 169.

177. "At twenty-four in Europe": Valmont Clinic medical report on Zelda Fitzgerald completed by Drs. Gross and Martell, Zelda Fitzgerald Papers, P.U.L.

177. "What it was all about I cannot say": Rosalind Smith, unpublished documentation on Zelda Fitzgerald, Mayfield Collection, University of Alabama.

178. "Six of us, oh the best and noblest relics": quoted in Mizener, *The Far Side of Paradise*, p. 181.

178. "I wanted you to swim with me": Letter from Zelda Fitzgerald to F. Scott Fitzgerald, late summer/early fall, 1930, quoted in Mellow, *Invented Lives*, p. 272.

178. "Zelda was a very extraordinary woman": Archibald MacLeish, interview with the author, August 1963, Uphill Farm, Conway, Massachusetts.

179. "He [Scott] really had the most appalling": Gerald Murphy, quoted in Calvin Tomkins, *Living Well Is the Best Revenge* (New York: New American Library, 1972), p. 125.

179. "Good writers are essentially muckrakers": Scottie Fitzgerald, Introduction to *Letters to His Daughter*, ed. Andrew Turnbull (New York: Charles Scribners' Sons, 1965), p. ix.

179. "We were swimming at the beach": Archibald MacLeish, interview with the author, August 1963, Uphill Farm, Conway, Massachusetts.

181. "Whenever they fought": Sara Murphy, quoted in Milford, *Zelda*, p. 123.

181. "One had to be a superb diver": Sara Murphy, quoted in Milford, *Zelda*, p. 124.

181. "The road from their villa had been built": Gilbert Seldes, quoted in Milford *Zelda*, p. 111.

181. "One particular night we had driven over": Archibald MacLeish, interview with the author.

182. "I have been deeply touched": Zelda Fitzgerald, quoted in Mayfield, *Exiles from Paradise*, p. 130.

184. "They collected people then as some collect pictures": Ernest Hemingway, quoted by Mellow in *Hemingway: A Life Without Consequences*, p. 334.

184. "Our life has gone to hell": Letter from Ernest Hemingway to F. Scott Fitz-

gerald, September 1926, quoted by Bernice Kert, *The Hemingway Women* (New York: W. W. Norton and Co., 1983), p. 179.

CHAPTER 5: ASCENT TO MADNESS

187. "This hotel is extraordinary": Letter from Carl Van Vechten to Fania Marinoff, January 19, 1927, *Letters of Carl Van Vechten*, ed. Bruce Kellner (New Haven, Conn.: Yale University Press, 1987), p. 91.

187. "Scott's basically a sweet, nice, person": Sara Haardt, quoted in Sara Mayfield, *The Constant Circle: H. L. Mencken and His Friends* (New York: Delacorte Press, 1969), p. 125.

187. "underneath it, as you and I both know": Ibid.

188. "like a breakfast food": Zelda Fitzgerald, quoted in Matthew J. Bruccoli, *Some Sort of Epic Grandeur* (New York: Harcourt Brace Jovanovich, 1981), p. 258.

188. "The weather here makes me think of Paris": Letter from Zelda Fitzgerald to Scottie Fitzgerald, quoted in Nancy Milford, *Zelda, a Biography* (New York: Harper & Row, 1970), p. 128.

188. "Everybody here is very clever": Letter from Zelda Fitzgerald to Scottie Fitzgerald, quoted in Andrew Mellow, *Invented Lives* (New York: Houghton Mifflin, 1984), p. 285.

189. "This is a tragic city of beautiful girls": Letter from F. Scott Fitzgerald to Cecilia Tancor, his cousin, quoted in Andrew Mellow, *Invented Lives*, p. 281.

189. "In California, though you would not": Zelda Fitzgerald, quoted in Eleanor Lanahan, *Scottie, the Daughter of . . .* (New York: HarperCollins, 1995), p. 43.

190. "Hollywood completely disrupted": Telegram from Lois Moran to F. Scott Fitzgerald, March 14, 1927, F. Scott Fitzgerald Papers, Col. 187, Box 51, Folder 12, P.U.L.

190. "Darling Scott—I miss you enormously": Letter from Lois Moran to F. Scott Fitzgerald, March 1927, ibid.

190. "Darling, dumbbell, upsetting adorable Scott": Letter from Lois Moran to F. Scott Fitzgerald, March 1927, ibid.

190. "I am crazy to own a house": Letter from Zelda Fitzgerald to Scottie Fitzgerald, quoted in Milford, *Zelda*, p. 130.

190. "Thank God you escaped alive": Letter from H. L. Mencken to F. Scott Fitzgerald, March 15 (no year), Fitzgerald Papers, Col. 187, Box 51, Folder 9, P.U.L.

191. "My earliest formal education": Scottie Fitzgerald, quoted in Lanahan, *Scottie, the Daughter of . . .*, p. 32.

191. "I wanted to go everywhere": Ibid.

191. "The rooms were high and full of": Zelda Fitzgerald, quoted in Milford, *Zelda*, p. 248.

192. "We used to have riotous parties": John Biggs, quoted in Seymour I. Toll, *A Judge Uncommon; A Life of John Biggs, Jr.* (Philadelphia, Legal Communications, Ltd., 1993), pp. 98–99, originally quoted in Lee Reese, *The House on Rodney Square* (Wilmington, Del.: The News Journal Company, 1977), pp. 174–175.

192. "From the depths of my polluted soul": Letter from Zelda Fitzgerald to Carl Van Vechten, May 27, 1927, quoted in Andrew Turnbull, *Scott Fitzgerald* (New York: Charles Scribner's Sons, 1962), p. 178.

192. "Carl is divine": Zelda Fitzgerald, quoted in Milford, *Zelda*, p. 249.

193. "Dearest Babykins, We had a wonderful time": Letter from Carl Van Vechten to Fania Marinoff, May 27, 1927, Kellner, *Letters of Carl Van Vechten*, p. 97.

193. "I am painting again": Letter from Zelda Fitzgerald to Carl Van Vechten, September 6, 1927, quoted in Turnbull, *Scott Fitzgerald*, p. 178.

193. "I think that Zelda saw the handwriting": Rosalind Smith, unpublished documentation on Zelda Fitzgerald, W. S. Hoole Special Collections Library, University of Alabama, Tuscaloosa, also quoted in Lanahan, *Scottie, the Daughter of . . .*, p. 185.

193. "David's success was his own": Zelda Fitzgerald, *Save Me the Waltz*, in *The Collected Writings*, ed. Matthew J. Bruccoli (New York: Charles Scribner's Sons, 1991), p. 56.

193. "I have often told you": Letter from Zelda Fitzgerald to F. Scott Fitzgerald, March 1932, quoted in *The Correspondence of F. Scott Fitzgerald*, ed. Matthew Bruccoli and Margaret Duggan (New York: Random House, 1980), p. 284.

194. "afterwards she sat a long time on the stairway": Zelda Fitzgerald quoted in Milford, *Zelda*, p. 249.

195. "I am so outrageously clever": Zelda Fitzgerald, *Save Me the Waltz*, in Bruccoli, *Collected Writings*, p. 80.

195. "Though it was my father": Scottie Fitzgerald, quoted in Lanahan, *Scottie, the Daughter of . . .*, p. 33.

196. "cardboard coach of Louis XIV": Ibid.

196. " 'Of course, it requires youth' ": Sara Haardt, "Zelda Fitzgerald," unpublished interview with Zelda Fitzgerald, p. 7, Enoch Pratt Free Library, Special Collections, Baltimore, Maryland.

196. "I joined the Philadelphia opera": Letter from Zelda Fitzgerald to Carl Van Vechten, October 4, 1927, quoted in Turnbull, *Scott Fitzgerald*, p. 179.

197. "One of the objects that caught her fancy": Anna Biggs, quoted in Toll, *A Judge Uncommon*, pp. 97–98, and in Milford, *Zelda*, p. 136.

197. "start at six or seven o'clock": John Biggs, quoted in Toll, *A Judge Uncommon*, p. 98, and in Reese, *House on Rodney Square*, p. 174.

198. "I really felt a little guilty": Letter from Harold Ober to F. Scott Fitzgerald, quoted in Bruccoli, *Some Sort of Epic Grandeur*, p. 273.

199. "She wanted to get her hands": Zelda Fitzgerald, "The Original Follies Girl," in Bruccoli, *Collected Writings*, p. 295.

199. "We'll be back Fri. night": Postcard from F. Scott Fitzgerald to Scottie Fitzgerald, January 25, 1929, F. Scott Fitzgerald Papers, P.U.L.

200. "Those delirious parties of theirs": John Dos Passos, quoted in Thomas J. Stavola, *Scott Fitzgerald: Crisis in an American Identity* (London: Vision Press, Ltd., London, 1979), p. 59.

200. "You were throwing": F. Scott Fitzgerald, taped conversation with Dr. Thomas Rennie at La Paix, May 28, 1933, Transcript in F. Scott Fitzgerald Papers, P.U.L.

200. "I knew there was only one way": Scottie Fitzgerald, quoted in Lanahan, *Scottie, the Daughter of . . .*, p. 71.

200. "Life at home was simply an existence": Zelda Fitzgerald, *Save Me the Waltz*, in Bruccoli, *Collected Writings*, p. 144.

201. "We want to go in May": Letter from Zelda Fitzgerald to Carl Van Vechten, quoted in Turnbull, *Scott Fitzgerald*, p. 179.

201. "With each new shipment of Americans": F. Scott Fitzgerald as quoted in Bruccoli, *Some Sort of Epic Grandeur*, p. 265.

201. "not a beautiful woman": Alan Tate, quoted in Mellow, *Invented Lives*, p. 346.

202. "reaching her goal": Zelda Fitzgerald, *Save Me the Waltz*, in Bruccoli, *Collected Writings*, p. 118.

202. "There was Marguerite": Ibid., p. 123.

203. "There's no use killing yourself": Ibid., p. 138.

203. "Alabama rubbed her legs": Ibid., p. 117.

204. "girls in the starkness of white": Ibid., p. 123.

204. "Zelda came to the door": Morley Callaghan, *That Summer in Paris* (Harmondsworth: Penguin Books, Ltd., 1979), p. 190.

204. "You were constantly drunk": Zelda Fitzgerald, quoted in Mellow, *Invented Lives*, p. 317.

205. "Scott and I had a row last week": Zelda Fitzgerald, quoted in Sara Mayfield, *Exiles from Paradise: Zelda and Scott Fitzgerald* (New York: Dell Publishing Co., 1971), p. 131.

205. "being carried home from the Ritz": F. Scott Fitzgerald, Facsimile of Ledger Book, P.U.L.

205. "I'm twenty-eight years old": Zelda Fitzgerald, quoted in Mayfield, *Exiles from Paradise*, p. 131.

205. "Don't try to be so damn tactful": Ibid.

206. "becoming unconscious when they drank": Ernest Hemingway, *A Moveable Feast* (New York: Bantam Books and Scribner's Sons, 1965), p. 179.

206. "There seemed to be more drinking": Malcolm Cowley, *Exile's Return* (New York: Viking Press, 1956), p. 291.

206. "Just when somebody's taken him up": F. Scott Fitzgerald, "A New Leaf," in Bruccoli, *Some Sort of Epic Grandeur*, p. 136.

206. "Why—for instance should you trample": Letter from Sara Murphy to F. Scott Fitzgerald, Fitzgerald Papers, Col. 187, Box 51, Folder 15, P.U.L.

207. "10 cigarettes a day": Zelda Fitzgerald, Spiral Loose-leaf Notebook, Zelda Fitzgerald Collection, P.U.L.

207. "We've been on a party": Zelda Fitzgerald, quoted in Mayfield, *Exiles from Paradise*, p. 138.

207. "She wished she could help David": Zelda Fitzgerald, *Save Me the Waltz*, in Bruccoli, *Collected Writings*, p. 155.

207. "I asked him to please try": John Biggs, quoted in Toll, *A Judge Uncommon*, p. 95, originally quoted by Rex Polier in "Fitzgerald in Wilmington, The 'Great Gatsby' at Bay," *Philadelphia Sunday Bulletin*, January 1974, Sec. 4.

208. "About the time I came into money": F. Scott Fitzgerald, "A New Leaf," quoted in Bruccoli, *Some Sort of Epic Grandeur*, p. 135.

208. "There was a kindliness": F. Scott Fitzgerald, *The Beautiful and Damned* (New York: Charles Scribner's Sons, 1950), p. 417.

208. "Two drinks puts him in a manic state": Zelda Fitzgerald quoted in Mayfield, *Exiles from Paradise*, p. 116.

208. "Am going on the water-wagon": Letter from F. Scott Fitzgerald to Maxwell Perkins, quoted in Ring Lardner Jr., *The Lardners: My Family Remembered* (New York: Harper Colophon Books, 1976), pp. 163–164.

208. "Nice life, sitting in a cafe all day": Zelda Fitzgerald, quoted in Mayfield, *Exiles from Paradise*, p. 138.

209. "First trip to jail": F. Scott Fitzgerald, Facsimile of Ledger Book, P.U.L.

209. "Scott had disappeared periodically": Gerald Murphy quoted in Honoria Murphy Donnelly, *Sara and Gerald: Villa America and After* (New York: Times Books, 1982), p. 149.

209. "He hated to be sober": F. Scott Fitzgerald, *The Beautiful and Damned*, p. 417.

209. "There was a grotesque intensity": Gerald and Sara Murphy, quoted in William Wiser, *The Crazy Years: Paris in the Twenties* (New York: Atheneum, 1983), p. 212.

209. "I was determined to find": Zelda Fitzgerald, summary of the important emotional events in her life, written for Dr. Oscar Forel (Prangins, 1931), quoted in Milford, *Zelda*, p. 175.

210. "I've seen that every time Zelda sees Egorova": F. Scott Fitzgerald, quoted in Mellow, *Invented Lives*, p. 359.

210. "I want you to have a lovely little Japanese room": Letter from Zelda Fitzgerald to Scottie Fitzgerald, quoted in Mellow, *Invented Lives*, p. 303.

211. "There was nothing in the commercial flat": Zelda Fitzgerald, quoted in Mellow, *Invented Lives*, p. 325, and in Milford, *Zelda*, p. 301.

211. "He [Scott] left me so much alone": Zelda Fitzgerald, quoted in Mellow, *Invented Lives*, p. 324, and in Milford, *Zelda*, pp. 300–301.

211. "had an air of being always startled": Zelda Fitzgerald, quoted in Milford, *Zelda*, p. 248.

211. "I'm a Federal Court Judge": John Biggs, quoted in Toll, *A Judge Uncommon*, p. 4.

211. "I do not know what Scott was doing": Zelda Fitzgerald, quoted in Milford, *Zelda*, p. 250.

212. "I am sorry I made, shall we say": Letter from Ernest Hemingway to F. Scott Fitzgerald, quoted in Mellow, *Invented Lives*, p. 326.

212. "There was the lone and lovely child": Zelda Fitzgerald quoted in Lanahan, *Scottie, the Daughter of . . .* , p. 34.

212. "Zelda never got along with anybody": John Biggs, quoted in Toll, *An Uncommon Judge*, p. 102.

213. "A bouillabaisse, to be served": Zelda Fitzgerald, recipe for bouillabaisse, Zelda Fitzgerald Papers, AM 20502, Folder 8, P.U.L.

213. "she [Egorova] seemed to me like a gardenia": Zelda Fitzgerald, quoted in Milford, *Zelda*, p. 250.

213. "She was very good and kind": Ibid.

214. *"Notre théâtre est magnifique":* Letter from Julie Sedova to Zelda Fitzgerald, September 29, 1929, Zelda Fitzgerald Papers, A.M. 20502, P.U.L.

215. "I have always felt that this frantic effort": Rosalind Smith, unpublished documentation on Zelda Fitzgerald, Mayfield Collection, University of Alabama.

215. "She had promise and should be given a bigger role": Zelda Fitzgerald, *Save Me the Waltz*, quoted in Scott Donaldson, *Fool for Love* (New York: Congdon & Weed, 1983), p. 80.

216. "Diaghilev died": Zelda Fitzgerald, *Save Me the Waltz*, quoted in Alice Hall Petry, "Women's Work: The Case of Zelda Fitzgerald," in *Literature-Interpretation-Theory* 1, no. 1–2 (December 1989), p. 82.

216. "We went [to] sophisticated places": Zelda Fitzgerald, quoted in Milford, *Zelda*, p. 156.

216. "peoples' arms too long": Letter from Zelda Fitzgerald to F. Scott Fitzgerald, Zelda Fitzgerald Papers, Box 42, Folder 51, P.U.L.

216. "I was there in the south of France": Tallulah Bankhead, quoted in Brendon Gill, *Tallulah* (New York: Holt, Rinehart and Winston, 1972), p. 122.

216. "There were all sorts and varieties of strange fish": Gerald Murphy, quoted in Milford, *Zelda*, p. 155.

216. "You don't even know what Zelda and Scottie are like": Sara Murphy, quoted in ibid., p. 155.

217. "Eleanor drew her horse up sharply": F. Scott Fitzgerald, *This Side of Paradise* (New York: Charles Scribner's Sons, 1970), p. 217.

217. "I worked constantly and was terribly superstitious": Zelda Fitzgerald, quoted in Milford, *Zelda*, p. 347.

218. "I found myself saying hateful things": F. Scott Fitzgerald, quoted in Tony Buttitta, *After the Good, Gay Times* (New York: Viking Press, 1974), p. 170.

218. "she no longer read or thought": F. Scott Fitzgerald, quoted in *Zelda: An Illustrated Life*, ed. Eleanor Lanahan (New York: Harry Abrams, 1996), p. 26.

218. "It was probably my fault": F. Scott Fitzgerald, quoted in Kaula Svokos Harnett, *Zelda Fitzgerald and the Failure of the American Dream for Women* (New York: Peter Lang Publishers, 1991), p. 172, initially quoted in Buttitta, *After the Good, Gay Times*, p. 123.

218. "We might all four": Letter from Gerald Murphy to F. Scott Fitzgerald, September 19, 1925, Fitzgerald Papers, Col. 187, Box 51, Folder 13, P.U.L.

219. "Altogether it was an unsuccessful attempt": Zelda Fitzgerald, quoted in Milford, *Zelda*, p. 251.

219. "It was a trying winter": Zelda Fitzgerald, quoted in Bruccoli, *Some Sort of Epic Grandeur*, p. 291.

219. "the Arabs fermenting in the vastness": Zelda Fitzgerald, quoted in Lane Yorke, "Zelda: A Worksheet," *The Paris Review* 25, no. 89 (Fall 1983), p. 22.

219. "impatience to get back": Ibid.

219. "I wanted to dance so well": Zelda Fitzgerald, quoted in Milford, *Zelda*, p. 168.

220. "first indications of lesbianism": F. Scott Fitzgerald, medical history about Zelda's condition, F. Scott Fitzgerald Papers, Craig House Files, Col. 745, P.U.L.

220. "In Paris again, I saw a great deal": Zelda Fitzgerald, quoted in Milford, *Zelda*, p. 252.

221. "At this time Zelda could drink": Ernest Hemingway, *A Movable Feast*, p. 179.

221. "In all that horror": Zelda Fitzgerald, quoted in Mellow, *Invented Lives*, p. 359.

221. "suddenly seemed to represent": Ibid.

221. "Since Eden man has been endowed": Letter from Zelda Fitzgerald to F. Scott Fitzgerald, Spring 1934, Zelda Fitzgerald Papers, Box 44, Folder 27, P.U.L.

222. "Women do nothing that they are disgusted by": Gertrude Stein, quoted in Mellow, *Invented Lives*, p. 265.

222. "I became aware that Scott kept his eye on her": Callaghan, *That Summer in Paris*, p. 152.

223. "For six months now she has been so exhausted Saturday night": F. Scott Fitzgerald, notes on Zelda's medical condition, F. Scott Fitzgerald Papers, P.U.L.

223. "In Paris, before I realized I was sick": Zelda Fitzgerald, Zelda Fitzgerald Papers, Col. 187, Box 42, Folder 52, P.U.L.

223. "When you saw in Paris that I was sick": Letter from Zelda Fitzgerald to F. Scott Fitzgerald, F. Scott Fitzgerald Papers, Col. 187, Box 42, Folder 53, P.U.L.

224. "We saw him and Zelda fairly often": Rosalind Smith, unpublished documentation about Zelda, Mayfield Collection, University of Alabama.

225. "it is a question of a *petite anxieuse*": Professor Claude, Malmaison, Report on Zelda Fitzgerald, in Craig House File, Col, 745, P.U.L., also quoted in Andre Le Vot, *F. Scott Fitzgerald: A Biography*, trans. William Byron (Garden City, N.Y.: Doubleday, 1983), p. 249.

225. "I went of my own free will": Letter from Zelda Fitzgerald to F. Scott Fitzgerald, May 1930, F. Scott Fitzgerald Papers, Col. 187, Box 42, Folder 57, P.U.L.

225. "I also went, practically voluntarily": Letter from Zelda Fitzgerald to F. Scott Fitzgerald, ibid.

226. "violent psychosis, wild homosexuality": F. Scott Fitzgerald, Summary of Zelda's psychological history written to Dr. Mildred Squires, April 4, 1932, in Craig House Records, Col. 745, P.U.L.

226. "Two sisters have nervous breakdowns": Malmaison Hospital and Valmont Clinic Patient Evaluation of Zelda's Condition, Craig House File, Zelda Fitzgerald Papers, Col. 745, P.U.L.

228. "Our ride to Switzerland": Letter from Zelda Fitzgerald to F. Scott Fitzgerald, quoted in Charter, *The Great Good Place*, p. 262.

229. "Now I see odd things": Letter from Zelda Fitzgerald to F. Scott Fitzgerald, F. Scott Fitzgerald Papers, AM 20502, Box 42, Folder 51, P.U.L.

229. "My first school was the Cours Dieterlen": Scottie Fitzgerald, quoted in Lanahan, *Scottie, the Daughter of . . .* , p. 39.

229. "I knew she was ill": Ibid., p. 48.

229. "daily visits of their two doctors": F. Scott Fitzgerald, "One Trip Abroad," in *The Short Stories of F. Scott Fitzgerald*, ed. Matthew J. Bruccoli (New York: Charles Scribner's Sons, 1989), p. 595.

229. "You say you place the beginning of the change": Letter from Rosalind Smith to F. Scott Fitzgerald, June 16, 1930, F. Scott Fitzgerald Papers, Box 53, Folder 14A, P.U.L.

230. "What I saw in her then": Letter from Rosalind Smith to F. Scott Fitzgerald, June 16, 1930, F. Scott Fitzgerald Papers, AM 20502, Box 53, Folder 14A, P.U.L.

230. "I would almost rather she die now": Letter from Rosalind Smith to F. Scott Fitzgerald, July 1930, F. Scott Fitzgerald Papers, Box 54, Folder 11, P.U.L.

230. "It was at this point": Scottie Fitzgerald, quoted in Lanahan, *Scottie, the Daughter of . . .* , p. 45.

231. "Scott sent me the transcript": Rosalind Smith, unpublished documentation on Zelda, Mayfield Collection, University of Alabama.

231. "I know your ineradicable impression": Letter from F. Scott Fitzgerald to Rosalind Smith, June 8, 1930, in Bruccoli, *Correspondence of F. Scott Fitzgerald*, p. 236.

231. "Do me a single favor": Draft of a letter from F. Scott Fitzgerald to Rosalind Smith, unsent, F. Scott Fitzgerald Papers, P.U.L.

231. "Please don't write to me about blame": Letter from Zelda Fitzgerald to F. Scott Fitzgerald, after June 1930, in Bruccoli, *Correspondence of F. Scott Fitzgerald*, p. 238.

231. "Scotty fell ill and I left at midnight": Letter from F. Scott Fitzgerald to Harold Ober, November 1930, quoted in *As Ever, Scott Fitzgerald*, ed. Matthew J. Bruccoli (New York: J.B. Lippincott Company, 1972), p. 172.

232. "I had begun dancing in Paris": Summary by Zelda of the important emotional moments in her life, written for Dr. Oscar Forel, quoted in Milford, *Zelda*, p. 175.

232. "I beg you to think twice": Letter from F. Scott Fitzgerald to Rosalind Smith, 1930, F. Scott Fitzgerald Papers, AM 20502, Box 53, Folder 14A, P.U.L.

232. "I'd like to discover the faintest basis": Letter from F. Scott Fitzgerald to Zelda Fitzgerald, quoted in Bruccoli, *Some Sort of Epic Grandeur*, pp. 481–482.

233. "I was terrified not exactly of, but for": Rebecca West, quoted in Turnbull, *Scott Fitzgerald*, pp. 343–344.

233. "The panic seems to have settled": Letter from Zelda Fitzgerald to F. Scott Fitzgerald, fall 1930, F. Scott Fitzgerald Papers, AM 20502, Box 42, Folder 64, P.U.L.

233. "The radio is a god-send": Letter from Zelda Fitzgerald to F. Scott Fitzgerald, F. Scott Fitzgerald Papers, Box 42, Folder 41, P.U.L.

233. "I gave word in Switzerland": Letter from F. Scott Fitzgerald to Dr. Jonathan Slocum, Craig House Files, Zelda Fitzgerald Papers, Col. 745, P.U.L.

233. "Dear Sweetheart—Walking along": Letter from Zelda Fitzgerald to F. Scott Fitzgerald, Zelda Fitzgerald Papers, AM 20502, Box 45, Folder 3, P.U.L.

234. "You have always had so much sympathy": Letter from Zelda Fitzgerald to F. Scott Fitzgerald, quoted in Harnett, *Zelda Fitzgerald and the Failure of the American Dream*, p. 192.

235. "Without hope or youth or money": Letter from Zelda Fitzgerald to F. Scott Fitzgerald, Zelda Fitzgerald Papers, AM 20502, Box 45, Folder 5, P.U.L.

236. "What I have, however, is not eczema but": Letter from Zelda Fitzgerald to F. Scott Fitzgerald, F. Scott Fitzgerald Papers, AM 20502, Box 42, Folder 66, P.U.L.

236. "after lunch she returned to the affectionate": F. Scott Fitzgerald, Notes on Zelda's condition at Prangins, F. Scott Fitzgerald Papers, P.U.L.

236. "in spite of tenderness": Ibid.

236. "They change the house of one girl": F. Scott Fitzgerald, Letter to Dr. Mildred Squires summarizing Zelda's symptoms between October 1 and February 1, 1930/31, F. Scott Fitzgerald Papers, P.U.L.

236. "The more I saw Zelda": Medical Commentary on Zelda's condition by Dr. Oscar Forel, Zelda Fitzgerald Papers, Craig House Files, Col. 745, P.U.L.

237. "The simple schizophrenics": Eugen Bleuler, *Dementia Praecox or The Group of Schizophrenias*, Monograph Series on Schizophrenia, No. 1, trans. Joseph Zinkin (New York: International Universities Press, 1950), p. 296.

237. "Let us openly say to ourselves": Eugen Bleuler, quoted in Elliot S. Valenstein, *Great and Desperate Cures: The Rise and Decline of Psychosurgery and Other Radical Treatments for Mental Illnesses* (New York: Basic Books, 1986), p. 246.

237. "*L'homosexualité est un symptome*": Oscar Forel, "Resume de La Consultation de M. Le Professeur Dr. Bleuler et de M. Le Forel," November 22, 1930, F. Scott Fitzgerald Papers, Craig House File, Col. 745, P.U.L.

239. "I can't help clinging to the idea": F. Scott Fitzgerald, quoted in Peter D. Kramer, "How Crazy Was Zelda?" *New York Times Magazine*, December 1, 1996, Sec. 6, p. 106.

239. "Dr. Forel told me to ask you": Letter from Zelda Fitzgerald to F. Scott Fitzgerald, fall 1930, F. Scott Fitzgerald Papers, AM 20502, Box 42, Folder 64, P.U.L.

240. "Can't you please explain to me": Letter from Zelda Fitzgerald to Dr. Oscar Forel, November 1930, Zelda Fitzgerald Papers, Box 5, File 3, P.U.L.

240. "Please, please let me out now": Letter from Zelda Fitzgerald to F. Scott Fitzgerald, Zelda Fitzgerald Papers, AM 20502, Box 42, Folder 65, P.U.L.

240. "I have not the slightest indication": Letter from Zelda Fitzgerald to F. Scott Fitzgerald, fall 1930, F. Scott Fitzgerald Papers, AM 20502, Box 42, Folder 63, P.U.L.

241. "Shall I write to daddy that he should": Ibid.

241. "Of course I realize that you have done all in your power": Letter from Zelda Fitzgerald to F. Scott Fitzgerald, Zelda Fitzgerald Papers, Col. 187, Box 42, Folder 56, P.U.L.

241. "If you want an idea of what it's like": Letter from Zelda Fitzgerald to F. Scott Fitzgerald, fall 1930, F. Scott Fitzgerald Papers, AM 20502, Box 42, Folder 63, P.U.L.

242. "You know I was much stronger": Letter from Zelda Fitzgerald to F. Scott Fitzgerald, quoted in Donaldson, *Fool for Love*, p. 56.

242. "but you said that she was too big": Ibid.

242. "He was leaning towards her": Ibid.

242. "You've got to make Dr. Forel arrange": Letter from Zelda Fitzgerald to F. Scott Fitzgerald, F. Scott Fitzgerald Papers, AM 20502, Box 42, Folder 65, P.U.L.

242. "What are you going to do?" : Letter from Zelda Fitzgerald to F. Scott Fitzgerald, Zelda Fitzgerald Papers, Col. 187, Box 43, Folder 54, P.U.L.

244. "I have been to a dance": Letter from Zelda Fitzgerald to F. Scott Fitzgerald, F. Scott Fitzgerald Papers, AM 20502, Box 42, Folder 41, P.U.L.

244. "Ages have passed since your last visit": Letter from Zelda Fitzgerald to F. Scott Fitzgerald, late spring 1931, Zelda Fitzgerald Papers, AM 20502, Box 43, Folder 9, P.U.L.

244. "I've made Scottie some wonderful paper dolls": Letter from Zelda Fitzgerald to F. Scott Fitzgerald, summer 1931, F. Scott Fitzgerald Papers, Box 43, Folder 12, P.U.L.

244. "Annecy is so blue that it tints the air": Postcard from Zelda Fitzgerald to her father, Judge Anthony Sayre, illustrated in *The Romantic Egoists*, ed. Matthew J. Bruccoli (New York: Charles Scribner's Sons, 1974), p. 180.

245. "First we lived at the Beau Rivage": Zelda Fitzgerald, "Show Mr. and Mrs. F. to Number ___," in Bruccoli, *Collected Writings*, p. 429.

245. "the good gone times": Ibid.

245. "Here is where Scott and I lunched yesterday": Postcard from Zelda Fitzgerald to her mother, "Mama" Sayre, illustrated in Lanahan, *Zelda: An Illustrated Life*, p. 27.

245. "the other day when I kissed her": Letter from Zelda Fitzgerald to F. Scott Fitzgerald, F. Scott Fitzgerald Papers, AM 20502, Box 44, Folder 47, P.U.L.

245. "Was the Madeleine pink": Letter from Zelda Fitzgerald to F. Scott Fitzgerald, quoted in Bruccoli, *Correspondence of F. Scott Fitzgerald*, p. 238; also in Harnett, *Zelda Fitzgerald and the Failure of the American Dream*, p. 153.

246. "I went to Geneva all by myself": Letter from Zelda Fitzgerald to F. Scott Fitzgerald, spring 1931, F. Scott Fitzgerald Papers, AM 20502, Box 43, Folder 8, P.U.L.

246. "Can't you possibly be just a little bit glad": Letter from Zelda Fitzgerald to F. Scott Fitzgerald, quoted in Donaldson, *Fool for Love*, p. 190.

247. "I am dependent on my husband": Zelda Fitzgerald, quoted in Milford, *Zelda*, p. 175.

Chapter 6: I Believed I Was a Salamander

248. "It was a year when": Malcolm Cowley, "Epilogue: New Year's Eve," *Exile's Return* (New York: Viking Press, 1956), p. 290.

250. "While all was serene on top": Letter from F. Scott Fitzgerald to Scottie Fitzgerald, July 1937, in *Letters of F. Scott Fitzgerald*, ed. Andrew Turnbull (New York: Charles Scribner's Sons, 1963), p. 17.

250. "The little mossy place on the back of your neck": Letter from Zelda Fitzgerald to F. Scott Fitzgerald, November 1931, Zelda Fitzgerald Papers, Box 4, Folder 23, P.U.L.

250. "I have stopped my dancing lessons": Letter from Zelda Fitzgerald to F. Scott Fitzgerald, Zelda Fitzgerald Papers, Box 43, Folder 49, P.U.L.

251. "I lost Scottie in a store": Letter from Zelda Fitzgerald to F. Scott Fitzgerald, Zelda Fitzgerald Papers, Box 43, Folder 23, P.U.L.

251. "When you are not here": Letter from Zelda Fitzgerald to F. Scott Fitzgerald, November 1931, Zelda Fitzgerald Papers, Box 43, Folder 38, P.U.L.

251. "Newman and I were in Europe": Rosalind Smith, unpublished documentation on Zelda Fitzgerald, W. S. Hoole Special Collections Library, University of Alabama, Tuscaloosa.

252. "I feel like a person lost in some Gregorian": Letter from Zelda Fitzgerald to F. Scott Fitzgerald, December 1931, Zelda Fitzgerald Papers, Box 43, Folder 39, P.U.L., also quoted in *The Correspondence of F. Scott Fitzgerald*, ed. Matthew J. Bruccoli and Margaret Duggan (New York: Random House, 1980), p. 274.

252. "If you mention one more time": Letter from Zelda Fitzgerald to F. Scott Fitzgerald, quoted in Nancy Milford, *Zelda, a Biography* (New York: Harper & Row, 1970), p. 198.

252. "I found myself almost desperate": Letter from Zelda Fitzgerald to F. Scott Fitzgerald, December 1931, Zelda Fitzgerald Papers, Box 43, Folder 37, P.U.L.

253. "It's fun thinking of Christmas": Letter from Zelda Fitzgerald to F. Scott Fitzgerald, December 1931, Zelda Fitzgerald Papers, Box 43, Folder 46, P.U.L.

253. "The . . . material which I will elect [to write about]": Letter from Zelda Fitzgerald to F. Scott Fitzgerald, April 1932, quoted in Bruccoli and Duggan, *Correspondence of F. Scott Fitzgerald*, p. 291.

254. "stretched lazily over the snubbed wilderness": Zelda Fitzgerald, "Show Mr. and Mrs. F. to Number ___," *The Collected Writings of Zelda Fitzgerald*, ed. Matthew J. Bruccoli (New York: Charles Scribner's Sons, 1991), p. 431.

255. "I am glad you and Scottie are getting some time": Letter from Zelda Fitzgerald to F. Scott Fitzgerald, spring 1932, Zelda Fitzgerald Papers, Box 44, Folder 3, P.U.L.

255. "I do not seem to be strong enough": Letter from Zelda Fitzgerald to F. Scott Fitzgerald, spring 1932, Zelda Fitzgerald Papers, Box 44, Folder 7, P.U.L.

256. "Liquor on my mouth is sweet to her": F. Scott Fitzgerald, quoted in Matthew J. Bruccoli, *Some Sort of Epic Grandeur* (New York: Harcourt Brace Jovanovich, 1981), p. 266.

257. "At no time have I been able to get any": Letter from Dr. Mildred Squires to F. Scott Fitzgerald, February 17, 1932, Zelda Fitzgerald Papers, Col. 187, Box 51, Folder 50, P.U.L.

257. "Our sexual relations have been good": Letter from F. Scott Fitzgerald to Dr. Mildred Squires, F. Scott Fitzgerald Papers, P.U.L.

257. "In the last analysis she is a stronger person": Letter from F. Scott Fitzgerald to Dr. Thomas Rennie, quoted in Thomas J. Stavrola, *Scott Fitzgerald: Crisis in an American Identity* (New York: Barnes & Noble, 1981), p. 65, and Milford, *Zelda*, p. 261.

258. "Thanks for the chess": Letter from Zelda Fitzgerald to F. Scott Fitzgerald, February 1932, Zelda Fitzgerald Papers, AM 20502, Box 44, Folder 2, P.U.L.

258. "I have got so fetid and constantly smell": Letter from Zelda Fitzgerald to F. Scott Fitzgerald, March 1932, quoted in Bruccoli and Duggan, *Correspondence of F. Scott Fitzgerald*, p. 285.

258. "I do not see how Dr. Squires": Letter from Zelda Fitzgerald to F. Scott Fitzgerald, March 1932, quoted in Bruccoli, *Collected Writings*, p. 466.

258. "This card was designed and printed": Dr. Frederick Wertham, handwritten note on the back of Dr. Mildred Squires's Christmas Card (made by Zelda), Wertham Collection, Harvard University.

259. "Please do not judge": Telegram from F. Scott Fitzgerald to Maxwell Perkins quoted in Bruccoli, *Some Sort of Epic Grandeur*, p. 325.

259. "I did not want a scathing criticism": Letter from Zelda Fitzgerald to F. Scott Fitzgerald, quoted in Milford, *Zelda*, p. 220.

259. "It would be throwing her broken": F. Scott Fitzgerald to Dr. Mildred Squires, quoted in Milford, *Zelda*, p. 222.

260. "The figures in her story whom I knew": Rosalind Smith, unpublished documentation on Zelda Fitzgerald, Mayfield Collection, University of Alabama.

260. "I am so outrageously clever": Zelda Fitzgerald, *Save Me the Waltz* (New York: Charles Scribner's Sons, 1932), p. 109.

261. " 'Those girls,' people said": Ibid., p. 1.

261. "wants to be told what she is like": Ibid., p. 4.

261. "I'm not glad Harlan's hair goes up": Ibid., p. 31.

261. "People can't live off the hair of Spanish Kings": Ibid.

261. "She's the wildest one of the Beggs' ": Ibid., p. 37.

261. "just sitting on the porch": Ibid., p. 39.

261. "Why am I this way": Ibid., p. 91.

262. "People who do not subscribe": Ibid., p. 73.

262. "The girl still looked all day long as if she'd": Ibid., p. 76.

262. "Oh, we are going to be so happy": Ibid., p. 105.

262. "I wish I could live in your pocket": Ibid., p. 155.

262. "Poor girl. I understand": Ibid., p. 157.

263. "It is better here than with Mummy's success": Ibid, p. 254.

263. "but it has brought us together again": Ibid., p. 262.

263. "Always, she thought, we will have to seek": Ibid., p. 284.

263. "We would be happier if Alabama": Ibid., p. 285.

263. "It's very expressive of myself": Ibid., p. 285.

264. "It is a pity that the publisher": *New York Times*, October 16, 1932, news clipping in Zelda Fitzgerald Scrapbook, P.U.L.

264. "Turning up in a novel signed by my wife": F. Scott Fitzgerald quoted in Turnbull, *Scott Fitzgerald*, p. 207.

264. "a gallery of unforgettable pictures": Gilbert Seldes, Review of Zelda's novel, Zelda Fitzgerald Scrapbook, P.U.L., also quoted in Koula Svokos Harnett, *Zelda Fitzgerald and the Failure of the American Dream for Women* (New York: Peter Lang Publishers, 1991), p. 137.

264. "a book constructive in thought": *Philadelphia Public Ledger*, October 15, 1932, news clipping in Zelda Fitzgerald Scrapbook, P.U.L.

264. "*Save Me the Waltz* is written in lively fashion": Frank Daniels, news clipping in Zelda Fitzgerald Scrapbook, P.U.L.

265. "You should go on writing": Letter from Maxwell Perkins to Zelda Fitzgerald, quoted in Harnett, *Zelda Fitzgerald and the Failure of the American Dream*, p. 138.

265. "We had a mad-man's ball": Letter from Zelda Fitzgerald to F. Scott Fitzgerald, spring 1932, Zelda Fitzgerald Papers, Box 44, Folder 9, P.U.L.

266. "We have black-gums": Letter from Zelda Fitzgerald to John Peale Bishop, quoted in Milford, *Zelda*, p. 258.

266. "We went to see her often. It was a strain, and so sad": Scottie Fitzgerald, quoted in Eleanor Lanahan, *Scottie, the Daughter of . . .* (New York: HarperCollins, 1995), p. 58.

266. "We are living near Baltimore": Letter from Scottie Fitzgerald to Fanny Myers, quoted in ibid., p. 59.

267. "There was always something of the magician": Andrew Turnbull, "Scott Fitzgerald at La Paix," *Publications in the Humanities*, M.I.T., Cambridge, Massachusetts, 1956, p. 7.

267. "at the deep, cool quarry": Turnbull, *Scott Fitzgerald*, pp. 230–231.

268. "Do go into my room": Letter from Zelda Fitzgerald to F. Scott Fitzgerald, February–March 1932, Zelda Fitzgerald Papers, Box 44, Folder 3, P.U.L.

268. "Six hours study, six hours work": Spiral Notebook belonging to Zelda Fitzgerald, Zelda Fitzgerald Papers, P.U.L.

268. "never believed I worked very hard": Letter from F. Scott Fitzgerald to Dr. Harry M. Murdoch, August 28, 1934, quoted in Bruccoli and Duggan, *Correspondence of F. Scott Fitzgerald*, p. 381.

269. "I consider myself driven": Document from Zelda Fitzgerald addressed to Dr. A. C. Rennie, October 10, 1932, F. Scott Fitzgerald Additional Papers, Col. 188, AM 10–10–32, Box 25, P.U.L.

269. "It is significant that last February": Letter from F. Scott Fitzgerald to Dr. A. C. Rennie, F. Scott Fitzgerald Papers, Col. 188, Box 25, File 1, P.U.L.

270. "he considered Scott as much in need": Rosalind Smith, unpublished documentation on Zelda Fitzgerald, Mayfield Collection, University of Alabama.

270. "the tranquillity of spirit necessary": Zelda Fitzgerald quoted in Andrew Le Vot, *Scott Fitzgerald*, trans. William Byron (Garden City, N.Y.: Doubleday, 1983), p. 266.

271. "The fundamental struggle continues": Letter from F. Scott Fitzgerald to Dr. A. C. Rennie, in F. Scott Fitzgerald, Additional Papers, Col. 188, Box 25, File 1, P.U.L.

271. "On the afternoon of my arrival": Malcolm Cowley, *The Dream of the Golden Mountains: Remembering the 1930's* (New York: Viking Press, 1964), p. 188.

272. "Zelda, looking vastly younger": Ibid., p. 191.

272. "Is Zelda more worth 'saving' than I am": Letter from F. Scott Fitzgerald to Dr. Adolf Meyer, April 10, 1933, F. Scott Fitzgerald Papers, Col. 187, Box 51, Folder 10A, P.U.L.

273. "Your complaint of the futility": Letter from Dr. Adolf Meyer to F. Scott Fitzgerald, April 18, 1933, Craig House Files, Col. 745, P.U.L.

274. "I wish I had a whole lot of money": Zelda Fitzgerald quoted in transcript of Dr. A. C. Rennie, F. Scott Fitzgerald Papers, p. 105, P.U.L.

274. "The evenings are so terrible": Taped conversation of the Fitzgeralds, La Paix,

Sunday, May 28, 1933, 2:30 P.M., Rennie Transcript, F. Scott Fitzgerald Papers, p. 82, P.U.L.

274. "He made it impossible for me to communicate": Ibid., p. 11.

275. "Zelda—had almost a hundred doctors": Ibid., pp. 11–12.

275. "I can think of—well, say fifty": Ibid., p. 12.

275. "a series of short observations": Rennie Transcript, quoted in Milford, *Zelda*, p. 273.

275. "It is the great humiliation of my life": Rennie Transcript, p. 104.

275. "Why do you think you met Léger?": Ibid., p. 27.

276. "because the girl seemed to be": Ibid., p. 86.

276. "As far as destroying you is concerned": Ibid., p. 6.

276. "Attack on all grounds": F. Scott Fitzgerald, quoted in Scott Donaldson, *Fool for Love* (New York: Congdon & Weed, 1983), p. 86.

276. "I want to write and I am going to write": Zelda Fitzgerald, quoted in Rennie Transcript, p. 88.

277. "So far as my own mood is concerned": Letter from F. Scott Fitzgerald to Dr. A. C. Rennie, F. Scott Fitzgerald Papers, Col. 188, Box 25, File 1, P.U.L.

277. "The situation has reduced itself": Letter from F. Scott Fitzgerald to Dr. A. C. Rennie, F. Scott Fitzgerald Papers, Col. 188, Box 25, File 1, P.U.L.

278. "the next day, he came up": Andrew Turnbull, "Further Notes on Fitzgerald at La Paix," *Publications in the Humanities*, No. 22, M.I.T., Cambridge, Massachusetts, 1956, p. 15.

279. "Anthony's trouble has been diagnosed": Letter from F. Scott Fitzgerald to Dr. Chilton Thorington, August 11, 1933, Craig House Files, 0745, Folder 1, P.U.L.

280. "I have just fully realized": Letter from F. Scott Fitzgerald to Dr. Rex Blankenship, May 4, 1934, Craig House Files, 0745, Folder 1, P.U.L.

280. "At no time did I feel that I had known him": F. Scott Fitzgerald, *The New Republic*, October 11, 1933, pp. 254–255.

280. "a man who never listened to anyone": Isabel Owens, quoted in Harnett, *Zelda Fitzgerald and the Failure of the American Dream*, p. 161.

280. "was just beaten down": Ibid.

281. "He must have realized that this phase": Turnbull, "Further Notes on Fitzgerald at La Paix," p. 15.

282. "Scott stayed with us at our Manhattan flat": Helen Hayes with Sanford Dody, *On Reflection: An Autobiography* (New York: M. Evans and Co., 1968), p. 198.

283. "Scott with his head down on the table": Edmund Wilson, *The Bit Between My Teeth: A Literary Chronicle of 1950–1965* (New York: Farrar, Straus and Giroux, 1965), p. 522.

283. "I assume full responsibility": Letter from F. Scott Fitzgerald to Edmund Wilson, quoted in *F. Scott Fitzgerald: A Life in Letters*, ed. Matthew J. Bruccoli (New York: Simon & Schuster, 1995), p. 227.

283. "How could he know people except on the surface": Letter from Ernest Hemingway to Malcolm Cowley, quoted in Morrill Cody, *Women of Montparnasse* (New York: Cornwall Books, 1984), p. 161.

283. "We are cooking ourselves and feeling very happy": Postcard from Zelda Fitzgerald to her mother, "Mama Sayre," posted from St. Catherine's Bathing Beach, St. Georges, Bermuda, Zelda Fitzgerald Scrapbook, P.U.L.

283. "For years we had wanted to go to Bermuda": Zelda and F. Scott Fitzgerald, "Show Mr. and Mrs. F. to Number—," in Bruccoli, *Collected Writings*, p. 431.

284. "The first installment of the novel confirms": Letter from John Peale Bishop to F. Scott Fitzgerald, quoted in Andrew Mellow, *Invented Lives* (New York: Houghton Mifflin, 1984), p. 415.

284. "an achievement which no student": Review of *Tender Is the Night*, in *Journal of Nervous and Mental Diseases*, quoted in Bruccoli, *Some Sort of Epic Grandeur*, p. 370.

284. "What made me so mad": Letter from Zelda Fitzgerald to Dr. A. C. Rennie, quoted in Mellow, *Invented Lives*, p. 425.

285. Would you be kind enough": Letter from Zelda Fitzgerald to Dr. Adolf Meyer, Zelda Fitzgerald Papers, Box 5, File 7, P.U.L.

285. "When the first signs of a relapse": Letter from F. Scott Fitzgerald to Dr. C. Jonathan Slocum, Craig House Files, 0745, April 1934, P.U.L.

286. "It's so pretty here": Letter from Zelda Fitzgerald to F. Scott Fitzgerald, Zelda Fitzgerald Papers, Box 44, Folder 30, P.U.L.

286. "It has been our observation that she tires": Letter from Dr. Clarence J. Slocum to F. Scott Fitzgerald, March 19, 1934, Craig House Files, 0745, P.U.L.

287. "I would not like to make even a tentative diagnosis": Letter from Dr. Clarence Slocum to F. Scott Fitzgerald, April 11, 1934, Craig House Files, 0745, P.U.L.

287. "She [Zelda] wished to give up the massage": Letter from Dr. Clarence Slocum to F. Scott Fitzgerald, April 11, 1934, Craig House Files, 0745, P.U.L.

287. "I am knitting myself": Letter from Zelda Fitzgerald to F. Scott Fitzgerald, Zelda Fitzgerald Papers, Box 42, Folder 41, P.U.L.

287. "Roaming nostalgically": Letter from Zelda Fitzgerald to F. Scott Fitzgerald, Zelda Fitzgerald Papers, Box 44, Folder 35, P.U.L.

288. "That's how a ballet dancer feels": Zelda Fitzgerald, quoted in Milford, *Zelda*, p. 381; and in Henry Dan Piper, *F. Scott Fitzgerald: A Critical Portrait* (New York, Holt, Rinehart & Winston, 1965), p. 201.

288. "Zelda was having a show of her paintings": James Thurber, "Scott in Thorns," *Credos and Curios* (New York: Harper & Row, 1962), pp. 157–159.

288. "I have about ten catalogs": Ibid., pp. 160–161.

289. "They are so lonely and magnificent": Letter from Zelda Fitzgerald to Dr. A. C. Rennie, Zelda Fitzgerald Papers, P.U.L.

289. "I went to see the O'Keeffes": Letter from Zelda Fitzgerald to *New York Post*, April 3, 1934, Zelda Fitzgerald Papers, P.U.L.

290. "Yes, it was good. The eyelashes": John Biggs, quoted in Milford, *Zelda*, p. 291.

290. "I couldn't have stood having them hang in the house": Dorothy Parker, quoted in Milford, *Zelda*, pp. 290–291.

290. "The work of a brilliant introvert": *Time* magazine exhibition review quoted in Jeffrey Meyer, *Scott Fitzgerald* (New York: HarperCollins, 1994), p. 234.

291. "The exhibition, as she may have told you": Letter from F. Scott Fitzgerald to Dr. Clarence Slocum, April 2, 1934, Craig House Files, 0745, P.U.L.

291. "Your pictures have been a success": Letter from F. Scott Fitzgerald to Zelda Fitzgerald, April 26, 1934, quoted in *F. Scott Fitzgerald: A Life in Letters*, ed. Matthew J. Bruccoli (New York: Simon & Schuster, 1995), p. 257, also quoted in Milford, *Zelda*, p. 295.

292. "Aristotle: he said that all emotions": Letter from Zelda Fitzgerald to F. Scott

Fitzgerald, quoted in Eleanor Lanahan, *Zelda: An Illustrated Life* (New York: Harry N. Abrams, 1996), p. 29.

292. "She will never be able to build a house": F. Scott Fitzgerald, quoted in Bruccoli, *Some Sort of Epic Grandeur*, p. 322.

293. "I cannot see why I should sit in luxury": Letter from Zelda Fitzgerald to F. Scott Fitzgerald, Zelda Fitzgerald Papers, Box 44, Folder 4, P.U.L.

293. "You must realize that to one as ill as I am": Letter from Zelda Fitzgerald to F. Scott Fitzgerald, Zelda Fitzgerald Papers, Box 44, Folder 46, P.U.L.

293. "I do not feel as you do": Letter from Zelda Fitzgerald to F. Scott Fitzgerald, Craig House Files, 0745, Box 44, Folder 42, P.U.L.

294. "During the period of her residence": Letter from Dr. Clarence Slocum to Mrs. Anthony Sayre, May 7, 1934, Craig House Files, P.U.L.

294. "I hope Mrs. Fitzgerald reached Baltimore": Letter from Dr. Clarence Slocum to F. Scott Fitzgerald, May 19, 1934, Craig House Files, 0745, P.U.L.

295. "I think that the transfer was made": Letter from Dr. Clarence Slocum to Mrs. Anthony Sayre, June 4, 1934, Craig House Files, Folder 1, P.U.L.

298. "It's my only strength": Zelda Fitzgerald quoted in Sara Mayfield, *Exiles from Paradise: Zelda and Scott Fitzgerald* (New York: Delacorte Press, 1971), p. 275.

298. "I have done nothing but turn over": Letter from Zelda Fitzgerald to F. Scott Fitzgerald, Zelda Fitzgerald Papers, P.U.L.

299. "The sadness of the past": Letter from F. Scott Fitzgerald to Zelda Fitzgerald, April 26, 1934, quoted in Bruccoli and Duggan, *Correspondence of F. Scott Fitzgerald*, p. 356.

299. "He gave back to me both times a woman": Letter from F. Scott Fitzgerald to Dr. Harry Murdoch, August 28, 1934, F. Scott Fitzgerald Papers, Box 51, P.U.L.

300. "I had Scott and Zelda in my car": John O'Hara quoted in Mellow, *Invented Lives*, p. 429.

300. "The wife acted as if her husband were backing out": Charles Warren, quoted in Arnold Latham, *Crazy Sundays: F. Scott Fitzgerald in Hollywood* (New York: Viking Press, 1971), p. 183.

301. "It meant so much to Zelda": Letter from F. Scott Fitzgerald to Gertrude Stein, December 29, 1934, quoted in Harnett, *Zelda Fitzgerald and the Failure of the American Dream*, p. 143.

302. "I did like being with you all in Baltimore": Letter from Gertrude Stein to Scottie Fitzgerald, undated, Zelda Fitzgerald Papers, AM 20502, Box 6, File 31, P.U.L.

303. "Living alone leaves so many loopholes": Letter from F. Scott Fitzgerald to Margaret Turnbull in Turnbull, *Letters of F. Scott Fitzgerald*, p. 439.

303. "There is no way to ask you to forgive me": Letter from Zelda Fitzgerald to F. Scott Fitzgerald, spring 1935, F. Scott Fitzgerald Papers, Box 45, Folder 5, P.U.L.

303. "It is Dr. Meyer's feeling": Letter from Dr. A. C. Rennie to F. Scott Fitzgerald, May 27, 1935, F. Scott Fitzgerald Papers, Box 53, Folder 14A, P.U.L.

303. "patients were capable of accepting guidance": Dr. A. C. Rennie, *Archives of Neurology and Psychiatry* 46 (August 1941): 197–229.

304. "Mrs. Fitzgerald has been moved to a closed ward": Letter from Isabel Owens to F. Scott Fitzgerald, F. Scott Fitzgerald Papers, Col. 187, Box 51, Folder 33, P.U.L.

304. "I don't need anything": Letter from Zelda Fitzgerald to F. Scott Fitzgerald, 1936, Zelda Fitzgerald Papers, Box 45, Folder 14, P.U.L.

304. "Scott had interfered so persistently with their care of Zelda": Interview with Rosalind Smith by the author, August 12, 1963.

304. "Her present condition was a great shock to me": Letter from Rosalind Smith to F. Scott Fitzgerald, June 4, 1935, F. Scott Fitzgerald Papers, Box 53, Folder 14A, P.U.L.

304. "My dear Scott, Poor Sara": Letter from H. L. Mencken to F. Scott Fitzgerald, May 30, 1935, F. Scott Fitzgerald Papers, Col. 187, Box 51, Folder 9, P.U.L.

305. "He was nervous and I thought": Lottie Stephens quoted in Tony Buttitta, *After the Good, Gay Times* (New York: Viking Press, 1974), p. 135.

305. "I have just emerged not totally unscathed": Letter from F. Scott Fitzgerald to James Boyd, August 1935, in Turnbull, *Letters of F. Scott Fitzgerald*, p. 528.

305. "The fortune teller did a good job on Scott": Letter from Rosalind Smith to the author, December 3, 1964. Collection of the author.

306. "I don't think the world is a very nice place": Letter from Sara Murphy to F. Scott Fitzgerald, August 20, 1935, in Bruccoli and Duggan, *Correspondence of F. Scott Fitzgerald*, p. 423.

306. "It occurs to me that you alone knew": Letter from Gerald Murphy to F. Scott Fitzgerald, August 11, 1935, F. Scott Fitzgerald Papers, Col. 187, Box 51, Folder 13, P.U.L.

307. "I suppose that we are two blatherskites": Letter from Gerald Murphy to F. Scott Fitzgerald, December 31, 1935, F. Scott Fitzgerald Collection, Col. 187, Box 51, Folder 13, P.U.L.

307. "I get a pretty highly developed delirium tremens": Letter from F. Scott Fitzgerald to Mabel Dodge Luhan, May 10, 1934, in Bruccoli, *F. Scott Fitzgerald: A Life in Letters*, p. 258.

308. "You have been cheated": Letter from Sara Murphy to F. Scott Fitzgerald, undated, F. Scott Fitzgerald Papers, Col. 187, Box 51, Folder 15, P.U.L.

308. "Scott first took Zelda to Highland": Rosalind Smith, unpublished documentation on Zelda Fitzgerald, Mayfield Collection, University of Alabama.

309. "One of the saddest memories": Rosalind Smith, unpublished documentation on Zelda Fitzgerald, Mayfield Collection, University of Alabama.

309. "I realize that I am at the end of my resources": Letter from F. Scott Fitzgerald to Harold Ober, May 1936, in Bruccoli, *F. Scott Fitzgerald: A Life in Letters*, p. 330.

Chapter 7: The End of the Story

312. "faithful weekly letters continued to be couched": Rosalind Smith, undocumented material on Zelda Fitzgerald, W. S. Hoole Special Collections Library, University of Alabama, Tuscaloosa.

312. "an enthusiastic person with an active mind": Graphological Analysis prepared by Dr. Robert Carroll for Mrs. Anthony Sayre, Zelda Fitzgerald Papers, P.U.L.

312. "While having a scientific mind": Ibid.

312. "At Asheville, where much of the institutional": Rosalind Smith, unpublished documentation on Zelda Fitzgerald, Mayfield Papers, University of Alabama.

313. "trying to show off for Zelda": Letter from F. Scott Fitzgerald to Xandra Kalman, September 1936, quoted in Arthur Mizener, *The Far Side of Paradise* (New York: Houghton Mifflin, 1949), p. 264.

313. "It was too bad on your birthday": Letter from F. Scott Fitzgerald to Zelda

Fitzgerald, July 27, 1936, in *The Correspondence of F. Scott Fitzgerald*, ed. Matthew J. Bruccoli and Margaret Duggan (New York: Random House, 1980), p. 440.

313. "As for life (as they call it)": Letter from Gerald Murphy to F. Scott Fitzgerald, October 1936, F. Scott Fitzgerald Papers, Col. 187, Box 51, Folder 28, P.U.L.

314. "In memory of another amusing": F. Scott Fitzgerald inscription, related to the author by Laura Kahler, daughter of Gerald and Pauline Brownell, interview with the author, August 12, 1994.

314. "To George Brownell—From His Friend F. Scott Fitzgerald": Ibid.

314. "My lilies died; they just plain died": Zelda Fitzgerald, Two-Ring Binder, Zelda Fitzgerald Papers, AM 20502, Box 4, P.U.L.

316. "I wish you had a little house with hollyhocks": Letter from Zelda Fitzgerald to F. Scott Fitzgerald, June 1935, quoted in Scott Donaldson, *Fool for Love* (New York: Congdon & Weed, 1983), p. 96.

316. "Friendship, conviviality, the right of choice": Letter from Zelda Fitzgerald to F. Scott Fitzgerald, Christmas, 1939, Zelda Fitzgerald Papers, Box 48, Folder 1, P.U.L.

316. "I assured him that either": Helen Northup, quoted in "F in Wolfe's Clothing," Note reprinted from the University of Wisconsin Library News, in the *Fitzgerald Newsletter*, Microcard Editions, Washington, D.C., No. 19, Fall 1962, pp. 102–103.

317. "The choosing of what was then one of the five or six": Scottie Fitzgerald, quoted in Eleanor Lanahan, *Scottie, the Daughter of . . .* (New York: HarperCollins, 1995), p. 76.

318. "There would be episodes": Letter from F. Scott Fitzgerald to Dr. Robert Carroll, *A Life in Letters: F. Scott Fitzgerald*, ed. Matthew J. Bruccoli (New York: Simon & Schuster, 1995), p. 354.

319. "I was busy surviving": Scottie Fitzgerald, Introduction to *Letters to His Daughter*, ed. Andrew Turnbull (New York: Charles Scribner's Sons, 1963), p. xii.

319. "after the ghastly tea dance": Ibid.

319. "Scottie writes me vague notes": Letter from Zelda Fitzgerald to F. Scott Fitzgerald, Zelda Fitzgerald Papers, Box 42, Folder 42, P.U.L.

320. "Self-preservation being the strongest": Scottie Fitzgerald, Introduction to Turnbull, *Letters to His Daughter;* p. xii.

320. "The telegram came today": Letter from F. Scott Fitzgerald to Sara and Gerald Murphy, January 1937, F. Scott Fitzgerald Papers, P.U.L.

320. "We will have to make a mass pilgrimage": Letter from F. Scott Fitzgerald to Anne Ober, March 4, 1938, Bruccoli, *A Life in Letters*, p. 352.

321. "I didn't want my mother at graduation": Scottie Fitzgerald, quoted in Lanahan, *Scottie, the Daughter of . . .* , p. 89.

321. "A friend . . . asked me to bum a ride": Ibid., p. 90.

321. "It seems that the dreaded Latin teacher": Ibid.

321. "It is going to be great fun": Letter from Anne Ober to F. Scott Fitzgerald, F. Scott Fitzgerald Papers, Col. 187, Box 51, Folder 27, P.U.L.

322. "What I need is a substantial sum 1st to pay a percentage on the bills": Letter from F. Scott Fitzgerald to Harold Ober, May 13, 1937, in Bruccoli, *A Life in Letters*, p. 322.

322. "I was to have lunch with Edmund Wilson": Carl Van Vechten, quoted in Andrew Le Vot, *F. Scott Fitzgerald*, trans. William Byron (Garden City, N.Y.: Doubleday, 1983), p. 318.

323. "I must be very tactful": Letter from F. Scott Fitzgerald to Scottie Fitzgerald, July 1937, in Turnbull, *Letters to His Daughter*, pp. 25–26.

324. "Scott has so lousy much talent": Ernest Hemingway, quoted in Andrew Mellow, *Hemingway: A Life Without Consequences* (New York: Houghton Miffin, 1992), p. 435.

324. "I talk with the authority of failure": F. Scott Fitzgerald, Notebooks, #1915, also quoted in Matthew J. Bruccoli, *Some Sort of Epic Grandeur* (New York: Harcourt Brace Jovanovich, 1981), p. 425.

324. "Smiling faintly at him": F. Scott Fitzgerald, *The Last Tycoon* (New York: Charles Scribner's Sons, 1941) p. 26; also quoted in Bruccoli, *Some Sort of Epic Grandeur*, p. 429.

324. "I've become hard here": Letter from F. Scott Fitzgerald to Sara Murphy, F. Scott Fitzgerald Papers, Box 51, Folder 12, P.U.L.

325. "Life ended for me when Zelda and I crashed": F. Scott Fitzgerald, quoted in Andrew Turnbull, *Scott Fitzgerald* (New York: Charles Scribner's Sons, 1962), p. 261.

325. "I now realize that during the time I knew Scott": Sheilah Graham, *The Real F. Scott Fitzgerald* (New York: Grosset & Dunlap, 1976), p. 50.

325. "The first Hollywood visit was fabulous": Scottie Fitzgerald, quoted in Lanahan, *Scottie, the Daughter of . . .* , pp. 83–84.

325. "So far Scottie is having the time of her young life": Letter from F. Scott Fitzgerald to Maxwell Perkins, quoted in Aaron Latham, *Crazy Sundays: F. Scott Fitzgerald in Hollywood* (New York: Viking Press, 1971), p. 127.

326. "rather unsure of himself": Letter from Edmund Wilson to Christian Gauss, quoted in Andrew Mellow, *Invented Lives* (New York: Houghton Mifflin, 1984), p. 478.

326. "Your mother was better": Letter from F. Scott Fitzgerald to Scottie Fitzgerald, quoted in Bruccoli, *Some Sort of Epic Grandeur*, p. 329.

326. "The pattern was always repeated": Scottie Fitzgerald, quoted in Lanahan, *Scottie, the Daughter of . . .* , p. 86.

326. "I think your chief trouble is a lack of sympathy": Letter from Rosalind Smith to Scottie Fitzgerald, quoted in Lanahan, *Scottie, the Daughter of . . .* , p. 154.

327. "Each time that I see her": Letter from F. Scott Fitzgerald to Dr. Robert Carroll, quoted in Jeffrey Meyer, *Scott Fitzgerald: A Biography* (New York: HarperCollins, 1994), p. 300.

327. "The outworn pretense": Letter from F. Scott Fitzgerald to Dr. Robert Carroll, quoted in Turnbull, *Scott Fitzgerald*, p. 291.

327. "She was the first girl I ever loved": Letter from F. Scott Fitzgerald to Scottie Fitzgerald, quoted in Mellow, *Invented Lives*, p. 462.

328. "People are either good for each other or not": Letter from F. Scott Fitzgerald to Sheilah Graham, quoted in Sheilah Graham, *Beloved Infidel* (New York: Henry Holt and Co., 1958), pp. 300–301.

328. "I don't know how this job is going": Letter from F. Scott Fitzgerald to Zelda Fitzgerald, quoted in *Letters of F. Scott Fitzgerald*, ed. Andrew Turnbull (New York: Charles Scribner's Sons, 1963), p. 144.

328. "I really don't want you out here for the whole summer": Letter from F. Scott Fitzgerald to Scottie Fitzgerald, August 18, 1938, in Turnbull, *Letters to His Daughter*, p. 42.

328. "the first of several distressing reunions with my father": Scottie Fitzgerald, quoted in Lanahan, *Scottie, the Daughter of . . .* , p. 92.

329. "He had a wife who couldn't live with him": Ibid., p. 95.

329. "I confess I didn't like the heroine": Letter from Zelda Fitzgerald to Margaret Turnbull, quoted in Mizener, *The Far Side of Paradise*, p. 301.

329. "This girl had a life": F. Scott Fitzgerald, end note in *The Last Tycoon: An Unfinished Novel* (New York: Charles Scribner's Sons, 1941), p. 152.

330. "What you have done to please me": Letter from F. Scott Fitzgerald to Scottie Fitzgerald, July 7, 1938, quoted in Turnbull, *Letters of F. Scott Fitzgerald*, p. 34.

330. "He didn't want me to have the fun": Scottie Fitzgerald, quoted in Meyer, *Scott Fitzgerald*, p. 299.

330. "Dr. Carroll is taking a car load of people": Letter from Zelda Fitzgerald to F. Scott Fitzgerald, December 1937, Zelda Fitzgerald Papers, Box 45, Folder 75, P.U.L.

330. "I'm tanning myself and exploiting my soul": Letter from Zelda Fitzgerald to F. Scott Fitzgerald, Zelda Fitzgerald Papers, Box 47, Folder 7, P.U.L.

330. "Thanks for the trip": Postcard from Zelda Fitzgerald to F. Scott Fitzgerald, Zelda Fitzgerald Papers, P.U.L.

331. "Meanwhile: what is your actual address?": Letter from Zelda Fitzgerald to F. Scott Fitzgerald, December 1938, Zelda Fitzgerald Papers, Box 46, Folder 51, P.U.L.

331. "Havana is probably a substantial sort of place": Letter from Zelda Fitzgerald to F. Scott Fitzgerald, in Nancy Milford, *Zelda, a Biography* (New York: Harper & Row, 1970), p. 327.

331. "I wish we were astride the tops": Letter from Zelda Fitzgerald to F. Scott Fitzgerald, Zelda Fitzgerald Papers, Box 45, Folder 82, P.U.L.

331. "cook and so forth, and maybe discover gold": Note from Zelda Fitzgerald to F. Scott Fitzgerald, written alongside pencil drawing of Scott by Zelda (titled *Do-Do in Guatemala*), Zelda Fitzgerald Papers, P.U.L.

332. "I wish things had been so that we were going on together somewhere": Letter from Zelda Fitzgerald to F. Scott Fitzgerald, late April 1939, Zelda Fitzgerald Papers, Box 47, Folder 29, P.U.L.

332. "You were a peach": Letter from F. Scott Fitzgerald to Zelda Fitzgerald, quoted in Bruccoli, *Some Sort of Epic Grandeur*, p. 456.

332. "Zelda was a finer wife to Scott": Interview with Archibald MacLeish by the author.

333. "There is an arresting and imaginative quality": Exhibition Review, "The Asheville Citizen," reprinted in *The Romantic Egoists*, ed. Matthew J. Bruccoli (New York: Charles Scribner's Sons, 1974), p. 237; and Koula Svokos Hartnett, "Zelda Fitzgerald and the Failure of the American Dream," paper presented at Southern Atlantic Modern Language Association annual meeting, 1981, p. 142.

333. "To waste a professional talent": Letter from Zelda Fitzgerald to F. Scott Fitzgerald, quoted in Milford, *Zelda*, p. 335.

334. "The shock wasn't so much at your refusal": Letter from F. Scott Fitzgerald to Harold Ober, July 19, 1939, Bruccoli, *A Life in Letters: F. Scott Fitzgerald*, p. 400.

334. "My unwritten debt to you": Ibid.

334. "Harold Ober and I are parting company": Letter from F. Scott Fitzgerald to Max Perkins, July 19, 1939, F. Scott Fitzgerald Papers, Col. 187, Box 51, Folder 37, P.U.L.

334. "Mrs. Ober and I had a run-in": Letter from F. Scott Fitzgerald to Maxwell Perkins, August 3, 1939, F. Scott Fitzgerald Papers, Col. 187, Box 51, Folder 37, P.U.L.

334. "I want to keep the lampshades": Letter from F. Scott Fitzgerald to Isabel Owens, May 29, 1940, quoted in Bruccoli and Duggan, *Correspondence of F. Scott Fitzgerald*, pp. 596–597.

335. "I hope you will find it possible": Letter from F. Scott Fitzgerald to Dr. R. H. Suitt, September 27, 1939, F. Scott Fitzgerald Papers, Box 53, Folder 14A, P.U.L.

335. "If you can't pay her board": Letter from Marjorie Brinson to F. Scott Fitzgerald, October 20, 1939, F. Scott Fitzgerald Papers, Box 55, P.U.L.

336. "The facts remain unchanged—": Letter from F. Scott Fitzgerald to Mrs. Anthony Sayre, October 15, 1939, F. Scott Fitzgerald Papers, AM 20502, Col. 183, Box 6, Folder 24, P.U.L.

336. "I think if there is any way to stop": Letter from F. Scott Fitzgerald to Dr. Robert Carroll, October 20, 1939, quoted in Bruccoli and Duggan, *Correspondence of F. Scott Fitzgerald*, p. 554.

336. "I have taken this whole thing": Unsent letter from F. Scott Fitzgerald to Marjorie Brinson, 1939, F. Scott Fitzgerald Papers, Box 55, P.U.L.

337. "There is no favorable prognosis": Letter from F. Scott Fitzgerald to Mrs. Anthony Sayre, January 3, 1939, F. Scott Fitzgerald Papers, Box 53, Folder 14A, P.U.L.

337. "I would like her [Scottie] to know": Letter from F. Scott Fitzgerald to Dr. R. H. Burke Suitt, July 5, 1939, F. Scott Fitzgerald Papers, Box 53, Folder 14A, P.U.L.

337. "I'm having a controversy with Highland Hospital": Letter from F. Scott Fitzgerald to Scottie Fitzgerald, quoted in Turnbull, *Letters to His Daughter*, pp. 46–47.

337. "What do you think of letting her go home": Letter from Dr. Robert Carroll to F. Scott Fitzgerald, March 8, 1940, quoted in Bruccoli and Duggan, *The Correspondence of F. Scott Fitzgerald*, p. 587.

338. "This morning I have a letter from Dr. Carroll": Letter from F. Scott Fitzgerald to Mrs. Anthony Sayre, quoted in Bruccoli and Duggan, *Correspondence of F. Scott Fitzgerald*, p. 587.

338. "It is wonderful to be able to write you this": Letter from F. Scott Fitzgerald to Zelda Fitzgerald, March 8, 1940, Zelda Fitzgerald Papers, Vol. 187, Box 41, Folder 14, P.U.L.

338. "I am moving into town": Letter from F. Scott Fitzgerald to Mrs. Anthony Sayre, April 1940, quoted in Bruccoli and Duggan, *Correspondence of F. Scott Fitzgerald*, p. 593.

339. "I do hope this goes well": Letter from F. Scott Fitzgerald to Zelda Fitzgerald, April 11, 1940, in Bruccoli, *A Life in Letters: F. Scott Fitzgerald*, p. 442.

339. "Zelda is home since this week Tuesday": Letter from F. Scott Fitzgerald to Gerald and Sara Murphy, summer 1940, in Bruccoli, *A Life in Letters: F. Scott Fitzgerald*, p. 458.

339. "Dear, I have had a very depressed letter": Letter from F. Scott Fitzgerald to Scottie Fitzgerald, June 6, 1940, F. Scott Fitzgerald Papers, Box 40, Folder 5, P.U.L.

339. "I don't know what is going to happen": Letter from F. Scott Fitzgerald to Scottie Fitzgerald, June 7, 1940, in Turnbull, *Letters of F. Scott Fitzgerald*, p. 77.

340. "I won't be able to stick this out": Telegram from Zelda Fitzgerald to F. Scott Fitzgerald, F. Scott Fitzgerald Papers, P.U.L.

340. "I have been an angel with mama": Letter from Scottie Fitzgerald to F. Scott Fitzgerald, quoted in Lanahan, *Scottie, the Daughter of . . .* , p. 127.

340. "I always forget how people": Scottie Fitzgerald, quoted in Lanahan, *Scottie, the Daughter of . . .* , p. 127.

340. "Ten years ago Paris": Letter from F. Scott Fitzgerald to Zelda Fitzgerald, June 14, 1940, Turnbull, *Letters of F. Scott Fitzgerald*, p. 119.

340. "What little I've accomplished": Letter from F. Scott Fitzgerald to Scottie Fitzgerald, June 12, 1940, Turnbull, *Letters to His Daughter*, p. 128.

340. "The police have just called": Letter from F. Scott Fitzgerald to Scottie Fitzgerald, June 20, 1940, Turnbull, *Letters to His Daughter*, p. 132.

341. "I do not like to feel that you consider yourself ill": Letter from Sara Murphy to F. Scott Fitzgerald, August 26, 1940, F. Scott Fitzgerald Papers, Col. 187, Box 51, Folder 13, P.U.L.

341. "You saved me—Scottie and me": Letter from F. Scott Fitzgerald to Gerald and Sara Murphy, quoted in Bruccoli and Duggan, *Correspondence of F. Scott Fitzgerald*, p. 554.

341. "She is nicer now than she has been since": Letter from F. Scott Fitzgerald to Gerald Murphy, September 14, 1940, F. Scott Fitzgerald Papers, Box 51, Folder 13, P.U.L.

341. "I find, after a long time out here": Letter from F. Scott Fitzgerald to Gerald Murphy, September 14, 1940, F. Scott Fitzgerald Papers, Box 51, Folder 13, P.U.L.

341. "We share in retrospect your feelings about Hollywood": Letter from Gerald Murphy to F. Scott Fitzgerald, March 10, 1940, F. Scott Fitzgerald Papers, Col. 187, Box 51, Folder 13, P.U.L.

341. "I'm sorry you can't sleep": Letter from Zelda Fitzgerald to F. Scott Fitzgerald, no date, F. Scott Fitzgerald Papers, Col. 187, Box 46, Folder 17, P.U.L.

342. "Take care of yourself": Letter from Zelda Fitzgerald to F. Scott Fitzgerald, no date, Zelda Fitzgerald Papers, Box 42, Folder 38, P.U.L.

342. "This part of the world is far more conducive": Letter from Zelda Fitzgerald to F. Scott Fitzgerald, no date. Zelda Fitzgerald Papers, Box 47, Folder 55, P.U.L.

342. "You have two beautiful bad examples": Letter from F. Scott Fitzgerald to Scottie Fitzgerald, quoted in Lanahan, *Scottie, the Daughter of . . .* , p. 130.

342. "All correspondence in a file": Final Will of F. Scott Fitzgerald, F. Scott Fitzgerald Papers, Box 55, Folder 22, P.U.L.

343. "No news except that the novel progresses": Letter from F. Scott Fitzgerald to Zelda Fitzgerald, December 6, 1940, in Turnbull, *Letters of F. Scott Fitzgerald*, p. 131.

344. "I made repeated requests": John Biggs, quoted in Seymour A. Toll, *A Judge Uncommon: A Life of John Biggs, Jr.* (Philadelphia: Legal Communications, Ltd., 1993), p. 185.

345. "About everybody who could have been reasonably expected": Rosalind Smith, unpublished material about Zelda, Mayfield Collection, University of Alabama.

345. "Of course I was upset": Scottie Fitzgerald, quoted in Lanahan, *Scottie, the Daughter of . . .* , pp. 132–133.

345. "sort of ashamed": Ibid., p. 11.

345. "In retrospect, it seems as if he was always": Letter from Zelda Fitzgerald to Harold Ober, quoted in Milford, *Zelda*, p. 350.

345. "I always feel that daddy was": Letter from Zelda Fitzgerald to Scottie Fitzgerald, in Milford, *Zelda*, p. 373.

346. "If it weren't for you": Letter from Scottie Fitzgerald to John Biggs, January 7, 1941, F. Scott Fitzgerald Papers, Box 5, Folder 8, P.U.L

349. "Down here, the little garden": Letter from Zelda Fitzgerald to Ludlow Fowler, 1946, Zelda Fitzgerald Papers, Box 5, File 4, P.U.L.

349. "I find the description of her as 'frail' ": Letter from Rosalind Smith to the author, December 3, 1964. Collection of the author.

349. "They are in no way ordinary paper dolls": "Zelda Fitzgerald Exhibits Dolls at Museum," *Montgomery Advertiser,* August 1941, Zelda Fitzgerald Papers, P.U.L.

349. "I have painted . . . King Arthur's roundtable": Letter from Zelda Fitzgerald to Maxwell Perkins, quoted in *Zelda: An Illustrated Life,* ed. Eleanor Lanahan (New York: Harry Abrams, 1996), p. 83.

350. "I am glad you are going to Princeton": Letter from F. Scott Fitzgerald to Scottie Fitzgerald, April 27, 1940, Turnbull, *Letters to His Daughter,* p. 114.

351. "I felt guilty about having left": Scottie Fitzgerald, quoted in Lanahan, *Scottie, the Daughter of . . .* , p. 150.

351. "She once became so envious": Interview with Landon Ray at Highland Hospital by the author, June 21, 1963.

352. "There's no place else to go and think": Zelda Fitzgerald quoted in Sara Mayfield, *Exiles from Paradise: Zelda and Scott Fitzgerald* (New York: Dell Publishing, 1971), p. 275.

352. "she became a person of the utmost rectitude": Rosalind Smith quoted in Lanahan, *Scottie, the Daughter of . . .* , p. 185.

353. "The pictures consisted of non-representational": Brendon Gill, quoted in *A New York Life: Of Friends and Others* (New York, Poseidon Press, 1990), p. 315.

353. "There was a great collection of eccentrics": Scottie Fitzgerald, quoted in Lanahan, *Scottie, the Daughter of . . .* , p. 160.

353. "the telegrams which we exchanged": Letter from Zelda Fitzgerald to Ludlow Fowler, Zelda Fitzgerald Papers, Box 5, file 4, P.U.L.

354. "This work-or-not issue": Scottie Fitzgerald, quoted in Lanahan, *Scottie, the Daughter of . . .* , p. 174.

354. "Zelda said we didn't need to worry": Anna Biggs, quoted in Milford, *Zelda,* p. 375.

354. "To Larchmont—gruesome day": Scottie Fitzgerald, quoted in Lanahan, *Scottie, the Daughter of . . .* , p. 175.

354. "Mother got quite drunk": Letter from Scottie Fitzgerald to John Biggs, January 7, 1946, F. Scott Fitzgerald Papers, Box 5, Folder 12, P.U.L.

354. "They know that she simply cannot drink": Marjorie Brinson, quoted in Helen Blackshear, "Mama Sayre, Scott Fitzgerald's Mother-in-Law," *Georgia Review,* Winter 1965.

355. "I remember one she came to": Nancy Milford, "The Golden Dreams of Zelda Fitzgerald," *Harper's Magazine,* January 1969, p. 52.

356. "Zelda returned to Montgomery": Letter from Mrs. H .L. Weatherby to the author, March 1964. Collection of the author.

356. "While I was conversing": C. Lawton Campbell, "The Fitzgeralds Were My Friends," unpublished essay, p. 29. Collection of the author.

356. "I have tried so hard and prayed": Letter from Zelda Fitzgerald to Rosalind Smith, quoted in Meyer, *Scott Fitzgerald,* p. 340.

357. "I'm distressed Zelda does not improve": Letter from Mrs. Anthony Sayre to Scottie Fitzgerald, January 17, 1944, quoted in Lanahan, *Scottie, the Daughter of . . .* , pp. 179–180.

357. "To-day there is promise of spring": Letter from Zelda Fitzgerald to Scottie Fitzgerald, quoted in Lanahan, *Scottie, the Daughter of . . .* , p. 181.

357. "There is hardly time to live at all anymore": Letter from Zelda Fitzgerald to Ludlow Fowler, 1946, Zelda Fitzgerald Papers, Box 5, File 4, P.U.L.

359. "Had she not been asleep": Dr. Irving Pine, quoted in Koula Svokos Harnett, *Zelda Fitzgerald and the Failure of the American Dream for Women* (New York: Peter Lang Publishers, 1991), p. 185, and in interviews with Dr. Basil T. Bennett by the author, August 11, 1963, and February and March 1964.

359. "There were many floral remembrances": Rosalind Smith, unpublished documentation on Zelda Fitzgerald, Mayfield Collection, University of Alabama.

359. "Scott loved Zelda with his last breath": John Biggs as quoted in Lanahan, *Scottie, the Daughter of . . .* , p. 182.

359. "Dearest Grandma—I am sure by now everyone": Letter from Scottie Fitzgerald to Mrs. Anthony Sayre, March 19, 1948, F. Scott Fitzgerald Papers, Col. AM 20502, Box 25, P.U.L.

361. "Jack decided to become a specialist in tax law": Scottie Fitzgerald quoted in Lanahan, *Scottie, the Daughter of . . .* , p. 184.

362. "I don't like putting them to bed": Ibid., p. 193.

362. "My mother sent us to camps": Eleanor Lanahan, as quoted in *Scottie, the Daughter of . . .* , p. 253.

362. "Her management strategy was to be nice": Ibid.

362. "I'm not trying to rationalize": Scottie Fitzgerald, quoted in Lanahan, *Scottie, the Daughter of . . .* , p. 223.

363. "She would give you the skin off her back": Clayton Fritchey, quoted in Lanahan, *Scottie, the Daughter of . . .* , p. 227.

363. "I am especially lucky": Scottie Fitzgerald, quoted in Lanahan, *Scottie, the Daughter of . . .* , p. 213.

363. "I kept my feelings aloof": Eleanor Lanahan quoted in Lanahan, *Scottie, the Daughter of . . .* , p. 256.

363. "I can't seem to give them anything": Scottie Fitzgerald, quoted in Lanahan, *Scottie, the Daughter of . . .* , p. 197.

364. "I can remember nothing except the troubles": Scottie Fitzgerald, quoted in Introduction to Turnbull, *Letters to His Daughter*, p. xi.

364. "In my next incarnation": Ibid., p. ix.

364. "You once made the astounding statement": Letter from F. Scott Fitzgerald to Scottie Fitzgerald, May 7, 1940, Turnbull, *Letters to His Daughter*, p. 118.

364. "You will be interviewed again": Ibid.

364. "I lent her the letters": Scottie Fitzgerald, quoted in Lanahan, *Scottie, the Daughter of . . .* , pp. 335–336.

364. "My mother was so distressed": Eleanor Lanahan, quoted in *Scottie, the Daughter of . . .* , p. 336.

364. "If I had no daughters": Scottie Fitzgerald, quoted in Lanahan, *Scottie, the Daughter of . . .* , p. 337.

365. "She is eighty years old now": Scottie Fitzgerald, quoted in *The Sunday Star*, July 19, 1970, Sec. G, p. 2.

365. "We got married in a great big rush": Scottie Fitzgerald, quoted in Lanahan, *Scottie, the Daughter of . . .* , p. 355.

366. "I just think that we were mis-mated": Ibid., p. 280.

366. "through the smoky twilight": Eleanor Lanahan, quoted in *Scottie, the Daughter of . . .* , p. 214.

366. "There was the odor of tobacco": F. Scott Fitzgerald, *The Beautiful and Damned* (New York: Charles Scribner's Sons, 1922), p. 295–296.

366. "I do wish the house could be saved": Scottie Fitzgerald, quoted in Lanahan, *Scottie, the Daughter of . . .* , p. 412.

367. "I didn't begin to be a heavy smoker": Letter from F. Scott Fitzgerald to Scottie Fitzgerald, quoted in Turnbull, *Letters to His Daughter*, p. 79.

368. "What a shame that someone": Jack Lanahan, quoted in Lanahan, *Scottie, the Daughter of . . .* , p. 529.

368. "My parents were always very circumspect": Scottie Fitzgerald, quoted in Lanahan, *Scottie, the Daughter of . . .* , p. 3.

368. "The fact that my father became a difficult parent": Scottie Fitzgerald, quoted in Introduction to Turnbull, *Letters to His Daughter*, p. xi.

369. "He [McKaig] is hopelessly and completely insane": Letter from John Peale Bishop to Edmund Wilson, quoted in Mellow, *Invented Lives*, p. 443.

369. "In New York the year was one of nervous breakdowns": Malcolm Cowley, "Epilogue: New Year's Eve," in *Exile's Return* (New York: Viking Press, 1956), p. 290.

369. "A classmate killed his wife": F. Scott Fitzgerald, "Echoes of the Jazz Age," in *The Crack-Up*, ed. Edmund Wilson (New York: New Directions, 1956), p. 22.

369. "She didn't have the strength for the big stage": quoted in Turnbull, *The Letters of F. Scott Fitzgerald*, p. 32.

370. "She realized too late": Letter from F. Scott Fitzgerald to Scottie Fitzgerald, quoted in Graham, *The Real F. Scott Fitzgerald*, p. 59.

372. "It was my mother's misfortune": Scottie Fitzgerald, Introduction to catalog for Zelda Fitzgerald exhibition at Montgomery Museum of Fine Arts, September 1974, p. 5.

372. "We ruined ourselves": Letter from F. Scott Fitzgerald to Zelda Fitzgerald, summer 1930, quoted in Bruccoli and Duggan, *Correspondence of F. Scott Fitzgerald*, p. 241.

372. "Nothing could have survived our life . . . Zelda Fitzgerald, quoted in Mellow, *Invented Lives*, p. 470.

BIBLIOGRAPHY

Aaron, Daniel. "The Legend of the Golden Couple," *Virginia Quarterly Review* 48 (1972): 157–160.

Allen, Frederick Lewis. *Only Yesterday: An Informal History of the 1920s.* New York: Harper & Row, 1964.

Allen, Joan. *Candies and Carnival Lights: The Catholic Sensibility of F. Scott Fitzgerald.* New York: New York University Press, 1978.

Amory, Cleveland, and Frederick Bradlee, eds. *Vanity Fair: A Cavalcade of the 1920's and 1930's.* New York: Viking Press, 1960.

Angoff, Charles. *H. L. Mencken: A Portrait from Memory.* New York: Yoseloff, 1956.

Arlen, Michael J. *Exiles.* New York: Farrar, Straus & Giroux, 1970.

Arieti, Silvano, M.D. *Interpretation of Schizophrenia.* New York: Basic Books, 1955; second edition, 1974.

Armitage, Shelley. *John Held Jr., Illustrator of the Jazz Age.* Syracuse, N.Y.: Syracuse University Press, 1987.

Baker, Carlos. *Ernest Hemingway: A Life Story.* New York Charles Scribner's Sons, 1969.

Berg, A. Scott. *Max Perkins: Editor of Genius.* New York: Pocket Books, 1979.

Blackshear, Helen F. "Mama Sayre, Scott Fitzgerald's Mother-in-Law," *Georgia Review,* Winter 1965; 445 ff.

Bode, Carl. *Mencken.* Carbondale and Edwardsville: Southern Illinois University Press, 1969.

Boyd, Ernest. *Portraits: Real and Imaginary.* London: Jonathan Cape, 1924.

Brown, Dorothy M. *American Women in the 1920s: Setting a Course.* Boston: Twayne Publishers, 1987.

Bruccoli, Matthew J., ed. *As Ever, Scott Fitzgerald.* Philadelphia: J.B. Lippincott & Co., 1972.

———. *The Romantic Egoists: A Pictorical Autobiography from the Scrapbooks and Albums of F. Scott and Zelda Fitzgerald.* New York: Charles Scribner's Sons, 1974.

———. *Scott and Ernest.* Carbondale and Edwardsville: Southern Illinois University Press. 1978.

Bruccoli, Matthew J., and Margret M. Duggan, eds. *Correspondence of F. Scott Fitzgerald.* New York: Random House, 1980.

———. *Some Sort of Epic Grandeur: The Life of F. Scott Fitzgerald.* New York: Harcourt Brace Jovanovich, 1981.

———, ed. *A Life in Letters: F. Scott Fitzgerald.* New York: Simon and Schuster, 1995.

Bruccoli, Matthew J., and Jackson R. Bryer, eds. *F. Scott Fitzgerald in His Own Time.* New York: Popular Library, 1971.

Bruccoli, Matthew J., and C. F. Frazer Clark Jr., eds. *F. Scott Fitzgerald and Ernest Hemingway in Paris.* Columbia, S.C.: University of South Carolina Press, 1972.

———. *Fitzgerald/Hemingway Annual 1973.* Washington, D.C.: Microcard Editions Books, 1974.

———. *Scott and Ernest: The Authority of Failure and the Authority of Success.* New York: Random House, 1978.

Bullock, Alan, and R. B. Woodings. *20th Century Culture; A Biographical Companion.* New York: Harper & Row, 1983.

Burgess, Anthony. *Ernest Hemingway and His World.* New York: Charles Scribner's Sons, 1985.

Buttitta, Tony. *After the Good, Gay Times—Asheville '35: A Season of F. Scott Fitzgerald.* New York: Viking Press, 1974.

Callaghan, Morley. *That Summer in Paris: Memories of Tangled Friendships with Hemingway, Fitzgerald, and Some Others.* New York: Coward-McCann, 1963.

Carey, Gary. *Anita Loos.* New York: Alfred A. Knopf, 1988.

Chesler, Phyllis. *Women & Madness.* New York: Doubleday, 1972.

Clemens, Anne Valdene. "Zelda Fitzgerald: An Unromantic Vision," *Dalhousie Review* 62, no. 2 (Summer 1982): 196–211.

Cody, Morrill, with Hugh Ford. *The Woman of Montparnasse.* New York: Cornwall Books, 1984.

Cooper, Douglas Marshall. "Form and Fiction: The Writing Style of Zelda Sayre Fitzgerald." Dissertation, University of Michigan, 1979.

Courbin-Tavernier, Jacqueline. "Art as Women's Response and Search: Zelda Fitzgerald's *Save Me the Waltz,*" *Southern Liberty Journal,* 11, no. 2 (Spring 1979): 22–42.

Cowley, Malcolm. *Exile's Return: A Literary Odyssey of the 1920s.* London: The Bodley Head, 1951.

———. *A Second Flowering: Works and Days of the Lost Generation.* New York: Viking Press, 1973.

———. *After the Genteel Tradition.* New York: W .W. Norton & Co., 1973.

Cowley, Malcolm, and Robert Cowley, eds. *Fitzgerald and the Jazz Age.* New York: Charles Scribner's Sons, 1966.

Diehl, Gaston. *Pascin.* New York: Crown Publishers, 1984.

Diliberto, Gioia. *Hadley.* New York: Ticknor & Fields, 1992.

Donaldson, Scott. *Fool for Love: F. Scott Fitzgerald*. New York: Congdon & Weed, 1983.

Donnelly, Honoria Murphy. *Sara and Gerald: Villa America and After*. New York: Times Books, 1982.

Dos Passos, John. *The Fourteenth Chronicle: Letters and Diaries of John Dos Passos*. Edited by Townsend Ludington. Boston: Gambit, Inc., 1973

Eble, Kenneth. *F. Scott Fitzgerald*. New Haven, Conn.: Yale University Press, 1963.

Eicher, Terry, and Jesse Geller. *Fathers and Daughters; Portraits in Fiction*. New York: Penguin Group, 1990.

Elder, Donald. *Ring Lardner*. Garden City, N.Y.: Doubleday, 1956.

Fels, Florent. *Drawings by Pascin*. New York: Book Adventures, Inc., 1967.

Fenton, Charles A. *The Apprenticeship of Ernest Hemingway*. New York: Viking Press, 1958.

Field, Andrew. *Djuna; the Formidable Miss Barnes*. Austin: University of Texas Press, 1985.

Fitzgerald, F. Scott. *Taps at Reveille*. New York: Charles Scribner's Sons, 1935.

———. *The Beautiful and Damned*. New York: Charles Scribner's Sons, 1950.

———. *The Stories of F. Scott Fitzgerald*. Selected and with an introduction by Malcolm Cowley. New York: Charles Scribner's Sons, 1953.

———. *The Crack-Up*. Edited by Edmond Wilson. New York: New Directions, 1956.

———. *Afternoon of an Author*. Edited by Arthur Mizener. New York: Charles Scribner's Sons, 1957.

———. *Flappers and Philosophers*. New York: Charles Scribner's Sons, 1959.

———. *Tender Is the Night*. New York: Charles Scribner's Sons, 1962.

———. *The Letters of F. Scott Fitzgerald*. Edited by Andrew Turnbull. New York: Charles Scribner's Sons, 1963.

———. *Thought Book of Francis Scott Key Fitzgerald*. Princeton, N.J.: Princeton University Library, 1965.

———. *The Great Gatsby*. New York: Charles Scribner's Sons, 1969.

———. *The Last Tycoon*. New York: Charles Scribner's Sons, 1969.

———. *This Side of Paradise*. New York: Charles Scribner's Sons, 1970.

———. *Babylon Revisited and Other Stories*. New York: Charles Scribner's Sons, 1971.

———. *Dear Scott/Dear Max: The Fitzgerald-Perkins Correspondence*. Edited by John Kuehl and Jackson R. Bryher. New York: Charles Scribner's Sons, 1971.

———. *As Ever Scott Fitz: Letters Between F. Scott Fitzgerald and His Literary Agent, Harold Ober*. Edited by Matthew J. Bruccoli. Philadelphia and New York: J.B. Lippincott Company, 1972.

———. *F. Scott Fitzgerald's Ledger: A Facsimile*. Washington, D.C.: Microcard Editions, 1972.

———. *The Vegetable*. New York: Charles Scribner's Sons, 1976.

———. *Correspondence of F. Scott Fitzgerald*. Edited by Matthew J. Bruccoli and Margaret M. Duggan. New York: Random House, 1980.

———. *The Notebook of F. Scott Fitzgerald*. Edited by Matthew J. Bruccoli. New York: Harcourt Brace Jovanovich, 1980.

Fitzgerald, F. Scott, and Zelda Fitzgerald. *Bits of Paradise*. New York: Charles Scribner's Sons, 1973.

Fitzgerald, Zelda. *Save Me the Waltz*. Carbondale and Edwardsville: Southern Illinois University Press, 1967.

———. *The Collected Writings*. Edited by Matthew J. Bruccoli. New York: Charles Scribner's Sons, 1991.

"Zelda Fitzgerald Exhibits Dolls at Museum." *Montgomery Advertiser,* August 1941.

"Zelda Sayre Fitzgerald's Pictures on View at Museum." *Montgomery Advertiser,* May 10, 1942.

"Zelda Sayre Fitzgerald." Montgomery Museum of Fine Arts Bulletin, September 1989.

"The Far Side of Zelda Fitzgerald." *Esquire* 62, no. 6 (December 1964): 158–159.

Flanner, Janet. *Paris Was Yesterday.* New York: Viking Press, 1972.

Ford, Hugh. *Publishing in Paris: A Literary Chronicle of Paris in the 1920s and 1930s.* New York: Collier Books, 1975.

Francillon, Robert E. *Zelda's Fortune.* Boston: James R. Osgood and Company, 1874.

Fryer, Sarah Beebe. *Fitzgerald's New Women: Harbingers of Change.* Ann Arbor, Mich.: U.M.I., Research Press, 1988.

Garafolo, Lynn. *Diagilev's Russes Ballets.* New York: Oxford University Press, 1989.

Gerald Murphy: Toward an Understanding of His Art and Inspiration. Washington, D.C.: Board of Governors of the Federal Reserve Board System, program of art exhibit, September 21–December 1, 1983.

Gill, Brendon. *A New York Life: Of Friends and Others.* New York: Poseidon Press, 1990.

Gilman, A. G. Goodman. *The Standard Textbook of Pharmacology for M.D.'s.*

Gish, Lillian. *The Movies, Mr. Griffith, and Me.* Englewood Cliffs, N.J.: Prentice Hall, 1969.

Going, William T. "Two Alabama Writers: Zelda Sayre Fitzgerald and Sara Haardt Mencken." *Alabama Review,* 23 (January 1970): 3–29.

Goldhurst, William. *F. Scott Fitzgerald and His Contemporaries.* New York: World, 1963.

Graham, Sheilah, *College of One.* New York: Viking Press, 1967.

———. *The Garden of Allah.* New York: Crown Publishers, Inc., 1970.

———. *Beloved Infidel.* New York: Grosset & Dunlap. 1976.

———. *The Real F. Scott Fitzgerald: Thirty-Five Years Later.* New York: Grosset & Dunlap, Inc., 1976.

Haardt, Sara. *The Making of a Lady.* New York: Doubleday, 1930.

Haney, Lynn. *Naked as the Feast: A Biography of Josephine Baker.* New York: Dodd, Mead & Company, 1981.

Hansen, Arlen J. *Expatriate Paris; A Cultural and Literary Guide to Paris of the 1920s.* New York: Arcade Publishing, Little Brown, 1990.

Hardwick, Elizabeth. *Seduction and Betrayal: Women and Literature.* New York: Vintage Press, 1975.

Harrison, Gilbert A. *The Enthusiast: A Life of Thornton Wilder.* New Haven, Conn.: Ticknor & Fields, 1983.

Hart, Livye Ridgeway. "A Profile of Zelda," original manuscript. Sara Mayfield Collection, University of Alabama, Tuscaloosa.

Harnett, Koula Svokos. *Zelda Fitzgerald and the Failure of the American Dream for Women.* New York: Peter Lang Publishers, 1991.

Hayes, Helen, with Sanford Dody. *On Reflection: An Autobiography.* New York: M. Evans and Company, 1968.

Heilbrun, Carolyn G. "Discovering the Lost Lives of Woman." *New York Times, Book Review,* June 24, 1984, pp. 1, 26, 27.

———. *Writing a Woman's Life.* New York: W. W. Norton & Co., 1988.

Heller, Adele, and Lois Rudnick. *1915; The Cultural Moment,* New Brunswick, N.J.: Rutgers University Press, 1991.

Hellman, Lillian. *An Unfinished Woman.* New York: Bantam Books, 1980.

Hemingway, Ernest. *The Sun Also Rises.* New York: Charles Scribner's Sons, 1926.

———. *A Moveable Feast.* New York: Charles Scribner's Sons, 1964.

———. *Ernest Hemingway: Selected Letters, 1917–1961.* Edited by Carlos Baker. New York: Charles Scribner's Sons, 1981.

———. *The Garden of Eden.* New York: Charles Scribner's Sons. 1986.

Hemingway, Mary Welsh. *How It Was.* New York: Alfred A. Knopf, 1976.

Hergesheimer, Joseph. *Cythrea.* New York: Alfred A Knopf, 1922.

Hotchner, A. E. *Papa Hemingway.* New York: Random House, 1966.

Hudgins, Andrew. "Zelda Sayre in Montgomery." *Southern Review* 20 (1984): 882–884.

Israel, Lee. *Miss Tallulah Bankhead.* New York: G. P. Putnam's Sons, 1972.

Jacobson, E. "The Early History of Psychotherapeutic Drugs," *Psychopharmacology* 89 (1986): 138.

Kazin, Alfred, ed. *F. Scott Fitzgerald: The Man and His Work.* New York: Collier Books, 1951.

Kellner, Bruce. *Carl Van Vechten and the Irreverent Decades.* Norman: University of Oklahoma Press, 1968.

Kelly, John. "Memories of Scott and Zelda," *Pittsburgh Press,* Vol. 6 (February 1983): 16, 18.

Kert, Bernice. *The Hemingway Women: Those Who Loved Him—the Wives and Others.* New York: W. W. Norton & Co., 1983.

Kluver, Billy, and Julie Martin. *Kiki's Paris: Artists and Lovers, 1900–1930.* New York: Harry N. Abrams, Inc., 1989.

Kokotailo, Philip. *John Glassco's Richer World: Memoirs of Montparnasse.* Toronto: ECW Press, 1988.

Kuel, John, and Jackson R. Bryer, eds. *Dear Scott/Dear Max.* New York: Charles Scribner's Sons, 1963.

Lanahan, Eleanor. *Scottie, the Daughter of . . . : The Life of Frances Scott Fitzgerald Lanahan Smith.* New York. Harper Collins, 1995.

———. *Zelda: An Illustrated Life. The Private World of Zelda Fitzgerald.* New York: Harry N. Abrams., 1996.

Lanoux, Armand. *Paris in the Twenties.* Translated by E. S. Seldon. New York: Golden Griffin Books/Essential Encyclopedia Arts, Inc., 1960.

Lardner, Ring. *What of It?* New York: Charles Scribner's Sons, 1925.

Lardner, Ring, Jr. *The Lardners: My Family Remembered.* New York: Harper Colophon Books, 1977.

Latham, Aaron. *Crazy Sundays: F. Scott Fitzgerald in Hollywood.* New York: Viking Press, 1971.

Le Vot, Andre. *F. Scott Fitzgerald: A Biography.* Translated by William Byron. Garden City, N.Y.: Doubleday, 1983.

Lewis, Janet. "The Cruise of the Rolling Junk; The Fictionalized Joys of Motoring," Fitzgerald/Hemingway Annual, 1978: 69–81.

Loos, Anita. *A Girl Like I.* New York: Viking Press. 1966.

———. *The Talmadge Girls.* New York: Viking Press, 1978.

Luce, William. *Zelda.* Off-Broadway one-woman show, New York, November 1984.

Ludington, Townsend. *John Dos Passos: A Twentieth Century Odyssey.* New York: E. P. Dutton, 1980.

MacLeish, Archibald. *Letters of Archibald MacLeish.* Edited by R. H. Winnick. Boston: Houghton Mifflin, 1983.

MacShane, Frank. *The Life of John O'Hara.* New York: E. P. Dutton, 1980. Collier Books, 1967.

McLendon, Winzola. "Scott and Zelda." *Ladies' Home Journal* 91 (November 1974): 58–171.

Mayfield, Sara. *The Constant Circle: H. L. Mencken and His Friends.* New York: Dell Publishing Co., 1968.

———. *Exiles from Paradise: Zelda and Scott Fitzgerald.* New York: Delacorte Press, 1971.

Mellow, James. *Charmed Circle: Gertrude Stein & Company.* New York: Praeger Publishers, 1974.

———. *Invented Lives: A Study of F. Scott and Zelda Fitzgerald.* New York: Houghton Mifflin, 1984.

———. *Hemingway: A Life Without Consequences.* Reading, Mass.: Addison-Wesley Publishing Company, 1992.

Mencken, H. L. *In Defense of Women.* New York: Alfred A. Knopf, 1927.

———. *The Vintage Mencken.* Gathered by Alistair Cooke. New York: Vintage Books, 1955.

Merkin, Richard. *The Jazz Age as Seen Through The Eyes of Ralph Barton, Miguel Covarrubias, and John Held, Jr.,* Providence: Museum of Art, Rhode Island School of Design, 25 September–November 10, 1968.

Meyers, Jeffrey. *Scott Fitzgerald.* New York: HarperCollins, 1994.

Milford, Nancy. *Zelda, a Biography.* New York: Harper & Row, 1970.

Mizener, Arthur. *The Far Side of Paradise.* New York: Houghton Mifflin Co., 1949.

Mizener, Arthur, ed. *F. Scott Fitzgerald: A Collection of Critical Essays.* Englewood Cliffs, N.J.: Prentice-Hall, Inc., 1963.

———. *The Fitzgerald Reader.* New York: Charles Scribner's Sons, 1963.

———. *Scott Fitzgerald and His World.* New York: G. P. Putnam's Sons, 1972.

Nathan, George Jean. *The Theater, the Drama, the Girls.* New York: Alfred A. Knopf, 1921.

———. *The World of George Jean Nathan.* Edited by Charles Angoff. New York: Alfred A. Knopf, 1952.

———. "Memories of Fitzgerald, Lewis and Dreiser." *Esquire,* October 1958, pp. 148–149.

Neret, Gilles. *The Arts of the Twenties.* New York: Rizzoli, 1986.

Nijinsky, Romola. *Nijinsky.* New York: Simon & Schuster, 1980.

O'Hara, John. *Selected Letters of John O'Hara.* Edited by Matthew J. Bruccoli. New York: Random House, 1978.

Pattillo, Edward. *Zelda: Zelda Sayre Fitzgerald Retrospective.* Montgomery: Montgomery Museum of Fine Arts, 1974.

Perkins, Maxwell E. *Editor to Author: The Letters of Maxwell E. Perkins.* Edited by John Hall Wheelock. New York: Charles Scribner's Sons, 1979.

Petry, Alice Hall. "Women's Work: The Case of Zelda Fitzgerald." *Literature-Interpretation-Theory,* December 1989, pp. 69–83.

Piper, Henry Dan. *F. Scott Fitzgerald: A Critical Portrait.* New York: Carbondale: Southern Illinois Press, 1968.

———, ed. *Fitzgerald's The Great Gatsby: The Novel, the Critics, the Background.* New York: Charles Scribner's Sons, 1970.

Pozharskaya, Militsa, and Tatiana Volodina. *The Art of the Ballet Russes: The Russian Seasons in Paris, 1908–1929.* New York: Abbeville Press, 1988.

Ring, Frances Kroll. *Against the Current: As I Remember F. Scott Fitzgerald*. Berkeley: Creative Arts Book Co., 1985.

Rogers, Marion Elizabeth, ed. *Mencken and Sara: A Life in Letters—The Private Correspondence of H. L. Mencken and Sara Haardt*. New York: McGraw-Hill Book Company, 1987.

Schouvaloff, Alexandre. *Léon Bakst: The Theatre Art*. London: Sotheby's Publications, 1991.

Schulberg, Budd. *The Disenchanted*. New York: Random House, 1950.

Showalter, Elaine. *The Female Malady: Women, Madness and English Culture, 1830–1980*. New York: Pantheon Books, 1985.

Sklar, Robert, ed. *F. Scott Fitzgerald: The Last Tycoon*. New York: Oxford University Press, 1967.

Smith (Lanahan), Frances (Scottie) Fitzgerald. Introduction to *Scott Fitzgerald's Letters to His Daughter*. New York, 1965.

———. "*My Father's Letters*: Advice Without Consent." *Esquire*, October 1965, pp. 93–99.

———. Foreword to *As Ever, Scott Fitz.*, Philadelphia, 1972.

———. *Bits of Paradise*. London: Bodby Head, 1973.

———. Foreword to *Zelda*. Exhibition Catalog. Montgomery, Ala.: Museum of Fine Arts, 1974.

———. Foreword to *Scott and Zelda Fitzgerald's Bits of Paradise*. 1974; New York, 1976.

Spencer, Charles. *Leon Bakst*. New York: Rizzoli, 1973.

———. *The World of Serge Diaghilev*. Chicago: Henry Regenery Co., 1974.

Spencer, Madera. "Museum Show to Feature Zelda Fitzgerald Art." *Montgomery Advertiser Journal*, September 29, 1974, section C.

Stavola, Thomas J. *Scott Fitzgerald: Crisis in an American Identity*. New York: Barnes & Noble, 1981.

Stein, Gertrude. *Selected Writings of Gertrude Stein*. Edited by Carl Van Vechten. New York: Random House, 1946.

Tate, Allen. *Memoirs and Opinions, 1926–1974*. Chicago: Swallow Press, 1975.

Taylor, Frances Finne (Kendall Taylor). "The Fitzgerald Myth: A Study of Zelda Sayre Fitzgerald." Master's thesis, Vanderbilt University, 1964.

Thurber, James. *Credos and Curios*. New York: Harper and Row, 1962.

Tighe, Mary Ann. "Painting on the Other Side of Paradise." *House and Garden* (October 1983), p. 204.

Tillotson, Jery, and Robbie Tillotson. "Zelda Fitzgerald Still Lives." *Feminist Art Journal* 4 (Spring 1975): 31–33.

Toklas, Alice B. *What Is Remembered*. New York: Holt, Rinehart, and Winston, 1963.

Tomkins, Calvin. *Living Well Is the Best Revenge*. New York: E. P. Dutton, 1962.

Turnbull, Andrew. *Scott Fitzgerald*. New York: Charles Scribner's Sons, 1962.

———, ed. *The Letters of F. Scott Fitzgerald*. New York: Charles Scribner's Sons, 1963.

Tytell, John. *Passionate Lives*. New York: Birch Lane Press Book, 1991.

Vaill, Amanda. *Everybody Was So Young*. New York: Houghton Mifflin, 1998.

Van Vechten, Carl. *Parties*. New York: Avon Books, 1977.

Warren, Carol A. B. *Madwives: Schizophrenic Women in the 1950s*. New Brunswick, N.J.: Rutgers University Press, 1987.

Weissman, Myrna M., and Eugene S. Paykel. *The Depressed Woman; A Study of Social Relationships*. Chicago: University of Chicago Press, 1974.

Wilson, Edmund. *The Shores of Light*. New York: Farrar, Straus & Young, 1952.

———. *The Twenties*. Edited by Leon Edel. New York: Farrar, Straus & Giroux, 1975.

———. *Letters on Literature and Politics, 1912–1972*. Edited by Elena Wilson. New York: Farrar, Straus & Giroux, 1977.

———. *The Thirties*. Edited by Leon Edel. New York: Farrar, Straus & Giroux, 1980.

Wiser, William. *The Crazy Years: Paris in the Twenties*. New York: Atheneum, 1983.

———. *The Great Good Place: American Expatriate Women in Paris*. New York: W.W. Norton and Company, 1991.

Wolfe, Travis. "Scott, Zelda: Fitzgerald Home in Montgomery Is Now Museum," *Chattanooga Times*, June 9, 1989, section D.

Wolff, Geoffery. *Black Sun: The Brief Transit and Violent Eclipse of Harry Crosby*. New York: Random House, 1976.

Woolcott, Alexander. *The Letters of Alexander Woolcott*. Edited by Beatrice Kaufman. New York: Viking Press, 1944.

Yardley, Jonathan. *Ring: A Biography of Ring Lardner*. New York: Random House, 1977.

Yorke, Lane. "Zelda: A Worksheet," *Paris Review*, Fall 1983, pp. 210–263.

Zickerman, George. *The Last Flapper*. Boston: Little, Brown & Co., 1969.

Unpublished Materials

Alabama State Department of Archives and History, historic materials on early residents of Montgomery, Alabama.

American Psychiatric Association Library, Archives on Schizophrenia, Washington, D.C.

Campbell, Lawton, "The Fitzgeralds Were My Friends." A thirty-page reminiscence concerning Zelda and Scott Fitzgerald. Collection of the author.

Fitzgerald, F. Scott, Papers, Special Collections Division, Manuscript Collections, Firestone Library, Princeton University, Princeton, New Jersey.

Fitzgerald, Zelda, Papers, #010116, Special Collections Division, Manuscript Collections, Firestone Library, Princeton University, Princeton, New Jersey.

Fitzgerald, Zelda, Collection of Zelda Fitzgerald artwork, Montgomery Museum of Fine Arts, Montgomery, Alabama.

Haardt, Sara, interview of Zelda Fitzgerald for *Good Housekeeping* magazine, unpublished. Now in the Sara Haardt Collection, Goucher College, also in the H. L. Mencken Collection at the Enoch Pratt Free Library, Baltimore, Maryland.

W. S. Hoole Special Collections Library, University of Alabama, Tuscaloosa.

Lanahan, Scottie, letters to the author from Zelda and Scott Fitzgerald's only child.

McKaig, Alexander, the diary of F. Scott Fitzgerald's Princeton classmate, now in the possession of his nephew, Attorney Robert Taft, Brighton, Fernald, Taft and Hampsey, Peterborough, New Hampshire.

George Jean Nathan Collection, Rare Book Department, Cornell University, Ithaca, New York.

New York State Psychiatric Hospital, Archives on Schizophrenia, Ogdensburg, New York.

Shafer, Carolyn, "To Spread a Human Aspiration: The Art of Zelda Fitzgerald," Submitted in partial fulfillment of the requirements for the degree of master of arts in the Department of Art, University of South Carolina, 1994.

Rosalind Smith, letters, in W. S. Hoole Special Collections Library, University of Alabama, Tuscaloosa.

Sheppard Pratt Hospital Archives, Baltimore, Maryland.

Frances Finne Taylor (Kendall Taylor), "The Fitzgerald Myth: A Study of Zelda Sayre
    Fitzgerald," master's thesis submitted to the Faculty of the Graduate School,
    Vanderbilt University, Nashville, Tennessee, August 1964.
Dr. Frederic Wertham, collection of Zelda Fitzgerald artwork, Wertham Collection,
    Fogg Art Museum, Harvard University, Boston, Massachusetts.
Weatherby, Mrs. H. L., letters to the author from one of Zelda's high school classmates.

INTERVIEWS BY THE AUTHOR

Charles Angoff, Rutherford, New Jersey, April 11, 1963.
Dr. Basil T. Bennett, former director of Highland Hospital, Nashville, Tennessee, Au-
    gust 22, 1963, and February 11 and March 3, 1964.
Dr. Otto Billig, Nashville, Tennessee, February 13, 1963.
Helen Blackshear, Montgomery, Alabama, telephone interview, December 14, 1994.
C. Lawton Campbell, Princeton classmate of F. Scott Fitzgerald, Bronxville, New York,
    January 28–29, 1964.
Tom Daniels, telephone interview, March 17, 1994.
Lillian Gish, San Francisco, California, February 12, 1966.
Mrs. George Hickson, employee, Highland Hospital, Asheville, North Carolina,
    June 21, 1963.
Helen Hopkins, nurse, Highland Hospital, Asheville, North Carolina, June 21, 1963.
Tom Johnson, West Point, New York, March 11, 1963.
Laura Kahler, Hagerstown, Maryland, August 12–13, 1994.
Scottie Fitzgerald Lanahan, daughter of Zelda and F. Scott Fitzgerald, Washington,
    D.C., January 24–29, 1964.
Mary McCahon, Westport Historical Society, Westport, Connecticut, April 11, 1995.
Archibald MacLeish, Conway, Massachusetts, August 14–15, 1963.
Dorothea Malm, Westport Historic District Commission, Westport, Connecticut,
    April 11, 1995.
James Mellow, telephone interview, April 23, 1995.
Arthur Mizener, Nashville, Tennessee, February 6, 1964, and Ithaca, New York, Janu-
    ary 23, 1966.
Richard and Nat Ober, telephone interviews, May 14, 2001, and June 10, 2001.
Mark Palmer, Montgomery, Alabama, February 7, 1995.
Ed Patillo, Montgomery Museum of Fine Art, Montgomery, Alabama, April 3, 1995.
Mary Porter, Asheville, North Carolina, June 21, 1963.
Landon Ray, employee, Highland Hospital, Asheville, North Carolina, June 21–22, 1963.
Carolyn Shafer, telephone interviews, February 15 and April 10, 1993.
Rosalind Smith, Zelda's sister, Montgomery, Alabama, July 12–14, 1963.
Robert Taft, Peterborough, New Hampshire, May 15–17, 1995.
Anne Tillinghast, Asheville, North Carolina, June 20–21, 1963.
Andrew Turnbull, Cambridge, Massachusetts, August 21–27, 1963.
Harold Weatherby, Nashville, Tennessee, March 21–24, 1964.

INDEX

From *This Side of Paradise* by F. Scott Fitzgerald (New York: Charles Scribner's Sons, 1920).

From *The Beautiful and Damned* by F. Scott Fitzgerald (New York: Charles Scribner's Sons, 1922).

ILLUSTRATION CREDITS

Alabama State Archives, Montgomery, Alabama
Montgomery's young women welcoming the 4th Alabama

Copyright 1948. Ashville (N.C.) *Citizen-Times.* Reprinted with permission.
The fire at Highland Hospital

Collection of the author
Pulitzer fountain; Washington Square fountain; The site of the Union Square fountain; *Female Patient;* Self-portrait as a paper doll with costume; The author in front of the Alabama Historical Commission plaque

Division of Rare and Manuscript Collections, Cornell University Library
Zelda and Scott in her front yard; Cover of *The Smart Set;* Zelda in front of the White Bear Yacht Club

F. Scott and Zelda Fitzgerald Museum, Montgomery, Alabama
Minnie Sayre; Judge Anthony Sayre; Anthony Sayre; Marjorie Sayre; Clothilde Sayre; Zelda in costume for "Folly"; Dust jacket for *Save Me the Waltz;* Zelda in her ballet costume; Postcard of the F. Scott and Zelda Fitzgerald Museum, Montgomery, Alabama

Library of Congress, Motion Picture Division
Actress Ruth Findlay in *The Salamander*

Montgomery Museum of Fine Arts, Montgomery, Alabama, Gift of Mrs. Frances Fitzgerald Smith
Ballerinas; Candler, North Carolina; Deposition; Scottie at Zelda's retrospective exhibition

Courtesy of Nathaniel Ober
Jack Lanahan and Scottie Fitzgerald at their wedding

Photograph of Harold Ober by Dorothy Compton, courtesy of Nathaniel Ober
Harold Ober

Photos from the F. Scott Fitzgerald Archives at the Princeton University Library used by permission of Harold Ober Associates as agents for the Fitzgerald Trustees; reproduction arranged through the Princeton University Library
Zelda at the time she met Scott; Swimming at Compo Beach; Zelda relaxing on the grass; Drawings of Zelda and Scott; Zelda in knickers; The Fitzgeralds on their auto trip; Zelda holding Scottie; Original cover of *The Beautiful and Damned;* Original cover of *The Great Gatsby;* The Fitzgeralds on the grass; Zelda, Scott, and Scottie with Scottie's nanny; The Fitzgeralds kicking up their heels; Zelda, Scott, and Scottie on the beach; The Fitzgeralds with Scottie out for a walk; The Fitzgeralds, arms linked; Zelda and Scott with Scottie on the steps; The Fitzgerald family passport; The Fitzgerald family aboard ship; Photo from Scott's French identity card; Photo from Zelda's French identity card; Scott and Zelda assessing damage; *Do-Do in Guatemala*

Private collection
Magnolia

Courtesy of Rosalind Smith
Zelda, her face showing effects of the treatments for her illness

Courtesy of Robert Taft, photos from Alex McKaig's logbook
Photo from Alex McKaig's naval logbook showing Scott and Zelda with friends; Alex McKaig; John Peale Bishop; Sap Donahoe

ABOUT THE AUTHOR

KENDALL TAYLOR, PH.D., a cultural historian and Fulbright scholar, has been a professor and a museum curator. Her interest in Zelda Fitzgerald began thirty years ago when she was a graduate student at Vanderbilt University and read Arthur Mizener's biography of F. Scott Fitzgerald. Noting that Mizener's study left Zelda's life largely undocumented, Taylor began her own research by speaking with many of the Fitzgeralds' acquaintances and conducting interviews with Zelda's friends and family. She has continued that investigation over the past decades. She lives with her daughter, Sophie, in New York and Washington.

Sometimes Madness Is Wisdom

KENDALL TAYLOR

A Reader's Guide

A Conversation with Kendall Taylor

Marion Meade: Kendall, you begin your book by saying you were fascinated by Zelda's legend for many years. What first attracted you to her, and did you alter your opinion of her as you proceeded with the research and writing?

Kendall Taylor: I read Arthur Mizener's biography of F. Scott Fitzgerald, *The Far Side of Paradise*, and my interest was ignited by Mizener's omission of Zelda's story after Scott's death. It was an oversight corrected in his second edition. By then, I was well along in my own research. At first I considered Zelda a woman thwarted by outside circumstances, not the least being that she was the wife of F. Scott Fitzgerald, but my interpretation of her life expanded through an extensive study of her work and the nature of mental illness.

MM: I remember watching a television documentary in which Zelda and Scott's granddaughter Eleanor called their marriage "a great love story." To me, it seems more like a marriage made in hell. But I would love to hear your opinion on their relationship.

KT: A great love story? Eleanor expressed the same sentiment to me and there is an ironic truth to what she says. By its unending interest, the public has mythologized their marriage into a great love story, but with nothing to sustain this notion, the premise would not hold our attention. Clearly, they were captivated by one another: Fitzgerald with Zelda's quick intelligence, courage and spirit; she with his talent and resulting fame. It was a marriage built on compromise, made in heaven but lived out in hell—not dissimilar from other celebrity marriages.

MM: There are moments in the book when Zelda's mental illness becomes almost unbearable to read about. Certainly it is the most detailed discussion of it I've seen. What particular problems were involved in writing about this aspect of your subject?

KT: The challenge was to make Zelda's mental illness understandable and interesting to the general public. A summary of medicines and treatment wouldn't do it, so I describe her descent into madness quite graphically, taking readers into the sanitariums where she was incarcerated. Certain scenes were so disturbing they got deleted from the final publication. My aim was to have readers experience some of what Zelda did. Initially, I didn't know much about manic-depression and schizophrenia, so it took substantial research at medical libraries.

MM: As we know now, schizophrenia is an inherited disease. Did Zelda have any chance of escaping it? Had she not married Scott, what kind of life do you think she might have had?

KT: Given her marital and family history, not really. The stressors were too severe and her first depressive episode triggered too early. When you consider how unprepared she was for overnight celebrity, and how totally dependent she was on Fitzgerald for financial and emotional stability, her breakdown seemed unavoidable. Had she married one of her early beaux, Peyton Matthis, proprietor of the Montgomery Marble Works, or Leon Ruth, who wound up owning a Montgomery jewelry shop, the story might have ended differently. But she was determined to leave the South and live life on a grand scale, and that path—as the wife of F. Scott Fitzgerald—led only in one direction.

MM: What part, if any, did Scott's alcoholism play in her breakdown?

KT: Being married to an abusive alcoholic is never pretty, and Scott was a heavy drinker from prep school days. By his mid-twenties, he was well on his way to becoming the mean-spirited drunk he so vividly describes in stories like "A New Leaf." If Zelda ever harbored illusions that he could provide a stable base, she was quickly disappointed. Her father, an Alabama supreme court judge, foresaw the disaster and tried stopping the marriage, but the lure of fame and fortune was too seductive. No matter what the cost, Zelda was determined to live life on a grand scale. Theirs was a "*folie á deux,*" with Fitzgerald requiring as much psychological help as Zelda. The fact that Scott never acted on that knowledge ultimately destroyed the marriage and Zelda.

MM: More conjecture: Were Zelda living today, and treated with antipsychotic drugs, would she have left an abusive relationship with an alcoholic? Gone to Al-Anon? Or what?

KT: Antipsychotic drugs only go so far and have numerous side effects. They are seldom a cure-all. Zelda's basic problem was her inability to focus on something long enough to excel at it—a typical symptom of manic-depression. Were she to have been born later in the century and diagnosed and treated early—and educated to acquire a skill that could have rendered her independent and self-supporting—she might have left Fitzgerald, or never married him at all. But Scottie was part of the equation. Zelda didn't trust Fitzgerald to bring her up, and Fitzgerald, though alcoholic, was famous and might have won custody against a mother with a history of mental illness.

MM: In her autobiographical novel *Save Me the Waltz*, her heroine is a sane, strong, intelligent, and creative woman. Is Alabama the person Zelda might have been without mental illness and an alcoholic husband?

KT: Yes, Alabama is Zelda before Fitzgerald entered her life, but also the result of that marriage with all the advantages it afforded. Alabama's opportunity to dance in Naples is a direct result of her study in Paris, just as Zelda's dancing skill was advanced through study with Lubov Egorova, trained in the Maryinsky Imperial Theater. Through writing *Save Me the Waltz*, Zelda hoped to reclaim her earlier personality and shed her mental illness—just as the salamander proverbially could shed its skin and emerge unscathed by fire.

MM: Zelda, a woman of several talents, happened to be an accomplished writer in her own right. And yet she was also Scott's muse—he regularly used her experiences, her thoughts, even her diaries verbatim in his fiction. What's more, he considered them his property. Isn't that a classic feminist horror story?

KT: Yes, and all too common. Fitzgerald paid the bills. How many times have women listened to boring men drone over dinner because *they* were paying the tab? Scott certainly believed he "owned" their life story because he'd paid for it. Today's woman wouldn't relinquish those rights. She might pick up her fair share with a separate income or demand equitable worth with sweat equity as a homemaker. The feminist movement changed attitudes in this regard, not to mention the law.

MM: Of the half dozen or so short stories she published— many were lost, of course—which ones do you think represent her best writing?

KT: I love the clever, witty stories about the twenties women Zelda wrote for *College Humor* including: "The Original Follies Girl," "Southern Girl," "The Girl the Prince Liked," "The Girl with Talent," and "Poor Working Girl." They contain varied aspects of Zelda's character and illuminate her true nature. Her best stories are "A Couple of Nuts" published by *Scribner's Magazine* in August 1932, and "A Millionaire's Girl" which appeared in the *Saturday Evening Post* on May 7, 1930 with F. Scott Fitzgerald's byline, but it actually was written by Zelda.

MM: I can't help feeling that Zelda was probably a far more accomplished dancer than anyone gave her credit for. She did after all receive at least one offer to dance professionally in Europe. Why didn't she take it?

KT: In 1929, Julia Sedova wrote Zelda inviting her to join the San Carlo Opera Ballet Company in Naples, Italy. As a debut piece, she offered her the solo in *Aida*. Zelda's sister Rosalind surmised Scott responded as he had eight years earlier when Zelda wanted to become a film actress. Either he forbade her, or made life so miserable she gave up on the idea. There was also the question of who would supervise Scottie. Fitzgerald rejected that responsibility, and would never have allowed Scottie to live with Zelda's sister, Rosalind. Zelda felt very conflicted. Influencing her decision was the fact that she disliked Italians and viewed Naples as a step down from London and Paris. At twenty-nine, she had never been anywhere alone, and without Fitzgerald's support was afraid of failing. Accepting the offer would also have meant relinquishing comforts she had come to expect in life, and reversing a pattern of dependent behavior. Turning down the offer was a decision she always regretted.

MM: Not until she was twenty-seven did she desire an identity for herself beyond being the wife of F. Scott Fitzgerald, or so it appears. Why was it so difficult for her to reach this point, in a period when more and more women were working outside the home? Or did she have some professional ambition before she met Scott?

KT: She was undereducated, unskilled, and from the Deep South where women of her social class seldom worked outside the home. She had no role models before arriving in New York, where actresses like Tallulah Bankhead and Ruth Findley first inspired her to embark on a stage and film career. But Fitzgerald would have none of it. The turning point came in Hollywood during 1927, when Scott began an affair with actress Lois Moran and touted her talents to Zelda. From this point, she determined to build an independent life and chose dance as the avenue to obtain that goal.

MM: In so many ways, Scott was a disaster as a human being and a husband. I'm curious if you had any particular problems in writing about him sympathetically.

KT: Not at all. Actually, I never viewed him as a disastrous human being, only a flawed one. It was Zelda's misfortune to have chosen him a husband, and his error to marry a girl whose psychological makeup demanded stability.

MM: Which novel—or short story—of Scott's would you recommend to readers interested in the lives of the Fitzgeralds?

KT: Scott and Zelda seldom wrote from imagination, and their writing generally reflects what is happening in their lives. Zelda's article "Show Mr. and Mrs. F. to Number—" and "Auction—Model 1934" are heavily autobiographical, and Scott's *Tender Is the Night* is drawn from the Fitzgeralds' stay in Europe and friendship with the Murphys. That's a particularly fascinating book to read after this biography.

MM: An interesting thread in your narrative concerns Zelda's relationships with women. Since she seemed to have little real affection for people of her own sex, it is a bit startling to read about her sudden sexual attraction to women in her later twenties. One psychiatrist (Eugen Bleuler) said that her homosexual interests were a symptom of her illness. Do you agree? In view of the fact that she probably never had any actual sexual contact with a woman, what is one to make of all this?

KT: I wouldn't rule out Zelda's sexual contact with women. While there is no direct proof, we have Zelda's writing about homosexuality being a natural act. And given how passionate she was, I think it's entirely possible she was intimate with some of the lesbian women she met in Paris during the late twenties. As far as it being a symptom of her mental illness, it seems more an indication of her loneliness in the marriage and aversion to becoming involved with another man.

MM: On this issue of her sexuality, much has been made about whether she did or she didn't have an extramarital affair with a hunky French aviator. Considering the dreadful, dysfunctional sex life she had with her husband, why would an affair be so surprising? I know I was rooting for her.

KT: To me it's quite clear her affair with Edouard Jozan was sexual. His disclaiming was a gentlemanly gesture. Zelda never admitted one way or the other how far she had gone—with him or any other man. At twenty-four she was very beautiful, largely ignored by her young husband, and desperate for affection. Jozan was eager to oblige and with his good looks, French manner, and allure as a pilot, he was a powerful sexual animal. Had Scottie not been born, Zelda might have run away with him. It was her first real sexual awakening—brimming with passion and excitement, and the thought of leaving Scott must surely have crossed her mind.

MM: One of the people in the book I found fascinating was their daughter Scottie. Given the chaos in which she must have grown up—mental illness and alcoholism—her claims that it never affected her are quite amazing. In fact, I believe she was severely damaged. So what do you think of the Fitzgeralds as parents?

KT: Scottie could not help but be emotionally damaged. To distance herself from the pain, she wrapped the experience in a protective membrane, but that didn't erase what had happened. She never really felt connected to her mother or father. Though Zelda and Scott loved their daughter, employed competent people to supervise her, bought Scottie exquisite gifts, and enrolled her in the best schools, they were distracted by personal demons. Their emotional distance took its toll, and was later perpetuated by Scottie on her own children.

MM: What comes across so clearly in your book is Zelda's strength, something not really emphasized in previous biographies. With the exceptions of Nancy Milford, Sara Mayfield, and Eleanor Lanahan, just about all the many, many writers on the Fitzgeralds have been men. Do you think male bias has affected the way she is regarded today?

KT: Not bias so much as unwillingness to delve into her character. For numerous reasons, the focus has always been on Scott, with Zelda an afterthought. When Nancy Milford researched her Zelda book in the late sixties, much of the material available today still was in Scottie's hands or unavailable to scholars. The other two Zelda biographers, her girlhood friend Sara Mayfield and granddaughter Eleanor Lanahan, both were unable to maintain objectivity.

MM: Despite everything, it seems her fate to be remembered as the wife of a famous novelist, or more precisely the crazy wife of a famous novelist. What are the chances of ever changing this kind of deeply imbedded image?

KT: Very good—given the critical response to *Sometimes Madness Is Wisdom* and continuing interest in Zelda's life and work.

Another study is due out in England next year, and I know she is one of four authors you are writing about in *The Last Flappers*. After all this literary consideration, it's unlikely she will primarily be viewed as the crazy wife of a famous novelist.

MM: To me Zelda is inspirational. Did writing her life change yours in any way?

KT: Not so much in the content of her life, but in the writing about that experience. Starting this book in my twenties and finishing in my fifties, I believe the biography reflects my own growing maturation in being able to tell Zelda's story with increasing depth and understanding. I'm grateful I had those decades to refine my ideas and write the biography Zelda deserved.